THE NEW AIR FRYER COOKBOOK FOR BEGINNERS 2022

1100+ Days of Easy, Tasty and Budget-Friendly Recipes to Learn How to Fry, Bake and Grill Your Favourite Meals

Corinne Jones

Introduction...1

Chapter 1: Breakfast................................3

1. Breakfast Spinach Quiche 3
2. Strawberry Dutch Pancakes 3
3. Cheesy Tomato and Egg 4
4. Mexican Waffles 4
5. Egg and Bacon Pie 4
6. Healthy Banana Pancakes....................4
7. Egg and Bacon Muffins........................4
8. Oat and Vanilla Pudding 4
9. Tropical French Toast 5
10. Mushroom Frittata 5
11. Cheese and Broccoli Quiche 5
12. Egg and Sausage Casserole 5
13. German Pancakes 5
14. Kale and Cottage Cheese Omelet.............6
15. Cheese Scones 6
16. Egg Muffins..6
17. Kale Egg Muffins 6
18. Zucchini Muffins 6
19. Breakfast Quinoa 7
20. Cauliflower and Avocado Toast............7
21. Fennel Frittata 7
22. Zucchini Gratin 7
23. Breakfast Broccoli Muffins..................7
24. Tomato Frittata 8
25. Onion and Cheese Omelet....................8
26. Perfect Scrambled Eggs 8
27. Tofu Omelet 8
28. Coconut Cream Cheese Pancakes 8
29. Florentine Eggs 9
30. Sausage Quiche 9
31. Smoked Salmon Omelet 9
32. Creamy Risotto 9
33. Veggie Toast..9
34. Avo-Eggs..10
35. Mixed Vegetable Frittata 10
36. Peanut Oats and Chia Porridge 10
37. Nutmeg Cranberry Scones..................10
38. Egg and Ham Cups 10
39. Breakfast Stuffed Poblanos 11
40. Bell Pepper Eggs 11
41. French Toast Sticks 11
42. Sweet Potato Hash 11
43. Cornflakes and Blackberries 11
44. Cinnamon Apple Pancakes 12
45. Super Cheesy Hash Browns 12
46. Pear and Walnut Oatmeal..................12
47. Cheesy Ham Pastries 12
48. Healthy Carrot Oatmeal 12
49. Herbed Omelet 12
50. Vanilla Steel Cut Oats 13
51. Milky French Toast 13
52. Creamy Bacon Omelet........................13
53. Mixed Berries Oatmeal 13
54. Paprika Egg Souffle 14
55. Cheesy Zucchini Frittata....................14
56. Breakfast Egg Sandwich 14
57. Chorizo Parmesan Rolls 14
58. Queso Crumpets 14
59. Parmesan Egg Clouds 15
60. Breakfast Egg Puffs 15
61. Breakfast Hash 15
62. Peanut Butter Muffins 15
63. Greek Egg Muffins 15
64. Sausage Balls 16
65. Strawberry Parfait 16
66. Churro-Banana Oats 16
67. Super Nutty French Toast 16
68. Radish Hash Browns 17
69. Toad in the Hole 17

70. Mozzarella and Cherry Tomato Pastries ...17
71. Air Fried Shirred Eggs........................17
72. Breakfast Blueberry Cobbler 18
73. Mixed Berries Muffins 18
74. Breakfast Bagels 18
75. Avocado Toast with Poached Eggs 18
76. Morning Burrito 19
77. Breakfast Egg Pastries 19
78. Baked Eggs with Kale and Ham................19
79. Chicken, Chive and Feta Frittata 19
80. Spinach Muffins 20
81. Vegetable Quiche 20
82. Cinnamon Rolls 20
83. Mushroom and Leeks Frittata............20
84. Carrot and Potato Hash Browns.............21
85. Nutty Bread Pudding 21
86. Japanese Tofu Omelet........................21
87. Mini Smoked Salmon Quiche..............21
88. Cheddar Cheese English Muffins............21
89. Cranberry Bran Muffins 22
90. Brown Rice and Salmon Frittata.............22
91. Cali Breakfast Melt 22
92. Chia Pudding......................................22
93. Flax Meal Porridge 23
94. Southern Buttermilk Biscuits 23
95. Salami and Prosciutto Omelet 23
96. Savory Pearl Barley 23
97. Espresso Oatmeal 23
98. Coconut Blueberry Oatmeal 23
99. Mexican Salsa Eggs 24
100. Pineapple French Toast......................24
101. Cranberry Bread Pudding 24
102. Chocolate Banana Muffins 24
103. Breaded Spam Steaks 25
104. Corn Flakes Casserole 25
105. Jalapeno Breakfast Muffins 25
106. Spinach Cheese Pie............................25
107. Pumpkin Spice Oats 25
108. Pizza Omelet 26
109. Zucchini Omelet 26
110. Streusel Donuts 26
111. Pesto Omelet 26
112. Berry and Nuts Granola 27
113. Spinach and Cheese Toast 27
114. Vanilla Apple Quinoa 27
115. Savory Feta Oats 27
116. Zucchini and Fruits Breakfast Plate..........28
117. Peach and Nuts Millet........................28
118. Pistachio and Pineapple Oats............28
119. Apricot and Vanilla Porridge 28
120. Seasoned Omelet with Croutons.............28
121. Kale Muffins 29
122. Creamy Mac and Cheese 29
123. Cacao Banana Leather 29
124. Squash Oatmeal Muffins 29
125. Sweet Potato Frittata 30
126. Mexican Chilis Frittata......................30
127. Amish Baked Oatmeal 30
128. Banana and Peach Bake Oatmeal 30
129. Cranberry Pumpkin Oatmeal 31
130. Coconut Blueberry Oatmeal 31
131. Papaya Coconut Oatmeal...................31
132. Dried Cranberry Farro 31
133. Lime Coconut Breakfast Quinoa.............31
134. Chocolate Cherry Oatmeal 32

Chapter 2: Sides and Appetizer 33

135. Jacket Potatoes 33
136. Queso Fundido....................................33
137. Spicy Mango Okra 34
138. Cajun Red Rice and Beans 34
139. Bacon Cheeseburger Dip 34

140. Roasted Potato Salad 34
141. Roasted Brussel Sprouts with Parmesan ... 35
142. Tortellini Pasta Salad 35
143. Spicy Pimento Cheese Dip 35
144. Pesto Tomatoes 35
145. Potato Poutine 35
146. Indian Style Sweet Potato Fries 36
147. Spiced Mozza Sticks 36
148. Sea Salt Parsnip Fries 36
149. Hot Mexican Bean Dip........................36
150. Sweet Potato with Broccoli 36
151. Cauliflower Florets 37
152. Lemon Flavored Green Beans............37
153. Crispy Avocado Wedges 37
154. Portobello Mushroom Pizza 37
155. Olive and Calamari Rings 37
156. Air Fried Leeks 37
157. Eggplant Surprise 38
158. Berbere-Spiced Fries 38
159. Chickpea Fries....................................38
160. Mushrooms and Sour Cream 38
161. Wild Rice Spinach Balls 38
162. Dill Mashed Potato 39
163. Loaded Disco Fries 39
164. Breaded Artichoke Fries 39
165. Cheesy Fingerling Potatoes 39
166. Zucchini Curly Fries 40
167. Coleslaw Stuffed Wontons 40
168. Jalapeno Cheese Balls 40
169. Black Bean Egg Rolls 40
170. Cheese and Salsa Mushrooms 41
171. Buffalo Cauliflower Bites 41
172. Twice Baked Potatoes 41
173. Apricots Stuffed with Walnuts 41
174. Breaded Okra......................................42
175. Cajun Sweet Potato Tots 42
176. Bacon and Cheese Jalapeno Poppers 42
177. Coriander Potatoes 42
178. Ricotta Balls 42
179. Falafel with Tahini Sauce 43
180. Roasted Paprika Carrots 43
181. Garlic Mashed Turnips........................43
182. Bacon Scallops 43
183. Spring Salad 43
184. Healthy Beet Hummus 44
185. Chicken Jalapeno Popper Dip 44
186. Turmeric Potatoes 44
187. Carrot Balls 44
188. Goat Cheese and Figs........................44
189. Corn with Cheese and Lime 45
190. Chicken Buffalo Dip............................45
191. Cheeseburger Dip 45
192. Prosciutto Wrapped Asparagus 45
193. Vegetable Spring Rolls 45
194. Baked Yams with Dill 46
195. Ranch Potatoes 46
196. Spinach Balls......................................46
197. Baked Mushrooms..............................46
198. Honey Dill Carrots 46
199. Mushroom and Cheese Hasselback Potatoes 47
200. Rosemary and Garlic Fries 47
201. Zucchini Fries 47
202. Roasted Garlic Zucchini 47
203. Indian Spiced Okra 47
204. Crunchy Almond & Kale Salad with Roasted Chicken................................48
205. Pakoras 48
206. Sweetened Onions 48
207. Lemon Lentils 49
208. Baba Ghanoush 49
209. Corn and Egg Salad............................49
210. Porcini Risotto....................................50

211.	Peas and Bacon	50
212.	Mini Peppers with Goat Cheese	50
213.	Roasted Pepper and Greens Salad	50
214.	Asparagus Fries	50
215.	Sautéed Pumpkin and Potatoes	51
216.	Beans in Tomato Sauce	51
217.	Roasted Corn on the Cob	51
218.	Southwest Egg Rolls	51
219.	Mac and Cheese Balls	52
220.	Pigs in a Blanket	52
221.	Kale and Brussels Sprouts	52
222.	Kale and Black Olives	52
223.	Bacon -Wrapped Onion Rings	52
224.	Potato -Kale Croquettes	52
225.	Spicy Arancini	53
226.	Gorgonzola Stuffed Mushrooms with Horseradish Mayo	53
227.	Sweet Corn Fritters	53
228.	Colby Potato Patties	53
229.	Asian Chicken and Peas Salad	54
230.	Roasted Hot Corn	54
231.	Cheesy Lemon Rice	54
232.	Mexican Black Beans and Corn	54
233.	Couscous with Raisins	55
234.	Celeriac Fries	55
235.	Balsamic Cherry Tomato Skewers	55
236.	Sesame Mustard Greens	55
237.	Cheesy Fennel	55
238.	Arugula and Beets Salad	56
239.	Simple Broccoli Side Dish	56
240.	Paprika Cucumber Chips	56
241.	Cheesy Sticks with Sweet Thai Sauce	56
242.	Easy Cheese Sticks	56
243.	Spicy Acorn Squash Wedges	57
244.	Spicy Tomato Chutney	57
245.	Mexican Rice	57
246.	Sweetcorn Risotto	57
247.	Potato and Kale Croquettes	57
248.	Arancini with Jerked Tomatoes & Mozzarella	58
249.	Scotch Eggs with Spicy Pepper Sauce	58
250.	Fiery Bacon Nibbles	58
251.	Goat Cheese Balls	58
252.	Grilled Endive with Yogurt Sauce	59
253.	Roasted Tomato Salsa	59
254.	Italian Fried Ravioli	59
255.	Roasted Grape Dip	59
256.	Rumaki Balls	60
257.	Cumin Tortilla Chips with Guacamole	60

Chapter 3: Soup, Stews and Vegetable Dishes . 61

258.	Mexican Beef Soup	61
259.	Spicy Vegetable Soup	62
260.	Caramelized Carrot Soup	62
261.	Chicken Orzo Soup	62
262.	Stuffed Eggplants	62
263.	Ratatouille Soup with Quinoa	63
264.	Italian Eggplant Stew	63
265.	Cauliflower Fried Rice	63
266.	Eggplant Parmesan	63
267.	Creamy Parsnip Soup	63
268.	Szechuan Pork Soup	64
269.	Tomato and Fennel Stew	64
270.	Zucchini Fritters	64
271.	Hasselback Zucchini	64
272.	Cream of Asparagus Soup	65
273.	Mexican Baked Potato Soup	65
274.	Roasted Veggie Tacos	65
275.	Creamy Cauliflower Pasta	65
276.	Vegetable Wontons	66
277.	Healthy Cheese Pockets	66
278.	Chinese Orange Tofu	66
279.	Asparagus Strata	67
280.	Lemon Tofu	67
281.	Zucchini Enchiladas	67
282.	Eggplant stacks	68
283.	Korean Cauliflower "Wings"	68

284.	Vegetables and Couscous	68
285.	Roasted Vegetable Pasta	68
286.	Cabbage Diet Soup	69
287.	Moroccan Vegetable Stew	69
288.	Baked Parsnip and Potato	69
289.	Sweet Potato Casserole	69
290.	Vegetable and Fruit Skewers	70
291.	Vegan Chili and Cheese Fries	70
292.	Roasted Bell Peppers with Spicy Mayo	70
293.	Baked Vegetables with Cheese and Olives	70
294.	Mushroom and Asparagus Cakes	71
295.	Rosemary Veggie Gratin	71
296.	Eggplant Caprese	71
297.	Beef Mushroom Soup	71
298.	Curry Zucchini Soup	71
299.	Squash Risotto	72
300.	Cheese Broccoli Pasta	72
301.	Crispy Noodle Vegetable Salad	72
302.	Baked Root Vegetables	72
303.	BBQ Tofu	73
304.	Vegan Taco Bowls	73
305.	Italian Tofu Steaks	73
306.	Pine-Pumpkin Puree	73
307.	Buttered Garlic Squash	74
308.	Roasted Rainbow Vegetable	74
309.	Julienne Vegetables with Chicken	74
310.	Bell Pepper Gratin	74
311.	Eggplant Boats	74
312.	Tex Mex Peppers	75
313.	Bell Pepper and Tomato Sauce	75
314.	Chery Tomato and Rutabaga Pasta	75
315.	Italian Eggplant Stew	75
316.	Spanish Greens	76
317.	Swiss Chard Salad	76
318.	Creamy Zucchini Mix	76
319.	Stuffed Tomatoes	76
320.	Spiced Turnip Salad	77
321.	Fiery Cabbage	77
322.	Tomatoes and Brussel Sprouts Mix	77
323.	Cheesy Zucchini Fritters	77
324.	Thai Peanut Tofu	77
325.	Rice Flour Coated Tofu	78
326.	Stuffed Okra	78
327.	Green Beans and Mushroom Casserole	78
328.	Salsa Eggplants	78
329.	Curried Eggplant	79
330.	Tofu with Capers Sauce	79
331.	Winter Beef Soup	79
332.	Fennel Risotto	79
333.	Cheddar Cheese Sliced Cauliflower	80
334.	Cream of Carrot Potato Soup	80
335.	Nutty Carrot Soup	80
336.	Summer Vegetable Soup	81
337.	Spiced Sweet Potato Soup	81
338.	Curry Lentil Soup	81
339.	Mushroom Soup	82
340.	Meatless Ziti Pasta	82
341.	Creamy Eggplant Gratin	82
342.	Creamy Cauliflower Gratin	83
343.	Cauliflower Fritters	83
344.	Avocado Asparagus Soup	83
345.	Pumpkin Gnocchi	83
346.	Pumpkin Lasagna	84
347.	Rustic Baked Halloumi with Fennel Salad	84
348.	Celeriac Potato Gratin	84
349.	Red Chard and Kalamata Olives	84
350.	Tomato Corn Risotto	85
351.	Red Cabbage Avocado Bowls	85
352.	Pesto Zucchini Salad	85
353.	Cream Cheese Zucchini	85
354.	Traditional Italian Rice & Parmesan Balls	85
355.	Mozzarella and Radish Salad	86
356.	Avocado and Crispy Tofu Salad	86
357.	Vegan Smoked Bacon	86
358.	Tomato and Bell Pepper Soup	86
359.	Chicken Corn Zucchini Soup	87
360.	Potato Parsley Soup	87

361.	Curried Cauliflower Soup	87
362.	Burrata-Stuffed Tomatoes	87
363.	Tuscan White Bean Soup	87
364.	Eggplant Satay	88
365.	Okra Corn Medley	88
366.	Mexican Avocado Fry	88
367.	Curried Zucchini	88
368.	Sunny Lentils	88
369.	Black Bean and Sausage Soup	88
370.	Fusilli with Broccoli in Pesto	89
371.	Khao Pad Fried Rice	89
372.	Minestrone Soup	89
373.	Wheat Berry Pilaf	89
374.	Hot Pumpkin Rendang	90
375.	Coconut Soup with Chive	90
376.	Tofu Red Curry Noodle	90

Chapter 4: Beef and Lamb | 91

377.	Beef Schnitzel	91
378.	Lamb Kebabs	91
379.	Spiced Beef Fajitas	92
380.	Greek Kafta Kabobs	92
381.	Classic Beef Ribs	92
382.	Spicy Short Ribs in Red Wine Reduction	92
383.	Coffee Rubbed Steaks	93
384.	Beef Roll-ups	93
385.	Beef Chimichangas	93
386.	Mushroom and Beef Meatballs	93
387.	Beef Broccoli	93
388.	Greek Lamb Patties	94
389.	Mustard and Lemon Lamb Chops	94
390.	Spicy Lamb Chops	94
391.	Ground Beef Yuca Balls	94
392.	Roast Beef Lettuce Wraps	94
393.	Beef Mozzarella	95
394.	Leg of Lamb with Brussel Sprouts	95
395.	Italian Beef Meatballs	95
396.	Beef Pot Pie	95
397.	Bacon-Wrapped Filet Mignon	96
398.	Winter Vegetables & Lamb Stew	96
399.	Air Fryer Lamb Leg	96
400.	Buttered Filet Mignon	96
401.	Lamb Korma	96
402.	Beer-Braised Short Loin	97
403.	Spicy Beef Spaghetti	97
404.	Classic Beef Stroganoff	97
405.	Crusted Fillet Mignon	97
406.	Sichuan Spiced Lamb	98
407.	Cumin-Paprika Rubbed Beef Brisket	98
408.	Herbed Pulled Beef	98
409.	Pesto Beef Rolls	98
410.	Beef Schnitzel	98
411.	Beef and Napa Cabbage Mix	99
412.	Mint Lamb with Red Potatoes	99
413.	Beef and Avocado Pan	99
414.	Spicy Lamb Balls	99
415.	Beef Tenderloin with Green Sauce	99
416.	Beef Cabbage Rolls	100
417.	Sweet and Sour Lamb Chops	100
418.	Glazed Skirt Steak	100
419.	Beef Adobo	100
420.	Mushroom Beef Steak	101
421.	Chili Ground Beef	101
422.	Steak & Bread Salad	101
423.	Paprika-Cumin Beef Brisket	101
424.	Beef Hamburger Casserole	101
425.	Pesto Lamb Ribs	102
426.	Oriental Lamb Shoulder	102
427.	Marinated Rib Eye Steak	102
428.	Beef, Carrot and Herbs Meatballs	102
429.	Beef Bolognese Sauce	103
430.	Beef Taco Fried Egg Rolls	103
431.	Moroccan Lamb Balls	103
432.	Delicious Beef Tips	103
433.	Beef BBQ Cubes with Onions	104
434.	Beef Spanish Casserole	104
435.	Turkish Lamb Liver	104

436. Wine Roasted Beef............104
437. Holiday Beef Roast 105
438. Russian Beef Gratin 105
439. Steak A La Mushrooms 105
440. Smoked Crispy Ribs 105
441. Moroccan Beef Roast 106
442. Basic Taco Meat 106
443. Tangy Beef Steak 106
444. Ginger-Orange Beef Strips 106
445. Hungarian Beef Goulash 106
446. Cheesy Beef Enchiladas 107
447. Lamb with Madeira Sauce 107
448. Suya-spiced Flank Steak 107
449. Kheema Burgers 108
450. Swedish Meatloaf 108
451. Swedish Meatballs 108
452. Hanger Steak in Mole Rub 109

Chapter 5: Pork 110

453. Mexican Pork Carnitas 110
454. Chinese Char Siu 111
455. Country Style Ribs 111
456. Crispy Pork Chops 111
457. Jamaican Meatballs 111
458. Pork Chops in Lemon Sage Sauce .111
459. Sweet and Spicy Pork Chops ...111
460. Lime-Chili Pork Tenderloin ...112
461. Parmesan Spiced Pork Chops ...112
462. Pork Chops and Mushrooms 112
463. Outback Ribs 112
464. Mexican Pork Chops 113
465. Chinese Style Meatballs 113
466. Chinese Five-Spice Pork Belly .113
467. Vietnamese Pork Chops 113
468. Pork Taquitos 113
469. Pork Egg Rolls 114
470. Pork Fricassee 114
471. Caramelized Pepper Pork 114
472. Bacon Carbonara 114
473. Country Meatloaf 115
474. Pineapple Spareribs 115
475. Pork Neck with Salad 115
476. Southern Pulled Pork 115
477. Smoked Ham and Pears 116
478. Stuffed Pork Chops 116
479. Pork Sausage Ratatouille 116
480. Italian Style Pork Chops 116
481. Sticky Pork Ribs 116
482. Pork Sausage with Mashed Cauliflower .117
483. Spicy Pork Meatballs 117
484. Hoisin Pork Loin 117
485. Pork Kebabs 117
486. Bacon Wrapped Hotdogs 117
487. Cheesy Pork Casserole 117
488. Sherry-Braised Ribs 118
489. Air-fried Pork with Sweet and Sour Glaze 118
490. Coconut Curry Pork Roast 118
491. Chinese Pork Dumplings 118
492. Five Spicy Crispy Roasted Pork .119
493. Tuscan Pork Chops 119
494. Thai Basil Pork 119
495. Hamburger Pasta Casserole 119
496. Noodle Ham Casserole 119
497. Pork Apple Meatballs 120
498. Pork Brunch Sticks 120
499. Pork Posole 120
500. Creamy Pork Curry 120
501. Texas Baby Back Ribs 121
502. Bratwurst Bites with Spicy Mustard .121
503. Oriental Pork Meatballs 121
504. Pork Bun and Liver Souffle ...121

Chapter 6: Chicken and Other Poultry 122

505. Garlic Honey Chicken 122
506. Asian Chicken Noodles 122
507. Chicken Sausage with Nestled Eggs .123

508. Thai Chicken Satay 123
509. Sweet and Sour Chicken 123
510. Dry-Rubbed Chicken Wings 123
511. Thanksgiving Turkey with Mustard Gravy 124
512. Butter and Orange Fried Chicken .124
513. Chicken Alfredo 124
514. Turkey Loaf 124
515. Cheesy Turkey Calzone 124
516. Mozzarella Turkey Rolls 125
517. Korean Chicken Wings 125
518. Curry Chicken Wings 125
519. Roasted Duck Breasts with Endives .125
520. Herbed Roast Chicken 125
521. Apricot-Glazed Turkey 126
522. Grilled Chicken and Radish Mix Recipe .126
523. Quail in White Wine Sauce 126
524. Hawaiian Roasted Quail 126
525. Caribbean Chicken Thighs 127
526. Chicken Coconut Meatballs 127
527. Chicken Pasta Salad 127
528. Chicken Marinara 127
529. Southern Fried Chicken 128
530. Mexican Chicken Burrito 128
531. Parmesan Garlic Wings 128
532. Creamy Coconut Chicken 128
533. Chinese Duck Legs 128
534. Dijon Lime Chicken 129
535. Parmesan Chicken Nuggets 129
536. Black Bean and Tater Tots 129
537. Cheese Herb Chicken Wings 129
538. Bourbon Peach Wings 129
539. Chicken Fried Rice 130
540. Chicken Curry 130
541. Coconut Chicken Tenders 130
542. Creamy Chicken Alfredo 130
543. Garlic Lemon Chicken with Green Olives 130
544. Tikka Masala Chicken 131
545. Cottage Cheese -Stuffed Chicken Breast .131
546. Creamy Cajun Chicken 131
547. Turkey with Mushrooms and Peas Casserole 131
548. Duck with Cherries Recipe 132
549. Chive and Cheese Chicken Rolls .132
550. Chicken Bruschetta 132
551. Chicken Tandoori 132
552. Tex Mex Stir-fried Chicken ...133
553. Juicy & Spicy Chicken Wings ..133
554. Southern Chicken Stew 133
555. Honey Glazed Chicken 133
556. Beer-Coated Duck Breast 134
557. Duck and Tea Sauce Recipe 134
558. Chinese Style Chicken Wings ..134
559. Tequila Orange Chicken 134
560. Lebanese Chicken 135
561. Turkey Shepherd's Pie 135
562. California Style Grilled Chicken .135
563. Blackened Baked Chicken 135
564. Brined Turkey Breast 136
565. Thyme Chicken Balls 136
566. Chicken Parmesan Meatballs ...136
567. Chicken with Chanterelle Mushrooms .136
568. Roasted Chicken with Tomato Salsa .137
569. Sautéed Duck with Asian Vegetables .137
570. Roasted Duck with Orange-Date Stuffing 137
571. Chicken Breasts with Passion Fruit Sauce 138
572. Tangy Orange Chicken Wings ...138
573. Indonesian Chicken Drumettes .138
574. Louisiana Chicken Drumettes ..139
575. Super Cheesy Chicken Mac and Cheese .139
576. Creamy Turmeric Chicken 139
577. Chicken Tikka Kebab 139
578. Chicken Tenders 140
579. Sticky BBQ Chicken 140

580. Tender and Juicy Whole Chicken ..140
581. Crispy Fried Whole Chicken ...140
582. Turkey Wings with Collard Greens .141
583. Fried Duck Thighs 141
584. Taco Turkey Casserole 141
585. Fiery Citrus Chicken 141
586. Air-Fried Lemon Olive Chicken .141
587. Fried Chicken with Salsa Verde .142
588. Rotisserie Chicken 142
589. Italian Parmesan Chicken Wings .142
590. Crispy Buttered Chicken 142
591. Chicken Fillets, Brie & Ham ..142
592. Old Bay Chicken Wings 143
593. Caesar Marinated Grilled Chicken .143
594. Boneless Air Fryer Turkey Breasts .143
595. Disney Land Turkey Legs 143
596. Mustard Chicken Fingers 143
597. Doritos Chicken Bites 143
598. Cottage Cheese Chicken 144
599. Turkey Breast Rolls 144
600. Bahian Seasoned Chicken 144
601. Salt and Pepper Chicken Wings .144
602. Western Chicken Wings 144
603. Fiery Hasselback Chicken 145
604. Fried Chicken Livers 145
605. Juicy Turkey Legs 145
606. Ranch Taco Wings 145
607. Honey Lime Chicken wings.. ...145
608. Sriracha Chicken Wings 145
609. Thyme Turkey Nuggets 146
610. Crispy Buttered Chicken 146
611. Buttermilk Chicken 146
612. Alfredo Chicken Wings 146
613. Citrus Rosemary Chicken 146
614. Crunchy Curry Chicken Strips .146
615. Simple Spiced Chicken Legs ...147
616. Pizza Stuffed Chicken 147
617. Texas Chicken Chili 147
618. Chicken Cordon Bleu 147
619. Lunch Chicken Fajitas 148
620. Turkey Breast with Maple Mustard Glaze 148
621. Chickpea Chicken Stew 148
622. Holiday Roasted Goose 148
623. Chicken Wontons 149
624. Chicken Luncheon Salad 149

Chapter 7: Fish and Seafood 150

625. Buttered Fish Scampi 150
626. Japanese Steamed Tuna 150
627. Cheese and Crab Souffle 151
628. Lobster Wontons 151
629. Shrimp Stuffed Peppers 151
630. Coconut Tilapia 151
631. Oriental Red Snapper 152
632. Blackberry-glazed Salmon 152
633. Salmon with Avocado Sauce 152
634. Salmon in Honey Chili Sauce ..152
635. Swordfish Steak with Avocado Salsa .152
636. Mustard Salmon 153
637. Miso Trout 153
638. Turmeric Flavored Shrimps 153
639. Tuna with Olives and Spinach .153
640. Cod in Jalapeno Sauce 153
641. Shrimp & Sausage Paella 154
642. Tuna and Capers 154
643. Tuna Au Gratin 154
644. Red Hot Chili Fish Curry 154
645. Pesto and Almond Crusted Salmon .154
646. Shrimp Nuggets 155
647. Shrimp Stroganoff 155
648. Breaded Prawns 155
649. Shrimp with Palm of Hearts ...155
650. Crab Balls 156
651. Crab Pastries 156
652. Cod and Vegetable Gratin 156
653. Lemon Pepper Shrimp 156

654. Sesame Tuna Steak 157
655. Panko-Crusted Tilapia 157
656. Cod Tortilla Wraps 157
657. Mexican Fish Tacos 157
658. Coriander Shrimp Cakes 157
659. Tuna Patties 158
660. Wasabi Crab Cakes 158
661. Shrimp Egg Rolls 158
662. Buttered Baked Cod with Wine 158
663. Louisiana Catfish 159
664. Thai Fish Cake with Mango Sauce 159
665. Salmon with Carrots and Fennel 159
666. Lemongrass Tuna Steaks 159
667. Tropical Shrimps 160
668. Scallops with Spring Veggies 160
669. Cajun Shrimps 160
670. Parmesan Crusted Clams 161
671. Crispy Halibut 161
672. Honey and Sriracha Calamari 161
673. Teriyaki Halibut Steak 161
674. Steamed Salmon and Summer Greens 162
675. Asian Steamed Salmon 162
676. Sesame Cabbage & Prawns Egg
     Roll Wraps 162
677. Fish Fillet in Pesto Sauce 162
678. Ranch Fish Fillet 163
679. Herbed Fish Fingers 163
680. Spicy Steamed Mussels 163
681. Quick and Easy Lobster Tails 163
682. Cajun Lemon-Shrimp Kebabs 164
683. Tuna Niçoise Salad 164
684. Broiled Tilapia 164
685. Lemon Parmesan Halibut 164
686. Cheesy Fish Balls 165
687. Creole Veggie-Shrimp Bake 165
688. Wine Poached Clams 165
689. Taiwan Cod Fillets 165
690. Tomato Basil Tilapia 165
691. Buttered Salmon with Dill 166
692. Garam Masala Shrimps 166
693. Cajun Lobster Tails 166
694. Haddock and Spinach 167
695. Sesame Crusted White Fish 167
696. Snapper Scampi 167
697. Teriyaki Salmon Noodles 167
698. Crispy Ranch Fish Fillets 168
699. Bang Bang Shrimp 168
700. Easy Shrimp Paella 168
701. Indian Spiced Fish Fingers 168
702. Balsamic and Shallots Cod 168
703. Alaskan Cod with Apple Slaw 169
704. Almond Crusted Shrimps 169
705. Buttered Cod and Chives 169
706. Spicy Lime and Basil Clams 169
707. Cornmeal Battered Fish 169
708. Citrus Balsamic Salmon 169
709. Paprika Fish Nuggets 170
710. Dijon Mustard 'n Parmesan
     Crusted Tilapia 170
711. Drunken Skewered Shrimp,
     Tomatoes 'n Sausages 170
712. Yuzu Soy Squid 170
713. Salted Tequila 'n Lime Shrimp 171
714. Roasted Parsley Cod 171
715. Baked Cod 171
716. Garlic Parsley Scallops 171
717. Spicy Vinegar Prawns 171
718. Halibut with Eggs and Veggies 172
719. Air-fried Green Herbs Scallop 172
720. Mustard Tuna Cakes 172
721. Hot Bacon Shrimps 172
722. Creamy Baked Cod 173
723. Fresh Shrimp Salad 173
724. Salmon with Kohlrabi and Asparagus 173
725. Asian Style Chicken Strips
     with Asparagus 174
726. Oriental Shrimps 174

727. Trout with Butter Sauce 174
728. Tuna Stuffed Potatoes 174
729. Flying Fish 175
730. Pistachio Crusted Salmon 175
731. Quick and Easy Air-fried Catfish 175
732. Tomato Parchment Cod 175
733. Oreganata Clams 175
734. Ahi Tuna Steaks 176
735. Hake in Creamy Red Pepper Sauce 176
736. Hake Fillet with Green Salad 176
737. Fish Sticks with Chili Ketchup Sauce 176
738. Baked Seafood Gratin 177
739. Shrimp Fajitas 177
740. Sea Bass and Fennel 177
741. Horseradish Salmon 177
742. Oriental Shrimp Fried Rice 177
743. Shrimp Mac and Cheese 178
744. Great Air-Fried Soft-Shell Crab 178
745. Salmon Rice Pilaf 178
746. Cajun Shrimp Boil 178
747. Crab Filled Mushrooms 178
748. Tuna Mushroom Pasta 179
749. Garlic Chili Fried Fish 179
750. Sea Bay Tilapia 179
751. Quick Crab Sticks 179
752. Italian Grilled Sardines 179
753. Caramelized Ginger Salmon 180
754. Sea Salt Salmon 180
755. Breaded Hake 180
756. Potato Fish Cakes 180
757. Prosciutto Wrapped Ahi Ahi 180
758. Prosciutto Wrapped Tuna Bites 181
759. Black Pepper Flounder 181
760. Buttered Crab Legs 181
761. Foil Packet Salmon 181
762. Parmesan Butter Flounder 181
763. Salmon & Eggs 182
764. Red Chili Mackerel 182
765. Buttered Thyme Scallops 182
766. Xinyan Cod 182
767. Delicious Red Mullet 182
768. Grilled Turbot 182
769. Citrusy Branzini on the Grill 183
770. Cheesy Breaded Salmon 183
771. Rice Flour Shrimps 183
772. Sriracha and Honey Calamari 183
773. 3-Ingredient Air Fryer Catfish 183
774. Creamy Air Fryer Salmon 183
775. Barbecued Lime Shrimp 184
776. Spicy Air-Fried Cheese Tilapia 184
777. Pesto Scallops 184
778. Dijon Fish Fillets 184
779. Steamed Clams 184
780. Shrimp A La Boom 184
781. Portuguese Bacalao Tapas 185
782. Creamy Coconut Sauce on
     Jamaican Salmon 185
783. Garlic and Black Pepper Shrimp Grill 185
784. Salmon with Lemon-Parsley Relish 185
785. Fried Stuffed Oysters on the Half Shell
     with Crawfish Stuffing 186
786. Hawaiian Salmon 186
787. Cod with Grape and Fennel Relish 186
788. Mahi Mahi in Dill Lemon Sauce 186
789. Crab Rangoon 186
790. Scallops Gratin 187
791. Pesto Fish Pie 187
792. Tuna Melt Croquettes 187

**Chapter 8: Snacks, Sandwiches &
     Savory Breads** 188

793. Pub Burgers 188
794. Buffalo Chicken Sliders 188
795. Bacon Pizza 189
796. Mexican Style Pizza 189
797. Paprika Sweet Potato Chips 189
798. Cheddar Muffins 189

799. Kale Chips 189
800. Mediterranean Turkey Burgers 190
801. Spiced Mixed Nuts 190
802. Tomato Quick Bread 190
803. Beef Jerky 190
804. Hawaiian Pork Sliders 190
805. Beef and Blue Cheese Burgers 191
806. Hoisin Turkey Burgers 191
807. Pepperoni Chips 191
808. Caramel Popcorn 191
809. Chicken Sandwich 191
810. Mushroom Pizza 192
811. Herbed Pork Burgers 192
812. Ham Pinwheels 192
813. Sunflower Seed Bread 192
814. Bow Tie Chips 193
815. Dinner Rolls 193
816. Shrimp Po'boy 193
817. Smoked Bacon Bread 193
818. Mushroom Pie 194
819. Cheese and Tuna Sandwich 194
820. Spicy Beet Chips 194
821. Zucchini Chips 194
822. Apple Chips 194
823. Spiced Edamame 194
824. Cajun Peanuts 195
825. Vegan Cornbread 195
826. Taro Chips 195
827. Lime and Garlic Tortilla Chips 195
828. English Muffin Tuna Sandwiches 195
829. Rosemary Sweet Potato Chips 196
830. Salted Corn Nuts 196
831. Fish Finger Sandwich 196
832. Honey BBQ Bacon Sandwiches 196
833. Korean Burgers 197
834. Garlic Cheese Bread 197
835. Pizza Hot Dog Buns 197
836. Philly Chicken Stromboli 197
837. Chicken and Avocado Sliders 198
838. Cheddar and Mustard Twists 198
839. Basil Keto Crackers 198
840. Paprika Pickle Chips 198
841. Cornbread with Pulled Pork 198
842. Spicy Cheese Crisps 199
843. Chickpea Cauliflower Tacos 199
844. Chili Cheese Curds 199
845. Orange Turkey Burgers 199
846. Cheese Vegan Sandwich 200
847. Smoked Paprika Pumpkin Seeds 200
848. Vegetable Tuna Melt 200
849. Veggie Pita 200
850. Green Vegetable Pizza 200
851. Salmon Nachos 201
852. Turkey Quesadillas 201
853. Salmon Jerky 201
854. Creamy Salmon Pie 201
855. Pizza Egg Rolls 202
856. Chicken Skin Crisps 202
857. Rustic Mushroom and Pork Burgers 202
858. Guilt-free Sloppy Joes 202
859. Croque Monsieur 203
860. Pita Pizza 203
861. Mexican Fish Quesadilla 203
862. Beef Empanadas 204
863. Pulled BBQ Beef Sandwiches 204
864. Indian Brunch Wrap 204
865. Greek Spinach Parcels 205
866. Polenta Pie 205
867. Black Bean Burger with Garlic-Chipotle 205
868. Spiced Veggie Burger 205
869. Basil and Garlic Crackers 205
870. Lamb Burgers 206
871. Mexican Chicken Burgers 206
872. Mixed Vegetable Chips 206
873. Chocolate Banana Chips 206
874. Healthy Turkey Lettuce Wraps 207
875. Ranch Pretzels 207

876. Dehydrated Strawberries 207
877. Chili Cheese Sandwich 207
878. Cranberry Spinach Turnovers 207
879. Mushroom Toast with Ginger and Sesame 208
880. Thai Style Pizza 208
881. Green Tomato BLT 208
882. Cheese-stuffed Burgers 209
883. Flax Mozza Wraps 209
884. Chives and Lamb Burgers 209
885. Kohlrabi Chips 209
886. Sourdough Bread 210
887. BBQ Vegetable Sandwich 210
888. Fruit Soft Tacos 210
889. Hummus Mushroom Pizza 210
890. Burger Taco Wrap 211
891. Smoky Cheeseburgers 211
892. Cinnamon Roasted Chickpeas 211
893. Taco Bell Crunch Wrap 211
894. Brussel Sprout Pizza 212
895. Tofu Crunch Wraps 212
896. Chili Cheese Dogs 212
897. Chicken Jerky 212
898. Mushroom Chips 212
899. Pear Chips 213
900. Honey Mango Slices 213
901. Dried Pineapple Chunks 213
902. Dried Dragon Fruit Chips 213
903. Candied Pecans 213
904. Meatloaf Wraps 213
905. Shrimp Grilled Cheese Sandwich 213
906. Fried Pork Quesadilla 214
907. Spicy Shrimp Pizza 214
908. All Meat Pizza 214
909. Waffle Cheese Fries 215
910. Creole Jalapeno Coins 215
911. Apple Turkey Burgers 215
912. Creamy Mushroom Pie 215
913. Cheese and Spinach Muffins 215
914. Zucchini Yogurt Bread 216
915. Cream Cheese and Sausage Biscuits 216
916. Eggs Benedict 216
917. Parmesan and Scallion Sandwich 216
918. Portobello Pesto Burgers 217
919. Brunch Mini Sliders 217
920. Air Fryer Sausage Wraps 217
921. Bacon and Brown Sugar Little Smokies . 217
922. Garlic Cheese Bread 217
923. Potato Bread Rolls 217
924. Grilled Gruyere Cheese Sandwich 218
925. Mozzarella -Spinach Stuffed Burgers 218
926. Flax Chips 218
927. Cheesy-Bacon Stuffed Pastry Pie 218
928. Fish Chicharron 219
929. Homemade Peanut Corn Nuts 219
930. Roasted Lima beans 219
931. Garlic Mozzarella Sticks 219
932. Seasoned Pork Rinds 219
933. Chocolate-Covered Maple Bacon 219
934. Dehydrated Candied Bacon 220
935. Taco Flavored Kale Chips 220
936. Ranch Flavored Kale Chips 220
937. Corn Dogs 220
938. Spiced Lentils Nibblers 220
939. Chia Seed Crackers 221
940. Baked Eggplant Chips 221
941. Toasted Coconut Flakes 221
942. Buttered Bagels 221
943. Salt Roasted Hazelnuts 221
944. Cheddar Mustard Toast 221
945. Yam Chips 222
946. Roasted Pine nuts 222
947. Cheesy Beef Puffs 222
948. Pao de Queijo 222
949. Mac and Cheese Toast 222
950. Classic Tortilla Pizza 222
951. Pizza Margherita 223

952. Hawaiian Pizza 223
953. Bacon and Cheese Popcorn 223
954. Kalamata Mozzarella Pita Melts 223
955. Squash and Zucchini Mini Pizza 223
956. Seven-Layer Tostadas 224
957. Morning Pizza 224
958. Honey Ham and Cheese Bagels 224
959. Jackfruit Taquitos 224
960. Keto Air Bread 225
961. Tomato Cake 225
962. Avocado Cinnamon Bread 225
963. Quinoa Burger 225
964. Chick Fil A Burgers 226
965. Classic Cheese Pizza 226
966. Breaded Deviled Eggs 226
967. Garlic Cheese Rolls 227
968. Provolone Egg Sandwich 227
969. Simple Shredded Beef Tacos 227
970. Cheesy Grape Pizza 227
971. Cashew Masala 227
972. Cajun Snack Mix 228
973. Apple and Ham Panini 228
974. Kenny Rogers Corn Muffins 228
975. Mini Sweet Corn Pakodas 228

Chapter 9: Desserts 229

976. Lemon Blueberry Cake 229
977. Pomegranate and Chocolate Bars 230
978. Red Wine Pears 230
979. Peanut Butter Custard 230
980. Chocolate Peanut Butter and Jelly S'mores 230
981. Creamy Leche Flan 230
982. Marbled Cheesecake 231
983. Peanut Butter and Chocolate Cupcakes ... 231
984. Low Sugar Spiced Plums 231
985. Raspberries and Avocado Cake 231
986. Dessert Fries 231
987. Deep Fried Cookie Dough Balls 232
988. Dark Chocolate Muffins 232
989. Fudgy Brownies 232
990. Low-fat Mug Cake 232
991. Stuffed Apples with Vanilla Sauce 232
992. Strawberry Cream cheese Chimichangas 233
993. S'mores 233
994. Fried Oreos 233
995. Cinnamon Fried Bananas 233
996. Soft Doughnuts 234
997. Vanilla Bread Pudding 234
998. Semolina Milk Cake 234
999. Snow White's Cake 234
1000. Caramel Muffins 235
1001. Cinnamon Churros 235
1002. Chocolate Oatmeal Cookies 235
1003. Cashew Cookies 235
1004. Apricot Nutmeg Muffins 236
1005. Sugar Free Coconut Cookies 236
1006. Moist Chocolate Cake 236
1007. Healthy Pecan Brownies 236
1008. Best Carrot Cake 236
1009. Autumn Pumpkin Cake 237
1010. Chocolate Zucchini Bread 237
1011. Moist Date Bread 237
1012. Cherry Pie 237
1013. Chocolate Chip Muffins 238
1014. Tropical Bananas 238
1015. Apple Cider Donuts 238
1016. Sugar Free Cheesecake 239
1017. Sesame Banana Dessert 239
1018. Flourless Chocolate Coconut Cupcakes ..239
1019. Lemon Sugar Cookies 239
1020. Irish Butter Cookies 240
1021. PB & J Doughnuts 240
1022. Zebra Cake 240
1023. Roasted Pears 240
1024. Chocolate and Ricotta Cake 241
1025. Cardamom Tapioca Pudding 241

1026. Chia Blackberry Jam 241
1027. Apple Dumplings 241
1028. Banana Fritters 241
1029. Chocolate Walnut Cake 241
1030. Moist Vanilla Cupcake 242
1031. Lemon Chiffon Cake 242
1032. Honey Pineapples 242
1033. Pink Champagne Cupcakes 242
1034. Pumpkin Muffins 243
1035. Apple Fries with Caramel 243
1036. Cinnamon Peaches 243
1037. Apple Crumble 243
1038. Raisin and Cranberry Beignet 244
1039. Vanilla Almond Cookies 244
1040. Latte Crème Brûlée 244
1041. Pecan Pie 244
1042. Cream and Coconut Cups 244
1043. Mixed Berries and Lemon Crumble 245
1044. Citrus Sponge Cake 245
1045. Black and White Brownies 245
1046. Salted Caramel Beignets 245
1047. Raspberry Cream Rolls 246
1048. Angel Cake 246
1049. Blueberry Turnovers 246
1050. Leche Flan 247
1051. Mint Baked Alaska 247
1052. Coconut Chocolate Fondue 247
1053. Sweet Pumpkin Cream 248
1054. Mixed Berries Cream Puffs 248
1055. Holiday Gingerbread Cake 248
1056. Triple Berry Pavlova 248
1057. Chocolate Chip Cookies 249
1058. Sweet Potato Dessert 249
1059. Lime Cheesecake 249
1060. Vanilla Oat Sandwiches 250
1061. Blueberry Cheesecake 250
1062. Sweet Potato Cheesecake 250
1063. Nutmeg Apple Jam 250
1064. Currant and Plum Tarts 251
1065. Red Velvet Cupcakes 251
1066. Fruity Oreo Cupcakes 251
1067. Raspberry Cupcakes 251
1068. Baked Apples 252
1069. White and Black Brownies 252
1070. Cocoa Banana Brownies 252
1071. Apple Empanadas 252
1072. Sweetened Plantains 253
1073. Coffee Cake 253
1074. Chocolate Smarties Cookies 253
1075. Tangy Lemon Mousse 253
1076. Fudgy Nutella Brownies 253
1077. Toffee Cookies 254
1078. Marshmallow Turnovers 254
1079. Soft Sugar Cookies 254
1080. Lemon Pound Cake 254
1081. Strawberry Souffle 255
1082. Puff Pastry Pears 255
1083. Vanilla Strawberry Mix 255
1084. Apricot Blackberry Crumble 255
1085. Lemon Cupcakes 255
1086. Quick Oatmeal Cake 256
1087. Vanilla Crème Brulee 256
1088. Baked Almond Donuts 256
1089. Coconut Caramel Cream 256
1090. Autumn Pumpkin Pie 257
1091. Tropical Rice Pudding 257
1092. Rich Chocolate Pudding 257
1093. Spiced Orange Slices 257
1094. Cinnamon Pear Crisps 257
1095. Spiced Mandarin and Apple Sauce 257
1096. Coconut-Coated White Chocolate Cookies 258
1097. Vegan Chocolate Vanilla Bars 258
1098. Coconut Raspberry Bars 258
1099. Sweet Blueberry Jam 258
1100. Chocolate Avocado Pudding 258
1101. Autumn Fruit Bowl 258

1102. Summer Fruit Bowl 259
1103. Zesty Strawberry Jam 259
1104. Cream Cheese Stuffed Strawberries........259
1105. Sweet Grape and Pear Compote..............259
1106. Peanut Butter Bars...................................259
1107. Cinnamon Cappuccino Muffins 259
1108. Dark Rum Cake 260
1109. Toffee Apple Upside-Down Cake...........260

1110. Creamy Vanilla Berry Mini Pies 260
1111. Tangerine Cake 260
1112. Sweet Walnut Fritters 261
1113. Chocolate Chip Bread 261
1114. Soft Cinnamon Donuts........................... 261
1115. Double-Dipped Mini Cinnamon Biscuits 261
1116. Peach Hand Pies..................................... 262
1117. Moist Banana Bread................................ 262

1118. Banana Foster 262
1119. Middle Eastern Toast and Milk 262
1120. Spiced Pears with Honey Lemon Ricotta 263
1121. Lemon Tart Macaroons 263

Conclusion 264

Index 265

INTRODUCTION

An Air Fryer serves you fried crispy food, but it does not fry the food; instead, it cooks it through an entirely different heating mechanism. When it comes to cooking quality food, you cannot take risks; you know all about the appliance you are using. It is worth mentioning here that various Air fryer models are now available, and each varies in size and control settings according to its brand.

In general, an Air Fryer consists of:

- *The Cooking Chamber*: This is the actual chamber where the cooking takes place. The difference between various models usually comes in the form of holding capacity. Some air fryers have the capacity to hold two cooking baskets, while some can hold only one.
- *Heating Element:* The heating element of an air fryer is the coil inside the fryer that produces the heat once electricity passes through it. Once the heating element reaches the desired temperature, the air is passed through this coil, where it gets heated up and is passed towards the fan and grill.
- *Exhaust System:* The exhaust system of an air fryer is responsible for maintaining a stable internal pressure and preventing the buildup of any harmful air. Some air fryer models tend to have a filter installed with the exhaust that cleans the exhausting air, freeing it from any harmful particles or unpleasant odors.
- *Transferable Food Tray:* The food tray is also known as the cooking basket. This is where you place the food in the air fryer to be cooked. Some newer models of air fryers tend to include a cooking basket with multiple walls built inside. This makes the cooking baskets much more versatile and allows the users to cook multiple items in one go. Some models even include a universal handle that allows the cooking basket to be easily handled.

Air Fryer Basket and the Fryer Drawer:

The cooking chamber in the Air Fryer is just an empty space in which a removable drawer is placed. This drawer is used to add food to the air fryer while handling it with ease. This drawer has a handle on the outside and a pull-out button on top of the handle to press and pull; otherwise, it keeps locked and fixed in the Air Fryer. The food is not directly placed in the drawer; rather, an air fryer basket is placed in the drawer in which the food is placed. The basket has a porous base that allows the hot air to pass through the food easily. The basket is removable and washable as well. You can also use and place other cooking accessories in this basket, like:

- Baking pan
- Casserole dish
- Ramekins
- Air fryer rack

Control Panel and Control dials:

There is a control panel that is present on the front top portion of an air fryer. This control panel is usually designed to allow better control over the time and temperature settings of the machine. There are two control dials present on the panel:

- The temperature dial:

The temperature dial can be used to increase or decrease the temperature values on the control panel display. You can select any value from 175 F to 400 F.

- The timer dial:

The timer dial is used to increase or decrease the cooking time according to the need. Usually, there is a 60-minutes timer dial fixed on any Air fryer.

Then there is a control panel display, which shows the cooking operations. It has different lights to represent different functions. For instance, there are usually:

- RED LIGHT: To indicate that the machine is working.
- BLUE LIGHT: To indicate that the heating or cooking function is over.

Note: These are commonly found features in almost all Air fryers. There are a number of other side or optional features that are available in different and new models of Air fryers, which are not discussed here.

What Kind of Meals Can You Prepare?

Air Fryers were first launched to provide oil-free crispy food to people looking for low-fat meals. But as the air fryers came more widely in use, new and better uses of the Air fryers came to light. As of today, there are a variety of options on the menu that you can cook in your air fryer, which may include:

- All Crispy Snacks: Rolls, fries, fat bombs, crisps, etc.
- Breakfast Meals: frittata, bread, omelet, bacon, sausages, etc.
- Seafood and Fish: Coated crispy cod, salmon, shrimp, etc.
- Poultry and Meat: steaks, chops, drumettes, chicken wings, etc.
- Vegetables Sides and Mains: Crispy broccoli, Brussel sprouts, cauliflower florets, potato cups, zucchini boat, etc.
- Desserts and Fruits: muffins, souffle, dried fruits, cookies, biscuits, etc.

CHAPTER 1: BREAKFAST

1.   Breakfast Spinach Quiche

Preparation Time: 10 minutes
Cooking Time: 15 minutes
Servings: 2

Ingredients:
- 3 tbsp heavy whipping cream
- Non-stick cooking spray
- ½ cup feta cheese
- 4 large eggs
- 2 cups coarsely chopped spinach leaves
- Salt and ground black pepper to taste

Directions:
- Preheat an air fryer to 350°F. Use non-stick spray to coat a 6-inch cake pan.
- In a mixing dish, whisk together eggs and cream. Combine spinach, feta cheese, salt, and pepper in a large mixing bowl until thoroughly blended. Cover securely with foil after pouring into the prepared cake pan.
- Air-fry for 10 minutes. Remove foil and continue air-frying for 2 to 4 minutes longer, or until the top begins to brown.

2.   Strawberry Dutch Pancakes

Preparation Time: 15 minutes
Cooking Time: 15-20 minutes
Servings: 4

Ingredients:
- 2 (scant) tbsp unsalted butter
- 3 eggs
- ½ cup flour
- ½ cup milk
- ½ tsp vanilla
- 1½ cups sliced fresh strawberries
- 2 tbsp powdered sugar

Directions:
- Set to 380°F Bake. The baking pan will need to be sprayed with a non-stick spray. Put in the butter and let it melt. Now, the eggs, milk, flour, and vanilla must be combined well until it is mixed well and frothy.
- Once done, get the basket from the fryer and ensure all the parts are covered with butter. Pour the batter, then bring it back to the fryer to cook. Let it cook for around 12-16 minutes or until the pancake is golden brown and puffed.

3. Cheesy Tomato and Egg

Preparation Time: 10 minutes
Cooking Time: 20 minutes
Servings: 4

Ingredients:

- 2 tomatoes
- 4 eggs
- 1 cup mozzarella cheese, shredded
- Salt and pepper to taste
- 1 tbsp olive oil
- A few basil leaves

Directions:

- Preheat your air fryer to 360°F. Cut each tomato into two halves and place them in a bowl. Season with salt and pepper. Place cheese around the bottom of the tomatoes and add the basil leaves. Break one egg into each tomato slice. Garnish with cheese and drizzle with olive oil. Set the temperature to 360°F and bake for 20-minutes.

4. Mexican Waffles

Preparation Time: 15 minutes
Cooking Time: 20 minutes
Servings: 4

Ingredients:

- 1 ½ cups almond flour
- 3 eggs
- 2 tsp. dried basil
- 2 tsp. dried parsley
- Salt and pepper to taste
- 3 tbsp. Butter
- 1 cup pickled Jalapeño
- 1 cup green olives
- 1 cup black olives
- 2 tbsp. salsa

Directions:

- Preheat the air fryer to 250°F.
- In a small bowl, mix the ingredients, except the Jalapeños.
- Take a waffle shape and grease it with butter. Pour the batter and cook till both sides have browned.
- Top with Jalapeños.

5. Egg and Bacon Pie

Preparation Time: 20 minutes
Cooking Time: 30 minutes
Servings: 6

Ingredients:

- 1 ½ cup plain flour
- 3 tbsp. unsalted butter
- 2 tbsp. powdered sugar
- 2 cups cold water
- 1 tbsp. sliced cashew
- **Filling:**
- 1 cup scrambled egg
- 8 slices bacon
- 3 tbsp. butter

Directions:

- Mix the first four ingredients together to create a dough.
- Roll the batter out into 2 large circles.
- Press one circle into the pie tin and prick the sides with a fork.
- Cook the filling ingredients over low heat and pour them into the tin.
- Cover the pie tin with the second circle.
- Preheat the air fryer to 300°F for 5 minutes. Cook until golden brown, then let it cool.
- Slice and serve with a dab of cream.

6. Healthy Banana Pancakes

Preparation Time: 10 minutes
Cooking Time: 15-20 minutes
Servings: 6

Ingredients:

- 4 ripe bananas (shredded)
- 1 ½ cups almond flour
- 3 eggs
- 2 tsp. cinnamon
- Salt and pepper to taste
- 3 tbsp. Butter

Directions:

- Preheat the air fryer to 250°F.
- In a small bowl, combine the ingredients. Mix well.
- Cook till both sides of the pancake has browned.
- Serve with maple syrup.

7. Egg and Bacon Muffins

Preparation Time: 10 minutes
Cooking Time: 30 minutes
Servings: 6

Ingredients:

- 6 eggs, lightly beaten
- 1 tbsp fresh parsley, chopped
- 1/4 tsp dry mustard powder
- 1/4 cup coconut milk
- 2 tbsp green onion, chopped
- 4 bacon slices, cooked and crumbled
- Pepper
- Salt

Directions:

- Spray a muffin tray with cooking spray and set aside.
- In a bowl, whisk eggs with coconut milk, mustard, pepper, and salt until well combined.
- Add bacon, green onion, and parsley to the egg mixture and whisk well.
- Pour the egg mixture into the silicone muffin molds and place it in an air fryer basket. Place basket in the air fryer.
- Seal the pot with an air fryer basket and select bake mode, and cook at 375°F for 20-25 minutes.
- Serve and enjoy.

8. Oat and Vanilla Pudding

Preparation Time: 15 minutes
Cooking Time: 15-20 minutes
Servings: 4

Ingredients:

- 2 cups vanilla powder
- 2 cups milk
- 1 cup oats
- 2 tbsp. custard powder
- 3 tbsp. powdered sugar
- 3 tbsp. unsalted butter

Directions:

- Heat the milk and sugar and add the custard powder, then oats and vanilla powder and mix till you get a thick blend.
- Preheat the air fryer to 300°F for 5 minutes.
- Place the dish in the fryer and lower the temperature to 250°F.
- Cook for ten minutes and set aside to cool.

9. Tropical French Toast

Preparation Time: 10 minutes
Cooking Time: 5 minutes
Servings: 1

Ingredients:

- 2 slices of gluten-free bread
- 1/2 cup shredded coconut
- 1 tbsp baking powder
- 1/2 cup coconut milk
- Maple syrup

Directions:

- In a large bowl, mix coconut milk and baking powder.
- Spread shredded coconut on a baking sheet.
- Dip each piece of bread in coconut milk, then dredge in shredded coconut.
- Place covered bread in the air fryer bin and air fry at 175°C for 4 minutes.
- Top with maple syrup.

10. Mushroom Frittata

Preparation Time: 15 minutes
Cooking Time: 10 minutes
Servings: 4-6

Ingredients:

- 8 eggs
- ½ cup heavy cream
- Salt and black pepper to taste
- 2 cups mushrooms, sliced
- 1 red onion, chopped
- ½ cup tomatoes, diced
- 1 cup mozzarella cheese, shredded
- 2 tsp fresh parsley for garnishing

Directions:

- Preheat the air fryer to 330°F. Grease a baking dish that fits in your air fryer with cooking spray.
- In a bowl, whisk the eggs, and add in heavy cream, mushrooms, onion, tomatoes, mozzarella cheese, salt, and pepper. Mix to combine. Pour the mixture into the baking dish and cook in the air fryer for 8 minutes, or until the eggs are set. Sprinkle with parsley and cut into wedges to serve.

11. Cheese and Broccoli Quiche

Preparation Time: 20 minutes
Cooking Time: 15 minutes
Servings: 4

Ingredients:

- 4 eggs
- 1 cup whole milk
- 2 cups broccoli florets, steamed
- 2 tomatoes, diced
- 1 steamed carrot, diced
- ¼ cup feta cheese, crumbled
- 1 cup cheddar cheese, grated
- Salt and pepper to taste
- 1 tsp chopped parsley
- 1 tsp dried thyme

Directions:

- In a bowl, beat the eggs with parsley, salt, pepper, and thyme. Add the milk gradually and whisk until a pale mixture is attained.
- In a quiche dish, add carrots and broccoli. Put the tomatoes on top, then the feta, and finish with half of the cheddar cheese. Pour the egg mixture over the layering and top with the remaining cheddar cheese. Place the dish in the air fryer and cook at 350°F for 14 minutes. Serve sliced.

12. Egg and Sausage Casserole

Preparation Time: 20 minutes
Cooking Time: 15 minutes
Servings: 6

Ingredients:

- 1 lb. ground sausages
- 6 eggs
- 1 red pepper, diced
- 1 green pepper, diced
- 1 yellow pepper, diced
- 1 sweet onion, diced
- 2 cups cheddar cheese, shredded
- Salt and black pepper to taste
- 2 tbsp fresh parsley, chopped

Directions:

- Place a skillet over medium heat on a stovetop, add the sausages, and cook until brown, turning occasionally. Once done, drain any excess fat derived from cooking and set it aside.
- Arrange the sausages on the bottom of a greased casserole dish that fits in your air fryer. Top with onion, red pepper, green pepper, and yellow pepper. Sprinkle the cheese on top.
- In a bowl, beat the eggs with salt and pepper. Pour the mixture over the cheese. Place the casserole dish in the air fryer basket and bake at 360°F for 15 minutes. Serve warm, garnished with fresh parsley.

13. German Pancakes

Preparation Time: 15 minutes
Cooking Time: 12-16 minutes
Servings: 4

Ingredients:

- 3 eggs, beaten
- 2 tbsp butter, melted
- 1 cup flour
- 2 tbsp sugar, powdered
- ½ cup milk
- 1 cup fresh strawberries, sliced

Directions:

- Preheat the air fryer to 330°F. In a bowl, mix flour, milk, and eggs until fully incorporated. Grease a baking pan that fits in your air fryer with the butter and pour in the mixture.
- Place the pan in the air fryer's basket and Air Fry for 12-16 minutes until the pancake is fluffy and golden brown. Drizzle powdered sugar and arrange sliced strawberries on top to serve.

14. Kale and Cottage Cheese Omelet

Preparation Time: 10 minutes
Cooking Time: 10 minutes
Servings: 3

Ingredients:

- 5 eggs
- 3 tbsp cottage cheese
- 1 cup kale, chopped
- ½ tbsp basil, chopped
- ½ tbsp fresh parsley, chopped
- Salt and black pepper to taste

Directions:

- Beat the eggs, salt, and pepper in a bowl. Stir in the rest of the ingredients. Pour the mixture into a greased baking pan and fit in the air fryer. Bake for 10 minutes at 330°F until slightly golden and set.

15. Cheese Scones

Preparation Time: 30 minutes
Cooking Time: 20 minutes
Servings: 4

Ingredients:

- 1 cup flour
- A pinch of salt
- 1 tsp baking powder
- 2 oz butter, cubed
- 1 tsp fresh chives, chopped
- 1 egg
- ¼ cup milk
- ½ cup cheddar cheese, shredded

Directions:

- Preheat the air fryer to 360°F. Sift flour in a bowl and add in butter, baking powder, and salt; mix until a breadcrumb mixture is formed. Add cheese, chives, milk, and egg, and mix to get a sticky dough. Roll the dough into small balls. Place the balls in the frying basket and Air Fry for 20 minutes. Serve warm.

16. Egg Muffins

Preparation Time: 10 minutes
Cooking Time: 15 minutes
Servings: 4

Ingredients:

- 4 eggs
- 2 tbsp olive oil
- 3 tbsp milk
- 3 ounces white flour
- 1 tbsp baking powder
- 2 ounces parmesan, grated
- A splash of Worcestershire sauce

Directions:

- In a bowl, mix egg with flour, oil, baking powder, milk, Worcestershire, and parmesan, whisk well and divide into 4 silicone muffin cups. Arrange cups in your air fryer's cooking basket, cover, and cook at 392°F for 15 minutes. Serve warm for breakfast. Enjoy!

17. Kale Egg Muffins

Preparation Time: 10 minutes
Cooking Time: 35 minutes
Servings: 6

Ingredients:

- 5 eggs
- 1/2 cup coconut milk
- 2 tbsp sausage, sliced
- 2 tbsp kale, chopped
- 2 tbsp sun-dried tomatoes, chopped
- Pepper
- Salt

Directions:

- In a bowl, put in all the ingredients and whisk until well combined.
- Pour the egg mixture into the silicone muffin molds and place it in an air fryer basket. Place basket in the pot.
- Seal the pot with an air fryer basket and select bake mode, and cook at 350°F for 30-35 minutes.
- Serve and enjoy.

18. Zucchini Muffins

Preparation Time: 10 minutes
Cooking Time: 20 minutes
Servings: 6

Ingredients:

- 4 eggs
- 1 tbsp parsley, chopped
- 1/2 cup baby spinach, chopped
- 1/2 red bell pepper, diced
- 1/8 cup green onion, chopped
- 6 bacon slices, cooked and crumbled
- 1 small zucchini, sliced
- 1/8 cup coconut milk
- 1/2 tbsp olive oil
- Pepper
- Salt

Directions:

- Heat olive oil in a pan.
- Add parsley, spinach, green onion, red bell pepper, and sauté until spinach is wilted.
- In a bowl, whisk eggs with coconut milk, pepper, and salt.

- Add sautéed vegetables, bacon, and zucchini to the egg mixture and stir well.
- Into the silicone muffin molds, pour the egg mixture, and place it in an air fryer basket. Place basket in the pot.
- Seal the pot with an air fryer basket and select bake mode, and cook at 350°F for 20 minutes.
- Serve and enjoy.

19.   Breakfast Quinoa

Preparation Time: 10 minutes
Cooking Time: 5-10 minutes
Servings: 4

Ingredients:

- 1/2 cup walnuts, soaked and chopped
- 4 ounces sesame seeds, soaked
- 2 ounces hemp seeds, soaked overnight
- 1 tsp date sugar
- 1/2 tsp ground cinnamon
- 5 ounces quinoa puff
- 1 tsp hemp seed oil
- 1 cup of coconut milk

Directions:

- Take a bowl and mix in all the seeds and spices
- Add hemp seed oil
- Stir well until the mixture is thick
- Flatten the mixture on your cooking basket
- Preheat your Air Fryer to 330°F.
- Transfer to your Air fryer and cook for 2-3 minutes until light brown
- Transfer mix to a serving bowl
- Add quinoa puff, stir well and add coconut milk stir again
- Serve and enjoy!

20.   Cauliflower and Avocado Toast

Preparation Time: 15 minutes
Cooking Time: 10-15 minutes
Servings: 2

Ingredients:

- ¼ cup cauliflower
- ½ cup shredded mozzarella cheese
- 1 large egg.
- 1 ripe medium avocado
- ½ tsp. garlic powder.
- ¼ tsp. ground black pepper

Directions:

- Cook the cauliflower as per the package directions. Remove from bag and squeeze excess moisture out using cheesecloth or a clean towel.
- In a large mixing basin, combine cauliflower, egg, and cheddar. Cut a parchment paper sheet to the size of your air fryer basket. Divide the cauliflower mixture in half and arrange it on the parchment paper in two mounds. Form the cauliflower mounds into a 1/4-inch-thick rectangle. Insert the parchment paper into the air fryer basket.
- Preheat the oven to 400°F and set the timer for 8 minutes.
- Halfway through the cooking time, flip the cauliflower.

- Remove the paper and let the cauliflower cool for 5 minutes after the timer goes off.
- Remove the pit from the avocado by slicing it in half. Scoop out the insides and mash them with garlic powder and pepper in a medium bowl. Spread the mixture over the cauliflower.

21.   Fennel Frittata

Preparation Time: 15 minutes
Cooking Time: 10-15 minutes
Servings: 6

Ingredients:

- 1 fennel bulb; shredded
- 6 eggs; whisked
- 2 tsp. Cilantro; chopped.
- 1 tsp. sweet paprika
- Cooking spray
- A pinch of salt and black pepper

Directions:

- Take a bowl and mix all the ingredients except the cooking spray and stir well.
- Grease a baking pan with the cooking spray, pour the frittata mix, and spread well
- Put the pan in the Air Fryer and cook at 370°F for 15 minutes. Divide between plates and serve them for breakfast.

22.   Zucchini Gratin

Preparation Time: 15 minutes
Cooking Time: 24 minutes
Servings: 6

Ingredients:

- 1 large egg, lightly beaten
- 1 1/4 cup unsweetened almond milk
- 3 medium zucchinis, sliced
- 1 tbsp Dijon mustard
- 1/2 cup nutritional yeast
- 1 tsp sea salt

Directions:

- Preheat the air fryer to 370°F.
- Arrange zucchini slices in the air fryer baking dish.
- In a saucepan, heat almond milk over low heat and stir in Dijon mustard, nutritional yeast, and sea salt. Add beaten egg and whisk well.
- Pour sauce over zucchini slices.
- The dish must be put in the air fryer and let cook for 20-24 minutes.
- Serve and enjoy.

23.   Breakfast Broccoli Muffins

Preparation Time: 20 minutes
Cooking Time: 20-24 minutes
Servings: 6

Ingredients:

- 2 large eggs
- 1 cup broccoli florets, chopped
- 1 cup unsweetened almond milk
- 2 cups almond flour
- 1 tsp baking powder

- 2 tbsp nutritional yeast
- 1/2 tsp sea salt

Directions:
- Preheat the air fryer to 325°F.
- In a bowl, put in all the ingredients and mix until well combined.
- Pour the mixture into the silicone muffin molds and place them into the air fryer basket.
- Cook muffins for 20-24 minutes.
- Serve and enjoy.

24.   Tomato Frittata

Preparation Time: 10 minutes
Cooking Time: 15 minutes
Servings: 2

Ingredients:
- 1 cup egg whites
- 1/4 cup tomato, sliced
- 2 tbsp coconut milk
- 2 tbsp chives, chopped
- 1/4 cup mushrooms, sliced
- Pepper
- Salt

Directions:
- Preheat the air fryer to 320°F.
- In a bowl, whisk together all ingredients.
- Spray the air fryer baking pan with cooking spray.
- Pour the egg mixture into the prepared pan and place it in the air fryer.
- Cook frittata for 15 minutes.
- Serve and enjoy.

25.   Onion and Cheese Omelet

Preparation Time: 5 minutes
Cooking Time: 10 minutes
Servings: 2

Ingredients:
- 2 eggs
- 2 tbsp. grated cheddar cheese
- 1 tsp. soy sauce
- 1/2 onion, sliced
- 1/4 tsp. pepper
- 1 tbsp. olive oil

Directions:
- Whisk the eggs along with the pepper and soy sauce.
- Preheat the air fryer to 350°F.
- Heat the olive oil and add the egg mixture and the onion.
- Cook for 8 to 10 minutes.
- Top with the grated cheddar cheese.

26.   Perfect Scrambled Eggs

Preparation Time: 10 minutes
Cooking Time: 6 minutes
Servings: 2

Ingredients:
- 4 eggs
- 1/4 tsp garlic powder

- 1/4 tsp onion powder
- 1 tbsp parmesan cheese
- Pepper
- Salt

Directions:
- Whisk eggs with garlic powder, onion powder, parmesan cheese, pepper, and salt.
- Pour the egg mixture into the air fryer baking dish.
- The dish must be put in the air fryer and let cook at 360°F for 2 minutes. Stir quickly and cook for 3-4 minutes more.
- Stir well and serve.

27.   Tofu Omelet

Preparation Time: 10 minutes
Cooking Time: 10 minutes
Servings: 2

Ingredients:
- 3 eggs, lightly beaten
- ¼ cup onion, chopped
- 2 tbsp green onion, chopped
- 2 tbsp soy sauce
- 1 tsp cumin
- 1 tsp coriander
- 1 /4 cup tofu, cubed
- Pepper
- Salt

Directions:
- Add all ingredients into the large bowl and stir until well combined.
- Spray the air fryer baking pan with cooking spray.
- Pour bowl mixture into the prepared baking pan and place into the air fryer.
- Cook at 400°F for 10 minutes.
- Serve and enjoy.

28.   Coconut Cream Cheese Pancakes

Preparation Time: 10 minutes
Cooking Time: 5-10 minutes
Servings: 1

Ingredients:
- ½ cup coconut flour
- 1 ⅕ tsp baking powder
- ¼ tsp baking soda
- 1 ⅕ tbsp sugar
- ½ cup low-fat milk
- 1 egg
- ⅕ tsp vanilla extract
- 1 ½ tbsp butter, melted

Directions:
- While mixing the pancake batter, preheat the air fryer to 330°F.
- Sift together the flour, baking powder, and soda in a large mixing basin.
- Add the sugar and stir to combine. Place aside.
- Combine the milk, egg, vanilla, and butter in a mixing bowl.
- Whisk the milk-flour mixture until smooth.

- Spray four 4-inch round springform pans lightly with oil. Fill each tin with 1/2 cup batter and set it on the air fryer tray.
- Cook for 10 to 12 minutes in the air fryer. Allow the pancakes to rest for 2-3 minutes in the pan before removing and cooling on a cooling rack.
- Now serve the pancakes with a drizzle of maple syrup and fresh berries on top.

29.   Florentine Eggs

Preparation Time: 15 minutes
Cooking Time: 10 minutes
Servings: 4

Ingredients:
- ¼ cup heavy cream
- 1 tbsp unsalted butter
- 6 ounces baby spinach, chopped
- 2 tbsp minced white onion
- 4 slices of Canadian bacon
- 4 large eggs
- 2 ounces aged cheddar, grated
- Salt and pepper to taste

Directions:
- Preheat the Air Fryer to 280°F.
- Butter 4 (about 6-ounce) ramekins and set aside.
- In a frying pan over medium heat, melt 1 tbsp of butter. Season the onion with pepper-salt and sauté until cooked, about 2 minutes. Cook until the spinach has wilted.
- Layer Canadian bacon, spinach, and onions on the bottom of each ramekin.
- Fill each ramekin with 1 tbsp of heavy cream and crack an egg into each.
- Distribute the cheese evenly among the ramekins.
- Bake in the Air Fryer, monitoring every minute until the whites are set, but the yolks are still liquid.
- Serve with buttered sourdough bread.

30.   Sausage Quiche

Preparation Time: 15 minutes
Cooking Time: 30 minutes
Servings: 4

Ingredients:
- 12 large eggs
- 1 cup heavy cream
- 1 tsp black pepper
- 12 oz sugar-free breakfast sausage
- 2 cups shredded cheddar cheese

Directions:
- Preheat your air fryer to 375°F/190°C.
- In a large bowl, whisk the eggs, heavy cream, salad, and pepper together.
- Add the breakfast sausage and cheddar cheese.
- Pour the mixture into a greased casserole dish.
- Bake for 25 minutes.
- Cut into 12 squares and serve hot.

31.   Smoked Salmon Omelet

Preparation Time: 10 minutes
Cooking Time: 10 minutes
Servings: 2

Ingredients:
- 3 eggs
- 1 smoked salmon
- 3 links pork sausage
- ¼ cup onions
- ¼ cup provolone cheese

Directions:
- Whisk the eggs and pour them into a skillet.
- Follow the standard method for making an omelet.
- Add the onions, salmon, and cheese before turning the omelet over.
- Sprinkle the omelet with cheese and serve with the sausages on the side.
- Serve!

32.   Creamy Risotto

Preparation Time: 20 minutes
Cooking Time: 35 minutes
Servings: 2

Ingredients:
- 1 onion, diced
- 2 cups chicken stock, boiling
- ½ cup parmesan OR cheddar cheese, grated
- 1 clove of garlic, minced
- ¾ cup Arborio rice
- 1 tbsp. olive oil
- 1 tbsp. unsalted butter

Directions:
- Set the Air Fryer at 390°F for 5 minutes to heat up.
- With oil, grease a round baking tin, small enough to fit inside the fryer, and stir in the garlic, butter, and onion.
- Transfer the tin to the Air Fryer and allow it to cook for 4 minutes. Add in the rice and cook for a further 4 minutes, giving it a stir three times throughout the cooking time.
- Turn the fryer down to 320°F and add in the chicken stock before gently mixing it. Leave to cook for 22 minutes with the fryer uncovered. Before serving, throw in the cheese and give it one more stir. Enjoy!

33.   Veggie Toast

Preparation Time: 15 minutes
Cooking Time: 15 minutes
Servings: 4

Ingredients:
- 4 slices bread
- 1 red bell pepper, cut into strips
- 1 cup sliced button or cremini mushrooms
- 1 small yellow squash, sliced
- 2 green onions, sliced
- 1 tbsp. olive oil
- 2 tbsp. softened butter
- ½ cup soft goat cheese

Directions:

- Drizzle the Air Fryer with the olive oil and pre-heat to 350°F.
- Put the red pepper, green onions, mushrooms, and squash inside the fryer give them a stir and cook for 7 minutes, shaking the basket once throughout the cooking time. Ensure the vegetables become tender.
- Remove the vegetables and set them aside.
- Spread some butter on the slices of bread and transfer to the Air Fryer, butter side-up. Brown for 2 to 4 minutes.
- Remove the toast from the fryer and top with goat cheese and vegetables. Serve warm.

34.   Avo-Eggs

Preparation Time: 5 minutes
Cooking Time: 10 minutes
Servings: 2

Ingredients:

- 2 large avocados, sliced
- 1 cup breadcrumbs
- ½ cup flour 2 eggs, beaten
- ¼ tsp. paprika
- Salt and pepper to taste

Directions:

- Pre-heat your Air Fryer at 400°F for 5 minutes.
- Sprinkle some salt and pepper on the slices of avocado. Optionally, you can enhance the flavor with a half-tsp of dried oregano.
- Lightly coat the avocados with flour. Dredge them in the eggs before covering them with breadcrumbs. Transfer to the fryer and cook for 6 minutes.

35.   Mixed Vegetable Frittata

Preparation Time: 20 minutes
Cooking Time: 30 minutes
Servings: 6

Ingredients:

- ¼ cup milk
- 1 zucchini
- ½ bunch asparagus
- ½ cup mushrooms
- ½ cup spinach or baby spinach
- ½ cup red onion, sliced
- 4 eggs
- ½ tbsp. olive oil
- 5 tbsp. feta cheese, crumbled
- 4 tbsp. cheddar, grated
- ¼ bunch of chives, minced
- Sea salt and pepper to taste

Directions:

- In a bowl, mix together the eggs, milk, salt, and pepper.
- Cut up the zucchini, asparagus, mushrooms, and red onion into slices. Shred the spinach using your hands.
- Over medium heat, stir-fry the vegetables for 5 – 7 minutes with the olive oil in a non-stick pan.
- Place some parchment paper in the base of a baking tin. Pour in the vegetables, followed by the egg mixture. Top with the feta and grated cheddar.
- Set the Air Fryer at 320°F and allow it to warm for five minutes.

- Transfer the baking tin to the fryer and allow to cook for 15 minutes. Take care when removing the frittata from the Air Fryer and leave to cool for 5 minutes.
- Top with the minced chives and serve.

36.   Peanut Oats and Chia Porridge

Preparation Time: 10 minutes
Cooking Time: 5 minutes
Servings: 4

Ingredients:

- 4 cups milk
- 2 tbsp. peanut butter
- 2 cups oats
- 1 cup chia seeds
- 4 tbsp. honey
- 1 tbsp. butter, melted

Directions:

- Preheat the Air Fryer to 390°F.
- Put the peanut butter, honey, butter, and milk in a bowl and mix together using a whisk. Add in the oats and chia seeds and stir.
- Transfer the mixture to a fryer-proof bowl that is small enough to fit inside the fryer and cook for 5 minutes. Give another stir before serving.

37.   Nutmeg Cranberry Scones

Preparation Time: 5 minutes
Cooking Time: 10 minutes
Servings: 4

Ingredients:

- 1 cup of fresh cranberries
- ⅓ cup of sugar
- One tbsp of orange zest
- ¾ cup of half and half cream
- 2 cups of flour
- ¼ tsp of ground nutmeg
- ¼ tsp of salt
- ¼ cup of butter, chilled and diced
- ¼ cup of brown sugar
- One tbsp of baking powder
- One egg

Directions:

- Set an Air fryer to 365°F for 10 minutes. Strain nutmeg, flour, baking powder, salt, and sugar in a bowl. Blend in the cream and egg. Fold in the orange zest and cranberries to form a smooth dough. Roll the dough and cut it into scones. Place the scones on the cooking tray. Insert the cooking tray in the Air fryer when it displays "Add Food." Flip the sides when it shows "Turn Food." Remove from the oven when cooking time is complete. Serve warm.

38.   Egg and Ham Cups

Preparation Time: 15 minutes
Cooking Time: 15 minutes
Servings: 2

Ingredients:

- 4 large eggs.
- 4: 1-oz. slices deli ham

- ½ cup shredded medium Cheddar cheese.
- ¼ cup diced green bell pepper.
- 2 tbsp. Diced red bell pepper.
- 2 tbsp. Diced white onion.
- 2 tbsp. Full-fat sour cream.

Directions:
- Place one slice of ham on the bottom of four baking cups.
- Take a large bowl, whisk eggs with sour cream. Stir in green pepper, red pepper, and onion
- Pour the egg mixture into ham-lined baking cups. Top with Cheddar. Place cups into the air fryer basket. Adjust the temperature to 320°F and set the timer for 12 minutes or until the tops are browned. Serve warm.

39. Breakfast Stuffed Poblanos

Preparation Time: 30 minutes
Cooking Time: 15-20 minutes
Servings: 2

Ingredients:
- ½ lb. spicy ground pork breakfast sausage
- 4 large poblano peppers
- 4 large eggs.
- ½ cup full-fat sour cream.
- 4 oz. full-fat cream cheese
- ¼ cup diced tomatoes and green chiles, drained
- 8 tbsp. shredded pepper jack cheese

Directions:
- On a heated pan, brown the sausage that has been ground and let it cook until there's no more pink in color. Take it out and remove excess fat. Put the eggs in the same pan, and cook them like scrambled eggs.
- Place cooked sausage in a large bowl and fold in cream cheese. Mix in diced tomatoes and chiles. Gently fold in eggs
- Cut a 4"–5" slit in the top of each poblano, removing the seeds and white membrane with a small knife. Separate the filling into four and spoon carefully into each pepper. Top each with 2 tbsp. pepper jack cheese.
- Place each pepper into the air fryer basket. Adjust the temperature to 350°F and set the timer for 15 minutes. The cheese is golden brown, and the peppers will be soft when the mixture is done. Now, serve it with sour cream on top.

40. Bell Pepper Eggs

Preparation Time: 20 minutes
Cooking Time: 15 minutes
Servings: 4

Ingredients:
- 4 medium green bell peppers
- ¼ medium onion; peeled and chopped
- 3 oz. cooked ham; chopped
- 8 large eggs.
- 1 cup mild Cheddar cheese

Directions:
- Cut the tops off each bell pepper. Remove the seeds and the white membranes with a small knife. Place ham and onion into each pepper

- Crack 2 eggs into each pepper. Top with ¼ cup cheese per pepper. Place into the air fryer basket
- Adjust the temperature to 390°F and set the timer for 15 minutes. When fully cooked, peppers will be tender, and eggs will be firm. Serve immediately.

41. French Toast Sticks

Preparation Time: 10 minutes
Cooking Time: 5 minutes
Servings: 4

Ingredients:
- 4 bread, sliced into sticks
- 2 tbsp soft butter or margarine
- 2 eggs, gently beaten
- Salt, to taste
- 1 pinch cinnamon
- 1 pinch nutmeg
- 1 pinch of ground cloves

Directions:
- Preheat the Air fryer to 365°F and grease an Air fryer pan with butter.
- Whisk eggs with salt, cinnamon, nutmeg, and ground cloves in a bowl.
- Dip the bread in the egg mixture and place it in the pan.
- Cook for about 5 minutes, flipping in between, and remove from the air fryer.
- Dish out and serve warm.

42. Sweet Potato Hash

Preparation Time: 10 minutes
Cooking Time: 15 minutes
Servings: 6

Ingredients:
- 2 large sweet potatoes, cut into small cubes
- 2 slices of bacon, cut into small pieces
- 2 tbsp olive oil
- 1 tbsp smoked paprika
- 1 tsp sea salt
- 1 tsp ground black pepper
- 1 tsp dried dill weed

Directions:
- Preheat the Air Fryer to 400°F and grease an Air fryer pan.
- Mix together sweet potato, bacon, olive oil, paprika, salt, black pepper, and dill in a large bowl.
- Transfer the mixture into the preheated air fryer pan and cook for about 15 minutes, stirring in between.
- Dish out and serve warm.

43. Cornflakes and Blackberries

Preparation Time: 5 minutes
Cooking Time: 10 minutes
Servings: 3

Ingredients:
- 3 cups milk
- 1/4 cup blackberries
- 2 eggs; whisked
- 1 tbsp. sugar

- 1/4 tsp. nutmeg; ground
- 4 tbsp. cream cheese; whipped
- 1½ cups corn flakes

Directions:

- In a bowl, mix all ingredients and stir well.
- Heat up your air fryer at 350°F, add the corn flakes mixture, spread, and cook for 10 minutes. Divide between plates, serve and enjoy

44. Cinnamon Apple Pancakes

Preparation Time: 20 minutes
Cooking Time: 15 minutes
Servings: 4

Ingredients:

- 1¾ cups white flour
- 1 cup apple; peeled, cored, and chopped.
- 1¼ cups milk
- 1 egg; whisked
- 2 tbsp. sugar
- 2 tsp. baking powder
- 1/4 tsp. vanilla extract
- 2 tsp. cinnamon powder
- Cooking spray

Directions:

- In a bowl, mix all ingredients: except cooking spray and stir until you obtain a smooth batter
- Grease your air fryer's pan with the cooking spray and pour in 1/4 of the batter; spread it into the pan.
- Cover and cook at 360°F for 5 minutes, flipping it halfway
- Repeat steps 2 and 3 with 1/4 of the batter 3 more times, and then serve the pancakes right away.

45. Super Cheesy Hash Browns

Preparation Time: 20 minutes
Cooking Time: 20 minutes
Servings: 6

Ingredients:

- 1½ lbs. hash browns
- 6 bacon slices; chopped.
- 8 oz. cream cheese; softened
- 1 yellow onion; chopped.
- 6 eggs
- 6 spring onions; chopped.
- 1 cup cheddar cheese; shredded
- 1 cup almond milk
- A drizzle of olive oil
- Salt and black pepper to taste

Directions:

- Heat up your air fryer with the oil at 350°F. In a bowl, mix all other ingredients except the spring onions and whisk well
- Add this mixture to your air fryer, cover, and cook for 20 minutes
- Divide between plates, sprinkle the spring onions on top, and serve.

46. Pear and Walnut Oatmeal

Preparation Time: 10 minutes
Cooking Time: 12 minutes
Servings: 2

Ingredients:

- 1 cup milk
- 1/4 cups brown sugar
- 1/2 cup walnuts; chopped.
- 2 cups pear; peeled and chopped.
- 1 cup old fashioned oats
- 1/2 tsp. cinnamon powder
- 1 tbsp. butter; softened

Directions:

- In a heat-proof bowl that fits your air fryer, mix all ingredients and stir well. Place in your fryer and cook at 360°F for 12 minutes. Divide into bowls and serve

47. Cheesy Ham Pastries

Preparation Time: 20 minutes
Cooking Time: 10 minutes
Servings: 8

Ingredients:

- 8 ham slices; chopped.
- 4 handfuls of mozzarella cheese; grated
- 1 puff pastry sheet
- 4 tsp. mustard

Directions:

- Roll out puff pastry on a working surface and cut it into 12 squares. Divide cheese, ham, and mustard on half of them and top with the other halves and seal the edges
- Place all the patties in your air fryer's basket and cook at 370°F for 10 minutes. Divide the patties between plates and serve

48. Healthy Carrot Oatmeal

Preparation Time: 5 minutes
Cooking Time: 15 minutes
Servings: 3

Ingredients:

- 2 cup steel-cut oats
- 2 cups almond milk
- 1 cup carrots; shredded
- 2 tsp. sugar
- 1 tsp. cardamom; ground
- Cooking spray

Directions:

- Spray your air fryer with cooking spray, add all ingredients, toss and cover. Cook at 365°F for 15 minutes. Divide into bowls and serve

49. Herbed Omelet

Preparation Time: 10 minutes
Cooking Time: 15 minutes
Servings: 4

Ingredients:

- 6 eggs; whisked
- 2 tbsp. parmesan cheese; grated

- 4 tbsp. heavy cream
- 1 tbsp. Parsley; chopped.
- 1 tbsp. Tarragon; chopped.
- 2 tbsp. Chives; chopped.
- Salt and black pepper to taste

Directions:

- In a bowl, mix all ingredients except for the parmesan and whisk well. Pour this into a pan that fits your air fryer, place it in the preheated fryer and cook at 350°F for 15 minutes
- Divide the omelet between plates and serve with the parmesan sprinkled on top

50.   Vanilla Steel Cut Oats

Preparation Time: 5 minutes
Cooking Time: 17 minutes
Servings: 2

Ingredients:

- 1 cup steel-cut oats
- 1 cup milk
- 2½ cups water
- 2 tsp. vanilla extract
- 2 tbsp. brown sugar

Directions:

- In a pan that fits your air fryer, mix all ingredients and stir well. Place the pan in your air fryer and cook at 360°F for 17 minutes. Divide into bowls and serve

51.   Milky French Toast

Preparation Time: 15 minutes
Cooking Time: 5 minutes
Servings: 2

Ingredients:

- 1 egg
- 4 bread slices
- 1 tsp vanilla extract
- 2 tbsp milk
- 1 tbsp sugar
- 2 tsp butter

Directions:

- Beat the egg in the bowl and whisk it until smooth.
- Then mash the butter with the help of the spoon.
- Add the vanilla extract to the mashed butter.
- After this, sprinkle the whisked egg with milk and sugar. Stir it until sugar is dissolved.
- After this, spread the bread slices with the mashed butter mixture from both sides.
- Put the bread slices in the egg-milk mixture and let them soak all the egg liquid.
- Preheat the air fryer to 400°F.
- Transfer the bread slices to the air fryer rack.
- Cook the toasts for 2 minutes from one side.
- After this, turn the bread slices to another side and cook for 3 minutes more.
- Cut the cooked toasts into triangles.
- Enjoy!

52.   Creamy Bacon Omelet

Preparation Time: 10 minutes
Cooking Time: 30 minutes
Servings: 4

Ingredients:

- 2 eggs
- 3 tbsp heavy cream
- 3 bacon slices
- ¼ tsp oregano
- 1 pinch salt
- ¼ tsp cayenne pepper
- 1 tsp butter
- 1 oz fresh dill, chopped

Directions:

- Crack the eggs into the mixing bowl and whisk them.
- Then pour the heavy cream and keep whisking the mixture for 30 seconds more.
- Preheat the air fryer to 360°F.
- Place the bacon slices on the air fryer rack and cook it for 5 minutes from each side.
- When the bacon is cooked – chill it a little and chop.
- Then sprinkle the egg mixture with the oregano, salt, cayenne pepper, and chopped dill.
- Spread 2 muffin molds with the butter.
- Pour the egg mixture there.
- Sprinkle it with the chopped bacon.
- Preheat the air fryer to 360°F.
- Cook the omelet for 14 minutes.
- When the meal is cooked – let it chill a little.
- Enjoy

53.   Mixed Berries Oatmeal

Preparation Time: 10 minutes
Cooking Time: 30 minutes
Servings: 2

Ingredients:

- ½ cup milk
- 1 egg
- 1 tsp vanilla extract
- 3 tbsp brown sugar
- 6 tbsp oatmeal
- 1 pinch salt
- 1 oz blackberry
- 1 oz strawberry
- 1 oz raspberry
- 1 pinch of ground cinnamon
- 1 tsp honey
- 1 tsp butter

Directions:

- Crack the egg into the bowl and whisk it.
- Add the salt, vanilla extract, and milk. Stir it carefully.
- Then combine the oatmeal and ground cinnamon together. Add the brown sugar and stir it.
- Combine the blackberries, strawberries, and raspberries in the bowl. Shake them a little.
- Put the oatmeal in the air fryer basket.
- Then pour the egg mixture and add berries.
- Preheat the air fryer to 370°F and cook the meal for 30 minutes.

- When the oatmeal is cooked – add butter and honey.
- Mix it up and serve.

54.   Paprika Egg Souffle

Preparation Time: 5 minutes
Cooking Time: 5 minutes
Servings: 2

Ingredients:
- 3 eggs
- 2 tbsp heavy cream
- 1 pinch salt
- ¼ tsp paprika
- ¼ tsp ground turmeric

Directions:
- Preheat the air fryer to 360°F.
- Crack the eggs into the bowl and whisk them.
- Add the heavy cream.
- Then sprinkle the egg mixture with salt, paprika, and ground turmeric.
- Stir it carefully.
- Pour the egg mixture into 2 ramekins.
- Put the ramekins in the air fryer basket and cook the soufflé for 5 minutes.
- When the soufflé is cooked – chill it for 3 minutes.
- Enjoy!

55.   Cheesy Zucchini Frittata

Preparation Time: 10 minutes
Cooking Time: 15 minutes
Servings: 2

Ingredients:
- 1 zucchini
- 3 oz. Cheddar cheese, shredded
- 1 pinch salt
- ½ white onion, diced
- 2 eggs
- 2 tbsp milk
- ¼ tsp paprika
- ¼ tsp butter

Directions:
- Cut the zucchini into the strips and combine them with the diced onion.
- Preheat the air fryer to 360°F and toss butter there.
- When the butter is melted – put the zucchini mixture in the air fryer basket.
- Cook the zucchini mixture for 8 minutes.
- Meanwhile, beat the eggs in the bowl and whisk them.
- Add the salt, paprika, and milk. Stir it.
- When the time is over – pour the egg mixture into the air fryer and stir it.
- Cook the frittata for 5 minutes at 360°F.
- Then add the shredded cheese and cook it for 5 minutes more at 370°F.
- Serve the cooked frittata immediately.

56.   Breakfast Egg Sandwich

Preparation Time: 10 minutes
Cooking Time: 8 minutes
Servings: 2

Ingredients:
- 4 slices of sandwich bread
- 4 eggs
- 1 pinch salt
- 1 tsp dried dill
- ¼ tsp dried oregano
- 1 tsp butter

Directions:
- Make the holes in the sandwich bread slices.
- Preheat the air fryer to 360°F.
- Melt the butter and put the bread slices in the air fryer basket.
- Then beat the eggs in the bread holes.
- Sprinkle the eggs with the dried dill, salt, and dried oregano.
- Cook the eggs in holes for 5 minutes.
- After this, turn the eggs into holes on another side and cook for 2 minutes more.
- Serve the cooked meal hot.
- Enjoy!

57.   Chorizo Parmesan Rolls

Preparation Time: 10 minutes
Cooking Time: 11 minutes
Servings: 2

Ingredients:
- 3 oz puff pastry
- 3 oz chorizo
- 1 tbsp fresh parsley
- 1 tsp tomato sauce
- 2 oz Parmesan, shredded
- 1 tsp butter
- ¼ tsp ground thyme

Directions:
- Roll the puff pastry.
- Spread it with the tomato sauce and sprinkle it with the shredded cheese.
- Then chop the fresh parsley and put it over the cheese.
- After this, sprinkle the dough with the ground thyme.
- Chop the chorizo and add it to the dough too.
- Roll the dough and cut it into 4 small rolls.
- Melt the butter.
- Brush the rolls with the butter.
- Preheat the air fryer to 365°F.
- Put the chorizo rolls on the air fryer rack and cook them for 11 minutes.
- When the meal is cooked – serve it immediately.

58.   Queso Crumpets

Preparation Time: 30 minutes
Cooking Time: 12 minutes
Servings: 2

Ingredients:
- 2 oz. Queso Fresco
- 2 tbsp milk
- 3 tbsp flour
- ¼ tsp sugar
- 1 pinch of dried yeast
- ¼ tsp butter

- 2 oz. Cheddar cheese, shredded

Directions:
- Melt Queso Fresco and preheat the milk.
- Combine the ingredients together and stir until you get a smooth mixture.
- Then combine flour, sugar, and yeast in the bowl.
- Start to add the milk mixture gradually.
- Stir it constantly.
- Leave the mixture for 10 minutes in a warm place.
- After this, add shredded Cheddar cheese and stir it.
- Melt the butter and add it to the dough too.
- Stir it well and leave it for 5 minutes more.
- Then pour the smooth dough into the ramekins.
- Preheat the air fryer to 370°F.
- Put the ramekins in the air fryer basket and cook for 12 minutes.
- When the crumpets are cooked – they will still be soft but with a crunchy surface.
- Let the crumpets chill a little.

59. Parmesan Egg Clouds

Preparation Time: 8 minutes
Cooking Time: 4 minutes
Servings: 2

Ingredients:
- 2 egg whites
- ¼ tsp olive oil
- ¼ tsp salt
- 1 oz Parmesan, shredded

Directions:
- Pour the egg whites into the bowl and mix them with the help of the hand mixer for 3 minutes or till you get the stiff peaks.
- Add salt and stir gently.
- Preheat the air fryer to 400°F.
- Spray the air fryer basket with the olive oil inside.
- Then make the medium clouds from the egg whites and place them in the air fryer basket.
- Cook the egg whites' clouds for 3 minutes. Then sprinkle the meal with the shredded cheese and cook for 1 minute more.
- When the egg whites' clouds are cooked – chill them to room temperature and serve.

60. Breakfast Egg Puffs

Preparation Time: 15 minutes
Cooking Time: 15 minutes
Servings: 4

Ingredients:
- 4 Eggs
- 1 tsp taco seasoning
- ½ tsp Baking powder
- 2 tbsp Parmesan cheese, grated
- 2 tbsp Onion, minced
- 1 tbsp Bell pepper, diced
- 1 small tomato, diced
- ½ cup Squash puree
- 1 tbsp Cornstarch

Directions:
- Spray 4 ramekins with cooking spray and set aside. In a mixing bowl, whisk eggs with the remaining ingredients until well combined. Pour egg mixture into the prepared ramekins. Place the dehydrating tray into the multi-level air fryer basket and place the basket into the air fryer. Place ramekins on the dehydrating tray. Seal the pot with the air fryer lid. Select bake mode and cook at 380°F for 15 minutes or until set. Serve.

61. Breakfast Hash

Preparation Time: 20 minutes
Cooking Time: 30 minutes
Servings: 4

Ingredients:
- 1 Sweet potato, diced
- 2 tbsp Olive oil
- 1 tsp thyme
- 2 tsp Garlic powder
- ½ tsp Black pepper
- 1 Onion, diced
- 2 medium potatoes, diced
- Pepper & salt, to taste

Directions:
- Add all sweet potatoes and potatoes into the mixing bowl. Add remaining ingredients and toss well. Add sweet potato mixture into the multi-level air fryer basket and place the basket into the air fryer. Seal pot with air fryer lid. Select air fry mode and cook at 400°F for 30 minutes. Stir 2-3 times. Serve.

62. Peanut Butter Muffins

Preparation Time: 30 minutes
Cooking Time: 16 minutes
Servings: 6

Ingredients:
- 1 Egg
- ¼ cup Peanut butter
- ¼ cup Sugar
- 6 tbsp Yogurt
- 1 cup Rolled oats
- 1 Banana
- ¼ tsp Baking soda
- ½ tsp Baking powder
- ½ tsp Vanilla
- Pinch of salt

Directions:
- Add all ingredients into the blender and blend until a smooth batter is formed. Pour batter into the 6 silicone muffin molds. Place the dehydrating tray into the multi-level air fryer basket and place the basket into the air fryer. Place muffin molds on the dehydrating tray. Seal the pot with the air fryer lid. Select bake mode and cook at 380°F for 16 minutes or until set. Serve.

63. Greek Egg Muffins

Preparation Time: 20 minutes
Cooking Time: 20 minutes
Servings: 3

Ingredients:

- 2 Eggs
- 4 Egg whites
- ¼ cup Feta cheese, crumbled
- 1 tbsp Fresh parsley, chopped
- ¼ cup Olives, diced
- ¼ cup Onion, diced
- ¼ cup Tomatoes, diced
- ½ cup Milk
- Pepper & salt, to taste

Directions:

- In a mixing bowl, whisk eggs, egg whites, milk, pepper, and salt. Add remaining ingredients and stir well. Pour egg mixture into the 6 silicone muffin molds. Place the dehydrating tray into the multi-level air fryer basket and place the basket into the air fryer. Place 6 muffin molds on the dehydrating tray. Seal pot with air fryer lid. Select bake mode and cook at 350°F for 20 minutes. Serve.

64. Sausage Balls

Preparation Time: 20 minutes
Cooking Time: 15 minutes
Servings: 6

Ingredients:

- 4 oz. Ground sausage meat
- ½ tsp Garlic, minced
- 1 tsp Sage
- 3 tbsp Breadcrumbs
- 1 Small onion, chopped
- Pepper & salt, to taste

Directions:

- In a bowl, put in all the ingredients and mix until well combined.
- Make small balls from the meat mixture and place them into the multi-level air fryer basket and place the basket into the air fryer. Seal pot with air fryer lid. Select air fry mode and cook at 360°F for 15 minutes. Serve.

65. Strawberry Parfait

Preparation Time: 10 minutes
Cooking Time: 40 minutes
Servings: 4

Ingredients:

- 2 cups Strawberries
- 2 tbsp Turbinado sugar
- 2 cups Greek yogurt
- 2 tbsp Honey
- ¼ cup granola

Directions:

- Set the air fryer at 400°F. In an air fryer basket, place parchment paper and add the strawberries and 2 tbsp of turbinado sugar. Warm for 8 minutes.
- Meanwhile, in a mixing bowl, add 2 cups of greek yogurt and 2 tbsp of honey and mix well.
- Now for serving in a glass, pour one layer of yogurt mixer, then strawberries, then granola
- Repeat until you have the desired number of layers. Enjoy warm so as to preserve the crunch of the granola.

66. Churro-Banana Oats

Preparation Time: 5 minutes
Cooking Time: 10 minutes
Servings: 2

Ingredients:

- For the churros:
- 1 large yellow banana, peeled, cut in half lengthwise, then cut in half widthwise
- 2 tbsp whole-wheat pastry flour (see Substitution Tip)
- ⅛ tsp sea salt
- 2 tsp oil (sunflower or melted coconut)
- 1 tsp water
- Cooking oil spray (refined coconut, sunflower, or safflower)
- 1 tbsp coconut sugar
- ½ tsp cinnamon
- For the oatmeal:
- ¾ cup rolled oats
- 1½ cups water
- Nondairy milk of your choice (optional)

Directions:

- To make the churros:
- Place the 4 banana pieces in a medium-size bowl and add the flour and salt. Stir gently. Add the oil and water. Stir gently and evenly mixed. You may need to press some of the coatings onto the banana pieces.
- Spray the air fryer basket with the oil spray. Place the banana pieces in the air fryer basket and fry at 350°F for 5 minutes. Remove, gently turn over, and cook for another 5 minutes (or until nicely browned).
- In a medium bowl, add the coconut sugar and cinnamon and stir to combine. When the banana pieces are nicely browned, spray with the oil and place in the cinnamon-sugar bowl. Toss gently with a spatula to coat the banana pieces with the mixture.
- To make the oatmeal:
- While the bananas are cooking, make your oatmeal. In a medium pot, bring the oats and water to a boil, then reduce to low heat. Simmer, often stirring, until all of the water is absorbed, about 5 minutes. Place the oatmeal into two bowls. If desired, pour a small amount of non-dairy milk on top (but not too much, or the banana pieces will get soggy when you add them).
- Top your oatmeal with the coated banana pieces and serve immediately

67. Super Nutty French Toast

Preparation Time: 20 minutes
Cooking Time: 10 minutes
Servings: 4

Ingredients:

- 1 cup (99g) of rolled oats
- 1 cup (113g) of pecans or nut of your choice
- 2 tbsp (12g) of ground flax seed
- 1 tsp (2g) of ground cinnamon
- 8 pieces of whole-grain vegan bread, regular or cinnamon raisin (use gluten-free bread)
- ¾ cup of non-dairy milk (plain or vanilla)
- maple syrup, for serving

Directions:
- Build the topping by combining your food processor with the oats, nuts, flaxseed, and cinnamon, and pulse until it looks similar to bread crumbs. Don't overmix. Pour into a shallow pan that is wide enough to dip the slices of your bread in.
- In a second container, add the non-dairy milk, then soak one or two pieces of bread for about 15 seconds, and turn and soak the other side. You don't want to let it go long enough to get mushy.
- Place the amount that fits in your air fryer basket at once, without overlapping. Cook for 3 minutes at 350°F, then flip over the bread and cook for 3 more minutes.
- Repeat until all of the cooked bread is coated.
- Serve with maple syrup on top.

68. Radish Hash Browns

Preparation Time: 20 minutes
Cooking Time: 15 minutes
Servings: 6

Ingredients:
- 1 pound of Radishes washed
- 1 medium of Yellow/Brown Onion
- 1 tsp of Garlic Powder
- 1 tsp of Granulated Onion Powder
- 3/4 tsp of Pink Himalayan Salt (or Sea Salt)
- 1/2 tsp of Paprika
- 1/4 tsp of Freshly Ground Black Pepper
- 1 Tbsp of Pure Virgin Coconut Oil

Directions:
- Wash the radishes, and cut off the roots. Remove the steam, and leave 1/4-1/2 inch.
- Use a food processor or mandolin, then slice the onions and radishes.
- Coconut oil is added and blends well. Grease Basket Air Fryer.
- Add Air Fryer Basket with Radishes and Onions.
- Cook for 8 minutes at 360°F, then turn a few times.
- Dump Radishes and Onions into Mixing Bowl again. Attach seasonings to the radishes and onions and cook for five minutes at 400°F, shaking halfway through.

69. Toad in the Hole

Preparation Time: 20 minutes
Cooking Time: 45 minutes
Servings: 4

Ingredients:
- 8 sausages
- 8 slices of bacon
- 100 g onion
- Thyme to taste
- Ingredients for donut dough:
- 130 g flour
- 2 g baking powder
- 1 whole egg
- 1 egg yolk
- 200 ml of milk
- 100 ml of water
- Salt to taste

- Pepper to taste

Directions:
- Prepare the donut dough. Beat all the ingredients together until you get a homogeneous mixture without lumps. Cover with the film and let stand for about 10 minutes.
- Chop the onion and pour it into the tank with the oil; Wrap each sausage with a slice of bacon and place on the onions with a few sprigs of fresh thyme. Pour 100 ml of water.
- Cook for 15 minutes at 160°C.
- Turn the sausages and cook for 10 minutes. At the end of cooking, pour the donut dough over the sausages, turn off the bottom element, and close.
- Cook for 15 to 20 minutes, depending on the degree of cooking desired.
- Serve the toad in the still-hot hole with a side sauce

70. Mozzarella and Cherry Tomato Pastries

Preparation Time: 20 minutes
Cooking Time: 30 minutes
Servings: 2

Ingredients:
- 1 roll of puff pastry
- ½ yellow pepper
- 100 g mozzarella
- 5 cherry tomatoes
- 2 eggs
- 20 g Parmesan
- 50 ml of milk
- Salt and pepper to taste

Directions:
- Beat the eggs, milk, and Parmesan in a bowl with a little salt and pepper.
- Unroll the puff pastry (leaving the baking paper) and then prick the bottom with a fork.
- Arrange the chopped mozzarella, pepper, and sliced tomatoes; pour the prepared preparation.
- Fold the edges of the dough in and cut the excess baking paper with scissors (keep the ends cut so you can easily rotate and extract the cake).
- Set the temperature to 160°C and cook another 15 minutes.
- Turn to 180°C and cook for another 12 minutes (using the baking paper).

71. Air Fried Shirred Eggs

Preparation Time: 6 minutes
Cooking Time: 14 minutes
Servings: 2

Ingredients:
- 2 tsp. butter, for greasing
- 4 eggs, divided
- 2 tbsp. heavy cream
- 4 slices ham
- 3 tbsp. parmesan cheese
- 1/4 tsp. paprika
- 3/4 tsp. salt
- 1/4 tsp. pepper
- 2 tsp. chopped chives

Directions:

- The air fryer must be heated to 320°F. Put butter in the pan and lay down the slices of ham on the pan. Then in a bowl, mix in cream, salt, one egg, and pepper. This mixture must be poured in over the slices of ham. Eggs must then be cracked, the ham then topped with parmesan cheese. Season it with paprika, then garnish with chive. Serve with bread.

72.   Breakfast Blueberry Cobbler

Preparation Time: 5 minutes
Cooking Time: 15 minutes
Servings: 2

Ingredients:

- ⅓ cup whole-wheat pastry flour
- ¾ tsp baking powder
- Dash sea salt
- ½ cup 2% milk
- 2 tbsp pure maple syrup
- ½ tsp vanilla extract
- Cooking oil spray
- ½ cup fresh blueberries
- ¼ cup store-bought granola

Directions:

- In a medium bowl, whisk the flour, baking powder, and salt. Add the milk, maple syrup, and vanilla and gently whisk just until thoroughly combined.
- Preheat the unit by selecting BAKE, setting the temperature to 350°F, and setting the time to 3 minutes. Select START/STOP to begin.
- Spray a 6-by-2-inch round baking pan with cooking oil and pour the batter into the pan. Top evenly with the blueberries and granola.
- Once the unit is preheated, place the pan into the basket.
- Select BAKE, set the temperature to 350°F, and set the time to 15 minutes. Select START/STOP to begin.
- When the cooking is complete, the cobbler should be nicely browned, and a knife inserted into the middle should come out clean. Enjoy plain or topped with a little vanilla yogurt.

73.   Mixed Berries Muffins

Preparation Time: 15 minutes
Cooking Time: 17 minutes
Servings: 8

Ingredients:

- 1⅓ cups plus 1 tbsp all-purpose flour, divided
- ¼ cup granulated sugar
- 2 tbsp light brown sugar
- 2 tsp baking powder
- 2 eggs
- ⅔ cup whole milk
- ⅓ cup safflower oil
- 1 cup mixed fresh berries

Directions:

- In a medium bowl, stir together 1⅓ cups of flour, the granulated sugar, brown sugar, and baking powder until mixed well.
- In a small bowl, whisk the eggs, milk, and oil until it is mixed well. The egg mixture will then be stirred with

the dry ingredients. The 1 tbsp of flour will be tossed with the berries, then stir it into the batter.

- Insert the crisper plate into the basket and the basket into the unit. Preheat the unit by selecting BAKE, setting the temperature to 315°F, and setting the time to 3 minutes. Select START/STOP to begin.
- Once the unit is preheated, place 4 cups into the basket and fill each three-quarters full with the batter.
- Select BAKE, set the temperature to 315°F, and set the time for 17 minutes. Select START/STOP to begin.
- After about 12 minutes, check the muffins. If they spring back when lightly touched with your finger, they are done. If not, resume cooking.
- When the cooking is done, transfer the muffins to a wire rack to cool.
- Repeat steps 6, 7, and 8 with the remaining muffin cups and batter.
- Let the muffins cool for 10 minutes before serving.

74.   Breakfast Bagels

Preparation Time: 10 minutes
Cooking Time: 10 minutes
Servings: 2

Ingredients:

- ½ cup self-rising flour, plus more for dusting
- ½ cup plain Greek yogurt
- 1 egg
- 1 tbsp water
- 4 tsp everything bagel spice mix
- Cooking oil spray
- 1 tbsp butter, melted

Directions:

- In a large bowl, using a wooden spoon, stir together the flour and yogurt until a tacky dough forms. Transfer the dough to a lightly floured work surface and roll the dough into a ball.
- Cut the dough into 2 pieces and roll each piece into a log. Form each log into a bagel shape, pinching the ends together.
- In a small bowl, whisk the egg and water. Brush the egg wash on the bagels.
- Sprinkle 2 tsp of the spice mix on each bagel and gently press it into the dough.
- Next, put the crisper plate into the basket of the fryer unit. Set the unit heat up by selecting BAKE, setting the temperature to 330°F, and setting the time to 3 minutes. Select START/STOP to begin.
- The CRISPER will need to be sprayed with a nonstick spray
- Drizzle the bagels with the butter and place them into the basket.
- Select BAKE, set the temperature to 330°F, and set the time to 10 minutes. Select START/STOP to begin.
- When the cooking is complete, the bagels should be lightly golden on the outside. Serve warm.

75.   Avocado Toast with Poached Eggs

Preparation Time: 7 minutes
Cooking Time: 10 minutes
Servings: 1

Ingredients:
- 2 eggs
- 1/2 avocado
- 2 slices bread
- 1 bunch spinach
- Pinch of salt
- Pinch of pepper

Directions:
- Preheat the air fryer oven to 350°F.
- Bring a pan of water to a boil.
- Place bread on a pan and toast it in the oven for 10 minutes. Once the water is boiling, whisk it around in a circle.
- Drop one egg in the hole and turn the heat to low, and then poach for 2 minutes.
- Repeat with the second egg.
- Mash avocado and spread it over the toast while the eggs poach.
- Add the eggs to the toast and top with spinach.

76.   Morning Burrito

Preparation Time: 15 minutes
Cooking Time: 15 minutes
Servings: 8

Ingredients:
- 16 oz. cooked bacon ends and pieces
- 16 eggs
- 1 tbsp. butter
- 8 hash brown squares
- 8 large soft flour tortillas
- 2 diced jalapeños
- 2 cups shredded sharp cheddar

Directions:
- Place bacon on a baking sheet in the air fryer oven.
- Bake at 450°F until it reaches the desired level of crispiness and set aside.
- Whisk together eggs in a bowl and set aside. Melt butter into a saucepan and mix in eggs until they start to cook but are not fully hardened.
- While eggs are cooking, microwave and cool hash brown squares. Roll out tortillas and top them with hash browns, bacon, jalapeños, and cheese.
- Wrap up the burritos and place them seam-down on a baking sheet.
- Bake at 375°F for 15 minutes

77.   Breakfast Egg Pastries

Preparation Time: 10 minutes
Cooking Time: 20 minutes
Servings: 2

Ingredients:
- ⅓ sheet frozen puff pastry, thawed
- Cooking oil spray
- ½ cup shredded Cheddar cheese
- 2 eggs
- ¼ tsp salt, divided
- 1 tsp minced fresh parsley (optional)

Directions:
- Put the crisper plate into the basket of the fryer unit. Set the unit by heating it up, select
- BAKE, setting the temperature to 390°F and setting the time to 3 minutes. Select START/STOP to begin.
- Lay the puff pastry sheet on a piece of parchment paper and cut it in half.
- The CRISPER PLATE will need to be sprayed with a nonstick spray
- Transfer the 2 squares of pastry to the basket, keeping them on the parchment paper.
- Select BAKE, set the temperature to 390°F, and set the time to 20 minutes. Select START/STOP to begin.
- After 10 minutes, use a metal spoon to press down the center of each pastry square to make a well. Divide the cheese equally between the baked pastries. Carefully crack an egg on top of the cheese, and sprinkle each with the salt. Resume cooking for 7 to 10 minutes.
- When the cooking is complete, the eggs will be cooked through. Sprinkle each with parsley (if using) and serve.

78.   Baked Eggs with Kale and Ham

Preparation Time: 10 minutes
Cooking Time: 15 minutes
Servings: 2

Ingredients:
- 2 eggs
- 1/4 tsp dried or fresh marjoram
- 2 tsp chili powder
- 1/3 tsp kosher salt
- ½ cup steamed kale
- 1/4 tsp dried or fresh rosemary
- 4 pork ham slices
- 1/3 tsp ground black pepper, or more to taste

Directions:
- Divide the kale and ham among 2 ramekins; crack an egg into each ramekin. Sprinkle with seasonings.
- Cook for 15 minutes at 335 °F or until your eggs reach desired texture.
- Serve warm with spicy tomato ketchup and pickles. Bon appétit!

79.   Chicken, Chive and Feta Frittata

Preparation Time: 10 minutes
Cooking Time: 8-10 minutes
Servings: 4

Ingredients:
- 1/3 cup Feta cheese, crumbled
- 1 tsp dried rosemary
- ½ tsp brown sugar
- 2 tbsp fish sauce
- 1 ½ cup cooked chicken breasts, boneless and shredded
- 1/2 tsp coriander sprig, finely chopped
- 3 medium-sized whisked eggs
- 1/3 tsp ground white pepper
- 1 cup fresh chives, chopped
- 1/2 tsp garlic paste
- Fine sea salt, to taste
- Nonstick cooking spray

Directions:
- Grab a baking dish that fits in your air fryer.
- Lightly coat the inside of the baking dish with a nonstick cooking spray of choice. Stir in all ingredients, minus Feta cheese. Stir to combine well.
- Set your machine to cook at 335°F for 8 minutes; check for doneness. Scatter crumbled feta over the top and eat immediately!

80.   Spinach Muffins

Preparation Time: 10 minutes
Cooking Time: 20 minutes
Servings: 8

Ingredients:
- 4 eggs
- 1/2 tsp baking powder
- 1 zucchini, grated
- 1/4 cup parmesan cheese, grated
- 1/2 cup feta cheese, crumbled
- 4 onion spring, chopped
- 1/3 cup coconut flour
- 1/4 cup butter, melted
- 4 tbsp parsley, chopped
- 1/2 tsp nutmeg
- 1/4 cup water
- 1/2 cup spinach, cooked
- 1/4 tsp pepper
- 1/4 tsp salt

Directions:
- Preheat the air fryer to 370°F.
- In a bowl, whisk together eggs, water, butter, and salt.
- Add baking soda and coconut flour and mix well.
- Add onions, nutmeg, parsley, spinach, and zucchini. Mix well.
- Add parmesan cheese and feta cheese and stir well. Season with pepper and salt.
- Pour batter into the silicone muffin molds and place in the air fryer basket.
- Cook muffins for 20 minutes.
- Serve and enjoy

81.   Vegetable Quiche

Preparation Time: 10 minutes
Cooking Time: 30 minutes
Servings: 6

Ingredients:
- 8 eggs
- 1 cup coconut milk
- 1 cup tomatoes, chopped
- 1 cup zucchini, chopped
- 1 tbsp butter
- 1 onion, chopped
- 1 cup Parmesan cheese, grated
- 1/2 tsp pepper
- 1 tsp salt

Directions:
- Preheat the air fryer to 370°F.
- Melt butter in a pan over medium heat, then add onion and sauté until onion is lightly brown.

- Add tomatoes and zucchini to the pan and sauté for 4-5 minutes.
- Transfer cooked vegetables into the air fryer baking dish.
- Beat eggs with cheese, milk, pepper, and salt in a bowl.
- Pour egg mixture over vegetables in a baking dish.
- Place dish in the air fryer and cook for 24 minutes or until eggs are set.
- Slice and serve.

82.   Cinnamon Rolls

Preparation Time: 10 minutes
Cooking Time: 10 minutes
Servings: 4

Ingredients:
- 8 oz. container crescent rolls, refrigerated
- 1 tbsp. ground cinnamon
- 2 oz. raisins
- 1/3 cup butter
- 2 tbsp. sugar, granulated
- 1/3 cup pecans, chopped
- Cooking spray (olive oil)
- Maple syrup – 2 tbsp.
- 1/3 cup brown sugar

Directions:
- In a saucepan, dissolve the butter completely. Transfer to a dish and blend the maple syrup and brown sugar.
- Layer one 8-inch pan with olive oil spray.
- Distribute the sugar into the pan and empty the raisins and pecans inside, stirring to incorporate.
- In a glass dish, whisk the sugar and ground cinnamon.
- Open the can of crescent rolls and place them on a cutting board.
- Slice the entire log of dough into eight individual pieces.
- Cover the top and bottom of the dough pieces in cinnamon and sugar, and transfer the pan to the air fryer.
- Adjust the settings to air fryer at 345°F for 5 minutes.
- Turn over the individual buns and steam for another 5 minutes.
- Take the pan out and move the buns to a serving plate.
- Drizzle the remaining sugar liquid on the buns and serve immediately.

83.   Mushroom and Leeks Frittata

Preparation Time: 10 minutes
Cooking Time: 30 minutes
Servings: 4

Ingredients:
- 6 eggs
- 6 oz mushrooms, sliced
- 1 cup leeks, sliced
- Salt

Directions:
- Preheat the air fryer to 325°F.
- Spray the air fryer baking dish with cooking spray and set aside.
- Heat another pan over medium heat. Spray pan with cooking spray.

- Add mushrooms, leeks, and salt to a pan sauté for 6 minutes.
- Break eggs in a bowl and whisk well.
- Transfer sautéed mushroom and leek mixture into the prepared baking dish.
- Pour egg over mushroom mixture.
- Place dish in the air fryer and cook for 32 minutes.
- Serve and enjoy.

84. Carrot and Potato Hash Browns

Preparation Time: 30 minutes
Cooking Time: 20 minutes
Servings: 4

Ingredients:
- 4 large potatoes, peeled, finely grated, and steamed
- 1 large carrot, peeled and finely grated
- 2 tbsp cornflour
- Salt and black pepper to taste
- 1 tsp garlic powder
- 1 tsp onion powder
- 2 tsp red chili flakes
- 2 tsp olive oil, divided

Directions:
- In a medium bowl, mix all the ingredients except the olive oil until well combined.
- Oil the inner part of a 6-inch glass casserole dish with 1 tsp of olive oil and spread in the potato mixture. Use a spoon to level the top evenly.
- Refrigerate the mixture for 20 minutes or until firm.
- After 20 minutes, insert the drip pan at the bottom rack of the device and preheat the air fryer at Air Fryer mode at 350°F for 3 to 4 minutes.
- Remove the dish from the refrigerator; divide the dough into 4 or 6 pieces and shape it into rounds.
- Grease the cooking tray with the remaining olive oil and arrange the hash browns patties on top. Fit the cooking tray on the middle rack of the oven and close the oven.
- Set the timer for 15 minutes and air fry until the timer reads to the end. Open the oven and carefully flip the hash browns. Cook further with the timer set for 6 minutes or until uniformly air fried.
- Open the lid and remove the hash browns.

85. Nutty Bread Pudding

Preparation Time: 15 minutes
Cooking Time: 30 minutes
Servings: 4

Ingredients:
- 8 slices of bread
- ½ cup buttermilk
- ¼ cup honey
- 1 cup milk
- 2 eggs
- ½ tsp vanilla extract
- 2 tbsp butter, softened
- ¼ cup sugar
- 4 tbsp raisins
- 2 tbsp chopped hazelnuts
- Cinnamon for garnish

Directions:
- Preheat the Air fryer oven to 310°F.
- Beat the eggs along with the buttermilk, honey, milk, vanilla, sugar, and butter.
- Stir in raisins and hazelnuts.
- Cut the bread into cubes and place them in a bowl.
- Pour the milk mixture over the bread. Let soak for 10 minutes. Cook the pudding for 30 minutes and garnish with cinnamon.

86. Japanese Tofu Omelet

Preparation Time: 10 minutes
Cooking Time: 10 minutes
Servings: 2

Ingredients:
- 1 small Japanese tofu, cubed
- 3 whole eggs
- Pepper to taste
- 1 tsp coriander
- 1 tsp cumin
- 2 tbsp soy sauce
- 2 tbsp green onion, chopped
- Olive oil
- 1 whole onion, chopped

Directions:
- In a bowl, mix eggs, soy sauce, cumin, pepper, oil, and salt.
- Add cubed tofu to baking forms and pour the egg mixture on top.
- Place the prepared forms in the frying basket and cook for 10 minutes at 400°F.
- Serve with a sprinkle of coriander and green onion.

87. Mini Smoked Salmon Quiche

Preparation Time: 15minutes
Cooking Time: 10 minutes
Servings: 7

Ingredients:
- 15 mini tart cases
- 4 eggs, lightly beaten
- ½ cup heavy cream
- Salt and black pepper
- 3 oz smoked salmon
- 6 oz cream cheese, divided into 15 pieces
- 6 fresh dill

Directions:
- Mix together eggs and cream in a pourable measuring container. Arrange the tarts into the basket. Pour the mixture into the tarts, about halfway up the side, and top with a piece of salmon and a piece of cheese. Cook for 10 minutes at 340°F on the Bake function; regularly check to avoid overcooking. Sprinkle with dill and serve chilled.

88. Cheddar Cheese English Muffins

Preparation Time: 20 minutes
Cooking Time: 20 minutes
Servings: 16 muffins

Ingredients:
- 4 tbsp cornmeal
- 3 to 3-1/4 cups bread flour
- 1 package (1/4 ounce) active dry yeast
- 1 tbsp sugar
- 1 tsp salt
- 2 tbsp canola oil
- 3/4 cup warm water (120° to 130°)
- 1/2 cup shredded cheddar cheese
- 1 egg
- 1 tbsp cider vinegar

Directions:
- Mix 2 cups of flour, yeast, salt, and sugar in a large mixing basin. Mix in the water and oil for 2 minutes on medium speed. Beat in the egg and vinegar for 2 minutes on high. Stir in the cheese and the remaining flour to make a firm dough.
- Then, on a floured surface, work the dough until it's smooth and no longer sticky, approximately 2 minutes total.
- Roll dough to about 1/2-inch thickness. Using a 3-inch circular cutter, cut out the shapes. If desired, roll scraps. Coat baking sheets with cooking spray and top with 2 tbsp cornmeal. Sprinkle the remaining cornmeal over the muffins. Let it rise for 1 hour, covered.
- Preheat the air fryer to 325°F. Cook for 20 to 25 minutes, or until golden brown, turning every 5 minutes. Place on wire racks to cool. Toast if desired after splitting with a fork.

89.   Cranberry Bran Muffins

Preparation Time: 15 minutes
Cooking Time: 15 minutes
Servings: 8

Ingredients:
- 1½ cups bran cereal flakes
- 1 cup plus 2 tbsp whole-wheat pastry flour
- 3 tbsp packed brown sugar
- 1 tsp low-sodium baking powder
- 1 cup 2 percent milk
- 3 tbsp safflower oil or peanut oil
- 1 egg
- ½ cup dried cranberries

Directions:
- In a medium bowl, mix the cereal, pastry flour, brown sugar, and baking powder.
- In a small bowl, whisk the milk, oil, and egg until combined.
- The dry ingredients must be stirred with the egg mixture until just combined
- Stir in the cranberries.
- Pour 4 cups into the air fryer and fill each three-fourths full with batter. Bake for about 15 minutes at 350°F, or until the muffin tops spring back when lightly touched with your finger.
- Let cool on a wire rack for 10 minutes before serving.

90.   Brown Rice and Salmon Frittata

Preparation Time: 15 minutes
Cooking Time: 15 minutes
Servings: 4

Ingredients:
- Olive oil, for greasing the pan
- 1 egg
- 4 egg whites
- ½ tsp dried thyme
- ½ cup cooked brown rice
- ½ cup cooked, flaked salmon (about 3 ounces)
- ½ cup fresh baby spinach
- ¼ cup chopped red bell pepper
- 1 tbsp grated Parmesan cheese

Directions:
- Preheat the air fryer to 350°F.
- Rub a 6-by-2-inch pan with a bit of olive oil and set aside.
- In a small bowl, beat the egg, egg whites, and thyme until well mixed.
- In the prepared pan, stir together the brown rice, salmon, spinach, and red bell pepper.
- Pour the egg mixture over the rice mixture and sprinkle with the Parmesan cheese.
- Bake for about 15 minutes, or until the frittata is puffed and golden brown. Serve.

91.   Cali Breakfast Melt

Preparation Time: 10 minutes
Cooking Time: 4-5 minutes
Servings: 2

Ingredients:
- 2 low-sodium whole-wheat English muffins, split
- 2 tbsp nonfat Greek yogurt
- 8 fresh baby spinach leaves
- 1 ripe tomato, cut into 4 slices
- ½ ripe avocado, peeled, pitted, and sliced lengthwise (see Tip)
- 8 fresh basil leaves
- 4 tbsp crumbled fat-free low-sodium feta cheese, divided

Directions:
- Put the English muffin halves into the air fryer. At 400°F, toast for 2 minutes, or until light golden brown. Transfer to a work surface.
- Spread each muffin half with 1½ tsp of yogurt.
- Top each muffin half with 2 spinach leaves, 1 tomato slice, one-fourth of the avocado, and 2 basil leaves. Sprinkle each with 1 tbsp of feta cheese.
- Toast the sandwiches in the air fryer for 3 to 4 minutes (still at 400°F), or until the cheese softens and the sandwich is hot. Serve immediately.

92.   Chia Pudding

Preparation Time: 10 minutes
Cooking Time: 7 minutes
Servings: 7

Ingredients:
- 1 cup chia seeds
- 1 cup unsweetened coconut milk
- 1 tsp. liquid Stevia
- 1 tbsp. coconut oil
- 1 tsp. butter

Directions:
- Pre-heat the fryer at 360°F.
- In a bowl, gently combine the chia seeds with the milk and Stevia before mixing the coconut oil and butter. Spoon seven equal-sized portions into seven ramekins and set these inside the fryer.
- Cook for four minutes. Take care when removing the ramekins from the fryer and allow them to cool for four minutes before serving.

93.   Flax Meal Porridge

Preparation Time: 10 minutes
Cooking Time: 12-15 minutes
Servings: 1

Ingredients:
- ½ Tsp Vanilla Extract
- 1 Tbsp Butter
- 1 Tsp Stevia
- 3 Tbsp Flax Meal
- 1 cup Almond Milk
- 2 Tbsp Sesame Seeds
- 4 Tbsp Chia Seeds

Directions:
- Preheat your air fryer to 375°F.
- Place your chia seeds, sesame seeds, flax meal, almond milk, butter, and stevia into your tray. Add in your vanilla, and then cook for eight minutes.
- Stir well, and allow it to sit for five minutes before serving.

94.   Southern Buttermilk Biscuits

Preparation Time: 20 minutes
Cooking Time: 8-10 minutes
Servings: 4

Ingredients:
- 1 ¼ cups flour, plus some for dusting
- ½ tsp baking soda
- ½ cup cake flour
- ¾ tsp salt
- ½ tsp baking powder
- 4 tbsp butter, chopped
- 1 tsp sugar
- ¾ cup buttermilk

Directions:
- Preheat the Air fryer to 400°F and combine all dry ingredients in a bowl. Place the chopped butter in the bowl, and rub it into the flour mixture until crumbed. Stir in the buttermilk.
- Flour a flat and dry surface and roll out until half-inch thick. Cut out 10 rounds with a small cookie cutter. Arrange the biscuits on a lined baking sheet. Cook for 8 minutes.

95.   Salami and Prosciutto Omelet

Preparation Time: 10 minutes
Cooking Time: 12 minutes
Servings: 2

Ingredients:
- 1 beef sausage, chopped
- 4 slices prosciutto, chopped
- 3 oz salami, chopped
- 1 cup grated mozzarella cheese
- 4 eggs
- 1 tbsp chopped onion
- 1 tbsp ketchup

Directions:
- Preheat the air fryer to 350°F. Whisk the eggs with the ketchup in a bowl. Stir in the onion. Brown the sausage in the air fryer for 2 minutes. Meanwhile, combine the egg mixture, mozzarella cheese, salami, and prosciutto. Pour the egg mixture over the sausage and give it a stir. Cook for 10 minutes.

96.   Savory Pearl Barley

Preparation Time: 10 minutes
Cooking Time: 18-20 minutes
Servings: 2

Ingredients:
- 1 cup pearl barley
- 4 oz baby kale
- 4 cups vegetable broth
- 1/4 cup onion, chopped
- 1 tbsp olive oil
- 1/2 tsp sea salt

Directions:
- Let the air fryer preheat at 350°F, add oil to the pan of the fryer, then sauté barley and onion for around 3 minutes. Put in the salt and broth, and stir. Cook it for 15 minutes.
- Add kale and stir until kale is wilted.
- Serve and enjoy.

97.   Espresso Oatmeal

Preparation Time: 10 minutes
Cooking Time: 10 minutes
Servings: 2

Ingredients:
- 1 cup steel-cut oats
- 1 1/2 tsp vanilla
- 1 tsp espresso powder
- 2 tbsp Sugar
- 1 cup milk
- 2½ cups of water
- 1/4 tsp salt

Directions:
- Add oats, espresso powder, Sugar, milk, water, and salt into the air fryer and stir well.
- Let it cook for around 17 minutes at 360°F.
- Stir in vanilla and serve.

98.   Coconut Blueberry Oatmeal

Preparation Time: 10 minutes
Cooking Time: 30 minutes
Servings: 4

Ingredients:
- 2 1/4 cups oats
- 1 cup blueberries

- 1/4 cup gluten-free flour
- 1/2 tsp vanilla
- 3 cups of water
- 14 oz coconut milk
- 6 tbsp Brown Sugar
- 1/8 tsp salt

Directions:
- Mix and add all ingredients into the air fryer and mix it well. Set the air fryer to 300°F and cook the meal for 30 minutes on the air fryer setting.
- Stir well and serve.

99. Mexican Salsa Eggs

Preparation Time: 10 minutes
Cooking Time: 20 minutes
Servings: 2

Ingredients:
- ½ green bell pepper, chopped
- ½ red bell pepper, chopped
- 2 eggs, whisked
- 1 tbsp mild salsa
- Cooking spray
- ½ tbsp chives, chopped
- Salt and black pepper, to taste
- ¼ cup cheddar cheese, grated

Directions:
- Grease 2 ramekins with Cooking spray and divide the bell peppers into each.
- In a bowl, mix the eggs with the salsa, chives, salt, and pepper, and whisk well.
- Divide the egg mixture between each ramekin and sprinkle the cheese on top.
- Preheat the air fryer at 360°F. Arrange the ramekins in the frying basket.
- Cook for 20 minutes at 360°F. Serve well.

100. Pineapple French Toast

Preparation Time: 10 minutes
Cooking Time: 15 minutes
Servings: 5

Ingredients:
- 10 bread slices
- 1/4 cup of Sugar
- 1/4 cup milk
- 3 large whole eggs
- 1 cup of coconut milk
- 10 slices pineapple, peeled
- 1/2 cup coconut flakes
- Cooking spray as needed

Directions:
- Take a mixing bowl and whisk in coconut milk, sugar, eggs, milk, and stir well
- Dup breads in the mixture and keep them on the side for 2 minutes
- Pre-heat the air fryer by pressing the "grill" option and setting it to "med" and the timer to 15 minutes
- Let it pre-heat until you hear a beep

- Arrange bread slices over grill grate, lock lid, and cook for 2 minutes. Flip and cook for 2 minutes more. Let them cook until the timer reads 0
- Repeat with remaining slices, serve and enjoy!

101. Cranberry Bread Pudding

Preparation Time: 20 minutes
Cooking Time: 45 minutes
Servings: 4

Ingredients:
- 1-1/2 cups milk
- 2-1/2 eggs
- 1/2 cup cranberries
- 1 tsp butter
- 1/4 cup and 2 tbsp white sugar
- 1/4 cup golden raisins
- 1/8 tsp ground cinnamon
- 3/4 cup heavy whipping cream
- 3/4 tsp lemon zest
- 3/4 tsp kosher salt
- 3/4 French baguettes, cut into 2-inch slices
- 3/8 vanilla bean, split and seeds scraped away

Directions:
- Lightly grease the baking pan of the Air Fryer with cooking spray. Spread baguette slices, cranberries, and raisins.
- In a blender, blend well vanilla bean, cinnamon, salt, lemon zest, eggs, sugar, and cream. Pour over baguette slices. Let it soak for an hour.
- Cover pan with foil.
- Close the air fryer Lid. Select Bake and cook for 35 minutes; cook at 330°F.
- Let it rest for 10 minutes.
- Serve and enjoy.

102. Chocolate Banana Muffins

Preparation Time: 20 minutes
Cooking Time: 30 minutes
Servings: 12

Ingredients:
- ¾ cup whole wheat flour
- ¾ cup plain flour
- ¼ cup cocoa powder
- ¼ tsp baking powder
- 1 tsp baking soda
- ¼ tsp salt
- 2 large bananas, peeled and mashed
- 1 cup sugar
- 1/3 cup canola oil
- 1 egg
- ½ tsp vanilla essence
- 1 cup mini chocolate chips

Directions:
- . In a large bowl, mix together flour, cocoa powder, baking powder, baking soda, and salt.
- In another bowl, add bananas, sugar, oil, egg, and vanilla extract and beat till well combined.
- Slowly, add flour mixture to egg mixture and mix till just combined.
- Fold in chocolate chips.

- Preheat the Air Fryer to 345 °F. Grease 12 muffin molds.
- Transfer the mixture into prepared muffin molds evenly, and close the air fryer Lid. Select Bake, set the temperature to 390°F, and set the time to 20 minutes or till a toothpick inserted in the center comes out clean. Select Start to begin. Remove the muffin molds from Air Fryer and keep them on a wire rack to cool for about 10 minutes. Carefully turn on a wire rack to cool completely before serving.

103. Breaded Spam Steaks

Preparation Time: 10 minutes
Cooking Time: 5 minutes
Servings: 4

Ingredients:
- 12 Oz Can Luncheon Meat
- 1 cup All-Purpose Flour
- 2 Eggs, beaten
- 2 Cups Italian Seasoned Breadcrumbs

Directions:
- Preparing the Ingredients. Preheat the Air Fryer to 380°F.
- Cut the luncheon meat into 1/4-inch slices.
- Gently press the luncheon meat slices into the flour to coat and shake off the excess flour. Dip into the beaten egg, then press into breadcrumbs.
- Place the batter slices into the Air Fryer tray, close the air fryer lid and cook for 3 to 5 minutes until golden brown.
- Serve with chili or tomato sauce

104. Corn Flakes Casserole

Preparation Time: 10 minutes
Cooking Time: 8 minutes
Servings: 5

Ingredients:
- 1/3 cup milk
- 4 tbsp. cream cheese; whipped
- 1/4 tsp. nutmeg; ground
- 1/4 cup blueberries
- 1 ½ cups corn flakes; crumbled
- 3 tsp. sugar
- 2 eggs; whisked
- 5 bread slices

Directions:
- In a bowl, mix eggs with sugar, nutmeg, and milk and whisk well.
- In another bowl, mix cream cheese with blueberries and whisk well.
- Put corn flakes in a third bowl.
- Spread blueberry mix on each bread slice; then dip in eggs mix and dredge in corn flakes at the end.
- Place bread in your air fryer's basket, heat up at 400°F, and bake for 8 minutes. Divide among plates and serve for breakfast.

105. Jalapeno Breakfast Muffins

Preparation Time: 10 minutes
Cooking Time: 15 minutes
Servings: 8

Ingredients:
- 5 eggs
- 1/3 cup coconut oil, melted
- 2 tsp baking powder
- 3 tbsp erythritol
- 3 tbsp jalapenos, sliced
- 1/4 cup unsweetened coconut milk
- 2/3 cup coconut flour
- 3/4 tsp sea salt

Directions:
- Preheat the air fryer to 325°F.
- In a large bowl, stir together coconut flour, baking powder, erythritol, and sea salt.
- Stir in eggs, jalapenos, coconut milk, and coconut oil until well combined.
- Pour batter into the silicone muffin molds and place it into the air fryer basket.
- Cook muffins for 15 minutes.
- Serve and enjoy.

106. Spinach Cheese Pie

Preparation Time: 10 minutes
Cooking Time: 20 minutes
Servings: 4

Ingredients:
- 1 cup frozen chopped spinach, drained
- ¼ cup heavy whipping cream.
- 1 cup shredded sharp Cheddar cheese.
- ¼ cup diced yellow onion
- 6 large eggs.

Directions:
- Take a medium bowl, whisk eggs and add cream. Add the remaining ingredients to the bowl.
- Pour into a 6-inch round baking dish. Place into the air fryer basket. Adjust the temperature to 320°F and set the timer for 20 minutes
- Eggs will be firm and slightly browned when cooked. Serve immediately.

107. Pumpkin Spice Oats

Preparation Time: 10 minutes
Cooking Time: 20 minutes
Servings: 2

Ingredients:
- 1½ cups Water
- ½ cup Pumpkin puree
- 1 tsp Pumpkin pie spice
- ½ cup Steel-cut oats

Directions:
- Heat the Air Fryer at 360°F to preheat.
- Toss in and mix the fixings into the Air Fryer.
- Set the timer for 20 minutes.
- When it's ready, portion the oatmeal into bowls and serve.

108. Pizza Omelet

Preparation Time: 15 minutes
Cooking Time: 12 minutes
Servings: 2

Ingredients:
- 4 eggs
- 2 tbsp milk
- Pinch of salt
- Ground black pepper, as required
- 8-10 turkey pepperoni slices

Directions:
- In a bowl, crack the eggs and beat them well.
- Add the remaining ingredients and gently stir to combine.
- Place the mixture into a baking pan.
- Press the "Power Button" of Air Fry and turn the dial to select the "Air Fry" mode.
- Press the Time button and again turn the dial to set the cooking time to 12 minutes.
- Now push the Temp button and rotate the dial to set the temperature at 355 °F.
- Press the "Start/Pause" button to start.
- When the unit beeps to show that it is preheated, open the lid.
- Arrange the pan over the "Wire Rack" and insert it into the oven.
- Cut into equal-sized wedges and serve hot.

109. Zucchini Omelet

Preparation Time: 15 minutes
Cooking Time: 15 minutes
Servings: 2

Ingredients:
- 1 tsp butter
- 1 zucchini, julienned
- 4 eggs
- ¼ tsp fresh basil, chopped
- ¼ tsp red pepper flakes, crushed
- Salt and ground black pepper, as required

Directions:
- In a skillet, melt the butter over medium heat and cook the zucchini for about 3-4 minutes.
- Remove from the heat and set aside to cool slightly.
- Meanwhile, in a bowl, mix together the eggs, basil, red pepper flakes, salt, and black pepper.
- Add the cooked zucchini and gently stir to combine.
- Place the zucchini mixture into a small baking pan.
- Press the "Power Button" of the Air Fryer and turn the dial to select the "Air Fry" mode.
- Press the Time button and again turn the dial to set the cooking time to 10 minutes.
- Now push the Temp button and rotate the dial to set the temperature at 355 °F.
- Press the "Start/Pause" button to start.
- When the unit beeps to show that it is preheated, open the lid.
- Arrange the pan over the "Wire Rack" and insert it into the oven.
- Cut the omelet into 2 portions and serve hot.

110. Streusel Donuts

Preparation Time: 15 minutes
Cooking Time: 15 minutes
Servings: 6

Ingredients:
- 1 cup plus 2 tbsp all-purpose flour, divided, plus additional to dust the work surface
- 5 tbsp dark brown sugar, divided
- 1 tsp baking powder
- Pinch sea salt
- ¼ cup whole milk
- 1 large egg, yolk and white separated
- 3 tbsp granulated sugar
- ½ tsp ground cinnamon
- ¼ cup butter, melted
- Cooking oil spray

Directions:
- In a medium bowl, combine 1 cup of flour, 2 tbsp of brown sugar, the baking powder, and salt, and mix well.
- In a small bowl, whisk together the milk and egg yolk. Add this to the flour mixture and mix just until a dough forms.
- In another small bowl, combine the remaining 3 tbsp of brown sugar, granulated sugar, cinnamon, remaining 2 tbsp of flour, and butter and mix until a crumbly streusel forms. Set aside.
- Dust the work surface with some flour. Turn the dough out onto the surface and pat it to ⅓-inch thickness. Using a 3-inch cookie cutter, cut out 6 rounds. We'll skip the donut holes so we can have more streusel on top.
- Beat the egg white until frothy in a small bowl, then brush the tops of the rounds with some of the egg white.
- Sprinkle each dough round with some of the streusel toppings, patting the topping onto the dough, so it sticks.
- Cut two pieces of parchment paper to fit in your air fryer basket. Place a parchment paper round into the air fryer basket and add the donuts, three at a time, depending on the size of your air fryer. Spray the tops with cooking oil.
- Set or preheat the air fryer to 350°F. Fry the donuts for 4 to 6 minutes or until they are light golden brown. Remove and cool on a wire rack. Remove and discard the parchment paper and replace it with a fresh round. Air fry the remaining donuts.

111. Pesto Omelet

Preparation Time: 15 minutes
Cooking Time: 15 minutes
Servings: 3

Ingredients:
- 1 tbsp olive oil
- 1 shallot, minced
- 1 garlic clove, minced
- ½ cup diced red bell pepper
- ¼ cup chopped fresh tomato
- 4 large eggs
- 2 tbsp light cream
- ¼ tsp sea salt
- ½ cup shredded mozzarella cheese

- 3 tbsp basil pesto

Directions:
- In a 6-inch round pan, place the olive oil. Add the shallot, garlic, bell pepper, and tomato and toss to coat in the oil.
- Set or preheat the air fryer to 350°F. Put the pan with the vegetables in the basket and the basket in the air fryer. Cook for 3 to 5 minutes, stirring once halfway through cooking time until the veggies are tender.
- Meanwhile, whisk together the eggs, cream, and salt until smooth.
- When the vegetables are done, remove the basket. Pour the egg mixture into the pan. Return the basket to the air fryer and cook for 8 minutes.
- Sprinkle with the cheese and cook another 2 minutes or until the cheese is melted and the eggs are set. Top with the pesto and serve immediately.

112.   Berry and Nuts Granola

Preparation Time: 15 minutes
Cooking Time: 12 minutes
Servings: 6

Ingredients:
- 1½ cups rolled oats (not quick-cooking oats)
- 1 cup chopped pecans or walnuts, or a combination
- 3 tbsp flaxseed
- ½ tsp cinnamon
- ⅛ tsp nutmeg
- ¼ cup maple syrup
- 3 tbsp vegetable oil
- 1 tsp vanilla
- ¼ tsp sea salt
- ½ cup dried blueberries
- ½ cup dried cherries

Directions:
- In a large bowl, combine the oats, nuts, flaxseed, cinnamon, and nutmeg and mix well.
- In a 2-cup glass measuring cup, combine the maple syrup, oil, vanilla, and salt and mix well. Pour this over the oat mixture and stir to combine.
- Spread the mixture in a 7-inch round pan.
- Set or preheat the air fryer to 350°F. Place the pan in the air fryer basket and the basket in the air fryer. Bake for 12 minutes, stirring halfway through cooking time until the granola is golden brown and fragrant.
- Transfer the granola to a serving bowl and let cool for 3 minutes. Stir in the dried blueberries and cherries. Let stand until cool, then serve, or store in an airtight container at room temperature for up to 4 days.

113.   Spinach and Cheese Toast

Preparation Time: 15 minutes
Cooking Time: 8 minutes
Servings: 4

Ingredients:
- ½ cup shredded Havarti cheese
- ½ cup frozen spinach, thawed and well-drained
- 4 tbsp (2 ounces) cream cheese, at room temperature
- 2 scallions, chopped
- 1 garlic clove, minced

- ½ tsp dried marjoram
- ¼ tsp sea salt
- ⅛ tsp freshly ground black pepper
- 4 (1¼-inch-thick) slices of French bread
- 2 large eggs
- ¼ cup whole milk
- ½ cup dried bread crumbs

Directions:
- In a medium bowl, combine the Havarti, spinach, cream cheese, scallions, garlic, marjoram, salt, and pepper and mix well.
- Cut a slit in the side of each piece of French bread about 2 inches wide. Do not go through to the other side; you are creating a pocket.
- Stuff the pockets with the spinach mixture. Press the slices gently to close.
- In a shallow bowl, beat the eggs with the milk until smooth. Place the French bread slices into the egg mixture, turning once, letting the bread absorb most of the egg mixture.
- Place the bread crumbs on a plate. Dip the egg-soaked bread slices into the bread crumbs; pat down on them, so they adhere to the slices.
- Set or preheat the air fryer to 350°F. Put the bread slices in the air fryer basket and the basket in the air fryer. Cook for 3 to 4 minutes on each side, turning once until the bread is browned and crisp. Serve.

114.   Vanilla Apple Quinoa

Preparation Time: 10 minutes
Cooking Time: 30 minutes
Servings: 4

Ingredients:
- 1 cup of quinoa, rinsed
- 2 cups of water
- 4 sweet apples, seeded and diced
- 2 tbsp white sugar
- 3 tsp vanilla
- ¼ tsp citric acid

Directions:
- Sprinkle the diced apples with vanilla and citric acid and place them in the fridge for 10 minutes. Soak the quinoa in warm water for a total of 15 minutes. Then once done, put all the ingredients in the air fryer.
- Cook at 400°F for 15 minutes.
- Release the pressure naturally over 10 minutes.
- Portion the apples and vanilla quinoa mix into bowls or mugs and dollop each bowl with the white sugar. Serve the apple quinoa with the cappuccino.

115.   Savory Feta Oats

Preparation Time: 10 minutes
Cooking Time: 30 minutes
Servings: 4

Ingredients:
- 2 cups of old-fashioned rolled oats
- ¼ cup of Feta cheese, crumbled
- 2 cups of water
- ¼ tsp paprika
- 3 oz scallion, chopped

- kosher salt, to taste
- black pepper, to taste

Directions:
- All the ingredients except the Feta cheese and chopped scallion must be put in the air fryer.
- Let it cook for 25 minutes at 350°F.
- Stir in the crumbled Feta cheese to melt it.
- Portion the oatmeal into four mugs and bowls then, scoop in each bowl then top with the scallion

116.   Zucchini and Fruits Breakfast Plate

Preparation Time: 10 minutes
Cooking Time: 20 minutes
Servings: 3

Ingredients:
- 2 melons, sliced
- 1 medium zucchini, sliced
- 1 cup of walnuts
- 2 apples, sliced
- ¼ cup of maple syrup
- 4 tbsp unsalted butter
- 1 tsp vanilla extract
- 3 tbsp pomegranate seeds

Directions:
- Roast the walnut in a preheated oven, set aside when it becomes light brown Then grind the walnuts using a food processor or blender.
- In a bowl, combine the maple syrup, unsalted butter, and vanilla extract and mix well until there is a smooth consistency and homogenous mass, then add in the melon and zucchini. Combine these ingredients and add them to your Air fryer.
- Close the lid and cook on a LOW pressure for 10 minutes.
- Quick-release the pressure. Portion the melon breakfast mix into three bowls or mugs and dollop each bowl with the apples, walnuts, and pomegranate seeds.

117.   Peach and Nuts Millet

Preparation Time: 10 minutes
Cooking Time: 20 minutes
Servings: 3

Ingredients:
- 2 cups of millet, rinsed
- 4 peaches, sliced
- 1 cup of peanuts
- 3 cups of milk
- 5 tbsp white sugar
- 2 bananas, peeled and sliced
- ½ tsp pure vanilla extract

Directions:
- Roast the peanuts in a preheated oven, set aside when it becomes light brown Then grind the walnuts using a food processor or blender.
- Soak the millet in warm water for around 10 minutes. Then add the millet to your air fryer.
- Add the peaches, peanuts, milk, and pure vanilla extract to your pot and stir well.
- Let it cook for 25 minutes at 355°F.

- Portion the millet into three bowls or mugs. Serve the millet with orange juice.

118.   Pistachio and Pineapple Oats

Preparation Time: 15 minutes
Cooking Time: 30 minutes
Servings: 6

Ingredients:
- 4 cups of oatmeal
- 2 pineapples, peeled and diced
- 4 tbsp cherry jam
- 1 cup of water
- 4 tbsp unsalted butter
- 1 tsp cherry extract
- 1 cup of pistachios

Directions:
- In a bowl, combine the water and cherry extract and mix well until there is a smooth consistency and homogenous mass; then, add the oatmeal, pineapples, butter, and cherry jam to your Air fryer and toss. Pour the cherry water into your air fryer.
- Close the instant pot air fryer lid and cook on a LOW pressure for 25 minutes.
- Portion the pineapple oatmeal into four bowls or mugs and dollop each bowl with the pistachios.

119.   Apricot and Vanilla Porridge

Preparation Time: 10 minutes
Cooking Time: 35 minutes
Servings: 2

Ingredients:
- 1 cup of dried apricots
- 1 cup of millet
- 1 cup of water
- 1 cup of milk
- 1 cup of peanuts, chopped
- 1 tbsp of flaxseeds, ground
- 1 tbsp pure vanilla extract

Directions:
- Roast the walnut in a preheated oven, set aside when it becomes light brown Then grind the peanuts using a food processor or blender.
- Wash the millet a few times.
- Soak the flaxseeds in warm water overnight. Chop the dried apricots.
- In a bowl, combine the water, apricots, millet, milk, flaxseeds, peanuts, and pure vanilla extract and add them to your Air fryer and mix well.
- Let it cook for 25 minutes at 350°F.
- Portion the vanilla-flavored millet porridge into two bowls or mugs and dollop each bowl with some flaxseeds. Remember that this dish should be served warm. Serve the millet porridge with the cocoa.

120.   Seasoned Omelet with Croutons

Preparation Time: 14 minutes
Cooking Time: 30 minutes
Servings: 3

Ingredients:
- 4 eggs
- 1 baguette
- 1 cup of milk
- 3 tbsp Olive oil
- 2 tbsp unsalted butter or baking spray
- 1 tsp herbs
- salt, to taste
- pepper, to taste
- basil, to taste

Directions:
- Grease ramekin with unsalted butter or baking spray.
- Combine the eggs and the milk. In a bowl, beat the eggs, the milk, and the salt using an electric hand mixer until there is a smooth and creamy consistency and homogenous mass.
- Cut the baguette into small cubes and toss them with salt, Olive oil, and herbs. Preheat the oven to 250-270 °F and spread the baguette cubes on a baking sheet. Bake the croutons for 10-15 minutes until golden brown and crispy.
- Combine all the ingredients with the croutons and pour the egg mixture into the ramekin.
- Add some water to your pot and place a steamer basket.
- Then place the ramekin inside and close the lid.
- Cook on a LOW pressure for 15 minutes and then release the pressure naturally.
- Sprinkle the salt and pepper to taste, and you are free to serve the omelet in separate dishes.

121. Kale Muffins

Preparation Time: 10 minutes
Cooking Time: 12-15 minutes
Servings: 8

Ingredients:
- 6 large eggs
- 1/2 cup almond milk
- 1 cup kale, chopped
- 1/4 cup chives, chopped
- Pepper
- Salt

Directions:
- Add all ingredients into the bowl and whisk well.
- Pour egg mixture into the 8 silicone muffin molds.
- Place the dehydrating tray in a multi-level air fryer basket and place the basket in the air fryer.
- Place 6 muffin molds on dehydrating tray.
- Seal pot with air fryer lid and select bake mode, then set the temperature to 350°F and timer for 30 minutes.
- Bake remaining muffins using the same method.
- Serve and enjoy.

122. Creamy Mac and Cheese

Preparation Time: 10 minutes
Cooking Time: 15 minutes
Servings: 4

Ingredients:
- 2 1/2 cups macaroni
- 1/4 tsp garlic powder
- 2 cups crackers, crushed
- 1/3 cup parmesan cheese, shredded
- 2 2/3 cups cheddar cheese, shredded
- 8 tbsp butter
- 1 1/4 cup heavy cream
- 2 cups vegetable stock
- Pepper
- Salt

Directions:
- Add heavy cream, 4 tbsp butter, and stock into the air fryer and stir well.
- Add macaroni and stir well.
- Seal the pot with a pressure cooking lid and cook on high pressure for 4 minutes.
- Once done, release pressure using quick release. Remove lid.
- Add 2 cups of cheese and stir until cheese is melted.
- Mix together the remaining butter and crushed crackers.
- Spread remaining cheddar cheese, parmesan cheese, and crushed crackers.
- Seal pot with air fryer lid and select air fry mode, then set the temperature to 400°F and timer for 5 minutes.
- Serve and enjoy.

123. Cacao Banana Leather

Preparation Time: 10 minutes
Cooking Time: 10 hrs
Servings: 3

Ingredients:
- 1 banana
- 1/4 tbsp brown sugar
- 1/2 tbsp cocoa powder

Directions:
- Add banana, brown sugar, and cocoa powder into the blender and blend until smooth.
- Place the dehydrating tray in a multi-level air fryer basket and place the basket in the air fryer.
- Line dehydrating tray with parchment paper.
- Spread banana mixture on dehydrating tray.
- Seal pot with air fryer lid and select dehydrate mode, then set the temperature to 130°F and timer for 10 hours.
- Serve and enjoy.

124. Squash Oatmeal Muffins

Preparation Time: 10 minutes
Cooking Time: 20 minutes
Servings: 12

Ingredients:
- 2 eggs
- 1 tbsp pumpkin pie spice
- 2 tsp baking powder
- 1 cup oats
- 1 cup all-purpose flour
- 1 tsp vanilla
- 1/3 cup olive oil
- 1/2 cup yogurt
- 1/2 cup maple syrup
- 1 cup butternut squash puree
- 1/2 tsp sea salt

Directions:

- Line 12 cups muffin pan with cupcake liners.
- Insert wire rack in rack position 6. Select bake, set temperature 390°F, and timer for 20 minutes. Press start to preheat the air fryer.
- In a large bowl, whisk together eggs, vanilla, oil, yogurt, maple syrup, and squash puree.
- In a small bowl, mix together flour, pumpkin pie spice, baking powder, oats, and salt.
- Add flour mixture into the wet mixture and stir to combine.
- Scoop the batter into the prepared muffin pan and bake for 20 minutes.
- Serve and enjoy.

125.   Sweet Potato Frittata

Preparation Time: 20 minutes
Cooking Time: 12 minutes
Servings: 5

Ingredients:

- 10 eggs
- 1/4 cup goat cheese, crumbled
- 1 onion, diced
- 1 sweet potato, diced
- 2 cups broccoli, chopped
- 1 tbsp olive oil
- Pepper
- Salt

Directions:

- Spray a baking dish with cooking spray and set aside.
- Insert wire rack in rack position 6. Select bake, set temperature 390°F, and timer for 20 minutes. Press start to preheat the air fryer.
- Heat oil in a pan over medium heat. Add sweet potato, broccoli, and onion, and cook for 10-15 minutes or until sweet potato is tender.
- In a large mixing bowl, whisk eggs with pepper and salt.
- Transfer cooked vegetables into the baking dish. Pour egg mixture over vegetables. Sprinkle with goat cheese and bake for 15-20 minutes.
- Slice and serve.

126.   Mexican Chilis Frittata

Preparation Time: 15 minutes
Cooking Time: 30 minutes
Servings: 3

Ingredients:

- 6 eggs
- 20 oz hash brown potatoes, shredded
- 1/4 tsp ground cumin
- 1/2 cup milk
- 2 cups Mexican cheese, shredded
- 1 lb. pork sausage, cooked and crumbled
- 1 cup chunky salsa
- 28 oz. can of whole green chiles
- Pepper
- Salt

Directions:

- Spray a 13*9-inch baking dish with cooking spray and set aside.
- Insert wire rack in rack position 6. Select bake, set temperature 350°F, timer for 40 minutes. Press start to preheat the oven.
- Layer half potatoes, chilis, salsa, half sausage, and half cheese into the prepared baking dish. Cover with remaining sausage, potatoes, and cheese.
- In a bowl, whisk eggs with milk, cumin, pepper, and salt and pour over potato mixture and bake for 40 minutes.
- Serve and enjoy.

127.   Amish Baked Oatmeal

Preparation Time: 10 minutes
Cooking Time: 30 minutes
Servings: 6

Ingredients:

- 2 eggs
- 3 cups rolled oats
- 1 tsp cinnamon
- 1 1/2 tsp vanilla
- 1 1/2 tsp baking powder
- 1/4 cup butter, melted
- 1/2 cup maple syrup
- 1 1/2 cups milk
- 1/4 tsp salt

Directions:

- Spray an 8*8-inch baking dish with cooking spray and set aside.
- Insert wire rack in rack position 6. Select bake, set temperature 350°F, timer for 30 minutes. Press start to preheat the air fryer.
- In a large bowl, whisk eggs with milk, cinnamon, vanilla, baking powder, butter, maple syrup, and salt. Add oats and mix well.
- Pour the mixture into the baking dish and bake for 30 minutes.
- Slice and serve with warm milk and fruits.

128.   Banana and Peach Bake Oatmeal

Preparation Time: 10 minutes
Cooking Time: 30 minutes
Servings: 4

Ingredients:

- 2 eggs
- 1 tsp vanilla
- 1 1/2 cups milk
- 1/2 tsp cinnamon
- 3/4 tsp baking powder
- 1/4 cup ground flax seed
- 2 1/2 cups steel-cut oats
- 2 bananas, sliced
- 1 peach, sliced
- 1/2 tsp salt

Directions:

- Spray an 8*8-inch baking dish with cooking spray and set aside.

- Insert wire rack in rack position 6. Select bake, set temperature 350°F, timer for 35 minutes. Press start to preheat the air fryer.
- Add all ingredients except one banana into the mixing bowl and mix until well combined.
- Pour the mixture into the baking dish and spread well. Spread the remaining banana slices on top and bake for 35 minutes.
- Serve and enjoy.

129. Cranberry Pumpkin Oatmeal

Preparation Time: 10 minutes
Cooking Time: 5 minutes
Servings: 2

Ingredients:
- 1 cup steel-cut oats
- 2 tbsp honey
- 1/2 cup dried cranberries
- 3/4 cup pumpkin puree
- 1 cup milk
- 2 cups of water
- 1 1/2 tsp pumpkin pie spice
- Pinch of salt

Directions:
- At the start, add all of the dry ingredients to a large mixing basin.
- Then stir in the pumpkin, milk, and water until fully combined.
- Fold in the cranberries.
- Place them in your air fryer.
- Set your temperature to 360°F for 10 minutes.
- Allow cooling before dusting with confectionery sugar if desired.
- Serve and have fun!

130. Coconut Blueberry Oatmeal

Preparation Time: 10 minutes
Cooking Time: 15 minutes
Servings: 2

Ingredients:
- 1/4 cup blueberries
- 3/4 cup rolled oats
- 1/2 tsp ground cinnamon
- 1/2 tsp baking powder
- 1/2 tsp pure vanilla extract
- 1 small egg
- 1/8 cup melted butter
- 1/3 cup coconut milk
- 1/8 cup maple syrup or brown sugar
- 1/4 tsp salt

Directions:
- Combine the oats, salt, powdered cinnamon, baking powder, pure vanilla extract, melted butter, maple syrup, egg, and milk in a large mixing bowl. Fold in the blueberries.
- Combine thoroughly. Then, coat your casserole dish or ramekins with nonstick cooking spray.
- Fill the oiled dish or ramekin halfway with the oatmeal mixture. Filling approximately halfway.

- Place your filled dish in the air fryer basket, set the temperature to 300°F, and cook for 10-15 minutes.
- Plate, serve, and have fun!

131. Papaya Coconut Oatmeal

Preparation Time: 10 minutes
Cooking Time: 5-10 minutes
Servings: 2

Ingredients:
- 1 cup steel-cut oats
- 3 tbsp hemp seeds
- 1/2 papaya, chopped
- 1/2 cup coconut cream
- 2 cups of water

Directions:
- Add oats, coconut cream, and water into the air fryer and let it cook for 4 minutes at 300°F.
- Stir in hemp seeds and papaya.
- Serve and enjoy.

132. Dried Cranberry Farro

Preparation Time: 10 minutes
Cooking Time: 20 minutes
Servings: 6

Ingredients:
- 15 oz farro
- ½ cup dried cranberries
- 1 tsp lemon extract
- ½ cup brown sugar
- 4 ½ cups of water
- ¼ tsp salt

Directions:
- Add farro, lemon extract, brown sugar, water, and salt into the air fryer and let it cook for 20 minutes at 250°F.
- Add cranberries and stir well.
- Serve and enjoy.

133. Lime Coconut Breakfast Quinoa

Preparation Time: 10 minutes
Cooking Time: 5 minutes
Servings: 4

Ingredients:
- 1 cup quinoa, rinsed
- 1/2 tsp coconut extract
- 1 lime juice
- 1 lime zest
- 2 cups of coconut milk
- 1 cup of water

Directions:
- Add all ingredients into the air fryer and let it cook for 5 minutes at 300°F.
- Stir well and serve.

134. Chocolate Cherry Oatmeal

Preparation Time: 10 minutes
Cooking Time: 15 minutes
Servings: 4

Ingredients:
- 2 cups steel cuts oats
- 3 tbsp honey
- 2 cups of water
- 2 cups of milk
- 3 tbsp chocolate chips
- 1 1/2 cups cherries
- 1/4 tsp cinnamon
- Pinch of salt

Directions:
- The air fryer insides will need to be sprayed with a nonstick spray. Put in all ingredients and let it cook for 15 minutes at 240°F.
- Stir well and serve.

CHAPTER 2: SIDES AND APPETIZER

135. Jacket Potatoes

Preparation Time: 10 minutes
Cooking Time: 20 minutes
Servings: 4

Ingredients:
- 4 Medium potatoes
- ½ tsp Salt
- ½ tsp Garlic powder
- Cooking spray

Directions:
- Add the potatoes to the Air Fryer basket and sprinkle both sides with cooking spray.
- Sprinkle sea salt and garlic on both sides of the potatoes, turning them as you go.
- Rub the potatoes with your hands to ensure that they are uniformly covered.
- Cook in the Air Fryer at 400°F for 40 to 50 minutes, or until fork-tender.

136. Queso Fundido

Preparation Time: 20 minutes
Cooking Time: 10 minutes
Servings: 4

Ingredients:
- 4 ounces fresh Mexican chorizo, casings removed
- 1 medium onion, chopped
- 3 cloves garlic, minced

- 1 cup chopped tomato
- 2 jalapeños, seeded and diced
- 2 tsp ground cumin
- 2 cups shredded Oaxaca or mozzarella cheese
- ½ cup half-and-half
- Celery sticks or tortilla chips for serving

Directions:
- In an ovenproof pan, combine the chorizo, onion, garlic, tomato jalapeños, and cumin. Stir to combine.
- Place the pan in the air fryer basket. Set the air fryer to 400°F for 15 minutes, or until the sausage is cooked, stirring halfway through the cooking time to break up the sausage. Add the cheese and half-and-half; stir to combine. Set the air fryer to 325°F for 10 minutes or until the cheese has melted. Serve with celery sticks or tortilla chips.

137.   Spicy Mango Okra

Preparation Time: 5 minutes
Cooking Time: 11 minutes
Servings: 2

Ingredients:
- 30 okra pods (whole)
- 1 and 1/4 tbsp rice flour
- 1 tsp ground coriander
- 3 tbsp chickpea flour
- 3/4 tsp salt
- 1 tsp red chili powder
- 1/2 tsp ground cumin
- 1 tbsp lemon juice
- 1 tsp mango powder
- 3.5 tbsp oil of choice

Directions:
- Rinse the okra, drain it, and pat it dry with a kitchen towel. The okra should be totally dry before cooking. Remove the stem ends and tips. Cut each okra into four thin, long slices.
- Except for the okra and lemon juice, combine 2.5 tbsp oil with the remaining ingredients. Stir everything together thoroughly. The residual oil will be rubbed within the air fryer basket.
- Place the sliced okra in the marinade and coat thoroughly.
- When you're ready to cook, rub the leftover oil within the air fryer basket.
- Preheat the air fryer to 350°F for about 5 minutes.
- Once warmed, place the okra in a single layer in the air fryer basket.
- Air fry at 350°F for approx. 7 minutes. Toss and cook for another 4 minutes at 380°F.
- When the okra is done, take it from the air fryer, sprinkle with lemon juice, and serve.

138.   Cajun Red Rice and Beans

Preparation Time: 20 minutes
Cooking Time: 45-50
Servings: 10-12

Ingredients:
- 1 onion, diced
- 1 bell pepper, diced

- 3 celery stalks, diced
- 1 tsp. fresh thyme
- 2 leaves bay
- 7 cups water
- 1-pound chicken andouille sausage cut into thin slices
- 10 cups cooked rice
- 3 cloves garlic, minced
- 1-pound dry red kidney beans
- 1 tsp. salt
- 1/2 tsp. black pepper
- 1/4 tsp. white pepper
- 1 tsp. hot sauce

Directions:
- Put all ingredients, except for sausage and rice, in the air fryer Pot.
- Select the High-pressure option and cook at High Pressure for 28 minutes and remove.
- Cook chicken andouille sausage at High Pressure for 15 minutes.
- Serve the bean mixture with cooked rice

139.   Bacon Cheeseburger Dip

Preparation Time: 5 minutes
Cooking Time: 5 minutes
Servings: 10

Ingredients:
- ½ cup chopped Tomatoes
- 10 oz shredded Monterey Jack Cheese
- 10 oz Cream Cheese
- 10 Bacon Slices, chopped roughly
- 1 cup Water

Directions:
- Turn on the cooker and select Air Fry mode. Set the temperature to 370°F and the time to 8 minutes.
- Add the bacon pieces and close the crisping lid. Press Start.
- When ready, open the lid and add the water, cream cheese, and tomatoes. Do Not Stir.
- Close the lid, secure the pressure valve, and select Pressure mode on High for 5 minutes. Press Start.
- As soon as the timer has ended, do a quick pressure release, and open the lid.
- Stir in the cheddar cheese and mix to combine. Serve with a side of chips.

140.   Roasted Potato Salad

Preparation Time: 30 minutes
Cooking Time: 25-30 minutes
Servings: 4

Ingredients:
- 2 pounds tiny red or creamer potatoes, cut in half
- 1 tbsp plus ⅓ cup olive oil
- Pinch salt
- Freshly ground black pepper
- 1 red bell pepper, chopped
- 2 green onions, chopped
- ⅓ cup lemon juice
- 3 tbsp Dijon or yellow mustard

Directions:
- Set to 350°F. Roast. Place the potatoes in the air fryer basket and drizzle with 1 tbsp of the olive oil. Sprinkle with salt and pepper.
- Roast for 25 minutes, shaking twice during the cooking time, until the potatoes are tender and light golden brown.
- Meanwhile, place the bell pepper and green onions in a large bowl.
- In a small bowl, combine the remaining ⅓ cup of olive oil, lemon juice, and mustard, and mix well with a whisk.
- When the potatoes are cooked, add them to the bowl with the bell peppers and top with the dressing. Toss gently to coat.
- Let cool for 20 minutes. Stir gently again and serve or refrigerate and serve later

141. Roasted Brussel Sprouts with Parmesan

Preparation Time: 10 minutes
Cooking Time: 20 minutes
Servings: 4

Ingredients:
- 1-pound fresh Brussels sprouts
- 1 tbsp olive oil
- ½ tsp salt
- ⅛ tsp pepper
- ¼ cup grated Parmesan cheese

Directions:
- Set air fryer to 350°F Roast. Trim the bottoms from the Brussels sprouts and pull off any discolored leaves. Toss with the olive oil, salt, and pepper, and place in the air fryer basket.
- Roast for 20 minutes, shaking the air fryer basket twice during the cooking time until the Brussels sprouts are dark golden brown and crisp.
- Transfer the Brussels sprouts to a serving dish and toss them with the Parmesan cheese. Serve immediately.

142. Tortellini Pasta Salad

Preparation Time: 5 minutes
Cooking Time: 30 minutes
Servings: 2

Ingredients:
- 1 pack cheese tortellini, freshly refrigerated
- 1 cucumber, finely chopped
- 2 finely chopped red bell peppers
- 1/2 cup Italian salad dressing
- 1/2 cup Parmesan cheese, shredded

Directions:
- Cook pasta in the air fryer for prospect minutes at 150°C. Let cool.
- In a large bowl, combine pasta, cucumber, bell pepper, a serving of mixed greens dressing, and cheese, and blend well.
- Refrigerate for 2 hours or more.

143. Spicy Pimento Cheese Dip

Preparation Time: 5 minutes
Cooking Time: 45 minutes
Servings: 4

Ingredients:
- 2 tbsp hot sauce
- 8 oz. block cheddar cheese, shredded
- 4 oz. jar sweet pimentos, drained
- ¼ cup onion, chopped
- 2 tsp jarred garlic
- ½ cup mayonnaise
- 8 oz. cream cheese
- ½ tsp salt
- ½ tsp pepper

Directions:
- Add all ingredients to a bowl and mix well with a hand blender. Transfer mixture to a baking dish.
- Position the oven rack in Rack Position 1 and place the dish on top. Select the Bake setting. Set the air fryer to 350°F and the time to 45 minutes.

144. Pesto Tomatoes

Preparation Time: 5 minutes
Cooking Time: 10 minutes
Servings: 4

Ingredients:
- 3 large heirloom tomatoes, cut into ½ inch thick slices.
- 1 cup Pesto
- 8 oz. Feta cheese, cut into ½ inch thick slices
- ½ cup Red onion, sliced thinly
- 1 tbsp Olive oil

Directions:
- Spread some pesto on each slice of tomato. Top each tomato slice with a feta slice and onion and drizzle with oil. Arrange the tomatoes onto the greased rack and spray with cooking spray. Arrange the drip pan in the bottom of the Instant Air fryer Oven cooking chamber. Select "Air Fry" and then set the temperature to 390 °F. Set the time for 14 minutes and press "Start." When the display shows "Add Food," insert the rack in the center position. When the display shows "Turn Food," turn the food. When Cooking Time is complete, remove the rack from the Air fryer Oven. Serve warm.

145. Potato Poutine

Preparation Time: 10 minutes
Cooking Time: 20 minutes
Servings: 4

Ingredients:
- 2 cups frozen waffle cut fries
- 2 tsp olive oil
- 1 red bell pepper, chopped
- 2 green onions, sliced
- 1 cup shredded Swiss cheese
- ½ cup bottled chicken gravy

Directions:
- Set the air fryer to 380°F Fry. Toss the waffle fries with olive oil and place them in the air fryer basket. Air-fry

for 10 to 12 minutes or until the fries are light golden brown and crisp. You also need to shake the basket in the middle of the cooking time.

- Beat the fries must be transferred to a pan and then topped with cheese, pepper, and green onions. Let it cook for 3 minutes. Take it out from the air fryer and pour gravy over it.
- Air-fry for 2 minutes or until the gravy is hot. Serve immediately.

146.   Indian Style Sweet Potato Fries

Preparation Time: 10 minutes
Cooking Time: 15-20 minutes
Servings: 4-6

Ingredients:
- ½ cup sour cream
- ½ cup mango chutney
- 3 tsp curry powder, divided
- 4 cups frozen sweet potato fries
- 1 tbsp olive oil
- Pinch salt
- Freshly ground black pepper

Directions:
- Set the air fryer to 380°F fry. In a small bowl, combine sour cream, chutney, and 1½ tsp of the curry powder. Mix well and set aside.
- Put the sweet potatoes in a medium bowl. Drizzle with the olive oil and sprinkle with the remaining 1½ tsp curry powder, salt, and pepper.
- Put the potatoes in the air fryer basket. Cook for 8 to 12 minutes or until crisp, hot, and golden brown, shaking the basket once during cooking time.
- Place the fries in a serving basket and serve with the chutney dip.

147.   Spiced Mozza Sticks

Preparation Time: 15 minutes
Cooking Time: 10 minutes
Servings: 4

Ingredients:
- 8-ounces mozzarella cheese, cut into strips
- 2 tbsp olive oil
- ½ tsp salt
- 1 cup pork rinds
- 1 egg
- 1 tsp garlic powder
- 1 tsp paprika

Directions:
- Cut the mozzarella into 6 strips. Whisk the egg along with salt, paprika, and garlic powder. Dip the mozzarella strips into the egg mixture first, then into the pork rinds. Arrange them on a baking platter and place them in the fridge for 30-minutes.
- Preheat your air fryer to 360°F. Drizzle olive oil into the air fryer.
- Arrange the mozzarella sticks in the air fryer and cook for about 5-minutes. Make sure to turn them at least twice to ensure they will become golden on all sides.

148.   Sea Salt Parsnip Fries

Preparation Time: 10 minutes
Cooking Time: 12-15 minutes
Servings: 2

Ingredients:
- 2 tbsp of olive oil
- A pinch of sea salt
- 1 large bunch of parsnips

Directions:
- Wash and peel the parsnips, then cut them into strips. Place the parsnips in a bowl with olive oil and sea salt and coat well.
- Preheat your air fryer to 360°F. Place the parsnip and oil mixture into the air fryer basket. Cook for 12-minutes. Serve with sour cream or ketchup.

149.   Hot Mexican Bean Dip

Preparation Time: 5 minutes
Cooking Time: 15 minutes
Servings: 4

Ingredients:
- ½ cup of salsa
- ½ cup sour cream
- 2 cans (15 oz. each) of black beans, well-drained
- 8 oz. Monterey Jack cheese, shredded
- 1 tsp hot pepper sauce

Directions:
- Add half of the cheese, black beans, sour cream, salsa, and hot pepper sauce to a blender and blend until slightly chunky.
- Add to a casserole dish. Add remaining cheese on top.
- Position the oven rack in Rack Position 1 and place the dish on top. Select the Bake setting to 350°F and the time to 15 minutes.

150.   Sweet Potato with Broccoli

Preparation Time: 5 minutes
Cooking Time: 20 minutes
Servings: 4

Ingredients:
- 2 medium sweet potatoes, peeled and cut into 1-inch cubes
- 1 Broccoli head, cut into 1-inch florets
- 2 tbsp Vegetable oil
- Salt and ground black pepper, as required

Directions:
- Grease a baking dish that will fit in the Air Fryer Oven. Gather all of the ingredients into a bowl and toss to coat well. Place the veggie mixture into the prepared baking dish in a single layer.
- Arrange the drip pan at the bottom of the Air Fryer Oven cooking chamber. Select "Roast" and then adjust the temperature to 415 °F. Set the time for 20 minutes and press "Start." When the display shows "Add Food," insert the baking dish in the center position.
- When the display shows "Turn Food," turn the vegetables. When Cooking Time is complete, remove the baking dish from the fryer. Serve hot.

151.   Cauliflower Florets

Preparation Time: 10 minutes
Cooking Time: 10 minutes
Servings: 4

Ingredients:
- 1/4 cup sultanas or golden raisins
- ¼ tsp salt
- 1 tbsp curry powder
- 1 head cauliflower, broken into small florets
- ¼ cup pine nuts

Directions:
- In a cup of boiling water, soak your sultanas to rehydrate.
- Preheat your air fryer to 350°F. Add oil and pine nuts to the air fryer and toast for a minute or so. In a bowl, toss the cauliflower and curry powder as well as salt, then add the mix to the air fryer mixing well.
- Cook for 10-minutes. Drain the sultanas, toss with cauliflower, and serve.

152.   Lemon Flavored Green Beans

Preparation Time: 10 minutes
Cooking Time: 12 minutes
Servings: 4

Ingredients:
- 1 lb. green beans washed and destemmed
- Sea salt and black pepper to taste
- 1 lemon
- ¼ tsp extra virgin olive oil

Directions:
- Preheat your air fryer to 400°F. Place the green beans in the air fryer basket. Squeeze lemon over beans and season with salt and pepper. Cover ingredients with oil and toss well. Cook green beans for 12-minutes and serve!

153.   Crispy Avocado Wedges

Preparation Time: 5 minutes
Cooking Time: 20 minutes
Servings: 2

Ingredients:
- 1 tbsp garlic pepper
- 1/2 cup all-purpose flour
- 2 eggs, beaten
- 1 cup Breadcrumbs
- 2 avocados, cut into 4 wedges each

Directions:
- Mix flour and garlic pepper in a large bowl or container.
- Add eggs to another bowl.
- Place Breadcrumb pieces in the third bowl.
- Coat avocado wedges in flour blend, eggs, then breadcrumbs.
- Spray the air fryer crate with cooking oil and place avocado wedges in it. Splash once more.
- Cook at 200°C for 8 minutes, turning partway through.

154.   Portobello Mushroom Pizza

Preparation Time: 20 minutes
Cooking Time: 6-10 minutes
Servings: 2

Ingredients:
- 2 Portobello mushrooms of large size
- ⅓ cup sliced black olives
- ⅓ cup pizza sauce
- ⅓ cup mozzarella cheese
- ⅓ cup pepperoni sliced
- ⅓ cup green capsicum (bell pepper)
- 1 teaspoon dried oregano

Directions:
- Set the air fryer to 180°C/350°F for 10 minutes.
- Remove the mushroom stems with a knife.
- Place the mushrooms in the Air Fryer, stem side down, and cook for 1-2 minutes.
- Spread pizza sauce over the surface of the mushroom's stems side up.
- Sprinkle with dried oregano and pepperoni
- Top with mozzarella cheese, capsicum, and olives.
- Cook for 8 almost minutes, or until the cheese is completely melted.

155.   Olive and Calamari Rings

Preparation Time: 20 minutes
Cooking Time: 20-30 minutes
Servings: 4

Ingredients:
- 1 lb. calamari rings
- 2 tbsp cilantro, chopped
- 1 chili pepper, minced
- 2 tbsp olive oil
- 1 cup pimiento-stuffed green olives
- Salt and black pepper to taste

Directions:
- In a bowl, add calamari rings, chili pepper, salt, black pepper, olive oil, and fresh cilantro. Marinate for 10 minutes. Pour the calamari into a baking dish and place it inside the fryer. Air Fry for 15 minutes, stirring every 5 minutes at 400°F. Serve warm with pimiento-stuffed olives.

156.   Air Fried Leeks

Preparation Time: 10 minutes
Cooking Time: 7 minutes
Servings: 2

Ingredients:
- 2 leeks, washed, ends cut, and halved
- Salt and black pepper, to taste
- ½ tbsp butter, melted
- ½ tbsp lemon juice

Directions:
- Rub leeks with melted butter and season with salt and pepper.
- Lay it inside the air fryer and cook at 350°F for 7 minutes.

- Arrange on a platter. Drizzle with lemon juice and serve.

157.   Eggplant Surprise

Preparation Time: 10-20 minutes
Cooking Time: 17 minutes
Servings: 4

Ingredients:

- 1 eggplant, roughly chopped
- 3 zucchinis, roughly chopped
- 3 tbsp. extra virgin olive oil
- 3 tomatoes, sliced
- 2 tbsp. lemon juice
- 1 tsp. thyme; dried
- 1 tsp. oregano; dried
- Salt and black pepper to the taste

Directions:

- Put eggplant pieces in your air fryer.
- Add zucchinis and tomatoes.
- In a bowl, mix lemon juice with salt, pepper, thyme, oregano, and oil and stir well
- Pour these over veggies, toss to coat, seal the air fryer lid and cook at 400°F for 14 minutes.
- Quick-release the pressure, carefully open the lid; divide among plates and serve.

158.   Berbere-Spiced Fries

Preparation Time: 10 minutes
Cooking Time: 20 minutes
Servings: 2

Ingredients:

- 1 large (about ¾ pound) potato (preferably Yukon Gold, but any kind will do)
- Cooking oil spray (sunflower, safflower, or refined coconut)
- 1 tbsp neutral-flavored cooking oil (sunflower, safflower, or refined coconut)
- 1 tsp coconut sugar
- 1 tsp garlic granules
- ½ tsp berbere
- ½ tsp sea salt
- ¼ tsp turmeric
- ¼ tsp paprika

Directions:

- Scrub the potato and cut it into French fry shapes (about ¼-inch thick) in relatively uniform pieces. The air frying pan will need to be sprayed with a nonstick spray
- In a medium bowl, toss the potato pieces with the oil, sugar, garlic, berbere, salt, turmeric, and paprika and stir very well (I use a rubber spatula). Place in the air fryer basket and fry for 8 minutes at 350°F.
- Remove the air fryer basket and shake (or gently stir) well. Fry for another 8 minutes at the same temperature.
- Remove one last time, stir or shake, and fry for another 3 to 5 minutes, or until tender and nicely browned. Enjoy while still hot or warm.

159.   Chickpea Fries

Preparation Time: 10 minutes
Cooking Time: 30 minutes
Servings: 4

Ingredients:

- 2 tbsp extra virgin olive oil
- 4 cups alkaline water
- 2 cups chickpea flour
- 1/2 tsp ground clove
- 1 tsp salt
- 2 tsp fresh oregano, chopped

Directions:

- Take parchment paper and line the loaf pan, mush chickpea, and grease pan. Add water to a large saucepan and let it boil. Add salt, add chickpea flour and keep whisking gently until no lumps are visible
- Add oregano and cloves, and stir. Cook for 1 minute 1. Remove the heat, and transfer to the loaf pan. Let it chill for 2 hours.
- Preheat your Air Fryer to 420°F.
- Remove pan from fridge and cut a half-inch thick fry. Use olive oil to brush the fries and sprinkle salt. Transfer them to the Air Fryer cooking basket and cook for 20-25 minutes
- Serve once golden; Enjoy!

160.   Mushrooms and Sour Cream

Preparation Time: 10 minutes
Cooking Time: 10 minutes
Servings: 6

Ingredients:

- 2 bacon strips, chopped
- 1 yellow onion, chopped
- 1 green bell pepper, chopped
- 24 mushrooms, stems removed
- 1 carrot, grated
- ½ cup sour cream
- 1 cup cheddar cheese, grated
- Salt and black pepper to the taste

Directions:

- Heat the air fryer, add bacon, onion, bell pepper, and carrot, stir and cook for 1 minute.
- Add salt, pepper, and sour cream, stir, cook for 1 minute more, take off the heat and cool down.
- Stuff mushrooms with this mix, sprinkle cheese on top, and cook at 360 °F for 8 minutes.
- Serve and Enjoy!

161.   Wild Rice Spinach Balls

Preparation Time: 10 minutes
Cooking Time: 20 minutes
Servings: 4

Ingredients:

- Juice of 1 key lime
- 1/4 cup Greek olives pitted
- 3/4 tsp salt
- 4 and 1/2 cups spinach leaves
- 1 tsp onion powder
- 1/2 cup chickpea flour

- 1/2 cup almonds, ground
- 1 and 1/4 cup cooked wild rice

Directions:
- Preheat your Air Fryer to 340°F
- Add lime, olives, salt, spinach leaves, onion powder to a food processor, a process well
- Add mix to a large bowl and add remaining ingredients; mix well
- Scoop mix into balls
- Transfer them to your Air Fryer cooking basket (Lined with parchment)
- Cook for 10-20 minutes until balls are golden
- Repeat if needed
- Serve and enjoy!

162.   Dill Mashed Potato

Preparation Time: 10 minutes
Cooking Time: 15 minutes
Servings: 2

Ingredients:
- 2 potatoes
- 2 tbsp fresh dill, chopped
- 1 tsp butter
- ½ tsp salt
- ¼ cup half and half

Directions:
- Preheat the air fryer to 390°F.
- Rinse the potatoes thoroughly and place them in the air fryer.
- Cook the potatoes for 15 minutes.
- After this, remove the potatoes from the air fryer.
- Peel the potatoes.
- Mash the potatoes with the help of the fork well.
- Then add chopped fresh dill and salt.
- Stir it gently and add butter and half and half.
- Take the hand blender and blend the mixture well.
- When the mashed potato is cooked – serve it immediately.
- Enjoy!

163.   Loaded Disco Fries

Preparation Time: 10 minutes
Cooking Time: 30 minutes
Servings: 4

Ingredients:
- 1 (28-ounce) bag of frozen steak fries
- Cooking oil
- Salt
- Pepper
- ½ cup beef gravy
- 1 cup shredded mozzarella cheese
- 2 scallions, green parts only, chopped

Directions:
- Set the air fryer to 400°F. Place the frozen steak fries in the air fryer. Cook for 10 minutes.
- The air fryer must be opened and shake the basket. Spray the fries with cooking oil. Sprinkle with salt and pepper to taste. Cook for an additional 8 minutes.

- Pour the beef gravy into a medium, microwave-safe bowl. Microwave for 30 seconds or until the gravy is warm.
- Open the air fryer and sprinkle the fries with the cheese. Cook for an additional 2 minutes until the cheese is melted.
- Transfer the fries to a serving dish. Drizzle the fries with gravy and sprinkle the scallions on top for a green garnish. Serve.

164.   Breaded Artichoke Fries

Preparation Time: 20 minutes
Cooking Time: 15 minutes
Servings: 4

Ingredients:
- 1 14-oz can of artichoke hearts, quartered
- For Wet Mix:
- 1 cup all-purpose flour
- 1 cup almond milk
- ½ tsp garlic powder
- ¾ tsp salt
- ¼ tsp black pepper, or to taste
- For Dry Mix:
- 1 ½ cup panko breadcrumbs
- ½ tsp paprika
- ¼ tsp salt

Directions:
- Let your Air Fryer preheat at 400°F. Whisk all the wet ingredients in one bowl and dry ingredients in another. Dip the artichoke quarters in the wet mixture, then coat them with the dry mixture. Place the quarters in the greased Air Fryer's Basket. Return the fryer basket to the Air Fryer and cook on bake mode for 13 minutes at 340°F. Enjoy.

165.   Cheesy Fingerling Potatoes

Preparation Time: 20 minutes
Cooking Time: 18-20 minutes
Servings: 4

Ingredients:
- 1 lb. fingerling potatoes, cut into wedges
- 1 tsp olive oil
- ½ tsp salt
- 1 tsp black pepper ground
- 1 ½ tsp dry garlic powder
- Cheese sauce
- Raw cashews
- 1 tsp turmeric
- 1 tsp paprika
- 2 tbsp nutritional yeast
- 1 tsp lemon juice
- 2 tbsp water

Directions:
- Preheat your Air Fryer machine to 400°F. Wash and cut the potatoes in half, lengthwise. Place the fingerling potatoes wedges in a bowl and add oil, salt, pepper, and garlic powder. Toss well and transfer the potatoes to the Air Fryer's Basket. Cook for 16 minutes and stir well when halfway through. Blend all the ingredients for cheese sauce in a blender Place the potatoes in the Air

Fryer's Basket. Pour over the cheese sauce. Cook for 2 minutes in the fryer. Serve warm.

166. Zucchini Curly Fries

Preparation Time: 20 minutes
Cooking Time: 10-15 minutes
Servings: 2

Ingredients:
- 1 zucchini
- 1 egg, whisked
- 1 cup panko bread crumbs
- 1 tsp Italian seasoning
- ½ cup Parmesan cheese, grated
- nonstick cooking spray

Directions:
- Preheat an Air Fryer to 400°F. Cut zucchini into spirals using a spiralizer fitted with a large blade. Place egg in a shallow dish. Mix bread crumbs, with Italian seasoning and Parmesan cheese, in a large Ziplock plastic bag.
- Coat 1/2 of the spiralized zucchini in the whisked egg and then transfer them to the breadcrumbs bag to coat. Spray the Air Fryer's basket with cooking spray. Spread the breaded zucchini fries in the prepared basket in a single layer.
- Spray the fries with cooking spray. Cook for about 10 minutes until crispy; flip them when cooked halfway through.
- Prepare and cook the remaining fries in a similar way. Serve warm.

167. Coleslaw Stuffed Wontons

Preparation Time: 20 minutes
Cooking Time: 20 minutes
Servings: 4

Ingredients:
- 1 package wonton of wrappers
- 1 package coleslaw mix
- 2 tbsp soy sauce
- 2 tbsp butter

Directions:
- Add butter to a cast iron pan and toss in coleslaw; thoroughly mix. Sauté it for 5 minutes, then add soy sauce. Adjust seasoning with black pepper and salt, then turn off the heat. Spread the wonton wrapper over a sheet of wax paper.
- Add a tbsp of coleslaw to the center of each wrap. Wet the edges of all the wonton wrappers and fold them into a triangle to seal the filling. Set the wontons in the Air Fryer basket.
- Let your Air Fryer preheat at 375°F. Return the basket to its fryer, then cook for 10 minutes approximately. Flip the wontons and cook for another 4 minutes. Serve warm.

168. Jalapeno Cheese Balls

Preparation Time: 30 minutes
Cooking Time: 15 minutes
Servings: 12

Ingredients:
- 4 ounces cream cheese
- ⅓ cup shredded mozzarella cheese
- ⅓ cup shredded Cheddar cheese
- 2 jalapeños, finely chopped
- ½ cup bread crumbs
- 2 eggs
- ½ cup all-purpose flour
- Salt
- Pepper
- Cooking oil

Directions:
- Set the air fryer to 380°F. In a medium bowl, combine the cream cheese, mozzarella, Cheddar, and jalapeños. Mix well.
- Form the cheese mixture into balls about an inch thick. Using a small ice cream scoop works well.
- Arrange the cheese balls on a sheet pan and place them in the freezer for 15 minutes. This will help the cheese balls maintain their shape while frying.
- The air fryer basket/pan needs to be sprayed with a nonstick spray
- Place the bread crumbs in a small bowl. In another small bowl, beat the eggs. In a third small bowl, combine the flour with salt and pepper to taste, and mix well.
- Remove the cheese balls from the freezer. Dredge cheese balls in the flour, then the eggs, and then the bread crumbs.
- Place the cheese balls in the air fryer. (It is okay to stack them.) Spray with cooking oil. Cook for 8 minutes.
- Open the air fryer and flip the cheese balls. I recommend flipping them instead of shaking them, so the balls maintain their form. Cook an additional 4 minutes.
- Cool before serving.

169. Black Bean Egg Rolls

Preparation Time: 20 minutes
Cooking Time: 15 minutes
Servings: 4

Ingredients:
- 1 can of black beans,
- 1 (13.5 oz) spinach,
- 1 1/3 cups shredded jalapeno Jack cheese
- 2 cups frozen corn, thawed
- 1 cup shredded Cheddar cheese
- 1 (4 oz) can dice green Chile, drained
- 4 green onions, sliced1 tsp salt
- 1 tsp ground cumin
- 1 tsp chili powder
- 1 (16 oz) package egg roll wrappers
- cooking spray

Directions:
- Toss corn with spinach with beans, cheese, green onions, cumin, salt, chili powder, and green Chile in a large bowl. Spread an egg roll wrapper and wet all the edges. Add ¼ cup of the spinach filling at the center and fold into a roll to seal the filling.

- Repeat the same cooking steps with the rest of the wrappers. Set the wrappers in the air basket and spray them with cooking oil.
- Return the basket to the Air Fryer and cook at 390°F for 8 minutes approximately. Flip all the wrappers and cook for another 4 minutes. Serve warm.

170.   Cheese and Salsa Mushrooms

Preparation Time: 10 minutes
Cooking Time: 10 minutes
Servings: 5

Ingredients:
- 8 ounces large portobello mushrooms
- ⅓ cup salsa
- ½ cup shredded Cheddar cheese
- Cooking oil

Directions:
- Set the air fryer to 370°F. Cut the stem out of the mushrooms: First, chop off the end of the stem, and then make a circular cut around the area where the stem was. Continue to cut until you have removed the rest of the stem.
- Stuff the mushrooms with the salsa. Sprinkle the shredded cheese on top.
- Place the mushrooms in the air fryer. Cook for 8 minutes.
- Cool before serving.

171.   Buffalo Cauliflower Bites

Preparation Time: 10 minutes
Cooking Time: 25-30 minutes
Servings: 3

Ingredients:
- 1 cup all-purpose flour
- 1 cup water
- 1 tsp garlic powder
- 1 large head cauliflower, cut into florets (4 cups)
- Cooking oil
- ⅓ cup Frank's Red-Hot Buffalo Wings sauce

Directions:
- Air fryer temperature set to 370°F. In a large bowl, combine the flour, water, and garlic powder. Mix well. The mixture should resemble pancake batter.
- Put the cauliflower into the batter and stir for it to coat. Transfer the cauliflower to another large bowl to drain the excess batter.
- Spray the air fryer with cooking oil.
- Transfer the cauliflower to the air fryer. Do not stack. Cook in batches. Spray the cauliflower with cooking oil. Cook for 6 minutes (Same Temp.)
- Open the air fryer and transfer the cauliflower to a large bowl. Drizzle with the Buffalo sauce. Mix well.
- Return the cauliflower to the air fryer. Cook for an additional 6 minutes, or until crisp.
- Remove the cooked cauliflower from the air fryer, then repeat steps 4 through 6 for the remaining cauliflower batches.
- Cool before serving.

172.   Twice Baked Potatoes

Preparation Time: 15 minutes
Cooking Time: 50 minutes
Servings: 8

Ingredients:
- 4 large russet potatoes
- 4 slices bacon
- 2 tbsp butter
- ½ cup milk
- 1 tsp garlic powder
- Salt
- Pepper
- 2 scallions, green parts (white parts optional), chopped
- 2 tbsp sour cream
- 1¼ cups shredded Cheddar cheese, divided

Directions:
- Set your fryer to 400°F. Using a fork, poke three holes into the top of each potato.
- Place the potatoes in the air fryer. Cook for 40 minutes.
- Meanwhile, in a skillet over medium-high heat, cook the bacon for about 5 to 7 minutes, flipping to evenly crisp. Drain on paper towels, crumble, and set aside.
- Remove the cooked potatoes from the air fryer and allow them to cool for 10 minutes. While the potatoes cool, heat a saucepan over medium-high heat. Add the butter and milk. Stir. Allow the mixture to cook for 2 to 3 minutes until the butter has melted.
- Halve each of the potatoes lengthwise. Scoop half of the flesh out of the middle of each potato half, leaving the flesh on the surrounding edges. This will hold the potato together when you stuff it.
- Place the potato flesh in a large bowl and mash with a potato masher. Add the warm butter and milk mixture and stir to combine. Season with garlic powder and salt and pepper to taste.
- Add the cooked bacon, scallions, sour cream, and 1 cup of Cheddar cheese. Stir to combine.
- Stuff each potato half with 1 to 2 tbsp of the mashed potato mixture. Sprinkle the remaining ¼ cup of Cheddar cheese on top of the potato halves.
- Place 4 potato halves in the air fryer. Do not stack. Cook for 2 to 3 minutes, or until the cheese has melted.
- Remove the cooked potatoes from the air fryer, then repeat step 10 for the remaining 4 potato halves.

173.   Apricots Stuffed with Walnuts

Preparation Time: 10 minutes
Cooking Time: 15 minutes
Servings: 6

Ingredients:
- 6 Fresh Apricots
- 2 Tbsp mini semi-sweet chocolate chips
- 1/4 cup walnuts
- 1/2 cup apple cider vinegar

Directions:
- Cut each apricot in half. Combine the chocolate chips, walnuts, and apple cider vinegar in a small bowl. Put about 2 tsp of the filling mixture in each half of the apricots.

- Place the assembled mold in the oven on the wire rack. Position 2. Set Air Fry at 200 ° C for 15 minutes. Cook golden brown and crispy.

174.   Breaded Okra

Preparation Time: 15 minutes
Cooking Time: 10 minutes
Servings: 4

Ingredients:
- 1½ cups okra, cut into ¼-inch pieces
- 3 tbsp buttermilk
- 2 tbsp all-purpose flour
- 2 tbsp cornmeal
- Salt
- Pepper
- Cooking oil

Directions:
- Set your air fryer to 380°F. Make sure the okra pieces are dry, using paper towels if needed.
- Pour the buttermilk into a small bowl. In another small bowl, combine the flour and cornmeal, and season with salt and pepper to taste.
- The air fryer basket/pan needs to be sprayed with a nonstick spray
- Dip the okra in the buttermilk, then the flour and cornmeal.
- Place the okra in the air fryer basket. It is okay to stack it. Spray the okra with cooking oil. Let it cook for 5 minutes.
- The air fryer must be opened and shake the basket.
- Cook for an additional 5 minutes or until the okra is crisp.

175.   Cajun Sweet Potato Tots

Preparation Time: 10 minutes
Cooking Time: 30 minutes
Servings: 4-5

Ingredients:
- 2 sweet potatoes, peeled
- 1 tsp Cajun seasoning
- Salt

Directions:
- Put some water in a pot, then boil it together with the sweet potatoes. After boiling, drain it, then after which smash it. Season with Cajun seasoning and combine. Add some oil. Put tot in the air fryer basket
- Cook at 400°F for 8 minutes. Turn tots to another side and cook for 8 minutes more.
- Serve and enjoy.

176.   Bacon and Cheese Jalapeno Poppers

Preparation Time: 20 minutes
Cooking Time: 5-10 minutes
Servings: 5

Ingredients:
- 10 fresh jalapeno peppers, cut in half, and remove seeds
- 2 bacon slices, cooked and crumbled
- 1/4 cup cheddar cheese, shredded
- 6 oz cream cheese, softened

Directions:
- In a bowl, combine together bacon, cream cheese, and cheddar cheese.
- Stuff each jalapeno half with bacon cheese mixture.
- Spray the air fryer basket with cooking spray.
- Place stuffed jalapeno halved in an air fryer basket and cooked at 370°F for 5 minutes.
- Serve and enjoy.

177.   Coriander Potatoes

Preparation Time: 10 minutes
Cooking Time: 30 minutes
Servings: 4

Ingredients:
- 1-pound gold potatoes, peeled and cut into wedges
- Salt and black pepper to the taste
- 1 tbsp tomato sauce
- 2 tbsp coriander, chopped
- ½ tsp garlic powder
- 1 tsp chili powder
- 1 tbsp olive oil

Directions:
- In a bowl, combine the potatoes with the tomato sauce and the other ingredients, toss, and transfer to the air fryer's basket.
- In the air fryer, cook at 370 °F for 25 minutes, divide between plates and serve as a side dish.

178.   Ricotta Balls

Preparation Time: 15 minutes
Cooking Time: 20 minutes
Servings: 6

Ingredients:
- ½ lb. ricotta
- 2 tbsp of flour
- 1 egg, separated and clear yolk
- Freshly ground black pepper
- ½ oz. fresh basil, finely chopped
- 1 tbsp chives, finely chopped
- 3 slices of stale white bread

Directions:
- Mix the ricotta in a bowl with the flour, the egg yolk, 1 tsp of salt, and freshly ground black pepper. Add the basil, chives, and orange zest to the mixture. Divide the mixture into 20 equal portions and form the balls with wet hands. Let the balls rest for a while.
- Grind the bread slices until obtaining a fine bread crumb with the food processor and mix with the olive oil. Put the mixture in a deep container. Lightly beat the egg white in another deep bowl.
- Preheat the fryer to 400°F. Carefully roll the ricotta balls into the egg whites and breadcrumbs. Place ten balls in the basket and slide them into the fryer. Set the timer for 8 to 10 minutes. Bake the balls until golden. Bake the rest of the balls in the same way.
- Serve the ricotta.

179.   Falafel with Tahini Sauce

Preparation Time: 30 minutes
Cooking Time: 20 minutes
Servings: 4

Ingredients:

- Falafel:
- chickpea nuggets
- 1 lb. chickpeas
- Fresh mint leaves
- 2 or 3 Syrian loaves
- Milk to moisten
- 1 tbsp of pasta dessert
- crushed garlic
- Salt and pepper to taste
- Lemon drops
- Tahini sauce:
- 1 tbsp of tahini
- ½ squeezed lemon
- ½ cup of water
- ½ crushed garlic clove

Directions:

- Falafel:
- Preheat the fryer to 400°F for 4 to 6 minutes. Drain the chickpeas. In a bowl, combine the minced bread, mint leaves, chickpeas, and beaten garlic.
- Add the pepper and drops of lemon juice. Moisten the mixture with a little milk and let it rest for half an hour so that the milk is absorbed.
- Then mix the mixture in a processor. The consistency must be smooth but firm to form balls. Make medium balls and flatten them out a bit.
- Put a layer of balls in the fryer basket and leave it for about 15 minutes, turning it half the time so that it browns evenly. If necessary, leave another 5 minutes. Place them in the center of a plate. When you serve, place the garnishes around.
- Tahini Sauce:
- Mix all ingredients and serve.

180.   Roasted Paprika Carrots

Preparation Time: 10 minutes
Cooking Time: 20 minutes
Servings: 1

Ingredients:

- 1 carrot
- Salt to taste
- Black pepper to taste
- Smoked paprika to taste
- Olive oil

Directions:

- Start by cutting the carrots into small strips. Cut it in half.
- Season well and mix with olive oil.
- Take the air fryer at 360°F for 20 minutes or until golden brown; this is the secret, as they are crispy on the outside and soft on the inside.
- Serve with a little sauce.

181.   Garlic Mashed Turnips

Preparation Time: 10 minutes
Cooking Time: 10 minutes
Servings: 4

Ingredients:

- 2 medium turnips, peeled off and cut into cubes
- 1/4 tsp garlic powder
- 1/4 tsp onion powder
- 1 tbsp olive oil
- Pinch of salt

Directions:

- In a bowl, combine turnip cubes. Toss in the olive oil to coat.
- Toss in the onion powder, garlic powder, and salt.
- Brush the air fryer basket with oil and arrange the seasoned turnip cubes in a single layer on it.
- Cook for 10-15 minutes in an Air Fryer set to 380°F. After 5 minutes, shake the basket.

182.   Bacon Scallops

Preparation Time: 15 minutes
Cooking Time: 5 minutes
Servings: 4

Ingredients:

- 16 large sea scallops, pat dry with paper towels
- 16 toothpicks
- 8 slices of center-cut bacon
- olive oil spray
- Freshly ground black pepper, to taste

Directions:

- Set the air fryer for 3 minutes at 400°F.
- Place the bacon in the air fryer for 3 minutes, flipping halfway through.
- Remove from fryer and put on a paper towel to cool.
- Remove any scalloped side muscles. To eliminate any moisture, pat the scallops dry with paper towels.
- Wrap each scallop with a bacon slice and fasten with a toothpick.
- Spritz olive oil over scallops and season with black pepper to taste.
- Cook the scallops in a single layer in the air fryer for 8 minutes, flipping halfway, until soft and opaque and the bacon is cooked through. Serve immediately.

183.   Spring Salad

Preparation Time: 10 minutes
Cooking Time: 10 minutes
Servings: 4

Ingredients:

- 6 plum tomatoes, halved
- 2 large red onions, sliced
- 4 long red pepper, sliced
- 2 yellow pepper, sliced
- 6 cloves of garlic, crushed
- 1 tbsp. extra-virgin olive oil
- 1 tsp. paprika
- ½ lemon, juiced
- Salt and pepper to taste
- 1 tbsp. baby capers

Directions:

- Pre-heat the Air Fryer to 420°F. Put the tomatoes, onions, peppers, and garlic in a large bowl and cover with the extra virgin olive oil, paprika, and lemon juice. Sprinkle with salt and pepper as desired.
- Line the inside of your fryer with aluminum foil. Place the vegetables inside and allow them to cook for 10 minutes, ensuring the edges turn brown.
- Serve in a salad bowl with the baby capers. Make sure all the ingredients are well combined.

184. Healthy Beet Hummus

Preparation Time: 10 minutes
Cooking Time: 40 minutes
Servings: 16

Ingredients:

- 1 cup chickpeas
- 1/3 cup water
- 1/4 cup olive oil
- 1/4 cup fresh lemon juice
- 3 beets, peeled and diced
- 2 garlic cloves, peeled
- 1/4 cup sunflower seeds
- 1 1/2 tsp kosher salt

Directions:

- Add beets, chickpeas, 1 tsp salt, 3 cups water, garlic, and sunflower seeds into the air fryer.
- Cook it for 40 minutes at 375°F.
- Strain beet, chickpeas, garlic, and sunflower seeds and place in a food processor along with lemon juice and remaining salt and process until smooth.
- Add oil and 1/3 cup water and process until smooth.
- Serve and enjoy.

185. Chicken Jalapeno Popper Dip

Preparation Time: 10 minutes
Cooking Time: 14 minutes
Servings: 10

Ingredients:

- 1 lb. chicken breast, boneless
- 1/2 cup water
- 1/2 cup breadcrumbs
- 3/4 cup sour cream
- 3 jalapeno pepper, sliced
- 8 oz cream cheese
- 8 oz cheddar cheese

Directions:

- Add chicken, jalapeno, water, and cream cheese into the air fryer.
- Let it cook for 12 minutes at 350°F.
- Stir in cream and cheddar cheese.
- Transfer the air fryer mixture to the baking dish and top with breadcrumbs, and broil for 2 minutes.
- Serve and enjoy.

186. Turmeric Potatoes

Preparation Time: 10 minutes
Cooking Time: 30 minutes
Servings: 2

Ingredients:

- 1 tsp ghee
- 2 big potatoes
- 1 sweet yellow pepper
- 1 white onion, sliced
- ½ tsp salt
- ½ tsp ground black pepper
- ½ tsp onion powder
- ½ tsp turmeric

Directions:

- Wash the potatoes carefully and cut them into medium cubes.
- Preheat the air fryer to 365°F.
- Put the potato cubes in the big bowl. Add water and leave the vegetables for 10 minutes.
- After this, drain the potatoes and dry them with the help of a paper towel.
- Place the potato cubes in the air fryer and add ghee.
- Cook the potatoes for 15 minutes.
- Then shake the potatoes and cook for 4 minutes more.
- Meanwhile, remove the seeds from the sweet yellow pepper and cut them into the strips.
- Combine the pepper strips with the sliced onion.
- After this, combine the turmeric, onion powder, ground black pepper, and salt in the shallow bowl. Stir it gently.
- Put the pepper-onion mixture in the air fryer.
- Sprinkle the mixture with spices and shake gently.
- Cook the meal for 6 minutes at 370°F.
- Then shake the cooked meal again.
- Enjoy!

187. Carrot Balls

Preparation Time: 10 minutes
Cooking Time: 4 minutes
Servings: 2

Ingredients:

- 2 carrots, boiled
- ½ tsp salt
- 1 tbsp turmeric
- 1 tbsp dried oregano
- 1 egg white
- 2 tbsp flour
- 1 tsp olive oil
- 3 tbsp plain yogurt

Directions:

- Grate the carrot and combine it together with salt, turmeric, dried oregano, egg white, flour, and plain yogurt.
- Form the small balls from the carrot mixture.
- Preheat the air fryer to 400°F.
- Place the carrot balls in the air fryer and sprinkle them with olive oil.
- Cook the carrot balls for 4 minutes.
- When the meal is cooked – chill it till the room temperature.

188. Goat Cheese and Figs

Preparation Time: 10 minutes
Cooking Time: 7 minutes
Servings: 2

Ingredients:
- 3 oz goat cheese
- 4 figs
- ½ tsp minced garlic
- 1 tbsp olive oil
- 1 tbsp fresh lemon juice
- ½ tsp ground ginger

Directions:
- Make the cross cuts in the figs.
- Remove ½ of all flesh from the figs.
- Combine the minced garlic, olive oil, and ground ginger in the bowl.
- Stir the mixture.
- Add the goat cheese and stir it.
- Then fill the figs with the goat cheese mixture well.
- Preheat the air fryer to 360°F and put the figs in the air fryer basket.
- Sprinkle the figs with the fresh lemon juice and cook for 7 minutes.
- When the figs are cooked – serve them hot.

189. Corn with Cheese and Lime

Preparation Time: 10 minutes
Cooking Time: 15 minutes
Servings: 2

Ingredients:
- 2 Corns on the cob, husks removed
- A drizzle of olive oil
- ½ cup Feta cheese, grated
- 2 tsp sweet paprika
- 2 limes Juice

Directions:
- Rub corn with oil and paprika. Place in the air fryer basket and cook at 400°F for 15 minutes. Flip once.
- Divide corn among plates and sprinkle cheese on top. Drizzle with lime juice and serve.

190. Chicken Buffalo Dip

Preparation Time: 15 minutes
Cooking Time: 10 minutes
Servings: 4

Ingredients:
- 1 cup cooked chicken breast, diced
- 8 ounces of full-fat cream cheese, softened
- ½ cup Buffalo sauce
- 1/3 cup Full-fat ranch dressing
- 1/3 cup Chopped pickled jalapenos
- 1½ cups Shred the cheddar cheese, divided
- 2 Scallions, sliced

Directions:
- Place chicken into a large bowl. Add buffalo sauce, cream cheese, and ranch dressing. Stir to mix well. Fold in jalapenos and 1-cup cheddar. Pour the mixture into a round baking dish and place the remaining cheddar on top.
- Place dish into the air fryer basket. Cook at 350°F for 10 minutes. Top with sliced scallions and serve warm.

191. Cheeseburger Dip

Preparation Time: 20 minutes
Cooking Time: 10 minutes
Servings: 6

Ingredients:
- 8 ounces of Full-fat cream cheese
- ¼ cup Full-fat mayonnaise
- ¼ cup Full-fat sour cream
- ¼ cup Chopped onion
- 1 tsp Garlic powder
- 1 tbsp Worcestershire sauce
- 1¼ cups Shredded cheddar cheese, divided
- ½ pound Cooked 80/20 ground beef
- 6 slices of bacon, cooked and crumbled
- 2 Large pickle spears, chopped

Directions:
- Place cream cheese in a bowl and microwave for 45 seconds. Stir in sour cream, mayonnaise, onion, garlic powder, 1-cup cheddar, and Worcestershire sauce. Add cooked bacon and ground beef. Sprinkle remaining cheddar on top.
- Place in a bowl and put into the air fryer basket. Cook at 400°F for 10 minutes. The dip is done when the top is golden and bubbling. Sprinkle pickles over the dish. Serve warm.

192. Prosciutto Wrapped Asparagus

Preparation Time: 15 minutes
Cooking Time: 10 minutes
Servings: 4

Ingredients:
- 1 lb Asparagus
- 12 slices of Prosciutto
- 1 tbsp Coconut oil melted
- 2 tsp Lemon juice
- 1/8 tsp Red pepper flakes
- 1/3 cup grated Parmesan cheese
- 2 tbsp salted butter, melted

Directions:
- On a clean work surface, place a few asparagus spears onto the sliced prosciutto. Drizzle with lemon juice and coconut oil. Sprinkle Parmesan and red pepper flakes across the asparagus. Roll prosciutto around asparagus spears.
- Place into the air fryer basket. Repeat. Cook at 375°F and 10 minutes. Drizzle the asparagus rolls with butter before serving.

193. Vegetable Spring Rolls

Preparation Time: 20 minutes
Cooking Time: 25minutes
Servings: 4

Ingredients:
- 2 cups Green cabbage, shredded
- 2 Yellow onions, chopped
- 1 Carrot, grated
- ½ Chili pepper, minced
- 1 tbsp Ginger
- 3 Garlic cloves, minced

- 1 tsp Sugar
- Salt and black pepper to taste
- 1 tsp Soy sauce
- 2 tbsp Olive oil
- 10 Spring roll sheets
- 2 tbsp Cornflour
- 2 tbsp Water

Directions:
- Heat oil in the Air fryer pan on Sauté. Add soy sauce, pepper, salt, sugar, garlic, ginger, chili pepper, carrots, onions, and cabbage. Stir-fry for 2 to 3 minutes. Remove and cool down. Cut spring roll sheets into squares, divide cabbage mix on each, and roll them.
- In a bowl, mix cornflour with water, stir well and seal spring rolls with this mix.
- Place spring rolls in the air fryer basket and cook at 360°F for 10 minutes. Flip rolls and cook them for 10 minutes more. Serve.

194.   Baked Yams with Dill

Preparation Time: 10 minutes
Cooking Time: 8 minutes
Servings: 2

Ingredients:
- 2 yams
- 1 tbsp fresh dill
- 1 tsp coconut oil
- ½ tsp minced garlic

Directions:
- Wash the yams carefully and cut them into halves.
- Sprinkle the yam halves with the coconut oil and then rub with the minced garlic.
- Place the yams in the air fryer basket and cook for 8 minutes at 400°F.
- After this, mash the yams gently with a fork and then sprinkle with the fresh dill.
- Serve the yams immediately.

195.   Ranch Potatoes

Preparation Time: 15 minutes
Cooking Time: 30 minutes
Servings: 6

Ingredients:
- 1 lb Potatoes, cut into chunks
- ½ tsp Dried tarragon
- 1/8 tsp Celery seed
- ¼ tsp Onion powder
- ½ tsp Garlic powder
- ¼ tsp Dried dill
- ½ tsp Dried parsley
- ½ tsp Dried chives
- 1 tsp Olive oil
- ½ tsp Kosher salt

Directions:
- In a large bowl, toss potatoes with remaining ingredients until coated thoroughly. Add potatoes into the multi-level air fryer basket and place the basket into the air fryer.

- Seal the pot with the air fryer lid. Select air fry mode and cook at 400°F for 30 minutes. Stir potatoes halfway through. Serve.

196.   Spinach Balls

Preparation Time: 35 minutes
Cooking Time: 30 minutes
Servings: 4

Ingredients:
- 3 Eggs, lightly beaten
- ½ Onion, chopped
- 1 cup Breadcrumb
- 6 oz. Frozen spinach, thawed
- ¼ cup Butter, melted
- ¼ cup Mozzarella cheese, shredded
- Pepper & salt, to taste

Directions:
- Put all ingredients into the mixing bowl and mix until combined thoroughly. Make small balls from the mixture and place them into the multi-level air fryer basket and then place the basket into the air fryer. Seal the pot with the air fryer lid.
- Select bake mode and cook at 350°F for 25 minutes. Serve.

197.   Baked Mushrooms

Preparation Time: 10 minutes
Cooking Time: 15 minutes
Servings: 6

Ingredients:
- 1 lb. Mushrooms, clean & stems trimmed
- 2 Garlic cloves, chopped
- 1 tbsp Olive oil
- 1/8 tsp Garlic powder
- 2 tbsp Chives, chopped
- Pepper & salt, to taste

Directions:
- Add mushrooms into the bowl. Add remaining ingredients and toss well. Add mushrooms into the multi-level air fryer basket and place the basket into the air fryer.
- Seal the pot with the air fryer lid. Select bake mode and cook at 380°F for 15 minutes. Serve.

198.   Honey Dill Carrots

Preparation Time: 10 minutes
Cooking Time: 12 minutes
Servings: 4

Ingredients:
- ½ lb. Baby carrots
- ½ tsp Dried dill
- ½ tbsp Honey
- ½ tbsp Olive oil
- Pepper & salt, to taste

Directions:
- Add all ingredients into the bowl and toss well and transfer carrots into the multi-level air fryer basket and

place the basket into the air fryer. Seal the pot with the air fryer lid.
- Select air fry mode and cook at 350°F for 12 minutes. Stir halfway through. Serve.

199. Mushroom and Cheese Hasselback Potatoes

Preparation Time: 30 minutes
Cooking Time: 40 minutes
Servings: 2

Ingredients:
- 2 Potatoes, Using a sharp knife, make slits on top
- 2 tbsp Butter, melted
- 3 tbsp Mushrooms, sliced
- 4 tbsp Parmesan cheese, grated
- Pepper & salt, to taste

Directions:
- Slide mushroom slices into each slit on the potatoes. Brush Potatoes with melted butter and season with pepper and salt. Place potatoes into the multi-level air fryer basket and place the basket into the air fryer. Seal the pot with the air fryer lid.
- Select air fry mode and cook at 350°F for 20 minutes. Sprinkle parmesan cheese on top of potatoes and air fry for 20 minutes more. Serve.

200. Rosemary and Garlic Fries

Preparation Time: 10 minutes
Cooking Time: 16 minutes
Servings: 4

Ingredients:
- 2 cups cubed potato (small cubes from 2 medium potatoes)
- 1½ tsp oil (olive or sunflower)
- 3 medium cloves garlic, minced or pressed
- ¼ tsp sea salt
- ¼ tsp onion granules
- ⅛ tsp freshly ground black pepper
- Cooking oil spray (sunflower, safflower, or refined coconut)
- ½ tbsp dried rosemary or fresh rosemary, minced

Directions:
- In a medium bowl, toss the potatoes with the oil, garlic, salt, onion granules, and black pepper. Stir to evenly coat the potatoes with the seasonings. Place the potato mixture in the air fryer basket and roast for 8 minutes at 400°F. Set the bowl aside.
- Remove, shake the basket or stir the contents and cook for another 8 minutes at 400°F, or until the potatoes are tender and nicely browned. Add the potatoes back to the bowl and spray with oil. Add the rosemary, toss, and serve immediately.

201. Zucchini Fries

Preparation Time: 10 minutes
Cooking Time: 14 minutes
Servings: 4

Ingredients:
- 2 small zucchinis (about ½ pound)

- ½ tsp garlic granules
- ¼ tsp sea salt
- ⅛ tsp freshly ground black pepper
- 2 tsp arrowroot (or cornstarch)
- 3 tbsp chickpea flour
- 1 tbsp water
- Cooking oil spray (sunflower, safflower, or refined coconut)

Directions:
- Trim the ends off the zucchini and then cut into sticks about 2 inches long and ½ inch wide. You should end up with about 2 cups of sticks.
- In a medium bowl, combine the zucchini sticks with garlic, salt, pepper, arrowroot, and flour. Stir well. Add the water and stir again, using a rubber spatula if you have one.
- Spray the air fryer basket with oil and add the zucchini sticks, spreading them out as much as possible. Spray the zucchini with oil. Fry for 7 minutes at 400°F.
- Remove the basket, gently stir or shake so the zucchini cooks evenly, and spray again with oil. Cook for another 7 minutes at 400°F, or until tender, nicely browned, and crisp on the outside. Enjoy the sticks plain or with your preferred dipping sauce.

202. Roasted Garlic Zucchini

Preparation Time: 10 minutes
Cooking Time: 14 minutes
Servings: 4

Ingredients:
- Cooking oil spray (sunflower, safflower, or refined coconut)
- 2 zucchinis, sliced in ¼- to ½-inch-thick rounds (about 2 cups)
- ¼ tsp garlic granules
- ⅛ tsp sea salt
- Freshly ground black pepper (optional)

Directions:
- Spray the air fryer basket with oil. Place the zucchini rounds in the basket and spread them out as much as you can. Sprinkle the tops evenly with the garlic, salt, and pepper, if using. Set the air fryer to 350°F. Spray with the oil and roast for 7 minutes.
- Remove the basket from the air fryer, toss or flip the zucchini with a spatula to cook evenly, and spray with oil again. Roast an additional 5 minutes at the same settings or until the zucchini rounds are nicely browned and tender.

203. Indian Spiced Okra

Preparation Time: 5 minutes
Cooking Time: 20 minutes
Servings: 4

Ingredients:
- ½ pound okra (3 cups)
- 1 tbsp coconut oil, melted
- 1 tsp cumin
- 1 tsp coriander
- 1 tsp garlic granules
- ¼ tsp sea salt

- ¼ tsp turmeric
- ⅛ tsp cayenne
- 1 tsp fresh lime juice

Directions:
- Place the okra in a medium bowl and toss with the oil. Add the cumin, coriander, garlic, salt, turmeric, and cayenne. Stir well, preferably with a rubber spatula, until the okra is well coated with the seasonings. Preheat the air fryer to 400°F.
- Put the okra in the air fryer basket and fry for 7 minutes. Set the seasoning bowl aside. Remove the air fryer basket, stir or toss to evenly cook the okra, and place it back in the air fryer, frying for another 7 minutes. Remove the basket, toss, and check for doneness. At this point, you'll most likely need to fry your okra for another 6 minutes, but it depends on the size of your okra (smaller pieces cook more quickly). Remove when the pieces feel crisp rather than "squishy." If you have a variety of sizes in your okra, you may need to remove smaller pieces, as they'll finish cooking before larger pieces.
- Once all of the okra is crisp, place it back into the seasoning bowl. Sprinkle the lime juice on top, give the okra one last stir, and serve immediately.

204. Crunchy Almond & Kale Salad with Roasted Chicken

Preparation Time: 10 minutes
Cooking Time: 20 minutes
Servings: 1

Ingredients:
- Salad
- 1 tsp extra virgin olive oil
- 100g Lacinato kale, sliced into thin strips
- 1/4 cup roasted almonds
- Pinch of sea salt
- Pinch of pepper
- Roasted Chicken
- 100g chicken thighs
- Pinch of sea salt
- Pinch of pepper
- 1 tsp apple cider vinegar
- 1/2 tsp extra-virgin olive oil
- 1 tbsp rosemary
- 1 tbsp cup sage

Directions:
- Place kale in a bowl and add olive oil; massage olive oil with hands into the kale until kale is tender; sprinkle with salt and pepper and toss with toasted almonds.
- Preheat your air fryer toast oven to 360°F.
- Sprinkle chicken with salt and pepper; add vinegar and olive oil and season with rosemary and sage.
- Roast in the basket of your air fryer toast oven for about 20 minutes, turning the chicken halfway through or until the chicken is cooked through.
- Serve chicken with kale and almond salad.

205. Pakoras

Preparation Time: 10 minutes
Cooking Time: 16 minutes
Servings: 5

Ingredients:
- ⅔ cup chickpea flour
- 1 tbsp arrowroot (or cornstarch)
- 1½ tsp sea salt
- 2 tsp cumin powder
- ½ tsp coriander powder
- ½ tsp turmeric
- ⅛ tsp baking soda
- ⅛ tsp cayenne powder
- 1½ cups minced onion
- ½ cup chopped cilantro
- ½ cup finely chopped cauliflower
- ¼ cup fresh lemon juice
- Cooking oil spray (coconut, sunflower, or safflower)

Directions:
- In a medium bowl, combine the chickpea flour, arrowroot, salt, cumin, coriander, turmeric, baking soda, and cayenne. Stir well.
- Add the onion, cilantro, cauliflower, and lemon juice to the flour mixture. Stir very well. Set aside.
- The air fryer basket/pan needs to be sprayed with a nonstick spray
- Grab a plate and set it aside as well.
- Using your hands, stir the mixture together again, massaging the flour and spices into the vegetables. Then begin to form the pakoras: Take small bits (about 1 tbsp—the idea is to keep them small, so they'll cook all the way through) and smash them together in your palm to form into a 1-inch ball. Place in the air fryer.
- Repeat with the remaining batter, making pakoras and placing them in the basket, making sure to leave room in between each one, so they don't touch. You'll most likely end up placing half of the mixture in the air fryer basket and half on a plate to cook later.
- Spray the tops of the pakoras in the air fryer with oil (use a generous amount) and fry for 4 minutes at 180°C. Remove the air fryer basket, spray generously with oil again and fry for another 4 minutes.
- Remove the basket and spray the pakoras again with oil. Gently turn each one over. Spray the tops with oil and fry for 4 minutes. Remove the basket, spray generously with oil one last time, and fry for a final 4 minutes, or until very browned and crisp. Serve immediately, plain or with some Cilantro Chutney.
- Repeat steps 4 to 7 with the remaining batter, or store in the fridge for future use (the batter will last about 5 days in an airtight container, refrigerated).

206. Sweetened Onions

Preparation Time: 10 minutes
Cooking Time: 20 minutes
Servings: 2

Ingredients:
- 2 large white onions
- 1 tbsp raw honey
- 1 tsp water
- 1 tbsp paprika

Directions:
- Peel the onions and, using a knife, make cuts in the shape of a cross.
- Then combine the raw honey and water; stir.
- Add the paprika and stir the mixture until smooth.

- Place the onions in the air fryer basket and sprinkle them with the honey mixture.
- Cook the onions for 16 minutes at 380°F.
- When the onions are cooked, they should be soft.
- Transfer the cooked onions to serving plates and serve.

207.   Lemon Lentils

Preparation Time: 10 minutes
Cooking Time: 30 minutes
Servings: 4

Ingredients:
- 1 cup of red lentils
- 4 cups water
- Cooking oil spray (coconut, sunflower, or safflower)
- 1 medium-size onion, peeled and cut into ¼-inch-thick rings
- Sea salt
- ½ cup kale stems removed, thinly sliced
- 3 large garlic cloves, pressed or minced
- 2 tbsp fresh lemon juice
- 2 tsp nutritional yeast
- 1 tsp sea salt
- 1 tsp lemon zest (see Ingredient Tip)
- ¾ tsp freshly ground black pepper

Directions:
- In a medium-large pot, bring the lentils and water to a boil over medium-high heat. Reduce the heat to low and simmer, uncovered, for about 30 minutes (or until the lentils have dissolved completely), making sure to stir every 5 minutes or so as they cook (so that the lentils don't stick to the bottom of the pot).
- While the lentils are cooking, get the rest of your dish together. Spray the air fryer basket with oil and place the onion rings inside, separating them as much as possible. Spray them with the oil and sprinkle them with a little salt. Fry for 5 minutes at 350°F. Remove the air fryer basket, shake or stir, spray again with oil, and fry for another 5 minutes. (Note: You're aiming for all of the onion slices to be crisp and well browned, so if some of the pieces begin to do that, transfer them from the air fryer basket to a plate.)
- Remove the air fryer basket, spray the onions again with oil, and fry for a final 5 minutes or until all the pieces are crisp and browned.
- To finish the lentils: Add the kale to the hot lentils, and stir very well, as the heat from the lentils will steam the thinly sliced greens. Stir in the garlic, lemon juice, nutritional yeast, salt, zest, and pepper. Stir very well and then distribute evenly in bowls. Top with the crisp onion rings and serve.

208.   Baba Ghanoush

Preparation Time: 40 minutes
Cooking Time: 1 hr. 15 minutes
Servings: 6

Ingredients:
- 1 medium-sized eggplant around 13 ounces
- 2 tsp of organic canola oil
- 3 tbsp tahini
- 1 Tbsp of lemon juice
- 1 clove of garlic minced

- 1/8 tsp of cumin
- 1/4 tsp of smoked salt
- 1/8 tsp of regular salt
- Drizzle extra virgin olive oil optional garnish

Directions:
- Cut the stem off the end of the Aubergine. Slice the eggplant lengthwise down the center. Place one tsp of canola oil on each half of the eggplant and rub it uniformly over the entire eggplant, including the cut side, and peel. Prick with a fork into several holes in the eggplant peel.
- Place halves of the eggplant cut side down in the bucket of the air fryer. Air for 20 minutes, cook at 400°F. (If you don't have an air fryer, then roast the eggplant in the oven. Preheat the oven to 400°F and place the eggplant halves cut-side-down on the baking sheet lined with parchment paper. Roast for 45 minutes. Test for doneness at about 35 minutes because cooking times can vary.) The cut side is crispy and toasty, and the peel is wrinkled. Take half of the eggplant from the air fryer bowl, push it onto a plate and allow it to cool.
- Once the eggplant half is cool enough to touch, scoop out the soft eggplant from its peel and place the eggplant in a food processor. You will be able to scoop out all the soft white eggplant with ease. You can have the peel discarded.
- To the food processor, add the tahini, lemon juice, garlic, cumin, smoked salt, and standard salt. Food processor pulse 4 or 5 times. Baba ghanoush is best when there's still a bit of body to it, as opposed to being absolutely smooth. The baba ghanoush can be served at once, but it is best if the flavors have an opportunity to meld for at least a few hours. (It's even better if you can make it the day before you want to serve it.) Move it into a covered container and place it in the fridge until you're ready to serve it.
- Serve the baba ghanoush for a dipping with pita bread and/or sliced vegetables. Before serving, pour a little extra virgin olive oil over the baba ghanoush, if you like.

209.   Corn and Egg Salad

Preparation Time: 60 minutes
Cooking Time: 40 minutes
Servings: 8

Ingredients:
- 6 large Eggs
- 3 ears of Corn cut into smaller pieces
- 2 tsp of Canola or Vegetable Oil
- Salt and Pepper to taste
- ¼ cup of sliced Red Onion
- ½ cup of julienned Carrots
- ½ cup of julienned Red Bell Pepper
- ½ cup of julienned Green Pepper
- Dressing
- 1 cup of Mayonnaise
- 1 tbsp of Yellow or Dijon Mustard
- 1 tsp of Maple Syrup or Honey
- Salt and Pepper to taste

Directions:
- Place the trivet in the basket of your air fryer. Stir the eggs in.

- Air-fry at 250°F for 20 minutes.
- Submerge the eggs in an ice bath as soon as the fryer beeps, using tongs.
- Then, cut and dice them into large chunks.
- Cut the corn cobs into small pieces in the air fryer to fit them in.
- Coat the corns in vegetable oil and sprinkle salt and pepper over them.
- Fry air for 10 minutes at 400°F, then flip once.
- Once the corn is finished and slightly cooled, the kernels are carefully cut out from the cob using a knife.
- Combine the air-fried corn kernels, the diced eggs, sliced onions, julienned carrots, and red and green peppers in a large bowl. Good shoot it. The mayonnaise, mustard, maple syrup, salt, and pepper are mixed in a small bowl. Whisk to merge.
- Attach egg and corn salad to the dressing and toss to blend properly.
- Cover and let the flavors evolve for about an hour to chill.
- Serve with grilled meat as a hand.
- Refrigerate the leftovers right away.

210. Porcini Risotto

Preparation Time: 10 minutes
Cooking Time: 25-30 minutes
Servings: 6

Ingredients:
- 320 g of basmati rice
- 200 g of porcini mushrooms
- 1250ml of broth
- 1 clove garlic
- Parsley to taste
- Grated cheese to taste
- Butter to taste

Directions:
- Grease the basket and add the garlic clove.
- Set the temperature to 150°C and brown for 2 minutes.
- Remove the garlic, add the porcini mushrooms and simmer for another 5 minutes.
- Add the rice, half the amount of the broth, and simmer for another 10 minutes.
- Pour the rest of the broth and finish cooking for another 13 minutes. Mix 2-3 times with a ladle at the end of cooking.

211. Peas and Bacon

Preparation Time: 20 minutes
Cooking Time: 45 minutes
Servings: 8

Ingredients:
- 750 g of frozen peas
- 100 g smoked bacon
- 2 shallots
- Salt and pepper to taste
- 200ml broth

Directions:
- Preheat the air fryer to 160°C for 5 minutes.
- Pour the chopped onion, bacon, oil into the basket
- Brown for 5 min.

- Add the peas, broth, salt, pepper, and simmer for additional 30 minutes.

212. Mini Peppers with Goat Cheese

Preparation Time: 10 minutes
Cooking Time: 8 minutes
Servings: 4

Ingredients:
- 8 mini peppers
- ½ tbsp olive oil
- ½ tbsp dried Italian herbs
- 1 tsp freshly ground black pepper
- 100 g soft goat cheese in eight portions

Directions:
- Preheat the air fryer to 200°C.
- Cut the top of the mini peppers and remove the seeds and the membrane.
- Mix the olive oil in a deep dish with the Italian herbs and pepper. Pour the portions of goat cheese into the oil.
- Press a serving of goat cheese against each mini pepper and place the mini peppers in the basket next to each other. Insert the basket into the air fryer and set the timer to 8 minutes. Bake the mini peppers until the cheese is melted.
- Serve mini peppers in small dishes such as snacks or snacks.

213. Roasted Pepper and Greens Salad

Preparation Time: 15 minutes
Cooking Time: 10 minutes
Servings: 4

Ingredients:
- 1 red pepper
- 1 tbsp lemon juice
- 3 tbsp yogurt
- 2 tbsp olive oil
- Freshly ground black pepper
- 1 romaine lettuce in wide strips
- 50 g arugula leaves

Directions:
- Preheat the air fryer to 200°C.
- Place the pepper in the basket and place it in the air fryer. Set the timer to 10 minutes and roast the pepper until the skin is slightly burned.
- Place the pepper in a bowl and cover it with a lid or with transparent film. Let stand for 10 to 15 minutes.
- Next, cut the pepper into four parts and remove the seeds and skin. Cut the pepper into strips.
- Mix a dressing in a bowl with 2 tbsp of the pepper juice, lemon juice, yogurt, and olive oil. Add pepper and salt to taste.
- Pour the lettuce and arugula leaves into the dressing and garnish the salad with the pepper strips.

214. Asparagus Fries

Preparation Time: 10 minutes
Cooking Time: 15 minutes
Servings: 5

Ingredients:
- Two tbsp parsley, chopped
- ½ tsp garlic powder
- ¼ cup almond flour
- ½ tsp smoked paprika
- Salt and pepper to taste
- Ten medium asparagus stems trimmed
- Two large eggs, beaten

Directions:
- Preheat the air fryer to 350°F for 5 minutes.
- In a mixing bowl, combine the parsley, garlic powder, almond flour, and smoked paprika. Season with salt and pepper to taste.
- Soak the asparagus in the beaten eggs and then dredge in the almond flour mixture.
- Place in the air fryer basket.
- Cook for 15 minutes at 350°F.
- Serve and enjoy!

215. Sautéed Pumpkin and Potatoes

Preparation Time: 20 minutes
Cooking Time: 30 minutes
Servings: 4

Ingredients:
- 450 g of potatoes
- 550 g pumpkin
- 20 g of breadcrumbs
- Coarse salt

Directions:
- Preheat the air fryer to 180°C for 5 minutes.
- Thoroughly clean the pumpkin and potatoes and cut them into large pieces. Pour all ingredients into the basket.
- Cook for 30 minutes or until you get the crispy you want.

216. Beans in Tomato Sauce

Preparation Time: 10 minutes
Cooking Time: 30 minutes
Servings: 8

Ingredients:
- 500g canned beans
- 300g of tomato puree
- ½ carrot
- 1 onion
- ½ sprig of rosemary
- Salt and pepper to taste
- 1 tsp olive oil

Directions:
- Prepare a chopped carrot and onion and place them inside the cooking tray with rosemary. Grease the basket with the oil.
- Set the air fryer to 150°C and brown for 4 min.
- Add the drained beans from your vegetable water and rinse thoroughly, simmer for another 3 min.
- Add the tomato, ½ glass of water, salt, and pepper, and continue cooking for another 13 minutes.

217. Roasted Corn on the Cob

Preparation Time: 10 minutes
Cooking Time: 6 minutes
Servings: 4

Ingredients:
- 4 ears of corn, shucked and halved crosswise
- 1 tbsp extra-virgin olive oil
- Salt
- Freshly ground black pepper
- Cooking oil spray

Directions:
- Insert the crisper plate into the basket and the basket into the unit. Preheat the unit by selecting AIR ROAST, setting the temperature to 390°F, and setting the time to 3 minutes. Select START/STOP to begin.
- Place the corn in a large bowl. Coat with the olive oil and season with salt and pepper to taste.
- Once the unit is preheated, spray the crisper plate with cooking oil. Place the corn into the basket.
- Select AIR ROAST, set the temperature to 390°F, and set the time to 6 minutes. Select START/STOP to begin.
- When the cooking is complete, let the corn cool for 5 minutes before serving.

218. Southwest Egg Rolls

Preparation Time: 30 minutes
Cooking Time: 16-20 minutes
Servings: 10

Ingredients:
- 2 cups frozen corn
- 15 oz. canned Black beans
- 13.5 oz. can of Spinach
- 1½ cups Jalapeno Jack cheese
- 1 cup sharp cheddar cheese
- 4 oz. can of Diced green chiles
- 4 Green onions
- 1 bunch of Scallions/Green onions
- 1 tsp Salt
- 1 tsp ground cumin
- 1 tsp Chili powder
- 16 oz. Egg roll wrappers

Directions:
- Preheat the Air Fryer to 390°F.
- Do the prep. Drain and rinse the beans. Drain the chiles and spinach. Shred the cheese and sliced the onions. Thaw and mix the corn, beans, spinach, both types of cheese, salt, green chiles, green onions, cumin, and chili powder in a large bowl.
- Lay an egg roll wrapper at an angle. Moisten all four edges with water - lightly. Place about 1/4 cup of the filling in the middle of the wrapper.
- Fold one corner over the filling and tuck in the sides to form a roll. Repeat with remaining wrappers and mist the egg roll with cooking spray.
- Arrange the egg rolls in the basket, making sure they are not touching
- Fry for 8 minutes; flip and cook until skins are crispy (4 min.).

219. Mac and Cheese Balls

Preparation Time: 35 minutes
Cooking Time: 10 minutes
Servings: 4

Ingredients:

- 2 cups Macaroni and cheese – leftovers are good
- ¼ cup Shredded cheddar cheese
- 2 cups Milk
- 3 Eggs
- ¾ cup White flour
- 1 cup Plain breadcrumbs

Directions:

- Heat the Air Fryer at 360°F.
- Combine the leftovers with shredded cheese.
- Add the breadcrumbs to a dish.
- Measure the flour into another bowl.
- Combine the milk and eggs.
- Make two balls from the mac n cheese.
- Roll the balls in the flour, eggs, and lastly, the breadcrumbs.
- Arrange the balls in the fryer basket. Press 'M' and go to the chicken icon.
- Set the timer for 10 minutes – rotating halfway through the cooking cycle.

220. Pigs in a Blanket

Preparation Time: 20 minutes
Cooking Time: 10 minutes
Servings: 4

Ingredients:

- 8 oz. can of Crescent rolls
- 12 oz. Cocktail franks

Directions:

- Warm the Air Fryer at 330°F.
- Rinse and dry the franks using paper towels.
- Slice the dough into rectangular strips (1.5 inches x 1-inch).
- Roll the dough around the franks, but leave the ends open.
- Place them in the freezer for approximately five minutes.
- Transfer them to the fryer for 6-8 minutes.
- Raise the temperature setting to 390° Fahrenheit. Continue cooking for approximately three more minutes.

221. Kale and Brussels Sprouts

Preparation Time: 5 minutes
Cooking Time: 15 minutes
Servings: 8

Ingredients:

- 1-pound Brussels sprouts, trimmed
- 2 cups kale, torn
- 1 tbsp olive oil
- Salt and black pepper to the taste
- 3 ounces mozzarella, shredded

Directions:

- In a pan that fits the air fryer, combine all the ingredients except the mozzarella and toss.
- Put the pan in the air fryer and cook at 380°F for 15 minutes.
- Divide between plates, sprinkle the cheese on top, and serve.

222. Kale and Black Olives

Preparation Time: 5 minutes
Cooking Time: 15 minutes
Servings: 4

Ingredients:

- 1 and ½ pounds kale, torn
- 2 tbsp olive oil
- Salt and black pepper to the taste
- 1 tbsp hot paprika
- 2 tbsp black olives, pitted and sliced

Directions:

- In a pan that fits the air fryer, combine all the ingredients and toss.
- Put the pan in your air fryer, cook at 370°F for 15 minutes, divide between plates and serve.

223. Bacon -Wrapped Onion Rings

Preparation Time: 40 minutes
Cooking Time: 17-20 minutes
Servings: 4

Ingredients:

- 12 rashers back bacon
- 1/2 tsp ground black pepper
- Chopped fresh parsley to taste
- 1/2 tsp paprika
- 1/2 tsp chili powder
- 1/2 tbsp soy sauce
- ½ tsp salt

Directions:

- Start by preheating your air fryer to 355°F.
- Season the onion rings with paprika, salt, black pepper, and chili powder. Simply wrap the bacon around the onion rings; drizzle with soy sauce.
- Bake for 17 minutes, garnish with fresh parsley and serve. Bon appétit!

224. Potato -Kale Croquettes

Preparation Time: 20 minutes
Cooking Time: 10 minutes
Servings: 6

Ingredients:

- 4 eggs, slightly beaten
- 1/3 cup flour
- 1/3 cup goat cheese, crumbled
- 1 ½ tsp fine sea salt
- 4 garlic cloves, minced
- 1 cup kale, steamed
- 1/3 cup breadcrumbs
- 1/3tsp red pepper flakes
- 3 potatoes, peeled and quartered

- 1/3 tsp dried dill weed

Directions:
- Firstly, boil the potatoes in salted water. Once the potatoes are cooked, mash them; add the kale, goat cheese, minced garlic, sea salt, red pepper flakes, dill, and one egg; stir to combine well.
- Now, roll the mixture to form small croquettes.
- Grab three shallow bowls. Place the flour in the first shallow bowl.
- Beat the remaining 3 eggs in the second bowl. After that, throw the breadcrumbs into the third shallow bowl.
- Dip each croquette in the flour; then, dip them in the eggs bowl; lastly, roll each croquette in the breadcrumbs.
- Air fry at 335°F for 7 minutes or until golden. Tate, adjust for seasonings, and serve warm.

225. Spicy Arancini

Preparation Time: 35 minutes
Cooking Time: 30 minutes
Servings: 4

Ingredients:
- 3 ounces cooked rice
- 1 /2 cup roasted vegetable stock
- 1 egg, beaten
- 1 cup white mushrooms, finely chopped
- 1/2 cup seasoned breadcrumbs
- 3 garlic cloves, peeled and minced
- 1/2 yellow onion, finely chopped
- 1/3 tsp ground black pepper, or more to taste
- 1 ½ bell peppers, seeded minced
- 1/2 chipotle pepper, seeded and minced
- 1/2 tbsp Colby cheese, grated
- 1 ½ tbsp canola oil
- Sea salt, to savor

Directions:
- Heat a saucepan over moderate heat; now, heat the oil and sweat the garlic, onions, bell pepper, and chipotle pepper until tender. Throw in the mushrooms and fry until they are fragrant and the liquid has almost evaporated.
- Throw in the cooked rice and stock; boil for 18 minutes. Now, add the cheese and spices; mix to combine.
- Allow the mixture to cool completely. Shape the risotto mixture into balls. Dip the risotto balls in the beaten egg, then roll them over the breadcrumbs.
- Air-fry risotto balls for 6 minutes at 400°F. Serve with marinara sauce, and enjoy!

226. Gorgonzola Stuffed Mushrooms with Horseradish Mayo

Preparation Time: 30 minutes
Cooking Time: 15 minutes
Servings: 5

Ingredients:
- 1/2 cup of breadcrumbs
- 2 cloves garlic, pressed
- 2 tbsp fresh coriander, chopped
- 1/3 tsp kosher salt
- 1/2 tsp crushed red pepper flakes

- 1 ½ tbsp olive oil
- 20 medium-sized mushrooms, cut off the stems
- 1/2 cup Gorgonzola cheese, grated
- 1/4 cup low-fat mayonnaise
- 1 tsp prepared horseradish, well-drained
- 1 tbsp fresh parsley, finely chopped

Directions:
- Mix the breadcrumbs together with the garlic, coriander, salt, red pepper, and olive oil; mix to combine well.
- Stuff the mushroom caps with the breadcrumb filling. Top with grated Gorgonzola.
- Place the mushrooms in the Air Fryer grill pan and slide them into the machine. Grill them at 380 °F for 8 to 12 minutes or until the stuffing is warmed through.
- Meanwhile, prepare the horseradish mayo by mixing the mayonnaise, horseradish, and parsley. Serve with warm fried mushrooms. Enjoy!

227. Sweet Corn Fritters

Preparation Time: 30 minutes
Cooking Time: 11 minutes
Servings: 4

Ingredients:
- 1 medium-sized carrot, grated
- 1 yellow onion, finely chopped
- 4 ounces canned sweet corn kernels, drained
- 1 tsp sea salt flakes
- 1 heaping tbsp fresh cilantro, chopped
- 1 medium-sized egg, whisked
- 2 tbsp plain milk
- 1 cup of Parmesan cheese, grated
- 1/4 cup of self-rising flour
- 1/3 tsp baking powder
- 1/3 tsp brown sugar

Directions:
- Press down the grated carrot in the colander to remove excess liquid. Then, spread the grated carrot between several sheets of kitchen towels and pat it dry.
- Then, mix the carrots with the remaining ingredients in the order listed above.
- Roll 1 tbsp of the mixture into a ball; gently flatten it using the back of a spoon or your hand. Now, repeat with the remaining ingredients.
- Spray the balls with nonstick cooking oil. Cook in a single layer at 350 °For 8 to 11 minutes or until they're firm to touch in the center. Serve warm, and enjoy!

228. Colby Potato Patties

Preparation Time: 20 minutes
Cooking Time: 10 minutes
Servings: 8

Ingredients:
- 2 pounds white potatoes, peeled and grated
- 1/2 cup scallions, finely chopped
- 1/2 tsp freshly ground black pepper or more to taste
- 1 tbsp fine sea salt
- 1/2 tsp hot paprika
- 2 cups Colby cheese, shredded
- 1/4 cup canola oil

- 1 cup crushed crackers

Directions:
- Firstly, boil the potatoes until fork-tender. Drain, peel and mash your potatoes.
- Thoroughly mix the mashed potatoes with scallions, pepper, salt, paprika, and cheese. Then, shape the balls using your hands. Now, flatten the balls to make the patties.
- In a shallow bowl, mix canola oil with crushed crackers. Roll the patties over the crumb mixture.
- Next, cook your patties at 360°F for approximately 10 minutes, working in batches. Serve with tabasco mayo if desired. Bon appétit!

229.   Asian Chicken and Peas Salad

Preparation Time: 10 minutes
Cooking Time: 30 minutes
Servings: 4
- **Ingredients**
- 4 tsp sesame oil
- 4 tbsp rice vinegar
- 1 tbsp soy sauce
- 1 tbsp water
- ½ tsp red pepper
- 1 cup sesame seeds
- 8 oz chicken
- 1 tbsp flour
- 1 egg white
- 12 cups lettuce
- 2 cups coleslaw mix
- 1 cup peas
- 1 cup canned mandarin oranges
- ¼ cup sliced almonds
- **Directions**
- Boil Chicken.
- Mix all ingredients.
- Then mix in chicken.
- Cook it for 20 minutes in Air Fryer at 375°F.
- Spray oil on it.
- Again, cook for 5 min.

230.   Roasted Hot Corn

Preparation Time: 5 minutes
Cooking Time: 15 minutes
Servings: 4

Ingredients:
- 2 cups frozen corn kernels, thawed and drained
- 1 small onion, diced
- 2 garlic cloves, sliced
- 2 tbsp butter, melted
- 1 tsp chili powder
- ½ tsp cayenne pepper
- ½ tsp sea salt
- ⅛ tsp freshly ground black pepper
- ¼ cup heavy (whipping) cream

Directions:
- Combine the corn, onion, garlic, butter, chili powder, cayenne pepper, salt, and black pepper in a 6-inch metal bowl that fits into your air fryer basket.

- Set or preheat the air fryer to 400°F. Place the bowl in the basket and roast for 10 minutes, shaking the basket once during the cooking time until some of the kernels start to turn gold around the edges.
- Remove the basket and pour the cream over the corn; stir to mix. Return the basket to the air fryer and roast for another 5 minutes or until the cream has thickened slightly. Serve.

231.   Cheesy Lemon Rice

Preparation Time: 5 minutes
Cooking Time: 15 minutes
Servings: 4

Ingredients:
- 4 tbsp of parmesan cheese, grated freshly
- 2 cups of white rice, boiled
- 6 tbsp of fresh lemon juice
- 2 tsp of fresh lemon zest, grated finely
- 4 tbsp of fresh mint leaves, chopped
- Salt and black pepper, to taste
- 2 tbsp of vegetable broth

Directions:
- Set the air fryer on an air fryer to 375 °F for 12 minutes. Place the rice in the cooking tray along with the vegetable broth, lemon juice, salt, and black pepper. Insert the cooking tray in the air fryer when it displays "add food." Remove from the air fryer when cooking time is complete. Fold in the lemon zest and parmesan cheese. Cook again in the air fryer for about 3 minutes and serve garnished with mint.

232.   Mexican Black Beans and Corn

Preparation Time: 10 minutes
Cooking Time: 10 minutes
Servings: 4

Ingredients:
- 1 (15-ounce) can of black beans, drained and rinsed
- 1 cup frozen corn kernels
- 1 red bell pepper, seeded and chopped
- 1 jalapeño pepper, sliced
- 2 garlic cloves, sliced
- 1 tbsp olive oil
- 1 tbsp freshly squeezed lime juice
- 2 tsp chili powder
- ½ tsp sea salt
- ⅛ tsp cayenne pepper

Directions:
- Combine the black beans, corn, bell pepper, jalapeño pepper, and garlic in the air fryer basket.
- Drizzle with the olive oil and lime juice and toss to coat. Sprinkle with the chili powder, salt, and cayenne pepper, and toss again. Place the basket in the air fryer.
- Set or preheat the air fryer to 350°F. Roast the vegetables for 10 minutes, shaking the basket halfway through cooking time until hot and tender. Serve.

233. Couscous with Raisins

Preparation Time: 30 minutes
Cooking Time: 30 minutes
Servings: 2

Ingredients:
- 2 cups of couscous, rinsed
- 4 cups of water
- ¼ tsp salt
- 2 tbsp brown sugar
- 1 cup of raisins
- 1 tsp cinnamon
- ¼ tsp citric acid

Directions:
- Soak the raisins in warm water for 10 minutes.
- Soak the couscous in the warm water for around 10-15 minutes. Mix in all the listed ingredients and spoon them into your Air fryer. Then pour the water.
- Lock up the air fryer lid, select the medium pressure setting and cook on a MEDIUM pressure for 30 minutes.
- Release the pressure naturally over 10 minutes.
- Portion the couscous into two bowls or mugs. Remember that this dish should be served warm. Serve the couscous with the coffee.

234. Celeriac Fries

Preparation Time: 30 minutes
Cooking Time: 25-30 minutes
Servings: 3

Ingredients:
- 3 cups water
- 1 tbsp lime juice
- ½ celeriac (celery root), peeled and cut into ½-inch sticks
- Mayo Sauce:
- 1 tsp powdered horseradish
- 1/3 cup vegan mayonnaise
- 1 tbsp brown mustard
- 1 tbsp olive oil
- 1 pinch salt
- Ground black pepper to taste

Directions:
- In a bowl, add water and lime juice to cel-ery roots. Stir the mixture together and leave it for a third of an hour
- Heat the air fryer to the heat of 390°F.
- Prepare vegan mayo sauce by adding to-gether horseradish powder, vegan mayon-naise, and mustard in a bowl. Cover the mixture and keep it in the refrigerator.
- Remove water from the celery root sticks and allow them to dry before putting them in a sep-arate bowl. Add some oil to the fries and sprinkle salt and pepper over them. Turn the fries over to allow a uniform coating to form.
- Place the drained and dried celery root sticks in the air fryer basket and cook for about 10 minutes, after which you can check to see how cooked it is. Shake the basket and cook for eight more minutes till the fries take on a crisp texture and brown color.

- Now bring out the vegan mayo sauce from the refrigerator and serve alongside the fries.

235. Balsamic Cherry Tomato Skewers

Preparation Time: 10 minutes
Cooking Time: 6 minutes
Servings: 4

Ingredients:
- 3 tbsp balsamic vinegar
- 24 cherry tomatoes
- 1 tbsp thyme, cleaved
- Salt and dark pepper to the taste
- For the dressing:
- 2 tbsp balsamic vinegar
- Salt and dark pepper to the taste
- 4 tbsp olive oil

Directions:
- In a bowl, blend 2 tbsp oil with 3 tbsp vinegar, 3 garlic cloves, thyme, salt, and dark pepper, and whisk well.
- Add tomatoes, hurl to cover, and leave aside for 30 minutes.
- Arrange 6 tomatoes on one stick and rehash with the remainder of the tomatoes.
- Introduce them to the air fryer cooker and cook at 360°F for about 6 minutes.
- In another bowl, blend 2 tbsp vinegar in with salt, pepper, and 4 tbsp oil and whisk well.
- Arrange tomato sticks on plates and present with the dressing showered on top. Enjoy!

236. Sesame Mustard Greens

Preparation Time: 10 minutes
Cooking Time: 10 minutes
Servings: 4

Ingredients:
- 2 garlic cloves, minced
- 1-pound mustard greens, torn
- 1 tbsp of olive oil
- ½ cup yellow onion, cut
- Salt and dark pepper to the taste
- 3 tbsp veggie stock
- ¼ tsp dull sesame oil

Directions:
- Heat up a dish that accommodates the air fryer cooker with the oil over medium heat, include onions, mix, and dark-colored them for 5 minutes.
- Add garlic, stock, greens, salt, and pepper, mix, present in the air fryer cooker, and cook at 350°F for about 6 minutes.
- Add sesame oil, hurl to cover, separate among plates and serve.
- Enjoy the recipe!

237. Cheesy Fennel

Preparation Time: 10 minutes
Cooking Time: 10 minutes
Servings: 4

Ingredients:
- 2 fennel bulbs, cut into quarters

- 3 tbsp olive oil
- Salt and dark pepper to the taste
- 1 garlic clove, minced
- 1 red bean stew pepper, hacked
- ¾ cup veggie stock
- Juice from ½ lemon
- ¼ cup white wine
- ¼ cup parmesan, ground

Directions:

- Heat up a container that fits the air fryer cooker with the oil over medium-high heat, put in garlic and stew pepper, mix and cook for 2 minutes.
- Add fennel, salt, pepper, stock, wine, lemon juice, and parmesan, hurl to cover, present in the air fryer cooker, and cook at 350°F for about 6 minutes.
- Divide among plates and serve immediately. Enjoy the recipe!

238. Arugula and Beets Salad

Preparation Time: 10 minutes
Cooking Time: 10 minutes
Servings: 4

Ingredients:

- 1 and ½ pounds beets, stripped and quartered
- A sprinkle of olive oil
- 1 tsp orange pizzazz, ground
- 2 tbsp juice vinegar
- ½ cup squeezed orange
- 2 tbsp dark colored sugar
- 2 scallions, hacked
- 2 tsp mustard
- 2 cups arugula

Directions:

- Rub beets with the oil and squeezed orange, place them in the air fryer cooker and cook at 350 °F for about 10 minutes.
- Transfer beet quarters to a bowl, including scallions, arugula, orange pizzazz, and hurl.
- In a different bowl, blend sugar in with mustard and vinegar, whisk well, add to a plate of mixed greens, and serve.

239. Simple Broccoli Side Dish

Preparation Time: 10 minutes
Cooking Time: 8 minutes
Servings: 4

Ingredients:

- 1 broccoli head, florets isolated
- 1 tbsp nut oil
- 6 garlic cloves, minced
- 1 tbsp of the Chinese rice wine vinegar
- Salt and dark pepper to the taste

Directions:

- In a bowl, blend broccoli in with salt, pepper, and half of the oil, hurl, move to the air fryer cooker and cook at 350 °F for about 8 minutes, shaking the fryer midway.
- Transfer broccoli to a plate of mixed greens bowl, including the remainder of the nut oil, garlic, and rice vinegar, hurl truly well and serve. Enjoy the recipe!

240. Paprika Cucumber Chips

Preparation Time: 10 minutes
Cooking Time: 11 minutes
Servings: 10

Ingredients:

- 1-pound cucumber
- 1 tsp salt
- 1 tbsp smoked paprika
- ½ tsp garlic powder

Directions:

- Wash the cucumbers carefully and slice them into chips.
- Sprinkle the chops with salt, smoked paprika, and garlic powder.
- Preheat the air fryer to 370°F.
- Place the cucumber slices in the air fryer rack.
- Cook the cucumber chips for 11 minutes.
- Transfer the cucumber chips to a paper towel and allow them to cool.
- Serve the cucumber chips immediately or keep them in a paper bag.

241. Cheesy Sticks with Sweet Thai Sauce

Preparation Time: 2 hours
Cooking Time: 20 minutes
Servings: 4

Ingredients:

- 12 mozzarella string cheese
- 2 cups breadcrumbs
- 3 eggs
- 1 cup sweet Thai sauce
- 4 tbsp skimmed milk
- **Directions**
- Pour the crumbs into a medium bowl. Break the eggs into a different bowl and beat with the milk. One after the other, dip each cheese stick in the egg mixture, in the crumbs, then the egg mixture again, and then in the crumbs again.
- Place the coated cheese sticks on a cookie sheet and freeze for 1 to 2 hours. Preheat the Air Fryer to 380°F. Arrange the sticks in the fryer without overcrowding. Cook for 5 minutes, flipping them halfway through cooking to brown evenly. Cook in batches. Serve with a sweet Thai sauce.

242. Easy Cheese Sticks

Preparation Time: 5 minutes
Cooking Time: 10 minutes
Servings: 4

Ingredients:

- 6 -6 oz bread cheese
- 2 tbsp butter
- 2 cups panko crumbs
- **Directions**
- Place the butter in a dish and melt it in the microwave for 2 minutes; set aside. With a knife, cut the cheese into equal-sized sticks. Brush each stick with butter and dip into panko crumbs. Arrange the cheese sticks in a single layer on the fryer basket. Cook at 390°F for 10 minutes. Flip them halfway through to brown evenly; serve warm.

243.   Spicy Acorn Squash Wedges

Preparation Time: 10 minutes
Cooking Time: 18 minutes
Servings: 2

Ingredients:
- 11 oz Acorn squash
- ½ tsp salt
- tbsp olive oil
- ½ tsp chili pepper
- ½ tsp paprika

Directions:
- Cut Acorn squash into the serving wedges.
- Sprinkle the wedges with salt, olive oil, chili pepper, and paprika.
- Massage the wedges gently.
- Preheat the air fryer to 400°F.
- Put Acorn squash wedges in the air fryer basket and cook for 18 minutes.
- Flip the wedges into another side after 9 minutes of cooking.
- Serve the cooked meal hot.
- Enjoy!

244.   Spicy Tomato Chutney

Preparation Time: 10 minutes
Cooking Time: 6 minutes
Servings: 4

Ingredients:
- 4 green tomatoes, chopped
- 1/2 tsp mustard seeds
- 1 tbsp brown sugar
- 2 jalapeno pepper, chopped
- 1/2 tsp turmeric
- 1 tbsp olive oil
- 1 tsp salt

Directions:
- Add oil into the air fryer duo fresh and set the pot on sauté mode.
- Once the oil is hot, then add mustard seeds and let them pop.
- Add remaining ingredients and stir well.
- Cook at 400°F for 5 minutes.
- Mash the tomato mixture using a potato masher until getting the desired consistency.
- Serve and enjoy.

245.   Mexican Rice

Preparation Time: 10 minutes
Cooking Time: 3 minutes
Servings: 2

Ingredients:
- 1 cup rice, long grain
- 1/4 cup green hot sauce
- 1/2 cup fresh cilantro, chopped
- 1/2 avocado flesh
- 1 1/4 cup vegetable broth
- Pepper
- Salt

Directions:
- Add soup and rice to the air fryer duo crisp and stir well.
- Seal the pot with a pressure cooking lid and cook at 400°F for 3 minutes.
- Once done, allow to release pressure naturally. Remove lid.
- Fluff the rice using a fork.
- Add green sauce, avocado, and cilantro to a blender and blend until smooth.
- Pour the blended mixture into the rice and stir well to combine. Season with pepper and salt.
- Serve and enjoy.

246.   Sweetcorn Risotto

Preparation Time: 10 minutes
Cooking Time: 13 minutes
Servings: 4

Ingredients:
- 1 cup arborio rice
- 1/2 cup sweet corn
- 1 tsp mix of herbs
- 3 cups vegetable stock
- 1 tbsp olive oil
- 1 tsp garlic, minced
- 1/2 cup peas
- One red pepper, diced
- One large onion, chopped
- 1/4 pepper
- 1/2 tsp salt

Directions:
- Add oil into the air fryer duo fresh and set the pot on sauté mode.
- Sauté for 5 minutes
- Add rice and stir to combine.
- Add remaining ingredients and stir well.
- Seal the pot with a pressure cooking lid and 400°F for 8 minutes.
- Once done, release pressure using a quick release. Remove lid.
- Serve and enjoy.

247.   Potato and Kale Croquettes

Preparation Time: 5 Minutes
Cooking Time: 7 Minutes
Servings: 6

Ingredients:
- 4 beaten eggs
- 1/3 cup flour
- 1/3 cup crumbled goat cheese
- 1-1/2 tsp. sea salt
- 4 minced garlic cloves
- 1 cup steamed kale
- 1/3 cup breadcrumbs
- 1/3 tsp. red pepper flakes
- 3 quartered potatoes
- 1/3 tsp. dried dill weed

Direction:
- Firstly, boil the potatoes in salted water.

- Mash the potatoes once cooked through; add the kale, goat cheese, minced garlic, sea salt, red pepper flakes, dill, and one egg; stir to combine well.
- Now, roll the mixture to form small croquettes.
- Grab three shallow bowls. Place the flour in the first shallow bowl.
- Beat the remaining three eggs in the second bowl.
- After that, throw the breadcrumbs into the third shallow bowl.
- Dip each croquette in the flour; then, dip them in the eggs bowl; lastly, roll each croquette in the breadcrumbs.
- Air fry at 335 °F for 7 minutes or until golden.
- Taste, adjust for seasonings and serve warm. Enjoy!

248. Arancini with Jerked Tomatoes & Mozzarella

Preparation Time: 10 Minutes
Cooking Time: 10-15 Minutes
Servings: 5-6

Ingredients:
- 1 cup Arborio rice, cooked
- ½ small onion, chopped
- 2 large eggs
- 3 oz Mozzarella cheese
- ⅓ cup Parmigiano-Reggiano cheese, grated
- ¼ cup oil-packed jerked tomatoes, chopped
- 1½ cups Italian seasoned breadcrumbs
- 1 tbsp olive oil
- Salt and ground black pepper
- Marinara sauce for garnish

Directions:
- In the large mixing bowl, combine warm cooker Arborio rice and Parmigiano-Reggiano cheese. Season with salt and pepper. Then, spread the rice mixture out onto a baking sheet to chill.
- Meanwhile, cut the Mozzarella into ¾-inch cubes.
- When the rice has chilled, combine it with beaten eggs, jerked tomatoes, and ½ cup of breadcrumbs. The remaining breadcrumbs place on a plate.
- Shape the rice into 10-12 equal balls. Make a hole in the center of a rice ball with your finger and push one or two cubes of Mozzarella cheese into the hole. Mold the rice back into a ball, enclosing the cheese.
- Roll the finished rice balls in the breadcrumbs and place them on a baking sheet. Lightly spray the rice balls with olive oil.
- Preheat the air fryer to 380°F.
- Working in batches, cook half of the Arancini for 13-15 minutes, turning once while cooking.
- While your rice balls cook, warm the marinara sauce in a small saucepan. Pool the sauce on the bottom of the serving plate and place the Arancini on the top of the marinara. Enjoy!

249. Scotch Eggs with Spicy Pepper Sauce

Preparation Time: 20 minutes
Cooking Time: 25-30 minutes
Servings:

Ingredients:
- 4 (4) hard-boiled eggs, peeled

- 1 cup Parmesan cheese
- 2 tbsp of fresh parsley, finely chopped
- 1 pound (453.59 g) of bulk pork sausage
- 1/8 tsp of Ground Nutmeg
- 2 tsp of Coarse-Ground Mustard
- 1/8 tsp of Kosher Salt
- 1 tbsp of chives, finely chopped
- 1/8 tsp of Ground Black Pepper
- **Instructions**
- With your huge bowl, mix your parsley, mustard, chives, sausage, black pepper, salt, and nutmeg. Shape combination in four equivalent-size patties.
- Place every egg on your sausage patty, then shape sausage all-round the egg. Immerse each of them into shredded Parmesan cheese so that it will totally cover.
- Organize eggs into your air fryer basket. Lightly spray with your stick-free vegetable oil. Heat your air fryer for 15minutes to 400°F. Cook Halfway, then turn eggs, then spray with your vegetable oil.
- After that, dish up your coarse-ground mustard.

250. Fiery Bacon Nibbles

Preparation Time: 10 minutes
Cooking Time: 10-15 minutes
Servings: 2

Ingredients:
- 1/4 cup of hot sauce
- 1/2 cup of crushed pork rinds
- 4 strips of bacon

Directions:
- Cut your raw bacon dice into 6 uniform pieces, then place them into a bowl.
- Put your hot sauce into your bowl; make sure equally sides of your bacon obtain sauce.
- Dip your bacon pieces into minced pork rinds, coating equally sides.
- After that, allow cooking in your air fryer for 10 minutes at 350°F. Check after 8 minutes to make sure it is not burning.

251. Goat Cheese Balls

Preparation Time: 40 minutes
Cooking Time: 8-10 minutes
Servings: 4

Ingredients:
- 2 Tbsp. flour
- 1 egg beaten
- 8 oz. log soft goat cheese
- 1/2 c. Panko bread crumbs
- 1/4 c. Honey

Directions:
- The goat cheese must be sliced into pieces and rolled into balls
- Put them in a tray and freeze for 30 minutes
- Crack the egg into a bowl
- After 30 minutes, take them out, and one by one, dip them into the flour, then into the cracked egg, and finally into the panko bread crumbs
- Then set them into the air fryer basket and pray the balls with non-stick cooking spray

- Set the air fryer to cook at 380°F for about 8 minutes, until they are brown
- Serve and enjoy

252. Grilled Endive with Yogurt Sauce

Preparation Time: 20 minutes
Cooking Time: 10 minutes
Servings: 6

Ingredients:
- 6 pcs Belgian endive
- 125 ml yogurt
- 1 tsp. garlic powder 2 cloves minced garlic)
- 1/2 tsp. curry powder
- 1/2 tsp. salt (or salt sub)
- 1/2 tsp. ground black pepper
- 3 tsp. Lemon juice

Directions:
- Wash, then slice into halve the endives lengthwise through the root end and set aside.
- Mix all the rest of the ingredients. If desired, thin with more lemon juice.
- Toss the endive halves in the marinade with a clean pair of hands.
- Cover and let it marinate and refrigerate for at least 30 minutes, but up to a day ahead is fine.
- Cook for 10 minutes
- Serve hot or warm.

253. Roasted Tomato Salsa

Preparation Time: 20 minutes
Cooking Time: 20 minutes
Servings: 4

Ingredients:
- 4pcs Tomatoes, red, ripe, raw
- 1 Pepper, jalapeno, raw
- ½ red onions
- 1 serving Pam Butter Cooking Spray
- 4 cloves Garlic, raw
- ½ cup Cilantro, raw
- 1 Lime, raw
- 1 pinch of Stable salt

Directions:
- Preheat the air fryer to 390°F (200°C).
- Put tomatoes and jalapeno skin-side down into the air fryer basket with red onion. Spray vegetables with cooking spray to help the roasting process.
- Air fry vegetables for 5 minutes. Open the basket and add garlic cloves. Spray lightly with cooking spray and air fry for another 5 minutes.
- Place vegetables on a cutting board and wait to cool for 10 minutes.
- Remove tomatoes and jalapeno skins; if desired, they should slip right off.
- Then Chop tomatoes, jalapeno, and onion into large chunks and add them to the bowl of a food processor.
- Add lime juice, garlic, cilantro, and salt. Blend several times until vegetables are finely chopped; do not over-process.
- Serve and enjoy.

254. Italian Fried Ravioli

Preparation Time: 20 minutes
Cooking Time: 10-15 minutes
Servings: 4

Ingredients:
- 1/2 tsp. Italian seasoning
- 1/2 tsp. salt
- Marinara sauce for dipping
- Alfredo sauce for dipping
- 1 (20 Oz) package of refrigerated cheese ravioli
- 2 large eggs
- 1/2 cup breadcrumbs
- 1/2 cup panko
- 1/4 cup grated parmesan
- 1 tsp. onion powder
- 1 tsp. Garlic powder
- 1 tsp. Dried basil

Directions:
- Crack the egg and mix together in a bowl and set it aside
- Mix parmesan, onion powder, garlic powder, panko, breadcrumbs, dried basil, Italian seasoning, and salt together in another bowl
- Dip the ravioli in the mixed egg and stir to coat
- Then put it in the breadcrumb mixture. Allow it to cover all the ravioli and set aside
- Preheat the air fryer to 400°F and spray the air fryer basket with cooking spray
- Put the coated ravioli in the air fryer in a single layer and air fry for 4 minutes or until crispy
- Repeat with the remaining ones

255. Roasted Grape Dip

Preparation Time: 20 minutes
Cooking Time: 12 minutes
Servings: 4

Ingredients:
- 2 cups seedless red grapes, rinsed and patted dry
- 1 tbsp apple cider vinegar
- 1 cup low-fat Greek yogurt
- 2 tbsp 2% milk
- 2 tbsp fresh basil, minced
- 2 tbsp sugar

Directions:
- The air fryer must be heated to 193°C
- In a large bowl, combine the red grapes with sugar and apple cider vinegar. Toss to coat well.
- Put the red grapes in the air fryer basket. Roast in the preheated air fryer for 8 to 12 minutes, shaking the basket halfway through the cooking time or until the grapes are slightly shriveled.
- Meanwhile, whisk together the yogurt and milk in a medium bowl until creamy.
- Transfer the grapes to the bowl of yogurt and milk. Mix in the minced basil and stir to incorporate.
- Serve immediately, or refrigerate to chill for about 2 hours.

256. Rumaki Balls

Preparation Time: 20 minutes
Cooking Time: 20 minutes
Servings: 6

Ingredients:
- 10 ounces (284 g) of raw chicken livers, cut into 1½-inch pieces
- 1 (8-ounce / 227-g) can of sliced water chestnuts, drained
- ¼ cup low-sodium teriyaki sauce
- 12 slices of turkey bacon, cut in half
- 24 toothpicks, soaked for at least 30 minutes

Directions:
- Put the livers and water chestnuts in a small bowl, then pour the teriyaki sauce over them. Make sure they are fully dunked in the sauce. Refrigerate for 1 hour.
- The air fryer will be heated to 193°C. Spritz the air fryer basket with cooking spray.
- Make the rumaki: Wrap a piece of chicken liver and a slice of water chestnut with a slice of bacon half. Secure with a toothpick. Repeat with the remaining ingredients.
- Arrange the rumaki in the air fryer basket and cook for 10 to 12 minutes or until the bacon is well browned and the internal temperature of the chicken pieces reads at least 165°F (74°C). You may need to work in batches to avoid overcrowding.
- Remove the rumaki from the basket. Discard the toothpick and serve.

257. Cumin Tortilla Chips with Guacamole

Preparation Time: 5 minutes
Cooking Time: 15 minutes
Servings: 4

Ingredients:
- 12 corn tortillas
- 2 tbsp. olive oil
- 1 tbsp. cumin powder
- 1 tbsp. paprika powder
- Salt and black pepper to taste
- For the guacamole:
- 1 large avocado, pitted and peeled
- 1 small firm tomato, chopped
- A pinch dried parsley

Directions:
- Preheat Air Fry mode at 375°F for 2 to 3 minutes.
- In a bowl, mix the ingredients for the tortilla chips well and pour the mixture into the rotisserie basket. Close to sealing.
- Fix the basket onto the lever.
- Time to 15 minutes, choose Start and cook until the tortillas are golden brown.
- Take out the basket using the rotisserie lift and transfer the chips to serving bowls.
- Meanwhile, as the chips are cooked, in a small bowl, mash the avocados and mix with the tomato and parsley until well combined.
- Serve the tortilla chips with guacamole.

CHAPTER 3: SOUP, STEWS AND VEGETABLE DISHES

258. Mexican Beef Soup

Preparation Time: 20 minutes
Cooking Time: 25-30 minutes
Servings: 10-12

Ingredients:

- 1-pound beef stew meat
- 3/4-pound potatoes cut into 3/4-inch cubes
- 2 cups frozen corn, thawed
- 2 medium carrots, cut into 1/2-inch slices
- 1 medium onion, chopped
- 2 garlic cloves, minced
- 1-1/2 tsp. dried oregano
- 1 tsp. ground cumin
- 1/2 tsp. salt
- 1/4 tsp. crushed red pepper flakes
- 2 cups beef stock
- 1 can diced tomatoes and green chilies

Directions:

- In the pressure cooker, combine the first 12 ingredients.
- Adjust to pressure-400°F for 15 minutes.
- If desired, serve with sour cream and chips.

259. Spicy Vegetable Soup

Preparation Time: 5 minutes
Cooking Time: 35 minutes
Servings: 4

Ingredients:

- One cup celery
- 1/2 cup carrots
- One medium onion
- One fresh jalapeno
- 2 tbsp olive oil
- 1/2 tsp coriander seeds
- 1/4 tsp cumin seed
- Three big russet potatoes
- 2 tbsp vegetable broth
- 4 cups of water
- 1/4 tsp ground turmeric
- 1/4 tsp ground cumin
- 2 tbsp chopped jalapenos
- Optional: chopped cilantro

Directions:

- Set pressure cooker on Sauté. Add olive oil and heat for a minute.
- Drop-in cumin seeds and coriander seeds, and heat until the coriander seeds pop. Add the chopped celery, carrots, onion, and jalapeno.
- Sauté until the onions become translucent, about 5 minutes. Add the pickled jalapenos, turmeric, and cumin. When you fill in some pleasant aroma, put in the chicken broth and potatoes.
- Change the setting to soup and set it for 30 minutes. Let the pressure come to normal. Before serving, add the chopped cilantro. Serve with good bread.

260. Caramelized Carrot Soup

Preparation Time: 15 minutes
Cooking Time: 15-20 minutes
Servings: 4

Ingredients:

- 1 tbsp. unsalted butter
- 1 tbsp. oil
- 1 onion, chopped
- ¼ tsp. Kosher salt
- ¼ tsp. pepper
- 2 cups low-sodium chicken broth
- 13.5 oz. can unsweetened coconut milk
- 1 tbsp. Sriracha
- 1 clove of garlic, minced
- 1 tbsp. minced ginger
- 1-pound carrots, chopped
- 1/4 tsp. brown sugar

Directions:

- Sauté onions in butter and oil for 2-3 minutes.
- Cook garlic, carrots, salt, pepper, brown sugar, and ginger for 4 minutes.
- Add chicken broth, coconut milk, and 1 tbsp. Sriracha sauce.
- Cook at High Pressure for 6 minutes.
- Purée the soup.
- Serve garnished with coriander.

261. Chicken Orzo Soup

Preparation Time: 5 minutes
Cooking Time: 40 minutes
Servings: 10

Ingredients:

- 2 chicken thighs, skinless, boneless, and cut into chunks
- 2 cups fresh baby spinach
- 2 tbsp fresh lemon juice
- 1/2 cup orzo pasta, uncooked
- 1/2 tsp lemon zest
- 5 cups chicken stock
- 1 tsp fresh rosemary, chopped
- 2 garlic cloves, minced
- 1 cup carrots, chopped
- 1 celery stalk, chopped
- 1 onion, chopped
- 2 tbsp olive oil
- 1/4 tsp black pepper
- 1/4 tsp salt

Directions:

- Add olive oil into the air fryer and set the container on sauté mode.
- Add onion to the pot and sauté until onion is softened, about 3 minutes.
- Add garlic, carrots, celery, and sauté for a minute.
- Add chicken, pepper, rosemary, and salt and stir well.
- Add stock, pasta, and lemon zest and stir well.
- Seal pot with lid and cook on manual high pressure for 3 minutes.
- Release pressure using the quick-release method, then open the lid.
- Add spinach and lemon juice and stir well.
- Serve and enjoy.

262. Stuffed Eggplants

Preparation Time: 30 minutes
Cooking Time: 15-20 minutes
Servings: 4

Ingredients:

- 4 small eggplants, halved lengthwise
- Salt and black pepper to the taste
- 10 tbsp olive oil
- 2 and ½ pounds tomatoes, cut into halves and grated
- 1 green bell pepper, chopped
- 1 yellow onion, chopped
- 1 tbsp garlic, minced
- ½ cup cauliflower, chopped
- 1 tsp oregano, chopped
- ½ cup parsley, chopped
- 3 ounces feta cheese, crumbled

Directions:

- Season eggplants with salt, pepper, and 4 tbsp oil, toss, put them in your air fryer, and cook at 350 °F for 16 minutes. Meanwhile, heat up a pan with 3 tbsp oil over medium high heat, add onion, stir and cook for 5 minutes. Add bell pepper, garlic and cauliflower, stir, cook for 5 minutes, take off heat, add parsley, tomato, salt, pepper, oregano, and cheese, and whisk everything. Stuff eggplants with the veggie mix, drizzle the rest of the oil over them, put them in your air fryer and cook at

350 °F for 6 minutes more. Divide among plates and serve right away. Enjoy!

263. Ratatouille Soup with Quinoa

Preparation Time: 10 minutes
Cooking Time: 30 minutes
Servings: 10

Ingredients:
- ½ cup quinoa
- 1 ½ cups eggplants, peeled, diced
- 1 ½ cups zucchini, quartered and sliced
- 1 ½ cups sweet onion, chopped
- 6 cups vegetable stock
- ¼ cup hot peppers, chopped
- 3 cups tomatoes, crushed
- 1 ½ tsp dry thyme leaves
- One tbsp olive oil

Directions:
- Heat olive oil in an air fryer. Add onions, zucchini, garlic, and eggplant. Cook for 2 minutes.
- Add quinoa and cook, stirring for an additional 8 minutes. Pour in vegetable stock and bring the mixture to a boil.
- Lower heat to a simmer. Add hot pepper and tomatoes. Let it simmer for 20 minutes.
- Garnish each serving with fresh basil.

264. Italian Eggplant Stew

Preparation Time: 10 minutes
Cooking Time: 15 minutes
Servings: 6

Ingredients:
- 1 red onion, chopped
- 2 garlic cloves, chopped
- 1 bunch parsley, chopped
- Salt and black pepper to the taste
- 1 tsp oregano, dried
- 2 eggplants, cut into medium chunks
- 2 tbsp olive oil
- 2 tbsp capers, chopped
- 1 handful of green olives, pitted and sliced
- 5 tomatoes, chopped
- 3 tbsp herb vinegar

Directions:
- Heat up a pan that fits your air fryer with the oil over medium heat, add eggplant, oregano, salt, and pepper, stir and cook for 5 minutes. Add garlic, onion, parsley, capers, olives, vinegar, and tomatoes, stir, introduce in your air fryer and cook at 360 °F for 15 minutes. Divide into bowls and serve. Enjoy!

265. Cauliflower Fried Rice

Preparation Time: 20 minutes
Cooking Time: 30 minutes
Servings: 4

Ingredients:
- 2 large eggs
- 1 (12 ounces) package of frozen cauliflower rice
- 2 slices Ham, sliced, regular
- 2 tablespoons soy sauce
- ¼ cup chopped green onions

Directions:
- Microwave the cauliflower rice for 5 to 6 minutes. Allow for one minute before carefully opening the bag.
- Preheat your air fryer to 400°F (200 degrees C). Use aluminum foil to cover the basket's bottom and the bottom 1/2 inch of the basket's sides.
- Combine the cauliflower rice, eggs, ham, green onions, and soy sauce in a mixing bowl.
- Air fry for 5 minutes. Remove the basket from the oven and toss the cauliflower mixture. Return to the air fryer and cook for another 5 minutes.

266. Eggplant Parmesan

Preparation Time: 15 minutes
Cooking Time: 20 minutes
Servings: 4

Ingredients:
- 1 medium eggplant, peeled
- 2 eggs
- ½ cup all-purpose flour
- ¾ cup Italian bread crumbs
- 2 tbsp grated Parmesan cheese
- Salt
- Pepper
- ¾ cup marinara sauce
- ½ cup shredded Parmesan cheese
- ½ cup shredded mozzarella cheese

Directions:
- Cut the eggplant into ½-inch-thick rounds. Blot the eggplant with paper towels to dry completely. You can also sprinkle with a tsp of salt to sweat out the moisture.
- In a small bowl, beat the eggs. Place the flour in another small bowl. In a third small bowl, combine the bread crumbs, grated Parmesan cheese, and salt and pepper to taste, and mix well.
- Set the air fryer temperature to 400°F. Spray the air fryer basket with cooking oil.
- Dip each eggplant round in the flour, then the eggs, and then the bread crumb mixture.
- Place the eggplant rounds in the air fryer basket. Do not stack. Cook in batches. Spray the eggplant with cooking oil. Cook for 7 minutes.
- Open the air fryer. Top each of the rounds with 1 tsp of marinara sauce and ½ tbsp each of shredded Parmesan and mozzarella cheese. Cook for an additional 2 to 3 minutes until the cheese has melted.
- Remove the cooked eggplant from the air fryer, then repeat steps 5 and 6 for the remaining eggplant.

267. Creamy Parsnip Soup

Preparation Time: 5 minutes
Cooking Time: 30 minutes
Servings: 4-5

Ingredients:
- 6 slices bacon
- 5 parsnips, peeled and chopped
- 1/2 onion, chopped
- 1 small celery stalk, chopped

- 1 small potato, peeled and chopped
- 2 garlic cloves, minced
- 4 cups vegetable broth
- 2 tbsp extra virgin olive oil
- 1 tsp salt
- black pepper, to serve
- 1 tbsp fresh thyme leaves, to serve
- 1 cup croutons, to serve

Directions:
- In a skillet, cook bacon until crisp. Drain on paper towels; put aside. Coarsely chop bacon and place it on a microwave-safe plate. Drizzle bacon with honey; cover with wrapping. Just before serving, cook in the microwave for 30 seconds.
- Heat olive oil in the air fryer and gently sauté the onion, celery, and garlic until fragrant. Stir in vegetable broth, parsnips, and salt, and bring to a boil.
- Reduce heat and simmer for 30 minutes. Set aside to cool and blend until smooth. Garnish with croutons, fresh thyme, and chopped bacon.

268. Szechuan Pork Soup

Preparation Time: 10 minutes
Cooking Time: 30 minutes
Servings: 6

Ingredients:
- Soy sauce-2 tbsp
- Szechuan peppers-2 tsp, crushed
- Cloves of garlic-6, minced
- Ginger-minced
- Boneless pork shoulder-1 pound, cut into chunks
- Salt-1 tsp
- Onion-½, sliced
- Olive oil-2 tbsp
- Cilantro-¼ cup
- Water-3 cups
- Bok choy-¾ cup, chopped

Directions:
- Set the Air fryer to sauté mode and pour in the oil. Allow it to warm up.
- Combine the garlic and ginger. Stir constantly for a minute.
- Add the soy sauce, peppers, pork, salt, and onion. Mix thoroughly.
- Close the lid and set the timer for 20 minutes as you turn the Air fryer to high pressure.
- Naturally, release the pressure.
- Add the bok choy and cilantro. Combine the ingredients well.
- Cover the lid and let the soup simmer for 10 minutes before serving.

269. Tomato and Fennel Stew

Preparation Time: 15 minutes
Cooking Time: 15 minutes
Servings: 4

Ingredients:
- 2 fennel bulbs; shredded
- ½ cup chicken stock
- 1 red bell pepper; chopped.

- 2 garlic cloves; minced
- 2 cups tomatoes; cubed
- 2 tbsp. tomato puree
- 1 tsp. rosemary; dried
- 1 tsp. sweet paprika
- Salt and black pepper to taste.

Directions:
- In a pan that fits your air fryer, mix all the ingredients, toss, introduce them to the fryer and cook at 380°F for 15 minutes
- Divide the stew into bowls.

270. Zucchini Fritters

Preparation Time: 20 minutes
Cooking Time: 12 minutes
Servings: 4

Ingredients:
- 2 medium zucchini, grated, and squeeze out all liquid
- ¼ tsp Black pepper
- ¼ tsp Paprika
- ¼ tsp Onion powder
- 1 tsp Garlic powder
- 3 tbsp All-purpose flour
- 1 Egg, lightly beaten
- Pepper & salt, to taste

Directions:
- Line multi-level air fryer basket with parchment paper and set aside. Add all ingredients into the mixing bowl and mix until well combined. Make small fritters from the mixture and place them on parchment paper in the air fryer basket. Place the air fryer basket into the air fryer. Seal the pot with the air fryer lid. Select air fry mode and cook at 360°F for 12 minutes. Turn fritters halfway through. Serve.

271. Hasselback Zucchini

Preparation Time: 10 minutes
Cooking Time: 20 minutes
Servings: 3

Ingredients:
- Three medium zucchinis
- Three tbsp olive oil
- Four tbsp coconut cream
- One tbsp lemon juice
- Salt and pepper to taste
- Three slices of bacon, fried and crumbled

Directions:
- The air fryer should preheat at 350°F for 5 minutes.
- Line up chopsticks on both facets of the zucchini and slice thinly till you hit the stick. Brush the zucchinis with olive
- Place the zucchini in the air fryer. Bake for 20 minutes at 350°F.
- Meanwhile, combine the coconut cream and lemon juice in a mixing bowl. Season with salt and pepper to taste.
- Once the zucchini is cooked, scoop the coconut cream mixture and drizzle on top.
- Sprinkle with bacon bits.

- Serve and enjoy!

272.   Cream of Asparagus Soup

Preparation Time: 20 minutes
Cooking Time: 17 minutes
Servings: 4

Ingredients:

- 12 Oz. Asparagus, trimmed and chopped
- 2½ cups Vegetable stock
- 1 tsp Garlic, chopped
- 1 tsp onion, chopped
- 1 tsp Olive oil
- 1 tsp Nutritional yeast
- 2 tbsp fresh lemon juice
- ¼ tsp Lemon zest.
- ¼ tsp Dried mint
- Pepper & salt, to taste
- For Croutons:
- 1 Croissant, cut into 1/2-inch cubes
- ½ tsp Dried oregano
- 2 tbsp Parmesan cheese, grated
- 1 tbsp Olive oil
- Pepper & salt, to taste

Directions:

- Add oil to the air fryer and set the pot on sauté mode. Add garlic and onion and sauté for 2 minutes. Add asparagus, lemon zest, mint, pepper, and salt, and sauté for a minute. Add stock and stir well. Seal the pot with the pressure-cooking lid and 400°F for 3 minutes. Release pressure using quick release. Remove lid. Puree the soup using a blender until smooth. Add nutritional yeast and lemon juice and stir well.
- For Croutons:
- In a bowl, toss bread cubes with the remaining ingredients. Add bread cubes into the multi-level air fryer basket and place the basket into the air fryer. Seal the pot with the air fryer lid. Select bake mode and cook at 350°F for 10 minutes. Stir halfway through. Top soup with croutons and serve.

273.   Mexican Baked Potato Soup

Preparation Time: 10 minutes
Cooking Time: 40 minutes
Servings: 4

Ingredients:

- 4 – 5 cloves garlic, diced
- One large onion, diced
- 1/8 -1/2 cup jalapeno seeded, diced (to taste)
- 4 cups vegetable broth
- 4 cups potatoes, diced
- ½ cup of salsa of choice
- 1 tsp cumin
- ¼ tsp oregano
- ¼ tsp garlic powder
- green onions, to taste
- ½ cup nutritional yeast (or to taste)
- Tofutti is Better than sour cream, to taste (optional)
- black pepper and white pepper, to taste

Directions:

- Press the Sauté button. Add onion, garlic, and jalapenos and sauté until brown.
- Turn off the Sauté. Add the vegetable broth, potatoes, salsa, cumin, oregano, and garlic powder – stir well.
- Lock the lid and put it on "Sealed." Click the Manual button and set the timer for 10 minutes.
- When the beeper sounds, allow the pressure to come down naturally. After about 20 minutes, you can release any remaining pressure and open the lid carefully – away from you.
- If you want the chunky soup, stop now and stir in the green onions, nutritional yeast, and pepper. Top each serving with Tofutti if desired.
- If you want the creamy soup
- Carefully transfer the soup to a blender. Add the nutritional yeast and pepper to the blender. Blend until smooth. Stir in the green onions. Top each serving with Tofutti if desired.
- Serve warm or cold

274.   Roasted Veggie Tacos

Preparation Time: 10 minutes
Cooking Time: 12 minutes
Servings: 3

Ingredients:

- Cooking oil spray (sunflower, safflower, or refined coconut)
- 1 small zucchini
- 1 small-medium yellow onion
- ¼ tsp garlic granules
- ⅛ tsp sea salt
- Freshly ground black pepper
- 1 (15-ounce) can of vegan refried beans
- 6 corn tortillas
- Fresh salsa of your choice
- 1 avocado, cut into slices, or fresh guacamole

Directions:

- Spray the air fryer basket with the oil. Spray with more oil and sprinkle evenly with the garlic, salt, and pepper to taste. Roast for 6 minutes at 350°F. Remove, shake or stir well, and cook for another 6 minutes, or until the veggies are nicely browned and tender.
- In a small pan, warm the refried beans over low heat. Stir often. Once to temperature, remove from the heat and set aside.
- To prepare the tortillas, sprinkle them individually with a little water, then place them in a hot skillet (in a single layer; you may need to do this in batches), turning over as each side becomes hot.
- To make the breakfast tacos: Place a corn tortilla on your plate and fill it with beans, roasted vegetables, salsa, and avocado slices.

275.   Creamy Cauliflower Pasta

Preparation Time: 10 minutes
Cooking Time: 18 minutes
Servings: 4

Ingredients:

- 4 cups cauliflower florets
- Cooking oil spray (sunflower,

- safflower, or refined coconut)
- 1 medium onion, chopped
- 8 ounces pasta, your choice (about 4 cups cooked; use gluten-free pasta if desired)
- Fresh chives or scallion tops, for garnish
- ½ cup raw cashew pieces (see Ingredient Tip)
- 1½ cups water
- 1 tbsp nutritional yeast
- 2 large garlic cloves, peeled
- 2 tbsp fresh lemon juice
- 1½ tsp sea salt
- ¼ tsp freshly ground black pepper

Directions:

- Place the cauliflower in the air fryer basket, spritz the tops with oil spray, and roast for 8 minutes at 330°F. Remove the air fryer basket, stir, and add the onion. Spritz with oil again and roast for another 10 minutes, or until the cauliflower is browned, and the onions are tender.
- While the vegetables are roasting in the air fryer, cook the pasta according to the package directions and mince the chives or scallions. Set aside.
- In a blender jar, place the roasted cauliflower and onions along with the cashews, water, nutritional yeast, garlic, lemon, salt, and pepper. Blend well until very smooth and creamy. Serve a generous portion of the sauce on top of the warm pasta, and top with the minced chives or scallions. The sauce will store refrigerated in an airtight container for about a week.

276. Vegetable Wontons

Preparation Time: 35 minutes
Cooking Time: 20 minutes
Servings: 12

Ingredients:

- 30 Wonton of Wrappers
- ¾ cup of Grated Cabbage
- ½ cup of Grated White Onion
- ½ cup of Grated Carrot
- ½ cup of Finely Chopped Mushrooms
- ¾ cup Finely Chopped Red Pepper
- 1 tbsp Chili Sauce
- 1 tsp of Garlic Powder
- 1/2 tsp of White Pepper
- Pinch of Salt
- ¼ cup of Water (for sealing wontons)
- Spray Olive Oil

Directions:

- In a hot skillet or medium-heat wok, throw all your vegetables in. Cook until all the mushroom and onion moisture has released and cooked out of the saucepan.
- Remove from heat and add salt, garlic powder, white pepper, and chili sauce. Let the mixture cool before having your wontons assembled.
- Remove from the basket, and let cool before consuming. Serve alongside duck sauce or soy!
- Place a wonton wrapper onto your work surface. Add 1 spoonful of your veggie mixture to the wonton wrapper center.

- Dip your finger in 1/4 cup of water and run your finger along with the square wrapper's exposed top half to get it.
- Push the bottom half carefully up and over the mixture making the corners rest offset.
- Spray your palm again, and spray the wonton's lower corners. Fold gently over the wonton's bottom corners so that one sits on top of the other and exerts slight pressure to seal it. Make sure the seals along your wonton are not open. Do another 29 times.
- Remove from the basket, and let cool before consuming. Serve alongside duck sauce or soy!
- Preheat your air-fryer for 3 minutes to 320°F. While spritzing your wontons with a little olive oil, preheats them.

277. Healthy Cheese Pockets

Preparation Time: 8 hours
Cooking Time: 15 min
Servings: 6

Ingredients:

- For the Dough:
- ¾ cup Almond Flour
- ½ cup Coconut Oil
- ½ tsp Salt
- For the Filling:
- ½ cup Raw Cashews, soaked in water overnight
- 1 tbsp Nutritional Yeast
- ½ tsp Garlic Powder
- ¼ tsp Salt

Directions:

- All ingredients in a bowl combine for the dough. Knead into a smooth paste.
- Combine all ingredients for the filling in a food processor. Blend until smooth.
- Lightly dust your working counter with almond flour.
- Roll out the dough into an 8"x12" rectangle. Cut the dough into six squares.
- Fill each square with the cashew mixture. Fold the dough into triangles, pressing the sides to seal.
- Lightly coat the frying basket with non-stick spray.
- Arrange the cheese pockets inside and cook for 15 minutes at 380°F.

278. Chinese Orange Tofu

Preparation Time: 20 minutes
Cooking Time: 10-15 minutes
Servings: 4

Ingredients:

- 1 pound of extra-firm tofu, drained and pressed (or use super-firm tofu)
- 1 Tbsp of tamari
- 1 Tbsp of cornstarch (or arrowroot powder)
- For the sauce:
- 1 tsp of orange zest
- 1/3 cup of orange juice
- ½ cup of water
- 2 tsp of cornstarch, (or arrowroot powder)
- ¼ tsp of crushed red pepper flakes
- 1 tsp of fresh ginger, minced

- 1 tsp of fresh garlic, minced
- 1 Tbsp of pure maple syrup

Directions:
- Cut the cubed tofu.
- Place the cubes of tofu in a plastic quarter-size storage bag. Place the tamari in and seal the jar. Shake the bag until the tamari is all filled with tofu.
- Add the cornstarch spoonful to the bag. Again, shake until coated with tofu. Place the tofu aside to marinate for 15 minutes or more.
- In the meantime, add all the ingredients in the sauce to a small bowl and mix with a spoon. Deposit aside. Place the tofu into a single layer in the air fryer. This is probably going to have to be done in two batches.
- Cook the tofu for 10 minutes at 390°F, and shake after 5 minutes.
- Once the tofu batches have been prepared, add them all to a skillet over medium-high heat. Give a stir to the sauce, and pour over the tofu. Remove tofu and sauce until the sauce has thickened, and heat the tofu through.
- Serve with rice and steamed vegetables immediately, if you so wish.

279. Asparagus Strata

Preparation Time: 12 minutes
Cooking Time: 17 minutes
Servings: 4

Ingredients:
- 6 asparagus spears, cut into 2-inch pieces
- 2 slices whole-wheat bread, cut into ½-inch cubes
- 4 eggs
- 3 tbsp whole milk
- ½ cup grated Havarti or Swiss cheese
- 2 tbsp chopped flat-leaf parsley
- Pinch salt
- Freshly ground black pepper

Directions:
- Preparing the Ingredients. Place the asparagus spears and one tbsp water in a 6-inch baking pan and place in the air fryer basket. Bake for 3 to 5 minutes or until crisp and tender at 350°F. Remove the asparagus from the pan and drain it. Spray the pan with nonstick cooking spray. Arrange the bread cubes and asparagus into the pan and set them aside. In a medium bowl, beat the eggs with the milk until combined. Add the cheese, parsley, salt, and pepper. Pour into the baking pan. Bake for 11 to 14 minutes or until the eggs are set and the top starts to brown.

280. Lemon Tofu

Preparation Time: 30 minutes
Cooking Time: 15-20 minutes
Servings: 6

Ingredients:
- 1 pound of extra-firm tofu drained and pressed, or use super-firm tofu
- 1 tbsp of tamari
- 1 tbsp of cornstarch, or arrowroot powder
- For the sauce:
- 1 tsp of lemon zest

- 1/3 cup of lemon juice
- 1/2 cup of water
- 2 tbsp of organic sugar
- 2 tsp of cornstarch, or arrowroot powder

Directions:
- Place the cubes of tofu in a plastic quarter-size storage bag. Put the tamari in and seal the bag. Shake the bag until the tamari is all filled with tofu.
- Attach the cornstarch spoonful to the jar. Again, shake until coated with tofu. Set the tofu aside to marinate for 15 minutes or more.
- In the meantime, add all the ingredients in the sauce to a small bowl and mix with a spoon. Deposit back.
- Drop the tofu into a single layer in the air fryer. This is probably going to have to be done in two batches. Cook the tofu for 10 minutes at 390°F, and shake after 5 minutes.
- Once the tofu batches have been cooked, add them all to a skillet over medium-high heat. Give a stir to the sauce, and pour over the tofu. Remove tofu and sauce until the sauce has thickened, and heat the tofu through.
- Serve with rice and steamed vegetables immediately, if you so wish.

281. Zucchini Enchiladas

Preparation Time: 35 minutes
Cooking Time: 15 minutes
Servings: 4

Ingredients:
- 1 large Zucchini
- 1 cup of shredded Chicken
- 1 small Onion diced
- 1 tsp of ground Cumin
- 1 tsp of Chili Powder
- 1 tsp of Garlic Powder
- 1 tsp of Smoked Paprika
- 1 cup of red Enchilada Sauce
- ¼ cup of shredded Mexican Blend Cheese
- 2 tbsp of Olive Oil
- Salt and pepper to taste
- A drizzle of Sour Cream and Green Onion to garnish

Directions:
- Heat up the olive oil in a large frying pan over medium heat and brown the diced onion until translucent.
- Attach and blend well the seasoning–garlic powder, ground cumin, chili powder, smoked paprika, salt, and pepper.
- Add the shredded chicken next, and blend well.
- Add the enchilada sauce of 3/4 cup and let it simmer for 2 minutes until the chicken is covered by the sauce. Test any seasoning and change it if necessary. Hold on, cool aside.
- Cut the zucchini in half while the chicken cools in a lengthwise direction. Render thin strips of the zucchini using a Y-shaped vegetable peeler. Of each half, you can easily get 6 to 8 slices.
- Layout three slices of zucchini, each overlapping.
- Place on one end of the zucchini strips about a tbsp of the chicken mixture. Roll it up and place it on a greased baking dish that can fit in a basket with an air fryer.
- Repeat with remaining strips of zucchini and a mixture of chicken.

- Add the remaining 1/4 cup enchilada sauce over the strips of rolled zucchini.
- Sprinkle with scrambled cheese.
- In an air fryer, cook for 10 minutes at 330°F.
- Serve hot with sour cream chips and a sprinkle of sliced green onion.

282. Eggplant stacks

Preparation Time: 5 minutes
Cooking Time: 15 minutes
Servings: 4

Ingredients:
- 2 large tomatoes; cut into ¼-inch slices
- ¼ cup fresh basil, sliced
- 4 oz. Fresh mozzarella; cut into ½-oz. Slices
- 1 medium eggplant; cut into ¼-inch slices
- 2 tbsp. Olive oil

Directions:
- In a 6-inch round baking dish, place four slices of eggplant on the bottom. Put a slice of tomato on each eggplant round, then mozzarella, then eggplant. Repeat as necessary.
- Drizzle with olive oil. Cover dish with foil and place dish into the air fryer basket. Adjust the temperature to 350 °F and set the timer for 12 minutes.
- When done, the eggplant will be tender. Garnish with fresh basil to serve.

283. Korean Cauliflower "Wings"

Preparation Time: 20 minutes
Cooking Time: 15-20 minutes
Servings: 6

Ingredients:
- 1 cauliflower cut up into smaller pieces
- For the batter
- 1 cup of flour
- 1/2 cup of cornstarch
- 2 tsp of baking soda
- 1 tbsp of garlic powder
- 1 tbsp of paprika
- 1 cup of water
- For the sauce
- 6 tbsp of Gochujang (pepper paste)
- 4 tbsp of soy sauce
- 2 tbsp of honey
- 4 tbsp of water

Directions:
- Combine the food, cornstarch, baking soda, garlic powder, and paprika into a large bowl. Give it a mix, and then add the batter to the surface.
- Dip the cauliflower into the batter and ensure it is thoroughly coated. Let it sit on a rack and let extra batter dip off for a minute.
- When ready, put it in a single layer in the air fryer and set it to 350°F for 12 minutes (no preheating required!) While the cauliflower is "frying" in the air fryer, prepare your sauce by mixing all the ingredients in the sauce into a saucepan. Mix it well, and then turn off the heat to a simmer on low heat. Once the cauliflower is

done in the air fryer, put it in the saucepan before setting it aside to cover the cauliflower.
- Keep until all of the cauliflower is fried.

284. Vegetables and Couscous

Preparation Time: 20 minutes
Cooking Time: 45 minutes
Servings: 6

Ingredients:
- 50g carrot
- Eggplant 250g
- 50g cherry tomatoes
- 1 shallot
- 150g broth
- 250g zucchini
- Salt to taste
- 1 clove garlic
- Chili pepper
- 375g couscous
- 400 ml of water
- Butter taste
- 1 ml of olive oil

Directions:
- Peel the garlic cut the chili into pieces, chop the shallot and place everything on the baking sheet, distributing it well through the bottom; add the oil. Before you start cooking, wash and cut eggplants, zucchini, carrots, and small diced tomatoes (the latter should be reserved as they will be added to couscous when they are cold).
- Set the air fryer to 150°C and brown for 3 minutes. Add carrots and broth, and simmer for another 6 min. Finally, pour the eggplant and zucchini, salt and pepper, and simmer for another 25 minutes.
- In addition to preparing the semolina, put the water in a saucepan, boil, and pour a small spoonful of salt. Add the couscous to the rain, oil, mix, and stop the fire. Let swell for 3 min. Add a pinch of butter and cook again for another 3 min. Regularly mix with a fork to shell properly.
- As soon as the vegetables have cooled, add the small tomatoes, and pour everything into a bowl with the couscous.

285. Roasted Vegetable Pasta

Preparation Time: 20 minutes
Cooking Time: 15 minutes
Servings: 8

Ingredients:
- 1 Yellow squash
- 4 oz. Brown mushrooms
- 1 Zucchini
- 1 each Red - Green - Orange bell peppers
- 1 Red onion
- 1 pinch of each Freshly cracked black pepper and salt
- 1 tsp Italian seasoning
- 1 cup Grape tomatoes
- ½ cup Pitted Kalamata olives
- 1 lb. Cooked Rigatoni or Penne Rigate
- ¼ cup Olive oil
- 2 tbsp Fresh chopped basil
- 3 tbsp Balsamic vinegar

Directions:

- Set the Air Fryer temperature to 380°F.
- Cut the peppers into large chunks and slice the red onion. Slice the tomatoes and olives into halves. Cut the squash and zucchini into half-moons.
- Toss the red onion, mushrooms, peppers, squash, and zucchini in a large mixing container. Drizzle with a spritz of oil, tossing well using the black pepper, salt, and Italian seasoning.
- Prepare in the Air Fryer until the veggies are softened - not mushy (12 to 15 min.). Toss the fixings in the basket about halfway through the cooking cycle for even frying.
- Combine the cooked pasta, roasted veggies, olives, and tomatoes into a large container. Pour in the vinegar, and toss.
- Keep it refrigerated until ready to serve. Garnish using the fresh basil as serving time.

286. Cabbage Diet Soup

Preparation Time: 5 minutes
Cooking Time: 30 minutes
Servings: 5-6

Ingredients:

- 1/2 head cabbage, chopped
- 2-3 leeks, carefully cleaned and chopped
- 2 tbsp coconut oil
- 3-4 ribs of celery, diced
- 1 bell pepper, diced
- 2-3 carrots, diced
- 2/3 cloves of garlic, minced
- 4 cups vegetable broth
- 1 tsp Italian seasoning
- 1 tsp Creole seasoning
- black pepper to taste
- 2-3 cups of mixed salad greens

Directions:

- Heat coconut oil on a sauté setting in the Air fryer.
- Add prepared vegetables (except salad greens) one at a time, starting with carrots, stirring well after each addition.
- Save garlic for last, so it doesn't burn.
- Season with black pepper, Creole seasoning, and Italian seasoning.
- Add vegetable broth.
- Close vent and cook on soup setting for 20 minutes.
- Once the cooking is complete, open the vent and remove the lid.
- Add salad greens, stir well and let sit a few minutes to wilt.
- Taste and adjust seasonings if needed.

287. Moroccan Vegetable Stew

Preparation Time: 35 minutes
Cooking Time: 40 minutes
Servings: 6

Ingredients:

- 1 finely sliced red onion
- 3 cloves garlic chopped finely
- 2 sticks of celery diced
- 20 ml olive oil

- 1 tsp cumin
- ½ tsp turmeric
- 1 tsp ground coriander
- 1 tsp smoked paprika
- 1 tin cooked chickpea
- 200ml vegetable stock
- 10 x dried apricots/halved
- 1x tin 450g peeled chopped tomato
- 8 baby eggplants/sliced in
- half lengthways
- ½ cup picked Coriander leaves

Directions:

- Touch the SAUTÉ/SEAR menu to select SAUTÉ/SEAR LOW TEMP program, set the cooking time for 5 minutes, and press START Heat olive oil in the cooker.
- Add onion, garlic, celery, and spices. Cook with the lid open until fragrant.
- Add in chickpeas, tomato, stock, apricots, and eggplant and touch the MULTI COOK menu to select the STEW/CURRY program, set the cooking time for 30 minutes, and press START.
- Serve on a bed of steamed couscous drizzled with yogurt and toasted slivered almonds.

288. Baked Parsnip and Potato

Preparation Time: 15 minutes
Cooking Time: 30 minutes
Servings: 8

Ingredients:

- 28 oz potato, cubed
- 3 tbsp pine nuts
- 28 oz parsnips, chopped
- 1 ¾ oz Parmesan cheese, shredded
- 6 ¾ oz crème Fraiche
- 1 slice bread
- 2 tbsp sage
- 4 tbsp butter
- 4 tsp mustard

Directions:

- Preheat the Air Fryer to 360°F, and boil salted water in a pot over medium heat. Add potatoes and parsnips. Bring to a boil. In a bowl, mix mustard, crème Fraiche, sage, salt, and pepper. Drain the potatoes and parsnips and mash them with butter using a potato masher. Add mustard mixture, bread, cheese, and nuts to the mash and mix.
- Add the batter to your cooking tray and cook for 25 minutes. Serve and enjoy!

289. Sweet Potato Casserole

Preparation Time: 15 minutes
Cooking Time: 15 minutes
Servings: 4

Ingredients:

- 2 c. sweet potatoes
- ¼ c. melted butter
- 1½ tbsp. milk
- ¼ c. honey
- vanilla

- 1 large egg
- ¼ c. brown sugar
- ¼ c. wheat flour
- 2 tbsp. butter
- ½ c. chopped pecans
- Cooking spray

Directions:
- Spray baking sheet with cooking spray.
- In a large mixing bowl, combine milk, honey, sweet potatoes, vanilla, melted butter, and egg. Mix well.
- In another mixing bowl, combine brown sugar and flour. Cut in 3 tbsp butter till crumbly. Add pecans and mix well.
- Sprinkle the mixture over sweet potatoes.
- Place on a 1-inch rack and cook for 25-30 minutes at 400°F (High) or until golden brown.
- Serve Immediately.

290. Vegetable and Fruit Skewers

Preparation Time: 60 minutes
Cooking Time: 20 minutes
Servings: 2

Ingredients:
- 4 tbsp virgin olive oil
- 3 tbsp. lemon juice
- 1 garlic clove, minced
- 2 tbsp. chopped parsley
- ½ tsp. salt
- ½ tsp. black pepper
- 1 sliced zucchini
- 1 sliced yellow squash
- ½ red bell pepper
- ½ c. cherry tomatoes
- ½ c. pineapple chunks
- 4 wooden skewers

Directions:
- In a large mixing bowl, combine olive oil, garlic, parsley, lemon juice, pepper, and salt. Pour into a large resealable plastic bag. Add zucchini, squash, bell pepper, and tomatoes. Seal bag, shake to coat vegetables and place in refrigerator for a minimum of 1 hour.
- Remove vegetables from marinade and thread onto skewers, along with pineapple, alternating among each item.
- Line the bottom of the air fryer Oven with foil for easier clean-up.
- Place skewers on the 4-inch rack. Cook on High Power (400°F) for 8 minutes.
- Flip skewers over and cook for another 6-8 minutes until veggies are desired level of doneness.
- Remove from the air fryer Oven, transfer to a plate, and serve

291. Vegan Chili and Cheese Fries

Preparation Time: 10 minutes
Cooking Time: 20 minutes
Servings: 4

Ingredients:
- 300 grams Jicama, cut into sticks

- 2 tbsp Olive Oil
- 1 tbsp Nutritional Yeast
- ½ tsp Cayenne
- ½ tsp Salt
- For Dipping:
- ½ cup Tofu Mayo
- 1 tbsp Sriracha

Directions:
- Toss together jicama sticks, olive oil, cayenne, nutritional yeast, and salt in a bowl.
- Arrange in layers inside the frying basket using cooling racks and cook for 20 minutes at 400°F.
- Whisk together tofu mayo and sriracha in a bowl.
- Serve jicama fries with sriracha dip.

292. Roasted Bell Peppers with Spicy Mayo

Preparation Time: 10 minutes
Cooking Time: 15 minutes
Servings: 2

Ingredients:
- 4 bell peppers, seeded and sliced
- ½ tsp rosemary, dried
- 1 tbsp olive oil
- 1 onion, sliced
- ½ tsp basil, dried
- 1/3 cup mayo
- 1/3 tsp sriracha
- ¼ tsp black pepper, to taste
- Kosher salt

Directions:
- Preheat your Air Fryer to 400 °F
- Toss bell pepper and onion with olive oil, basil, salt, rosemary, salt, and black pepper
- Place the peppers and onion to make a layer in the cooking basket
- Cook for 12 to 15 minutes
- Make the sauce by whisking the mayonnaise and sriracha
- Serve warm, and enjoy!

293. Baked Vegetables with Cheese and Olives

Preparation Time: 15 minutes
Cooking Time: 15-20 minutes
Servings: 4

Ingredients:
- ½ pound cauliflower, cut into 1-inch florets
- ¼ pound zucchini, cut into 1-inch chunks
- 1 red onion, sliced
- 2 bell pepper, cut into 1-inch chunks
- 2 tbsp extra virgin olives
- 1 cup dry white wine vinegar
- 1 tsp dried rosemary
- Salt and pepper to taste
- ½ tsp dried basil
- ½ cup tomato, pureed
- ½ cup cashew cheese
- 1-ounce kalamata olives pitted and halved

Directions:
- Preheat your Air Fryer to 390 °F

- Toss vegetables with olive oil, vinegar, rosemary, salt, pepper, and basil until coated
- Add pureed tomatoes to a lightly greased baking dish, spread to cover the bottom of the baking dish
- Add vegetables and top with cashew cheese; scatter kalamata olives on top
- Transfer to Air Fryer and cook for 20 minutes, making sure to shake halfway through
- Serve and enjoy!

294.   Mushroom and Asparagus Cakes

Preparation Time: 30 minutes
Cooking Time: 15 minutes
Servings: 4

Ingredients:

- ¾ pound asparagus spears
- 1 tbsp canola oil
- 1 tsp paprika
- Salt and pepper to taste
- 1 tsp garlic powder
- 3 tbsp scallions, chopped
- 1 cup button mushrooms, chopped
- ½ cup cheese
- 2 tbsp flax seeds
- 2 eggs
- 4 tbsp cream

Directions:

- Preheat your Air Fryer to 400 °F
- Place asparagus spears in a lightly greased Air Fryer cooking basket, toss asparagus with canola oil, paprika, salt, pepper
- Cook for 5 minutes
- Chop asparagus, add garlic powder, scallions, mushrooms, flax seeds, cashew cream, flax eggs
- Mix well until everything is incorporated well, form patties with the mixture
- Transfer to Air Fryer and cook for 5 minutes, making sure to flip halfway through
- Serve and enjoy!

295.   Rosemary Veggie Gratin

Preparation Time: 10 minutes
Cooking Time: 20 minutes
Servings: 4

Ingredients:

- ¾ pound cauliflower, steamed
- 1 onion, sliced
- 2 garlic cloves, minced
- 1 bell pepper, deveined
- 2 eggs, whipped
- 1 cup cream
- Salt and pepper to taste
- 1 tsp cayenne pepper
- 1 tbsp fresh rosemary

Directions:

- Preheat your Air Fryer to 325 °F
- Place vegetables in a lightly greased casserole dish, add remaining ingredients, and stir
- Spoon cream on top
- Transfer to Air Fryer and cook for 20 minutes

- Serve and enjoy!

296.   Eggplant Caprese

Preparation Time: 15 minutes
Cooking Time: 12 minutes
Servings: 2

Ingredients:

- 1 medium eggplant, cut into ¼-inch slices
- 2 large tomatoes cut into ¼-inch slices
- 4 oz. fresh mozzarella cut into ½-oz slices
- 2 tbsp. olive oil
- A few sprigs of fresh basil

Directions:

- Cover the bottom of a baking dish with eggplant slices. Place a tomato slice on top, followed by the mozzarella, and top with another piece of eggplant. Continue in this way until you have used all the ingredients.
- Splash some olive oil on top and wrap some foil around the dish. Place it into your fryer.
- Cook at 350°F for twelve minutes.
- Check the eggplants have softened before serving. Top with some fresh basil.

297.   Beef Mushroom Soup

Preparation Time: 20 minutes
Cooking Time: 1 hr. 35 minutes
Servings: 8

Ingredients:

- 2 tbsp of clarified butter or ghee
- 2 pounds of stew beef (cut it into bite-sized pieces)
- 1 chopped onion
- 1 quart of beef broth
- 1 16-ounce can of cremini mushrooms

Directions:

- Start with the sauté option on your pressure cooker and start melting the butter in it. Brown, the meat for 2-3 minutes, making sure it's seared on all sides. (Work in smaller batches to prevent overcrowding the pot.) Take each batch out, put it on a plate, and set it aside.
- Into the pot, add the onion, sprinkle it with a bit of salt, and let it sauté. The liquid it releases will help you deglaze the pot of any browned bits.
- When the onions are caramelized, add the beef back into the pot along with the rest of the ingredients. Close the lid and the valve. Use the meat/stew option or the pressure cook function and set the timer for 35 minutes.
- After the time is up, let the pressure release on its own (it should take 30-35 minutes). Remove the lid – if it seems like there's too much liquid, simply ladle out a bit.
- Serve in warm bowls with a little parsley garnish.

298.   Curry Zucchini Soup

Preparation Time: 10 minutes
Cooking Time: 30 minutes
Servings: 8

Ingredients:

- 10 chopped zucchinis
- 1 tbsp of Thai curry paste

- 1 tbsp of low-carb sweetener (such as stevia, stevia, sucralose)
- 13 ½ ounces of coconut milk
- 2 cups of stock or chicken bone broth

Directions:

- Add all of the ingredients into the air fryer, close the lid and seal the vent.
- Make sure the valve is closed. Use the option for manual pressure and set the timer for 10 minutes.
- Perform a quick release of the pressure once the time is up. Carefully open the lid and use a blender to cream the veggies until the soup is smooth (be careful of splashing!).

299.   Squash Risotto

Preparation Time: 10 minutes
Cooking Time: 13 minutes
Servings: 2

Ingredients:

- 1 small yellow onion, chopped
- A drizzle of olive oil
- 1 garlic clove, minced
- ½ red bell pepper, chopped
- 1 cup butternut squash, chopped
- 1 cup Arborio rice
- 1 and ½ cups veggie stock
- 3 tbsp dry white wine
- 4 ounces mushrooms, chopped
- A pinch of salt and black pepper
- A pinch of oregano, dried
- ¼ tsp coriander, ground
- 1 and ½ cups mixed kale and spinach
- 1 tbsp nutritional yeast

Directions:

- Set your air fryer on sauté mode, add the oil, and heat it up.
- Add onion, bell pepper, squash, and garlic, stir and cook for 5 minutes.
- Add rice, stock, wine, salt, pepper, mushrooms, oregano, and coriander, stir, cover, and at 400°F for 5 minutes.
- Add mixed kale and spinach, parsley and yeast, stir and leave aside for 5 minutes.
- Divide between 2 plates and serve as a side dish.

300.   Cheese Broccoli Pasta

Preparation Time: 10 minutes
Cooking Time: 10 minutes
Servings: 2

Ingredients:

- 2 cups water
- ½ pound pasta
- 8 ounces cheddar cheese, grated
- ½ cup broccoli
- ½ cup half and half

Directions:

- Put the water and the pasta in your air fryer.
- Add the steamer basket, add the broccoli, and cover the cooker and 400°F for 4 minutes.

- Drain the pasta, transfer it as well as the broccoli, and clean the pot.
- Set it on sauté mode, add pasta and broccoli, cheese and a half and half, stir well, cook for 2 minutes, divide between plates and serve as a side dish for chicken.

301.   Crispy Noodle Vegetable Salad

Preparation Time: 30 minutes
Cooking Time: 20 minutes
Servings: 3

Ingredients:

- 1 carrot, sliced thinly
- 1 cup cabbage, sliced thinly
- 1 green bell pepper, sliced thinly
- 1 onion, sliced thinly
- 1 package of wheat noodles
- 1 sprig of coriander, chopped
- 1 tbsp cooking oil
- 1 tbsp lime juice
- 1 tbsp red chili sauce
- 1 tbsp tamari
- 1 tomato, chopped
- salt to taste

Directions:

- In a big pot, boil water and add a tsp of salt. Bring the water to a boil and add the noodles. Boil the noodles until it is half-cooked. Drain.
- In a mixing bowl, pour oil over the noodles and mix until the noodles are coated evenly.
- Place a tin foil on the base of the air fryer basket and place the noodles inside.
- Cook in a preheated air fryer at 395°F for 15 to 20 minutes or until crisp.
- Meanwhile, mix together the tamari, red chili sauce, and lime juice. Season with salt and pepper to taste.
- Once the noodles are cooked, assemble the salad by placing the air-fried noodles in a bowl. Add the vegetables and pour over the sauce.

302.   Baked Root Vegetables

Preparation Time: 20 minutes
Cooking Time: 45 minutes
Servings: 6

Ingredients:

- ¼ cup olive oil
- 1 head broccoli, cut into florets
- 1 tbsp dry onion powder
- 2 sweet potatoes, peeled and cubed
- 4 carrots, cut into chunks
- 4 zucchinis, sliced thickly
- salt and pepper to taste

Directions:

- Preheat the air fryer to 400°F.
- In a baking dish that can fit inside the air fryer, mix all the ingredients and bake for 45 minutes or until the vegetables are tender and the sides have browned.

303.   BBQ Tofu

Preparation Time: 15 minutes
Cooking Time: 26 minutes
Servings: 3

Ingredients:

- 1 (16-ounce) block of extra-firm tofu
- 2 tbsp low-sodium soy sauce
- 1 tbsp ketchup
- 1 tbsp honey
- 1 cup store-bought barbecue sauce, divided, plus more for serving

Directions:

- Drain the tofu, then cut it into 1-by-4-inch slices. Put the slices on layers of paper towel. Put more paper towels on top and press down to remove as much moisture from the tofu as possible. Put the tofu into a glass baking dish.
- In a small bowl, whisk together the soy sauce, ketchup, and honey. Brush over the tofu on both sides. Set aside for 10 minutes.
- Put half the tofu slices in the bottom of the air fryer basket. Place a raised rack over the slices and put the remaining tofu slices on it.
- Set or preheat the air fryer to 400°F. Grill the tofu slices for 10 minutes, turn them over, and grill for another 6 minutes. Remove the tofu from the air fryer.
- Brush the tofu with ½ cup of barbecue sauce and put it back into the air fryer basket. Grill for 5 minutes. Then turn the tofu, brush with the remaining barbecue sauce, and grill for 4 to 5 minutes or until the tofu is glazed and deep golden brown.
- Serve the riblets with more barbecue sauce.

304.   Vegan Taco Bowls

Preparation Time: 15 minutes
Cooking Time: 9 minutes
Servings: 4

Ingredients:

- 2 (10-ounce) packages of frozen cooked brown rice
- 1 tbsp olive oil
- 1 onion, chopped
- 3 garlic cloves, minced
- 1 (15-ounce) can of pinto beans, drained and rinsed
- 1 cup frozen corn kernels
- ⅔ cup mild salsa, divided
- ⅓ cup sour cream
- 2 tbsp freshly squeezed lime juice
- 1⅓ cups grated pepper Jack cheese

Directions:

- Prepare the rice as directed on the package and set it aside.
- In a 6-inch metal bowl, drizzle the olive oil over the onion and garlic and toss to combine.
- Set or preheat the air fryer to 375°F. Put the bowl into the air fryer basket. Bake for 3 to 4 minutes or until the vegetables are tender.
- Remove the basket from the air fryer and add the beans, corn, and ⅓ cup of salsa to the bowl; stir to combine. Return the basket to the air fryer. Bake for another 4 to 5 minutes or until the ingredients are hot.

- Meanwhile, combine the remaining ⅓ cup of salsa, sour cream, and lime juice in a small bowl until well mixed.
- Divide the rice equally among four bowls. Divide the bean mixture on top. Drizzle with the sour cream mixture and sprinkle with the cheese. Serve.

305.   Italian Tofu Steaks

Preparation Time: 20 minutes
Cooking Time: 20 minutes
Servings: 4

Ingredients:

- 1 (16-ounce) package of firm tofu
- 1 tbsp olive oil
- 1 tsp dried Italian seasoning
- ½ tsp smoked paprika
- ¼ tsp garlic powder
- ¼ tsp sea salt
- ⅛ tsp red pepper flakes

Directions:

- Drain the liquid from the tofu. Place the tofu on some paper towels. Top with more paper towels and press gently but firmly to remove more liquid. Repeat this step, then cut the tofu into four equal-size slices.
- In a glass baking dish large enough to hold the tofu slices, whisk together the olive oil, Italian seasoning, paprika, garlic powder, salt, and red pepper flakes. Add the tofu to the dish and turn to coat. Let stand for 10 minutes.
- Put two of the tofu slices in the air fryer basket. Add a raised rack and put the other two tofu slices on the rack.
- Set or preheat the air fryer to 375°F. Bake for 15 to 20 minutes or until the tofu is golden brown. Serve.

306.   Pine-Pumpkin Puree

Preparation Time: 15 minutes
Cooking Time: 30 minutes
Servings: 4

Ingredients:

- 4 pounds pumpkin, seeded and diced
- 2 tbsp pure pineapple extract
- 1 tbsp orange zest
- 1 cup of water
- salt and pepper to taste

Directions:

- Add the water to your Pot and place the steamer rack at the bottom of your pot.
- Pour the water and place the diced pumpkin in a steamer basket and place it on top of the steamer rack and close the lid to cook on HIGH pressure for 30 minutes.
- Quick-release the pressure and let the pumpkin cool; mix in the orange zest and pure pineapple extract.
- Then, scoop out the flesh into a bowl.
- Mash the pumpkin and raisins using the potato masher and season with salt and pepper to taste.
- Portion the pumpkin puree into two bowls or mugs; serve the pumpkin puree with the tea or coffee.

307. Buttered Garlic Squash

Preparation Time: 15 minutes
Cooking Time: 30 minutes
Servings: 4

Ingredients:

- 2.5 pounds of medium-sized butternut squash, seeded and diced
- 1 cup of garlic taste butter
- 3 cloves of garlic, minced
- 1 cup of cream
- 1 cup of water
- Salt and pepper to taste

Directions:

- In a pot, melt the garlic butter for 5 minutes.
- Add the water to your Air fryer and place the steamer rack at the bottom of your pot.
- Place the diced squash and the butter in a steamer basket and place it on top of the steamer rack and close the lid to cook on HIGH pressure for 15-20 minutes.
- Quick-release the pressure and let the squash cool.
- Blend the squash with garlic butter and minced garlic. Then mix in the cream and blend using the blender, and season with the salt and pepper to taste.
- Portion the squash puree into four bowls or mugs. Remember that this dish should be served warm. Serve the squash puree with the bread.

308. Roasted Rainbow Vegetable

Preparation Time: 15 minutes
Cooking Time: 10 minutes
Servings: 4

Ingredients:

- 1 zucchini, cut into 1-inch pieces
- 4 ounces fresh mushrooms, cleaned and halved
- 1 red bell pepper, seeded and cut inch pieces
- 1 tablespoon extra-virgin olive oil
- ½ sweet onion, cut into 1-inch wedges
- salt and pepper to taste
- 1 yellow summer squash, cut into inch pieces

Directions:

- Preheat an air fryer to 330 °F.
- In a large bowl, add the red bell pepper, summer squash, zucchini, mushrooms, and onion. Toss in the olive oil, salt, and black pepper to taste.
- In the air fryer basket, arrange the veggies in a uniform layer. Cook until the veggies are roasted, approximately 20 minutes, stirring halfway through.

309. Julienne Vegetables with Chicken

Preparation Time: 30 minutes
Cooking Time: 15-20 minutes
Servings: 2

Ingredients:

- 2 chicken breast fillets á 250 g
- 100 g carrots
- 100 g parsley root
- 50 g leek
- 50 g red pepper
- 2 - 3 sprigs of thyme

- 2 tbsp butter
- Himalayan salt
- pepper
- 1 tsp olive oil

Directions:

- Preheat the air fryer to 400°F. Peel, wash, and clean carrots and parsley roots.
- Cut the peppers in half, remove and wash the seeds.
- Halve and wash the leeks.
- Cut the whole vegetables into thin julienne strips.
- Pluck the thyme leaves
- Rinse off the chicken breast and dab dry; massage the chicken breast with oil, salt, pepper, and thyme, then fry in a coated Air Fryer for 5 minutes or until golden brown.
- Blanch the vegetables and place them on plates together with the chicken breast fillet.

310. Bell Pepper Gratin

Preparation Time: 30 minutes
Cooking Time: 15-20 minutes
Servings: 2

Ingredients:

- 2 big red peppers
- 600 g ground beef
- ½ zucchini
- 1 shallot
- 1 tbsp olive oil
- 200 g Gouda, grated
- 12 stems of thyme
- sea-salt
- pepper

Directions:

- Wash vegetables and herbs and drain
- Halve the peppers and remove the seeds
- Cut the courgette into small pieces
- Peel the shallot and finely dice
- Remove the leaves from 6 thyme stalks.
- Preheat your air fryer to 390°F. Heat the oil in the Air Fryer and sauté the shallot with zucchini.
- Take both out again and fry the minced meat.
- Season the minced meat with salt and pepper and mix with the thyme leaves, zucchini, and shallot.
- Pour minced meat mixture into the halves of the pepper and sprinkle with Gouda
- Put the peppers in a casserole dish and gratinate for 15 - 20 minutes in a preheated oven.
- Cover the paprika buns with thyme and serve.

311. Eggplant Boats

Preparation Time: 15 minutes
Cooking Time: 30 minutes
Servings: 4

Ingredients:

- 4 little eggplants split the long way
- Salt and dark pepper to the taste
- 10 tbsp olive oil
- 2 and ½ pounds tomatoes, cut into equal parts and ground
- 1 green ringer pepper

- 1 yellow onion
- 1 tbsp garlic, minced
- ½ cup cauliflower
- 1 tsp oregano
- ½ cup parsley
- 3 ounces feta cheddar,

Directions:
- Season eggplants with salt, pepper, and 4 tbsp oil, hurl, put them in the air fryer cooker and cook at 350 °F for about 16 minutes.
- Meanwhile, heat up a container with 3 tbsp oil over medium high heat, include onion, mix and cook for 5 minutes.
- Add chime pepper, garlic and cauliflower, mix, cook for 5 minutes, take off heat, include parsley, tomato, salt, pepper, oregano, and cheddar, and whisk everything.
- Stuff eggplants with the veggie blend, shower the remainder of the oil over them, put them in the air fryer cooker, and cook at 350 °F for about 6 minutes more.
- Divide among plates and serve immediately. Enjoy!

312. Tex Mex Peppers

Preparation Time: 10 minutes
Cooking Time: 20 minutes
Servings: 4

Ingredients:
- 4 ringer peppers, finish cut off, and seeds evacuated
- ½ cup tomato juice
- 2 tbsp jostled jalapenos, hacked
- 4 chicken bosoms
- 1 cup tomatoes, hacked
- ¼ cup yellow onion slashed
- ¼ cup green peppers, slashed
- 2 cups tomato sauce
- Salt and dark pepper to the taste
- 2 tsp onion powder
- ½ tsp red pepper, squashed
- 1 tsp bean stew powder
- ½ tsp garlic powder
- 1 tsp cumin, ground

Directions:
- In a skillet that accommodates the air fryer cooker, blend chicken bosoms in with tomato juice, jalapenos, tomatoes, onion, green peppers, salt, pepper, onion powder, red pepper, stew powder, garlic powder, oregano, and cumin; mix well, present in the air fryer cooker and cook at 350 °F for about 15 minutes,
- Shred meat utilizing 2 forks, mix, stuff ringer peppers with this blend, place them in the air fryer cooker and cook at 320 °F for about 10 minutes more.
- Divide stuffed peppers on plates and serve. Enjoy the recipe!

313. Bell Pepper and Tomato Sauce

Preparation Time: 10 minutes
Cooking Time: 15 minutes
Servings: 4

Ingredients:
- 2 red ringer peppers, slashed
- 2 garlic cloves, minced

- 1-pound cherry tomatoes, divided
- 1 tsp rosemary, dried
- 3 straight leaves
- 2 tbsp olive oil
- 1 tbsp balsamic vinegar
- Salt and dark pepper to the taste

Directions:
- In a bowl, blend tomatoes with garlic, salt, dark pepper, rosemary, straight leaves, half of the oil, and half of the vinegar, hurl to cover, present in the air fryer cooker, and meal them at 320 °F for about 15 minutes.
- Meanwhile, in your food processor, blend ringer peppers with a spot of ocean salt, dark pepper, the remainder of the oil, and the remainder of the vinegar, and mix well indeed.
- Divide cooked tomatoes among plates, shower the chime peppers sauce over them and serve. Enjoy the recipe!

314. Chery Tomato and Rutabaga Pasta

Preparation Time: 10 minutes
Cooking Time: 20 minutes
Servings: 4

Ingredients:
- 1 tbsp shallot, hacked
- 1 garlic clove, minced
- ¾ cup cashews splashed for a few hours and depleted
- 2 tbsp the nutritional facts yeast
- ½ cup veggie stock
- Salt and dark pepper to the taste
- 2 tsp lemon juice
- For the pasta:
- 1 cup cherry tomatoes, divided
- 5 tsp olive oil
- ¼ tsp garlic powder
- 2 rutabagas, stripped and cut into thick noodles

Directions:
- Place tomatoes and rutabaga noodles into a container that accommodates the air fryer cooker, shower the oil over them, season with salt, dark pepper, and garlic powder, and hurl to cover and cook in the air fryer cooker at 350 °F for about 15 minutes.
- Meanwhile, in a food processor, blend garlic with shallots, cashews, veggie stock, the nutritional facts yeast, lemon squeeze, a spot of ocean salt, and dark pepper to the taste and mix well.
- Divide rutabaga pasta among plates, top with tomatoes, sprinkle the sauce over them, and serve. Enjoy the recipe!

315. Italian Eggplant Stew

Preparation Time: 15 minutes
Cooking Time: 15-20 minutes
Servings: 4

Ingredients:
- 1 red onion, hacked
- 2 garlic cloves, hacked
- 1 bundle parsley, slashed
- Salt and dark pepper to the taste
- 1 tsp oregano, dried

- 2 eggplants, cut into medium pieces
- 2 tbsp olive oil
- 2 tbsp tricks, slashed
- 1 bunch of green olives, hollowed and cut
- 5 tomatoes, hacked
- 3 tbsp herb vinegar

Directions:
- Heat up a dish that fits the air fryer cooker with the oil over medium heat, including eggplant, oregano, salt, and pepper; mix and cook for 5 minutes.
- Add garlic, onion, parsley, tricks, olives, vinegar, and tomatoes, mix, present in the air fryer cooker, and cook at 360 °F for about 15 minutes.
- Divide into bowls and serve.
- Enjoy the recipe!

316.   Spanish Greens

Preparation Time: 10 minutes
Cooking Time: 10 minutes
Servings: 4

Ingredients:
- 1 apple, cored and slashed
- 1 yellow onion, cut
- 3 tbsp olive oil
- ¼ cup raisins
- 6 garlic cloves, slashed
- ¼ cup pine nuts, toasted
- ¼ cup balsamic vinegar
- 5 cups blended spinach and chard
- Salt and dark pepper to the taste
- A spot of nutmeg

Directions:
- Heat up a skillet that fits the air fryer cooker with the oil over medium-high heat, include onion, mix and cook for 3 minutes.
- Add apple, garlic, raisins, vinegar, blended spinach and chard, nutmeg, salt and pepper, mix, present in the preheated air fryer, and cook at 350 °F for about 5 minutes.
- Divide between the plates, sprinkle pine nuts on top, and serve.
- Enjoy the recipe!

317.   Swiss Chard Salad

Preparation Time: 10 minutes
Cooking Time: 12 minutes
Servings: 4

Ingredients:
- 1 bundle Swiss chard, torn
- 2 tbsp olive oil
- 1 little yellow onion, slashed
- A spot of red pepper chips
- ¼ cup pine nuts, toasted
- ¼ cup raisins
- 1 tbsp balsamic vinegar
- Salt and dark pepper to the taste

Directions:
- Heat up a skillet that fits the air fryer cooker with the oil over medium heat, include chard and onions, mix and cook for 5 minutes.
- Add salt, pepper, pepper drops, raisins, pine nuts, and vinegar, mix, present in the air fryer cooker, and cook at 350 °F for about 8 minutes.
- Divide among plates and serve.
- Enjoy the recipe!

318.   Creamy Zucchini Mix

Preparation Time: 10 minutes
Cooking Time: 15 minutes
Servings: 6

Ingredients:
- 6 zucchinis, split and afterward cut
- Salt and dark pepper to the taste
- 1 tbsp margarine
- 1 tsp oregano, dried
- ½ cup yellow onion, cleaved
- 3 garlic cloves, minced
- 2 ounces parmesan, ground
- ¾ cup overwhelming cream

Directions:
- Heat up a container that fits the air fryer cooker with the spread over medium-high heat, include onion, mix and cook for 4 minutes.
- Add garlic, zucchinis, oregano, salt, pepper, and overwhelming cream, and hurl, present in the air fryer cooker, and cook at 350 °F for about 10 minutes.
- Add parmesan, mix, partition among plates, and serve.

319.   Stuffed Tomatoes

Preparation Time: 10 minutes
Cooking Time: 15 minutes
Servings: 2

Ingredients:
- 4 tomatoes, finish cut off and mash scooped and hacked
- Salt and dark pepper to the taste
- 1 yellow onion, cleaved
- 1 tbsp spread
- 2 tbsp celery, cleaved
- ½ cup mushrooms, cleaved
- 1 tbsp bread pieces 1 cup curds
- ¼ tsp caraway seeds
- 1 tbsp parsley, cleaved

Directions:
- Heat up a container with the spread over medium heat, melt the oil, then include in onion and celery, mix and cook for 3 minutes.
- Add tomato mash and mushrooms, mix and cook for a brief more.
- Add salt, pepper, disintegrated bread, cheddar, caraway seeds, and parsley, mix, cook for 4 minutes more and take off the heat.
- Stuff tomatoes with this blend, place them in the air fryer cooker, and cook at 350 °F for about 8 minutes.
- Divide stuffed tomatoes into plates and serve. Enjoy the recipe!

320. Spiced Turnip Salad

Preparation Time: 10 minutes
Cooking Time: 12 minutes
Servings: 4

Ingredients:

- 20 ounces turnips, stripped and slashed
- 1 tsp garlic, minced
- 1 tsp ginger, ground
- 2 yellow onions slashed
- 2 tomatoes, cleaved
- 1 tsp cumin, ground
- 1 tsp coriander, ground
- 2 green chilies, slashed
- ½ tsp turmeric powder
- 2 tbsp margarine
- Salt and dark pepper to the taste
- A bunch of coriander leaves, slashed

Directions:

- Heat up a skillet that fits the air fryer cooker with the margarine, melt it, include green chilies, garlic, and ginger, mix and cook for a minute.
- Add onions, salt, pepper, tomatoes, turmeric, cumin, ground coriander, and turnips, mix, present in the air fryer cooker, and cook at 350 °F for about 10 minutes.
- Divide among plates, sprinkle new coriander on top, and serve.
- Enjoy the recipe!

321. Fiery Cabbage

Preparation Time: 10 minutes
Cooking Time: 8-10 minutes
Servings: 4

Ingredients:

- 1 cabbage, cut into 8 wedges
- 1 tbsp sesame seed oil
- 1 carrot, ground
- ¼ cup apple juice vinegar
- ¼ cups squeezed apple
- ½ tsp cayenne pepper
- 1 tsp red pepper drops, squashed

Directions:

- In a skillet that accommodates the air fryer cooker, join cabbage with oil, carrot, vinegar, squeezed apple, cayenne, and pepper chips, and hurl, present in the preheated air fryer and cook at 350 °F for about 8 minutes.
- Divide cabbage blend among plates and serve. Enjoy the recipe!

322. Tomatoes and Brussel Sprouts Mix

Preparation Time: 5 minutes
Cooking Time: 10 minutes
Servings: 4

Ingredients:

- Salt and dark pepper to the taste
- 6 cherry tomatoes, split
- ¼ cup green onions, cleaved
- 1 tbsp of olive oil

Directions:

- Season Brussels grows with salt and pepper, put them in the air fryer cooker, and cook at 350 °F for about 10 minutes.
- Transfer them to a bowl, include salt, pepper, cherry tomatoes, green onions, and olive oil, hurl well and serve.

323. Cheesy Zucchini Fritters

Preparation Time: 10 minutes
Cooking Time: 8 minutes
Servings: 7

Ingredients:

- 4 oz. Mozzarella
- 3 oz. Cheddar cheese
- 1 zucchini, grated
- 2 tbsp dried dill
- 1 tbsp coconut flour
- 1 tbsp almond flour
- ¼ tsp salt
- 1 tsp butter

Directions:

- Shred the Cheddar and Mozzarella.
- Combine the grated zucchini with the shredded cheese.
- Add dried dill and coconut flour.
- Add almond flour and salt.
- Stir carefully with a fork.
- Mix well to combine and leave to marinate for 3 minutes.
- Preheat the air fryer to 400°F.
- Melt the butter in the air fryer tray.
- Make the fritters from the zucchini mixture and put them in the melted butter.
- Cook the fritters for 5 minutes.
- Turn the zucchini fritters over and cook for 3 minutes more.

324. Thai Peanut Tofu

Preparation Time: 20 minutes
Cooking Time: 25-30 minutes
Servings:

Ingredients:

- For Tofu:
- 2 tbsp fresh lime juice
- 2 tbsp soy sauce
- 1 tbsp maple syrup
- 1 tsp Sriracha sauce
- 2 tsp fresh ginger, peeled
- 2 garlic cloves, peeled
- 1 (14-ounces) block tofu, pressed and cut into strips
- For Sauce:
- 1 (2-inches) piece of fresh ginger, peeled
- 2 garlic cloves, peeled
- ½ cup creamy peanut butter
- 1 tbsp soy sauce
- 1 tbsp fresh lime juice
- 1-2 tsp Sriracha sauce
- 6 tbsp of water

Directions:
- For the tofu: in a food processor, put all the ingredients except tofu and pulse until smooth.
- In a bowl, mix together the marinade and tofu.
- Set aside to marinate for about 20-30 minutes.
- Meanwhile, soak 6 bamboo skewers in the water for about 30 minutes.
- With a cutter, cut each skewer in half.
- Thread one tofu strip onto each little bamboo stick.
- Set the temperature of the air fryer to 370 °F. Grease an air fryer basket.
- Arrange tofu skewers into the prepared air fryer basket in a single layer.
- For the sauce: add all the ingredients to a food processor and pulse until smooth.
- Remove from the air fryer and transfer the tofu onto serving plates.
- **Top with the sauce and serve.**

325. Rice Flour Coated Tofu

Preparation Time: 15 minutes
Cooking Time: 28 minutes
Servings: 3

Ingredients:
- 1 (14-ounces) block of firm tofu, pressed and cubed into a ½-inch size
- 2 tbsp cornstarch
- ¼ cup rice flour
- Salt and ground black pepper, as required
- 2 tbsp olive oil

Directions:
- In a bowl, mix together cornstarch, rice flour, salt, and black pepper.
- Coat the tofu evenly with a flour mixture.
- Drizzle the tofu with oil.
- Set the temperature of the air fryer to 360 °F. Grease an air fryer basket.
- Arrange tofu cubes into the prepared air fryer basket in a single layer.
- Air fry for about 14 minutes per side.
- Remove from the air fryer and transfer the tofu onto serving plates.
- Serve warm.

326. Stuffed Okra

Preparation Time: 15 minutes
Cooking Time: 12 minutes
Servings: 3

Ingredients:
- 8 ounces large okra
- ¼ cup chickpea flour
- ¼ of onion, chopped
- 2 tbsp coconut, grated freshly
- 1 tsp garam masala powder
- ½ tsp ground turmeric
- ½ tsp red chili powder
- ½ tsp ground cumin
- Salt, to taste

Directions:
- With a knife, make a slit in each okra vertically without cutting in 2 halves.
- In a bowl, mix together the flour, onion, grated coconut, and spices.
- Stuff each okra with the mixture.
- Set the temperature of the air fryer to 390 °F. Grease an air fryer basket.
- Arrange stuffed okra into the prepared air fryer basket.
- Air fry for about 12 minutes.
- Remove from the air fryer and transfer the okra onto serving plates.
- Serve hot.

327. Green Beans and Mushroom Casserole

Preparation Time: 15 minutes
Cooking Time: 12 minutes
Servings: 4

Ingredients:
- 24 ounces fresh green beans, trimmed
- 2 cups fresh button mushrooms, sliced
- 3 tbsp olive oil
- 2 tbsp fresh lemon juice
- 1 tsp ground sage
- 1 tsp garlic powder
- 1 tsp onion powder
- Salt and ground black pepper, as required
- 1/3 cup French fried onions

Directions:
- In a bowl, add the green beans, mushrooms, oil, lemon juice, sage, and spices and toss to coat well.
- Set the temperature of the air fryer to 400 °F. Lightly grease an air fryer basket.
- Arrange mushroom mixture into the prepared air fryer basket.
- Air fry for about 10-12 minutes, shaking several times while frying.
- Remove from the air fryer and transfer the mushroom mixture into a serving dish.
- Top with fried onions and serve.

328. Salsa Eggplants

Preparation Time: 15 minutes
Cooking Time: 30 minutes
Servings: 2

Ingredients:
- 1 large eggplant
- 2 tsp olive oil, divided
- 2 tsp fresh lemon juice, divided
- 8 cherry tomatoes, quartered
- 2 tbsp tomato salsa
- ½ tbsp fresh parsley
- Salt and ground black pepper, as required

Directions:
- Set the temperature of the air fryer to 390 °F. Grease an air fryer basket.
- Place eggplant into the prepared air fryer basket.
- Air fry for about 15 minutes.
- Remove from the air fryer and cut the eggplant in half lengthwise.

- Drizzle the eggplant halves evenly with one tsp of oil.
- Now, set the temperature of the air fryer to 355 °F. Grease the air fryer basket.
- Arrange eggplant into the prepared air fryer basket, cut-side up.
- Air fry for another 10 minutes.
- Remove eggplant from the air fryer and set aside for about 5 minutes.
- Carefully scoop out the flesh, leaving it about ¼-inch away from the edges.
- Drizzle the eggplant halves with one tsp of lemon juice.
- Transfer the eggplant flesh into a bowl.
- Add the tomatoes, salsa, parsley, salt, black pepper, remaining oil, and lemon juice and mix well.
- Stuff the eggplant haves with salsa mixture and serve.

329.   Curried Eggplant

Preparation Time: 15 minutes
Cooking Time: 10 minutes
Servings: 2

Ingredients:
- 1 large eggplant, cut into ½-inch thick slices
- 1 garlic clove, minced
- ½ fresh red chili, chopped
- 1 tbsp vegetable oil
- ¼ tsp curry powder
- Salt, as required

Directions:
- Set the temperature of the air fryer to 300 °F. Grease an air fryer basket.
- In a bowl, add all the ingredients and toss to coat well.
- Arrange eggplant slices into the prepared air fryer basket in a single layer.
- Air fry for about 10 minutes, shaking once halfway through.
- Remove from the air fryer and transfer the eggplant slices onto serving plates.
- Serve hot.

330.   Tofu with Capers Sauce

Preparation Time: 20 minutes
Cooking Time: 20 minutes
Servings: 4

Ingredients:
- For Marinade:
- ¼ cup fresh lemon juice
- 2 tbsp fresh parsley
- 1 garlic clove, peeled
- Salt and ground black pepper, as required
- For Tofu:
- 1 (14-ounces) block of extra-firm tofu, pressed and cut into 8 rectangular cutlets
- ½ cup mayonnaise
- 1 cup panko breadcrumbs
- For Sauce:
- 1 cup vegetable broth
- ¼ cup lemon juice
- 1 garlic clove, peeled
- 2 tbsp fresh parsley
- 2 tsp cornstarch

- Salt and ground black pepper, as required
- 2 tbsp capers

Directions:
- For marinade:
- In a food processor, add all the ingredients and pulse until smooth.
- In a bowl, mix together the marinade and tofu.
- Set aside for about 15-30 minutes.
- In two shallow bowls, place the mayonnaise and panko breadcrumbs, respectively.
- Coat the tofu pieces with mayonnaise and then roll into the panko.
- Set the temperature of the air fryer to 375 °F. Grease an air fryer basket.
- Arrange tofu pieces into the prepared air fryer basket in a single layer.
- Air fry for about 20 minutes, shaking once halfway through.
- Meanwhile, for the sauce: add broth, lemon juice, garlic, parsley, cornstarch, salt, and black pepper in a food processor and pulse until smooth.
- Transfer the sauce to a small pan and stir in the capers.
- Place the sauce over medium heat and bring to a boil.
- Reduce the heat to low and simmer for about 5-7 minutes, stirring continuously.
- Remove the tofu from the air fryer and transfer it onto serving plates.
- Top with the sauce and serve.

331.   Winter Beef Soup

Preparation Time: 10 minutes
Cooking Time: 15 minutes
Servings: 4

Ingredients:
- 9 ounces tender beef, chopped
- 1/2 cup leeks, chopped
- 1/2 cup celery stalks, chopped
- 2 cloves garlic, smashed
- 2 tbsp red cooking wine
- 3/4 cup cream of celery soup
- 2 sprigs rosemary, chopped
- 1/4 tsp smoked paprika
- 3/4 tsp salt
- 1/4 tsp black pepper, or to taste

Directions:
- Add the beef, leeks, celery, and garlic to the baking dish of the air fryer; cook for about 5 minutes at 390 °F.
- Once the meat is starting to tender, pour in the wine and soup. Season with rosemary, smoked paprika, salt, and black pepper. Now, cook an additional 7 minutes.

332.   Fennel Risotto

Preparation Time: 10-20 minutes
Cooking Time: 20 minutes
Servings: 2

Ingredients:
- 1 ½ cups Arborio rice
- 1 yellow onion; chopped.
- 2 tbsp. butter
- 1 tbsp. extra-virgin olive oil

- 1/4 cup white wine
- 3 cups chicken stock
- 1 fennel bulb, trimmed and chopped.
- 1/2 tsp. thyme; dried
- 3 tbsp. tomato paste
- 1/3 cup parmesan cheese, grated
- Salt and black pepper to the taste

Directions:

- Set your air fryer on Sauté mode; add butter and melt it.
- Add fennel and onion; then stir well. sauté for 4 minutes and transfer to a bowl.
- Add oil to your pot and heat it up
- Add rice, stir and cook for 3 minutes
- Add tomato paste, stock, fennel, onions, wine, salt, pepper, and thyme; then stir well. Close the air fryer lid and cook at 400°F for 8 minutes.
- Quick-release the pressure, carefully open the lid; add cheese; then stir well. Divide among plates and serve.

333.   **Cheddar Cheese Sliced Cauliflower**

Preparation Time:15 minutes
Cooking Time: 10 minutes
Servings: 6

Ingredients:

- 14 oz. cauliflower
- 6 oz. Cheddar cheese, sliced
- 1 tsp salt
- 1 tsp ground black pepper
- 1 tsp butter, frozen
- 1 tsp dried dill
- 1 tbsp olive oil

Directions:

- Wash the cauliflower head carefully and slice it into the servings.
- Sprinkle the sliced cauliflower with salt, ground black pepper, and dried dill.
- Grate the frozen butter.
- Then sprinkle the cauliflower with the olive oil from both sides.
- Preheat the air fryer to 400°F.
- Place the cauliflower slices in the air fryer rack and cook it for 7 minutes.
- After this, turn the cauliflower slices into another side and sprinkle them with the grated frozen butter.
- Cook the cauliflower for 3 minutes more.
- Then place the cheese slices over the cauliflower and cook it for 1 minute more.
- Transfer the cooked cauliflower to the serving plates with the help of the spatula.
- Serve the dish immediately.

334.   **Cream of Carrot Potato Soup**

Preparation Time: 20 minutes
Cooking Time: 25-30 minutes
Servings: 6

Ingredients:

- 3 lbs. russet potatoes, peeled and diced
- 2 carrots, peeled and sliced
- 3 garlic cloves, minced
- 1 onion, chopped

- 15 oz can coconut milk
- 3 cups chicken broth
- 1/2 tsp dried thyme
- 2 tbsp olive oil
- Pepper
- Salt
- For Caesar Croutons:
- 2 cup bread cubes
- 1/8 tsp dried thyme
- 1/4 tsp dried oregano
- 1/4 tsp garlic powder
- 1/2 tsp dried parsley
- 1 tbsp parmesan cheese, grated
- 1 tbsp olive oil
- Pepper
- Salt

Directions:

- Add oil to the air fryer and set the pot on sauté mode.
- Add onion and garlic and sauté for 3-4 minutes.
- Add remaining ingredients except for coconut milk and stir well.
- Seal pot with pressure cooking lid and 400°F for 9 minutes.
- Once done, release pressure using quick release. Remove lid.
- Puree the soup using a blender until smooth.
- Add coconut milk and stir well. Season soup with pepper and salt.
- For Croutons:
- In a bowl, toss bread cubes with the remaining ingredients.
- Spray air fryer multi-level air fryer basket with cooking spray.
- Add bread cubes into the air fryer basket and place the basket into the air fryer.
- Seal pot with air fryer lid and select bake mode then set the temperature to 375°F and timer for 10 minutes. Stir halfway through.
- Top soup with croutons and serve.

335.   **Nutty Carrot Soup**

Preparation Time: 15 minutes
Cooking Time: 20 minutes
Servings: 10

Ingredients:

- 8 carrots, peeled and chopped
- 1 1/2 cup chicken stock
- 1/4 cup peanut butter
- 1 tbsp curry paste
- 1 onion, chopped
- 3 garlic cloves, peeled
- 14 oz coconut milk
- Pepper
- Salt
- For Parmesan Croutons:
- 2 cups of bread cubes
- 2 tbsp parmesan cheese, grated
- 2 tbs butter, melted
- 1 garlic clove, minced
- 1 tbsp olive oil
- Pepper

- Salt

Directions:
- Add all ingredients into the air fryer and stir well.
- Seal pot with pressure cooking lid and 400°F for 15 minutes.
- Once done, release pressure using quick release. Remove lid.
- Puree the soup using a blender until smooth.
- Season soup with pepper and salt.
- For Croutons:
- In a bowl, toss bread cubes with butter, garlic, oil, pepper, and salt.
- Spray air fryer multi-level air fryer basket with cooking spray.
- Add bread cubes into the air fryer basket and place the basket into the air fryer.
- Seal pot with air fryer lid and select bake mode, then set the temperature to 375°F and timer for 15 minutes. Stir halfway through.
- Toss bread cubes with parmesan cheese until well coated.
- Top soup with croutons and serve.

336.   Summer Vegetable Soup

Preparation Time: 20 minutes
Cooking Time: 30 minutes
Servings: 4

Ingredients:
- 1 summer squash, sliced
- 1 onion, diced
- 1/4 cup basil, chopped
- 2 bell peppers, sliced
- 1/2 cup green beans, cut into pieces
- 8 cups vegetable broth
- 1 zucchini, sliced
- 2 tomatoes, sliced
- 1 eggplant, sliced
- 2 garlic cloves, smashed
- 3/4 cup corn
- Pepper
- Salt
- For Garlic Buttery Croutons
- 2 cups of bread cubes
- 1/2 tsp garlic powder
- 1 tbsp olive oil
- 1 tbsp butter, melted

Directions:
- Add all ingredients into the air fryer and stir well.
- Seal pot with pressure cooking lid and 400°F for 10 minutes.
- Once done, release pressure using quick release. Remove lid.
- Puree the soup using a blender until smooth.
- For Croutons:
- In a bowl, toss bread cubes, garlic powder, butter, and oil.
- Spray air fryer multi-level air fryer basket with cooking spray.
- Add bread cubes into the air fryer basket and place the basket into the air fryer.

- Seal pot with air fryer lid and select bake mode, then set the temperature to 350°F and timer for 15-20 minutes. Stir halfway through.
- Top soup with croutons and serve.

337.   Spiced Sweet Potato Soup

Preparation Time: 10 minutes
Cooking Time: 15 minutes
Servings: 4

Ingredients:
- 2 lbs. sweet potatoes, peeled and diced
- 2 cups of water
- 4 cups vegetable broth
- 1/2 onion, chopped
- 1 tbsp olive oil
- 1/2 tsp cinnamon
- 1 tsp paprika
- 3 garlic cloves, minced
- Pepper
- Salt
- For Croissant Croutons:
- 1 croissant, cut into 1/2-inch cubes
- 2 tbsp parmesan cheese, grated
- 1/2 tsp dried oregano
- 1 tbsp olive oil
- Pepper
- Salt

Directions:
- Add oil to the air fryer and set the pot on sauté mode.
- Add onion and sweet potato and sauté for 5 minutes.
- Add remaining ingredients and stir well.
- Seal pot with pressure cooking lid and 400°F for 10 minutes.
- Once done, release pressure using quick release. Remove lid.
- Puree the soup using a blender until smooth.
- For Croutons:
- In a bowl, toss croissant cubes with the remaining ingredients.
- Spray air fryer multi-level air fryer basket with cooking spray.
- Add croissant cubes into the air fryer basket and place the basket into the air fryer.
- Seal pot with air fryer lid and select bake mode, then set the temperature to 350°F and timer for 10 minutes. Stir halfway through.
- Top soup with croutons and serve.

338.   Curry Lentil Soup

Preparation Time: 10 minutes
Cooking Time: 15 minutes
Servings: 4

Ingredients:
- 1 cup red lentils, rinsed
- 1 tbsp fresh ginger, grated
- 14 oz can tomato
- 1 tsp garlic, sliced
- 3 1/2 cups vegetable stock
- 1 tsp turmeric
- 1 1/2 tsp curry powder

- 1 onion, chopped
- 1/2 tsp salt
- For Parmesan Croutons:
- 2 cups of bread cubes
- 2 tbsp parmesan cheese, grated
- 2 tbs butter, melted
- 1 garlic clove, minced
- 1 tbsp olive oil
- Pepper
- Salt

Directions:
- Add all ingredients into the air fryer and stir well.
- Seal pot with pressure cooking lid and 400°F for 8 minutes.
- Once done, release pressure using quick release. Remove lid.
- Puree the soup using a blender until smooth.
- For Croutons:
- In a bowl, toss bread cubes with butter, garlic, oil, pepper, and salt.
- Spray air fryer multi-level air fryer basket with cooking spray.
- Add bread cubes into the air fryer basket and place the basket into the air fryer.
- Seal pot with air fryer lid and select bake mode, then set the temperature to 375°F and timer for 15 minutes. Stir halfway through.
- Toss bread cubes with parmesan cheese until well coated.
- Top soup with croutons and serve.

339. Mushroom Soup

Preparation Time: 10 minutes
Cooking Time: 15 minutes
Servings: 3

Ingredients:
- 1 cup mushrooms, chopped
- 1 onion, chopped
- 1 1/2 tsp garam masala
- 2 tbsp olive oil
- 1 tsp fresh lemon juice
- 1/4 tsp chili powder
- 5 cups chicken stock
- 2 fresh celery stalks, chopped
- 2 garlic cloves, crushed
- For Croissant Croutons:
- 1 croissant, cut into 1/2-inch cubes
- 2 tbsp parmesan cheese, grated
- 1/2 tsp dried oregano
- 1 tbsp olive oil
- Pepper
- Salt

Directions:
- Add oil to the air fryer and set the pot on sauté mode.
- Add garlic and onion and sauté for 5 minutes at 400°F.
- Add chili powder and garam masala and cook for a minute.
- Add remaining ingredients and stir well.
- Seal the pot with a pressure cooking lid and cook on high pressure for 5 minutes.

- Once done, release pressure using quick release. Remove lid.
- Puree the soup using a blender until smooth.
- For Croutons:
- In a bowl, toss croissant cubes with the remaining ingredients.
- Spray air fryer multi-level air fryer basket with cooking spray.
- Add croissant cubes into the air fryer basket and place the basket into the air fryer.
- Seal pot with air fryer lid and select bake mode, then set the temperature to 350°F and timer for 10 minutes. Stir halfway through.
- Top soup with croutons and serve.

340. Meatless Ziti Pasta

Preparation Time: 10 minutes
Cooking Time: 20 minutes
Servings: 4

Ingredients:
- 16 oz ziti pasta
- 2 cups mozzarella cheese, shredded
- 1/2 cup sour cream
- 1 tsp garlic powder
- 1 tsp dried parsley
- 1 tsp dried basil
- 8 oz cream cheese
- 14 oz can tomato, diced
- 24 oz spaghetti sauce

Directions:
- Spray the air fryer from the inside using cooking spray.
- Cook pasta according to the packet instructions. Drain well.
- In a large bowl, mix together spaghetti sauce, garlic powder, parsley, basil, cream cheese, and tomatoes.
- Add cooked pasta into the spaghetti sauce and mix well.
- Pour half of the pasta mixture into the air fryer, then spread sour cream on top and sprinkle with half mozzarella cheese.
- Top with remaining pasta and remaining mozzarella cheese.
- Seal pot with air fryer lid and select bake mode, then set the temperature to 375°F and timer for 20-25 minutes.
- Serve and enjoy.

341. Creamy Eggplant Gratin

Preparation Time: 15 minutes
Cooking Time: 45 minutes
Servings: 6

Ingredients:
- 2 lbs. eggplant, cut into 1/2-inch slices
- 1 tbsp mint, dried
- 1/3 lb. feta cheese, crumbled
- 2 tbsp olive oil
- 2 onions, sliced
- 3/4 cup heavy whipping cream
- 6 tbsp cheese, shredded
- 6 tbsp fresh parsley, chopped
- Pepper
- Salt

Directions:

- Insert wire rack in rack position 6. Select bake, set temperature 390°F, timer for 30 minutes. Press start to preheat the air fryer.
- Brush eggplant slices with oil and place in baking dish. Season with salt.
- Bake eggplant slices until lightly golden brown.
- Meanwhile, heat oil in a pan over medium heat.
- Add onion and sauté until lightly brown.
- Sprinkle fried onion over baked eggplants, then sprinkle parsley and mint.
- Sprinkle with grated cheese and feta cheese.
- Pour heavy whipped cream over the eggplant and onion layer.
- Bake for 30 minutes or gratin lightly brown.

342. Creamy Cauliflower Gratin

Preparation Time: 10 minutes
Cooking Time: 20 minutes
Servings: 4

Ingredients:

- 1 cauliflower head, cut into florets
- 2 tbsp fresh lemon juice
- 1/2 cup cheddar cheese, shredded
- 1/2 cup mayonnaise
- 2 tsp Dijon mustard
- 1/4 cup sour cream

Directions:

- Insert wire rack in rack position 6. Select bake, set temperature 375°F, timer for 10 minutes. Press start to preheat the air fryer
- Spread cauliflower florets on a roasting pan and bake for 10 minutes.
- In a mixing bowl, stir together cauliflower, lemon juice, cheese, mayonnaise, mustard, and sour cream and pour into the casserole dish.
- Bake cauliflower mixture for 10 minutes.
- Serve and enjoy.

343. Cauliflower Fritters

Preparation Time: 10 minutes
Cooking Time: 14 minutes
Servings: 5

Ingredients:

- 5 cups chopped cauliflower florets
- 1/2 cup almond flour
- 1/2 tsp baking powder
- ½ tsp ground black pepper
- ½ tsp salt
- 2 eggs, pastured

Directions:

- Add chopped cauliflower to a blender or food processor, pulse until minced, and then tip the mixture into a bowl.
- Add remaining ingredients, stir well and then shape the mixture into 1/3-inch patties, an ice cream scoop of mixture per patty.
- Switch on the air fryer, insert the fryer basket, grease it with olive oil, then shut its lid, set the fryer at 390 °F and preheat for 5 minutes.

- Then open the fryer, add cauliflower patties in it a single layer, spray oil over the patties, close with its lid and cook for 14 minutes at 375 °F until nicely golden and cooked, flipping the patties halfway through the frying.
- Serve straight away with the dip.

344. Avocado Asparagus Soup

Preparation Time: 10 minutes
Cooking Time: 20 minutes
Servings: 4

Ingredients:

- 1 avocado, peeled, pitted, cubed
- 12 ounces asparagus
- ½ tsp ground black pepper
- 1 tsp garlic powder
- 1 tsp sea salt
- 2 tbsp olive oil, divided
- 1/2 of a lemon, juiced
- 2 cups vegetable stock

Directions:

- Switch on the air fryer, insert the fryer basket, grease it with olive oil, then shut its lid, set the fryer at 400°F, and preheat for 5 minutes.
- Meanwhile, place asparagus in a shallow dish, drizzle with 1 tbsp oil, sprinkle with garlic powder, salt, and black pepper, and toss until well mixed.
- Open the fryer, add asparagus to it, close with its lid and cook for 10 minutes until nicely golden and roasted, shaking halfway through the frying.
- When the air fryer beeps, open its lid and transfer asparagus to a food processor.
- Add remaining ingredients into a food processor and pulse until well combined and smooth.
- Tip the soup in a saucepan, pour in water if the soup is too thick, and heat it over medium-low heat for 5 minutes until thoroughly heated.
- Ladle soup into bowls and serve.

345. Pumpkin Gnocchi

Preparation Time: 10 minutes
Cooking Time: 45 minutes
Servings: 6

Ingredients:

- 26 oz. Potato gnocchi, cooked
- 1/3 cup olive oil
- 16 sage leaves
- 26 oz. Pumpkin, cut into slices
- 2 egg yolks
- 2 ½ cup cream
- 1/2 tsp finely grated nutmeg
- 3/4 cup coarsely grated mozzarella
- 3.5 oz. Blue cheese, crumbled
- Roasted chopped hazelnuts, to serve

Directions:

- Mix pumpkin with 1 tbsp oil in a bowl.
- Stir in egg yolks, cream, gnocchi, half of the sage, half of the blue cheese, nutmeg, cream, and mozzarella.
- Spread this mixture in the air fryer duo insert.
- Top the casserole with the remaining cheese.

- Put on the air fryer lid and seal it.
- Hit the "bake button" and select 45 minutes of cooking time, then press "start."
- Once the air fryer duo beeps, remove its lid.
- Heat ¼ cup in a frying pan and add sage. Sauté for 1 minute.
- Transfer the fried sage to a plate lined with a paper towel.
- Add this fried sage and nuts to the casserole.
- Garnish with sage oil.
- Serve.

346.   Pumpkin Lasagna

Preparation Time: 20 minutes
Cooking Time: 60 minutes
Servings: 6

Ingredients:
- 28 oz. Pumpkin, cut into slices
- 1 bunch sage, chopped
- 1/2 cup ghee, melted
- 1 leek, thinly sliced
- 4 garlic cloves, finely grated
- 3.5 oz. Kale and cavolo nero leaves shredded
- 270g semi-dried tomatoes, drained, chopped
- 17 0z. Quark
- 2 eggs, lightly beaten

Directions:
- Mix pumpkin slices with sage leaves, 2 tsp salt, and 2 tbsp ghee in a bowl.
- Toss leek separately with 2 tbsp ghee, garlic, and ½ tsp salt in another bowl.
- Mix kale with 1 tsp salt, tomato, and cavolo nero in a bowl.
- Now beat eggs with quark and sage in a bowl.
- Take a baking pan that can fit into the air fryer duo.
- Add 1/3 of the leek mixture to the base of the baking pan.
- Top the mixture with a layer of pumpkin slices.
- Add 1/3 of quark mixture on top, then add 1/3 of kale mixture over it.
- Top it with pumpkin slices and continue repeating the layer while ending at the pumpkin slice layer on top.
- Place the baking pan in the air fryer duo.
- Put on the air fryer lid and seal it.
- Hit the "bake button" and select 60 minutes of cooking time, then press "start."
- Once the air fryer duo beeps, remove its lid.
- Serve.

347.   Rustic Baked Halloumi with Fennel Salad

Preparation Time: 20 minutes
Cooking Time: 35 minutes
Servings: 4

Ingredients:
- Olive oil to brush
- 7 oz. Sweet potato, coarsely grated
- 10 oz. Potatoes, coarsely grated
- 10 oz. Carrots, coarsely grated
- 9 oz. Halloumi, coarsely grated
- 1/2 onion, coarsely grated

- 2 tbsp thyme leaves
- 2 eggs
- 1/3 cup plain flour
- 1/2 cup sour cream, to serve
- Fennel salad
- 2 celery stalks, thinly sliced
- 1 fennel, thinly sliced
- 1/2 cup olives, chopped
- Juice of 1 lemon
- 1 lemon quarter, chopped
- 1 tsp toasted coriander seeds, ground

Directions:
- Toss sweet potato, carrot, potato, onion, halloumi, thyme, flour, and eggs in a bowl.
- Spread this mixture in the air fryer duo insert.
- Put on the air fryer lid and seal it.
- Hit the "bake button" and select 35 minutes of cooking time, then press "start."
- Once the air fryer duo beeps, remove its lid.

Prepare the salad by mixing its ingredients: in a salad bowl.
- Serve the sweet potato rosti with the prepared salad.

348.   Celeriac Potato Gratin

Preparation Time: 20 minutes
Cooking Time: 60 minutes
Servings: 5

Ingredients:
- 2 cups cream
- 1 tsp caraway seeds, toasted
- 1 garlic clove, crushed
- 1 tsp fennel seeds, toasted
- 2 bay leaves
- 1/4 tsp ground cloves
- Zest of 1/2 a lemon
- 2 tsp melted butter
- 1kg potatoes, peeled
- 1 cup celeriac, peeled and minced
- 6 slices prosciutto, torn
- 3/4 cup fresh ricotta
- ¼ cup fontina cheese, grated

Directions:
- Add cream, garlic, caraway seeds, cloves, bay leaves, fennel, zest, and cloves to a saucepan.
- Stir cook this mixture for 3 minutes, then remove from the heat.
- Thinly slices potato by passing through the mandolin and spread the potatoes in the insert of the air fryer duo.
- Top the potato with celeriac, prepared white sauce, prosciutto, and ricotta.
- Put on the air fryer lid and seal it.
- Hit the "bake button" and select 60 minutes of cooking time, then press "start."
- Once the air fryer duo beeps, remove its lid.
- Serve.

349.   Red Chard and Kalamata Olives

Preparation Time: 10 minutes
Cooking Time: 20 minutes
Servings: 4

Ingredients:

- 2 cups red chard, torn
- 1 cup kalamata olives, pitted and halved
- ½ cup tomato sauce
- 1 tsp chili powder
- 2 tbsp olive oil
- Salt and black pepper to the taste

Directions:

- In a pan that fits the air fryer, combine the chard with the olives and the other ingredients and toss.
- Put the pan in your air fryer, cook at 370°F for 20 minutes, divide between plates and serve.

350. Tomato Corn Risotto

Preparation Time: 15 minutes
Cooking Time: 15-20 minutes
Servings: 4

Ingredients:

- 1 1/2 cups Arborio rice
- 1 cup cherry tomatoes, halved
- 1/4 cup basil, chopped
- 1/4 cup parmesan cheese, grated
- 1/4 cup half and half
- 32 oz vegetable broth
- 1 cup sweet corn
- 3 garlic cloves, minced
- 1/2 cup onion, chopped
- 2 tbsp olive oil
- 4 tbsp butter
- 1 tsp salt

Directions:

- Add butter into the air fryer and set the pot on sauté mode.
- Add garlic and onion and sauté for 5 minutes.
- Add rice and cook for 2-3 minutes.
- Add broth, corn, pepper, and salt and stir well.
- Seal pot with lid and cook on high pressure for 6 minutes.
- Once done, then release pressure using the quick-release method, then open the lid.
- Stir in cherry tomatoes, basil, parmesan, and a half and half.
- Serve and enjoy.

351. Red Cabbage Avocado Bowls

Preparation Time: 10 minutes
Cooking Time: 15 minutes
Servings: 4

Ingredients:

- 2 cups red cabbage; shredded
- 1 red bell pepper; sliced
- 1 small avocado, peeled, pitted, and sliced
- A drizzle of olive oil
- Salt and black pepper to taste.

Directions:

- Grease your air fryer with the oil, add all the ingredients, toss, cover, and cook at 400°F for 15 minutes.
- Divide into bowls and serve cold for breakfast

352. Pesto Zucchini Salad

Preparation Time: 10 minutes
Cooking Time: 15 minutes
Servings: 4

Ingredients:

- 4 oz. Mozzarella; shredded
- 2 cups zucchinis, cut with a spiralizer
- ½ cup coconut cream
- ¼ cup basil pesto
- 1 tbsp. Olive oil
- Salt and black pepper to taste.

Directions:

- In a pan that fits your air fryer, mix the zucchini noodles with the pesto and the rest of the ingredients, toss, introduce the pan to the fryer and cook at 370°F for 15 minutes
- Divide between plates and serve

353. Cream Cheese Zucchini

Preparation Time: 20 minutes
Cooking Time: 15 minutes
Servings: 3

Ingredients:

- 1 lb. Zucchinis; cut into wedges
- 1 green onion; sliced
- 1 cup cream cheese, soft
- 1 tbsp. Butter; melted
- 2 tbsp. Basil; chopped.
- 1 tsp. Garlic powder
- A pinch of salt and black pepper

Directions:

- In a pan that fits your air fryer, mix the zucchinis with all the other ingredients, toss, introduce them to the air fryer and cook at 370°F for 15 minutes
- Divide between plates and serve as a side dish.

354. Traditional Italian Rice & Parmesan Balls

Preparation Time: 15 minutes
Cooking Time: 27 minutes
Servings: 6

Ingredients:

- ½ cup olive oil + 1 tbsp
- 1 onion, diced
- 2 garlic cloves, minced
- 5 cups chicken stock
- ½ cup apple vinegar
- 2 cups rice
- 1½ cups grated Parmesan cheese
- 1 cup chopped green beans
- Salt and black pepper to taste
- 2 cups fresh panko breadcrumbs
- 2 eggs

Directions:

- Choose Sear/Sauté on the pot and add 1 tbsp of oil and onion. Sauté the onion until translucent, add the garlic and cook further for 2 minutes or until the garlic starts getting fragrant. Stir in the stock, vinegar, and rice. Seal the pressure lid, choose Pressure, set to High, and set the time to 7 minutes. Press Start.

- After cooking, perform a natural pressure release for 10 minutes.
- Stir in the Parmesan cheese, green beans, salt, and pepper to mash the rice until a risotto form. Spoon the mixture into a bowl and set it aside to cool completely.
- Clean the pot and in a bowl, combine the breadcrumbs and the remaining olive oil. In another bowl, lightly beat the eggs.
- Form 12 croquettes out of the rice mixture or as many as you can get. Dip each into the beaten eggs and coat in the breadcrumb mixture.
- Put the rice balls in the Cook & Crisp basket in a single layer.
- Close the crisping lid, choose Air Fry, set the temperature to 390°F, and set the time to 12 minutes. Choose Start to begin frying or until the balls are crisp and golden brown. At the 6-minute mark, turn the croquettes.
- Allow cooling before serving. Serve with a tangy relish.

355.   Mozzarella and Radish Salad

Preparation Time: 15 minutes
Cooking Time: 30 minutes
Servings: 4

Ingredients:
- 1 lb. radish, sliced into rounds
- 2 tbsp olive oil
- Salt and pepper to taste
- ½ lb. vegan mozzarella, sliced into rounds
- 2 tbsp balsamic glaze

Directions:
- Toss radish rounds in oil and season with salt and pepper.
- Cook in the air fryer at 350 °F for 30 minutes, shaking once or twice during cooking.
- Arrange on a serving platter with the vegan mozzarella.
- Drizzle cheese and radish with balsamic glaze before serving.

356.   Avocado and Crispy Tofu Salad

Preparation Time: 15 minutes
Cooking Time: 15 minutes
Servings: 6

Ingredients:
- Cooking spray
- 2 cups tofu, cubed
- 4 cups mixed greens
- 4 cups Romaine lettuce
- ½ cup onion, sliced
- 1 cup cherry tomatoes, sliced in half
- ½ avocado, sliced into cubes
- ½ cup red wine vinegar
- 1 cup avocado lime dressing

Directions:
- Spray the air fryer basket with oil.
- Cook the tofu cubes at 375°F for 15 minutes, shaking halfway through.
- In a bowl, arrange the salad by topping the lettuce and mixed greens with crispy tofu, onion, tomatoes, and avocado.

- Drizzle with red wine vinegar and avocado lime dressing.

357.   Vegan Smoked Bacon

Preparation Time: 10 minutes
Cooking Time: 30 minutes
Servings: 6

Ingredients:
- 4 ounces Tempeh, sliced thin (organic, non-gmo, preferred brand: Light life Organic Flax
- ¼ cup low-sodium soy sauce (or tamari if gluten-free)
- ½ tbsp Liquid Smoke
- 1 tsp oil
- 1 tbsp pure maple syrup
- ¼ tsp black pepper
- ¼ tsp garlic powder
- ¼ tsp smoked paprika

Directions:
- Line the air fryer basket with a round piece of parchment paper, just big enough to cover the bottom.
- Slice the tempeh thinly.
- Mix the marinade ingredients in a shallow bowl; add the tempeh slices and let sit for 10 minutes, flipping over halfway through.
- Place slices in the parchment-lined air fryer basket and drizzle half the remaining marinade over the slices.
- Slide the basket into the fryer and set the temperature to 350°F for 10 minutes.
- After 5 minutes have elapsed, remove the basket, flip slices over and drizzle the remaining marinade. Slide the basket back in, and the fryer will start up again and continue 'frying' for the remaining 5 minutes.

358.   Tomato and Bell Pepper Soup

Preparation Time: 10 minutes
Cooking Time: 20 minutes
Servings: 4

Ingredients:
- 1 yellow onion, chopped
- 2 tbsp olive oil
- 2 red bell peppers, roughly chopped
- 1-pound tomatoes, cubed
- 3 tbsp tomato paste
- 2 celery ribs, chopped
- 6 cups chicken stock
- 1 tsp garlic powder
- ½ tbsp basil, dried
- ½ tsp red pepper flakes

Directions:
- Set the air fryer on Sauté mode, add the oil, heat it up, add the onion, garlic powder, basil, and pepper flakes, and stir and sauté for 5 minutes.
- Add the rest of the ingredients, put the lid on, and 400°F for 15 minutes.
- Release the pressure naturally for 10 minutes, divide the soup into bowls and serve.

359. Chicken Corn Zucchini Soup

Preparation Time: 10 minutes
Cooking Time: 15 minutes
Servings: 4

Ingredients:
- 1 tbsp olive oil
- 1 celery stalk, chopped
- 1 yellow onion, chopped
- 2 cups corn
- 2 zucchinis, cubed
- 2 cups tomatoes, chopped
- 4 garlic cloves, minced
- 30 ounces chicken stock, low-sodium
- A pinch of salt and black pepper
- 2 tbsp basil, chopped

Directions:
- Set your air fryer on Sauté mode, add the oil, heat it up, add the onion, stir and sauté for 5 minutes.
- Add the rest of the ingredients except the basil, stir, and put the lid on and 400°F for 10 minutes.
- Release the pressure naturally for 10 minutes, add the basil, and divide the soup into bowls.

360. Potato Parsley Soup

Preparation Time: 5 minutes
Cooking Time: 20 minutes
Servings: 4

Ingredients:
- 6 cups gold potatoes, cubed
- 2 tbsp olive oil
- ½ cup yellow onion, chopped
- 6 cups chicken stock
- A pinch of salt and black pepper
- 2 tbsp parsley, chopped
- 2 cups coconut cream
- 1 cup cheddar cheese, grated

Directions:
- Set your air fryer on Sauté mode, add the oil, heat it up, add the onion, stir and sauté for 5 minutes
- Add the potatoes, stock, salt, and pepper, and put the lid on and 400°F for 10 minutes.
- Release the pressure fast for 5 minutes, add the cream, and blend the soup using an immersion blender.
- Set the pot on Sauté mode, add the cheese and parsley, cook the soup for 3 minutes more, divide into bowls, and serve.

361. Curried Cauliflower Soup

Preparation Time: 10 minutes
Cooking Time: 20 minutes
Servings: 4

Ingredients:
- 1-pound cauliflower florets
- 3 garlic cloves, minced
- 1 yellow onion, chopped
- 14 ounces coconut cream
- 2 cups chicken stock
- 1 tbsp red curry paste

- 2 tbsp chives, chopped

Directions:
- In your air fryer, combine all the ingredients, toss, and put the lid on and 400°F for 20 minutes.
- Release the pressure naturally for 10 minutes, blend using an immersion blender, ladle into bowls and serve.

362. Burrata-Stuffed Tomatoes

Preparation Time: 5 minutes
Cooking Time: 5 minutes
Servings: 4

Ingredients:
- 4 medium tomatoes
- ½ tsp fine sea salt
- 4 (2-ounce) Burrata balls
- Fresh basil leaves, for garnish
- Extra-virgin olive oil, for drizzling
- **Directions**
- Preparing the Ingredients. Preheat the air fryer to 300°F.
- Scoop out the tomato seeds and membranes using a melon baller or spoon. Sprinkle the insides of the tomatoes with the salt. Stuff each tomato with a ball of Burrata.
- Put it in the fryer and cook for 5 minutes or until the cheese has softened.
- Garnish with olive oil and basil leaves. Serve warm.

363. Tuscan White Bean Soup

Preparation Time: 15 minutes
Cooking Time: 15 minutes
Servings: 4

Ingredients:
- 1 cup diced celery
- 1 ½ cups diced onion (about 1 medium onion)
- 2 cups chopped leek, white and light green parts only
- 2 cups diced carrot
- 1 ½ cups diced zucchini (about 1 medium zucchini)
- 8 ounces cremini mushrooms, sliced
- 4 garlic cloves, minced
- 3 15-ounce cans of cannellini beans, drained and rinsed well
- 1 28 ounce can dice San Marzano tomatoes
- 4 cups of vegetable or chicken stock
- 1 tbsp dried Italian seasoning herb mix
- 1-pound Italian sausage links, left whole (optional)
- 1 bunch Lacinato kale, shredded
- 1/2 bunch fresh Italian parsley, chopped
- Thinly sliced rounds of lemon, chopped
- Salt and pepper, to taste

Directions:
- Combine the celery, onion, leek, carrot, zucchini, mushrooms, garlic, beans, tomatoes, stock, dried Italian herbs, and whole Italian sausage links, if using.
- Close and seal the Air fryer, and set for five minutes on high of the "Manual" setting.
- Let pressure release naturally. Remove sausage links if using, and slice them into bite-size pieces. Replace pieces into the soup.
- Stir the shredded kale, parsley, and chopped lemon into the soup. Season to taste and serve hot.

364. Eggplant Satay

Preparation Time: 10 minutes
Cooking Time: 20 minutes
Servings: 4

Ingredients:
- 1 red onion; chopped
- 2 garlic cloves; chopped
- 1 bunch parsley; chopped
- 1 tsp oregano; dried
- 2 eggplants; cut into medium chunks
- 2 tbsp olive oil
- 2 tbsp capers; chopped
- 1 handful of green olives; pitted and sliced
- Salt and black pepper to the taste
- 5 tomatoes; chopped
- 3 tbsp herb vinegar

Directions:
- Add oil to a greased skillet and place it over medium heat. Stir in oregano, eggplant, salt, and pepper. Cook for 5 minutes, then add parsley, onion, garlic, capers, vinegar, tomatoes, and olives. Mix well, then transfer this mixture to the Air fryer. Put on the Instant Air Fryer lid and cook on Bake mode for 15 minutes at 360 °F. Once done, remove the lid and serve warm.

365. Okra Corn Medley

Preparation Time: 10 minutes
Cooking Time: 12 minutes
Servings: 4

Ingredients:
- 1 pound okra; trimmed
- 28oz. canned tomatoes; chopped
- 6 scallions; chopped
- 2 tbsp olive oil
- 1 tsp sugar
- 1 cup of corn
- 3 green bell peppers; chopped
- Salt and black pepper to the taste

Directions:
- Take a baking dish suitable to fit in your Air fryer. Place it over medium heat and add oil, bell peppers, and scallions; sauté for 5 minutes. Stir in salt, pepper, okra, sugar, corn, and tomatoes.
- Transfer the dish to the Air fryer. Put on the Instant Air Fryer lid and cook on Bake mode for 7 minutes at 360 °F. Once done, remove the lid and serve warm.

366. Mexican Avocado Fry

Preparation Time: 5 minutes
Cooking Time: 20 minutes
Servings: 12 slices

Ingredients:
- 1 peeled avocado, sliced
- 1 beaten egg
- 1/2 cup panko bread crumbs
- Salt
- Tortillas and toppings

Directions:
- Using a bowl, add the egg.
- Using a separate bowl, set in the breadcrumbs.
- Dip the avocado into the bowl with the beaten egg and coat with the breadcrumbs. Sprinkle the coated wedges with a bit of salt.
- Arrange them in the cooking basket in a single layer.
- Set the Air Fryer to 392°F and cook for 15 minutes. Shake the basket halfway through the cooking process.
- Put them on tortillas with your preferred toppings.

367. Curried Zucchini

Preparation Time: 5 Minutes
Cooking Time: 8-10 Minutes

Ingredients:
- 2 Zucchinis, Washed & Sliced
- 1 Tbsp Olive Oil
- Pinch Sea Salt
- Curry Mix, Pre-Made

Directions:
- Turn on your air fryer to 390°F.
- Combine your zucchini slices, salt, oil, and spices.
- Put the zucchini into the air fryer, cooking for eight to ten minutes.
- You can serve it alone or with sour cream.

368. Sunny Lentils

Preparation Time: 10 minutes
Cooking Time: 12 minutes
Servings: 4

Ingredients:
- 1/3 cup of red bell pepper, chopped
- ½ tsp of dried tarragon
- 1 cup of tomatoes, diced
- 3 tbsp of sweetened coconut, shredded
- ¼ tsp of curry powder
- ¼ cup of water
- Salt and black pepper, to taste
- 1 cup of red lentils, boiled
- 1 tbsp of olive oil
- 1/3 cup of green bell pepper, chopped
- 1 tbsp of garlic, minced
- 1/3 cup of onions, chopped

Directions:
- Set the air fryer on roast to 375 °F for 8 minutes. Sauté onions, garlic, green bell pepper, red bell pepper, tarragon, and spices in the olive oil in a pan for about 4 minutes. Stir in the tomatoes, red lentils, and coconut. Transfer this mixture to the cooking dish and place it on the cooking tray. Insert the cooking tray in the air fryer when it displays "add food." Remove from the air fryer when cooking time is complete. Serve warm.

369. Black Bean and Sausage Soup

Preparation Time: 20 minutes
Cooking Time: 30 minutes
Servings: 4-5

Ingredients:
- 650g black-eyed peas, dried

- 5 cup chicken stock
- 340 grams sliced chicken sausage
- 2 leeks, chopped
- 3 bay leaves
- 1 cup diced tomatoes
- 4 garlic cloves, minced
- 3 tbsp Worcestershire sauce
- 2 medium spring fresh Rosemary

Directions:
- Select the Pressure Cook button of your air fryer and set it over a medium temperature of 350°F.
- Mix black-eyed peas and chicken stock in a pot
- Cook for 12 minutes.
- Open the pot and put the remaining ingredients.
- Cook for 12 minutes
- Serve with java rice.

370.   Fusilli with Broccoli in Pesto

Preparation Time: 15 minutes
Cooking Time: 30 minutes
Servings: 4

Ingredients:
- 1 medium head of broccoli (about 3 cups), cut into very small florets
- 1/2 cup walnuts, toasted
- 1/3 cup Parmesan, freshly grated
- 1 clove of garlic
- juice of 1/2 a lemon
- 1/4 tsp + fine grain sea salt
- 1/3 cup extra-virgin olive oil
- 1/2 pound (8 ounces) dried whole-wheat pasta (bite-sized - fusilli, penne, etc.)
- 3 handfuls of spinach orchard, well chopped
- a handful of black olives pitted

Directions:
- Put the pasta on the air fryer with 4 cups of cold water and 1 tsp of salt (if you want to use a different amount of pasta, use enough water to cover the pasta barely).
- Press the "Pressure Cook" or "Manual" button and set the time for 5 minutes on High pressure (or 2 minutes if you like al dente pasta). Drain and set aside.
- Press the sauté button on your Air fryer and allow the inner pot to heat up for 2-5 minutes at 300°F. Cook the broccoli by adding salt to the boiling water - Cook for just 3 minutes.
- Set aside a few of the small broccoli trees and puree the rest in a food processor along with walnuts, parmesan, garlic, lemon juice, and salt.
- Mix the pasta with broccoli and pesto mixture and serve.

371.   Khao Pad Fried Rice

Preparation Time: 30 minutes
Cooking Time: 30 minutes
Servings: 4

Ingredients:
- 5 cups of cooked Jasmine rice (cooled, better if a day old)
- 20 shrimps, deveined
- 2 onion

- 3 leaves of Chinese broccoli
- 3 cloves garlic
- 4 egg
- 2 tbsp soy sauce
- 2 tbsp oyster sauce
- 2 tbsp of oil
- Prik Nam Pla (spicy fish sauce)
- 5 Thai chilies
- 4 tbsp of fish sauce
- 1/4 cup lime juice

Directions:
- Set the air fryer to sauté function at 300°F and put the oil.
- Beat and scrambled the egg. Set aside.
- Mix all dry ingredients except rice, cooked egg, and fish sauce mixture. Cook thoroughly.
- Mix in all wet ingredients. Cook thoroughly.
- Mix in egg and rice. Cook until all parts are hot.
- Serve on a platter with the Prik Nam Pla sauce.

372.   Minestrone Soup

Preparation Time: 10 minutes
Cooking Time: 10 minutes
Servings: 4

Ingredients:
- 1/2 cup fresh spinach
- 4 cups vegetable stock
- 2 cups cooked cannellini beans
- 1 tsp basil, dried
- 28 oz tomatoes, chopped
- 1 cup dry pasta
- 1 tsp oregano
- Two garlic cloves, minced
- One carrot, diced
- One onion, diced
- Two celery stalks, diced
- 2 tbsps. olive oil
- One bay leaf
- Pepper
- Salt

Directions:
- Add olive oil into the air fryer and set the container on sauté mode at 300°F.
- Add onion, garlic, celery, and carrot and cook until softened.
- Add pepper, oregano, and basil. Stir well.
- Add tomatoes, paste, bay leaf, spinach, and stock. Stir well.
- Seal fryer with lid and cook on high pressure for 6 minutes.
- Release pressure using the quick-release method, then open the lid carefully.
- Add cooked cannellini beans and stir well.
- Serve and enjoy.

373.   Wheat Berry Pilaf

Preparation Time: 10 minutes
Cooking Time: 35 minutes
Servings: 6

Ingredients:
- 1 1/2 cups wheat berries, rinsed and drained
- 1/2 cup onion, minced
- 1 tsp coriander seeds
- 2 tsp cumin seeds
- 1 tbsp olive oil
- 3 cups of water
- 1 1/2 tsp turmeric
- 1 tbsp garlic, minced
- Salt

Directions:
- Add oil into the air fryer duo fresh and set the pot on sauté mode at 300°F.
- Add onion and cook until softened.
- Add turmeric, garlic, coriander, cumin, and sauté for 2 minutes.
- Add wheat berries and sauté for 2 minutes.
- Add water and stir everything well.
- Seal the pot with a pressure cooking lid and 400°F for 30 minutes.
- Once done, allow to release pressure naturally. Remove lid.
- Stir well and serve.

374. Hot Pumpkin Rendang

Preparation Time: 20 minutes
Cooking Time: 30 minutes
Servings: 4

Ingredients:
- 25 oz. pumpkin, cubed
- ½ lemon, peeled and cubed
- 2 onions, peeled and chopped
- 7-8 oz. vegan cheese, grated
- 1 tbsp of ginger, minced
- 1 small jalapeno pepper, chopped
- 5 tbsp sunflower oil
- 4 garlic cloves, minced
- 1 pack of rendang curry paste
- ½ a cup of water

Directions:
- In a bowl, combine the onions, jalapeno pepper, garlic, ginger, and rendang curry paste. Toss the pumpkin in the spices and vegetables. Then set the pumpkin aside to marinate it for at least a few hours, unrefrigerated at room temperature, or place it in the fridge overnight.
- Set the pot to a mode of sautéing, then put some sunflower oil at 300°F.
- Allow the oil to heat up, and add in the pumpkin and all the remaining ingredients (except the cheese). Pour the water and close the lid to cook on a MEDIUM pressure for about 30 minutes. Open the lid and spoon the pumpkin into the plates or bowls. Dollop each plate with some vegan cheese.
- Serve the spicy pumpkin with the beer and vegetable salad.

375. Coconut Soup with Chive

Preparation Time: 10 minutes
Cooking Time: 30 minutes
Servings: 3-4

Ingredients:
- 1 sweet yellow onion, diced
- 1 cup of coconut milk
- 3 cups of vegetable broth
- 1 pinch of sea salt
- 2 bunches of chives, chopped
- 1 bunch of greenery, chopped

Directions:
- On your instant pot, put all ingredients in and close the lid to select the soup function.
- Boil the soup on HIGH pressure for 30 minutes.
- Portion the coconut soup into three bowls or mugs and dollop each bowl with the greenery. Serve warm

376. Tofu Red Curry Noodle

Preparation Time: 20 minutes
Cooking Time: 20 minutes
Servings: 4

Ingredients:
- 1 pc. Tofu
- 1 (8-ounce) package of Thai rice noodles (preferably brown rice noodles)
- 2 tbsp Thai red curry paste
- 1 (14-ounce) can of full-fat coconut milk, divided
- 4 garlic cloves, minced
- 2 tbsp grated fresh ginger
- ¼ cup fresh lime juice
- 1 tsp of sea salt
- ⅓ cup chopped cilantro
- ⅓ cup chopped fresh basil
- ⅓ cup minced scallions
- ⅓ cup finely chopped red cabbage

Directions:
- Set to 392°F. Prepare the Tofu. While that's in the air fryer, get the rest of the dish together. Cook noodled following directions on their package.
- While the noodles are cooking, make the sauce: In a very large bowl, combine the curry paste and about ¼ cup of coconut milk.
- Whisk together until smooth, using a wire whisk or fork. Put coconut milk and let it emulsify by whisking. Add the garlic, ginger, lime juice, and salt. Stir or whisk well. Add the cilantro, basil, scallions, and cabbage to the bowl and stir.
- Once the noodles are al dente, drain thoroughly and add them to the bowl. Stir gently to combine with the sauce thoroughly.
- Serve the noodle-veggie mixture hot, topped with the Tofu.

CHAPTER 4: BEEF AND LAMB

377. Beef Schnitzel

Preparation Time: 15 minutes
Cooking Time: 12-15 minutes
Servings: 4

Ingredients:

- 4 thin beef schnitzels
- 2 tbsp paprika
- 1 cup breadcrumbs
- 1 tbsp sesame seeds
- 2 eggs, beaten
- 4 tbsp almond flour

- 3 tbsp olive oil
- Salt and pepper to taste

Directions:

- Preheat the air fryer to 350°F. Season schnitzel with pepper and salt. In a bowl, mix the flour, salt, and paprika. In another bowl, mix breadcrumbs, olive oil, and sesame seeds. Add beaten eggs into a third bowl. Dip the schnitzel into the flour mixture, then into the egg, and finally coat with breadcrumbs. Place coated schnitzel in an air fryer basket and cook for 12-minutes. Serve warm.

378. Lamb Kebabs

Preparation Time: 20 minutes
Cooking Time: 25-30 minutes
Servings: 6

Ingredients:

- 1 lb. of lamb
- 3- onions chopped
- 5- green chilies-roughly chopped
- 1 ½- tbsp. ginger paste
- 1 ½- tsp garlic paste
- 1 ½- tsp salt
- 3 tsp lemon juice

- 2 tsp garam masala
- 4 tbsp. chopped coriander
- 3 tbsp. cream
- 4 tbsp. fresh mint chopped
- 3 tbsp. chopped capsicum
- 3 eggs
- 2 ½- tbsp. white sesame seeds

Directions:
- Mix the lamb with the ground ginger and cut green chilies.
- Pound this blend until it turns into a thick paste. Add water if required.
- Add the onions, mint, breadcrumbs, and spices.
- Blend this well until you get a soft mixture.
- Form round kebabs with the dough.
- Pour a small amount of milk onto each kebab to wet it.
- Roll the kebab in the dry breadcrumbs.
- Preheat the Air Fryer for 5 minutes at 300°F and cook for 30 minutes.
- Recommended sides for this dish are mint chutney, tomato ketchup, or yogurt chutney.

379. Spiced Beef Fajitas

Preparation Time: 30 minutes
Cooking Time: 10 minutes
Servings: 8

Ingredients:
- 1 lb. beef sirloin steak, cut into strips
- 2 garlic cloves, minced
- 1 tbsp paprika
- 1 red bell pepper, sliced
- 1 orange bell pepper, sliced
- 2 shallots, sliced
- 2 tbsp cajun seasoning
- 2 tbsp olive oil
- 8 tortilla wraps
- ½ cup cheddar cheese, shredded
- Salt and black pepper to taste

Directions:
- Preheat the air fryer to 360°F.
- In a bowl, combine the beef, shallots, bell peppers, and garlic. Season with Cajun seasoning, paprika, salt, and black pepper; toss to combine. Transfer the mixture to a greased baking dish and place it in the air fryer basket. Bake for 10 minutes, shaking once or twice throughout cooking. Serve on tortillas, topped with cheddar cheese.

380. Greek Kafta Kabobs

Preparation Time: 15 minutes
Cooking Time: 10 minutes
Servings: 14

Ingredients:
- 1 tbsp coriander seed
- 1 tbsp cumin seeds
- 1 tsp peppercorns
- 1 tsp allspice
- 1/2 tsp cardamom seeds
- 1/2 tsp turmeric powder
- 1 tbsp oil
- 1 pound 85% ground beef

- 1/4 cup parsley
- One tbsp minced garlic

Directions:
- Grind the seeds and peppercorns into powder and combine with the turmeric and allspice.
- Put altogether of the ingredients together in a blender and blend until well mixed.
- Divide the meat into four equal parts and form a sausage around the skewers.
- Cook in the air fryer at 370°For 10 minutes.

381. Classic Beef Ribs

Preparation Time: 35 minutes
Cooking Time: 25-30 minutes
Servings: 8

Ingredients:
- 2 pounds beef back ribs
- 1 tbsp sunflower oil
- 1/2 tsp mixed peppercorns, cracked
- 1 tsp red pepper flakes
- 1 tsp dry mustard
- Coarse sea salt, to taste

Directions:
- Trim the excess fat from the beef ribs. Mix the sunflower oil, cracked peppercorns, red pepper, dry mustard, and salt. Rub over the ribs.
- Cook in the preheated air fryer at 395°F for 11 minutes. Turn the heat to 330°F and continue to cook for 18 minutes more. Serve warm.

382. Spicy Short Ribs in Red Wine Reduction

Preparation Time: 3 hrs.
Cooking Time: 20 minutes
Servings: 6

Ingredients:
- 1 ½ pound short ribs,
- 1 cup red wine
- 1/2 cup tamari sauce
- 1 lemon, juiced
- 1 tsp fresh ginger, grated
- 1 tsp salt
- 1 tsp black pepper
- 1 tsp paprika
- 1 tsp chipotle chili powder,
- 1 cup ketchup
- 1 tsp garlic powder,
- 1 tsp cumin

Directions:
- In a ceramic bowl, place the beef ribs, wine, tamari sauce, lemon juice, ginger, salt, black pepper, paprika, and chipotle chili powder. Cover and let it marinate for 3 hours in the refrigerator. Discard the marinade and add the short ribs to the air fryer basket.
- Cook in the preheated air fry at 380°F for 10 minutes, turning them over halfway through the cooking time. In the meantime, heat the saucepan over medium heat; add the reserved marinade and stir in the ketchup, garlic powder, and cumin. Cook until the sauce has thickened slightly. Pour the sauce over the warm ribs and serve immediately. Bon appétit!

383.   Coffee Rubbed Steaks

Preparation Time: 10 minutes
Cooking Time: 15 minutes
Servings: 4

Ingredients:
- 1 and ½ tbsp coffee, ground
- 4 rib-eye steaks
- ½ tbsp sweet paprika
- 2 tbsp chili powder
- 2 tsp garlic powder
- 2 tsp onion powder
- ¼ tsp ginger, ground
- ¼ tsp, coriander, ground
- A pinch of cayenne pepper
- Black pepper to the taste

Directions:
- In a bowl, mix coffee with paprika, chili powder, garlic powder, onion powder, ginger, coriander, cayenne, and black pepper, stir, rub steaks with this mix, and put in the preheated air fryer and cook at 360°F for 15 minutes.
- Divide steaks among plates and serve with a side salad. Enjoy!

384.   Beef Roll-ups

Preparation Time: 60 minutes
Cooking Time: 25-30 minutes
Servings: 6

Ingredients:
- 1½ pounds sirloin steak, cut into slices
- 2 tbsp Worcestershire sauce
- ½ tbsp garlic powder
- ½ tbsp onion powder
- 2 medium bell peppers of any color, cut into thin strips
- ½ cup shredded mozzarella cheese
- Salt
- Freshly ground black pepper
- Olive oil

Directions:
- Set to 370°F. Using a meat mallet, pound the steaks very thin.
- In a small bowl, combine the Worcestershire sauce, garlic powder, and onion powder to make a marinade.
- Place the steaks and marinade in a large zip-top plastic bag, seal, and refrigerate for at least 30 minutes. Soak 8 toothpicks in water for 15 to 20 minutes.
- Place ¼ of the bell peppers and ¼ of the mozzarella cheese in the center of each steak. Season with salt and black pepper. Roll each steak up tightly and secure it with 2 toothpicks.
- Spray a fryer basket lightly with olive oil. Place the beef roll-ups in the fryer basket, toothpick side down, in a single layer. You may need to cook the roll-ups in batches.
- Air fry for 10 minutes. Flip the steaks over and cook until the meat reaches an internal temperature of at least 150°F, an additional 7 to 10 minutes.
- Let the roll-ups rest for 10 minutes before serving.

385.   Beef Chimichangas

Preparation Time: 20 minutes
Cooking Time: 25-30 minutes
Servings: 4

Ingredients:
- Olive oil
- 1-pound lean ground beef
- 1 tbsp taco seasoning
- ½ cup salsa
- 1 (16-ounce) can of fat-free refried beans
- 4 large whole-wheat tortillas
- ½ cup shredded Cheddar cheese

Directions:
- Set to 370°F. Spray the fryer basket lightly with olive oil.
- In a large skillet over medium heat, cook the ground beef until browned, about 5 minutes. Add the taco seasoning and salsa and stir to combine. Set aside.
- Spread ½ cup of refried beans onto each tortilla, leaving a ½ inch border around the edge. Add ¼ of the ground beef mixture to each tortilla and sprinkle with 2 tbsp of Cheddar cheese.
- Fold the opposite sides of the tortilla in and roll-up.
- Place the chimichangas in the fryer basket, seam side down. Spray lightly with olive oil. You may need to cook the chimichangas in batches.
- Air fry until golden brown, 5 to 10 minutes.

386.   Mushroom and Beef Meatballs

Preparation Time: 20 minutes
Cooking Time: 30 minutes
Servings: 6

Ingredients:
- Olive oil
- 2 pounds lean ground beef
- ⅔ cups finely chopped mushrooms
- 4 tbsp chopped parsley
- 2 eggs, beaten
- 2 tsp salt
- 1 tsp freshly ground black pepper
- 1 cup whole-wheat bread crumbs

Directions:
- Set to 390°F. Spray a fryer basket lightly with olive oil.
- In a large bowl, mix together the beef, mushrooms, and parsley. Add the eggs, salt, and pepper and mix gently. Add the bread crumbs and mix until the bread crumbs are no longer dry. Be careful not to overmix.
- Using a small cookie scoop, form 24 meatballs.
- Place the meatballs in the fryer basket in a single layer and spray lightly with olive oil.
- Air fry until the internal temperature reaches at least 160°F, 10 to 15 minutes, shaking the basket every 5 minutes for even cooking.

387.   Beef Broccoli

Preparation Time: 10 minutes
Cooking Time: 15 minutes
Servings: 3

Ingredients:

- 1/2 lb. steak, cut into strips
- 1 tsp garlic, minced
- 1 tsp ginger, minced
- 2 tbsp sesame oil
- 2 tbsp soy sauce
- 4 tbsp oyster sauce
- 1 lb. broccoli florets
- 1 tbsp sesame seeds, toasted

Directions:

- Add all ingredients except sesame seeds into the large mixing bowl and toss well. Place bowl in the refrigerator for 1 hour.
- Add marinated steak and broccoli into the air fryer basket and cook at 350°F for 15 minutes.
- Shake basket 2-3 times while cooking.
- Garnish with sesame seeds and serve.

388. Greek Lamb Patties

Preparation Time: 10 minutes
Cooking Time: 20 minutes
Servings: 4

Ingredients:

- 1 1/2 lbs. ground lamb
- 1/3 cup feta cheese, crumbled
- 1 tsp oregano
- 1/4 tsp pepper
- 1/2 tsp salt

Directions:

- Preheat the air fryer to 375°F.
- Add all ingredients into the bowl and mix until well combined.
- Spray the air fryer basket with cooking spray.
- Make the equal shape of patties from the meat mixture and place them into the air fryer basket.
- Cook lamb patties for 10 minutes, then turn to another side and cook for 10 minutes more.
- Serve and enjoy.

389. Mustard and Lemon Lamb Chops

Preparation Time: 10 minutes
Cooking Time: 15 minutes
Servings: 8

Ingredients:

- 8 lamb chops
- 1 tbsp lemon juice
- 1 tsp tarragon
- 1/2 tsp olive oil
- 2 tbsp Dijon mustard
- Pepper
- Salt

Directions:

- Preheat the air fryer to 390°F.
- In a small bowl, mix together mustard, lemon juice, tarragon, and olive oil.
- Brush mustard mixture over lamb chops.
- Place lamb chops in an air fryer basket and cook for 15 minutes. Turn halfway through.
- Serve and enjoy.

390. Spicy Lamb Chops

Preparation Time: 40 minutes
Cooking Time: 10 minutes
Servings: 6

Ingredients:

- 1½ lbs. lamb chops
- 1 tbsp butter, melted
- 1 tbsp olive oil
- 1 ½ tsp cayenne pepper
- 1 tsp garlic powder
- 1 tsp onion powder
- ½ tsp red chili flakes
- 1 tsp chili pepper
- ½ tsp lime zest

Directions:

- In a large bowl, mix together oil, butter, lime zest, chili pepper, chili flakes, onion powder, garlic powder, and cayenne pepper.
- Add lamb chops to the bowl and coat well with the marinade, and place in the refrigerator for 30 minutes.
- Spray the air fryer basket with cooking spray.
- Place marinated pork chops into the air fryer basket and cook for 10 minutes at 375°F. Turn pork chops halfway through.
- Serve and enjoy.

391. Ground Beef Yuca Balls

Preparation Time: 20 minutes
Cooking Time: 20 minutes
Servings: 6

Ingredients:

- 1 lb. of ground beef
- ½ lb. Yuca, cooked and crushed
- 1 clove garlic
- ½ onion
- 1 tomato
- to taste green smell
- to taste Salt and pepper
- 1 tbsp of olive oil

Directions:

- Mix the meat, yucca, and olive oil.
- Put salt and pepper, and the green smell mixes well.
- When the mixture is homogeneous, add the onion, garlic, and tomato cut into small pieces.
- Make 12 balls with your hands and put them in the air fryer for 20 minutes at 400°F.

392. Roast Beef Lettuce Wraps

Preparation Time: 30 minutes
Cooking Time: 10 minutes
Servings: 4

Ingredients:

- 8 large iceberg lettuce leaves
- 8 oz (8 slices) rare roast beef
- ½ cup homemade mayonnaise
- 8 slices provolone cheese
- 1 cup baby spinach

Directions:
- In the air fryer basket, place the beef roast. Cook for 30 minutes at 375°F, turning halfway through.
- Take the roast steak out of the air fryer. Allow for a 20-minute rest before carving the roast.
- Wash the lettuce leaves and sake them dry. Try not to rip them.
- Place 1 slice of roast beef inside each wrap.
- Smother 1 tbsp of mayonnaise on top of each piece of roast beef.
- Top the mayonnaise with 1 slice of provolone cheese and 1 cup of baby spinach.
- Roll the lettuce up around the toppings.
- Serve & enjoy!

393. Beef Mozzarella

Preparation Time: 15 minutes
Cooking Time: 25-30 minutes
Servings: 6

Ingredients:
- 12 oz. beef brisket
- 2 tsp. Italian herbs
- 2 tsp. butter
- 1 onion, sliced
- 7 oz. mozzarella cheese, sliced

Directions:
- Pre-heat the fryer to 365°F.
- Cut up the brisket into four equal slices and season with the Italian herbs.
- Allow the butter to melt in the fryer. Place the slices of beef inside along with the onion. Put a piece of mozzarella on top of each piece of brisket and cook for twenty-five minutes.
- Enjoy!

394. Leg of Lamb with Brussel Sprouts

Preparation Time: 30 minutes
Cooking Time: 1 hr. 20 minutes
Servings: 8

Ingredients:
- 2¼ pounds leg of lamb
- 1 tbsp fresh rosemary, minced
- 1 tbsp fresh lemon thyme
- 1½ pounds Brussels sprouts, trimmed
- 3 tbsp olive oil, divided
- 1 garlic clove, minced
- Salt and ground black pepper, as required
- 2 tbsp honey

Directions:
- Preheat the Air fryer to 300°F and grease an Air fryer basket.
- Make slits in the leg of lamb with a sharp knife.
- Mix 2 tbsp of oil, herbs, garlic, salt, and black pepper in a bowl.
- Coat the leg of lamb with oil mixture generously and arrange in the Air fryer basket.
- Cook for about 75 minutes and set the Air fryer to 390°F.

- Coat the Brussels sprout evenly with the remaining oil and honey and arrange them in the Air fryer basket with the leg of lamb.
- Cook for about 15 minutes and dish out to serve warm.

395. Italian Beef Meatballs

Preparation Time: 20 minutes
Cooking Time: 15-20 minutes
Servings: 6

Ingredients:
- 2 large eggs
- 2 pounds of ground beef
- ¼ cup fresh parsley, chopped
- 1¼ cups panko breadcrumbs
- ¼ cup Parmigiano Reggiano, grated
- 1 tsp dried oregano
- 1 small garlic clove, chopped
- Salt and black pepper, to taste
- 1 tsp vegetable oil

Directions:
- Preheat the Air fryer to 350°F and grease an Air fryer basket.
- Mix beef with all other ingredients in a bowl until well combined.
- Make equal-sized balls from the mixture and arrange the balls in the air fryer basket.
- Cook for about 13 minutes and dish out to serve warm.

396. Beef Pot Pie

Preparation Time: 20 minutes
Cooking Time: 1 hr. 20 minutes
Servings: 6

Ingredients:
- 1-pound beef stewing steak, cubed
- 1 canned of ale mixed into 1 cup of water
- 2 beef bouillon cubes
- 1 tbsp plain flour
- 1 prepared shortcrust pastry
- 1 tbsp olive oil
- 1 tbsp tomato puree
- 2 tbsp onion paste
- Salt and black pepper, to taste

Directions:
- Preheat the Air fryer to 390°F and grease 2 ramekins lightly.
- Heat olive oil in a pan and add steak cubes.
- Cook for about 5 minutes and stir in the onion paste and tomato puree.
- Cook for about 6 minutes, and add the ale mixture, bouillon cubes, salt, and black pepper.
- Bring to a boil and reduce the heat to simmer for about 1 hour.
- Mix flour and 3 tbsp of warm water in a bowl and slowly add this mixture to the beef mixture.
- Roll out the shortcrust pastry and line 2 ramekins with pastry.
- Divide the beef mixture evenly in the ramekins and top with extra pastry.
- Transfer into the Air fryer and cook for about 10 minutes.

- Set the Air fryer to 335°F and cook for about 6 more minutes.
- Dish out and serve warm.

397. Bacon-Wrapped Filet Mignon

Preparation Time: 15 minutes
Cooking Time: 5-10 minutes
Servings: 2

Ingredients:
- 2 filet of mignon steaks
- 2 slices of bacon
- 2 toothpicks
- 1 tsp of freshly cracked peppercorns
- 1/2 tsp of kosher salt
- Avocado oil

Directions:
- Wrap the bacon around the mignon filet and secure it with a toothpick by pressing the toothpick through the bacon and into the filet, then to the bacon on the other end of the toothpick from the filet.
- Season the steak with the salt and pepper or the seasonings you prefer.
- Place the mignon filet wrapped with bacon on the air fryer rack.
- Sprinkle a small amount of avocado oil on the steak.
- Cook bacon-wrapped filet mignon. Air fry the steak at 375°F for about 10 minutes, and then flip as one side is nice and seared while the other is not.
- Fry air for another 5 minutes, or until the desired doneness is reached. We are pursuing a medium.

398. Winter Vegetables & Lamb Stew

Preparation Time: 35 minutes
Cooking Time: 45-50 minutes
Servings: 6

Ingredients:
- 500g stewing lamb, cubed
- 2 cloves garlic, chopped finely
- 1 tbsp. fresh thyme, chopped finely
- freshly ground pepper and salt
- 300g butternut squash, seeded and cubed
- 150g parsnip, sliced
- 150g sweet potato, cubed
- 125g celery, sliced
- 1 medium onion, chopped coarsely
- 100ml red wine
- 125ml beef stock
- 1 tbsp. olive oil

Directions:
- Mix the lamb with garlic, thyme, pepper, and salt to taste. Mix in the squash, parsnip, sweet potato, celery, and onion.
- Pour the red wine, beef stock, and olive oil over the lamb and vegetables. Close the lid.
- Touch the MULTI COOK menu to select the STEW/CURRY program, set cooking time for 45 minutes at 350°F, and press START Stir once or twice. Serve with rice or couscous.

399. Air Fryer Lamb Leg

Preparation Time: 40 minutes
Cooking Time: 60 minutes
Servings: 6

Ingredients:
- 8 pounds of the whole leg of lamb
- Salt to taste
- Ground black pepper to taste
- 6 ounces prepared mustard
- 1 dash Worcestershire sauce
- 2 tablespoons all-purpose flour
- 4 cloves garlic, sliced

Directions:
- Preheat the air fryer oven to 325°F.
- Season the lamb well with salt and pepper. Sprinkle the mustard all over the lamb and cover it with a thin layer of flour. Cut up garlic cloves and arrange them on top of the lamb leg in a roasting pan. To taste, sprinkle with Worcestershire sauce.
- Roast uncovered at 325°F until done to preference. For a pink roast, allow around 20 minutes per pound. Take from the pan to a hot plate. Make a gravy using the drippings and a little flour and water. Season with salt and pepper to taste.

400. Buttered Filet Mignon

Preparation Time: 10 minutes
Cooking Time: 14 minutes
Servings: 4

Ingredients:
- 2 (6-ounces) filet mignon steaks
- 1 tbsp butter, softened
- Salt and ground black pepper, as required

Directions:
- Coat each steak evenly with butter and then season with salt and black pepper.
- Set the temperature of the air fryer to 390°F. Grease an air fryer basket.
- Arrange steaks into the prepared air fryer basket.
- Air fry for about 14 minutes, flipping once halfway through.
- Remove from the air fryer and transfer onto serving plates.
- Serve hot.

401. Lamb Korma

Preparation Time: 35 minutes
Cooking Time: 30 minutes
Servings: 8

Ingredients:
- 1.5kg boned lamb shoulder, chopped coarsely
- 2 medium brown onions, sliced thinly
- 5cm piece of fresh ginger, grated
- 3 cloves garlic, crushed
- ⅔ cup korma paste
- 3 medium tomatoes, chopped coarsely
- ½ cup chicken stock
- 300ml pouring cream
- 1 cinnamon stick

- ½ cup loosely packed fresh coriander leaves
- 1 fresh long red chili, sliced thinly
- ⅓ cup toasted flaked almonds

Directions:
- Combine lamb, onion, ginger, garlic, paste, tomatoes, stock, cream, and cinnamon in a cooker.
- Seal the lid, cook on SLOW COOK LOW TEMP at 300°F for 6 hours, or touch the PRESSURE COOK menu to select the MEAT/POULTRY program for 25 minutes. Press START.
- Season to taste. Discard cinnamon stick. Serve korma sprinkled with coriander, chili, and almonds.

402.   Beer-Braised Short Loin

Preparation Time: 70 minutes
Cooking Time: 40 minutes
Servings: 4

Ingredients:
- 1 ½ pounds short loin
- 2 tbsp olive oil
- 1 bottle beer
- 2-3 cloves garlic, finely minced
- 2 Turkish bay leaves

Directions:
- Pat the beef dry; then tenderize the beef with a meat mallet to soften the fibers. Place it in a large-sized mixing dish.
- Add the remaining ingredients; toss to coat well, and let it marinate for at least 1 hour.
- Cook for about 30 minutes at 395 °F; after that, pause the Air Fryer. Flip the meat over and cook for another 8 minutes, or until it's done.

403.   Spicy Beef Spaghetti

Preparation Time: 35 minutes
Cooking Time: 40 minutes
Servings: 5

Ingredients:
- 3/4-pound ground chuck
- 1 onion, peeled and finely chopped
- 1 tsp garlic paste
- 1 bell pepper, chopped
- 1 small-sized habanero pepper, deveined and finely minced
- 1/2 tsp dried rosemary
- 1/2 tsp dried marjoram
- 1 ¼ cups crushed tomatoes, fresh or canned
- 1/2 tsp sea salt flakes
- 1/4 tsp ground black pepper, or more to taste
- 1 package of cooked spaghetti, to serve

Directions:
- In the Air Fryer baking dish, place the ground meat, onion, garlic paste, bell pepper, habanero pepper, rosemary, and marjoram.
- Air-fry, uncovered, for 10 to 11 minutes 375°F. Next step, stir in the tomatoes along with salt and pepper; cook for 17 to 20 minutes at 375°F. Serve over cooked spaghetti. Bon appétit!

404.   Classic Beef Stroganoff

Preparation Time: 65 minutes
Cooking Time: 30-35 minutes
Servings: 5

Ingredients:
- 3/4-pound beef sirloin steak, cut into small-sized strips
- 1/4 cup balsamic vinegar
- 1 tbsp brown mustard
- 2 tbsp all-purpose flour
- 1 tbsp butter
- 1 cup beef broth
- 1 cup leek, chopped
- 2 cloves garlic, crushed
- 1 tsp cayenne pepper
- Sea salt flakes and crushed red pepper, to taste
- 1 cup sour cream
- 2 ½ tbsp tomato paste

Directions:
- Place the beef along with the balsamic vinegar and the mustard in a mixing dish; cover and marinate in your refrigerator for about 1 hour.
- Then, coat the beef strips with the flour, butter the inside of a baking dish, and put the beef into the dish of the air fryer.
- Add the broth, leeks, and garlic. Cook at 380 °For 8 minutes. Pause the machine and add the cayenne pepper, salt, red pepper, sour cream, and tomato paste; cook for additional 7 minutes.
- Check for doneness and serve with warm egg noodles, if desired. Bon appétit!

405.   Crusted Fillet Mignon

Preparation Time: 15 minutes
Cooking Time: 20 minutes
Servings: 2

Ingredients:
- 1/2-pound filet mignon
- Sea salt and ground black pepper, to your liking
- 1/2 tsp cayenne pepper
- 1 tsp dried basil
- 1 tsp dried rosemary
- 1 tsp dried thyme
- 1 tbsp sesame oil
- 1 small-sized egg, well-whisked
- 1/2 cup seasoned breadcrumbs

Directions:
- Season the filet mignon with salt, black pepper, cayenne pepper, basil, rosemary, and thyme. Brush with sesame oil.
- Put the egg on a shallow plate. Now, place the breadcrumbs on another plate.
- Coat the filet mignon with the egg, then lay it into the crumbs. Set your Air Fryer to cook at 360 °F.
- Cook for 10 to 13 minutes or until golden. Serve with mixed salad leaves, and enjoy!

406. Sichuan Spiced Lamb

Preparation Time: 20 minutes
Cooking Time: 30 minutes
Servings: 4

Ingredients:

- For lamb:
- 2 tbsp Cumin
- 1 tsp Sichuan peppers
- 1 lb. Lamb shoulder (cut in 2-inch pieces)
- 2 tbsp Vegetable oil
- 1 tbsp Light soy sauce
- 1 tbsp Garlic (minced)
- 2 Red chili peppers
- 1 tsp Salt
- ¼ tsp Sugar
- For garnishing:
- 2 Scallions (chopped)
- 1 handful of Cilantro (chopped)

Directions:

- Start by preparing the spice mix to marinate the lamb. For this, you need to take a dry non-stick pan and add the cumin and Sichuan pepper. Roast them until they become fragrant.
- Empty the cumin and pepper into a mortar and pestle. Allow them to cool. Once cooled, grind them into a coarse powder.
- Poke holes into the lamb shoulder and place it in a shallow dish. Sprinkle the prepared spice mix on top and use your hand to massage the meat.
- Add the oil, light soy sauce, red chili peppers, garlic, sugar, cayenne pepper, and sugar. Mix and massage well into the pork shoulder.
- Turn on the air fryer and place the marinated pork into the basket.
- Cook the lamb for 30 minutes at 360°F.
- Transfer the lamb shoulder onto a serving platter.
- Finish by garnishing with chopped cilantro and scallions. Serve hot!

407. Cumin-Paprika Rubbed Beef Brisket

Preparation Time: 5 minutes
Cooking Time: 2 hours
Servings: 12

Ingredients:

- ¼ tsp cayenne pepper
- 1 ½ tbsp paprika
- 1 tsp garlic powder
- 1 tsp ground cumin
- 1 tsp onion powder
- 2 tsp dry mustard
- 2 tsp ground black pepper
- 2 tsp salt
- 5 pounds brisket roast
- 5 tbsp olive oil

Directions:

- Place all ingredients in a Ziploc bag and allow to marinate in the fridge for at least 2 hours.
- Remove the Grill Grate from the unit. Select BAKE, set the temperature to 350°F, and set the time to 30

minutes. Select START/STOP to begin preheating and cook for 2 hours at 350°F.

408. Herbed Pulled Beef

Preparation Time: 10 minutes
Cooking Time: 25-30 minutes
Servings: 6

Ingredients:

- 1 tsp. dried dill
- 1 tsp. dried thyme
- 1 tsp. garlic powder
- 2 lbs. beefsteak
- 3 tbsp. butter

Directions:

- Pre-heat your fryer at 360°F.
- Combine the dill, thyme, and garlic powder together, and massage into the steak.
- Cook the steak in the fryer for twenty minutes, then remove, shred, and return to the fryer. Add the butter and cook for a further two minutes at 365°F. Make sure the beef is coated in the butter before serving.

409. Pesto Beef Rolls

Preparation Time: 30 minutes
Cooking Time: 15 minutes
Servings: 4

Ingredients:

- 2 pounds beef steak, sliced
- 1 tsp pepper
- 3 tbsp pesto
- 1 tsp salt
- 6 slices cheese
- ¾ cup spinach, chopped
- 3 oz bell pepper, deseeded and sliced

Directions:

- Preheat your Air Fryer to 400°F. Top the steak slices with pesto, cheese, spinach, and bell pepper. Roll up the slices and secure them using a toothpick. Season with salt and pepper accordingly. Place the prepared slices in your Air Fryer's cooking basket and cook for 15 minutes. Serve and enjoy!

410. Beef Schnitzel

Preparation Time: 15 minutes
Cooking Time: 12 minutes
Servings: 1

Ingredients:

- 2 tbsp vegetable oil
- 2 oz breadcrumbs
- 1 whole egg, whisked
- 1 thin beef schnitzel, cut into strips
- 1 whole lemon

Directions:

- Preheat your fryer to 356°F. In a bowl, add breadcrumbs and oil and stir well to get a loose mixture. Dip schnitzel in egg, then dip in breadcrumbs coat well. Place the prepared schnitzel in your Air Fryer's cooking basket and cook for 12 minutes. Serve with a drizzle of lemon juice.

411. Beef and Napa Cabbage Mix

Preparation Time: 5 minutes
Cooking Time: 30 minutes
Servings: 4

Ingredients:
- 2 pounds beef, cubed
- ½ pound bacon, chopped
- 2 shallots, chopped
- 1 Napa cabbage, shredded
- 2 garlic cloves, minced
- A pinch of salt and black pepper
- 2 tbsp olive oil
- 1 tsp thyme, dried
- 1 cup beef stock

Directions:
- Heat up a pan that fits the air fryer with the oil at 350°F, and add the beef and brown for 3 minutes.
- Add the bacon, shallots, and garlic and cook for 2 minutes more.
- Add the rest of the ingredients, toss, put the pan in the air fryer and cook at 390 °F for 20 minutes.
- Divide between plates and serve.

412. Mint Lamb with Red Potatoes

Preparation Time: 10 minutes
Cooking Time: 14-15 minutes
Servings: 2

Ingredients:
- 2 lamb steaks
- 2 tbsp olive oil
- 2 garlic cloves, crushed
- Salt and black pepper to taste
- A handful of fresh mint, chopped
- 4 red potatoes, cubed

Directions:
- Rub the steaks with oil, garlic, salt, and black pepper. Put mint in the fryer, and place the steaks on top. Oil the potato chunks and sprinkle with salt and pepper. Arrange the potatoes next to the steaks, and cook at 360°F for 14 minutes, turning once halfway through cooking.

413. Beef and Avocado Pan

Preparation Time: 5 minutes
Cooking Time: 30 minutes
Servings: 4

Ingredients:
- 4 flank steaks
- 1 garlic clove, minced
- 1/3 cup beef stock
- 2 avocados, peeled, pitted, and sliced
- 1 tsp chili flakes
- ½ cup basil, chopped
- 2 spring onions, chopped
- 2 tsp olive oil
- A pinch of salt and black pepper

Directions:
- Heat up a pan that fits the air fryer with the oil over medium-high heat, add the steaks and cook for 2 minutes on each side.
- Add the rest of the ingredients except the avocados, put the pan in the air fryer, and cook at 380°F for 15 minutes.
- Add the avocado slices, cook for 5 minutes more, divide everything between plates and serve.

414. Spicy Lamb Balls

Preparation Time: 45 minutes
Cooking Time: 30-40 minutes
Servings: 12

Ingredients:
- 1 ½ lb. ground lamb
- ½ cup minced onion
- 2 tbsp chopped mint leaves
- 3 garlic cloves, minced
- 2 tsp paprika
- 2 tsp coriander seeds
- ½ tsp cayenne pepper
- 1 tsp salt
- 1 tbsp chopped parsley
- 2 tsp cumin
- ½ tsp ground ginger

Directions:
- Soak 24 skewers in water until ready to use. Preheat the air fryer to 330°F. Combine all ingredients in a large bowl. Mix well with your hands until the herbs and spices are evenly distributed, and the mixture is well incorporated.
- Shape the lamb mixture into 12 sausage shapes around 2 skewers. Cook for 12 to 15 minutes, or until it reaches the preferred doneness. Serve with tzatziki sauce, and enjoy.

415. Beef Tenderloin with Green Sauce

Preparation Time: 20 minutes
Cooking Time: 35 minutes
Servings: 4

Ingredients:
- 2 lb. beef tenderloin, cut into strips
- ½ cup flour
- Sauce:
- 1 tbsp minced ginger
- 1 tbsp minced garlic
- ½ cup chopped green onions
- 2 tbsp olive oil
- ½ cup soy sauce
- ½ cup water
- ¼ cup vinegar
- ¼ cup sugar
- 1 tsp cornstarch
- ½ tsp red chili flakes
- Salt and black pepper to taste

Directions:
- Pour the flour into a bowl, add the beef strips and dredge them in the flour. Spray the fryer basket with cooking spray and arrange the beef strips in it; spray

with cooking spray. Cook the beef at 400°F for 4 minutes. Slide out and shake the fryer basket to toss the beef strips. Cook further for 3 minutes; set aside.

- To make the sauce, pour the cornstarch into a bowl and mix it with 3 to 4 tsp of water until well dissolve; set aside. Place a wok or saucepan over medium heat on a stovetop and add olive oil, garlic, and ginger. Stir continually for 10 seconds. Add the soy sauce, vinegar, and remaining water.
- Stir well and bring to boil for 2 minutes. Stir in the sugar, chili flakes, and cornstarch mixture. Add the beef strips, stir and cook for 3 minutes. Stir in the green onions and cook for 1 to 2 minutes. Season with pepper and salt as desired. Turn off the heat. Serve with a side of steamed rice.

416.   Beef Cabbage Rolls

Preparation Time: 45 minutes
Cooking Time: 35-40 minutes
Servings: 4

Ingredients:
- ½ lb. ground beef
- 8 savoy cabbage leaves
- 1 small onion, chopped
- ¼ packet Taco seasoning
- 1 tbsp cilantro-lime rotel
- ⅔ cup shredded Mexican cheese
- 2 tsp olive oil
- Salt and black pepper to taste
- 2 cloves garlic, minced
- 1 tsp chopped cilantro

Directions:
- Preheat the Air Fryer to 400°F. Grease a skillet with cooking spray and place it over medium heat on a stovetop. Add the onions and garlic; sauté until fragrant. Add the beef, pepper, salt, and taco seasoning. Cook until the beef browns while breaking the meat with a vessel as it cooks. Add the cilantro Rotel and stir well to combine.
- Turn off the heat. Lay 4 of the savoy cabbage leaves on a flat surface and scoop the beef mixture in the center, and sprinkle with the Mexican cheese. Wrap diagonally and double wrap with the remaining 4 cabbage leaves.
- Arrange the 4 rolls in the fryer basket and spray with cooking spray. Close the fryer and cook for 8 minutes. Flip the rolls, spray with cooking spray, and continue to cook for 4 minutes. Remove, garnish with cilantro and allow them to cool. Serve with cheese dip.

417.   Sweet and Sour Lamb Chops

Preparation Time: 15 minutes
Cooking Time: 40 minutes
Servings: 3

Ingredients:
- 3 (8-ounce) lamb shoulder chops
- Salt and ground black pepper, as required
- ¼ cup brown Sugar
- 2 tbsp fresh lemon juice

Directions:
- Season the lamb chops with salt and black pepper generously.

- In a baking pan, place the chops and sprinkle with sugar, followed by the lime juice.
- Arrange the drip pan at the bottom of the air fryer.
- Place the baking pan over the drip pan.
- Select "bake" and then adjust the temperature to 376 °F.
- Set the timer for 40 minutes and press "start."
- When the display shows "turn food," flip the chops.
- When cooking time is complete, remove the baking pan from the toaster oven.
- Serve hot.

418.   Glazed Skirt Steak

Preparation Time: 10 minutes
Cooking Time: 15 minutes
Servings: 6

Ingredients:
- 1¼ pounds skirt steak
- ½ cup low-Sodium soy sauce
- ¼ cup white wine
- 3-4 tbsp fresh lemon juice
- 2 tbsp sesame oil
- 3 tbsp maple syrup
- 1 tbsp red pepper flakes, crushed
- 2 garlic cloves, minced

Directions:
- In a large resealable bag, place all the ingredients except for the sCallions.
- Seal the bag and shake to mix well.
- Refrigerate for up to 2 hours.
- Remove the steak from the bag and set it aside at room temperature for 20 minutes before Cooking.
- Place the skirt steak onto a greased baking pan.
- Arrange the drip pan at the bottom of the air fryer.
- Place the baking pan over the drip pan.
- Select "bake" and then adjust the temperature to 400 °F.
- Set the timer for 10 minutes and press "start."
- When the display shows "turn food," do nothing.
- When cooking time is complete, remove the baking pan from the toaster oven.
- Place the steak onto a cutting board for about 10-15 minutes before slicing.
- With a sharp knife, cut the steak into desired size slices and serve.

419.   Beef Adobo

Preparation Time: 10 minutes
Cooking Time: 15 minutes
Servings: 4

Ingredients:
- 1-pound beef roast, trimmed
- ½ tsp oregano, dried
- ¼ tsp garlic powder
- A pinch of salt and black pepper
- ½ tsp turmeric powder
- 1 tbsp olive oil

Directions:
- In a bowl, mix the roast with the rest of the ingredients, and rub well.
- Put the roast in the air fryer's basket and cook at 390 °F for 30 minutes.

- Slice the roast, divide it between plates and serve with a side salad.

420. Mushroom Beef Steak

Preparation Time: 15 minutes
Cooking Time: 30 minutes
Servings: 4

Ingredients:
- 4 beef steaks
- 1 tbsp olive oil
- A pinch of salt and black pepper
- 2 tbsp ghee, melted
- 2 garlic cloves, minced
- 5 cups wild mushrooms, sliced
- 1 tbsp parsley, chopped

Directions:
- Heat up a pan that fits the air fryer with the oil over medium-high heat, add the steaks and sear them for 2 minutes on each side.
- Add the rest of the ingredients, toss, transfer the pan to your air fryer and cook at 380 °F for 20 minutes.
- Divide between plates and serve.

421. Chili Ground Beef

Preparation Time: 15 minutes
Cooking Time: 20 minutes
Servings: 4

Ingredients:
- 1-pound beef, ground
- A pinch of salt and black pepper
- A drizzle of olive oil
- 2 spring onions, chopped
- 3 red chilies, chopped
- 1 cup beef stock
- 6 garlic cloves, minced
- 1 green bell pepper, chopped
- 8 ounces canned tomatoes, chopped
- 2 tbsp chili powder

Directions:
- Heat up a pan that fits your air fryer with the oil over medium-high heat, and add the beef and brown for 3 minutes.
- Add the rest of the ingredients, toss, put the pan in the fryer and cook at 380 °F for 16 minutes.
- Divide into bowls and serve.

422. Steak & Bread Salad

Preparation Time: 10 minutes
Cooking Time: 14 minutes
Servings: 4

Ingredients:
- 1 tbsp mustard
- 2 tsp packed brown sugar
- 1/2 tsp salt
- 1/2 tsp pepper
- 1 cup ranch salad dressing
- 1 beef top sirloin steak, diced
- 2 tsp chili powder

- 3 large tomatoes, diced
- 2 cups bread, cubed
- 2 tbsp olive oil
- 2 tbsp horseradish, finely grated
- 1 cucumber, chopped
- 1 red onion, thinly sliced

Direction:
- First, mix the chili powder with salt, pepper, and brown sugar in a bowl
- Sauté the bread cubes with oil in a skillet for 10 minutes until golden.
- Take a small bowl and mix horseradish with mustard and salad dressing.
- Prepare and preheat the air fryer to 400°F.
- Once it is preheated, open the lid and place the Steaks on the grill.
- Cover the air fryer lid and let it grill in the "Grilling Mode" for 4 minutes.
- Flip the steak and continue grilling for another 4 minutes.
- Toss the sautéed bread cubes with the rest of the ingredients and dressing mix in a salad bowl.
- Slice the grilled steak and serve on top of the salad.
- Enjoy.

423. Paprika-Cumin Beef Brisket

Preparation Time: 20 minutes
Cooking Time: 2 hrs.
Servings: 10

Ingredients:
- ¼ tsp cayenne pepper
- 1 ½ tbsp paprika
- 1 tsp garlic powder
- 1 tsp ground cumin
- 1 tsp onion powder
- 2 tsp dry mustard
- 2 tsp ground black pepper
- 2 tsp salt
- 5 pounds brisket roast
- 5 tbsp olive oil

Directions:
- Place all ingredients in a ziplock bag and allow to marinate in the fridge for at least 2 hours.
- Remove the grill grate from the unit. Select bake set the temperature to 350°F and set the time to 30 minutes. Select start/stop to begin preheating and cook for 2 hours at 350°F.

424. Beef Hamburger Casserole

Preparation Time: 30 minutes
Cooking Time: 35 minutes
Servings: 10

Ingredients:
- 1 tbsp of olive oil
- 2 pounds hamburger, ground
- 2 cups eggplant, cleaved
- Salt and dark pepper to the taste
- 2 tsp mustard
- 2 tsp gluten-free Worcestershire sauce
- 28 ounces canned tomatoes, cleaved

- 2 cups mozzarella, ground
- 16 ounces tomato sauce
- 2 tbsp parsley, cleaved
- 1 tsp oregano, dried

Directions:

- In a bowl, blend eggplant in with salt, pepper, and oil, and hurl to cover.
- In another bowl, blend meat in with salt, pepper, mustard, and Worcestershire sauce, mix well, and spread on the base of a skillet that accommodates the air fryer cooker.
- Add eggplant blend, tomatoes, tomato sauce, parsley, oregano, and sprinkle mozzarella toward the end.
- Introduce in the air fryer cooker and cook at 360 °F for about 35 minutes
- Divide among plates and serve hot.

425. Pesto Lamb Ribs

Preparation Time: 60 minutes
Cooking Time: 45 minutes
Servings: 8

Ingredients:

- 1 cup parsley
- 1 cup mint
- 1 little yellow onion, generally slashed
- 1/3 cup pistachios, hacked
- 1 tsp lemon pizzazz, ground
- 5 tbsp olive oil
- Salt and dark pepper to the taste
- 2 pounds lamb riblets
- ½ onion, slashed
- 5 garlic cloves, minced
- Juice from 1 orange

Directions:

- In your food processor, blend parsley with mint, onion, pistachios, lemon pizzazz, salt, pepper, and oil, and mix quite well.
- Rub lamb with this blend, place in a bowl, spread, and leave in the refrigerator for 60 minutes.
- Transfer lamb to a preparing dish that accommodates the air fryer cooker; likewise, include garlic, sprinkle squeezed orange, and cook in the air fryer cooker at 300 °F for about 45 minutes.
- Divide lamb into plates and serve.

426. Oriental Lamb Shoulder

Preparation Time: 20 minutes
Cooking Time: 40 minutes
Servings: 8

Ingredients:

- 2 and ½ pounds lamb shoulder, slashed
- 3 tbsp honey
- 2 ounces almonds, stripped and slashed
- 9 ounces plumps, pitted
- 8 ounces of veggie stock
- 2 yellow onions, slashed
- 2 garlic cloves, minced
- Salt and dark pepper to the preferences
- 1 tsp cumin powder
- 1 tsp of the turmeric powder,

- 1 tsp of ginger powder
- 1 tsp cinnamon powder
- 3 tbsp olive oil

Directions:

- In a bowl, blend the cinnamon powder with ginger, cumin, turmeric, garlic, olive oil, and lamb, hurl to cover, place in your preheated air fryer and cook at 350 °F for about 8 minutes.
- Transfer meat to a dish that accommodates the air fryer cooker, including onions, stock, honey, and plums, mix, present in the air fryer cooker, and cook at 350 °F for about 35 minutes.
- Divide everything among plates and present with almonds sprinkled on top.
- Enjoy the recipe!

427. Marinated Rib Eye Steak

Preparation Time: 10 minutes
Cooking Time: 20 minutes
Servings: 4

Ingredients:

- 2 pounds rib-eye steak
- Salt and dark pepper to the taste
- 1 tbsp olive oil
- For the rib:
- 3 tbsp sweet paprika
- 2 tbsp onion powder
- 2 tbsp garlic powder
- 1 tbsp dark colored sugar
- 2 tbsp oregano, dried
- 1 tbsp cumin, ground
- 1 tbsp rosemary, dried

Directions:

- In a bowl, blend paprika in with the onion and garlic powder, sugar, oregano, rosemary, salt, pepper, and cumin; mix and rub steak with this blend.
- Season steak with salt and pepper, rub again with the oil, put in the air fryer cooker, and cook at 400 °F for about 20 minutes, flipping them midway.
- Transfer steak to a cutting board, cut, and present with a side plate of mixed greens. Enjoy the recipe

428. Beef, Carrot and Herbs Meatballs

Preparation Time: 10 minutes
Cooking Time: 20 minutes
Servings: 8

Ingredients:

- 1-pound ground beef
- 2 carrots
- 1 red onion, peeled and chopped
- 2 cloves garlic
- 1/2 tsp dried rosemary, crushed
- 1/2 tsp dried basil
- 1 tsp dried oregano
- 1 egg
- 3/4 cup breadcrumbs
- 1/2 tsp salt
- 1/2 tsp black pepper, or to taste
- 1 cup plain flour

Directions:

- Place ground beef in a large bowl. In a food processor, pulse the carrot, onion, and garlic; transfer the vegetable mixture to a large-sized bowl.
- Then, add the rosemary, basil, oregano, egg, breadcrumbs, salt, and black pepper.
- Shape the mixture into even balls; refrigerate for about 30 minutes. Roll the balls into the flour.
- Pour the balls into the Oven rack/basket. Place the rack on the middle shelf of the Cuisinart Air Fryer Oven. Set temperature to 350°F, and set time to 20 minutes, turning occasionally; work with batches. Serve with toothpicks.

429. Beef Bolognese Sauce

Preparation Time: 10 minutes
Cooking Time: 30 minutes
Servings: 2

Ingredients:

- 13 Oz Ground Beef
- 1 Carrot
- 1 Stalk of Celery
- 10 oz. Diced Tomatoes
- 1/2 Onion
- Salt and Pepper to taste

Directions:

- Preheat Air Fryer to 390°F.
- Finely dice the carrot, celery, and onions. Place into the oven-safe bowl along with the ground beef and combine well
- Place the bowl into the Air Fryer tray and cook for 12 minutes until browned.
- Pour the diced tomatoes into the bowl and replace them in the air fryer.
- Season with salt and pepper, then cook for another 18 minutes
- Serve over cooked pasta or freeze for later use.

430. Beef Taco Fried Egg Rolls

Preparation Time: 10 minutes
Cooking Time: 12 minutes
Servings: 8

Ingredients:

- 1 tsp. cilantro
- 2 chopped garlic cloves
- 1 tbsp. olive oil
- 1 C. shredded Mexican cheese
- ½ packet taco seasoning
- ½ can cilantro lime rotel
- ½ chopped onion
- 16 egg roll wrappers
- 1-pound lean ground beef

Directions:

- Ensure that your Air Fryer is preheated to 400°F.
- Add onions and garlic to a skillet, cooking till fragrant. Then add taco seasoning, pepper, salt, and beef, cooking till beef is broken up into tiny pieces and cooked thoroughly.
- Add Rotel and stir well.

- Layout egg wrappers and brush with water to soften a bit.
- Load wrappers with beef filling and add cheese to each.
- Fold diagonally to close and use water to secure edges.
- Brush-filled egg wrappers with olive oil and add to the air fryer.
- Pour into the Oven rack/basket. Place the rack on the middle shelf of the Air Fryer. Set temperature to 400°F, and set time to 8 minutes. Cook 8 minutes, flip, and cook another 4 minutes.
- Served sprinkled with cilantro.

431. Moroccan Lamb Balls

Preparation Time: 15 minutes
Cooking Time: 15 minutes
Servings: 6

Ingredients:

- 1 tsp cumin seeds
- 1 tsp coriander seeds
- 1 garlic clove, sliced
- 12 oz. ground lamb
- 2 tbsp fresh lemon juice
- 1 egg
- 1 tsp dried mint
- 2 tbsp heavy cream

Directions:

- Combine the ground lamb and sliced garlic in a bowl.
- Sprinkle the meat mixture with the coriander seeds and cumin seeds.
- Coat the ground lamb with fresh lemon juice and dried mint.
- Stir the ground lamb mixed with a fork.
- Crack the egg into the mixture.
- Stir well.
- Preheat the air fryer 360°F.
- Make the meatballs from the lamb mixture and place them in the air fryer.
- Cook for 8 minutes.
- Drizzle the lamb balls with the heavy cream and cook for 6 minutes.
- Place a cocktail stick in every lamb ball and serve them.

432. Delicious Beef Tips

Preparation Time: 15 minutes
Cooking Time: 10 minutes
Servings: 2

Ingredients:

- 1-pound top round beef, cut into 1½-inch cubes
- ½ yellow onion, chopped
- 2 tbsp Worcestershire sauce
- 1 tbsp avocado oil
- 1 tsp onion powder
- 1 tsp garlic powder
- Salt and ground black pepper, as required

Directions:

- In a bowl, mix together the beef tips, onion, Worcestershire sauce, oil, and spices.
- Set the temperature of the Air Fryer to 360 °F. Grease an Air Fryer basket.

- Arrange the beef mixture into the prepared Air Fryer basket.
- Air Fry for about 8-10 minutes.
- Remove from Air Fryer and transfer the steak mixture onto serving plates.
- Serve hot.

433.   Beef BBQ Cubes with Onions

Preparation Time: 15 minutes
Cooking Time: 40 minutes
Servings: 4

Ingredients:

- 1 cup red onions, cut into wedges
- 1 tbsp dry mustard
- 1 tbsp olive oil
- 1-pound boneless beef sirloin, cut into cubes
- Salt and pepper to taste

Directions:

- Preheat the air fryer to 390°F.
- Place the grill pan accessory in the air fryer.
- Toss all ingredients in a bowl and mix until everything is coated with the seasonings.
- Place on the grill pan and cook for 40 minutes.
- Halfway through the cooking time, give a stir to cook evenly.

434.   Beef Spanish Casserole

Preparation Time: 15 minutes
Cooking Time: 50 minutes
Servings: 4

Ingredients:

- 2 tbsp chopped green bell pepper
- 1 tbsp chopped fresh cilantro
- 1/2-pound lean ground beef
- 1/2 cup water
- 1/2 tsp salt
- 1/2 tsp brown sugar
- 1/2 pinch ground black pepper
- 1/3 cup uncooked long-grain rice
- 1/4 cup finely chopped onion
- 1/4 cup chile sauce
- 1/4 tsp ground cumin
- 1/4 tsp Worcestershire sauce
- 1/4 cup shredded Cheddar cheese
- 1/2 (14.5 ounces) of canned tomatoes

Directions:

- Lightly grease the baking pan of the air fryer with cooking spray. Add ground beef.
- For 10 minutes, cook at 360°F. Halfway through cooking time, stir and crumble beef. Discard excess fat,
- Stir in pepper, Worcestershire sauce, cumin, brown sugar, salt, chile sauce, rice, water, tomatoes, green bell pepper, and onion. Mix well. Cover pan with foil and cook for 25 minutes. Stirring occasionally.
- Give it one last good stir, press down firmly, and sprinkle cheese on top.
- Cook uncovered for 15 minutes at 390°F until tops are lightly browned.
- Serve and enjoy with chopped cilantro.

435.   Turkish Lamb Liver

Preparation Time: 20 minutes
Cooking Time: 30 minutes
Servings: 4

Ingredients:

- 1 pound of fresh, deveined young lamb's liver
- 1 tsp of salt
- 1 tsp of black pepper
- 6 tbsp of flour
- ½ tsp of paprika
- 4 tbsp of butter
- ⅓ cup of olive oil
- 1 peeled, sliced and quartered red onion
- 1 tsp of sumac
- ⅓ cup of chopped fresh Italian parsley

Directions:

- First, prepare the liver by cutting it into dice-size cubes.
- Add the liver cubes to a colander, and under very cold running water, wash away any blood.
- Set the liver to one side to drain for 2-3 minutes. Turn the drained meat out onto a kitchen paper towel to absorb any excess moisture.
- In a clean resealable bag, combine the salt with the pepper, flour, and paprika. Seal and shake the bag gently to combine.
- Add the liver to the bag and shake to evenly coat.
- In an oven-safe bowl, melt the butter.
- When the butter is hot, add the floured cubes of the liver to the pan and set the air fryer at 400°F, and cook. Using a wooden spoon, make sure all of the cubes have even contact with the oil.
- When one side of each cube of meat is browned, turn them over and brown on the other side. Take care not to be too vigorous, or you may cause them to lose some of their coatings.
- While the liver cooks, add the red onion to the sumac and parsley and toss to coat. Season with salt.
- Spoon the liver on top of the red onion mixture and serve.

436.   Wine Roasted Beef

Preparation Time: 10 minutes
Cooking Time: 48 minutes
Servings: 5-6

Ingredients:

- 2 celery stalks, chopped
- 1 bell pepper, chopped
- 2 tbsp olive oil
- 2 tbsp Italian seasoning
- 2 ½ pounds beef roast
- 1 onion, sliced
- 2 garlic cloves, sliced
- 1 cup red wine
- 1 cup beef broth
- 2 tbsp steak sauce, sugar-free

Directions:

- Take your Air fryer; open the top lid. Plug it and turn it on.
- Press the "sauté" setting, and the pot will start heating up.

- In the cooking pot area, add the meat and half of the oil. Stir and cook at 375°F for 4-5 minutes until evenly brown from all sides.
- Set aside on a plate.
- Heat the remaining olive oil and add the onions, celery, and peppers. Cook at 300°F for 3 minutes to soften.
- Stir in the garlic and seasonings and cook for 1 minute. Return the beef to the pot.
- Add the broth, sauce, and red wine; whisk the mixture.
- Close the top lid and seal its valve.
- Press the "MANUAL" setting. Adjust cooking time to 40 minutes.
- Allow the recipe to cook for the set cooking time at 375°F.
- After the set cooking time ends, press "CANCEL" and then press "NPR (Natural Pressure Release)."
- The air fryer will slowly and naturally release the pressure.
- Open the top lid, and add the cooked recipe mix to the serving plates. Serve and enjoy!

437.   Holiday Beef Roast

Preparation Time: 10 minutes
Cooking Time: 8 hours
Servings: 2

Ingredients:
- 1-pound bottom round roast
- 1/2 tsp oregano, dried
- 1/2 tsp rosemary, crushed
- 1/2 tsp fennel seed
- 1 tsp garlic, sliced
- 1/4 cup water
- 1/4 cup onions, caramelized
- 1/2 tsp pepper
- 1/4 tsp salt

Directions:
- In a bowl, combine together rosemary, fennel seeds, pepper, oregano, and salt.
- Rub rosemary mixture all over meat and place in the refrigerator for 30 minutes.
- Place marinated roast into the inner pot of the air fryer duo crisp and top with garlic, onions, and water.
- Seal the pot with a pressure cooking lid and select slow cook mode and cook on low for 8 hours at 200°F.
- Remove roast from pot and slice.
- Serve and enjoy.

438.   Russian Beef Gratin

Preparation Time: 10 minutes
Cooking Time: 60 minutes
Serving: 6

Ingredients:
- 1 (2 pounds) beef tenderloin
- Salt and ground black pepper to taste
- 2 onions, sliced
- 1 1/2 cups Cheddar cheese, grated
- 1 cup milk
- 3 tbsp mayonnaise

Directions:
- Slice the beef into thick slices and pound them with a mallet.
- Place these pounded slices in the Air fryer Duo's pan.
- Top these slices with onion, salt, black pepper, cheese, milk, and mayonnaise.
- Put on the Air Fryer lid and seal it.
- Hit the "Bake Button" and select 60 minutes of cooking time at 350°F, then press "Start."
- Crush the crackers and mix them well with 4 tbsp melted butter.
- Once the Air fryer Duo beeps, remove its lid. Serve.

439.   Steak A La Mushrooms

Preparation Time: 10 minutes
Cooking Time: 18 minutes
Serving: 2

Ingredients:
- 1-pound Steaks, cubed
- 8 ounces of Mushrooms washed and halved
- 2 tbsp butter, melted
- 1 tsp Worcestershire sauce
- 1/2 tsp garlic powder, optional
- Salt, to taste
- Fresh cracked black pepper, to taste
- Minced parsley, garnish

Directions:
- Toss the steak cubes with mushrooms, melted butter, garlic powder, salt, black, Worcestershire sauce, black pepper, and salt in a bowl.
- Place the Air Fryer Basket in the Air fryer Duo.
- Spread the steak cubes and mushrooms in the basket.
- Put on the Air frying lid and seal it.
- Hit the "Air fryer Button" and select 18 minutes of cooking time at 325°F, then press "Start."
- Once the Air fryer Duo beeps, remove its lid.
- Garnish with parsley. Serve.

440.   Smoked Crispy Ribs

Preparation Time: 10 minutes
Cooking Time: 50 minutes
Serving: 2

Ingredients:
- 1 rack of pork ribs
- Rub
- 1 1/2 cup broth
- 3 tbsp Liquid Smoke
- 1 cup Barbecue Sauce

Directions:
- Rub the rib rack with spice rub generously.
- Pour the liquid into the Air fryer Duo Crisp.
- Set an Air Fryer Basket into the Pot and place the rib rack in the basket.
- Put on the pressure-cooking lid and seal it.
- Hit the "Pressure Button" and select 30 minutes of cooking time 350°F, then press "Start."
- Once the Air fryer Duo beeps, do a quick release and remove its lid.
- Remove the ribs and rub them with barbecue sauce.
- Empty the pot and place the Air Fryer Basket in it.

- Set the ribs in the basket and Air fry them for 20 minutes. Serve.

441.   Moroccan Beef Roast

Preparation Time: 10 minutes
Cooking Time: 10 hours
Servings: 4

Ingredients:
- 2 lbs. beef roast
- ½ cup sliced yellow onions
- 1 tbsp Olive oil
- Pepper and salt as desired
- 4 tbsp. garam masala seasoning

Directions:
- Preheat the air fryer to 390 °F.
- On a plate, mix the oil, salt, and pepper.
- Using paper towels, pat the beef roast dry. Place the beef roast on a platter and flip to coat the exterior with the oil-herb mixture.
- Peel the onion in half, then place the onion halves in the air fryer basket.
- In the air fryer basket, place the beef roast.
- Set the timer for 5 minutes to air-fry the steak.
- When the timer goes off, change the temperature to 360°F. If your air fryer requires it, flip the beef roast halfway through cooking time.
- Cook the beef for 30 minutes more. Check it early and cook it for another 5 minutes if you like it more done.
- Remove the beef from the air fryer, cover with foil, and set aside for at least ten minutes before serving.
- Serve the roast meat thinly sliced.

442.   Basic Taco Meat

Preparation Time: 5 minutes
Cooking Time: 10 minutes
Servings: 8

Ingredients:
- 2 pounds of ground beef
- ½ of a cup of diced onion
- ½ of a cup of diced bell pepper
- 1 cup of tomato sauce (unsalted)
- 3 tbsp of taco seasoning

Directions:
- Put the meat inside your cooker and set it to sauté at 325°F. Brown the meat thoroughly and turn off the sautéing.
- Add the rest of the ingredients to the meat and stir them together.
- Using the manual setting, set the timer for 8 minutes.
- After the beep, you can either release the pressure quickly or let it release naturally. Serve with the garnishes of your choice, for example, over some cauliflower rice.

443.   Tangy Beef Steak

Preparation Time: 5 minutes
Cooking Time: 40 minutes
Servings: 4

Ingredients:
- 4 medium beef steaks
- 3 garlic cloves; minced
- 1 cup balsamic vinegar
- 2 tbsp. olive oil
- Salt and black pepper to taste.

Directions:
- Take a bowl and mix steaks with the rest of the ingredients and toss.
- Transfer the steaks to your air fryer's basket and cook at 390°F for 35 minutes, flipping them halfway
- Divide among plates and serve with a side salad.

444.   Ginger-Orange Beef Strips

Preparation Time: 5 minutes
Cooking Time: 25 minutes
Servings: 3

Ingredients:
- 1 ½ pound stir fry steak slices
- 1 ½ tsp sesame oil
- One navel orange, segmented
- One tbsp olive oil
- One tbsp rice vinegar
- One tsp grated ginger
- Two scallions, chopped
- Three cloves of garlic, minced
- Three tbsp molasses
- Three tbsp soy sauce
- Six tbsp cornstarch

Directions:
- Preheat the air fryer to 330°F.
- Season the steak slices with soy sauce and dust with cornstarch.
- Place in the air fryer basket and cook for 25 minutes.
- Meanwhile, place in the skillet oil and heat over medium flame.
- Sauté the garlic and ginger until fragrant.
- Stir in the oranges, molasses, and rice vinegar. Season with salt and pepper to taste.
- Once the meat is cooked, place it in the skillet and stir to coat the sauce.
- Drizzle with oil and garnish with scallions

445.   Hungarian Beef Goulash

Preparation Time: 20 minutes
Cooking Time: 1 hr.
Servings: 6-8

Ingredients:
- Sea salt and cracked black pepper, to taste
- 1 tsp Hungarian paprika
- 1 ½ pound beef chuck roast, boneless, cut into bite-sized cubes
- 2 tsp sunflower oil
- 1 medium-sized leek, chopped
- 2 garlic cloves, minced
- 2 bay leaves
- 1 tsp caraway seeds.
- 2 cups roasted vegetable broth
- 1 ripe tomato, pureed
- 2 tbsp red wine

- 2 bell peppers, chopped
- 1 celery stalk, peeled and diced

Directions:

- Add the salt, black pepper, Hungarian paprika, and beef to a resealable bag; shake to coat well. Heat the oil in a Dutch oven over a medium-high flame; sauté the leeks, garlic, bay leaves, and caraway seeds for about 4 minutes or until fragrant. Transfer to a lightly greased baking pan. Then, brown the beef, occasionally stirring, working in batches. Add to the baking pan.
- Add the vegetable broth, tomato, and red wine. Lower the pan onto the Air Fryer basket. Bake at 325 °F for 40 minutes. Add the bell peppers and celery. Cook an additional 20 minutes. Serve immediately and enjoy!

446.   Cheesy Beef Enchiladas

Preparation Time: 20 minutes
Cooking Time: 5-10 minutes
Servings: 4

Ingredients:

- 1 lb. Ground Beef
- 2 tbsp Taco Seasoning
- 8 pcs corn or flour Tortillas
- 1 cup of black beans ins a can
- 1 ½ cup diced tomatoes
- 1 /3 cup green chilies in the can, chopped
- 1 ½ cup enchilada sauce
- 1 ½ Mexican Cheese
- ½ Cup Chopped Cilantro
- 1/2 Cup Sour Cream

Directions:

- Begin by browning the ground beef in a medium-sized skillet, and Add in the taco seasoning
- Stuff each tortilla by adding beef, beans, tomatoes, and chilies.
- Line the basket with foil and place each one inside the air fryer basket.
- When all the enchiladas are done, pour the enchilada sauce evenly over them.
- Then add the cheese on top.
- Cook at 350°F for 5 Minutes.
- Remove and add toppings, and serve.

447.   Lamb with Madeira Sauce

Preparation Time: 20 minutes
Cooking Time: 35 minutes
Servings: 12

Ingredients:

- 1 cup seasoned flour
- 3 tbsp sherry vinegar
- 1 tbsp tomato paste
- Salt and black pepper, to taste
- 24 small lamb ribs
- 1/2 tsp chili sauce
- 1 tsp cayenne pepper powder
- 1 tbsp soy sauce
- 1 tbsp brown sugar
- FOR THE MADEIRA SAUCE:
- 2 tbsp plain flour
- 1 medium onion, chopped

- 2 tbsp unsalted butter
- 1 cup beef stock
- Salt and black pepper, to taste
- 1 cup Madeira

Directions:

- Fill a bowl with 1 cup seasoned flour, put the ribs inside it, and mix thoroughly
- In another medium bowl, mix together the tomato paste, soy sauce, chili sauce, sugar, cayenne pepper, and sherry vinegar
- Then Dip the ribs with flour in this marinade and put it in the refrigerate for at least 20 minutes
- Take it out and put it in the air fryer, air fry at 350°F for 15 minutes, check and flip over the ribs 10 minutes through cooking time to cook equally.
- FOR THE SAUCE:
- Add butter and onion to a pan and cook on a medium heat
- Then pour the flour and beef stock inside it; Cook for 5 minutes on a low heat
- Then add the Madeira and continue to cook for about 4 minutes a 350°F.
- Serve the ribs and Madeira sauce

448.   Suya-spiced Flank Steak

Preparation Time: 20 minutes
Cooking Time: 25-30 minutes
Servings: 3

Ingredients:

- For the Suya Spice Mix
- ¼ cup dry-roasted peanuts
- 1 tsp cumin seeds
- 1 tsp garlic powder
- 1 tsp smoked paprika
- ½ tsp ground ginger
- 1 tsp kosher salt
- ½ tsp cayenne pepper
- For the Steak
- 1 pound flank steak
- **2 tbsp vegetable oil**

Directions:

- For the spice mix: In a clean coffee grinder or spice mill, combine the peanuts and cumin seeds. Process until you get a coarse powder. (Do not overprocess, or you will wind up with peanut butter! Alternatively, you can grind the cumin with ⅓ cup of ready-made peanut powder)
- Pour the peanut mixture into a small bowl, add the garlic powder, paprika, ginger, salt, and cayenne, and stir to combine. This recipe makes about ½ cup suya spice mix.
- For the steak: Cut the flank steak into ½-inch-thick slices, cutting against the grain and at a slight angle. Place the beef strips in a resealable plastic bag and add the oil and 2½ to 3 tbsp of the spice mixture. Massage to coat all of the meat with the oil and spice mixture. Then, marinate it
- The beef strips will be placed in the air fryer basket. Set the air fryer to 400°F for 8 minutes, turning the strips halfway through the cooking time.
- Transfer the meat to a serving platter. Sprinkle with additional spice mix, if desired.

449. Kheema Burgers

Preparation Time: 20 minutes
Cooking Time: 25-30 minutes
Servings: 4

Ingredients:

- 1 pound 85% lean ground beef or ground lamb
- 2 large eggs, lightly beaten
- 1 medium yellow onion, diced
- ¼ cup chopped fresh cilantro
- 1 tbsp minced fresh ginger
- 3 cloves garlic, minced
- 2 tsp Garam Masala
- 1 tsp ground turmeric
- ½ tsp ground cinnamon
- ⅛ tsp ground cardamom
- 1 tsp kosher salt
- 1 tsp cayenne pepper
- For the Raita Sauce
- 1 cup grated cucumber
- ½ cup sour cream
- ¼ tsp kosher salt
- ¼ tsp black pepper
- For Serving
- 4 lettuce leaves, hamburger buns, or naan bread

Directions:

- In a container, combine the ground beef, eggs, onion, cilantro, ginger, garlic, garam masala, turmeric, cinnamon, cardamom, salt, and cayenne. Gently mix until ingredients are thoroughly combined. Divide into four portions and make them into round patties. Make a slight depression in the middle of each patty with your thumb to prevent them from puffing up into a dome shape while cooking.
- Place the patties in the air fryer basket. Set the air fryer to 350°F for 12 minutes

450. Swedish Meatloaf

Preparation Time: 20 minutes
Cooking Time: 25-30 minutes
Servings: 8

Ingredients:

- 1½ pounds of ground beef (85% lean)
- ¼ pound ground pork or ground beef
- 1 large egg (omit for egg-free)
- ½ cup minced onions
- ¼ cup tomato sauce
- 2 tbsp dry mustard
- 2 cloves garlic, minced
- 2 tsp fine sea salt
- 1 tsp ground black pepper
- SAUCE:
- ½ cup (1 stick) unsalted butter
- ½ cup shredded Swiss or mild cheddar cheese (about 2 ounces)
- 2 ounces cream cheese (¼ cup), softened
- ⅓ cup beef broth
- ⅛ tsp ground nutmeg
- Halved cherry tomatoes for serving (optional)

Directions:

- Preheat the air fryer to 390°F.
- In a container, combine the ground beef, ground pork, egg, onions, tomato sauce, dry mustard, garlic, salt, and pepper. Using your hands, mix until well combined.
- Place the meatloaf mixture in a 9 by 5-inch loaf pan and place it in the air fryer. Cook for 35 minutes, or until cooked through and the internal temperature reaches 145°F. Check the meatloaf after 25 minutes; if it's getting too brown on the top, cover it loosely with foil to prevent burning.
- While the meatloaf cooks, make the sauce: Heat the butter in a saucepan over medium-high heat until it sizzles and brown flecks appear, constantly stirring to keep the butter from burning. Whisk in the Swiss cheese, cream cheese, broth, and nutmeg. Simmer for at least 10 minutes. When the meatloaf is done, transfer it to a serving tray and pour the sauce over it. Garnish with ground black pepper and serve with cherry tomatoes, if desired. Allow the meatloaf to rest for 10 minutes before slicing, so it doesn't crumble apart.

451. Swedish Meatballs

Preparation Time: 10 minutes
Cooking Time: 15 minutes
Servings: 4

Ingredients:

- For the meatballs
- 1 pound 93% lean ground beef
- 1 (1-ounce) packet Lipton Onion Recipe Soup & Dip Mix
- ⅓ cup bread crumbs
- 1 egg, beaten
- Salt
- Pepper
- For the gravy
- 1 cup beef broth
- ⅓ cup heavy cream
- 3 tbsp all-purpose flour

Directions:

- In a bowl, put in all ingredients and mix the ground beef, onion soup mix, bread crumbs, egg, and salt and pepper to taste. Mix thoroughly.
- Using 2 tbsp of the meat mixture, create each meatball by rolling the beef mixture around in your hands. This should yield about 10 meatballs.
- Place the meatballs in the Air Fryer. It is okay to stack them. Close the air fryer lid and cook for 14 minutes at 375°F. While the meatballs cook, prepare the gravy. Heat a saucepan over medium-high heat. Add the beef broth and heavy cream.
- Stir for 1 to 2 minutes. Add the flour and stir. Cover the pan and let it simmer for 3 to 4 minutes, or until thick. Drizzle the gravy over the meatballs and serve.

452. Hanger Steak in Mole Rub

Preparation Time: 15 minutes
Cooking Time: 1 hr.
Servings: 2

Ingredients:
- 1 tbsp ground black pepper
- 2 hanger steaks
- 2 tbsp coriander seeds
- 2 tbsp ground coffee
- 2 tbsp olive oil
- 2 tbsp salt
- 4 tsp unsweetened cocoa powder
- 4 tsp brown sugar

Directions:
- Preheat the air fryer to 390°F.
- Place the grill pan accessory in the air fryer. In a bowl, make the spice rub by combining the coriander seeds, ground coffee, salt, brown sugar, cocoa powder, and black pepper.
- Rub the steaks with the spice mixture and brush with oil. Grill for 30 minutes, and make sure to flip the meat every 10 minutes for even grilling and cook in batches.

CHAPTER 5: PORK

453. Mexican Pork Carnitas

Preparation Time: 20 minutes
Cooking Time: 35-40 minutes
Servings: 12

Ingredients:

- 3 lb. skinless, boneless pork shoulder, chopped into 2-inch chunks
- 1 1/2 cup orange juice
- 1 tsp. ground cumin
- 1 cinnamon stick
- 1 tbsp. dried oregano
- 1/2 tsp. ground cloves
- 2 1/2 tsp. kosher salt
- 12 tortillas
- 2 tsp. ancho chili powder
- 1 onion, quartered
- 3 jalapeños, halved
- 6 cloves garlic
- 2 tsp. black pepper

Directions:

- Put all ingredients except tortillas into the Air fryer.
- Cook at 400°F for 35 minutes.
- Discard spices.
- Shred meat.
- Pour ¾ cup of cooking liquid over the pork.
- Broil until deeply browned in spots.
- Serve with tortillas, thinly sliced cabbage, pickled red onion, sour cream, and hot sauce.

454. Chinese Char Siu

Preparation Time: 20 minutes
Cooking Time: 1 hr. 15 minutes
Servings: 10

Ingredients:
- 1/2 cup honey
- 1/2 cup hoisin sauce
- 1/4 cup soy sauce
- 1/4 cup ketchup
- 4 garlic cloves, minced
- 4 tsp. minced fresh gingerroot
- 1 tsp. Chinese five-spice powder
- 1 boneless pork shoulder butt roast
- 1/2 cup chicken broth
- ½ cup fresh cilantro leaves

Directions:
- Marinate chicken with the first 7 ingredients into a large shallow dish.
- Transfer pork, chicken broth, and marinade to the Air fryer.
- Adjust pressure-400°F for 75 minutes.
- Shred meat using 2 forks.
- Skim fat from cooking juices.
- Return pork to pressure cooker.
- Select Sauté on Low.
- Top pork with fresh cilantro and serve.

455. Country Style Ribs

Preparation Time: 10 minutes
Cooking Time: 15-20 minutes
Servings: 4

Ingredients:
- 4 country-style pork ribs, trimmed of excess fat
- Salt and black pepper to taste
- 1 tsp dried marjoram
- 1 tsp garlic powder
- 1 tsp thyme
- 2 tsp dry mustard
- 3 tbsp coconut oil
- 3 tbsp cornstarch

Directions:
- Preheat the air fryer to 400°F for 2 minutes. Place ingredients in a bowl, except pork ribs. Soak the ribs in the mixture and rub them in. Place the ribs into the air fryer for 12-minutes. Serve and enjoy!

456. Crispy Pork Chops

Preparation Time: 15 minutes
Cooking Time: 15-20 minutes
Servings: 2

Ingredients:
- 2 pork chops
- ½ cup breadcrumbs
- 1 tbsp olive oil
- 1 egg, beaten
- 1 tbsp almond flour
- Salt and pepper to taste

Directions:
- Season pork chops with salt and pepper. Add flour to the mixing bowl. In another small bowl, add beaten egg. In a third bowl, combine breadcrumbs with olive oil. Coat the pork chops with flour, dip in egg, and coat with breadcrumbs. Place chops into an air fryer basket and cook at 400°F for 10-minutes. Flip chops over and cook on the other side for an additional 5-minutes. Serve warm.

457. Jamaican Meatballs

Preparation Time: 20 minutes
Cooking Time: 20 minutes
Servings: 4

Ingredients:
- 2 tbsp Jerk Dry Rub
- 100g minced chicken
- 100g breadcrumbs
- 4 tbsp raw honey
- 1 tbsp soy sauce

Directions:
- In a bowl, place chicken and add breadcrumbs and 1 tbsp Jerk dry rub seasoning. Mix properly and press into meatball shapes using a meatball press.
- Place in the air fryer and cook at 180°C for 15 minutes.
- In a mixing bowl, combine soy sauce, honey, and remaining jerk seasoning and mix well.
- When meatballs are done, dip or, toss them in the sauce and serve.

458. Pork Chops in Lemon Sage Sauce

Preparation Time: 10 minutes
Cooking Time: 15 minutes
Servings: 2

Ingredients:
- 2 pork chops
- Salt and black pepper to the taste
- 1 tbsp olive oil
- 2 tbsp butter
- 1 shallot, sliced
- 1 handful sage, chopped
- 1 tsp lemon juice

Directions:
- Season pork chops with salt and pepper, rub with the oil, put in your air fryer, and cook at 370 °F for 10 minutes, flipping them halfway. Meanwhile, heat up a pan with the butter over medium heat, add shallot, stir and cook for 2 minutes. Add sage and lemon juice, stir well, cook for a few more minutes and take off the heat. Divide pork chops on plates, drizzle the sage sauce all over, and serve. Enjoy!

459. Sweet and Spicy Pork Chops

Preparation Time: 10 minutes
Cooking Time: 15 minutes
Servings: 4

Ingredients:
- 1 tbsp olive oil, plus more for spraying
- 3 tbsp brown sugar

- ½ tsp cayenne pepper
- ½ tsp garlic powder
- ½ tsp salt
- ¼ tsp freshly ground black pepper
- 4 thin boneless pork chops, trimmed of excess fat

Directions:

- Set the temperature to 370°F and spray a fryer basket lightly with olive oil.
- In a small bowl, mix together the brown sugar, 1 tbsp of olive oil, cayenne pepper, garlic powder, salt, and black pepper.
- Coat each pork chop with the marinade, shake them to remove any excess, and place them in the fryer basket in a single layer. You may need to cook them in batches.
- Air fry for 7 minutes. Flip the pork chops over and brush with more marinade. Cook until the chops reach an internal temperature of 145°F, an additional 5 to 8 minutes.

460.   Lime-Chili Pork Tenderloin

Preparation Time: 10 minutes
Cooking Time: 30 minutes
Servings: 4

Ingredients:

- 1 tbsp lime juice
- 1 tbsp olive oil,
- ½ tbsp soy sauce
- ½ tbsp chili powder
- ¼ tbsp minced garlic
- 1-pound boneless pork tenderloin

Directions:

- Set to 370°F. In a large zip-top plastic bag, mix together the lime juice, olive oil, soy sauce, chili powder, and garlic and mix well. Add the pork, seal, and refrigerate for at least 1 hour or overnight.
- Spray a fryer basket lightly with olive oil.
- Shake off any excess marinade from the pork and place it in the fryer basket.
- Air fry for 15 minutes. Flip the tenderloin over and cook until the pork reaches an internal temperature of at least 145°F for an additional 5 minutes. If necessary, continue to cook in 2- to 3-minute intervals until it reaches the proper temperature.
- Let the tenderloin rest for 10 minutes before cutting it into slices and serving.

461.   Parmesan Spiced Pork Chops

Preparation Time: 10 minutes
Cooking Time: 15 minutes
Servings: 4

Ingredients:

- 4 pork chops, boneless
- 4 tbsp parmesan cheese, grated
- 1 cup pork rind
- 2 eggs, lightly beaten
- 1/2 tsp chili powder
- 1/2 tsp onion powder
- 1 tsp paprika
- 1/4 tsp pepper

- 1/2 tsp salt

Directions:

- Preheat the air fryer to 400°F.
- Season pork chops with pepper and salt.
- Add pork rind to food processor and process until crumbs form.
- Mix together pork rind crumbs and seasoning in a large bowl.
- Place egg in a separate bowl.
- Dip pork chops in egg mixture, then coat with pork crumb mixture and place in the air fryer basket.
- Cook pork chops for 12-15 minutes.
- Serve and enjoy.

462.   Pork Chops and Mushrooms

Preparation Time: 10 minutes
Cooking Time: 20 minutes
Servings: 4

Ingredients:

- 1 lb. pork chops, rinsed and pat dry
- 1/2 tsp garlic powder
- 1 tsp soy sauce
- 2 tbsp butter, melted
- 8 oz mushrooms, halved
- Pepper
- Salt

Directions:

- Preheat the air fryer to 400°F.
- Cut pork chops into the 3/4-inch cubes and place them in a large mixing bowl.
- Add remaining ingredients into the bowl and toss well.
- Transfer pork and mushroom mixture into the air fryer basket and cook for 15-18 minutes. Shake basket halfway through.
- Serve and enjoy.

463.   Outback Ribs

Preparation Time: 20 minutes
Cooking Time: 60 minutes
Servings: 6

Ingredients:

- 2 ¼ lb. of pork ribs
- ½ lemon
- 1 cup tomato sauce
- ½ cup dark mustard
- ½ cup of vinegar
- 1 spoon of sugar
- Salt and black pepper to taste.

Directions:

- Spray the basket of the air fryer.
- Place the rib piece in half "folded" so that it fits into the pan.
- On top, place the tomato sauce, mustard, pepper, salt, sugar, and vinegar (or, if you want, replace these spices with a tube of prepared barbecue sauce).
- Add two glasses of water, cover the pan, and cook for about 50 minutes at 400°F.
- Remove from the pressure cooker being careful not to disassemble it.

- Place the piece on a greased baking sheet, drizzle with the sauce, or add more barbecue sauce.
- Place in the air fryer until you have a crispy crust.

464. Mexican Pork Chops

Preparation Time: 15 minutes
Cooking Time: 20 minutes
Servings: 2

Ingredients:
- ¼ tsp. dried oregano
- 1 ½ tsp. taco seasoning mix
- 2 x 4-oz. boneless pork chops
- 2 tbsp. unsalted butter, divided

Directions:
- Combine the dried oregano and taco seasoning to rub into the pork chops.
- In your fryer, cook the chops at 400°F for fifteen minutes, turning them over halfway through to cook on the other side.
- When the chops are a brown color, check the internal temperature has reached 145°F and remove them from the fryer. Serve with a garnish of butter.

465. Chinese Style Meatballs

Preparation Time: 15 minutes
Cooking Time: 20 minutes
Servings: 3

Ingredients:
- 1 egg, beaten
- 6-ounce ground pork
- ¼ cup cornstarch
- 1 tsp oyster sauce
- ½ tbsp light soy sauce
- ½ tsp sesame oil
- ¼ tsp five-spice powder
- ½ tbsp olive oil
- ¼ tsp brown sugar

Directions:
- Preheat the Air fryer to 390°F and grease an Air fryer basket.
- Mix all the ingredients in a bowl except cornstarch and oil until well combined.
- Shape the mixture into equal-sized balls and place the cornstarch in a shallow dish.
- Roll the meatballs evenly into the cornstarch mixture and arrange them in the air fryer basket.
- Cook for about 10 minutes and dish out to serve warm.

466. Chinese Five-Spice Pork Belly

Preparation Time: 15 minutes
Cooking Time: 20 minutes
Servings: 6

Ingredients:
- 1-pound pork belly
- 2 tbsp swerve
- 2 tbsp dark soy sauce
- 1 tbsp Shaoxing: cooking wine
- 2 tsp garlic, minced
- 2 tsp ginger, minced

- 1 tbsp hoisin sauce
- 1 tsp Chinese Five Spice

Directions:
- Preheat the Air fryer to 390°F and grease an Air fryer basket.
- Mix all the ingredients in a bowl and place them in the Ziplock bag.
- Seal the bag, shake it well and refrigerate to marinate for about 1 hour.
- Remove the pork from the bag and arrange it in the air fryer basket.
- Cook for about 15 minutes and dish out in a bowl to serve warm.

467. Vietnamese Pork Chops

Preparation Time: 30 minutes **plus marinating time**
Cooking Time: 15-20 minutes
Servings: 2

Ingredients:
- 1 tbsp. olive oil
- 1 tbsp. fish sauce
- 1 tsp. low-sodium dark soy sauce
- 1 tsp. pepper
- 3 tbsp. lemongrass
- 1 tbsp. chopped shallot
- 1 tbsp. chopped garlic
- 1 tbsp. brown sugar
- 2 pork chops

Directions:
- Add pork chops to a bowl along with olive oil, fish sauce, soy sauce, pepper, lemongrass, shallot, garlic, and brown sugar.
- Marinade pork chops for 2 hours.
- Ensure your air fryer is preheated to 400°F. Add pork chops to the basket.
- Cook for 7 minutes, making sure to flip after 5 minutes of cooking.
- Serve alongside steamed cauliflower rice!

468. Pork Taquitos

Preparation Time: 20 minutes
Cooking Time: 15 minutes
Servings: 5

Ingredients:
- 30 oz. of cooked shredded pork tenderloin
- 2 1/2 cups fat-free shredded mozzarella
- 10 small flour tortillas
- 1 lime, juiced
- Cooking spray
- Salsa for dipping (optional)
- Sour Cream (optional)

Directions:
- The air fryer preheats to 380°F.
- Sprinkle the lime juice over the pork, fry, and stir gently.
- Microwave 5 tortillas for 10 seconds at a time with a wet paper towel over them to soften.
- Then add 3 oz. Of pork, and 1/4 cup for tortilla cheese.

469.   Pork Egg Rolls

Preparation Time: 15 minutes
Cooking Time: 12 minutes
Servings: 12

Ingredients:
- Cooking oil spray
- 2 garlic cloves, minced
- 12 ounces ground pork
- 1 tsp sesame oil
- ¼ cup soy sauce
- 2 tsp grated peeled fresh ginger
- 2 cups shredded green cabbage
- 4 scallions, green parts (white parts optional), chopped
- 24 egg roll wrappers

Directions:
- Spray a skillet with the cooking oil and place it over medium-high heat. Add the garlic and cook for 1 minute until fragrant.
- Add the ground pork to the skillet. Using a spoon, break the pork into smaller chunks.
- In a small bowl, whisk the sesame oil, soy sauce, and ginger until combined. Add the sauce to the skillet. Stir to combine and continue cooking for about 5 minutes until the pork is browned and thoroughly cooked.
- Stir in the cabbage and scallions. Transfer the pork mixture to a large bowl.
- Lay the egg roll wrappers on a flat surface. Dip a basting brush in water and glaze each egg roll wrapper along the edges with the wet brush. This will soften the dough and make it easier to roll.
- Stack 2 egg roll wrappers (it works best if you double-wrap the egg rolls). Scoop 1 to 2 tbsp of the pork mixture into the center of each wrapper stack.
- Roll one long side of the wrappers up over the filling. Press firmly on the area with the filling, tucking it in lightly to secure it in place. Fold in the left and right sides. Continue rolling to close. Use the basting brush to wet the seam and seal the egg roll. Repeat with the remaining ingredients.
- Insert the crisper plate into the basket and the basket into the unit. Preheat the unit by selecting AIR FRY, setting the temperature to 400°F, and setting the time to 3 minutes. Select START/STOP to begin.
- Once the unit is preheated, spray the crisper plate with cooking oil. Place the egg rolls into the basket. It is okay to stack them. Spray them with cooking oil.
- Select AIR FRY, set the temperature to 400°F, and set the time to 12 minutes. Insert the basket into the unit. Select START/STOP to begin.
- After 8 minutes, use tongs to flip the egg rolls. Reinsert the basket to resume cooking.
- When the cooking is complete, serve the egg rolls hot

470.   Pork Fricassee

Preparation Time: 35 minutes
Cooking Time: 70 minutes
Servings: 6

Ingredients:
- 2 tbsp. olive oil
- 500g pork
- 1kg potatoes, chopped
- 1 onion, chopped
- 300g mushrooms
- 1 carrot grated
- 1 clove of garlic
- 1 tbsp. cumin
- salt and pepper to season

Directions:
- Add the oil, onion, and garlic into the inner pot.
- Touch the SAUTÉ/SEAR menu to select SAUTÉ/SEAR HIGH TEMP program, set the cooking time for 10 minutes at 400°F, and press START (Do not close the lid). Stir from time to time.
- After 5 minutes, add the carrot and continue for another 5 minutes.
- Add the meat cut into cubes, seasoning, and salt.
- Close the lid. Touch the MULTI COOK menu to select the STEW/CURRY program, set the cooking time for 35 minutes, and press START. After 15 minutes, add potatoes and mushrooms.

471.   Caramelized Pepper Pork

Preparation Time: 30 minutes
Cooking Time: 40 minutes
Servings: 4

Ingredients:
- 14 shallots chopped finely
- 3 cloves garlic chopped finely
- 45ml fish sauce
- 1 tbsp cracked black pepper
- 800g rindless/boneless pork belly
- 5g brown sugar
- 2 stalks of spring onion

Directions:
- Combine shallots, garlic, fish sauce, pepper, and pork in a bowl.
- Pour oil into the inner pot and touch the SAUTÉ/SEAR menu to select SAUTÉ/SEAR HIGH TEMP program. Set cooking time for 10 minutes at 400°F and press START (Do not close the lid).
- Sear pork until it begins to caramelize. Then add in sugar and water.
- Close lid and cook on SLOW COOK LOW TEMP for 6 hours or touch the PRESSURE COOK menu to select the MEAT/POULTRY program for 15 minutes. Press START.
- Serve with sliced spring onion and steamed rice.

472.   Bacon Carbonara

Preparation Time: 20 minutes
Cooking Time: 40 minutes
Servings: 2

Ingredients:
- 1 tbsp. olive oil
- ½ medium onion, chopped
- 1 garlic clove, crushed
- 100g bacon, chopped
- 180ml double cream
- salt and pepper to season
- 200g spaghetti
- 540ml water

Directions:
- Add the oil, onion, and garlic to the inner pot.
- Touch the SAUTÉ/SEAR menu to select SAUTÉ/SEAR HIGH TEMP program, set the cooking time for 10 minutes, and press START (Do not close the lid). Stir from time to time.
- Break the spaghetti in half and place it into the inner pot with the rest of the ingredients and water. Mix all the ingredients. Close the lid.
- Touch the MULTI COOK menu to select the STEW/CURRY program, set the cooking time for 30 minutes at 400°F, and press START.

473. Country Meatloaf

Preparation Time: 35 minutes
Cooking Time: 30 minutes
Servings: 6

Ingredients:
- 1/2-pound lean minced pork
- 1/3 cup breadcrumbs
- 1/2 tbsp minced green garlic
- 1½ tbsp fresh cilantro, minced
- 1/2 tbsp fish sauce
- 1/3 tsp dried basil
- 2 leeks, chopped
- 2 tbsp tomato puree
- 1/2 tsp dried thyme
- Salt and ground black pepper, to taste

Directions:
- Add all ingredients, except for breadcrumbs, to a large-sized mixing dish and combine everything using your hands.
- Lastly, add the breadcrumbs to form a meatloaf.
- Bake for 23 minutes at 365 °F. Afterward, allow your meatloaf to rest for 10 minutes before slicing and serving. Bon appétit!

474. Pineapple Spareribs

Preparation Time: 15 minutes
Cooking Time: 15 minutes
Servings: 4

Ingredients:
- 2 lb. cut spareribs
- 7 oz salad dressing
- 1 (5-oz) can of pineapple juice
- 2 cups water
- Garlic salt to taste
- Salt and black pepper

Directions:
- Sprinkle the ribs with salt and pepper, and place them in a saucepan. Pour water and cook the ribs for 12 minutes on high heat. Drain the ribs and arrange them in the frying basket; sprinkle with garlic salt. Cook for 15 minutes at 390°F on the Air Fry function. Prepare the sauce by combining the salad dressing and the pineapple juice. Serve the ribs drizzled with the sauce.

475. Pork Neck with Salad

Preparation Time: 10 minutes
Cooking Time: 15-20 minutes
Servings: 2

Ingredients:
- For Pork:
- 1 tbsp soy sauce
- 1 tbsp fish sauce
- ½ tbsp oyster sauce
- ½ pound pork neck
- For Salad:
- 1 ripe tomato, sliced tickly
- 8-10 Thai shallots, sliced
- 1 scallion, chopped
- 1 bunch of fresh basil leaves
- 1 bunch of fresh cilantro leaves
- For Dressing:
- 3 tbsp fish sauce
- 2 tbsp olive oil
- 1 tsp apple cider vinegar
- 1 tbsp palm sugar
- 2 bird eye chilies
- 1 tbsp garlic, minced

Directions:
- For pork in a bowl, mix together all ingredients except pork.
- Add pork neck and coat with marinade evenly. Refrigerate for about 2-3 hours.
- Preheat the Cuisinart Air Fryer Oven to 340°F.
- Place the pork neck onto a grill pan. Cook for about 12 minutes.
- Meanwhile, in a large salad bowl, mix together all salad ingredients.
- In a bowl, add all dressing ingredients and beat till well combined.
- Remove pork neck from the Air fryer and cut into desired slices.
- Place pork slices over salad.

476. Southern Pulled Pork

Preparation Time: 30 minutes
Cooking Time: 35 minutes
Servings: 4

Ingredients:
- ½ Tsp Paprika
- 1 Tsp Black Pepper
- 1 Tbsp Chili Flakes
- 1 Tsp Cayenne Pepper
- 1/3 Cup Cream
- 1 lb. Pork Tenderloin
- 1 Tsp Sea Salt, Fine
- 4 Cups Chicken Stock
- 1 Tsp Thyme, Ground
- 1 Tsp Butter

Directions:
- Place your chicken stock into your air fryer, and then get out your pork. Sprinkle it with black pepper, paprika, cayenne, salt, and chili flakes.
- Heat your air fryer to 370°F, and then cook for 20 minutes.

- Strain your liquid, and then shred your meat.
- Add your butter and cream to the mix, and then cook at 360°F for 4 minutes.
- Allow it to cool before serving.

477. Smoked Ham and Pears

Preparation Time: 20 minutes
Cooking Time: 20 minutes
Servings: 8

Ingredients:
- 15 oz pears, halved
- 8-pound smoked ham
- 1 ½ cups brown sugar
- ¾ tbsp allspice
- 1 tbsp apple cider vinegar
- 1 tsp black pepper
- 1 tsp vanilla extract

Directions:
- Preheat your Air Fryer to 330°F. In a bowl, mix pears, brown sugar, cider vinegar, vanilla extract, pepper, and allspice.
- Place the mixture in a frying pan and fry for 2-3 minutes. Pour the mixture over the ham. Add the ham to the Air Fryer cooking basket and cook for 15 minutes.
- Serve ham with hot sauce to enjoy!

478. Stuffed Pork Chops

Preparation Time: 30 minutes
Cooking Time: 25-30 minutes
Servings: 8

Ingredients:
- 8 pork chops
- ¼ tsp pepper
- 4 cups stuffing mix
- ½ tsp salt
- 2 tbsp olive oil
- 4 garlic cloves, minced
- 2 tbsp sage leaves

Directions:
- Preheat your Air Fryer to 350°F. Cut a hole in pork chops and fill chops with stuffing mix. In a bowl, mix sage leaves, garlic cloves, oil, salt, and pepper. Cover chops with marinade and let marinate for 10 minutes. Place the chops in your Air Fryer's cooking basket and cook for 25 minutes. Serve and enjoy!

479. Pork Sausage Ratatouille

Preparation Time: 40 minutes
Cooking Time: 50 minutes
Servings: 6

Ingredients:
- 4 pork sausages
- For Ratatouille
- 1 pepper, chopped
- 2 zucchinis, chopped
- 1 eggplant, chopped
- 1 medium red onion, chopped
- 1 tbsp olive oil
- 1-ounce butterbean, drained
- 15 oz tomatoes, chopped
- 2 sprigs of fresh thyme
- 1 tbsp balsamic vinegar
- 2 garlic cloves, minced
- 1 red chili, chopped

Directions:
- Preheat your Air Fryer to 392°F. Mix pepper, eggplant, oil, onion, and zucchinis, and add to the cooking basket. Roast for 20 minutes. Set aside to cool. Reduce Air Fryer temperature to 356 F. In a saucepan, mix prepared vegetables and the remaining ratatouille ingredients, and bring to a boil over medium heat.
- Let the mixture simmer for 10 minutes; season with salt and pepper. Add sausages to your Air Fryer's basket and cook for 10-15 minutes. Serve the sausages with ratatouille.

480. Italian Style Pork Chops

Preparation Time: 30 minutes
Cooking Time: 20 minutes
Servings: 4

Ingredients:
- 4 slices of pork chops, sliced
- 2-3 tbsp olive oil
- Salt and black pepper to taste
- 1 whole egg, beaten
- 1 tbsp flour
- Breadcrumbs as needed
- A bunch of Italian herbs

Directions:
- Preheat your Air Fryer to 400°F. Mix oil, salt, and pepper to form a marinade. Place the beaten egg on a plate. On a separate plate, add the breadcrumbs. Add pork to the marinade and allow to rest for 15 minutes.
- Add one slice to the egg and then to the breadcrumbs; repeat with all slices. Place the prepared slices in your Air Fryer's cooking basket and cook for 20 minutes. Season with your desired herbs and serve.

481. Sticky Pork Ribs

Preparation Time: 30 minutes
Cooking Time: 45 minutes
Servings: 6

Ingredients:
- 2 lb. pork ribs
- 2 tbsp char siew sauce
- 2 tbsp minced ginger
- 2 tbsp hoisin sauce
- 2 tbsp sesame oil
- 1 tbsp honey
- 4 garlic cloves, minced
- 1 tbsp soy sauce

Directions:
- Whisk together all marinade ingredients in a small bowl; coat the ribs well with the mixture. Place in a container with a lid, and refrigerate for 4 hours. Preheat the air fryer to 330°F.
- Place the ribs in the basket but do not throw away the liquid from the container; cook for 40 minutes. Stir in

the liquid, increase the temperature to 350°F, and cook for 10 more minutes.

482. Pork Sausage with Mashed Cauliflower

Preparation Time: 20 minutes
Cooking Time: 30 minutes
Servings: 6

Ingredients:
- 1-pound cauliflower, chopped
- 1/2 tsp tarragon
- 1/3 cup Colby cheese
- 1/2 tsp ground black pepper
- 1/2 onion, peeled and sliced
- 1 tsp cumin powder
- 1/2 tsp sea salt
- 3 beaten eggs
- 6 pork sausages, chopped

Directions:
- Boil the cauliflower until tender. Then, purée the cauliflower in your blender. Transfer to a mixing dish along with the other ingredients.
- Divide the prepared mixture among six lightly greased ramekins; now, place ramekins in your air fryer.
- Bake in the preheated Air Fryer for 27 minutes at 365°F. Eat warm.

483. Spicy Pork Meatballs

Preparation Time: 30 minutes
Cooking Time: 15 minutes
Servings: 4

Ingredients:
- 1-pound ground pork
- 1 cup scallions, finely chopped
- 2 cloves garlic, finely minced
- 1 ½ tbsp Worcester sauce
- 1 tbsp oyster sauce
- 1 tsp turmeric powder
- 1/2 tsp freshly grated ginger root
- 1 small sliced red chili for garnish

Directions:
- Mix all of the above ingredients, apart from the red chili. Knead with your hands to ensure an even mixture.
- Roll into equal balls and transfer them to the Air Fryer cooking basket.
- Set the timer for 15 minutes and push the power button. Air-fry at 350°F. Sprinkle with sliced red chili; serve immediately with your favorite sauce for dipping. Enjoy!

484. Hoisin Pork Loin

Preparation Time: 20 minutes
Cooking Time: 5-10 minutes
Servings: 4

Ingredients:
- 2 tbsp dry white wine
- 1/3 cup hoisin sauce
- 2 tsp smoked cayenne pepper
- 3 garlic cloves, pressed
- 1/2-pound pork loin steak, cut into strips

- 3 tsp fresh lime juice
- Salt and ground black pepper, to taste

Directions:
- Start by preheating your Air Fryer to 395°F.
- Toss the pork with other ingredients; let it marinate for at least 20 minutes in a fridge.
- Then, air-fry the pork strips for 5 minutes. Bon appétit!

485. Pork Kebabs

Preparation Time: 35 minutes
Cooking Time: 18-20 minutes
Servings: 6

Ingredients:
- 2 tbsp tomato puree
- 1/2 fresh serrano, minced
- 1/3 tsp paprika
- 1-pound pork, ground
- 1/2 cup green onions, finely chopped
- 3 cloves garlic, peeled and finely minced
- 1 tsp ground black pepper, or more to taste
- 1 tsp salt, or more to taste

Directions:
- Thoroughly combine all ingredients in a mixing dish. Then, form your mixture into sausage shapes.
- Cook for 18 minutes at 355°F in the air fryer. Mound salad on a serving platter, top with air-fried kebabs, and serve warm. Bon appétit!

486. Bacon Wrapped Hotdogs

Preparation Time: 20 minutes
Cooking Time: 10-12 minutes
Servings: 5

Ingredients:
- 10 thin slices of bacon
- 5 pork hot dogs, halved
- 1 tsp cayenne pepper
- Sauce:
- 1/4 cup mayo
- 4 tbsp ketchup, low-carb
- 1 tsp rice vinegar
- 1 tsp chili powder

Directions:
- Lay the slices of bacon on your working surface. Place a hot dog on one end of each slice; sprinkle with cayenne pepper and roll them over.
- Cook in the preheated Air Fryer at 390°F for 10 to 12 minutes.
- Whisk all ingredients for the sauce in a mixing bowl and store in your refrigerator, covered, until ready to serve.
- Serve bacon-wrapped hot dogs with the sauce on the side. Enjoy!

487. Cheesy Pork Casserole

Preparation Time: 30 minutes
Cooking Time: 16-20 minutes
Servings: 6

Ingredients:
- 1-pound lean ground pork
- 1/2-pound ground beef
- 1/4 cup tomato puree
- Sea salt and ground black pepper, to taste
- 1 tsp smoked paprika
- 1/2 tsp dried oregano
- 1 tsp dried basil
- 1 tsp dried rosemary
- 2 eggs
- 1 cup Cottage cheese, crumbled, at room temperature
- 1/2 cup Cotija cheese, shredded

Directions:
- Lightly grease a casserole dish with nonstick cooking oil. Add the ground meat to the bottom of your casserole dish.
- Add the tomato puree. Sprinkle with salt, black pepper, paprika, oregano, basil, and rosemary.
- In a mixing bowl, whisk the egg with cheese. Place on top of the ground meat mixture. Place a piece of foil on top.
- Bake in the preheated Air Fryer at 350°F for 10 minutes; remove the foil and cook for an additional 6 minutes. Bon appétit!

488.   Sherry-Braised Ribs

Preparation Time: 15 minutes
Cooking Time: 25-30 minutes
Servings: 4

Ingredients:
- 1 rack ribs, cut in half to fit the Air Fryer
- 1/4 cup sherry wine
- 2 tbsp coconut amino
- 1 tbsp Dijon mustard
- Sea salt and ground black pepper, to taste
- 1 cup grape tomatoes
- 1 tsp dried rosemary

Directions:
- Toss the pork ribs with sherry wine, coconut aminos, mustard, salt, and black pepper.
- Add the ribs to the lightly greased cooking basket. Cook in the preheated Air Fryer at 370°F for 25 minutes.
- Turn the ribs over, add the tomatoes and rosemary; cook an additional 5 minutes. Serve immediately.

489.   Air-fried Pork with Sweet and Sour Glaze

Preparation Time: 20 minutes
Cooking Time: 30 minutes
Servings: 6

Ingredients:
- ¼ cup rice wine vinegar
- ¼ tsp Chinese five-spice powder
- 1 cup potato starch
- 1 green onion, chopped
- 2 large eggs, beaten
- 2 pounds of pork chops cut into chunks
- 2 tbsp cornstarch + 3 tbsp water
- 5 tbsp Brown Sugar
- Salt and pepper to taste

Directions:
- Preheat the air fryer oven to 390°F.
- Season pork chops with salt and pepper to taste.
- Dip the pork chops in egg. Set aside.
- In a bowl, combine the potato starch and Chinese five-spice powder.
- Dredge the pork chops in the flour mixture.
- Place in the double layer rack and cook for 30 minutes.
- Meanwhile, place the vinegar and brown sugar in a saucepan. Season with salt and pepper to taste. Stir in the cornstarch slurry and allow to simmer until thick.
- Serve the pork chops with the sauce and garnish with green onions.

490.   Coconut Curry Pork Roast

Preparation Time: 15 minutes
Cooking Time: 60 minutes
Servings: 6

Ingredients:
- ½ tsp curry powder
- ½ tsp ground turmeric powder
- 1 can of unsweetened coconut milk
- 1 tbsp Sugar
- 2 tbsp fish sauce
- 2 tbsp soy sauce
- 3 pounds of pork shoulder
- Salt and pepper to taste

Directions:
- Place all ingredients in a bowl and allow the meat to marinate in the fridge for at least 2 hours.
- Preheat the air fryer to 390°F.
- Place the grill pan accessory in the air fryer.
- Grill the meat for 20 minutes making sure to flip the pork every 10 minutes for even grilling, and cook in batches.
- Meanwhile, pour the marinade into a saucepan and allow to simmer for 10 minutes until the sauce thickens.
- Baste the pork with the sauce before serving.

491.   Chinese Pork Dumplings

Preparation Time: 20 minutes
Cooking Time: 15 minutes
Servings: 8

Ingredients:
- ¼ tsp crushed red pepper
- ½ tsp Sugar
- 1 tbsp chopped fresh ginger
- 1 tbsp chopped garlic
- 1 tsp canola oil
- 1 tsp toasted sesame oil
- 18 dumpling wrappers
- 2 tbsp rice vinegar
- 2 tsp soy sauce
- 4 cups bok choy, chopped
- 4 ounces ground pork

Directions:
- Heat oil in a skillet and sauté the ginger and garlic until fragrant. Stir in the ground pork and cook for 5 minutes.
- Stir in the bok choy and crushed red pepper. Season with salt and pepper to taste. Allow cooling.

- Place the meat mixture in the middle of the dumpling wrappers. Fold the wrappers to seal the meat mixture in.
- Place the bok choy in the grill pan.
- Cook the dumplings in the air fryer at 330°F for 15 minutes.
- Meanwhile, prepare the dipping sauce by combining the remaining ingredients in a bowl.

492.   Five Spicy Crispy Roasted Pork

Preparation Time: 20 minutes
Cooking Time: 35 minutes
Servings: 6

Ingredients:
- 1 tsp Chinese five-spice powder
- 1 tsp white pepper
- 2 pounds pork belly
- 2 tsp garlic salt

Directions:
- Preheat the air fryer oven to 390°F.
- Mix all the spices in a bowl to create the dry rub.
- Score the skin of the pork belly with a knife and season the entire pork with the spice rub.
- Place in the air fryer basket and cook for 40 to 45 minutes until the skin is crispy.
- Chop before serving.

493.   Tuscan Pork Chops

Preparation Time: 20 minutes
Cooking Time: 10-15 minutes
Servings: 4

Ingredients:
- 1/4 cup all-purpose flour
- 1 tsp salt
- 3/4 tsp seasoned pepper
- 4 (1-inch-thick) boneless pork chops
- 1 tbsp olive oil
- 3 to 4 garlic cloves
- 1/3 cup balsamic vinegar
- 1/3 cup chicken broth
- 3 plum tomatoes, seeded and diced
- Tbsp capers

Directions:
- Combine flour, salt, and pepper
- Press pork chops into flour mixture on both sides until evenly covered.
- Cook in your air fryer oven at 360 °F for 14 minutes, flipping halfway through.
- While the pork chops cook, warm olive oil in a medium skillet.
- Add garlic and sauté for 1 minute; then mix in vinegar and chicken broth.
- Add capers and tomatoes and turn to high heat.
- Bring the sauce to a boil, stirring regularly, then add pork chops, cooking for one minute.
- Remove from heat and cover for about 5 minutes to allow the pork to absorb some of the sauce; serve hot.

494.   Thai Basil Pork

Preparation Time: 10 minutes
Cooking Time: 15 minutes
Servings: 4

Ingredients:
- 1 minced hot chili
- 1 minced shallot
- 1-pound ground pork
- 2 tbsp fish sauce
- 2 tbsp lime juice
- 3 tbsp basil
- Tbsp chopped mint
- 3 tbsp cilantro

Directions:
- In a shallow dish, mix well all ingredients with your hands. Form into 1-inch ovals.
- Thread ovals in skewers. Place on skewer rack in the air fryer.
- For 15 minutes, cook at 360°F. Halfway through Cooking time, turnover skewers. If needed, cook in batches.
- Serve and enjoy.

495.   Hamburger Pasta Casserole

Preparation Time: 10 minutes
Cooking Time: 15 minutes
Servings: 6

Ingredients:
- 1 lb. ground beef
- 8 oz milk
- 1 tbsp garlic powder
- 1 tbsp onion powder
- 1 cup cheddar cheese, shredded
- 8 oz Velveeta cheese, cut into cubes
- 2 cups chicken broth
- 16 oz elbow pasta

Directions:
- Add the meat into the air fryer and cook on sauté mode at 300°F until browned. Turn off the air fryer.
- Add noodles, milk, garlic powder, onion powder, and broth and stir well.
- Seal the pot with a pressure cooking lid and cook on high pressure at 400°F for 4 minutes.
- Once done, release pressure using quick release. Open the lid.
- Sprinkle cheddar cheese and Velveeta cheese on top.
- Seal pot with air fryer lid and select broil mode, then set the timer for 4 minutes.
- Serve and enjoy.

496.   Noodle Ham Casserole

Preparation Time: 10 minutes
Cooking Time: 30 minutes
Servings: 4

Ingredients:
- 10.5 oz cream of chicken soup
- 3 cups ham, cooked & diced
- 12 oz egg noodles, cooked and drained
- 2 cups Monterey jack cheese, shredded

- 1/2 tsp garlic powder
- 1 1/2 cups milk
- 1 cup sour cream
- Pepper
- Salt

Directions:
- Spray the air fryer from the inside with cooking spray.
- Add chicken soup, garlic powder, milk, sour cream, pepper, and salt into the air fryer and stir well.
- Add ham and cooked noodles and stir well.
- Sprinkle shredded cheese on top.
- Seal pot with air fryer lid and select bake mode, then set the temperature to 350°F and timer for 25 minutes.
- Serve and enjoy.

497. Pork Apple Meatballs

Preparation Time: 30 minutes
Cooking Time: 15 minutes
Servings: 8

Ingredients:
- 2 cups pork, minced
- 6 basil leaves, chopped
- 2 tbsp cheddar cheese, grated
- 4 garlic cloves, minced
- ½ cup apple, peeled, cored, chopped
- 1 large white onion, diced
- Salt and pepper to taste
- 2 tsp Dijon Mustard
- 1 tsp liquid Stevia

Directions:
- Add pork mince in a bowl, then add diced onion and apple into a bowl and mix well. Add the stevia, mustard, garlic, cheese, basil, salt, and pepper and combine well. Make small round balls from the mixture and place them into an air fryer basket. Cook at 350°F for 15-minutes. Serve and enjoy!

498. Pork Brunch Sticks

Preparation Time: 15 minutes
Cooking Time: 10 minutes
Servings: 4

Ingredients:
- 1 tsp dried basil
- ¼ tsp ground ginger
- 1 tsp nutmeg
- 1 tsp oregano
- 1 tsp apple cider vinegar
- 1 tsp paprika
- oz. pork fillet
- ½ tsp salt
- 1 tbsp olive oil
- 5 oz. Parmesan, shredded

Directions:
- Cut the pork fillet into the thick strips.
- Then combine the ground ginger, nutmeg, oregano, paprika, and salt in the shallow bowl. Stir it.
- After this, sprinkle the pork strips with the spice mixture.
- Sprinkle the meat with apple cider vinegar.

- Preheat the air fryer to 380°F.
- Sprinkle the air fryer basket with the olive oil inside and place the pork strips (sticks) there.
- Cook the dish for 5 minutes.
- After this, turn the pork sticks to another side and cook for 4 minutes more.
- Then cover the pork sticks with the shredded Parmesan and cook the dish for 1 minute more.
- Remove the pork sticks from the air fryer and serve them immediately. The cheese should be soft during the serving.

499. Pork Posole

Preparation Time: 10 minutes
Cooking Time: 30 minutes
Servings: 8

Ingredients:
- 1 lb. pork shoulder, cut into cubes
- 1 tsp dried oregano
- 3 tsp chili sauce
- 24 oz posole
- 1 cup of water
- 2 tsp chili powder
- 1 tsp ground cumin
- Two garlic cloves
- 1 tsp salt

Directions:
- Mix all ingredients into the instant fryer and stir well.
- Seal fryer with lid and cook on manual high pressure at a temperature of 400°F for 30 minutes.
- Once done, then allow to release pressure naturally, then open the lid.
- Stir and serve.

500. Creamy Pork Curry

Preparation Time: 10 minutes
Cooking Time: 37 minutes
Servings: 8

Ingredients:
- 4 lbs. pork shoulder, boneless and cut into chunks
- Two garlic cloves, minced
- One onion, chopped
- 3 cups chicken broth
- 2 cups of coconut milk
- 1/2 tsp turmeric
- 2 tbsp olive oil
- 1/2 tbsp ground cumin
- 1 1/2 tbsp curry paste
- 2 tbsp fresh ginger, grated
- Pepper
- Salt

Directions:
- Add oil into the pot and set the container on sauté mode.
- Season meat with pepper and salt. Add chicken to the pot and cook until browned.
- Add remaining ingredients and stir everything well.
- Seal the pot with a lid and cook on soup/stew mode for 30 minutes at 375°F.

- Once done, then release pressure using the quick-release method, then open the lid.
- Stir well and serve.

501. Texas Baby Back Ribs

Preparation Time: 20 minutes
Cooking Time: 30-40 minutes
Servings:

Ingredients:
- 1 rack of baby back ribs,
- 2 tbsp. Oil
- 1 tbsp. Liquid Smoke
- SEASONING:
- 1 tsp Chili powder
- 1 tsp Onion powder
- 2 tsp Kosher Salt
- 1 tsp Ground Black Pepper
- ½ tsp Brown Sugar
- ½ tsp Garlic powder

Directions:
- Use a kitchen paper towel to pat dry the ribs, and then rub oil and liquid smoke all over it
- All the seasonings must be mixed together in a bowl and spice the ribs with it
- Cut the rack of ribs into 4-5 sections to fit the air fryer.
- Depending on the rib thickens, set the air fryer to cook the ribs at 400°F for 30-40 minutes, and it's done

502. Bratwurst Bites with Spicy Mustard

Preparation Time: 20 minutes
Cooking Time: 10 minutes
Servings: 5-6

Ingredients:
- ⅛ Tsp. Spices, allspice, ground
- ½ cup German stone-ground mustard
- 6 pcs bell peppers, mini sweet peppers
- 5 links pork link sausage
- ½ cup dark beer
- 3 tbsp Honey, strained or extracted
- ½ tsp Spices, turmeric, ground

Directions:
- Mix honey, turmeric, beer, and allspice in a small saucepan and boil on low-medium heat, uncovered until the volume has reduced by half, about 8 minutes. Stir in mustard and set aside until ready to serve.
- Place sweet peppers and bratwurst chunks in a single layer in the air fryer basket.
- Let it cook at 400°F using an air fryer for about 10 minutes, tossing once halfway through cooking, until peppers are tender and bratwurst edges are golden brown and crisp.

- Serve warm with mustard sauce.

503. Oriental Pork Meatballs

Preparation Time: 20 minutes
Cooking Time: 9-10 minutes
Servings: 8

Ingredients:
- 1pound ground pork
- 2 large eggs
- ¼ cup chopped green onions
- ¼ cup chopped fresh cilantro or parsley
- 1 tbsp minced fresh ginger
- 3 cloves garlic, minced
- 2 tsp soy sauce
- 1 tsp oyster sauce
- ½ tsp kosher salt
- 1 tsp black pepper

Directions:
- In the bowl, combine the pork, eggs, green onions, cilantro, ginger, garlic, soy sauce, oyster sauce, salt, and pepper.
- Let it mix until ingredients are incorporated, 2 to 3 minutes. Form the mixture into 12 meatballs and arrange them in a single layer in the air fryer basket.
- Set the air fryer to 350°F for 10 minutes. U. Transfer the meatballs to a bowl and serve.

504. Pork Bun and Liver Souffle

Preparation Time: 20 minutes
Cooking Time: 25-30 minutes
Servings: 4

Ingredients:
- ½ pound (227 g) pork liver, cut into cubes
- 3 ounces (85 g) buns
- 1 cup of warm milk
- 3 eggs yolks
- Salt and ground black pepper, to taste
- 4 ramekins

Directions:
- Put the liver in a bowl and refrigerate for 15 minutes.
- Soak the buns in a separate bowl of warm milk for 10 minutes.
- The air fryer must be heated to 180°C
- Put the buns, liver, and remaining ingredients in a food processor. Pulse to combine well.
- Divide the mixture into the ramekins, then arrange the ramekins into the air fryer basket.
- Cook in the preheated air fryer for 20 minutes or until a toothpick inserted in the soufflé comes out clean.
- Serve the soufflé warm.

CHAPTER 6: CHICKEN AND OTHER POULTRY

505. Garlic Honey Chicken

Preparation Time: 10 minutes
Cooking Time: 20-30 minutes
Servings: 4

Ingredients:

- 1/3 cup water
- ¼ cup low sodium soy sauce
- ¼ cup honey
- 2 cloves garlic, minced
- ¼ tsp. black pepper
- 1 1/2-pound medium-size boneless skinless chicken breasts
- 2 tsp. cornstarch

Directions:

- Combine water, soy sauce, honey, garlic, chicken, and pepper in the air fryer.
- Cook at 400°F for 10 minutes.
- In a bowl, mix 2 tsp cornstarch and 1 tbsp water.
- Cook cornstarch mixture on Sauté mode for 2-3 minutes.
- Dip sliced chicken in sauce.
- Serve with rice and vegetable.

506. Asian Chicken Noodles

Preparation Time: 20 minutes
Cooking Time: 30-35 minutes
Servings: 6

Ingredients:

- 1 tbsp. olive oil
- 1 onion, diced
- 3 cloves of garlic, minced
- ½ tbsp. pepper
- 4 oz. of extra-wide egg noodles
- 1/4 cup of minced flat-leaf parsley
- 5 carrots, sliced into 1/2-inch chunks
- 2 celery sticks, sliced into 1/2-inch pieces
- 1 whole 5-pound chicken giblet removed and discarded
- 2 tbsp. soy sauce
- 8 cups water
- ½ tbsp. salt

Directions:

- In the air fryer at 300°F, cook onion in olive oil at Sauté for 2-3 minutes.
- Add garlic, carrots, celery, and sauté for 1 minute.
- Add whole chicken, soy sauce, 2 tsp of salt, and several turns of freshly ground pepper in Pot.
- Cook at 400°F for 20 minutes and remove.
- Turn the Air fryer back to Sauté and let the chicken broth come to a boil.
- Add egg noodles and let cook for about 5 minutes.
- Once noodles are cooked, add shredded chicken and fresh parsley and serve.

507.   Chicken Sausage with Nestled Eggs

Preparation Time: 20 minutes
Cooking Time: 17 minutes
Servings: 6

Ingredients:

- 6 eggs
- 2 bell peppers, seeded and sliced
- 1 tsp dried oregano
- 1 tsp hot paprika
- 1 tsp freshly cracked black pepper
- 6 chicken sausages
- 1 tsp sea salt
- 1 1/2 shallots, cut into wedges
- 1 tsp dried basil
- **Directions**
- Take four ramekins and divide chicken sausages, shallot, and bell pepper among those ramekins. Cook at 315 °F for about 12 minutes in the air fryer.
- Now, crack an egg into each ramekin. Sprinkle the eggs with hot paprika, basil, oregano, salt, and cracked black pepper. Cook for 5 more minutes at 405 °F.

508.   Thai Chicken Satay

Preparation Time: 20 minutes
Cooking Time: 20-30 minutes
Servings: 12

Ingredients:

- ½ cup crunchy peanut butter
- ⅓ cup chicken broth
- 3 tbsp low-sodium soy sauce
- 2 tbsp lemon juice
- 2 cloves garlic, minced
- 2 tbsp olive oil
- 1 tsp curry powder

- 1-pound chicken tenders

Directions:

- Set to 390°F Grill. In a medium bowl, combine the peanut butter, chicken broth, soy sauce, lemon juice, garlic, olive oil, and curry powder, and mix well with a wire whisk until smooth. Remove 2 tbsp of this mixture to a small bowl. Put the remaining sauce into a serving bowl and set aside.
- Add the chicken tenders to the bowl with the 2 tbsp sauce and stir to coat. Let stand for a few minutes to marinate, then run a bamboo skewer through each chicken tender lengthwise.
- Put the chicken in the air fryer basket and cook in batches for 6 to 9 minutes or until the chicken reaches 165°F on a meat thermometer. Serve the chicken with the reserved sauce.

509.   Sweet and Sour Chicken

Preparation Time: 15 minutes
Cooking Time: 20-30 minutes
Servings: 6

Ingredients:

- 6 chicken drumsticks
- 3 tbsp lemon juice, divided
- 3 tbsp low-sodium soy sauce, divided
- 1 tbsp peanut oil
- 3 tbsp honey
- 3 tbsp brown sugar
- 2 tbsp ketchup
- ¼ cup pineapple juice

Directions:

- Set to 350°F Bake. Sprinkle the drumsticks with 1 tbsp of lemon juice and 1 tbsp of soy sauce. Place in the air fryer basket and drizzle with the peanut oil. Toss to coat. Bake for 18 minutes or until the chicken is almost done.
- Meanwhile, in a 6-inch bowl, combine the remaining 2 tbsp of lemon juice, the remaining 2 tbsp of soy sauce, honey, brown sugar, ketchup, and pineapple juice.
- Add the cooked chicken to the bowl and stir to coat the chicken well with the sauce.
- Place the metal bowl in the basket. Cook for 5 to 7 minutes or until the chicken is glazed and registers 165°F on a meat thermometer.

510.   Dry-Rubbed Chicken Wings

Preparation Time: 5 minutes
Cooking Time: 30 minutes
Servings: 12

Ingredients:

- 12 chicken wings
- 1 tsp garlic powder
- 1 tsp chili powder
- 1/2 tsp kosher salt
- 1/2 black pepper, paprika

Directions:

- Preheat the air fryer to 180°C.
- Mix garlic powder, chili powder, paprika, salt, and pepper in a large bowl.

- Rinse and pat every chicken wing dry and toss into a bowl to cover uniformly.
- Place wings in air fryer crate and cook for 15 minutes, turning at interims.
- Cool again for an additional 5 minutes.
- Serve hot.

511. Thanksgiving Turkey with Mustard Gravy

Preparation Time: 50 minutes
Cooking Time: 45 minutes
Servings: 6

Ingredients:

- 2 tsp butter, softened
- 1 tsp dried sage
- 2 sprigs rosemary, chopped
- 1 tsp salt
- 1/4 tsp freshly ground black pepper or more to taste
- 1 whole turkey breast
- 2 tbsp turkey broth
- 2 tbsp whole-grain mustard
- 1 tbsp butter
- **Directions**
- Start by preheating your air fryer to 360°F.
- To make the rub, combine 2 tbsp of butter, sage, rosemary, salt, and pepper; mix well to combine and spread it evenly over the surface of the turkey breast.
- Roast for 20 minutes in an air fryer cooking basket. Flip the turkey breast over and cook for a further 15 to 16 minutes. Now, flip it back over and roast for 12 minutes more.
- While the turkey is roasting, whisk the other ingredients in a saucepan. After that, spread the gravy all over the turkey breast.
- Let the turkey rest for a few minutes before carving.

512. Butter and Orange Fried Chicken

Preparation Time: 20 minutes
Cooking Time: 13 minutes
Servings: 4

Ingredients:

- ½ tbsp Worcestershire sauce
- 1 tsp finely grated orange zest
- 2 tbsp melted butter
- ½ tsp smoked paprika
- 4 chicken drumsticks, rinsed and halved
- 1 tsp sea salt flakes
- 1 tbsp cider vinegar
- 1/2 tsp mixed peppercorns, freshly cracked
- **Directions**
- Firstly, pat the chicken drumsticks dry. Coat them with melted butter on all sides.
- Toss the chicken drumsticks with the other ingredients.
- Transfer them to the air fryer cooking basket and roast for about 13 minutes at 345 °F.

513. Chicken Alfredo

Preparation Time: 15 minutes
Cooking Time: 15-20 minutes
Servings: 4

Ingredients:

- 1 lb. chicken breasts, skinless and boneless
- ½ lb. button mushrooms, sliced
- 1 medium-sized onion, chopped
- 1 tbsp olive oil
- 2 cups cooked rice
- 1 jar (10-ounces) Alfredo sauce
- Salt and pepper to taste
- ½ tsp thyme, dried

Directions:

- Cut the chicken breasts into 1-inch cubes. Mix chicken, onion, and mushrooms in a large bowl. Season with salt and dried thyme and mix well. Preheat your air fryer to 370°F and sprinkle the basket with olive oil. Transfer chicken and vegetables to the fryer and cook for 12-minutes, and stir occasionally. Stir in the Alfredo sauce. Cook for another 4-minutes. Serve with cooked rice

514. Turkey Loaf

Preparation Time: 20 minutes
Cooking Time: 40 minutes
Servings: 4

Ingredients:

- 1 egg
- ½ tsp dried savory dill
- 2/3 cup walnuts, finely chopped
- 1 ½ lb. turkey breast, diced
- ½ tsp ground allspice
- ¼ tsp black pepper
- 1 garlic clove, minced
- 1 tbsp Dijon mustard
- 1 tbsp liquid Aminos
- 1 tbsp tomato paste
- 2 tbsp parmesan cheese, grated
- 1 tbsp onion flakes

Directions:

- Preheat your air fryer to 375°F. Grease a baking dish using cooking spray. Whisk dill, egg, tomato paste, liquid aminos, mustard, garlic, allspice, salt, and pepper. Mix well and add diced turkey. Mix again and add cheese, walnuts, and onion flakes. Put mixture into baking dish and bake for 40-minutes in the air fryer. Serve hot!

515. Cheesy Turkey Calzone

Preparation Time: 20 minutes
Cooking Time: 10-15minutes
Servings: 4

Ingredients:

- 1 free-range egg, beaten
- ¼ cup mozzarella cheese, grated
- 1 cup cheddar cheese, grated
- 1-ounce bacon, diced, cooked
- Cooked turkey, shredded
- 4 tbsp tomato sauce
- Salt and pepper to taste
- 1 tsp thyme
- 1 tsp basil
- 1 tsp oregano
- 1 package of frozen pizza dough

Directions:

- Roll the pizza dough out into small circles, the same size as a small pizza. Add thyme, oregano, and basil into a bowl with tomato sauce and mix well. Pour a small amount of sauce onto your pizza bases and spread it across the surface. Add the turkey, bacon, and cheese. Brush the edge of the dough with beaten egg, then fold over and pinch to seal. Brush the outside with more egg. Place into the air fryer and cook at 350°F for 10-minutes. Serve warm.

516. Mozzarella Turkey Rolls

Preparation Time: 15 minutes
Cooking Time: 10-15 minutes
Servings: 4

Ingredients:

- 4 slices of turkey breast
- 4 chive shoots (for tying rolls)
- 1 tomato, sliced
- ½ cup basil, fresh, chopped
- 1 cup mozzarella, sliced

Directions:

- Preheat your air fryer to 390°F. Place the slices of mozzarella cheese, tomato, and basil onto each slice of turkey. Roll up and tie with chive shoot. Place into the air fryer and cook for 10-minutes. Serve warm.

517. Korean Chicken Wings

Preparation Time: 10 minutes
Cooking Time: 15 minutes
Servings: 4

Ingredients:

- 8 chicken wings
- Salt to taste
- 1 tsp sesame oil
- Juice from half lemon
- ¼ cup sriracha chili sauce
- 1-inch piece ginger, grated
- 1 tsp garlic powder
- 1 tsp sesame seeds

Directions:

- Preheat the air fryer to 370°F. Grease the air fryer basket with cooking spray.
- In a bowl, mix salt, ginger, garlic, lemon juice, sesame oil, and chili sauce. Add in the wings and coat them well. Air Fry for 15 minutes, flipping once. Sprinkle with sesame seeds and serve.

518. Curry Chicken Wings

Preparation Time: 30 minutes
Cooking Time: 20 minutes
Servings: 4

Ingredients:

- 1 cup rice milk
- 1 tbsp soy sauce
- 1 tbsp red curry paste
- 1 tbsp sugar
- 8 chicken wings
- 2 tbsp fresh parsley, chopped

Directions:

- Preheat the air fryer to 380°F.
- In a bowl, mix all the ingredients, except for the parsley. Marinate for 20 minutes. Grease the air fryer basket with cooking spray. After 20 minutes, drain the wings and reserve the marinade.
- Place wings in the frying basket and Air Fry for 18-20 minutes, flipping once. Add the marinade to a saucepan over medium heat, and cook until thickened, 8 minutes. Pour this sauce over the chicken and top with parsley to serve

519. Roasted Duck Breasts with Endives

Preparation Time: 20 minutes
Cooking Time: 35 minutes
Servings: 4

Ingredients:

- duck breasts 2
- sugar-1 tbsp.
- Salt and black pepper to the taste
- olive oil-1 tbsp.
- endives; julienned-6
- cranberries-2 tbsp.
- White wine-8 oz.
- Garlic; minced-1 tbsp.

Directions:

- Score duck bosoms and season them with salt and pepper, place them in the preheated air fryer, and cook at 350 °F for 20 minutes, flipping them midway.
- On the other hand, heat a skillet with the oil over medium warmth, including sugar and endives; blend and cook for 2 minutes.
- Include salt, pepper, wine, garlic, cream, and cranberries; blend and cook for 3 minutes.
- Divide duck bosoms among plates; spread the endives sauce all finished, and serve.

520. Herbed Roast Chicken

Preparation Time: 35 minutes
Cooking Time: 1 hr. 30 minutes
Servings: 8

Ingredients:

- 1 (3.5 lb.) whole chicken
- 2 tbsp olive oil
- 1 tsp garlic powder
- 1 tsp paprika
- ½ tsp oregano
- Salt and black pepper to taste
- 1 lemon, cut into quarters
- 5 garlic cloves

Directions:

- In a bowl, combine olive oil, garlic powder, paprika, oregano, salt, and pepper, and mix well to make a paste. Rub the chicken with the paste and stuff lemon and garlic cloves into the cavity.
- Place the chicken in the air fryer, breast side down, and tuck the legs and wings tips under. Bake for 45 minutes at 360°F. Flip the chicken so the breast side up and cook for another 15-20 minutes. Let rest for 5-6 minutes, then carve and serve.

521. Apricot-Glazed Turkey

Preparation Time: 20 minutes
Cooking Time: 30 minutes
Servings: 4

Ingredients:
- Olive oil
- ¼ cup sugar-free apricot preserves
- ½ tbsp spicy brown mustard
- 1½ pound turkey breast tenderloin
- Salt
- Freshly ground black pepper

Directions:
- Set to 370°F. Spray a fryer basket lightly with olive oil.
- In a small bowl, combine the apricot preserves and mustard to make a paste.
- Season the turkey with salt and pepper. Spread the apricot paste all over the turkey.
- Place the turkey in the fryer basket and lightly spray with olive oil.
- Air fry for 15 minutes. Flip the turkey over and lightly spray with olive oil. Air fry until the internal temperature reaches at least 170°F, an additional 10 to 15 minutes.
- Let the turkey rest for 10 minutes before slicing and serving.

522. Grilled Chicken and Radish Mix Recipe

Preparation Time: 20 minutes
Cooking Time: 40 Minutes
Servings: 4

Ingredients:
- 4 bone-in chicken things
- Salt and black pepper to the taste
- 1 tbsp Olive oil
- 3 carrots; cut into thin sticks
- 2 tbsp Chopped chives
- 1 cup chicken stock
- 1 cup sugar
- 6 radishes, halved

Directions:
- Start by Heating a container that accommodates your air fryer over medium warmth, including stock, carrots, sugar, and radishes; mix delicately,
- Reduce warmth to medium, spread pot somewhat, and permit to stew for 20 minutes.
- Coat the chicken with olive oil, season with salt and pepper, put in your air fryer, and cook at 350 °F for 4 minutes.
- Introduce the chicken to radish blend and hurl appropriately
- Introduce everything in your air fryer, cook for 4 minutes more,
- Share among plates and serve.

523. Quail in White Wine Sauce

Preparation Time: 12 hrs.
Cooking Time: 90 minutes
Servings: 4

Ingredients:
- 4 large quail
- 1 bottle of dry white wine
- 1 tsp of sweet paprika
- 1 tsp of hot paprika
- ½ package fresh sage, chopped or 2 tbsp dehydrated sage
- 1 head minced garlic
- ¼ tsp of virgin olive oil
- 1.7 oz. of butter
- Salt to taste
- 4 rosemary sprigs

Directions:
- The recipe is very easy; it should only be prepared well in advance.
- Wash the quail well. Boil salted water in a skillet enough to cover the quail.
- When the water boils, place the quail in the pan and cover for 5 minutes.
- Drain and let cool. Put a little minced garlic inside each quail. Place the quail in a large bowl and top with white wine. Add sweet bell pepper, hot pepper, olive oil, and sage. Marinate in the seasoning in the refrigerator for at least 12 hours. Remove the quail from the seasoning and place it in a pan with butter.
- Take to the preheated air fryer to about 200°F and bake for 90 minutes.
- Open the oven every 15 minutes and turn the quails and sprinkle with the marinade.

524. Hawaiian Roasted Quail

Preparation Time: 20 minutes
Cooking Time: 30 minutes
Servings: 4

Ingredients:
- 1 cup champagne
- 1 cup of water
- ½ tbsp ground black pepper
- 2 tsp of salt
- 3 tsp of curry
- 3 tsp virgin olive oil
- 3 minced garlic
- 3 ½ tsp lemon vinegar
- 4 medium-size Hawaii pineapple slices
- 4 very clean quails, washed and dried
- 20 sliced endive leaves

Directions:
- Cut the pineapple curry slices. Reserve.
- Heat 2 tbsp of oil in a frying pan and brown the pineapple slices on both sides.
- Chop them and fill the quail. Tie well. Place on the baking sheet. Season with champagne, water, salt, and garlic.
- Bake in the air fryer for 40 minutes at 350°F or until golden brown.
- Arrange the quail on the plates. Add endive and reserve.
- Mix the vinegar, remaining oil, and pepper. Endive water. Pineapple, rosemary, and thyme leave to decorate.

525.   Caribbean Chicken Thighs

Preparation Time: 30 minutes
Cooking Time: 10 minutes
Servings: 8

Ingredients:

- 3 lbs. Chicken thigh fillets, boneless and skinless
- Ground black pepper
- 1 tbsp ground coriander seed
- Salt
- 1 tbsp ground cinnamon
- 1 tbsp Cayenne pepper
- 1½ tbsp Ground ginger
- 1½ tbsp Ground nutmeg
- 3 tbsp Coconut oil

Directions:

- Take chicken off the packaging and pat dry. To soak up any residual liquid, place it on a large baking sheet covered with paper towels. Chicken is salted and peppered on both sides. Let the chicken sit for 30 minutes, so when you go into the air fryer, it isn't that cold.
- Combine cilantro, cinnamon, cayenne, ginger, and nutmeg in a small bowl. Coat the spice mixture on each piece of chicken and brush both sides with coconut oil.
- Place four pieces of chicken in your air fryer basket (they shouldn't overlap). Air fry for 10 minutes at 390 °F. Remove the chicken from the basket and place it in a safe stove dish, tightly covered with foil.
- Keep the chicken in the oven to keep it warm until the remaining chicken is done — repeat the instructions for air frying with the rest of the chicken.

526.   Chicken Coconut Meatballs

Preparation Time: 10 minutes
Cooking Time: 10 minutes
Servings: 4

Ingredients:

- 1 lb. ground chicken
- 1 ½ tsp sriracha
- 1/2 tbsp soy sauce
- 1/2 tbsp hoisin sauce
- ¼ cup shredded coconut
- 1 tsp sesame oil
- ½ cup fresh cilantro, chopped
- 2 green onions, chopped
- Pepper
- Salt

Directions:

- Spray the air fryer basket with cooking spray.
- Add all ingredients into the large bowl and mix until well combined.
- Make small balls from the meat mixture and place them into the air fryer basket.
- Cook at 350°F for 10 minutes. Turn halfway through.
- Serve and enjoy.

527.   Chicken Pasta Salad

Preparation Time: 20 minutes
Cooking Time: 25-30 minutes
Servings: 4

Ingredients:

- 3 chicken breasts
- 1 medium bag of frozen vegetables of choice
- 1 cup rigatoni or pasta of choice; cooked
- Paprika
- Garlic and herb seasoning
- Italian dressing
- Black pepper
- Ground parsley
- Oil spray

Directions:

- Wash the chicken breasts and season with paprika, garlic, and herb seasoning and a tbsp of the Italian dressing. Top a little with black pepper and ground parsley. Mist the air fryer with oil, then add the marinated chicken breasts. Spray oil over the chicken as well. Cook at 360°F for 15 minutes
- Halfway through, flip the chicken breasts and season with pepper and parsley. Spray over with oil and allow to cook all the way
- While the chicken is cooking, empty a bag of frozen vegetables into a bowl and season with the garlic and herb dressing and some Italian dressing. Mix well. Spray another air fryer and add in the vegetables. Cook for 12 minutes at 380°F.
- Dice the cooked chicken while waiting for the vegetables to cook. Season the cooked with some garlic and herb seasoning, along with some parsley and Italian dressing
- Mix well, tasting to your preference. Add the diced chicken to the mix, mixing well. Once the vegetables have finished cooking, add to the chicken and pasta mixture and incorporate thoroughly. Serve

528.   Chicken Marinara

Preparation Time: 20 minutes
Cooking Time: 15 minutes
Servings: 2

Ingredients:

- ½ C. keto marinara
- 6 tbsp. mozzarella cheese
- 1 tbsp. melted ghee
- 2 tbsp. grated parmesan cheese
- 6 tbsp. gluten-free seasoned breadcrumbs
- 2 8-ounce chicken breasts

Directions:

- Ensure the air fryer is preheated to 360°F. Spray the basket with olive oil.
- Mix parmesan cheese and breadcrumbs together. Melt ghee.
- Brush melted ghee onto the chicken and dip into the breadcrumb mixture.
- Place coated chicken in the air fryer and top with olive oil.

- Cook 2 breasts for 6 minutes and top each breast with a tbsp of sauce and 1 ½ tbsp of mozzarella cheese. Cook another 3 minutes to melt the cheese.
- Keep cooked pieces warm as you repeat the process with the remaining breasts.

529.   Southern Fried Chicken

Preparation Time: 20 minutes
Cooking Time: 25-30 minutes
Servings: 4

Ingredients:
- 1 tsp. cayenne pepper
- 2 tbsp. mustard powder
- 2 tbsp. oregano
- 2 tbsp. thyme
- 3 tbsp. coconut milk
- 1 beaten egg
- ¼ C. cauliflower
- ¼ C. gluten-free oats
- 8 chicken drumsticks

Directions:
- Ensure the air fryer is preheated to 350°F.
- Layout chicken and season with pepper and salt on all sides.
- Add all other ingredients to a blender, blending till a smooth-like breadcrumb mixture is created. Place in a bowl and add a beaten egg to another bowl.
- Dip chicken into breadcrumbs, then into the egg and breadcrumbs once more.
- Place coated drumsticks into the air fryer and cook for 20 minutes. Bump up the temperature to 390 degrees and cook another 5 minutes till crispy.

530.   Mexican Chicken Burrito

Preparation Time: 20 minutes
Cooking Time: 10 minutes
Servings: 4

Ingredients:
- 4 chicken breast slices; cooked and shredded
- 2 tortillas
- 1 avocado; peeled, pitted, and sliced
- 1 green bell pepper; sliced
- 2 eggs; whisked
- 2 tbsp. mild salsa
- 2 tbsp. cheddar cheese; grated
- Salt and black pepper to taste

Directions:
- In a bowl, whisk the eggs with salt and pepper and pour them into a pan that fits your air fryer. Put the pan in the air fryer's basket, cook for 5 minutes at 400°F and transfer the mix to a plate
- Place the tortillas on a working surface, and between them, divide the eggs, chicken, bell peppers, avocado, and the cheese; roll the burritos
- Line your air fryer with tin foil, add the burritos and cook them at 300°F for 3-4 minutes. Serve for breakfast-or lunch or dinner!

531.   Parmesan Garlic Wings

Preparation Time: 20 minutes
Cooking Time: 30 minutes
Servings: 4

Ingredients:
- 2 pounds Raw chicken wings
- 1 tsp Salt
- ½ tsp Garlic powder
- 1 tbsp Baking powder
- 4 tbsp Unsalted butter, melted
- 1/3 cup grated Parmesan cheese
- ¼ tsp Dried parsley

Directions:
- Place chicken wings, salt, ½ tsp garlic powder, and baking powder in a bowl. Coat and place wings into the air fryer basket. Cook at 400°F for 25 minutes. Toss the basket two or 3 times during the cooking time. Combine butter, parmesan, and parsley in a bowl. Remove wings from the air fryer and place them into a bowl. Pour the butter mixture over the wings and toss to coat. Serve warm

532.   Creamy Coconut Chicken

Preparation Time: 20 minutes
Cooking Time: 30 minutes
Servings: 4

Ingredients:
- 4 Big chicken legs
- 5 tbsp Turmeric powder
- 2 tbsp Ginger, grated
- Salt and black pepper to taste
- 4 tbsp Coconut cream

Directions:
- In a bowl, mix salt, pepper, ginger, turmeric, and cream. Whisk. Add chicken pieces, coat, and marinate for 2 hours. Transfer chicken to the preheated air fryer and cook at 370°F for 25 minutes. Serve.

533.   Chinese Duck Legs

Preparation Time: 30 minutes
Cooking Time: 35 minutes
Servings: 2

Ingredients:
- 2 Duck legs
- 2 Dried chilies, chopped
- 1 tbsp Olive oil
- 2 Star anise
- 1 bunch Spring onions, chopped
- 4 slices Ginger
- 1 tbsp Oyster sauce
- 1 tbsp Soy sauce
- 1 tsp Sesame oil
- 14 ounce Water
- 1 tbsp Rice wine

Directions:
- Heat oil in a pan. Add water, soy sauce, oyster sauce, ginger, rice wine, sesame oil, star anise, and chili. Stir and cook for 6 minutes. Add spring onions and duck

legs, toss to coat, and transfer to a pan. Place the pan in the air fryer and cook at 370°F for 30 minutes. Serve.

534. Dijon Lime Chicken

Preparation Time: 20 minutes
Cooking Time: 35 minutes
Servings: 2

Ingredients:
- 4 Chicken drumsticks
- ½ tsp Dried parsley
- ¼ tsp Black pepper
- ½ Lime juice
- 1 Garlic clove, minced
- ½ tbsp Mayonnaise
- 1½ tbsp Dijon mustard
- Salt, to taste

Directions:
- Add chicken drumsticks into the large mixing bowl. Add remaining ingredients over chicken and toss until well coated. Add chicken drumsticks into the multi-level air fryer basket and place the basket into the air fryer. Seal pot with air fryer lid. Select bake mode and cook at 380°F for 35 minutes. Serve.

535. Parmesan Chicken Nuggets

Preparation Time: 30 minutes
Cooking Time: 30 minutes
Servings: 4

Ingredients:
- 1 ½ pound of Chicken breasts, cut into chunks
- ½ tsp Garlic powder
- 6 tbsp Parmesan cheese, shredded
- ¼ cup Mayonnaise
- ½ tsp Salt

Directions:
- Line the multi-level air fryer basket with parchment paper and set it aside. In a medium bowl, mix together mayonnaise, shredded cheese, garlic powder, and salt.
- Coat chicken chunks with the mayo mixture and place them into the air fryer basket and place the basket into the air fryer. Seal the pot with the air fryer lid.
- Select bake mode and cook at 380°F for 25-30 minutes. Serve.

536. Black Bean and Tater Tots

Preparation Time: 20 minutes
Cooking Time: 15 minutes
Servings: 3

Ingredients:
- 1 1/4 cups of tater tots
- 1 cup of black beans
- salsa
- sour cream (dairy-free / vegan)
- garlic lemon sauce (recipe follows)

Directions:
- Use an air fryer to prepare. Set temperatures to 400°F, and cook tater tots for seven minutes. Remove, shake, and add black beans to turn the tot's tater. Return to the air fryer and cook for another 5 minutes until the tots are fully cooked, and the beans are hot.
- If using an oven, preheat the oven to 425°F. Line parchment baking sheet.
- Arrange tater tots into a single layer on a lined (parchment) baking sheet. Bake for 15 minutes, and remove temperature from oven to 375°F. Move to one side of the baking sheet using a spatula, flip tater tots and keep in a single layer.
- Prepare the garlic lemon sauce, slice the green onion, and prep toppings while the tater tots bake.
- Assemble touches: pile tots on two plates, black beans, salsa, sour cream, and lemon sauce with garlic. Top with green onion and serve straight away.

537. Cheese Herb Chicken Wings

Preparation Time: 10 minutes
Cooking Time: 15 minutes
Servings: 4

Ingredients:
- 2 lbs. chicken wings
- 1 tsp herb de Provence
- ½ cup parmesan cheese, grated
- 1 tsp paprika
- Salt

Directions:
- Preheat the air fryer to 350°F.
- In a small bowl, mix together cheese, herb de Provence, paprika, and salt.
- Spray the air fryer basket with cooking spray.
- Toss chicken wings with cheese mixture and place into the air fryer basket, and cook for 15 minutes. Turn halfway through.
- Serve and enjoy.

538. Bourbon Peach Wings

Preparation Time: 20 minutes
Cooking Time: 30 minutes
Servings: 6

Ingredients:
- 1/2 cup of peach preserves
- 1 tbsp of brown sugar
- 1 garlic clove, minced
- 1/4 tsp of salt
- 2 tbsp of white vinegar
- 2 tbsp of bourbon
- 1 tsp of cornstarch
- 1-1/2 tsp of water
- 2 pounds of chicken wings

Directions:
- Preheat the fryer by air to 400°F. In a food processor, add peach preserves, brown sugar, garlic, and salt; process until blended. Transfer to a saucepan. Remove bourbon and vinegar, and bring it to a boil. Reduce heat; simmer, uncovered, for 4-6 minutes until slightly thickened.
- Mix the cornstarch and water in a small bowl until smooth; stir in the preserve mixture. Return to a boil, constantly stirring; cook and stir for 1-2 minutes, or until thick. Apply 1/4 cup sauce to drink.

Using a sharp knife, cut each chicken wing through the two joints; discard tips on the wing. Spray basket with cooking spray to the air fryer. Working in batches as needed, place wing pieces in the air fryer basket in a single layer. 6 minutes to cook; Turn over and clean the mixture with preserve. Return to air fryer and cook for 6-8 minutes, until browned and juices run free. Remove, and stay warm. Repeat on the remaining pieces of a wing. Serve wings with reserved sauce immediately.

539. Chicken Fried Rice

Preparation Time: 15 minutes
Cooking Time: 20 minutes
Servings: 5

Ingredients:
- 1 cup Packed cooked chicken
- 3 cups cold cooked white rice
- 1 cup frozen carrots and peas
- 1 tbsp Vegetable oil
- 6 tbsp Soy sauce
- ½ cup Diced onion
- Also Needed: 7 by 2-inch cake pan

Directions:
- Set the Air Fryer at 360°F.
- Cook and dice the chicken. Prepare the rice. Dice the onion.
- Add the chilled rice, soy sauce, and oil into a mixing bowl. Stir well.
- Toss in the onion, chicken, peas, and carrots. Combine the fixings in the Air Fryer and fry for 20 minutes.
- Enjoy as a luncheon treat or serve as a side with your favorite dinner-time meal.

540. Chicken Curry

Preparation Time: 20 minutes
Cooking Time: 15 minutes
Servings: 4

Ingredients:
- 1 lb. Chicken breast
- 1 tsp Olive oil
- 1 Onion
- 2 tsp Garlic
- 1 tbsp Lemongrass
- ½ cup Chicken stock
- 1 tbsp Apple cider vinegar
- ½ cup Coconut milk
- 2 tbsp Curry paste

Directions:
- Warm the air fryer to reach 365°F.
- Dice the chicken into cubes. Peel and dice the onion and combine in the Air Fryer basket. Cook for five minutes.
- Remove the basket and add the rest of the fixings. Mix well and air-fry for ten more minutes.
- Serve for a quick and easy meal.

541. Coconut Chicken Tenders

Preparation Time: 20 minutes
Cooking Time: 25-30 minutes
Servings: 4

Ingredients:
- 2 large eggs
- 2 garlic powder tsp
- 1 tsp of salt
- 1/2 tsp black pepper
- 3/4 cup panko breadcrumbs
- 3/4 cup grated sweet coconut
- 1-pound tender chicken around 8 tenders
- Cooking spray

Directions:
- Preheat the air fryer to 400°F. Spray a large baking sheet with an oil spray.
- Add the eggs, garlic powder, salt, and pepper to a large, shallow dish. Beat until homogeneous. In a second large, shallow dish, add the panko breadcrumbs and grated coconut Stir to combine.
- Dip the chicken fillets in the egg mixture and cover both sides. Lift the chicken from the egg and let the excess drip off. Place the egg-coated chicken in the coconut mixture. Press the coconut mixture into the chicken and make sure all sides are completely covered. Place the coconut-coated chicken on the prepared baking sheet. Discard the excess egg and the coconut mixture. Spray the top of the chicken tender with an oil spray.
- Bake 12 to 14 minutes on the fryer until the chicken is cooked through and the coating is crisp and golden.

542. Creamy Chicken Alfredo

Preparation Time: 10 minutes
Cooking Time: 22 minutes
Servings: 4

Ingredients:
- 2 chicken breasts, skinless, boneless, and cubed
- 8 button mushrooms, sliced
- 1 red bell pepper, chopped
- 1 tbsp olive oil
- ½ tsp thyme, dried
- 10 ounces alfredo sauce
- 6 bread slices
- 2 tbsp butter, soft

Directions:
- In your air fryer, mix chicken with mushrooms, bell pepper, and oil, toss to coat well, and cook at 350°F for 15 minutes.
- Transfer chicken mixture to a bowl, add thyme and alfredo sauce, toss, return to air fryer and cook at 350°F for 4 minutes more.
- Spread butter on bread slices, add it to the fryer, butter side up and cook for 4 minutes more.
- Arrange toasted bread slices on a platter, and top each with chicken mixture.

543. Garlic Lemon Chicken with Green Olives

Preparation Time: 30 minutes
Cooking Time: 45-50 minutes
Servings: 8

Ingredients:
- 2 tbsp soft butter
- 1 tbsp olive oil

- Zested Rind of 1 lemon
- 3 cloves garlic chopped finely
- 100 g pitted green olives
- chopped finely
- 2 tbsp flat-leaf parsley
- chopped coarsely
- 1 x 1.5kg whole chicken
- 1 lemon cut into quarters
- 1 whole garlic bulb cut in half

Directions:
- Combine soft butter with rind, garlic, olives, and parsley.
- Push lemons and garlic bulbs into the chicken carcass. Gently add half the butter mix under the skin and spread the remaining all over the top of the chicken.
- Gently add half the butter mix under the skin and spread the remaining all over the top of the chicken. Place chicken into the inner pot, seal the lid, and cook on SLOW COOK POT ROAST for 5 hours (touch the MULTI COOK menu to select this program) or touch the PRESSURE COOK menu to select MEAT/POULTRY program for 45 minutes, breast side down (this will allow the chicken to caramelize nicely).
- Remove chicken and cut into four to serve.

544.   Tikka Masala Chicken

Preparation Time: 30 minutes
Cooking Time: 4hrs
Servings: 6

Ingredients:
- 1kg skinless chicken thigh cutlets
- 800g canned diced tomatoes
- 2 large brown onions, sliced thinly
- ⅔ cup tikka masala paste
- ¼ cup pouring cream
- 1 cup loosely packed fresh
- coriander leaves

Directions:
- Combine chicken, tomatoes, onion, and paste in the inner pot.
- Seal the lid, touch the SLOW COOK menu to select the SLOW COOK HIGH TEMP program. Set cooking time for 4 hours. Press START.
- Season to taste.
- Serve drizzled with cream, topped with coriander.

545.   Cottage Cheese -Stuffed Chicken Breast

Preparation Time: 35 minutes
Cooking Time: 20 -30 minutes
Servings: 2

Ingredients:
- 1/2 cup Cottage cheese
- 2 eggs, beaten
- 2 medium-sized chicken breasts, halved
- 2 tbsp fresh coriander, chopped
- 1tsp fine sea salt
- Seasoned breadcrumbs
- 1/3tsp freshly ground black pepper, to savor
- 3 cloves garlic, finely minced

Directions:
- Firstly, flatten out the chicken breast using a meat tenderizer.
- In a medium-sized mixing dish, combine the Cottage cheese with garlic, coriander, salt, and black pepper.
- Spread 1/3 of the mixture over the first chicken breast. Repeat with the remaining ingredients. Roll the chicken around the filling; make sure to secure it with toothpicks.
- Now, whisk the egg in a shallow bowl. In another shallow bowl, combine the salt, ground black pepper, and seasoned breadcrumbs.
- Coat the chicken breasts with the whisked egg; now, roll them in the breadcrumbs.
- Cook in the air fryer cooking basket at 365 °F for 22 minutes. Serve immediately.

546.   Creamy Cajun Chicken

Preparation Time: 30 minutes
Cooking Time: 20 minutes
Servings: 6

Ingredients:
- 3 green onions, thinly sliced
- ½ tbsp Cajun seasoning
- 1 ½ cup buttermilk
- 2 large-sized chicken breasts, cut into strips
- 1/2 tsp garlic powder
- 1 tsp salt
- 1 cup cornmeal mix
- 1 tsp shallot powder
- 1 ½ cup flour
- 1 tsp ground black pepper, or to taste

Directions:
- Prepare three mixing bowls. Combine 1/2 cup of the plain flour together with the cornmeal and Cajun seasoning in your bowl. In another bowl, place the buttermilk.
- Pour the remaining 1 cup of flour into the third bowl.
- Sprinkle the chicken strips with all the seasonings. Then, dip each chicken strip in the 1 cup of flour, then in the buttermilk; finally, dredge them in the cornmeal mixture.
- Cook the chicken strips in the air fryer baking pan for 16 minutes at 365 °F. Serve garnished with green onions. Bon appétit!

547.   Turkey with Mushrooms and Peas Casserole

Preparation Time: 20 minutes
Cooking Time: 30 minutes
Servings: 4

Ingredients:
- 1 chopped yellow onion
- Salt and black pepper to the taste
- 1 chopped celery stalk
- 2 lbs. skinless, boneless turkey breasts
- ½ cup peas
- 1 cup cream of mushrooms soup
- 1 cup chicken stock
- 1 cup bread cubes

Directions:

- Mix turkey with salt, pepper, onion, celery, peas, and stock in a dish that accommodates your air fryer
- Introduce blend in your air fryer and cook at 360°F for 15 minutes.
- Include solid bread shapes and cream of mushroom soup; mix, hurl and cook at 360°F for 5 minutes more.
- Share the supper among plates and serve hot.

548.   Duck with Cherries Recipe

Preparation Time: 20 minutes
Cooking Time: 30 minutes
Servings: 4

Ingredients:

- 4 Duck breasts; boneless, skin on and scored
- 1 tbsp Ginger; grated
- 2 cups Rhubarb; sliced
- Salt and black pepper to the taste
- 1 tsp ground cumin
- 1 tsp Minced Garlic
- 2 cups Pitted cherries
- ½ cup Sugar
- ½ tsp Ground clove
- ¼ cup Honey
- ½ cup chopped yellow onion
- ½ tsp Cinnamon powder
- 1/3 cup Balsamic vinegar
- 4 Chopped sage leaves
- 1 Jalapeno

Directions:

- Start by spicing the duck bosom with salt and pepper, put it in your air fryer preheated to 350 °F, and cook for 5 minutes on each side.
- On the other hand; heat a dish to over medium warmth, include sugar, nectar, vinegar, garlic, ginger, cumin, clove, cinnamon, sage, jalapeno, rhubarb, onion, and fruits; blend appropriately; at that point, bring to a stew and cook for 10 minutes.
- Add duck bosoms and hurl well,
- Share everything among plates and serve.

549.   Chive and Cheese Chicken Rolls

Preparation Time: 40 minutes
Cooking Time: 30-40 minutes
Servings: 6

Ingredients:

- 2 eggs, well-whisked
- Tortilla chips, crushed
- 1½ tbsp extra-virgin olive oil
- 1½ tbsp fresh chives, chopped
- 3 chicken breasts, halved lengthwise
- 1½ cup soft cheese
- 2 tsp sweet paprika
- ½ tsp wholegrain mustard
- ½ tsp cumin powder
- 1/3 tsp fine sea salt
- 1/3 cup fresh cilantro, chopped
- 1/3 tsp freshly ground black pepper, or more to taste

Directions:

- Flatten out each piece of the chicken breast using a rolling pin. Then, grab three mixing dishes.
- In the first one, combine the soft cheese with the cilantro, fresh chives, cumin, and mustard.
- In another mixing dish, whisk the eggs together with the sweet paprika. In the third dish, combine the salt, black pepper, and crushed tortilla chips.
- Spread the cheese mixture over each piece of chicken. Repeat with the remaining pieces of the chicken breasts; now, roll them up.
- Coat each chicken roll with the whisked egg; dredge each chicken roll into the tortilla chips mixture. Lower the rolls onto the air fryer cooking basket. Drizzle extra-virgin olive oil over all rolls.
- Air fry at 345 °F for 28 minutes, working in batches. Serve warm, garnished with sour cream if desired.

550.   Chicken Bruschetta

Preparation Time: 30 minutes
Cooking Time: 30 minutes
Servings: 4

Ingredients:

- 3 ripe tomatoes, cubed
- 2 minced cloves of garlic
- ¼ cup chopped red onion
- 2 tbsps. chopped basil leaves
- 1 tbsp. balsamic vinegar
- 3 oz. diced mozzarella
- 8 thinly sliced chicken cutlets
- 1 tbsp. olive oil
- Salt and ground black pepper

Directions:

- Place cubed tomatoes in a bowl. Mix in balsamic, pepper, onion, basil, olive oil, and garlic. Set aside for 15-20 minutes to blend the flavors. Mix in the cheese when ready to serve.
- Preheat your air fryer to 360 °F.
- Apply black pepper and salt to the chicken.
- Coat the air fryer basket with cooking spray.
- Place the chicken cutlets in the basket and cook for 6 minutes, turning over halfway through the cooking time.
- Transfer to a plate.
- Top the cutlets with the tomato mixture and serve.

551.   Chicken Tandoori

Preparation Time: 30 minutes
Cooking Time: 30 minutes
Servings: 4

Ingredients:

- ⅔ cup plain low-fat yogurt
- 2 tbsp freshly squeezed lemon juice
- 2 tsp curry powder
- ½ tsp ground cinnamon
- 2 garlic cloves, minced
- 2 tsp olive oil
- 4 (5-ounce) low-sodium boneless skinless chicken breasts

Directions:
- In a medium bowl, whisk the yogurt, lemon juice, curry powder, cinnamon, garlic, and olive oil.
- With a sharp knife, cut thin slashes into the chicken. Add it to the yogurt mixture and turn to coat. Let stand for 10 minutes at room temperature. You can also prepare this ahead of time and marinate the chicken in the refrigerator for up to 24 hours.
- Remove the chicken from the marinade and shake off any excess liquid. Discard any remaining marinade.
- Roast the chicken for 10 minutes at 400°F. With tongs, carefully turn each piece. Roast for 8 to 13 minutes more, or until the chicken reaches an internal temperature of 165°F on a meat thermometer. Serve immediately.

552.   Tex Mex Stir-fried Chicken

Preparation Time: 15 minutes
Cooking Time: 20 minutes
Servings: 4

Ingredients:
- 1 pound low-sodium boneless skinless chicken breasts, cut into 1-inch cubes
- 1 medium onion, chopped
- 1 red bell pepper, chopped
- 1 jalapeño pepper, minced
- 2 tsp olive oil
- ⅔ cup canned low-sodium black beans, rinsed and drained
- ½ cup low-sodium salsa
- 2 tsp chili powder

Directions:
- In a medium metal bowl, mix the chicken, onion, bell pepper, jalapeño, and olive oil. Stir-fry in the air fryer for 10 minutes, stirring once during cooking.
- Add the black beans, salsa, and chili powder. Cook for 7 to 10 minutes more at 400°F, stirring once until the chicken reaches an internal temperature of 165°F on a meat thermometer. Serve immediately.

553.   Juicy & Spicy Chicken Wings

Preparation Time: 10 minutes
Cooking Time: 30 minutes
Servings: 4

Ingredients:
- 2 lbs. chicken wings
- 12 oz hot sauce
- 1 tsp Worcestershire sauce
- 1 tsp Tabasco
- 6 tbsp butter, melted

Directions:
- Spray the air fryer basket with cooking spray.
- Add chicken wings into the air fryer basket and cook at 380°F for 25 minutes. Shake the basket after every 5 minutes.
- Meanwhile, in a bowl, mix together hot sauce, Worcestershire sauce, and butter. Set aside.
- Add chicken wings into the sauce and toss well.
- Serve and enjoy.

554.   Southern Chicken Stew

Preparation Time: 15 minutes
Cooking Time: 20 minutes
Servings: 6

Ingredients:
- 1 Tsp Cilantro
- 8 Ounces Chicken Breast, Boneless & Skinless
- 1 Onion
- ½ Cup Spinach
- 2 Cups Chicken Stock
- 5 Ounces Cabbage
- 6 Ounces Cauliflower
- 1 Tsp Salt
- 1 Green Bell Pepper
- 1/3 Cup Heavy Cream
- 1 Tsp Paprika
- 1 Tsp Butter
- 1 Tsp Cayenne Pepper

Directions:
- Start by cubing your chicken breast and then sprinkling your cilantro, cayenne, salt, and paprika over it.
- Heat your air fryer to 365°F, and then melt your butter in your air fryer basket.
- Add your chicken cubes in, cooking it for four minutes.
- Chop your spinach, and then dice your onion.
- Shred your cabbage and cut your cauliflower into florets. Chop your green pepper next, and then add them to your air fryer.
- Pour your chicken stock and heavy cream in, and then reduce your air fryer to 360°F. Cook for eight minutes, and stir before serving.

555.   Honey Glazed Chicken

Preparation Time: 10 minutes
Cooking Time: 30 minutes
Servings: 3

Ingredients:
- 6 fresh chicken thighs (they should be skinless and boneless)
- 1/2 cup of runny honey
- ½ cup cornstarch
- 1/2 cup Worcestershire sauce
- 2 tbsp of tomato sauce
- 1 ½ tsp of fresh crushed garlic
- 1/2 tsp of ground ginger
- 4 portions of steamed wild rice
- 1 small onion finely chopped
- salt and fresh ground black pepper to taste

Directions:
- Place the crisper plate in the Air Fryer drawer.
- Use non-stick cooking spray to spray the crisper plate.
- Preheat the Air Fryer to 390°F. Use the Air Fry setting and set the preheat for 3 minutes.
- Pour the cornstarch into a large bowl.
- Cut the chicken into chunks or cubes.
- Place the cubed chicken in the bowl with the cornstarch and toss the chicken in order to coat it with cornstarch completely.
- Place the cornstarch-coated chicken cubes into the Air Fryer on top of the crisping plate.

- Set the Air Fryer for 25 minutes and use the Air Fry setting to start cooking the chicken.
- After 12 minutes, pause the Air Fryer in order to turn the chicken over using the food tongs.
- Once the chicken cubes have all been turned, start the Air Fryer to continue cooking the chicken cubes for the last 13 minutes.
- While the chicken is cooking, heat the honey, garlic, Worcestershire sauce, tomato sauce, and ginger, bring the mixture slowly to a boil and whisk in a tbsp of cornstarch to thicken the sauce.
- When the chicken has finished cooking in the Air Fryer, remove the drawer and put the chicken cubes into a heatproof bowl.
- Pour the honey sauce over the chicken cubes. Mix it around, so the chicken is coated.
- Serve on a bed of rice with some greens of your choice.

556.   Beer-Coated Duck Breast

Preparation Time: 15 minutes
Cooking Time: 20 minutes
Servings: 2

Ingredients:
- 1 tbsp olive oil
- 1 tsp mustard
- 1 tbsp fresh thyme, chopped
- 1 cup beer
- Salt and ground black pepper, as required
- 1 (10½-ounces) duck breast
- 6 cherry tomatoes
- 1 tbsp balsamic vinegar

Directions:
- In a bowl, mix together the oil, mustard, thyme, beer, salt, and black pepper.
- Add the duck breast and generously coat with marinade.
- Cover and refrigerate for about 4 hours.
- Set the temperature of the Air Fryer to 390 °F.
- With a piece of foil, cover the duck breast and arrange it into an Air Fryer basket.
- Air Fry for about 15 minutes.
- Remove the foil from the breast.
- Now, set the temperature of the Air Fryer to 355 °F. Grease the Air Fryer basket.
- Place duck breast and tomatoes into the prepared Air Fryer basket.
- Air Fry for about 5 minutes.
- Remove from Air Fryer and place the duck breast onto a cutting board for about 5 minutes before slicing.
- With a sharp knife, cut the duck breast into desired size slices and transfer onto serving plates.
- Drizzle with vinegar and serve alongside the cherry tomatoes.

557.   Duck and Tea Sauce Recipe

Preparation Time: 10 minutes
Cooking Time: 30 minutes
Servings: 2

Ingredients:
- 2 boneless duck breast halves
- ¾ cup chopped shallot
- Salt and black pepper to the taste

- 2¼ cups chicken stock
- 1½ cups orange juice
- 3 tsp Earl gray tea leaves
- 3 tbsp melted butter
- 1 tbsp Honey

Directions:
- Season duck bosom parts with salt and pepper, move to your preheated air fryer and cook at 360 °F for 10 minutes.
- On the other hand, heat a skillet with the margarine to over medium warmth, include shallot; mix and cook for 2-3 minutes.
- Include stock; mix and cook for one more moment.
- Include squeezed orange, tea leaves, and nectar; mix, cook for 2-3 minutes more, and strain into a bowl.
- Share duck on plates; spread tea sauce all finished, and serve.

558.   Chinese Style Chicken Wings

Preparation Time: 20 minutes
Cooking Time: 30 minutes
Servings: 2

Ingredients:
- 4 Chicken wings
- 1 tbsp Chinese spice
- 1 tbsp Mixed spices - your choice
- 1 tbsp Soy sauce

Directions:
- Warm the Air Fryer to 356°F.
- Add the seasonings into a large mixing bowl, stirring thoroughly. Pour it over the chicken wings until each piece is covered.
- Put some aluminum foil on the base of the fryer, and add the chicken, sprinkling any remnants over the chicken. Air-fry it for 15 minutes.
- Flip the chicken and air-fry for another 15 minutes at 392°F.

559.   Tequila Orange Chicken

Preparation Time: 30 minutes
Cooking Time: 50 minutes
Servings: 4

Ingredients:
- ¼ cup tequila
- 1 shallot, minced
- 1/3 cup orange juice
- 2 tbsp brown sugar
- 2 tbsp honey
- 2 tbsp whole coriander seeds
- 3 cloves of garlic, minced
- 3 pounds of chicken breasts
- Salt and pepper to taste

Directions:
- Place all ingredients in a Ziploc bag and allow to marinate for at least 2 hours in the fridge.
- Preheat the air fryer to 390°F.
- Place the grill pan accessory in the air fryer.
- Grill the chicken for at least 40 minutes
- Flip the chicken every 10 minutes for even cooking.

- Meanwhile, pour the marinade into a saucepan and simmer until the sauce thickens.
- Brush the chicken with the glaze before serving.

560. Lebanese Chicken

Preparation Time: 20 minutes
Cooking Time: 20 minutes
Servings: 4

Ingredients:
- 1 onion, cut into large chunks
- 1 small green bell pepper, cut into large chunks
- 1 tsp tomato paste
- 1/2 cup chopped fresh flat-leaf parsley
- 1/2 tsp dried oregano
- 1/3 cup plain yogurt
- 1/8 tsp ground allspice
- 1/8 tsp ground black pepper
- 1/8 tsp ground cardamom
- 1/8 tsp ground cinnamon
- 1-pound skinless, boneless chicken breast halves cut into 2-inch pieces
- 2 cloves garlic, minced
- 2 tbsp lemon juice
- 2 tbsp vegetable oil
- 3/4 tsp salt

Directions:
- In a resealable plastic bag, mix cardamom, cinnamon, allspice, pepper, oregano, salt, tomato paste, garlic, yogurt, vegetable oil, and lemon juice. Add chicken, remove excess air, seal, and marinate in the ref for at least 4 hours.
- Thread chicken into skewers, place on skewer rack, and cook in batches.
- For 10 minutes, cook at 360°F. Halfway through cooking time, turnover skewers.
- Serve and enjoy with a sprinkle of parsley.

561. Turkey Shepherd's Pie

Preparation Time: 30 minutes
Cooking Time: 50 minutes
Servings: 4

Ingredients:
- 1 tbsp butter, room temperature
- 1/2 clove garlic, minced
- 1/2 large carrot, shredded
- 1/2 onion, chopped
- 1/2 tsp chicken bouillon powder
- 1/2-pound ground turkey
- 1/8 tsp dried thyme
- 1-1/2 large potatoes, peeled
- 1-1/2 tsp all-purpose flour
- 1-1/2 tsp chopped fresh parsley
- 1-1/2 tsp olive oil
- 2 tbsp warm milk
- 4.5-ounce can slice mushrooms
- ground black pepper to taste
- salt to taste

Directions:
- Until tender, boil potatoes, drain, and transfer to a bowl. Mash with milk and butter until creamy. Set aside.

- Lightly grease the baking pan of the air fryer with olive oil. Add onion and for 5 minutes, cook at 360°F. Add chicken bouillon, garlic, thyme, parsley, mushrooms, carrot, and ground turkey. Cook for 10 minutes while stirring and crumbling halfway through cooking time.
- Season with pepper and salt. Stir in flour and mix well. Cook for 2 minutes.
- Evenly spread turkey mixture. Top with mashed potatoes evenly.
- Cook for 20 minutes or until potatoes are lightly browned.
- Serve and enjoy.

562. California Style Grilled Chicken

Preparation Time: 30 minutes
Cooking Time: 40 minutes
Servings: 4

Ingredients:
- ¾ cup balsamic vinegar
- 1 tsp garlic powder
- 2 tbsp extra virgin olive oil
- 2 tbsp honey
- 2 tsp Italian seasoning
- 4 boneless chicken breasts
- 4 slices mozzarella
- 4 slices of avocado
- 4 slices tomato
- Balsamic vinegar for drizzling
- Salt and pepper to taste

Directions:
- In a Ziploc bag, mix together the balsamic vinegar, garlic powder, honey, olive oil, Italian seasoning, salt, pepper, and chicken. Allow marinating in the fridge for at least 2 hours.
- Preheat the air fryer to 390°F.
- Place the grill pan accessory in the air fryer.
- Put the chicken on the grill and cook for 40 minutes.
- Flip the chicken every 10 minutes to grill all sides evenly.
- Serve the chicken with mozzarella, avocado, and tomato. Drizzle with balsamic vinegar.

563. Blackened Baked Chicken

Preparation Time: 10 minutes
Cooking Time: 18 minutes
Servings: 4

Ingredients:
- 4 chicken breasts
- 2 tsp olive oil
- Seasoning:
- 1 1/2 tbsp brown sugar
- 1 tsp paprika
- 1 tsp dried oregano
- 1/4 tsp garlic powder
- 1/2 tsp salt and pepper
- Garnish:
- Chopped parsley

Directions:
- Mix olive oil with brown sugar, paprika, oregano, garlic powder, salt, and black pepper in a bowl.

- Place the chicken breasts in the baking tray of the Oven.
- Pour and rub this mixture liberally over all the chicken breasts.
- Turn the dial to select the "Bake" mode.
- Hit the Time button and again use the dial to set the cooking time to 18 minutes.
- Now push the Temp button and rotate the dial to set the temperature at 425 °F.
- Once preheated, place the baking tray inside the oven.
- Serve warm.

564. Brined Turkey Breast

Preparation Time: 10 minutes
Cooking Time: 45 minutes
Servings: 10

Ingredients:
- 7 lb. bone-in, skin-on turkey breast
- Brine:
- 1/2 cup salt
- 1 lemon
- 1/2 onion
- 3 cloves garlic, smashed
- 5 sprigs of fresh thyme
- 3 bay leaves
- black pepper
- Turkey Breast:
- 4 tbsp butter, softened
- 1/2 tsp black pepper
- 1/2 tsp garlic powder
- 1/4 tsp dried thyme
- 1/4 tsp dried oregano

Directions:
- Mix the turkey brine ingredients in a pot and soak the turkey in the brine overnight.
- The next day, remove the soaked turkey from the brine.
- Whisk the butter, black pepper, garlic powder, oregano, and thyme.
- Brush the butter mixture over the turkey, then place it on a baking tray.
- Press the "Power Button" on Air Fry Oven and turn the dial to select the "Air Roast" mode.
- Press the Time button and again turn the dial to set the cooking time to 45 minutes.
- Now push the Temp button and rotate the dial to set the temperature at 370 °F.
- Once preheated, place the turkey baking tray in the oven and close its lid.
- Slice and serve warm.

565. Thyme Chicken Balls

Preparation Time: 10 minutes
Cooking Time: 10 minutes
Servings: 4

Ingredients:
- 1-lb. ground chicken
- 1/3 cup panko
- 1 tsp salt
- 2 tsp chives
- 1/2 tsp garlic powder
- 1 tsp thyme

- 1 egg

Directions:
- Toss all the meatball ingredients in a bowl and mix well.
- Make small meatballs out of this mixture and place them in the air fryer basket.
- Press the "Power Button" of the Air Fry Oven and turn the dial to select the "Air Fry" mode.
- Press the Time button and again turn the dial to set the cooking time to 10 minutes.
- Now push the Temp button and rotate the dial to set the temperature at 350 °F.
- Once preheated, place the air fryer basket inside and close its lid.
- Serve warm.

566. Chicken Parmesan Meatballs

Preparation Time: 15 minutes
Cooking Time: 12 minutes
Servings: 4

Ingredients:
- 1-lb. ground chicken
- 1 large egg, beaten
- ½ cup Parmesan cheese, grated
- ½ cup pork rinds, ground
- 1 tsp garlic powder
- 1 tsp paprika
- 1 tsp kosher salt
- ½ tsp pepper
- Crust:
- ½ cup pork rinds, ground

Directions:
- Toss all the meatball ingredients in a bowl and mix well.
- Make small meatballs out of this mixture and roll them in the pork rinds.
- Place the coated meatballs in the air fryer basket.
- Press the "Power Button" of the Air Fry Oven and turn the dial to select the "Bake" mode.
- Press the Time button and again turn the dial to set the cooking time to 12 minutes.
- Now push the Temp button and rotate the dial to set the temperature at 400 °F.
- Once preheated, place the air fryer basket inside and close its lid.
- Serve warm.

567. Chicken with Chanterelle Mushrooms

Preparation Time: 15 minutes
Cooking Time: 35 minutes
Servings: 2

Ingredients:
- 2 chicken legs á 200 g
- 100 g of chanterelles
- 50 g mushrooms
- 1 shallot
- ½ bunch of thyme
- Sea salt & pepper
- 2 tbsp olive oil

Directions:
- Rinse chicken thighs under warm water and dry
- Peel and dice shallot
- Remove thyme leaves from the stalk.
- In a large Air Fryer, heat 1 tbsp of olive oil and sauté chicken legs from all sides.
- Sprinkle chicken thighs with thyme and cook in preheated oven at 140 ° C for about 35 minutes.
- Brush mushrooms In a second Air Fryer, heat 1 tbsp of olive oil and fry the shallots.
- Add the mushrooms and fry for a short time.
- Season the mushroom Air Fryer with salt and pepper and add to the chicken.

568.   Roasted Chicken with Tomato Salsa

Preparation Time: 20 minutes
Cooking Time: 20 minutes
Servings: 2

Ingredients:
- 2 chicken breast fillets á 200 g
- ½ tsp of paprika
- ½ tsp turmeric
- Sea salt (Fleur de sel)
- pepper
- 1 tbsp olive oil
- For the salsa
- 2 tomatoes
- 50 g of zucchini
- 1 red onion
- ½ bunch of coriander
- 1 red chili pepper
- 1 clove of garlic
- Juice of a lime
- Sea salt
- pepper

Directions:
- Cut the tomatoes and zucchini into small cubes
- Peel the onion and garlic and cut them to size.
- Chop the chili and coriander.
- Pour lime juice into a bowl and add minced Ingredients
- Season with salt and pepper and leave to soak.
- For the chicken breast, mix spices in a small bowl and rub fillets with them.
- Heat olive oil in an Air Fryer and fry fillets from both sides at 375°F for 20 minutes.
- Remove chicken breast fillets from the Air Fryer, cut them up, and spread tomato salsa on top.

569.   Sautéed Duck with Asian Vegetables

Preparation Time: 24 minutes
Cooking Time: 30 minutes
Servings: 3

Ingredients:
- 500 g of duck breast fillets
- 200 g Chinese cabbage
- 200 g of broccoli
- 12 brown mushrooms
- 2 spring onions
- 2 cloves of garlic
- 2 red chili peppers
- ½ red pepper
- about 4 cm of fresh ginger
- Juice of a lemon
- 100 ml vegetable fond
- 6 tbsp soy sauce
- 1 tbsp. Sesame oil
- 1 tsp honey
- Bamboo salt
- pepper

Directions:
- Cut the duck breast fillets into strips
- Cut the Chinese cabbage into small pieces
- Cut the broccoli florets from the stalk
- Clean the pomegranates
- Brush the mushrooms and cut them in half.
- Clean the spring onions and cut them into wide rings
- Peel the garlic and ginger and cut into thin slices
- Cut the chili peppers into rings
- Cut the peppers into bite-sized pieces.
- Place the duck breast with onion in the air fryer basket, skin side up, and cook for 5 minutes at 390°F/ 195°C.
- Air-fry the duck breast for a further 10-12 minutes at a temperature of up to 320°F, 160°C, once the time is up.
- Put the paprika and broccoli in the hot wok and sauté.
- Add mushrooms, garlic, and ginger and sauté
- Chinese cabbage and chili peppers last
- Add the stock and add meat again.
- Add soy sauce, honey, and lemon juice and simmer briefly.
- Season with salt and pepper, and serve hot.

570.   Roasted Duck with Orange-Date Stuffing

Preparation Time: 30 minutes
Cooking Time: 2 hrs. 15 minutes
Servings: 8

Ingredients:
- 1 free-range duck, approx. 1.5 kg
- 2 oranges, organic quality
- 400 g Brussels sprouts
- 150 g of celeriac
- 3 shallots
- 2 carrots
- 6 dates, pitted
- 1 bunch of thyme
- 4 - 5 sprigs of rosemary
- 4 branches of oregano
- 1 L of poultry or vegetable fond
- 200 ml of red wine
- 50 g butter
- 2 tbsp olive oil
- 2-star anise
- 2 bay leaves
- 1 tsp Ras el hanout
- Pepper pink
- sea-salt
- pepper

Directions:
- Rinse the duck under running water and dab it dry
- Wash the orange hot and grate dry, then cut into pieces
- Wash and dry the herbs

- Crush the dates roughly and add the orange and duck to the duck along with the herbs and pieces. The skin of the duck rub in with salt and pepper.
- Peel the shallots and finely dice
- Peel and slice the carrots
- Peel the celeriac and cut it into small cubes
- Heat the oil in the roasting Air Fryer Roast the all-around duck brown. Add the shallots, carrots, celery, and sauté.
- Deglaze everything with wine and add the pieces of the second orange
- Add half of the fund to the duck and let it boil down briefly
- Add the star anise, bay leaves, Ras el hanout, and paprika, and stir.
- Duck in a roasting Air Fryer in a preheated oven at 150 °C. Roast air for 2 hours, and pour duck with the sauce from the roasting tin in between.
- After 20 minutes, add the remaining stock and continue to cook the duck.
- Whisk Brussels sprouts and remove the withered leaves
- Halve brussels sprouts and cover with steam over a little water. Cook for 5 minutes until firm.
- Put brussels sprouts in a sauce Air Fryer.

571.   Chicken Breasts with Passion Fruit Sauce

Preparation Time: 10 minutes
Cooking Time: 20 minutes
Servings: 4

Ingredients:
- passion fruits; halved, de-seeded and pulp reserved-4
- maple syrup-2 oz.
- Whiskey-1 tbsp.
- chicken breasts 4
- Anise-2-star
- chopped chives; -1 bunch
- Salt and black pepper to the taste

Directions:
- Start by warming a skillet with the enthusiasm natural product mash to over medium warmth, incorporate bourbon, star anise, maple syrup, and chives; mix well, stew for 5-6 minutes, and remove the heat.
- Season chicken with salt and pepper; put in a preheated air fryer and cook at 360 °F for 10 minutes; flipping most of the way during cooking.
- Share chicken on plates, heat the sauce a bit, spread it over the chicken, and serve.

572.   Tangy Orange Chicken Wings

Preparation Time: 10 minutes
Cooking Time: 25-30 minutes
Servings: 3

Ingredients:
- 6 chicken wings
- Orange juice from 1 orange
- 1 tsp orange zest
- 1½ tbsp Worcestershire sauce
- Country herbs (basil, oregano, mint, parsley, thyme, rosemary, and sage)
- 1 tbsp sugar
- Salt and ground black pepper to taste

Directions:
- Ensure that the chicken wings are washed well and pat dry.
- Mix juice and orange zest in a big clean bowl.
- Place the chicken wings inside the bowl and stir well until the wings are fully coated.
- Make a mixture of Worcestershire sauce, country herbs, sugar, salt, and black pep-per in another bowl.
- Rub all sides of the wing with this mix-ture.
- Ensure that the Air Fryer is preheated to 360°F.
- Wrap the rubbed/coated chicken wings, alongside the sauce, with an aluminum foil.
- Transfer the wrapped wings into the air fryer and let it cook for 20 minutes.
- Remove the cooked chicken wings with the sauce and place them in a bowl.
- Using the sauce, brush the wings be-fore returning them to the air fryer. Do not dispose of the remains of the orange sauce.
- Let the wings cook for another 15 minutes in the air fryer. Remove and brush again with the remains of the or-ange source.
- Cook for an additional ten minutes.
- Remove from the fryer and serve.

573.   Indonesian Chicken Drumettes

Preparation Time: 20 minutes
Cooking Time: 25-30 minutes
Servings: 4

Ingredients:
- 1½ lbs. chicken wing drumettes
- Olive oil cooking spray
- 1 tbsp lower-sodium soy sauce
- ½ tsp cornstarch
- 1 tsp finely chopped garlic
- ½ tsp finely chopped fresh ginger
- 1 tsp sambal oelek (ground fresh chili paste)
- ¼ tsp kosher salt
- 1 tsp fresh lime juice
- 2 tsp honey
- 2 tbsp chopped

Directions:
- Pat the rinsed chicken drumettes dry using paper towels and then spray with olive oil.
- Ensure that your air fryer is preheated to 400°F.
- Transfer the chicken drumettes to the air fryer, maintaining a single layer.
- Allow cooking in the air fryer for 22 min-utes while shaking twice or thrice.
- Withdraw the drumettes when crispy.
- With the drumettes in the air fryer, get a clean saucepan, and combine the soy sauce and cornstarch.
- Toss in the garlic, ginger, sambal, salt, lime juice, and honey.
- Stir the mixture thoroughly and transfer to medium-high heat.
- Cook until the mixture becomes thickened and starts to form bubbles.
- Remove the chicken drumettes and place them in a big bowl.
- Pour the sauce mixture over the drumettes and stir mildly.

- Add chopped scallions and toppings before serving.

574. Louisiana Chicken Drumettes

Preparation Time: 20 minutes
Cooking Time: 45 minutes
Servings: 4

Ingredients:

- 2 large slices of bread
- Salt and ground black pepper to taste
- 1 tbsp dried garlic and onion
- 1 tsp basil
- ½ tsp cayenne pepper
- 1 tbsp plain flour 2 tbsp paprika
- 5 oz buttermilk
- 4 chicken drumsticks
- 1 tbsp oregano
- 1 tbsp rosemary
- 1 tbsp thyme
- 1 tsp olive oil

Directions:

- Ensure that the Air Fryer is preheated to about 365°F - it takes about two minutes.
- In addition to the bread, add the salt, pep-per, dried garlic, onion, basil, and a pinch of cayenne. Blend the mixture in the blender until the blend looks like bread-crumbs. Put the blend into a separate bowl and set aside.
- In a new bowl, add flour and mix with ½ the paprika while adding pepper and salt to taste. Set aside this bowl also.
- Get a third bowl and make a mixture of the buttermilk, the chicken drumsticks, and the rest of the seasonings. Stir the mixture well while the drumsticks are submerged.
- Take out each chicken drumstick from the bowl and place it in the flour, and after that, in the breadcrumbs.
- Once you are done with the dipping for each, place them into the basket in your air fryer.
- After coating all the chicken drumsticks, sprinkle a bit of olive oil to ensure that they do not dry while improving their taste.
- Place all coated and oiled drumsticks in the air fryer and cook for about 30 minutes at 365°F. Reduce the heat to 345°F and cook for an extra two minutes.
- Remove from the air fryer and serve.

575. Super Cheesy Chicken Mac and Cheese

Preparation Time: 10 minutes
Cooking Time: 9 minutes
Servings: 6

Ingredients:

- 2 1/2 cup macaroni
- 2 cup chicken stock
- 1 cup cooked chicken, shredded
- 1 1/4 cup heavy cream
- 8 tbsp butter
- 2 2/3 cups cheddar cheese, shredded
- 1/3 cup parmesan cheese, shredded
- 1 bag of Ritz crackers
- 1/4 tsp garlic powder

- Salt and pepper to taste

Directions:

- Add chicken stock, heavy cream, chicken, 4 tbsp butter, and macaroni to the Air fryer Duo.
- Put on the pressure-cooking lid and seal it.
- Hit the "Pressure Button" and select 4 minutes of cooking time, then press "Start."
- Crush the crackers and mix them well with 4 tbsp melted butter.
- Once the Air fryer Duo beeps, do a quick release and remove its lid.
- Put on the Air Fryer lid and seal it.
- Hit the "Air Fryer Button" and select 5 minutes of cooking time, then press "Start."
- Once the Air fryer Duo beeps, remove its lid.
- Serve.

576. Creamy Turmeric Chicken

Preparation Time: 20 minutes
Cooking Time: 35 minutes
Servings: 2

Ingredients:

- 3 pcs whole chicken leg (de-skin or with skin is totally up to you)
- 4-5 tsp ground turmeric
- ½ tbsp salt
- 2 oz galangal
- 2 oz pure coconut paste (or coconut milk)
- 2 oz old ginger

Directions:

- Do not pound or blend the chicken meat; all other ingredients should be pounded or blended.
- With a focus on the thick parts, cut a few slits on the leg of the chicken. The cuttings will increase the absorption of the flavor during marinating.
- Add the blended ingredients to the chicken and allow to marinate for no less than four hours, or if possible, overnight. During the marinating process, the sea-soned chicken should be wrapped with a cling film and stored inside the refrigera-tor.
- Set the Air Fryer to 375°F and allow to pre-heat at this temperature, then air-fry the chicken for about 20-25 minutes, frying each side for half of the total time.
- Once you have a golden-brown chicken, you can proceed to serve.

577. Chicken Tikka Kebab

Preparation Time: 10 minutes
Cooking Time: 17 minutes
Servings: 4

Ingredients:

- 1 lb. chicken thighs, boneless skinless, cubed
- 1 tbsp oil
- 1/2 cup red onion, cubed
- 1/2 cup green bell pepper, cubed
- 1/2 cup red bell pepper, cubed
- lime wedges to garnish
- onion rounds to garnish
- For marinade:
- 1/2 cup yogurt Greek

- 3/4 tbsp ginger, grated
- 3/4 tbsp garlic, minced
- 1 tbsp lime juice
- 2 tsp red chili powder mild
- 1/2 tsp ground turmeric
- 1 tsp garam masala
- 1 tsp coriander powder
- 1/2 tbsp dried fenugreek leaves
- 1 tsp salt

Directions:

Prepare the marinade by mixing yogurt with all its Ingredients: in a bowl.

- Fold in chicken, then mix well to coat and refrigerate for 8 hours.
- Add bell pepper, onions, and oil to the marinade and mix well.
- Thread the chicken, peppers, and onions on the skewers.
- Set the Air Fryer Basket in the Air fryer Duo.
- Put on the Air Fryer lid and seal it.
- Hit the "Air Fry Button" and select 10 minutes of cooking time, then press "Start."
- Once the Air fryer Duo beeps and remove its lid.
- Flip the skewers and continue Air frying for 7 minutes.

578. Chicken Tenders

Preparation Time: 20 minutes
Cooking Time: 10-15 minutes
Servings: 3

Ingredients:

- 12 oz of chicken breasts
- Salt and ground black pepper to taste
- 1 oz flour
- 1 egg white
- 1¼ oz panko bread crumbs

Directions:

- Before you cut the chicken breast into ten-ders, remove any excess fat by trimming.
- Use the combination of salt and pepper to season each side.
- Get your flour, egg, and panko bread-crumbs into different clean bowls.
- Then dip the chicken tenders into flour, eggs, and panko breadcrumbs, respectively.
- Arrange the coated chicken into the bas-ket of your air fryer, and spray with olive spray.
- Set your air fryer to 350°F and cook.
- Let the chicken cook through - for about 10 minutes.

579. Sticky BBQ Chicken

Preparation Time: 5 minutes
Cooking Time: 24 minutes
Servings: 4

Ingredients:

- 2-pound Chicken Drumettes, bone in and skin in
- ½ cup Chicken Broth
- ½ tsp Dry Mustard
- ½ tsp Sweet Paprika
- ½ tbsp Cumin Powder
- ½ tsp Onion Powder
- ¼ tsp Cayenne Powder
- Salt and Pepper, to taste
- 1 stick of butter, sliced into 5 to 7 pieces
- BBQ Sauce to taste

Directions:

- Pour the chicken broth into the inner pot of the cooker and insert the reversible rack. In a zipper bag, pour in dry mustard, cumin powder, onion powder, cayenne powder, salt, and pepper. Add chicken, close the bag and shake to coat the chicken well with the spices.
- Then, remove the chicken from the bag and place it on the rack. Spread the butter slices on the drumsticks. Close the lid, secure the pressure valve, and select Pressure mode on High pressure for 10 minutes. Press Start.
- Once the timer has ended, do a quick pressure release, and open the lid.
- Remove the chicken onto a clean flat surface like a cutting board and brush them with the barbecue sauce using the brush. Return to the rack and close the crisping lid. Cook for 10 minutes at 400°F on Air Fry mode. Serve immediately.

580. Tender and Juicy Whole Chicken

Preparation Time: 10 minutes
Cooking Time: 30 minutes
Servings: 6

Ingredients:

- 3 pounds of whole chicken
- 1 tbsp garlic, minced
- 3 tbsp butter
- 8 cups of water
- 2 bay leaves
- 1 tsp dried thyme
- 1 tsp dried rosemary
- 1 tsp dried oregano
- 5 tsp sea salt

Directions:

- Add water, thyme, rosemary, oregano, bay leaves, and salt into the air fryer and stir well.
- Place chicken into the air fryer duo.
- Seal the pot with a pressure cooking lid and cook on high pressure for 20 minutes.
- Once done, allow to release pressure naturally. Remove lid.
- Remove chicken from pot and set aside. Clean the air fryer.
- In a pan, melt butter over medium heat. Add garlic and saute for 1 minute. Remove from heat.
- Brush chicken with garlic butter.
- Place steamer rack in the air fryer, then places chicken on top of the rack.
- Seal pot with air fryer lid and select broil mode, and set timer for 5 minutes. Serve and enjoy.

581. Crispy Fried Whole Chicken

Preparation Time: 5 minutes
Cooking Time: 1 hour and 10 minutes
Servings: 4

Ingredients:

- 1 Whole chicken

- 2 tbsp or spray of oil of choice
- 1 tsp garlic powder
- 1 tsp onion powder
- 1 tsp paprika
- 1 tsp Italian seasoning
- 2 tbsp Montreal Steak Seasoning (or salt and pepper to taste)
- 1.5 cup chicken broth

Directions:

- Truss and wash the chicken.
- Mix the seasoning and rub a little amount on the chicken.
- Pour the broth inside the Air fryer Duo Crisp Air Fryer.
- Place the chicken in the air fryer basket.
- Select the option Air Fry Close the Air Fryer lid and cook for 25 minutes.
- Spray or rub the top of the chicken with oil and rub it with half of the seasoning.
- Close the air fryer lid and air fry again at 400°F for 10 minutes.
- Flip the chicken, spray it with oil, and rub it with the remaining seasoning.
- Again, air fry it for another ten minutes.
- Allow the chicken to rest for 10 minutes.

582. Turkey Wings with Collard Greens

Preparation Time: 10 minutes
Cooking Time: 17 minutes
Servings: 2

Ingredients:

- 1 sweet onion; chopped
- 2 smoked turkey wings
- 1/2 tsp crushed red pepper
- 2 tbsp apple cider vinegar
- 1 tbsp brown sugar
- 2 tbsp olive oil
- 3 garlic cloves; minced
- 2 ½ pound collard greens; chopped
- Salt and black pepper to the taste

Directions:

- Add oil and onions to the dish and place it over medium heat to sauté for 2 minutes. Add vinegar, greens, salt, pepper, garlic, red pepper, smoked turkey, and sugar. Mix well, then transfer to the Air fryer. Put on the Instant Air Fryer lid and cook on Bake mode for 15 minutes at 350°F. Once done, remove the lid and serve warm.

583. Fried Duck Thighs

Preparation Time: 5 minutes
Cooking Time: 50 minutes
Servings: 4

Ingredients:

- 2 pcs. Duck legs
- 1 tsp salt
- 1 tsp spice mixture (for ducks and geese)
- 1 tsp olive oil

Directions:

- For the duck legs of the Air fryer, the duck legs wash and pat dry. Mix the oil with the salt and the spice mixture and rub the duck legs around with it.

- Place the spiced duck legs on the rack of the hot air fryer and cook at 200 ° C for 40 minutes. After 20 minutes, turn the legs once.
- The duck leg from the Air fryer with red cabbage and dumplings served by choice.

584. Taco Turkey Casserole

Preparation Time: 5 minutes
Cooking Time: 40 minutes
Servings: 6

Ingredients:

- 8 oz. shredded cheese
- 1 ½ - 2 lbs. ground turkey
- 1 cup salsa
- 2 tbsp. taco seasoning
- 16 oz. cottage cheese

Directions:

- Switch on the oven to 400°F.
- In a sizeable casserole dish, put in the ground meat and mix in the taco seasoning—Bake for 20 minutes.
- While ground turkey is baking, mix 1 cup of shredded cheese, cottage cheese, and salsa.
- Take the casserole from the oven and strain out any leftover juices from the ground meat.
- Pound and crush the meat into smaller pieces and then layer the cottage cheese and salsa combo over the meat. Sprinkle the remaining cheese on top of the ground meat.
- Put the casserole back into the oven and bake for 15-20 minutes until the meat cooks all the way through. And the cheese is melted and bubbling.

585. Fiery Citrus Chicken

Preparation Time: 10 minutes
Cooking Time: 28 minutes
Servings: 2

Ingredients:

- ½ cup hot sauce
- 2 tbsp butter
- ½ cup water
- 1/3 cup lemon juice
- 1-pound drumstick

Directions:

- Add all the ingredients into the cook and crisp basket and place the basket inside the air fryer duo.
- Place the pressure cooker lid on top of the pot and close the pressure valve to the seal position. Set the pressure cooker function to 400°F and set the timer for 5 minutes
- Immediately after the cooking is done, release the pressure quickly by carefully opening the steamer valve.
- Serve hot

586. Air-Fried Lemon Olive Chicken

Preparation Time: 10 minutes
Cooking Time: 15 minutes
Servings: 4

Ingredients

- 4 Boneless Skinless Chicken Breasts

- 1/2tsp organic cumin
- 1tsp sea salt
- 1/4tsp black pepper
- 1/2cup butter, melted
- 1 lemons1/2 juiced, 1/2 thinly sliced
- 1cup chicken bone-broth
- 1can pitted green olives
- 1/2cup red onions, sliced

Directions:
- Liberally season the chicken breasts with sea salt, cumin, and black pepper
- Preheat your air fryer toast oven to 370°F and brush the chicken breasts with melted butter.
- Cook in the pan of your air fryer toast oven for about 5 minutes until evenly browned.
- Add all remaining ingredients and cook at 320°For 10 minutes.
- Serve hot!

587.   Fried Chicken with Salsa Verde

Preparation Time: 5 minutes
Cooking Time: 25 minutes
Servings: 2

Ingredients:
- 10 ounces Salsa Verde
- 1 tbsp paprika
- 1-pound boneless chicken breasts
- 1 tsp ground coriander
- 1 tsp cilantro

Directions:
- Rub the boneless chicken breasts with paprika, ground black pepper, and cilantro. Set the pressure cooker to "Pressure" mode.
- Place the boneless chicken into the pressure cooker. Sprinkle the meat with the salsa Verde and stir well.
- Close the pressure cooker lid and cook for 30 minutes.
- When the Cooking Time ends, release the pressure and transfer the chicken to the mixing bowl. Shred the chicken well. Serve it.

588.   Rotisserie Chicken

Preparation Time: 5 minutes
Cooking Time: 1 hour
Servings: 4

Ingredients:
- 1 whole chicken, cleaned and patted dry
- 2 tbsp Olive oil
- 1 tbsp Seasoned salt

Directions:
- Remove the giblet packet from the cavity. Rub the chicken with oil and salt. Place in the air fryer basket, breast-side down. Cook at 350°F for 30 minutes. Then flip and cook another 30 minutes. Chicken is done when it reaches an internal temperature of 165°F.

589.   Italian Parmesan Chicken Wings

Preparation Time: 5 minutes
Cooking Time: 15 minutes
Servings: 4

Ingredients:
- 2 lbs. Chicken wings – 2 lbs. cut into drumettes, pat dried
- 7/8 cup Parmesan, grated
- 1 tsp Herbs de Provence
- 1 tsp Paprika
- Salt to taste

Directions:
- Combine the parmesan, herbs, paprika, and salt in a bowl and rub the chicken with this mixture. Preheat the air fryer to 350°F. Grease the basket with cooking spray. Cook for 15 minutes. Flip once at the halfway mark. Garnish with parmesan and serve.

590.   Crispy Buttered Chicken

Preparation Time: 5 minutes
Cooking Time: 15 minutes
Servings: 4

Ingredients:
- 2 (8-ounce) boneless, skinless chicken breasts
- 1 sleeve Ritz crackers
- 4 tbsp (½ stick) cold unsalted butter, cut into 1-tbsp slices

Directions:
- Preparing the Ingredients. Spray the Cuisinart air fryer basket with olive oil, or spray an air fryer–size baking sheet with olive oil or cooking spray.
- Dip the chicken breasts in water. Put the crackers in a resealable plastic bag. Using a mallet or your hands, crush the crackers. Place the chicken breasts inside the bag one at a time and coat them with the cracker crumbs.
- Place the chicken in the greased air fryer basket or on the greased baking sheet set into the air fryer basket. Put 1 to 2 dabs of butter onto each piece of chicken.
- Air Frying. Set the temperature of your Cuisinart AF to 370°F. Set the timer and bake for 7 minutes.
- Using tongs, flip the chicken. Spray the chicken generously with olive oil to avoid uncooked breading. Reset the timer and bake for 7 minutes more.
- Check that the chicken has reached an internal temperature of 165°F. Add Cooking Time if needed. Using tongs, remove the chicken from the air fryer and serve.

591.   Chicken Fillets, Brie & Ham

Preparation Time: 5 minutes
Cooking Time: 15 minutes
Servings: 4

Ingredients:
- 2 Large Chicken Fillets
- Freshly Ground Black Pepper
- 4 Small Slices of Brie (Or your cheese of choice)
- 1 Tbsp Freshly Chopped Chives
- 4 Slices Cured Ham

Directions:
- Preparing the Ingredients. Slice the fillets into four and make incisions as you would for a hamburger bun. Leave a little "hinge" uncut at the back. Season the inside and pop some brie and chives in there. Close

them, and wrap them each in a slice of ham. Brush with oil and pop them into the basket.

- Air Frying. Heat your fryer to 350°F. Roast the little parcels until they look tasty (15 min)

592.   Old Bay Chicken Wings

Preparation Time: 5 minutes
Cooking Time: 25 minutes
Servings:4

Ingredients:

- 16 pieces of chicken wings
- ¾ cup almond flour
- One tbsp old bay spices
- One tsp lemon juice, freshly squeezed
- Salt and pepper to taste
- ½ cup butter

Directions:

- Preheat the air fryer to 350°F for 5 minutes.
- In a mixing bowl, integrate all ingredients except for the butter.
- Place in the air fryer basket.
- Cook for 25 minutes at 350°F.
- Halfway through the cooking time, shake the fryer basket for even cooking.
- Once cooked, drizzle with melted butter.
- Serve and enjoy!

593.   Caesar Marinated Grilled Chicken

Preparation Time: 10 minutes
Cooking Time: 25 minutes
Servings: 4

Ingredients:

- ¼ cup crouton
- 1 tsp lemon zest. Form into ovals, skewer, and grill.
- 1/2 cup Parmesan
- 1/4 cup breadcrumbs
- 1-pound ground chicken
- 2 tbsp Caesar dressing and more for drizzling
- 2-4 romaine leaves

Directions:

- In a shallow dish, mix well chicken, 2 tbsp Caesar dressing, parmesan, and breadcrumbs. Mix well with hands. Form into 1-inch oval patties. Thread chicken pieces in skewers. Place on skewer rack in the air fryer.
- For 12 minutes, cook at 360°F. Halfway through Cooking Time, turnover skewers. If needed, cook in batches. Serve on a bed of lettuce and sprinkle with croutons and extra dressing.

594.   Boneless Air Fryer Turkey Breasts

Preparation Time: 10 minutes
Cooking Time: 50 minutes
Servings: 4

- **Ingredients**
- 3 lb. boneless breast
- ¼ cup mayonnaise
- 2 tsp poultry seasoning
- 1 tsp salt
- ½ tsp garlic powder

- ¼ tsp black pepper

Directions:

- Choose the Air Fry option on the Air fryer Duo Crisp Air fryer. Set the temperature to 360°F and push start. The preheating will start.
- Season your boneless turkey breast with mayonnaise, poultry seasoning, salt, garlic powder, and black pepper.
- Once preheated, Air Fry the turkey breasts at 360°F for 1 hour, turning every 15 minutes or until internal temperature has reached a temperature of 165°F.

595.   Disney Land Turkey Legs

Preparation Time: 5 minutes
Cooking Time: 40 minutes
Servings: 2

- **Ingredients**
- 2 large turkey legs
- 1 1/2 tsp smoked paprika
- 1 tsp brown sugar
- 1 tsp seasoned salt
- ½ tsp garlic powder
- oil for spraying avocado, canola, etc.

Directions:

- Mix the smoked paprika, brown sugar, seasoned salt, and garlic powder thoroughly.
- Wash and pat dry the turkey legs.
- Rub the made seasoning mixture all over the turkey legs making sure to get under the skin also.
- While preparing for cooking, select the Air Fry option. Press start to begin preheating.
- Once the preheating temperature is reached, place the turkey legs on the tray in the Air fryer Duo Crisp Air Fryer basket. Lightly spray them with oil.
- Air Fry the turkey legs at 400°F for 20 minutes. Then, open the Air Fryer lid and flip the turkey legs and lightly spray with oil. Close the Air fryer Duo Crisp Air Fryer lid and cook for 20 more minutes.
- Remove and Enjoy.

596.   Mustard Chicken Fingers

Preparation Time: 5 minutes
Cooking Time: 20 minutes
Servings: 4

Ingredients:

- ½ C. coconut flour
- 1 tbsp. spicy brown mustard
- 2 beaten eggs
- 1 pound of chicken tenders

Directions:

- Season tenders with pepper and salt.
- Place a thin layer of mustard onto tenders and then dredge in flour and dip in egg.
- Add to the Air fryer, set temperature to 390°F, and set time to 20 minutes.

597.   Doritos Chicken Bites

Preparation Time: 10 minutes
Cooking Time: 15 minutes
Servings: 4

Ingredients:

- ½ lb. boneless, skinless chicken breast
- ¼ lb. Doritos snack
- 1 cup of wheat flour
- 1 egg
- Salt, garlic, and black pepper to taste.

Directions:

- Cut the chicken breast in the width direction, 1 to 1.5 cm thick, so that it is already shaped like pips.
- Season with salt, garlic, black pepper to taste, and some other seasonings if desired.
- You can also season with those seasonings or powdered onion soup.
- Put the Doritos snack in a food processor or blender and beat until everything is crumbled, but don't beat too much; you don't want flour.
- Now bread, passing the pieces of chicken breast first in the wheat flour, then in the beaten eggs, and finally in the Doritos, without leaving the excess flour, eggs, or Doritos.
- Place the seeds in the Air Fryer basket and program for 15 minutes at 400°F, and half the time, they brown evenly.

598. Cottage Cheese Chicken

Preparation Time: 10 minutes
Cooking Time: 10-15 minutes
Servings: 4

Ingredients:

- ½ lb. seasoned and minced chicken
- 1 cup light cottage cheese
- 1 egg
- Condiments to taste
- Flaxseed or oatmeal

Directions:

- In a bowl, mix all of the ingredients together except flour.
- Knead well with your hands and mold into coxinha format.
- If you prefer, you can fill it, add chicken or cheese.
- Repeat the process until all the dough is gone.
- Pass the drumsticks in the flour and put them in the fryer.
- Bake for 10 to 15 minutes at 390°F or until golden.

599. Turkey Breast Rolls

Preparation Time: 5 minutes
Cooking Time: 10 minutes
Servings: 4

Ingredients:

- 1 box of cherry tomatoes
- ¼ lb. turkey blanket

Directions:

- Wrap the turkey and blanket in the tomatoes, and close with the help of toothpicks.
- Take to Air Fryer for 10 minutes at 390°F.
- You can increase the filling with ricotta and other preferred light ingredients.

600. Bahian Seasoned Chicken

Preparation Time: 2 hours
Cooking Time: 20 minutes
Servings: 4

Ingredients:

- 5 pieces of chicken
- 2 garlic cloves, crushed
- 4 tbsp of lemon juice
- 1 coffee spoon of Bahian spices
- salt and black pepper to taste

Directions:

- Place the chicken pieces in a covered bowl and add the spices. Add the lemon juice. Cover the container and let the chicken marinate for 2 hours.
- Place each piece of chicken in the basket of the air fryer without overlapping the pieces. Set the fryer for 20 minutes at 390°F. In half the time, brown evenly. Serve!

601. Salt and Pepper Chicken Wings

Preparation Time: 5 minutes
Cooking Time: 10 minutes
Servings: 4

Ingredients:

- 2 tsp salt
- 2 tsp fresh ground pepper
- 2 pounds of chicken wings

Directions:

- In a bowl, mix the salt and pepper.
- Add the wings to the bowl and mix with your hands to coat every last one.
- Put 8 to 10 wings in the air fryer basket that has been sprayed with nonstick cooking spray. Set for 350°F (there is no need to preheat) and cook for about 15 minutes, turning once at 7 minutes.
- Repeat with the rest of the wings and serve hot.

602. Western Chicken Wings

Preparation Time: 10 minutes
Cooking Time: 15 minutes
Servings: 4

Ingredients:

- 2 lbs. chicken wings
- 1 tsp Herb de Provence
- 1 tsp paprika
- 1/2 cup parmesan cheese, grated
- Salt and Pepper

Directions:

- Add cheese, paprika, herb de Provence, pepper, and salt into the large mixing bowl. Place the chicken wings into the bowl and toss well to coat.
- Preheat the air fryer to 350°F.
- Place the chicken wings into the air fryer basket. Spray top of chicken wings with cooking spray.
- Cook chicken wings for 15 minutes. Turn chicken wings halfway through.
- Serve and enjoy.

603.   Fiery Hasselback Chicken

Preparation Time: 10 minutes
Cooking Time: 15 minutes
Servings: 2

Ingredients:

- 2 chicken breasts, boneless and skinless
- 1/2 cup cheddar cheese, shredded
- 4 tbsp pickled jalapenos, chopped
- 2 oz cream cheese, softened
- 4 bacon slices, cooked and crumbled

Directions:

- Make five to six slits on top of chicken breasts.
- In a bowl, mix together 1/2 cheddar cheese, pickled jalapenos, cream cheese, and bacon.
- Stuff cheddar cheese mixture into the slits.
- Place chicken into the air fryer basket and cook at 350°F for 14 minutes.
- Sprinkle the remaining cheese on top of the chicken and air fry for 1 minute more.
- Serve and enjoy.

604.   Fried Chicken Livers

Preparation Time: 5 minutes
Cooking Time: 10 minutes
Servings: 4

Ingredients:

- 1 pound of chicken livers
- 1 cup flour
- 1/2 cup cornmeal
- 2 tsp of your favorite seasoning blend
- 3 eggs
- 2 tbsp milk

Directions:

- Clean and rinse the livers, pat dry.
- Beat eggs in a shallow bowl and mix in milk.
- In another bowl, combine flour, cornmeal, and seasoning, mixing until even.
- Dip the livers in the egg mix, then toss them in the flour mix.
- Pour into the Oven rack/basket. Place the rack on the middle shelf of the Air fryer oven. Set temperature to 375°F, and set time to 10 minutes. Toss at least once halfway through.

605.   Juicy Turkey Legs

Preparation Time: 10 minutes
Cooking Time: 27 minutes
Servings: 4

Ingredients:

- 4 turkey legs
- 1/4 tsp oregano
- 1/4 tsp rosemary
- 1 tbsp butter
- Salt and Pepper

Directions:

- Season turkey legs with pepper and salt.
- In a small bowl, mix together butter, oregano, and rosemary.

- Rub the butter mixture all over the turkey legs.
- Preheat the air fryer to 350°F.
- Place turkey legs into the air fryer basket and cook for 27 minutes.
- Serve and enjoy.

606.   Ranch Taco Wings

Preparation Time: 10 minutes
Cooking Time: 30 minutes
Servings: 4

Ingredients:

- 2 lbs. chicken wings
- 1 tsp ranch seasoning
- 1 1/2 tsp taco seasoning
- 1 tsp olive oil

Directions:

- Preheat the air fryer to 400°F.
- In a mixing bowl, add chicken wings, ranch seasoning, taco seasoning, and oil, and toss well to coat.
- Place chicken wings into the air fryer basket and cook for 15 minutes.
- Turn chicken wings to another side and cook for 15 minutes more.
- Serve and enjoy.

607.   Honey Lime Chicken wings

Preparation Time: 10 minutes
Cooking Time: 50 minutes
Servings: 6

Ingredients:

- 2 lbs chicken wings
- 2 tbsp fresh lime juice
- salt and black pepper
- 1/4 tsp white pepper powder
- 2 tbsp honey

Directions:

- In a bowl, place all the ingredients and coat well.
- Place marinated chicken wings into the refrigerator for 1-2 hours.
- Preheat the air fryer to 182°C/ 360°F.
- Place marinated chicken wings into the air fryer basket and cook for 12 minutes. Shake the air fryer basket halfway through.
- Turn temperature to 400°F / 204°C and cook for 3 minutes more.
- Serve and enjoy.

608.   Sriracha Chicken Wings

Preparation Time: 10 minutes
Cooking Time: 35 minutes
Servings: 2

Ingredients:

- 1 lb. chicken wings
- 1/2 lime juice
- 1 tbsp grass-fed butter
- 2 tbsp sriracha sauce
- 1/4 cup honey

Directions:
- Preheat the air fryer to 182°C/ 360°F.
- Add chicken wings to the air fryer basket and cook for 30 minutes.
- Meanwhile, in a pan, add all remaining ingredients and bring to a boil for 3 minutes.
- Once chicken wings are done then, toss with sauce and serve.

609. Thyme Turkey Nuggets

Preparation Time: 5 minutes
Cooking Time: 20 minutes
Servings: 4

Ingredients:
- 8 oz turkey breast
- 1 egg, beaten
- 1 cup breadcrumbs
- ½ tsp dried thyme
- Salt and black pepper to taste
- **Directions**
- Preheat Cuisinart on Air Fry function to 350°F. Pulse the turkey in a food processor and transfer it to a bowl. Stir in thyme, salt, and pepper.
- Form nugget-sized balls out of turkey mixture and dip them in breadcrumbs, then in egg, and finally in the breadcrumbs again. Place the nuggets on a greased Air Fryer basket and fit them in the baking tray. Cook for 10 minutes, shaking once until golden brown. Serve warm.

610. Crispy Buttered Chicken

Preparation Time: 5 minutes
Cooking Time: 20 minutes
Servings: 4

Ingredients:
- 1-pound turkey breast halved
- 2 cups panko breadcrumbs
- Salt and black pepper to taste
- ½ tsp cayenne pepper
- 1 stick butter, melted

Directions:
- In a bowl, combine the breadcrumbs, salt, cayenne, and black peppers. Brush the butter onto the turkey breast and coat in the crumb mixture. Transfer to a lined baking dish. Cook in your Cuisinart for 15 minutes at 390°F. Serve warm.

611. Buttermilk Chicken

Preparation Time: 10 minutes
Cooking Time: 25 minutes
Serving: 6

Ingredients:
- 3-lb. whole chicken
- 1 tbsp salt
- 1-pint buttermilk

Directions:
- Place the whole chicken in a large bowl and drizzle salt on top.

- Pour the buttermilk over it and leave the chicken soaked overnight.
- Cover the chicken bowl and refrigerate overnight.
- Remove the chicken from the marinade and fix it on the rotisserie rod in the air fryer oven.
- Turn the dial to select the "Air Roast" mode.
- Hit the Time button and again use the dial to set the Cooking Time to 25 minutes.
- Now push the Temp button and rotate the dial to set the temperature at 370°F.
- Close its lid and allow the chicken to roast.
- Serve warm.

612. Alfredo Chicken Wings

Preparation Time: 5 minutes
Cooking Time: 20 minutes
Servings: 4

Ingredients:
- 1 ½ lb. chicken wings, pat-dried
- Salt to taste
- ½ cup Alfredo sauce

Directions:
- Preheat the air fryer to 370°F.
- Season the wings with salt. Arrange them in the greased air fryer basket without touching, and air fry for 12 minutes until they are no longer pink in the center. Work in batches if needed.
- Flip them, increase the heat to 390°F and cook for 5 more minutes. Plate the wings and drizzle with Alfredo sauce to serve.

613. Citrus Rosemary Chicken

Preparation Time: 30 minutes
Cooking Time: 15 minutes
Servings: 2

Ingredients:
- 1 lb. chicken thighs
- 1/2 tsp rosemary, fresh, chopped
- 1/8 tsp thyme, dried
- ½ cup tangerine juice
- 2 tbsp white wine
- 1 tsp garlic, minced
- Salt and pepper to taste
- 2 tbsp lemon juice

Directions:
- Place the chicken thighs in a mixing bowl. In another bowl, mix tangerine juice, garlic, white wine, lemon juice, rosemary, pepper, salt, and thyme. Pour the mixture over the chicken thighs and place in the fridge for 20-minutes. Preheat your air fryer to 350°F and place your marinated chicken in the air fryer basket and cook for 15-minutes. Serve hot, and enjoy!

614. Crunchy Curry Chicken Strips

Preparation Time: 10 minutes
Cooking Time: 15 minutes
Servings: 4

Ingredients:
- 12 oz. chicken breast, cut into strips

- Salt and pepper to taste
- 1 egg, beaten
- ¼ cup whole wheat flour
- ½ cup panko breadcrumbs
- ¼ cup curry powder

Directions:
- Season the chicken strips with salt and pepper.
- Dip each of the chicken strips into the flour, then into the egg.
- In a bowl, mix the curry powder and breadcrumbs.
- Coat each of the chicken strips with the curry powder mixture.
- Cook in the air fryer at 350°F for 10 minutes.
- Flip and cook for another 5 minutes.

615. Simple Spiced Chicken Legs

Preparation Time: 5 minutes
Cooking Time: 30 minutes
Servings: 6

Ingredients:
- 2-2.5 lbs. chicken drumsticks 6-8 legs
- 2 tbsp olive oil
- 1 tsp kosher salt
- 1 tsp pepper
- 1 tsp garlic powder
- 1 tsp smoked paprika
- 1/2 tsp cumin

Directions:
- Take a large bowl and drizzle the drumsticks with olive oil and toss them to coat.
- Take a small bowl, stir together the remaining ingredients, followed by sprinkling over drumsticks, and toss to coat evenly.
- Divide the coated chicken onto cooking trays of the Air fryer Duo Crisp Air Fryer.
- Select Air Fry from the display panel, then adjust the temperature to 400°F and the time to 25 minutes and touch the start button.
- Once preheated, insert two cooking trays in the top-most position and in the bottom-most position, one in each.
- After half time, turn the food over and switch the cooking trays between the top and bottom positions.
- When the Air Fryer program is complete, check to make sure the thickest portion of the meat reads at least an internal temperature of 165°F.
- Remove and serve hot.

616. Pizza Stuffed Chicken

Preparation Time: 10 minutes
Cooking Time: 15 minutes
Servings: 4

Ingredients:
- 5 boneless skinless, chicken thighs
- ½ cup of pizza sauce
- 14 slices of turkey pepperoni
- ½ small red onion sliced
- 5 ounces of sliced mozzarella cheese

Directions:
- Open the chicken thighs and lay them flat on a piece of parchment paper.
- Place another piece of parchment paper on top of the chicken. Pound the chicken to create a thin piece.
- Spoon a tbsp of pizza sauce on each piece of the chicken and spread it equally. Put 3 pieces of turkey pepperoni on top of the sauce.
- Add a slice of Mozzarella cheese. Fold one side of the chicken over onto the other. Use a toothpick to hold the chicken together.
- Once cooked, it stays together on its own. Preheat your Air fryer to 370°F for about 2 minutes.
- Smear the tray with oil, and lay the pieces out in a single layer. Add the chicken and set your Air fryer to cook for about 6 minutes.
- After the 6 minutes, Flip the chicken and cook for another 6 minutes. Add the cheese to melt on the top for the last 3 minutes,
- Always check chicken thighs to ensure they are heated at an internal temperature of 165°F.
- When the time is up, serve and enjoy!

617. Texas Chicken Chili

Preparation Time: 20 minutes
Cooking Time: 30 minutes
Servings: 8

Ingredients:
- 1 tbsp Canola oil
- 2 cups yellow onion,
- 2 tbsp chili powder
- 1 tbsp minced garlic
- 2 tbsp ground cumin
- 1 tbsp oregano
- 15 oz beans
- 4 cups chicken broth
- 3 cups skinless chicken breast
- 14.5 oz diced tomatoes
- 1/3 cup fresh cilantro
- 2 tbsp fresh lime juice
- ½ tsp salt
- ½ tsp pepper

Directions:
- Add the onions and chili powder, garlic, and cumin and stir to coat the onions. Spray oil. Cook for 2 more minutes in the fryer.
- When cooked, add the oregano and beans, and cook for 5 minutes in a fryer at 350°F.
- Add the broth and reduce the heat to medium-low. Simmer for 20 minutes, stirring occasionally.
- When cooked, transfer this mixture to a blender and blend.
- Then add the chicken and tomatoes and cook over 350°F for another 30 minutes in the fryer. Add the cilantro, lime juice, salt & pepper and stir to combine before serving.

618. Chicken Cordon Bleu

Preparation Time: 20 minutes
Cooking Time: 45 minutes
Servings: 4

Ingredients:

- 4 skinless and boneless chicken breasts
- 4 slices of ham
- 4 slices of Swiss cheese
- 3 tbsp almond flour
- 1 cup of heavy whipping cream
- 1 tsp of chicken bouillon granules
- ½ cup dry white wine
- 5 tbsp butter
- 1 tsp paprika

Directions:

- Preheat your air fryer to 390°F. Pound the chicken breasts and put a slice of ham and Swiss cheese on each breast. Fold over the edges of the chicken; cover the filling, and secure the edges with toothpicks. In a bowl, combine flour and paprika. Coat chicken with this mixture. Set the air fryer to cook the chicken for 15-minutes. In a large skillet, heat the butter, bouillon, and wine, then reduce heat to low. Remove the chicken from the air fryer and add it to the skillet. Allow the components to simmer for around 30-minutes. Serve warm, and enjoy!

619. Lunch Chicken Fajitas

Preparation Time: 10 minutes
Cooking Time: 10 minutes
Servings: 4

Ingredients:

- 1 tsp garlic powder
- ¼ tsp cumin, ground
- ½ tsp chili powder
- Salt and black pepper to the taste
- ¼ tsp coriander, ground
- 1-pound chicken breasts, cut into strips
- 1 red bell pepper, sliced
- 1 green bell pepper, sliced
- 1 yellow onion, chopped
- 1 tbsp lime juice
- Cooking spray
- 4 tortillas, warmed up
- Salsa for serving
- Sour cream for serving
- 1 cup lettuce leaves, torn for serving

Directions:

- In a bowl, mix chicken with garlic powder, cumin, chili, salt, pepper, coriander, lime juice, red bell pepper, green bell pepper, and onion, toss, leave aside for 10 minutes, transfer to your air fryer and drizzle some cooking spray all over.
- Toss and cook at 400 °F for 10 minutes.
- Arrange tortillas on a working surface, divide chicken mix, also add salsa, sour cream, and lettuce, wrap and serve for lunch.

620. Turkey Breast with Maple Mustard Glaze

Preparation Time: 4 Minutes
Cooking Time: 49 Minutes
Servings: 6

Ingredients:

- 5 lbs. turkey breast

- 1 tbsp unsalted butter
- 2 tbsp Dijon mustard
- ¼ cup sugar-free maple syrup
- ½ tsp black pepper
- 1 tsp of sea salt
- ½ tsp paprika
- 1 tsp dried thyme
- 1 tbsp olive oil
- ½ tsp sage

Directions:

- Preheat your air fryer to 350°F. Prepare the turkey breast by brushing it with olive oil. Combine salt, pepper, paprika, sage, and thyme in a bowl. Cover the turkey breast with this mixture. Place the turkey breast inside the air fryer and cook for 25-minutes. Turn and prepare for another 12-minutes. Turn once more and cook for an additional 12-minutes. Use a small saucepan to mix mustard, melted butter, and maple syrup; stir well. When turkey breast is done cooking, cover with sauce. Then air-fry for another 5-minutes. Get the turkey out of the air fryer and set it aside for at least 5-minutes, covering it with aluminum foil. Slice turkey and serve.

621. Chickpea Chicken Stew

Preparation Time: 10 minutes
Cooking Time: 30 minutes
Servings: 4

Ingredients:

- 2 chicken breasts, boneless and skinless
- 15 oz can chickpeas, drained and rinsed
- 7 cups spinach
- 1 tsp garlic powder
- 1/4 tsp cinnamon
- 2 celery stalks, diced
- 1 onion, diced
- 8 cups chicken stock
- 1/4 cup fresh lemon juice
- 2 carrots, diced
- 1/2 tsp pepper
- 1/2 tsp sea salt

Directions:

- Add carrots, chickpeas, celery, and onions to the air fryer.
- Add chicken, stock, lemon juice, garlic powder, cinnamon, pepper, and salt.
- Seal pot with lid and cook on soup mode.
- Allow releasing pressure naturally, then open the lid.
- Remove chicken from pot and shred using a fork.
- Return shredded chicken to the pot along with spinach and stir for 1-2 minutes.
- Serve and enjoy.

622. Holiday Roasted Goose

Preparation Time: 10 minutes
Cooking Time: 60 minutes
Serving: 12

Ingredients:

- 2 goose
- 2 lemons, sliced

- 1 ½ lime, sliced
- ½ tsp Chinese five-spice powder
- ½ handful parsley, chopped
- ½ handful sprigs, chopped
- ½ handful thyme, chopped
- ½ handful sage, chopped
- 1 ½ tbsp clear honey
- ½ tbsp thyme leaves

Directions:
- Place the goose in a baking dish and brush it with syrup.
- Set the lemon and lime slices on top of the goose.
- Add all the herbs and spice powder over the lemon slices.
- Press the "Power Button" on Air Fry Oven and turn the dial to select the "Air Roast" mode.
- Press the Time button and again turn the dial to set the cooking time to 60 minutes.
- Now push the Temp button and rotate the dial to set the temperature at 375 °F.
- Once preheated, place the baking dish inside and close its lid.
- Serve warm.

623. Chicken Wontons

Preparation Time: 12 Minutes
Cooking Time: 25 Minutes
Servings: 4

Ingredients:
- 1 cup All-Purpose Flour
- 1/4-pound Boneless Skinless Chicken Breast
- 1 Egg
- 1 Green Onion
- 1 tbsp French beans
- 1 tbsp carrot
- 1/2 tsp Pepper Powder
- 1/4 tsp Soy Sauce
- 1/2 tsp Cornstarch
- 1 tsp Sesame Seed Oil

Direction:
- Finely dice all of your vegetables, beans, and chicken into the smallest pieces possible.
- Mix flour, salt, and a little hot water to create a stiff dough. Cover and set aside.
- Beat the egg in a large bowl.
- Add all other ingredients except for the sesame seed oil to the egg bowl and mix well.

- Add the sesame seed oil to the mix and mix again.
- Roll your dough flat and use a cookie cutter to cut it into circles about 6 inches in diameter.
- Preheat the fryer to 360°F.
- Scoop a little mixture into the center of each circle.
- Use your fingers to wet the edges of the circles.
- Fold them over the stuffing and press to close.
- Cook in the fryer for 12 minutes, flipping them after 7 minutes.

624. Chicken Luncheon Salad

Preparation Time: 10 minutes
Cooking Time: 20 minutes
Servings: 4

Ingredients:
- 2 ears of corn, hulled
- 1-pound chicken tenders, boneless
- Olive oil as needed
- Salt and black pepper to the taste
- 1 tsp sweet paprika
- 1 tbsp brown sugar
- ½ tsp garlic powder
- ½ iceberg lettuce head, cut into medium strips
- ½ romaine lettuce head, cut into medium strips
- 1 cup canned black beans, drained
- 1 cup cheddar cheese, shredded
- 3 tbsp cilantro, chopped
- 4 green onions, chopped
- 12 cherry tomatoes, sliced
- ¼ cup ranch dressing
- 3 tbsp BBQ sauce

Directions:
- Put corn in your air fryer, drizzle some oil, toss, cook at 400°F for 10 minutes, transfer to a plate and leave aside for now.
- Put chicken in your air fryer's basket, add salt, pepper, brown sugar, paprika, and garlic powder, toss, drizzle some more oil, cook at 400°F for 10 minutes, flipping them halfway, transfer tenders to a cutting board and chop them.
- Cur kernels off the cob, transfer corn to a bowl, add chicken, iceberg lettuce, romaine lettuce, black beans, cheese, cilantro, tomatoes, onions, BBQ sauce, and ranch dressing, toss well, and serve for lunch.

CHAPTER 7: FISH AND SEAFOOD

625.   Buttered Fish Scampi

Preparation Time: 15 minutes
Cooking Time: 15 minutes
Servings: 4

Ingredients:
- 1 tbsp olive oil
- 4 (6-ounce) skinless snapper or arctic char fillets
- 3 tbsp lemon juice, divided
- ½ tsp dried basil
- Pinch salt
- Freshly ground black pepper
- 2 tbsp butter
- 2 cloves garlic, minced

Directions:
- Set to 380°F Grill. Rub the fish fillets with olive oil and 1 tbsp of lemon juice. Sprinkle with the basil, salt, and pepper, and place in the air fryer basket.
- Grill the fish for 7 to 8 minutes or until the fish just flakes when tested with a fork. Remove the fish from the basket and put it on a serving plate. Cover to keep warm.
- In a 6x6x2-inch pan, combine the butter, remaining 2 tbsp lemon juice, and garlic. Cook in the air fryer for 1 to 2 minutes or until the garlic is sizzling. Pour this mixture over the fish and serve.

626.   Japanese Steamed Tuna

Preparation Time: 10 minutes
Cooking Time: 10-15 minutes
Servings: 4

Ingredients:

- 4 small tuna steaks
- 2 tbsp low-sodium soy sauce
- 2 tsp sesame oil
- 2 tsp rice wine vinegar
- 1 tsp grated fresh ginger
- ⅛ tsp pepper
- 1 stalk lemongrass, bent in half
- 3 tbsp lemon juice

Directions:

- Set to 380°F Steam. Place the tuna steaks on a plate. In a small bowl, combine the soy sauce, sesame oil, rice wine vinegar, and ginger, and mix well. Pour this mixture over the tuna and marinate for 10 minutes. Rub the soy sauce mixture gently into both sides of the tuna. Sprinkle with the pepper.
- Place the lemongrass on the air fryer basket and top with the steaks. Put the lemon juice and 1 tbsp water in the pan below the basket.
- Steam the fish for 8 to 10 minutes or until the tuna registers at least 145°F. Discard the lemongrass and serve the tuna.

627. Cheese and Crab Souffle

Preparation Time: 20 minutes
Cooking Time: 20 minutes
Servings: 2

Ingredients:

- 1 lb. cooked crab meat
- 1 capsicum
- 1 small onion, diced
- 1 cup cream
- 1 cup milk
- 4-ounces Brie
- Brandy to cover crab meat
- 3 eggs
- 5 drops of liquid stevia
- 3-ounces cheddar cheese, grated
- 4 cups bread, cubed

Directions:

- Soak the crammed meat in brandy and 4-parts water. Loosen the meat in brandy. Sauté onion and bread. Grate cheddar cheese and mix ingredients. In the same pan, add some of the butter and stir for a minute. Add the crab to the pan. Add ½ of the milk and 1 tbsp of brandy and cook for 2-minutes. Add the bread cubes to the frying pan and mix well. Sprinkle with cheese and pepper. Put the stuffing in 5 ramekins without brushing them with oil. Distribute the brie evenly. In a bowl, combine ½ cup of cream with stevia. Heat the cream in a pan and add the remaining milk. Pour mixture into ramekins. Preheat your air fryer to 350°F, add the dish and cook for 20-minutes.

628. Lobster Wontons

Preparation Time: 20 minutes
Cooking Time: 30 minutes
Servings: 8

Ingredients:

- For dough:

- 1 ½- cup all-purpose flour
- ½- tsp. salt
- 5- tbsp. water
- For filling:
- 2- cups minced lobster
- 2- tbsp. oil
- 2- tsp. ginger-garlic paste
- 2- tsp. soy sauce
- 2- tsp. vinegar

Directions:

- Mix the dough, cover it with saran wrap and set aside.
- Mix the filling ingredients.
- Fold the dough and cut it into a square.
- Place the filling in the middle.
- Wrap the dough to cover the filling and squeeze the edges together.
- Preheat the Air Fryer to 200°F for 5 minutes. Place in the fry bin and cook for 20 minutes.

629. Shrimp Stuffed Peppers

Preparation Time: 20 minutes
Cooking Time: 5-10 minutes
Servings: 6

Ingredients:

- 12 baby bell peppers, cut into halves lengthwise
- ¼ tsp red pepper flakes, crushed
- 1-pound shrimp, cooked, peeled, and deveined
- 6 tbsp jarred basil pesto
- Salt and black pepper to the taste
- 1 tbsp lemon juice
- 1 tbsp olive oil
- Handful parsley, chopped

Directions:

- In a bowl, mix shrimp with pepper flakes, pesto, salt, black pepper, lemon juice, oil, and parsley, whisk very well, and stuff bell pepper halves with this mix. Place them in your air fryer and cook at 320°F for 6 minutes; arrange peppers on plates and serve. Enjoy!

630. Coconut Tilapia

Preparation Time: 10 minutes
Cooking Time: 10 minutes
Servings: 4

Ingredients:

- 4 medium tilapia fillets
- Salt and black pepper to the taste
- ½ cup coconut milk
- 1 tsp ginger, grated
- ½ cup cilantro, chopped
- 2 garlic cloves, chopped
- ½ tsp garam masala
- Cooking spray
- ½ jalapeno, chopped

Directions:

- In your food processor, mix coconut milk with salt, pepper, cilantro, ginger, garlic, jalapeno, and garam masala, and pulse really well.

- Spray fish with cooking spray spread coconut mix all over, rub well, transfer to your air fryer's basket and cook at 400°F for 10 minutes.
- Divide among plates and serve hot.

631. Oriental Red Snapper

Preparation Time: 10 minutes
Cooking Time: 8-10 minutes
Servings: 6

Ingredients:
- 2 pounds red snapper fillets, boneless
- Salt and black pepper to the taste
- 3 garlic cloves, minced
- 1 yellow onion, chopped
- 1 tbsp tamarind paste
- 1 tbsp oriental sesame oil
- 1 tbsp ginger, grated
- 2 tbsp water
- ½ tsp cumin, ground
- 1 tbsp lemon juice
- 3 tbsp mint, chopped

Directions:
- In your food processor, mix garlic with onion, salt, pepper, tamarind paste, sesame oil, ginger, water, and cumin, pulse well, and rub fish with this mix.
- Place fish in your preheated air fryer at 320°F and cook for 12 minutes, flipping fish halfway.
- Divide fish on plates, drizzle lemon juice all over, sprinkle mint, and serve right away.

632. Blackberry-glazed Salmon

Preparation Time: 20 minutes
Cooking Time: 45 minutes
Servings: 4

Ingredients:
- 1 cup water
- 1-inch ginger piece
- Juice from ½ lemon
- 12 oz. blackberries
- 1 tbsp. olive oil
- ¼ cup sugar
- 4 medium salmon fillets
- Salt and black pepper

Directions:
- Heat pot with water over high heat. Add ginger, blackberries, and lemon juice and stir. Boil, then cook for 4-5 minutes, take off heat, strain and pour into pan mix with sugar.
- Stir the mix, simmer over low heat, then cook for 20 minutes.
- Allow blackberry sauce to cool. Brush salmon and season with pepper and salt, sprinkle olive oil over, then rub fish well.
- Place fish in the preheated air fryer at 350°F and cook for 10 minutes.
- Divide among plates, sprinkle some blackberry sauce over and serve.

633. Salmon with Avocado Sauce

Preparation Time: 15 minutes
Cooking Time: 10 minutes
Servings: 4

Ingredients:
- 1 avocado, pitted, peeled, and chopped
- 4 salmon fillets, boneless
- ¼ cup cilantro, chopped
- 1/3 cup coconut milk
- 1 tbsp lime juice
- 1 tbsp lime zest, grated
- 1 tsp onion powder
- 1 tsp garlic powder
- Salt and black pepper to the taste

Directions:
- Season salmon fillets with salt, black pepper, and lime zest, rub well, put in your air fryer, cook at 350°F for 9 minutes, flipping once and divide among plates.
- In your food processor, mix avocado with cilantro, garlic powder, onion powder, lime juice, salt, pepper, and coconut milk, blend well, drizzle over salmon, and serve right away.

634. Salmon in Honey Chili Sauce

Preparation Time: 10 minutes
Cooking Time: 15 minutes
Servings: 4

Ingredients:
- 1 and ¼ cups coconut, shredded
- 1-pound salmon, cubed
- 1/3 cup flour
- A pinch of salt and black pepper
- 1 egg
- 2 tbsp olive oil
- ¼ cup water
- 4 red chilies, chopped
- 3 garlic cloves, minced
- ¼ cup balsamic vinegar
- ½ cup honey

Directions:
- In a bowl, mix flour with a pinch of salt and stir.
- In another bowl, mix egg with black pepper and whisk.
- Put coconut in a third bowl.
- Dip salmon cubes in flour, egg, and coconut, put them in your air fryer's basket, cook at 370°F for 8 minutes, shaking halfway and divide among plates.
- Heat up a pan with the water over medium-high heat, add chilies, cloves, vinegar, and honey, stir very well, bring to a boil, simmer for a couple of minutes, drizzle over salmon and serve.

635. Swordfish Steak with Avocado Salsa

Preparation Time: 10 minutes
Cooking Time: 6-10 minutes
Servings: 2

Ingredients:
- 2 medium swordfish steaks
- Salt and black pepper to the taste
- 2 tsp avocado oil

- 1 tbsp cilantro, chopped
- 1 mango, chopped
- 1 avocado, pitted, peeled, and chopped
- A pinch of cumin
- A pinch of onion powder
- A pinch of garlic powder
- 1 orange, peeled and sliced
- ½ tbsp balsamic vinegar

Directions:
- Season fish steaks with salt, pepper, garlic powder, onion powder, and cumin, and rub with half of the oil; place in your air fryer and cook at 360°F for 6 minutes, flipping halfway.
- Meanwhile, in a bowl, mix avocado with mango, cilantro, balsamic vinegar, salt, pepper, and the rest of the oil and stir well.
- Divide fish on plates, top with mango salsa, and serve with orange slices on the side.

636.   Mustard Salmon

Preparation Time: 10 minutes
Cooking Time: 10 minutes
Servings: 1

Ingredients:
- 1 big salmon fillet, boneless
- Salt and black pepper to the taste
- 2 tbsp mustard
- 1 tbsp coconut oil
- 1 tbsp maple extract

Directions:
- In a bowl, mix maple extract with mustard, whisk well, season salmon with salt and pepper, and brush salmon with this mix.
- Spray some cooking spray over the fish, place it in your air fryer and cook at 370°F for 10 minutes, flipping halfway.
- Serve with a tasty side salad.

637.   Miso Trout

Preparation Time: 10 minutes
Cooking Time: 15 minutes
Servings: 4

Ingredients:
- 1-pound trout fillets, boneless
- 2 scallions, chopped
- 2 tbsp olive oil
- 1 tbsp ginger, grated
- ¼ cup miso
- 1 tsp mustard
- 1 tsp sugar

Directions:
- In your air fryer, combine the trout with the scallions, the oil, and the other ingredients, toss gently, and cook at 370°F for 14 minutes.
- Divide everything between plates and serve.

638.   Turmeric Flavored Shrimps

Preparation Time: 10 minutes
Cooking Time: 10 minutes
Servings: 4

Ingredients:
- 1-pound shrimp, peeled and deveined
- 4 asparagus spears, trimmed and halved
- 2 tbsp avocado oil
- 2 scallions, chopped
- 2 tbsp balsamic vinegar
- Salt and black pepper to the taste
- ¼ tsp turmeric powder
- 1 tbsp chives, chopped

Directions:
- In your air fryer, combine the shrimp with the asparagus, oil, and the other ingredients, toss and cook at 380°F for 10 minutes.
- Divide everything between plates and serve.

639.   Tuna with Olives and Spinach

Preparation Time: 10 minutes
Cooking Time: 15 minutes
Servings: 4

Ingredients:
- 4 tuna fillets, boneless and cubed
- 1 cup baby spinach
- 1 cup black olives, pitted and halved
- 2 tbsp olive oil
- Juice of 1 lime
- 4 garlic cloves, minced
- 2 tbsp cilantro, chopped

Directions:
- In your air fryer, combine the tuna with the spinach, olives, and the other ingredients, toss gently, and cook at 380°F for 15 minutes.
- Divide everything between plates and serve.

640.   Cod in Jalapeno Sauce

Preparation Time: 10 minutes
Cooking Time: 15 minutes
Servings: 4

Ingredients:
- 1-pound cod fillets, boneless
- 2 jalapenos, minced
- 2 tbsp butter, melted
- Salt and black pepper to the taste
- ½ cup heavy cream
- 1 tsp ginger, grated
- 1 tbsp parsley, chopped

Directions:
- In your air fryer's pan, combine the cod with the jalapenos and the other ingredients, toss and cook at 380°F for 15 minutes.
- Divide between plates and serve hot.

641. Shrimp & Sausage Paella

Preparation Time: 5 minutes
Cooking Time: 35 minutes
Servings: 4

Ingredients:

- 1 tbsp extra-virgin olive oil
- 1 onion, chopped
- 1 red bell pepper, chopped
- 4 ounces chicken chorizo, diced
- 2 cups long-grain white rice
- 5 cups Chicken Stock or low-sodium store-bought chicken stock
- Generous pinch saffron threads
- 1 pound fresh shrimp, peeled and deveined
- 1 cup pea, fresh or frozen
- ¼ cup fresh parsley
- Juice of 1 lemon
- Celtic sea salt or kosher salt

Directions:

- In a large huge fryer, 350°F, heat the olive oil.
- If the oil is medium hot, add the onion and red bell pepper. Sauté for 3 to 5 minutes to soften at 300°F.
- Add the chorizo. Cook for 5 minutes to brown.
- Stir in the rice, chicken stock, and saffron threads. Cook for 20 minutes at 375°F, or until most of the stock is absorbed and the rice is soft.
- Add the shrimp and peas. Wait for 5 minutes or until the shrimp are opaque and cooked through.
- Stir in the parsley and lemon juice. Season to taste with salt.

642. Tuna and Capers

Preparation Time: 10 minutes
Cooking Time: 12-15 minutes
Servings: 4

Ingredients:

- 2 tbsp olive oil
- 3 scallions, chopped
- 1-pound tuna fillets, boneless and cubed
- 1 tbsp capers, drained
- 3 tbsp balsamic vinegar
- 2 tbsp parsley, chopped
- 1 jalapeno pepper, chopped
- Salt and black pepper to the taste

Directions:

- Heat up the air fryer with the oil at 380°F, add the scallions, tuna, and the other ingredients, toss gently, and cook for 12 minutes.
- Divide the mix between plates and serve

643. Tuna Au Gratin

Preparation Time: 20 minutes
Cooking Time: 25-30 minutes
Servings: 6

Ingredients:

- 1 tbsp butter, melted
- 1 medium-sized leek, thinly sliced
- 1 tbsp chicken stock

- 1 tbsp dry white wine
- 1-pound tuna
- 1/2 tsp red pepper flakes, crushed
- Sea salt and ground black pepper, to taste
- 1/2 tsp dried rosemary
- 1/2 tsp dried basil
- 1/2 tsp dried thyme
- 2 small ripe tomatoes, pureed
- 1 cup Parmesan cheese, grated

Directions:

- Melt 1/2 tbsp of butter in a sauté pan over medium-high heat. Now, cook the leek and garlic until tender and aromatic. Add the stock and wine to deglaze the pan.
- Preheat your Air Fryer to 370°F.
- Grease a casserole dish with the remaining 1/2 tbsp of melted butter. Place the fish in the casserole dish. Add the seasonings. Top with the sautéed leek mixture.
- Add the tomato puree. Cook for 10 minutes in the preheated Air Fryer. Top with grated Parmesan cheese; cook an additional 7 minutes until the crumbs are golden. Bon appétit!

644. Red Hot Chili Fish Curry

Preparation Time: 20 minutes
Cooking Time: 25-30 minutes
Servings: 4

Ingredients:

- 2 tbsp sunflower oil
- 1 pound of fish, chopped
- 2 red chilies, chopped
- 1 tbsp coriander powder
- 1 tsp red curry paste
- 1 cup coconut milk
- Salt and white pepper, to taste
- 1/2 tsp fenugreek seeds
- 1 shallot, minced
- 1 garlic clove, minced
- 1 ripe tomato, pureed

Directions:

- Preheat your Air Fryer to 380°F; brush the cooking basket with 1 tbsp of sunflower oil.
- Cook your fish for 10 minutes on both sides. Transfer to the baking pan that is previously greased with the remaining tbsp of sunflower oil.
- Add the remaining ingredients and reduce the heat to 350°F. Continue to cook an additional 10 to 12 minutes or until everything is heated through. Enjoy!

645. Pesto and Almond Crusted Salmon

Preparation Time: 10 minutes
Cooking Time: 12 minutes
Servings: 2

Ingredients:

- 2 salmon fillets
- 2 tbsp butter, melted
- ¼ cup pesto
- ¼ cup almond, ground

Directions:

- Mix together pesto and almond.

- Brush salmon fillets with melted butter and place them into the air fryer baking dish.
- Top salmon fillets with pesto and almond mixture.
- Place dish in the air fryer and cook at 390°F for 12 minutes.
- Serve and enjoy.

646. Shrimp Nuggets

Preparation Time: 20 minutes
Cooking Time: 30 minutes
Servings: 4

Ingredients:
- 1 lb. medium shrimp with clean, washed shell
- ½ lemon
- 1 ½ tbsp of flour
- 2 garlic cloves, squeezed
- Salt to taste

Directions:
- Preheat the fryer to 400°F for 4 to 6 minutes. Season shrimp with salt, lemon, and squeezed garlic. Let drain in a strainer.
- Cover the bottom of a baking sheet with two layers of absorbent paper and spread the shrimp. Sprinkle the flour and mix well. Prawns should be without water when adding wheat flour because if they are with water, they will stick together.
- Place in the fryer basket and leave to work for 20 minutes, until golden brown, occasionally stirring for even cooking. Serve with white rice and a green salad.

647. Shrimp Stroganoff

Preparation Time: 15 minutes
Cooking Time: 10 minutes
Servings: 4

Ingredients:
- 1 tbsp butter
- 1 medium onion, grated
- 1 lb. of medium clean shrimp
- Salt and pepper
- 4 tbsp of brandy
- 3 ½ oz. minced pickled mushrooms
- 3 tbsp of tomato sauce
- 1 tbsp of mustard
- 1 can of cream

Directions:
- Clean the shrimp. Remove the peels and wash them very well with water and lemon, drain and set aside.
- Heat the butter and brown the onion. Remove from the heat and mix with the shrimp and stir well; season with salt and pepper.
- Put in the air fryer at 320°F for 5 minutes.
- Heat the cognac in a shell until it catches fire. And pour it over the shrimp, flaming them.
- Add the mushroom, tomato sauce, and mustard, and put back in the air fryer for about 5 minutes.
- When serving, add the cream, stir well, and heat without boiling.
- Serve the stroganoff with white rice and straw potatoes.

648. Breaded Prawns

Preparation Time: 20 minutes
Cooking Time: 15 minutes
Servings: 6

Ingredients:
- 12 large prawns
- 3 tbsp butter, melted
- 6 eggs
- Wheat flour to the point
- Salt to taste
- 1 tbsp of virgin olive oil

Directions:
- Cook the prawns in the air fryer at 320°F, being careful not to cook them for about 10 minutes. Remove.
- Then peel the prawns and place them in the melted butter, resting.
- Separate the whites from the yolks of the 6 eggs, beating the whites in the snow, then add the wheat flour until it sighs, season with salt and a spoon of oil.
- Then place the prawns in this pasta, and with a spoon, remove each shrimp, accompanied by a little pasta.
- Put back in the air fryer for 5 minutes.

649. Shrimp with Palm of Hearts

Preparation Time: 15 minutes
Cooking Time: 20 minutes
Servings: 12

Ingredients:
- 1 cup grated Parmesan cheese
- 1 tbsp butter
- 4 ½ lb. shrimp
- ½ cup of olive oil
- Very minced garlic
- Striped onion
- 1 can of sour cream
- 1 can of sliced palm heart
- Grated Parmesan cheese for sprinkling
- For White Sauce:
- 1 onion, sliced
- Margarine and butter
- 2 cups milk
- 2 tbsp of flour
- Salt to taste

Directions:
- Lightly brown the onion with margarine and butter.
- Put the milk and wheat flour in a blender.
- Add the stewed onion.
- Beat everything very well.
- Bring this mixture to the fire and cook until it forms a thick cream. Remove the white sauce from the heat and add the Parmesan cheese and butter. Reserve.
- Sauté the shrimp in olive oil with garlic and onion.
- Add the sautéed shrimp to the white sauce and gradually add the palm kernel and cream, mixing everything very well.
- Arrange in a greased refractory shape, and sprinkle plenty of Parmesan cheese on top.
- Bake in the air fryer at 360°F for 15-20 minutes.

650.   Crab Balls

Preparation Time: 20 minutes
Cooking Time: 30 minutes
Servings: 4

Ingredients:

- 1 lb. of crab
- Salt to taste
- Olive oil
- 2 cloves garlic, minced
- 1 chopped onion
- 3 tbsp of wheat flour
- 1 tbsp of parsley
- 1 fish seasoning
- 2 lemons
- 1 cup milk
- Tarnish:
- 1 beaten egg
- Bread crumbs
- Oil for frying

Directions:

- Wash the crab in the juice of 1 lemon.
- Season with the juice of the other lemon, along with the salt and the prepared fish seasoning.
- In a frying pan, sauté the onion and garlic with the sweet oil.
- Mix the crab meat with the stir fry.
- Let cook in this mixture for another 5 minutes.
- Add the parsley.
- Dissolve the flour in the milk and add it to the crab.
- Stir constantly until this mixture begins to come out of the pan.
- Let cool, shape the meatballs, and go through the beaten egg and breadcrumbs.
- Fry in the air fryer at 400°F for 25 minutes.

651.   Crab Pastries

Preparation Time: 20 minutes
Cooking Time: 30 minutes
Servings: 6

Ingredients:

- 1 small onion
- 1 tomato
- 1 small green pepper
- 1 lb of crab meat
- Seasoning ready for fish
- 1 tbsp of oil
- Pastry dough

Directions:

- Sauté the chopped onion, tomato, and pepper in oil.
- Add the crab meat and seasoning.
- Cook until very dry, without stirring, so that it does not stick to the bottom of the pan.
- Fill the cakes with the prepared crab meat.
- Fry in the air fryer at 400°F for 25 minutes.

652.   Cod and Vegetable Gratin

Preparation Time: 35 minutes
Cooking Time: 20 minutes
Servings: 6

Ingredients:

- 2 ¼ lb. cod
- 1 pound of potato
- 1-pound carrot
- 2 large onions
- 2 red tomatoes
- 1 bell pepper
- 1 tbsp of tomato paste
- Coconut milk
- Garlic, salt, coriander, and olive oil to taste.
- Olives
- Sauce:
- 2 cups milk
- 1 ½ tbsp all-purpose flour
- 1 tbsp butter
- 1 egg
- ½ cup sour cream
- Nutmeg, black pepper, and salt

Directions:

- Soak the cod for 24 hours, always changing the water. Blanch at a rapid boil, removing skin and pimples. Strain the water where the cod was cooked and reserve.
- Season the cod in French fries with garlic, salt, and coriander. Besides, put a saucepan on the fire with olive oil and sliced onions. Add the skinless and seedless tomatoes, pepper, and chopped olives. Add the cod, tomato extract, coconut milk, and a little of the water where the cod was cooked. Let everything cook a lot. It gets a lot of sauce. Test the salt. Cook sliced potatoes and carrots.
- Whisk together milk, wheat, and melted butter in a blender. Bring to the fire and stir until the mixture thickens. Finally, add the cream, nutmeg, black pepper, salt, and beaten egg.
- Grease a plate with olive oil after rubbing a clove of garlic inside. Arrange the cod, potato, and carrot in alternate layers. Cover everything with the sauce and bake in the air fryer at 380°F for 20 minutes.

653.   Lemon Pepper Shrimp

Preparation Time: 5 minutes
Cooking Time: 10 minutes
Servings: 2

Ingredients:

- 1 tbsp Olive oil
- 1 lemon Juice
- Lemon Pepper
- ¼ tsp Paprika
- ¼ tsp Garlic powder
- 12 ounces Uncooked medium shrimp, washed and deveined
- 1 Sliced Lemon

Directions:

- Preheat an air fryer to 400°F (200 °C).
- In a cup, mix olive oil with lemon juice, lemon pepper, paprika, and garlic powder. Add the shrimps and then toss in the mixture until fully coated.
- Open the air fryer and put the shrimp on the air fryer basket, and cook for 6 to 8 minutes until pink and strong. Serve with sliced lemon.

654.   Sesame Tuna Steak

Preparation Time: 15 minutes
Cooking Time: 8-10 minutes
Servings: 2

Ingredients:

- 1 tbsp. coconut oil, melted
- 2 x 6-oz. tuna steaks
- ½ tsp. garlic powder
- 2 tsp. black sesame seeds
- 2 tsp. white sesame seeds

Directions:

- Apply the coconut oil to the tuna steaks with a brunch, then season with garlic powder.
- Combine the black and white sesame seeds. Embed them in the tuna steaks, covering the fish all over. Place the tuna into your air fryer.
- Cook for eight minutes at 400°F, turning the fish halfway through.
- The tuna steaks are ready when they have reached a temperature of 145°F. Serve straight away.

655.   Panko-Crusted Tilapia

Preparation Time: 10 minutes
Cooking Time: 15 minutes
Servings: 3

Ingredients:

- 2 tsp. Italian seasoning
- 2 tsp. lemon pepper
- 1/3 C. panko breadcrumbs
- 1/3 C. egg whites
- 1/3 C. almond flour
- 3 tilapia fillets
- Olive oil

Directions:

- Place panko, egg whites, and flour into separate bowls. Mix lemon pepper and Italian seasoning with breadcrumbs.
- Pat tilapia fillets dry. Dredge in flour, then egg, then breadcrumb mixture. Add to air fryer basket and spray lightly with olive oil.
- Cook 10-11 minutes at 400°F, making sure to flip halfway through cooking.

656.   Cod Tortilla Wraps

Preparation Time: 30 minutes
Cooking Time: 15 minutes
Servings: 4

Ingredients:

- 4 cod fillets; skinless and boneless
- 4 tortillas
- 1 green bell pepper; chopped.
- 1 red onion; chopped.
- A drizzle of olive oil
- 1 cup corn
- 1/2 cup salsa
- 4 tbsp. parmesan cheese; grated
- A handful of baby spinach

Directions:

- Put the fish fillets in your air fryer's basket, cook at 350°F for 6 minutes and transfer to a plate.
- Heat up a pan with the oil over medium heat, add the bell peppers, onions and corn and stir
- Sauté for 5 minutes and take off the heat. Arrange all the tortillas on a working surface and divide the cod, salsa, sautéed veggies, spinach, and parmesan evenly between the 4 tortillas; then wrap/roll them
- Place the tortillas in your air fryer's basket and cook at 350°F for 6 minutes. Divide between plates, serve.

657.   Mexican Fish Tacos

Preparation Time: 20 minutes
Cooking Time: 15 minutes
Servings: 4

Ingredients:

- 4 big tortillas
- 1 yellow onion; chopped
- 1 cup corn
- 1 red bell pepper; chopped
- 1/2 cup salsa
- 4 white fish fillets; skinless and boneless
- A handful of mixed romaine lettuce; spinach, and radicchio
- 4 tbsp. parmesan; grated

Directions:

- Put fish fillets in your air fryer and cook at 350°F for 6 minutes
- Meanwhile; heat up a pan over medium-high heat, add bell pepper, onion, and corn; stir and cook for 1 - 2 minutes
- Arrange tortillas on a working surface, divide fish fillets, spread salsa over them; divide mixed veggies and mixed greens, and spread parmesan on each at the end.
- Roll your tacos; place them in the preheated air fryer and cook at 350°F for 6 minutes more. Divide fish tacos into plates and serve for breakfast

658.   Coriander Shrimp Cakes

Preparation Time: 20 minutes
Cooking Time: 25-30 minutes
Servings: 2

Ingredients:

- 6 oz shrimps, peeled
- 1 tsp ground coriander
- 2 tbsp semolina
- 1 egg
- 1 tbsp fresh parsley, chopped
- ¼ tsp chili flakes
- 1 tsp butter
- ½ tsp salt
- 1 tbsp oatmeal flour

Directions:

- Chop the peeled shrimps into the tiny pieces.
- Crack the egg in the chopped shrimps.
- Add semolina, chopped fresh parsley, ground coriander, chili flakes, salt, and oatmeal flour.
- Mix the shrimp mixture carefully until homogenous.

- Then preheat the air fryer to 400°F.
- Melt the butter in the air fryer basket.
- Make medium shrimp cakes and put them in the melted butter.
- Cook the shrimp cakes for 3 minutes on each side.
- When the shrimp cakes are cooked – chill them and serve.

659.   Tuna Patties

Preparation Time: 30 minutes
Cooking Time: 10 minutes
Servings: 4

Ingredients:
- 2 cans of tuna packed in water
- 1 and 1/2 tbsp of almond flour
- 1 and 1/2 tbsp of mayo
- 1 tsp of dried dill
- 1 tsp of garlic powder
- 1/2 tsp of onion powder
- Pinch of salt and pepper
- Juice of 1/2 lemon

Directions:
- Mix all the ingredients in a bowl and combine them well. For Air Fryer: Heat up to 400°F; tuna should still be wet but able to form into patties. Add an additional tbsp of almond flour if it is not dry enough to form into 4 patties.
- Place patties in the basket in a single layer, and cook for 10 minutes. Add an extra 3 minutes if you want them crisper

660.   Wasabi Crab Cakes

Preparation Time: 30 minutes
Cooking Time: 12 minutes
Servings: 6

Ingredients:
- 1 medium sweet red pepper, finely chopped
- 1 celery rib, finely chopped
- 3 green onions, finely chopped
- 2 large egg whites
- 3 tbsp of reduced-fat mayonnaise
- 1/4 tsp of prepared wasabi
- 1/4 tsp of salt
- 1/3 cup of plus 1/2 cup dry bread crumbs, divided
- 1-1/2 cups of lump crabmeat, drained
- Cooking spray
- SAUCE:
- 1 celery rib, chopped
- 1/3 cup of reduced-fat mayonnaise
- 1 green onion, chopped
- 1 tbsp of sweet pickle relish
- 1/2 tsp of prepared wasabi
- 1/4 tsp of celery salt

Directions:
- The air fryer preheats to 375°F. Spritz basket with spray for cooking fryer. Combine the first 7 ingredients; substitute crumbs for 1/3 cup of bread. Fold softly in crab.
- Place the remaining crumbs of the bread in a shallow bowl. Drop-in crumbs to heap tbsp of crab mixture.

Coat and form gently into 3/4-in.-thick patties. Working in batches as required, place crab cakes in a basket in a single layer. Spritz crab cakes with spray to cook. Cook for 8-12 minutes, until golden brown, turning carefully halfway through cooking and spritzing with additional spray. Replace, and stay warm. Repeat with leftover crab cakes. In the meantime, place sauce ingredients in a food processor; pulse to blend 2 or 3 times or until the desired consistency is achieved. Serve the crab cakes with a sauce to dip immediately.

661.   Shrimp Egg Rolls

Preparation Time: 35 minutes
Cooking Time: 40 minutes
Servings: 5

Ingredients:
- 1 tsp of toasted sesame oil
- 1 tsp of fresh ground ginger
- 3 garlic cloves, minced
- 1 cup of chopped carrots
- 1/2 cup of sliced green onion
- 2 tbsp of soy sauce
- 1/2 tbsp of sugar
- 1/4 cup of chicken or vegetable broth
- 3 cups of coleslaw mix or shredded cabbage
- 10 large cooked shrimp, cut into small pieces
- 10 egg roll wrappers
- 1 egg, beaten

Directions:
- Heat up the oil over medium heat in a large skillet. Cook for 30 seconds, and add the garlic and ginger.
- Stir in carrots and green onion, and sauté for 2 minutes.
- Alternatively, whisk the soy sauce, sugar, and broth together.
- Mix in a mixture of soy sauce, coleslaw mixture/cabbage, and shrimp into the vegetable pan and cook for 5 minutes.
- Remove the pan from heat and allow it to cool in a strainer for about 15 minutes.
- Preheat the air fryer to 390°F as the coleslaw or vegetable mixture is cooling.
- Place the wrappers of egg rolls on a work surface. Top each mixture with 3 spoonfuls of veggie or shrimp.
- Brush some egg onto the wrapper's bottom. Roll up the wrappers, and fold over the sides so that they hold the filling. Brush the egg on the outside of the roll of the egg right before you add it to the air fryer. When you brush it on and let the egg roll sit down, it gets soft, and it can rip.
- Sprinkle with a cooking spray on the air fryer basket. Carefully add 3-4 rolls of eggs to the basket of the air-fryer. Brush egg rolls to the tops with egg.
- Air fry for 8-9 minutes, or until the outside is crispy and crunchy.

662.   Buttered Baked Cod with Wine

Preparation Time: 10 minutes
Cooking Time: 12 minutes
Servings: 2

Ingredients:
- 1 tbsp butter

- 1 tbsp butter
- 2 tbsp dry white wine
- 1/2 pound thick-cut cod loin
- 1-1/2 tsp chopped fresh parsley
- 1-1/2 tsp chopped green onion
- 1/2 lemon, cut into wedges
- 1/4 sleeve buttery round crackers, crushed
- 1/4 lemon, juiced

Directions:

- In a small bowl, melt butter in the microwave. Whisk in crackers.
- Lightly grease the baking pan of the air fryer with the remaining butter. And melt for 2 minutes at 390°F.
- In a small bowl, whisk well lemon juice, white wine, parsley, and green onion.
- Coat cod filets in melted butter. Pour dressing. Top with butter-cracker mixture.
- Cook for 10 minutes at 390°F.
- Serve and enjoy with a slice of lemon.

663. Louisiana Catfish

Preparation Time: 15 minutes
Cooking Time: 30 minutes
Servings: 4

Ingredients:

- 4 catfish fillets
- 1/4 cup of seasoned fish fry. I used Louisiana
- 1 tbsp of olive oil
- 1 tbsp of chopped parsley optional

Directions:

- Preheat Air Fryer to 400°F.
- Rinse the catfish and dry brush.
- Pour the fried fish into a big Ziploc bag for seasoning.
- Add catfish, one at a time, into the bag. Seal, and shake the jar. Ensure seasoning coats the entire filet.
- Sprinkle the olive oil over each filet.
- Place the filet in the basket at Air Fryer. (Because of the size of my filets, I cooked each at a time). Open and simmer for 10 minutes.
- Flip over the shrimp. Cook for 10 minutes.
- Flip over the snake.
- Cook for another 2-3 minutes or until crispness is desired.
- Top with some parsley.

664. Thai Fish Cake with Mango Sauce

Preparation Time: 20 minutes
Cooking Time: 15 minutes
Servings: 4

Ingredients:

- 1 ripe mango
- 1 tsp and a half of red chili paste
- 3 tbsp fresh cilantro or parsley
- 1 lime juice and zest
- 500 g of white fish fillets
- 1 egg
- 1 chopped chive
- 50 g ground coconut

Directions:

- Peel the mango and cut it into small dice. Mix the mango dice in a bowl with ½ tsp of red chili paste, 1 tbsp of cilantro, and the juice and zest of a lime.
- Beat the fish in the kitchen robot and mix it with 1 egg, 1 tsp of salt, and the rest of the lime zest, red chili paste, and lime juice. Mix everything with the rest of the cilantro, chives, and 2 tbsp of coconut.
- Place the rest of the coconut on a deep plate. Divide the fish mixture into 12 portions, shape them into round cakes and coat them with the coconut.
- Place six fish cakes in the basket and place them in the air fryer at 180°C. Set the timer to 7 minutes and fry the cakes until golden brown and ready to drink. Fry in the same way as the rest of the fish cakes.
- Serve with mango sauce.

665. Salmon with Carrots and Fennel

Preparation Time: 15 minutes
Cooking Time: 15 minutes
Servings: 4

Ingredients:

- 1 fennel bulb, thinly sliced
- 2 large carrots, sliced
- 1 large onion, thinly sliced
- 2 tsp extra-virgin olive oil
- ½ cup sour cream
- 1 tsp dried tarragon leaves
- 4 (5-ounce) salmon fillets
- ⅛ tsp salt
- ¼ tsp coarsely ground black pepper

Directions:

- Insert the crisper plate into the basket and the basket into the unit. Preheat the unit by selecting AIR ROAST, setting the temperature to 400°F, and setting the time to 3 minutes. Select START/STOP to begin.
- In a medium bowl, toss together the fennel, carrots, and onion. Add the olive oil and toss again to coat the vegetables. Put the vegetables into a 6-inch round metal pan.
- Once the unit is preheated, place the pan into the basket.
- Select AIR ROAST, set the temperature to 400°F, and set the time to 15 minutes. Select START/STOP to begin.
- After 5 minutes, the vegetables should be crisp-tender. Remove the pan and stir in the sour cream and tarragon. Top with the salmon fillets and sprinkle the fish with salt and pepper. Reinsert the pan into the basket and resume cooking.
- When the cooking is complete, the salmon should flake easily with a fork, and a food thermometer should register at least 145°F. Serve the salmon on top of the vegetables.

666. Lemongrass Tuna Steaks

Preparation Time: 10 minutes
Cooking Time: 10 minutes
Servings: 4

Ingredients:

- 4 small tuna steaks
- 2 tbsp low-sodium soy sauce

- 2 tsp sesame oil
- 2 tsp rice wine vinegar
- 1 tsp grated peeled fresh ginger
- ⅛ tsp freshly ground black pepper
- 1 stalk lemongrass, bent in half
- 3 tbsp freshly squeezed lemon juice

Directions:

- Place the tuna steaks on a plate.
- In a small bowl, whisk the soy sauce, sesame oil, vinegar, and ginger until combined. Pour this mixture over the tuna and gently rub it on both sides. Sprinkle the fish with the pepper. Let marinate for 10 minutes.
- Insert the crisper plate into the basket and the basket into the unit. Preheat the unit by selecting BAKE, setting the temperature to 390°F, and setting the time to 3 minutes. Select START/STOP to begin.
- Once the unit is preheated, place the lemongrass into the basket and top it with the tuna steaks. Drizzle the tuna with lemon juice and 1 tbsp of water.
- Select BAKE, set the temperature to 390°F, and set the time to 10 minutes. Select START/STOP to begin.
- When the cooking is complete, a food thermometer inserted into the tuna should register at least 145°F. Discard the lemongrass and serve the tuna.

667.   Tropical Shrimps

Preparation Time: 10 minutes
Cooking Time: 18 minutes
Servings: 4

Ingredients:

- ½ cup light brown sugar
- 2 tsp cornstarch
- ⅛ tsp plus ½ tsp salt, divided
- 4 ounces crushed pineapple with syrup
- 2 tbsp freshly squeezed lemon juice
- 1 tbsp yellow mustard
- 1½ pounds raw large shrimp, peeled and deveined
- 2 eggs
- ½ cup all-purpose flour
- 1 cup unsweetened shredded coconut
- ¼ tsp granulated garlic
- Olive oil spray

Directions:

- In a medium saucepan over medium heat, combine the brown sugar, cornstarch, and ⅛ tsp of salt.
- As the brown sugar mixture melts into a sauce, stir in the crushed pineapple with syrup, lemon juice, and mustard. Cook for about 4 minutes until the mixture thickens and begins to boil. Boil for 1 minute. Remove the pan from the heat, set aside, and let cool while you make the shrimp.
- Put the shrimp on a plate and pat them dry with paper towels.
- In a small bowl, whisk the eggs.
- In a medium bowl, stir together the flour, shredded coconut, remaining ½ tsp of salt, and granulated garlic.
- Insert the crisper plate into the basket and the basket into the unit. Preheat the unit by selecting AIR FRY, setting the temperature to 400°F, and setting the time to 3 minutes. Select START/STOP to begin.

- Dip the shrimp into the egg and into the coconut mixture to coat.
- Once the unit is preheated, place a parchment paper liner into the basket. Place the coated shrimp on the liner in a single layer and spray them with olive oil.
- Select AIR FRY, set the temperature to 400°F, and set the time to 13 minutes. Select START/STOP to begin.
- After 6 minutes, remove the basket, flip the shrimp, and spray them with more olive oil. Reinsert the basket to resume cooking. Check the shrimp after 3 minutes more. If browned, they are done; if not, resume cooking.
- When the cooking is complete, serve with the prepared pineapple sauce.

668.   Scallops with Spring Veggies

Preparation Time: 10 minutes
Cooking Time: 10 minutes
Servings: 4

Ingredients:

- Cooking oil spray
- 1-pound asparagus ends trimmed, cut into 2-inch pieces
- 1 cup sugar snap peas
- 1-pound sea scallops
- 1 tbsp freshly squeezed lemon juice
- 2 tsp extra-virgin olive oil
- ½ tsp dried thyme
- Salt
- Freshly ground black pepper

Directions:

- Insert the crisper plate into the basket and the basket into the unit. Preheat the unit by selecting AIR FRY, setting the temperature to 400°F, and setting the time to 3 minutes. Select START/STOP to begin.
- Once the unit is preheated, spray the crisper plate with cooking oil. Place the asparagus and sugar snap peas into the basket.
- Select AIR FRY, set the temperature to 400°F, and set the time to 10 minutes. Select START/STOP to begin.
- Meanwhile, check the scallops for a small muscle attached to the side. Pull it off and discard it. In a medium bowl, toss together the scallops, lemon juice, olive oil, and thyme. Season with salt and pepper.
- After 3 minutes, the vegetables should just start to get tender. Place the scallops on top of the vegetables. Reinsert the basket to resume cooking. After 3 minutes more, remove the basket and shake it. Again, reinsert the basket to resume cooking.
- When the cooking is complete, the scallops should be firm when tested with your finger and opaque in the center, and the vegetables tender. Serve immediately.

669.   Cajun Shrimps

Preparation Time: 10 minutes
Cooking Time: 5 minutes
Servings: 4

Ingredients:

- 1 tbsp Olive oil
- ½ tsp Old Bay seasoning
- 1.25 lbs. Tiger shrimp
- ¼ tsp Smoked paprika

- ¼ tsp Cayenne pepper
- Pinch of Salt

Directions:
- Heat the Air Fryer to reach 390°F.
- Coat the shrimp using oil and spices.
- Toss the shrimp in the fryer basket and set the timer for five minutes.
- Serve with your favorite side dish.

670. Parmesan Crusted Clams

Preparation Time: 20 minutes
Cooking Time: 10 minutes
Servings: 6

Ingredients:
- 24 Shucked clams
- 1 cup of unseasoned breadcrumbs
- 4 tbsp melted butter
- 3 Garlic cloves
- 1 tsp Dried oregano
- ¼ cup Parsley
- ¼ cup Grated parmesan cheese
- For the Pan: sea salt

Directions:
- Heat the Air Fryer for a few minutes at 400°F.
- Mince the garlic. Chop the parsley to combine with the breadcrumbs, oregano, parmesan cheese, and melted butter in a medium mixing bowl.
- Use a heaping tbsp of the crumb mixture, and add it to the clams.
- Fill with the salt, arrange the clams inside, and air-fry for three minutes.
- Garnish them using lemon wedges and fresh parsley.

671. Crispy Halibut

Preparation Time: 15 minutes
Cooking Time: 20 minutes
Servings: 4

Ingredients:
- 4 Halibut fillets
- ¼ cup Fresh chives
- ½ cup Fresh parsley
- ¼ cup Fresh dill
- Black pepper & sea salt (to your liking)
- ¾ cup Pork rinds
- 1 tbsp Extra-virgin olive oil
- 1 tbsp Finely grated lemon zest

Directions:
- Warm the Air Fryer to reach 390°F.
- Chop the chives, dill, and parsley. Combine all of the dry fixings – parsley, pork rinds, chives, dill, lemon zest, black pepper, sea salt, and olive oil.
- Rinse the halibut thoroughly and let them drain well on paper towels.
- Prepare a baking tin to fit in the cooker. Spoon the rinds over the fish and press.

672. Honey and Sriracha Calamari

Preparation Time: 15 minutes
Cooking Time: 15 minutes
Servings: 3

Ingredients:
- 0.5 lbs. Calamari tubes - tentacles if you prefer
- 1 cup Club soda
- 1 cup Flour
- Salt - red pepper & black pepper (2 dashes each)
- ½ cup Honey + 1-2 tbsp Sriracha
- Red pepper flakes (2 shakes)

Directions:
- Thoroughly rinse the calamari and blot it dry using a bunch of paper towels. Slice into rings (.25-inch wide). Toss the rings into a bowl. Pour in the club soda and stir until all are submerged. Wait for about ten minutes.
- Sift the salt, flour, red pepper, and black pepper. Set aside for now.
- Dredge the calamari through the flour mixture, and place it on a platter until ready to fry.
- Spritz the basket of the Air Fryer with a small amount of cooking oil spray. Arrange the calamari in the basket, careful not to crowd it too much.
- Set the temperature at 375°F and the timer for 11 minutes.
- Shake the basket twice during the cooking process, loosening any rings that may stick.
- Remove from the basket, toss with the sauce and return to the Air Fryer for two more minutes.
- Serve with additional sauce as desired. Make the sauce by combining honey, sriracha, and red pepper flakes in a small bowl, and mix until combined.

673. Teriyaki Halibut Steak

Preparation Time: 40 minutes
Cooking Time: 15-20 minutes
Servings: 4

Ingredients:
- 1 lb. Halibut steak
- The Marinade:
- 3/5 cup Low-sodium soy sauce
- ½ cup Mirin Japanese cooking wine
- ¼ cup Sugar
- ¼ cup Orange juice
- 2 tbsp Lime juice
- ¼ tsp Ground ginger
- ¼ tsp Crushed red pepper flakes
- 1 Smashed garlic clove

Directions:
- Set the Air Fryer at 390°F.
- Combine all of the marinade components in a saucepan, bringing it to a boil. Lower the heat setting to medium and cool.
- Pour half of the marinade in a plastic bag with the halibut and zip it closed. Marinate in the fridge for about 30 minutes.
- Air-fry the halibut for 10 to 12 minutes. Brush using the remaining glaze over the steak.
- Serve with a bed of rice. Add a little basil or mint or basil for extra flavoring.

674. Steamed Salmon and Summer Greens

Preparation Time: 20 minutes
Cooking Time: 15-20 minutes
Servings: 4

Ingredients:
- 4 salmon steaks of 200g each
- 10g dill, keep a few sprigs to use
- for garnish
- 1 zucchini, finely sliced
- 200g green asparagus tips
- 150g broad beans (frozen)
- 150g garden peas (frozen)
- freshly ground pepper and salt
- lemon-flavored olive oil

Directions:
- Place 1 cup of water into the inner pot and add a steam tray.
- Layer all the vegetables on the steaming tray, trying to keep it a flat layer.
- Place the salmon fillets on top of the vegetable layer and season with salt, pepper, and lemon-flavored olive oil.
- Close the lid of the air fryer duo, touch the PRESSURE COOK to select a STEAM program, set the cooking time for 10 minutes, and press START.

675. Asian Steamed Salmon

Preparation Time: 10 minutes
Cooking Time: 5 minutes
Servings: 4

Ingredients:
- 800g skin-on salmon fillet
- 2 tbsp ginger, julienned
- Spring onion finely sliced
- 8 slices lime
- 200ml vegetable stock
- 30ml Shaoxing wine
- 25g sugar
- 30ml light soy sauce
- 5ml sesame oil
- 1 bunch Coriander
- Ground white pepper

Directions:
- Cut salmon into 4 even pieces
- Pour stock, sugar, Shaoxing, soy, and sesame oil into the cooker base.
- Lay salmon on a cabbage leaf in a steamer tray. Layer the lime, ginger, spring onion, and white pepper onto the salmon. Close the lid of the air fryer duo.
- Touch the PRESSURE COOK to select a STEAM program, and set the cooking time for 5 minutes. Press START.
- Use steaming liquid as a sauce with fish. Garnish with coriander leaves.

676. Sesame Cabbage & Prawns Egg Roll Wraps

Preparation Time: 30 minutes
Cooking Time: 18 minutes
Servings: 4

Ingredients:
- 2 tbsp vegetable oil
- 1-inch piece of fresh ginger, grated
- 1 tbsp minced garlic
- 1 carrot, cut into strips
- ¼ cup chicken broth
- 2 tbsp reduced-sodium soy sauce
- 1 tbsp sugar
- 1 cup shredded Napa cabbage
- 1 tbsp sesame oil
- 8 cooked prawns, minced
- 1 egg
- 8 egg roll wrappers

Directions:
- In a skillet over high heat, heat vegetable oil, and cook ginger and garlic for 40 seconds, until fragrant. Stir in carrot and cook for another 2 minutes. Pour in chicken broth, soy sauce, and sugar and bring to a boil.
- Add cabbage and let simmer until softened, for 4 minutes. Remove the skillet from the heat and stir in sesame oil. Let cool for 15 minutes. Strain cabbage mixture, and fold in minced prawns. Whisk an egg in a small bowl. Fill each egg roll wrapper with prawn mixture, arranging the mixture just below the center of the wrapper.
- Fold the bottom part over the filling and tuck it under. Fold in both sides and tightly roll-up. Use the whisked egg to seal the wrapper. Place the rolls into a greased frying basket, spray with oil and cook for 12 minutes at 370°F on the Air Fry function, turning once halfway through.

677. Fish Fillet in Pesto Sauce

Preparation Time: 15 minutes
Cooking Time: 8 minutes
Servings: 2

Ingredients:
- 2½ pound Whitefish fillets
- 1 tbsp Olive oil
- 1 tsp Pepper
- ½ tsp Salt
- Pesto sauce:
- 1 bunch of fresh basil
- 1 tbsp Pine nuts
- 1 tbsp Parmesan cheese, shredded
- 1 cup Extra-virgin olive oil
- 2 Garlic cloves

Directions:
- Chop the basil and keep it aside.
- Set the air fryer temperature to 180°C and preheat.
- Spray the fillet with olive oil and rub pepper and salt.
- Put the coated fillet in the air fryer basket and cook for 8 minutes.
- Flip the fillet halfway for even cooking.
- Put the chopped basil, pine nuts, garlic, olive oil, and Parmesan cheese into a food processor and make a sauce paste.
- Add salt as required.
- Drizzle pesto sauce over the fillets and serve hot.

678.   Ranch Fish Fillet

Preparation Time: 10 minutes
Cooking Time: 12 minutes
Servings: 4

Ingredients:
- 4 Tilapia or salmon fillets
- ¾ cup Bread crumbs
- 1-ounce Ranch-style dressing mix, dry
- 2½ tbsp Cooking oil
- 2 Eggs
- 1 Lemon wedges

Directions:
- In a medium bowl, beat eggs and keep them aside.
- Combine ranch dressing and breadcrumbs in a medium bowl.
- Pour cooking oil into it and stir until it becomes loose.
- Set the air temperature to 180°C and preheat the air fryer.
- Now start the cooking process.
- Dip the fish fillet into the beaten egg and let it drip off the excess liquid.
- Dredge the fish fillet into the crumb mixture.
- Place the coated fish fillet into the air fryer.
- Cook for 12 minutes.
- Serve along with lemon wedges.

679.   Herbed Fish Fingers

Preparation Time: 30 minutes
Cooking Time: 30 minutes
Servings: 4

Ingredients:
- 10½ ounces Seer fish
- ½ tsp Red chili flakes
- ¼ tsp Turmeric powder
- 2 tsp Garlic powder
- 1 tsp Ginger paste
- ½ tsp Black pepper, crushed
- 2 tsp Mixed herbs, powdered
- 2 tbsp Corn flour
- 2 Eggs
- ¼ tsp Baking soda
- 1 cup Breadcrumbs
- Cooking spray – as required
- 2 tbsp Lemon juice
- ½ tsp Salt

Directions:
- Wash, clean, and cut seer fish into a finger shape. Pat dry and keep it aside.
- Combine thoroughly lemon juice, turmeric powder, red chili flakes, crushed black pepper, 1 tsp garlic powder, ginger paste, 1 tsp mixed herbs, and salt in a medium bowl.
- Put seer fish fingers into it and gently combine to marinate. Keep it aside for 10 minutes.
- In another medium bowl, beat eggs and add corn flour.
- Dip the marinated fish into it and keep it aside for 10 minutes.
- Take another bowl and mix breadcrumbs, 1 tsp mixed herbs, and one tsp garlic powder.
- Dredge the fish into the flour mixture.

- Set the air fryer temperature to 180°C.
- Place an aluminum liner inside the air fryer basket.
- Layer the marinated fish inside the air fryer basket without overlapping one another.
- Spritz cooking oil over the fish.
- Cook for 10 minutes by flipping halfway.
- Serve hot along with your favorite sauce.

680.   Spicy Steamed Mussels

Preparation Time: 30 minutes
Cooking Time: 15 minutes
Servings: 6

Ingredients:
- 1 pound Seawater mussels with shell
- 1 cup Water
- 1 tbsp Butter
- 2 tsp Garlic, minced
- 1 tsp Black pepper ground
- ¼ tsp Red chili powder
- 1 tsp Chives
- 1 tsp Basil, finely chopped
- 1 tsp Parsley, finely chopped
- ½ tsp Salt
- Cooking spray – as required

Directions:
- Scrub, wash, clean the mussel and soak it for 30 minutes.
- Place it in a tray that can be put in the air fryer basket along with water.
- Set the temperature to 190°C and cook for 5 minutes.
- Transfer the mussels into a bowl. You can see all the shells opened.
- Take out the mussel's flesh from the shell with a spoon or fork.
- Remove the 'hair,' and also the dirt, which you can see in black color.
- After cleaning, wash gently and pat dry.
- In a bowl, combine butter, ground pepper, chili powder, garlic, chives, and basil with the cleaned mussels.
- Layer an aluminum foil inside the air fryer basket and place the mussels over it.
- Cook it for 5 minutes, intermittently shaking the basket at 200°C.
- Halfway through cooking, spritz some cooking oil.
- Serve hot garnishing with chopped parsley.

681.   Quick and Easy Lobster Tails

Preparation Time: 5 minutes
Cooking Time: 6 minutes
Servings: 2

Ingredients:
- 4 Lobster tails
- 2 tbsp melted butter
- 1 tsp ground pepper
- ½ tsp Salt

Directions:
- Cut the lobster lengthwise.
- Remove the shells and devein.
- Coat the lobster with melted butter, pepper, and salt.
- Set the air fryer temperature to 180°C and preheat.

- Put the coated lobster in the air fryer basket and cook for 6 minutes.
- Shake the air basket intermittently and sprinkle the remaining butter over it and continue cooking until it becomes crisp.
- Serve hot.

682. Cajun Lemon-Shrimp Kebabs

Preparation Time: 10 minutes
Cooking Time: 10 minutes
Servings: 2

Ingredients:
- 1 tsp cayenne
- 1 tsp garlic powder
- 1 tsp kosher salt
- 1 tsp onion powder
- 1 tsp oregano
- 1 tsp paprika
- 12 pcs XL shrimp
- 2 lemons, sliced thinly crosswise
- 2 tbsp olive oil

Directions:
- In a bowl, mix all ingredients except for sliced lemons. Marinate for 10 minutes.
- Thread 3 shrimps per steel skewer.
- Place in skewer rack.
- Cook for 5 minutes at 390°F.
- Serve and enjoy with freshly squeezed lemon.

683. Tuna Niçoise Salad

Preparation Time: 35 minutes
Cooking Time: 10 minutes
Servings: 2

Ingredients:
- 6 New baby potatoes (quartered)
- 2 tsp Vegetable oil
- Olive oil spray
- Salt – as per taste
- Black pepper (ground) – as per taste
- 1 cup Green beans (trim and snap in half)
- 2 Tuna fillets (4 ounces each)
- 1 cup cherry tomatoes
- 6 leaves of butter lettuce
- 2 Hard-boiled eggs (peel and cut in half)
- 10 Olives
- Vinaigrette Dressing
- 2 tbsp Olive oil
- 1 tbsp Red wine vinegar
- 1/8 tsp Salt
- 1 tsp Dijon mustard
- Black pepper (freshly ground) – as per taste

Directions:
- Start by tossing the potatoes, beans, tomatoes, salt, pepper, and 2 tsp of vegetable oil in a mixing bowl.
- Take the basket out of the air fryer and place the seasoned vegetables in the same. Make sure to arrange the vegetables in a single layer.
- Return the basket to the fryer and cook for about 10 minutes at 400°F.

- Grease both sides of the tuna fillets with olive oil spray. Generously season the fish with pepper and salt.
- Take out the air fryer basket and place the fillets over the vegetables. Let them cook for about 5 minutes. The tuna should be medium-well by now.
- Remove the tuna and set it aside for a few minutes. Cut into slices.
- Meanwhile, prepare the vinaigrette. For this, add the vinegar, mustard, salt, black pepper, and olive oil to a small glass jar and close the lid. Shake until well-combined.
- Place the butter lettuce leaves on a flat wooden surface and place equal amounts of tuna, tomatoes, potatoes, and green beans on the lettuce leaves.
- Take 2 serving platters and place 3 prepared lettuce salad bowls on each platter.
- Place 2 egg halves on each of the serving platters and sprinkle with chopped olives.
- Finish by drizzling vinaigrette on top of all the salad bowls. Serve fresh!

684. Broiled Tilapia

Preparation Time: 5 minutes
Cooking Time: 10 minutes
Servings: 4

Ingredients:
- 1-pound tilapia fillets
- Old bay seasoning as needed
- Canola oil as needed
- Lemon pepper as needed
- Salt to taste
- Butter

Directions:
- Preheat your Fryer to 400°F.
- Cover tilapia with oil.
- Take a bowl and mix in salt, lemon pepper, butter buds, and seasoning.
- Cover your fish with the sauce.
- Bake fillets for 10 minutes.
- Serve and enjoy!

685. Lemon Parmesan Halibut

Preparation Time: 10 minutes
Cooking Time: 15 minutes
Servings: 4

Ingredients:
- 1 lb. halibut fillet
- ½ cup butter
- 2 ½ tbsp. mayonnaise
- 2 ½ tbsp. lemon juice
- ¾ cup parmesan cheese, grated

Directions:
- Pre-heat your fryer at 375°F.
- Spritz the halibut fillets with cooking spray and season as desired.
- Put the halibut in the fryer and cook for twelve minutes.
- In the meantime, combine the butter, mayonnaise, and lemon juice in a bowl with a hand mixer. Ensure a creamy texture is achieved.
- Stir in the grated parmesan.

- When the halibut is ready, open the drawer and spread the butter over the fish with a butter knife. Allow to cook for a further two minutes, then serve hot.

686. Cheesy Fish Balls

Preparation Time: 30 minutes
Cooking Time: 16 minutes
Servings: 4

Ingredients:
- 1 cup smoked fish, flaked
- 2 cups cooked rice
- 2 eggs, lightly beaten
- 1 cup grated Grana Padano cheese
- ¼ cup finely chopped thyme
- Salt and black pepper to taste
- 1 cup panko crumbs

Directions:
- In a bowl, add fish, rice, eggs, Parmesan cheese, thyme, salt, and pepper into a bowl; stir to combine. Shape the mixture into 12 even-sized balls. Roll the balls in the crumbs, then spray with oil.
- Arrange the balls into the fryer and cook for 16 minutes at 400°F until crispy.

687. Creole Veggie-Shrimp Bake

Preparation Time: 10 minutes
Cooking Time: 20 minutes
Servings: 4
- **Ingredients**
- 1 Bag of Frozen Mixed Vegetables
- 1 Tbsp Gluten-Free Cajun Seasoning
- Olive Oil Spray
- Season with salt and pepper
- Small Shrimp Peeled & Deveined (Regular Size Bag about 50-80 Small Shrimp)
- **Directions**
- Lightly grease the baking pan of the air fryer with cooking spray. Add all ingredients and toss well to coat. Season with pepper and salt generously.
- For 10 minutes, cook at 330°F. Halfway through cooking time, stir.
- Cook for 10 minutes at 330°F.
- Serve and enjoy.

688. Wine Poached Clams

Preparation Time: 10 minutes
Cooking Time: 30 minutes
Servings: 4

Ingredients:
- 2 ½ pounds of littleneck clams
- 3 tbsp of butter
- 2 peeled and diced shallots
- 1 ¼ cup of chicken broth
- 2 tsp of white wine vinegar

Directions:
- Store the clams in a cool space before cooking. Before you begin, scrub them under the tap and put them in a large bowl filled with ice water. If you notice any clams with large pieces of shells missing, discard them. Place the bowl on the counter and lightly tap the surface close to the bowl. Discard any clams that don't close up as well.
- Let the clams sit in the water for about 20 minutes. This way, they will get rid of sand and grit.
- In the meantime, set your pressure cooker to sauté, and add the butter and a drizzle of olive oil. Sauté the shallots in the mixture for 1-2 minutes until it becomes slightly translucent.
- Add the broth to the air fryer and wait until it starts simmering. Carefully transfer the clams one by one into the pot and let it all simmer for about 8-10 minutes at 390°F. You can see which clams are done because they will open on their own. If you notice several closed ones, give them an extra minute or two, but they stay closed – throw them out.
- Use a spider or a slotted spoon to transfer the clams into a bowl. Keep simmering the liquid in the pot for 5 more minutes (or more, until it reduces as much as you like). Pour the liquid into the bowl over clams.
- To garnish, sprinkle some fresh herbs onto the clams (rosemary, parsley, thyme, or dill will work great) and drizzle them with the vinegar – this trick is the substitute for a white wine that would be normally used. Do not add any salt – the clams are naturally salty.
- Serve right after pouring the broth and garnishing!

689. Taiwan Cod Fillets

Preparation Time: 10 minutes
Cooking Time: 15 minutes
Servings: 4

Ingredients:
- 4 cod fillets, boneless
- Salt and black pepper to taste
- 1 cup water
- 4 tbsp light soy sauce
- 1 tbsp sugar
- 3 tbsp olive oil + a drizzle
- 4 ginger slices
- 3 spring onions, chopped
- 2 tbsp coriander, chopped

Directions:
- Season the fish with salt and pepper, then drizzle some oil over it and rub well.
- Put the fish in your air fryer and cook at 360°F for 12 minutes.
- Put the water in a pot and heat up over medium heat; add the soy sauce and sugar, stir, bring to a simmer, and remove from the heat.
- Heat up a pan with the olive oil over medium heat; add the ginger and green onions, stir, cook for 2-3 minutes, and remove from the heat.
- Divide the fish between plates and top with ginger, coriander, and green onions.
- Drizzle the soy sauce mixture all over, serve, and enjoy!

690. Tomato Basil Tilapia

Preparation Time: 10 minutes
Cooking Time: 5-10 minutes
Servings: 4

Ingredients:
- 4 4-ounce fillets of tilapia
- 3 Roma tomatoes
- 2 minced garlic cloves
- ¼ of a cup of chopped fresh basil
- 2 tbsp of olive oil

Directions:
- Pour ½ of a cup of water into the air fryer and place the steaming basket on the surface. Arrange the fish in the basket and sprinkle with salt and pepper.
- Close the lid and the valve and manually set the pressure to high.
- Cook fresh tilapia for 2 minutes at 400°F, or for 4 minutes if it's frozen.
- In the meantime, finely dice the tomatoes. Place them in a bowl and combine with garlic, olive oil, and basil. Gently stir them together and taste for seasoning. Add salt and pepper if necessary.
- After the timer beeps, open the valve to quickly release the pressure, carefully open the lid and test the fish. If you're using the thermometer, it should register a minimum of 145 °F. You can also test it with a fork – the meat should flake easily.
- Gently transfer the fish to the plates (be careful, it might crumble – a wide spatula is helpful here). Add about 1 spoonful of the tomatoes on top of each fillet and serve immediately.

691.   Buttered Salmon with Dill

Preparation Time: 5 minutes
Cooking Time: 5 minutes
Servings: 4

Ingredients:
- 1 pound of salmon (fresh or defrosted)
- 1 thinly sliced lemon
- zest of 1 lemon
- 1 tsp of chopped fresh dill
- 2 tbsp of room-temperature butter

Directions:
- First, prepare your compound butter. In a small mixing bowl, combine the soft butter with lemon zest and dill. Mix until everything is well blended.
- Cut the salmon into portions and spread an even layer of butter over the top of all of them. Sprinkle with salt and pepper to taste.
- Add 1 cup of water into the pressure cooker. For extra flavor, you can also place a couple of sprigs of fresh dill inside. Place the standard trivet in and arrange half of the fillets on it, placing 2 thin lemon slices on each of them. Then, stack a 3-inch trivet on top of that and arrange the remaining portions, seasoning them and topping with lemon as well.
- Close the lid of the air fryer duo and the valve, set the pressure to high, and cook for 34 minutes. Once it's done, quickly release the pressure and serve the fish immediately.

692.   Garam Masala Shrimps

Preparation Time: 10 minutes
Cooking Time: 10 minutes
Servings: 4

Ingredients:
- 1 pound of shelled and deveined shrimp
- 1 tbsp of minced fresh ginger
- 1 tbsp of minced fresh garlic
- ½ of a can of coconut milk, full-fat
- 1 tsp of garam masala

Directions:
- In a bowl, mix the coconut milk with garam masala, garlic and ginger. Then, add the shrimp and stir together, making sure they are well coated.
- Into the pressure cooker, pour 2 cups of water and place down the trivet.
- Transfer the shrimp and the sauce together into a heatproof dish. Make sure it will fit inside the cooker. Cover it with tinfoil and set it down on the trivet.
- Close the lid of the air fryer duo, secure the valve and set the cooker for low pressure for 4 minutes. Once it's done, quickly release the pressure and carefully open the lid.
- Take out the dish, remove the foil and stir everything together. Taste for seasoning and add coconut milk, salt or pepper as needed. For serving, you can garnish the shrimp with chopped herbs, such as parsley or cilantro or lime wedges.

693.   Cajun Lobster Tails

Preparation Time: 5 minutes
Cooking Time: 10 minutes
Servings: 4

Ingredients:
- 8 frozen lobster tails
- 1 cup of water
- 1 tbsp of Old Bay seasoning
- 1 cup of butter
- 1 tsp of minced garlic

Directions:
- First, prepare the lobster tails. Using sharp scissors, cut the shell down to the fin in a line. Lobster tails tend to curl without that step, which makes them harder to eat.
- Pour 1 cup of water into the air fryer and add the Old Bay seasoning to it. Then, put down the trivet and place 4 tails shell side down onto it. Use the pot's steam basket for the remaining four – simply place it over the tails that are on the trivet. Close the lid and seal the valve.
- Use the Manual button for pressure and set the timer for 4 minutes at 350°F. Remember that this time is applicable to frozen tails – if you're using fresh, they will need to be set for 7 minutes, as the pot will need a bit of time to heat when using frozen lobster.
- As the tails steam, prepare a butter sauce to dip them in. Brown 1 tbsp of butter on the stove in a skillet over medium heat. This should take about 3-4 minutes. Then, add the remaining butter and the garlic. Sauté the garlic until it's golden, but don't let it burn – it will become bitter.
- When the timer beeps, switch off the heat and quickly release the pressure. Take the tails out with tongs and serve immediately.
- Garnish with your preferred side dishes and herbs!

694.   Haddock and Spinach

Preparation Time: 10 minutes
Cooking Time: 5 minutes
Servings: 4

Ingredients:
- 1 pound of frozen haddock fillets (½-in. thick, cut into 4 pieces)
- 2 cups of frozen spinach
- 2 tbsp of mayonnaise
- 1 tsp of minced garlic
- 2 tsp of lemon juice

Directions:
- Before you begin, take the haddock out of the freezer and let it thaw in a bowl on the counter.
- Prepare 4 sheets of aluminum foil. Make sure they are each big enough to create a "pocket" for each of the fillets.
- Spread the foil on the counter. Place an equal amount of spinach on every one of them and place the fish on the spinach. Salt and pepper the fillets to taste and close the foil. Make sure to fold the edges to prevent leaking.
- Put the steaming basket inside the cooker and arrange the fillets on it. Make sure the pockets lie flat and don't overlap. Close the lid and valve, set the pressure to high and cook for 4 minutes at 400°F. After the beep, let the pressure release naturally for 10-12 minutes and release the rest quickly.
- In the meantime, mix together mayonnaise, garlic and lemon juice in a small bowl to create the sauce for the fish.
- Open the lid of the cooker, remove the packets and transfer the fish gently onto plates. Top each fillet with spinach. Make sure to also pour out any accumulated juices from inside the foil! Lastly, drizzle the top with the sauce you prepared.

695.   Sesame Crusted White Fish

Preparation Time: 10 minutes
Cooking Time: 8-10 minutes
Servings: 5

Ingredients:
- 3 tbsp plain flour
- 2 eggs
- ½ cup sesame seeds, toasted
- ½ cup breadcrumbs
- 1/8 tsp dried rosemary, crushed
- Pinch of salt
- Pinch of black pepper
- 3 tbsp olive oil
- 5 frozen fish fillets (white fish of your choice)

Directions:
- . In a shallow dish, place flour. In a second shallow dish, beat the eggs. In a third shallow dish, add remaining ingredients except for fish fillets and mix till a crumbly mixture forms.
- Coat the fillets with flour and shake off the excess flour.
- Next, dip the fillets in the egg.
- Then coat the fillets with sesame seeds mixture generously.
- Preheat the Air Fryer to 390 °F.
- Line an Air Fryer basket with a piece of foil. Arrange the fillets into the prepared basket. Close air fryer lid and cook for about 14 minutes, flipping once after 10 minutes.

696.   Snapper Scampi

Preparation Time: 10 minutes
Cooking Time: 10 minutes
Servings: 4

Ingredients:
- 4 (6-ounce) skinless snapper or arctic char fillets
- 1 tbsp olive oil
- 3 tbsp lemon juice, divided
- ½ tsp dried basil
- Pinch salt
- Freshly ground black pepper
- 2 tbsp butter
- cloves of garlic, minced

Directions:
- Rub the fish fillets with olive oil and 1 tbsp of lemon juice. Sprinkle with the basil, salt, and pepper, and place in the Air Fryer basket.
- Close the air fryer lid and grill the fish for 7 to 8 minutes at 400°F or until the fish just flakes when tested with a fork. Remove the fish from the basket and put it on a serving plate. Cover to keep warm. In a 6-by-6-by-2-inch pan, combine the butter, remaining 2 tbsp lemon juice, and garlic. Cook in the Air Fryer for 1 to 2 minutes or until the garlic is sizzling. Pour this mixture over the fish and serve.

697.   Teriyaki Salmon Noodles

Preparation Time: 10 minutes
Cooking Time: 16 minutes
Servings: 4

Ingredients:
- 1 Salmon Fillet
- 1 Tbsp Teriyaki Marinade
- 3 ½ Oz Soba Noodles, cooked and drained
- 10 Oz Firm Tofu
- 7 Oz Mixed Salad
- 1 cup Broccoli
- Olive Oil
- Salt and Pepper to taste

Directions:
- Season the salmon with salt and pepper to taste, then coat with the teriyaki marinate. Set aside for 15 minutes
- Preheat the Air Fryer to 350°F, close the air fryer lid and cook the salmon for 8 minutes.
- Whilst the Air Fryer is cooking the salmon, start slicing the tofu into small cubes.
- Next, slice the broccoli into smaller chunks. Drizzle with olive oil.
- Once the salmon is cooked, put the broccoli and tofu into the Air Fryer tray for 8 minutes.
- Plate the salmon and broccoli tofu mixture over the soba noodles. Add the mixed salad to the side and serve

698. Crispy Ranch Fish Fillets

Preparation Time: 10 minutes
Cooking Time: 12 minutes
Servings: 2

Ingredients:
- 2 fish fillets
- 1/2 packet ranch dressing mix
- 1/4 cup breadcrumbs
- 1 egg, lightly beaten
- 1 1/4 tbsp olive oil

Directions:
- In a shallow dish, mix together ranch dressing mix and breadcrumbs.
- Add oil and mix until the mixture becomes crumbly.
- Place the dehydrating tray in a multi-level air fryer basket and place the basket in the air fryer.
- Dip fish fillet in egg, then coats with breadcrumb and place on dehydrating tray.
- Seal pot with air fryer lid and select air fry mode, then set the temperature to 350°F and timer for 12 minutes. Turn fish fillets halfway through.
- Serve and enjoy.

699. Bang Bang Shrimp

Preparation Time: 10 minutes
Cooking Time: 8 minutes
Servings: 4

Ingredients:
- 1 tsp. paprika
- Montreal chicken seasoning
- ¾ C. panko bread crumbs
- ½ C. almond flour
- 1 egg white
- 1-pound raw shrimp (peeled and deveined)
- Bang Bang Sauce:
- ¼ C. sweet chili sauce
- 2 tbsp. sriracha sauce
- 1/3 C. plain Greek yogurt

Directions:
- Ensure your Air Fryer is preheated to 400°F.
- Season all shrimp with seasonings.
- Add flour to one bowl, egg white in another, and breadcrumbs to a third.
- Dip seasoned shrimp in flour, then egg whites, and then breadcrumbs.
- Spray coated shrimp with olive oil and add to Air Fryer basket.
- Close the air fryer lid. Set temperature to 400°F, and set time to 4 minutes. Cook 4 minutes, flip, and cook an additional 4 minutes.
- To make the sauce, mix together all sauce ingredients until smooth.

700. Easy Shrimp Paella

Preparation Time: 15 minutes
Cooking Time: 15 minutes
Servings: 4

Ingredients:
- 1 (10-ounce) package frozen cooked rice, thawed
- 1 (6-ounce) jar of artichoke hearts, drained and chopped
- ¼ cup vegetable broth
- ½ tsp turmeric
- ½ tsp dried thyme
- 1 cup frozen cooked small shrimp
- ½ cup frozen baby peas
- 1 tomato, diced

Directions:
- In a 6-by-6-by-2-inch pan, combine the rice, artichoke hearts, vegetable broth, turmeric, and thyme, and stir gently.
- Place in the Air Fryer, close the air fryer lid and bake for 8 to 9 minutes or until the rice is hot. Remove from the Air Fryer and gently stir in the shrimp, peas, and tomato. Cook for 5 to 8 minutes or until the shrimp and peas are hot and the paella is bubbling.

701. Indian Spiced Fish Fingers

Preparation Time: 35 minutes
Cooking Time: 15 minutes
Servings: 3

Ingredients:
- 1/2-pound fish fillet
- 1 tbsp finely chopped fresh mint leaves or any fresh herbs
- 1/3 cup bread crumbs
- 1 tsp ginger garlic paste or ginger and garlic powders
- 1 hot green chili finely chopped
- 1/2 tsp paprika
- Generous pinch of black pepper
- Salt to taste
- 3/4 tbsp lemon juice
- 3/4 tsp garam masala powder
- 1/3 tsp rosemary
- 1 egg

Directions:
- Start by removing any skin on the fish, washing it, and patting it dry. Cut the fish into fingers.
- In a medium bowl, mix together all ingredients except for fish, mint, and bread crumbs. Bury the fingers in the mixture and refrigerate for 30 minutes.
- Remove the bowl from the fridge and mix in mint leaves.
- In a separate bowl, beat the egg, and pour bread crumbs into a third bowl. Dip the fingers in the egg bowl, then toss them in the bread crumbs bowl.
- Close the air fryer lid. Cook at 360 °F for 15 minutes, toss the fingers halfway through.

702. Balsamic and Shallots Cod

Preparation Time: 5 minutes
Cooking Time: 12 minutes
Servings: 2

Ingredients:
- 2 cod fillets, boneless
- 2 tbsp lemon juice
- Salt and black pepper to taste
- ½ tsp garlic powder
- ⅓ cup water
- ⅓ cup balsamic vinegar

- 3 shallots, chopped
- 2 tbsp olive oil

Directions:
- In a bowl, toss the cod with the salt, pepper, lemon juice, garlic powder, water, vinegar, and oil; coat well.
- Transfer the fish to your fryer's basket and cook at 360°F for 12 minutes, flipping them halfway.
- Divide the fish between plates, sprinkle the shallots on top, and serve.

703. Alaskan Cod with Apple Slaw

Preparation Time: 20 minutes
Cooking Time: 15 minutes
Servings: 4

Ingredients:
- ¼ cup mayonnaise
- ½ red onion, diced
- 1 ½ pounds frozen Alaskan cod
- 1 box of whole-wheat panko bread crumbs
- 1 granny smith apple, julienned
- 1 tbsp vegetable oil
- 1 tsp paprika
- 2 cups Napa cabbage, shredded
- Salt and pepper to taste

Directions:
- Preheat the air fryer to 390°F.
- Place the grill pan accessory in the air fryer.
- Brush the fish with oil and dredge in the breadcrumbs.
- Place the fish on the grill pan and cook for 15 minutes. Make sure to flip the fish halfway through the cooking time.
- Meanwhile, prepare the slaw by mixing the remaining ingredients in a bowl.
- Serve the fish with the slaw.

704. Almond Crusted Shrimps

Preparation Time: 10 minutes
Cooking Time: 10 minutes
Servings: 4

Ingredients:
- ½ cup almond flour
- 1 tbsp yellow mustard
- 1-pound raw shrimps, peeled and deveined
- 3 tbsp olive oil
- Salt and pepper to taste

Directions:
- Place all ingredients in a Ziploc bag and give a good shake.
- Place in the air fryer and cook for 10 minutes at 400°F.

705. Buttered Cod and Chives

Preparation Time: 5 minutes
Cooking Time: 12 minutes
Servings: 4

Ingredients:
- 4 cod fillets, boneless
- Salt and black pepper to taste
- 3 tsp lime zest

- 2 tsp lime juice
- 3 tbsp chives, chopped
- 6 tbsp butter, melted
- 2 tbsp olive oil

Directions:
- Season the fish with salt and pepper, rub it with the oil, and then put it in your air fryer.
- Cook at 360°F for 10 minutes, flipping once.
- Heat up a pan with the butter over medium heat, and then add the chives, salt, pepper, lime juice, and zest, whisk; cook for 1-2 minutes.
- Divide the fish between plates, drizzle the lime sauce all over, and serve immediately.

706. Spicy Lime and Basil Clams

Preparation Time: 15 minutes
Cooking Time: 15 minutes
Servings: 4

Ingredients:
- ½ cup basil leaves
- ½ cup tomatoes, chopped
- 1 tbsp fresh lime juice
- 25 littleneck clams
- 4 cloves of garlic, minced
- 6 tbsp unsalted butter
- Salt and pepper to taste

Directions:
- Preheat the air fryer to 390°F.
- Place the grill pan accessory in the air fryer.
- On a large foil, place all ingredients. Fold over the foil and close by crimping the edges.
- Place on the grill pan and cook for 15 minutes.

707. Cornmeal Battered Fish

Preparation Time: 2 minutes
Cooking Time: 15 minutes
Servings: 3

Ingredients:
- ¼ cup flour
- ½ tsp garlic powder
- ¾ cup fine cornmeal
- 1 tsp paprika
- 2 tsp old bay seasoning
- 6 fish fillets cut in half
- Salt and pepper to taste

Directions:
- Preheat the air fryer to 330°F.
- Place the cornmeal, flour, and seasonings in a Ziploc bag.
- Add the fish fillets and shake until the fish is covered in flour.
- Place on the double layer rack and cook for 15 minutes.

708. Citrus Balsamic Salmon

Preparation Time: 5 minutes
Cooking Time: 15 minutes
Servings: 4

Ingredients:

- 4 salmon fillets, boneless and cubed
- 2 lemons, sliced
- ¼ cup balsamic vinegar
- ¼ cup orange juice
- A pinch of salt and black pepper

Directions:

- In a pan that fits your air fryer, mix all ingredients except the fish; whisk.
- Heat the mixture up over medium-high heat for 5 minutes, and add the salmon.
- Toss gently and place the pan in the air fryer and cook at 360°F for 10 minutes.

709. Paprika Fish Nuggets

Preparation Time: 30 minutes
Cooking Time: 35 minutes
Servings: 6

Ingredients:

- 1 ½ pounds fresh fish fillet, chopped finely
- 1 cup almond flour
- 1 tbsp lemon juice
- 1 tbsp olive oil
- 1 tsp chili powder
- 1 tsp smoked paprika
- 2 cloves of garlic, minced
- 2 eggs, beaten
- Salt and pepper to taste

Directions:

- Place all ingredients in a bowl and mix until well combined.
- Form small nuggets using your hands. Place in the fridge to set for 2 hours.
- Preheat the air fryer for 5 minutes.
- Carefully place the nuggets in the fryer basket.
- Cook for 25 minutes at 350°F.

710. Dijon Mustard 'n Parmesan Crusted Tilapia

Preparation Time: 20 minutes
Cooking Time: 15 minutes
Servings: 2

Ingredients:

- 1 tbsp lemon juice
- 1 tsp prepared horseradish
- 1/4 cup dry bread crumbs
- 2 tbsp grated Parmesan cheese, divided
- 2 tsp butter, melted
- 2 tsp Dijon mustard
- 2 tilapia fillets (5 ounces each)
- 3 tbsp reduced-fat mayonnaise

Directions:

- Lightly grease the baking pan of the air fryer with cooking spray. Place tilapia in a single layer.
- In a small bowl, whisk well mayo, lemon juice, mustard, 1 tbsp cheese and horseradish. Spread on top of fish.
- In another bowl, mix the remaining cheese, melted butter, and bread crumbs. Sprinkle on top of fish.

- For 15 minutes, cook at 390°F.
- Serve and enjoy.

711. Drunken Skewered Shrimp, Tomatoes 'n Sausages

Preparation Time: 30 minutes
Cooking Time: 20 minutes
Servings: 6

Ingredients:

- 1/2 tsp dried crushed red pepper
- 1/2 tsp freshly ground black pepper
- 12 1-inch-long pieces of andouille or other fully cooked smoked sausages
- 12 2-layer sections of red onion wedges
- 12 cherry tomatoes
- 12 uncooked extra-large shrimp (13 to 15 per pound), peeled, deveined
- 2 tbsp chopped fresh thyme
- 3/4 cup olive oil
- 3/4 tsp salt
- 4 large garlic cloves, pressed
- 4 tsp Sherry wine vinegar
- 5 tsp smoked paprika*
- Nonstick vegetable oil spray

Directions:

- In a medium bowl, mix well red pepper, black pepper, salt, wine vinegar, smoked paprika, thyme, garlic, and oil. Transfer half to a small bowl for dipping.
- Thread sausage and shrimp alternately in skewers. Place on skewer rack on the air fryer and baste with the paprika glaze. Cook in batches.
- For 10 minutes, cook at 360°F. Halfway through cooking time, baste and turnover skewers.
- Serve and enjoy with the reserved dip on the side.

712. Yuzu Soy Squid

Preparation Time: 10 minutes
Cooking Time: 10 minutes
Servings: 4

Ingredients:

- ½ cup mirin
- 1 cup soy sauce
- 1/3 cup yuzu or orange juice, freshly squeezed
- 2 cups water
- 2 pounds squid body, cut into rings

Directions:

- Place all ingredients in a Ziploc bag and allow the squid rings to marinate in the fridge for at least 2 hours.
- Preheat the air fryer to 390°F.
- Place the grill pan accessory in the air fryer.
- Grill the squid for 10 minutes.
- Meanwhile, pour the marinade over a sauce pan and allow to simmer for 10 minutes or until the sauce has reduced.
- Baste the squid rings with the sauce before serving

713. Salted Tequila 'n Lime Shrimp

Preparation Time: 15 minutes
Cooking Time: 16 minutes
Servings: 4

Ingredients:

- 1 large lime, quartered
- 1 pinch of garlic salt
- 1 pinch of ground cumin
- 1/4 cup olive oil
- 1-pound large shrimp, peeled and deveined
- 2 tbsp lime juice
- 2 tbsp tequila
- ground black pepper to taste

Directions:

- In a bowl, mix well pepper, cumin, salt, olive oil, tequila and lime juice. Stir in shrimp and marinate for at least an hour. Tossing every now and then.
- Thread shrimps in skewers. Place on skewer rack. If needed, cook in batches.
- For 8 minutes, cook at 360°F. Halfway through cooking time,
- Serve and enjoy.

714. Roasted Parsley Cod

Preparation Time: 10 minutes
Cooking Time: 10 minutes
Servings: 4

Ingredients:

- 3 tbsp parsley, chopped
- 4 medium cod filets, boneless
- ¼ cup butter, melted
- 2 garlic cloves, minced
- 2 tbsp lemon juice
- 1 shallot, chopped
- Salt and black pepper to taste

Directions:

- In a bowl, mix all ingredients except the fish; whisk well.
- Spread this mixture over the cod fillets.
- Put them in your air fryer and cook at 390°F for 10 minutes.
- Divide the fish between plates and serve.

715. Baked Cod

Preparation Time: 10 minutes
Cooking Time: 12 minutes
Servings: 2

Ingredients:

- 1/2 pound thick-cut cod loin
- Juice of 1/4 lemon
- 2 tbsp butter, melted
- 1/4 sleeve round crackers, crushed
- 1 1/2 tsp chopped parsley
- 1 1/2 tsp chopped green onion
- 1/2 lemon, cut into wedges
- 2 tbsp dry white wine

Directions:

- In a mixing bowl, add half butter and crackers. Combine to mix well with each other.
- In another bowl, add lemon juice, white wine, parsley, and green onion. Combine to mix well with each other. Coat cod with remaining butter.
- Place Air fryer over kitchen platform. Place Air Fryer Lid on top. Press Air Fry, set the temperature to 375°F and set the timer to 5 minutes to preheat. Press "Start" and allow it to preheat for 5 minutes.
- Take Air Fryer Basket, grease it with some cooking spray. In the basket, add cod. Top with the dressing and add the cracker mixture top.
- Place the basket in the inner pot of the Air fryer, and close Air Fryer Lid on top. Press the "Bake" setting. Set the temperature to 390°F and set the timer to 10 minutes. Press "Start."
- Open Air Fryer Lid after cooking time is over. Serve warm.

716. Garlic Parsley Scallops

Preparation Time: 10 minutes
Cooking Time: 10 minutes
Servings: 4

Ingredients:

- 5 cloves garlic, minced
- 2 shallots, chopped
- 16 sea scallops, rinsed and drained
- 5 tbsp butter, melted
- 3 pinches of ground nutmeg
- 1 cup bread crumbs
- 4 tbsp olive oil
- 1/4 cup chopped parsley
- Black pepper (ground) and salt to taste

Directions:

- In a mixing bowl, shallots, garlic, melted butter, scallops, salt, nutmeg, and pepper. Combine to mix well with each other.
- In another bowl, add oil and bread crumbs. Combine to mix well with each other.
- Place Air fryer over kitchen platform. Place Air Fryer Lid on top. Press Air Fry, set the temperature to 375°F and set the timer to 5 minutes to preheat. Press "Start" and allow it to preheat for 5 minutes.
- Take Air Fryer Basket, grease it with some cooking spray. In the basket, add a scallop mixture and top with the crumb mixture.
- Place the basket in the inner pot of the Air fryer, and close Air Fryer Lid on top.
- Press the "Bake" setting. Set the temperature to 390°F and set the timer to 10 minutes. Press "Start." Cook until the top is light brown.
- Open Air Fryer Lid after cooking time is over. Serve warm with the parsley on top.

717. Spicy Vinegar Prawns

Preparation Time: 5 minutes
Cooking Time: 8 minutes
Servings: 2

Ingredients:

- 1 tbsp ketchup

- 12 prawns, shelled and deveined
- 1 tbsp white wine vinegar
- ½ tsp black pepper
- ½ tsp sea salt
- 1 tsp chili flakes
- 1 tsp chili powder

Directions:

- Place Air fryer over kitchen platform. Place Air Fryer Lid on top. Press Air Fry, set the temperature to 375°F and set the timer to 5 minutes to preheat. Press "Start" and allow it to preheat for 5 minutes.
- Take Air Fryer Basket, grease it with some cooking spray. In the basket, add all ingredients and combine well.
- Place the basket in the inner pot of the Air fryer, and close Air Fryer Lid on top.
- Press the "Air Fry" setting. Set the temperature to 390°F and set the timer to 8 minutes. Press "Start." Stir mixture halfway down.
- Open Air Fryer Lid after cooking time is over. Serve warm.

718. Halibut with Eggs and Veggies

Preparation Time: 10 minutes
Cooking Time: 15 minutes
Servings: 6

Ingredients:

- 2 pounds of mixed vegetables
- 4 cups torn lettuce leaves
- 1 cup cherry tomatoes, halved
- 1 ½ pounds halibut fillets
- Black pepper (ground) and salt to taste
- 2 tbsp olive oil
- 4 large hard-boiled eggs, sliced

Directions:

- Rub the halibut with salt and black pepper. Coat fish with oil.
- Place Air fryer over kitchen platform. Place Air Fryer Lid on top. Press Air Fry, set the temperature to 375°F and set the timer to 5 minutes to preheat. Press "Start" and allow it to preheat for 5 minutes.
- Take Air Fryer Basket, grease it with some cooking spray. In the basket, add fish and arrange vegetables around.
- Place the basket in the inner pot of the Air fryer, and close Air Fryer Lid on top.
- Press the "Air Fry" setting. Set the temperature to 375°F and set the timer to 15 minutes. Press "Start." Stir the mixture halfway down.
- Open Air Fryer Lid after cooking time is over. Serve warm in a bowl mixed with eggs, lettuce, and tomatoes.

719. Air-fried Green Herbs Scallop

Preparation Time: 5 minutes
Cooking Time: 10 minutes
Servings: 2

Ingredients:

- 2 tbsp dried thyme
- 1 tbsp dried oregano
- 2 tsp chipotle pepper

- 1 tbsp ground coriander
- 1 tbsp ground fennel
- 1-pound sea scallops, cleaned and patted dry
- Black pepper (ground) and salt to taste
- 3 dried chilies

Directions:

- In a mixing bowl, add scallops and other ingredients. Combine to mix well with each other.
- Place Air fryer over kitchen platform. Place Air Fryer Lid on top. Press Air Fry, set the temperature to 375°F and set the timer to 5 minutes to preheat. Press "Start" and allow it to preheat for 5 minutes.
- Take Air Fryer Basket, grease it with some cooking spray. In the basket, add scallops.
- Place the basket in the inner pot of the Air fryer, and close Air Fryer Lid on top.
- Press the "Air Fry" setting. Set the temperature to 390°F and set the timer to 10 minutes. Press "Start."
- Open Air Fryer Lid after cooking time is over. Serve warm.

720. Mustard Tuna Cakes

Preparation Time: 10 minutes
Cooking Time: 6 minutes
Servings: 4

Ingredients:

- ¼ cup breadcrumbs
- 1 tbsp mustard
- 7 ounces of canned tuna
- 1 egg, large
- ¼ tsp salt
- ½ tsp ground black pepper

Directions:

- In a mixing bowl, add the egg, tuna, bread crumbs, pepper, salt, and mustard. Combine the ingredients to mix well with each other. Prepare 4 patties from the mixture.
- Grease Air Fryer Basket with some cooking spray. Add the patties.
- Place the Air fryer Crisp over the kitchen platform. Press Air Fry, set the temperature to 400°F and set the timer to 5 minutes to preheat. Press "Start" and allow it to pre-heat for 5 minutes.
- In the inner pot, place the Air Fryer basket.
- Close the Crisp Lid and press the "Broil" setting. Set the temperature to 400°F and set the timer to 6 minutes. Press "Start."
- Halfway down, open the Crisp Lid, flip the patties, and close the lid to continue cooking for the remaining time.
- Open the Crisp Lid after cooking time is over. Serve warm with your choice of dip or ketchup.

721. Hot Bacon Shrimps

Preparation Time: 10 minutes
Cooking Time: 10 minutes
Servings: 6

Ingredients:

- 1/2 tsp cayenne pepper
- 1/2 tsp ground cumin
- 1/2 tsp onion powder

- 1-pound shrimp
- 1 package bacon
- 1 tsp garlic powder
- 1/2 tsp lemon zest
- 1 tbsp lemon juice
- 1 tbsp Worcestershire sauce

Directions:
- In a mixing bowl, whisk the Worcestershire sauce, cayenne pepper, onion powder, cumin, lemon zest, and garlic powder. Add and combine the shrimp. Refrigerate for 1-2 hours to marinate.
- Take the bacon, slice it into two parts, and wrap each shrimp with them.
- Place Air fryer Crisp over kitchen platform. Press Air Fry, set the temperature to 400°F and set the timer to 5 minutes to preheat. Press "Start" and allow it to pre-heat for 5 minutes.
- In the inner pot, place the Air Fryer basket. In the basket, add the wrapped shrimps.
- Close the Crisp Lid and press the "Air Fry" setting. Set the temperature to 380°F and set the timer to 10 minutes. Press "Start."
- Halfway down, open the Crisp Lid, shake the basket and close the lid to continue cooking for the remaining time.
- Open the Crisp Lid after cooking time is over. Serve warm.

722.   Creamy Baked Cod

Preparation Time: 10 minutes
Cooking Time: 10 minutes
Servings: 4

Ingredients:
- 1 tbsp lemon juice
- ½ tsp ground black pepper
- ½ tsp salt
- 1-pound cod fillets
- 2 tbsp olive oil
- Sauce:
- 3 tbsp ground mustard
- 1 tbsp butter
- ½ cup heavy cream
- ½ tsp salt

Directions:
- Spread some olive oil on the fillets. Season with salt, pepper, and lemon juice.
- Grease Air Fryer Basket with some cooking spray. Place the fillets over.
- Place Air fryer Crisp over kitchen platform. Press Air Fry, set the temperature to 400°F and set the timer to 5 minutes to preheat. Press "Start" and allow it to pre-heat for 5 minutes.
- In the inner pot, place the Air Fryer basket.
- Close the Crisp Lid and press the "Air Fry" setting. Set the temperature to 350°F and set the timer to 10 minutes. Press "Start."
- Halfway down, open the Crisp Lid, flip the fillets, and close the lid to continue cooking for the remaining time.
- Open the Crisp Lid after cooking time is over. Add the fish to a serving plate.

- Press "Sauté," select the "Hi" setting and press "Start." In the inner pot, add the heavy cream, mustard sauce, heavy cream, and salt. Cook for 3-4 minutes.
- Pour it over the fish and serve warm.

723.   Fresh Shrimp Salad

Preparation Time: 15 minutes
Cooking Time: 10 minutes
Servings: 1

Ingredients:
- 250 g organic shrimp
- 125 g organic lettuce mix
- 6 cherry tomatoes
- ½ spring onion
- 1 tbsp olive oil
- 1 clove of garlic
- 1 organic lemon
- Sea salt
- pepper

Directions:
- Preheat the air fryer to 400°F.
- Brushing prawns Peel and chop the garlic. Rinse hot lemon, dry and grate the skin. Put the lemon, olive oil, garlic, a little salt and pepper in a bowl and mix. Add shrimp and leave for 10 minutes.
- Wash the salad and dry it in the salad spinner. Clean the spring onion and cut it into thin rings. Wash and halve the tomatoes. Squeeze out the lemon. Put the salad and vegetables in a salad bowl, season with salt and pepper and drizzle with a little lemon juice.
- Put prawns and lemon-oil mixture in a Hot Air Fryer and fry shrimp from all sides. Spread salad on two plates, serve hot shrimp and serve.

724.   Salmon with Kohlrabi and Asparagus

Preparation Time: 15 minutes
Cooking Time: 20 minutes
Servings: 2

Ingredients:
- 2 salmon fillets á 200 g
- 500 g green asparagus
- 50 g lamb's lettuce
- 1 large kohlrabi
- 2 - 3 branches dill
- 2 tbsp olive oil
- 1 tbsp butter
- 1 tsp pink berries
- sea-salt

Directions:
- Wash salmon and dry with a kitchen paper towel, pat salmon skin with your sharp knife, lettuce, and wash dill and drain.
- Cut off the asparagus leaves and peel the bottom as needed
- Peel and dice the kohlrabi
- Place the kohlrabi and asparagus in a large pot with a steamer insert and cook until crispy in the hot steam.
- Heat the butter and olive oil in the Air Fryer and fry the salmon on the skin side at 400°F.

- Then cover with the Air Fryer and cook the salmon covered over 350°F.
- Depending on how thick the filet is, the salmon must roast for 10 - 20 minutes.
- Arrange corn salad on both plates
- Add the asparagus and kohlrabi and lay the salmon on the plates
- Sprinkle salmon with chopped dill and sea salt and serve hot.

725.   Asian Style Chicken Strips with Asparagus

Preparation Time: 20 minutes
Cooking Time: 20 minutes
Servings: 2

Ingredients:
- 300 g chicken breast fillet, organic quality
- 500 g green asparagus
- 2 cloves of garlic
- 1 shallot
- 150 ml of water
- 40 ml organic soy sauce
- 2 tbsp of sesame oil
- 2 tsp honey
- Lemon zest from an organic lemon
- Bamboo salt
- Colorful pepper

Directions:
- Cut the meat into thin strips, making sure that the cuts are transverse to the longitudinal fibers. Wash the asparagus spears thoroughly and peel the lower third if necessary.
- Cut the green asparagus into pieces.
- Peel and cut the shallot and garlic.
- Heat the oil in an Air Fryer and fry the meat at 400°F.
- Remove the meat and set it aside.
- Put the shallot and garlic in the hot Air Fryer and sauté at 300°F.
- Add green asparagus and stir.
- Mix the honey and soy sauce with 150 ml of warm water and add to the asparagus.
- Put the meat strips back into the Air Fryer to the green asparagus and swing everything through. Add the lemon zest to the meat and season with salt and pepper.
- Place the chicken breast strips with green asparagus of the Asian style on two plates and serve.

726.   Oriental Shrimps

Preparation Time: 8 minutes
Cooking Time: 10 minutes
Servings: 4

Ingredients:
- 2 tbsp olive oil
- 2 tbsp scallions, finely chopped
- 2 cloves garlic, chopped
- 1 tsp fresh ginger, grated
- 1 tbsp dry white wine
- 1 tbsp balsamic vinegar
- 1/4 cup soy sauce
- 1 tbsp sugar
- 1-pound shrimp

- Salt and ground black pepper, to taste

Directions:
- To make the marinade, warm the oil in a saucepan; cook all ingredients except the shrimp, salt, and black pepper. Now, let it cool.
- Marinate the shrimp, covered for at least an hour, in the refrigerator.
- After that, pour into the Oven rack/basket. Place the rack on the middle shelf of the Air Fryer. Set temperature to 350°F, and set time to 10 minutes. Bake the shrimp at 350 °F for 8 to 10 minutes (depending on the size), turning once or twice. Season prepared shrimp with salt and black pepper and serve.

727.   Trout with Butter Sauce

Preparation Time: 10 minutes
Cooking Time: 10 minutes
Servings: 2

Ingredients:
- 2 trout fillets, boneless
- Salt and black pepper, to taste
- 1 ½ tsp lemon zest, grated
- 1 ½ tbsp chives, chopped
- 3 tbsp butter
- 1 tbsp olive oil
- 1 tsp lemon juice

Directions:
- Season trout with salt and pepper. Drizzle with oil and rub well.
- Cook in the air fryer at 360°F for 10 minutes. Flip once.
- Meanwhile, heat up a pan with the butter over medium heat. Add lemon juice, zest, chives, salt, and pepper. Whisk well and cook for 2 minutes, then remove from heat.
- Divide fish fillets on plates. Drizzle with butter sauce and serve.

728.   Tuna Stuffed Potatoes

Preparation Time: 10 minutes
Cooking Time: 30 minutes
Servings: 4

Ingredients:
- 4 starchy potatoes
- ½ tbsp olive oil
- 1 (6-ounce) can tuna, drained
- 2 tbsp plain Greek yogurt
- 1 tsp red chili powder
- Salt and freshly ground black pepper, to taste
- 1 scallion, chopped and divided
- 1 tbsp capers

Directions:
- In a large bowl of water, soak the potatoes for about 30 minutes. Drain well and pat dry with a paper towel.
- Preheat the air fryer to 355°F. Place the potatoes in a fryer basket.
- Cook for about 30 minutes.
- Meanwhile, in a bowl, add tuna, yogurt, red chili powder, salt, black pepper and half of the scallion and with a potato masher, mash the mixture completely.

- Remove the potatoes from the Air Fryer and place them onto a smooth surface.
- Carefully cut each potato from the top side lengthwise.
- With your fingers, press the open side of the potato halves slightly. Stuff the open potato portion with the tuna mixture evenly.
- Sprinkle with the capers and remaining scallion. Serve immediately.

729. Flying Fish

Preparation Time: 5 minutes
Cooking Time: 10 minutes
Servings: 4

Ingredients:
- 4 Tbsp Oil
- 3–4 oz Breadcrumbs
- 1 Whisked Whole Egg in a Saucer/Soup Plate
- 4 Fresh Fish Fillets
- Fresh Lemon (For serving)

Directions:
- Preheat the air fryer to 350° F. Mix the crumbs and oil until it looks nice and loose.
- Dip the fish in the egg and coat lightly, then move on to the crumbs. Make sure the fillet is covered evenly.
- Cook in the Air Fryer basket for roughly 12 minutes – depending on the size of the fillets you are using.
- Serve with fresh lemon & chips to complete the duo.

730. Pistachio Crusted Salmon

Preparation Time: 10 minutes
Cooking Time: 20 minutes
Servings:

Ingredients:
- 4 medium-sized salmon filets
- 2 raw eggs
- 3 ounces of melted butter
- 1 clove of garlic, peeled and finely minced
- 1 large-sized lemon
- 1 tsp of salt
- 1 tbsp of parsley, rinsed, patted dry and chopped
- 1 tsp of dill, rinsed, patted dry and chopped
- ½ cup of pistachio nuts shelled and coarsely crushed

Directions:
- Preheat the air fryer oven to 350°F.
- In a mixing bowl, beat the eggs until fluffy and until the yolks and whites are fully combined.
- Add the melted butter, the juice of the lemon, the minced garlic, the parsley and the dill to the beaten eggs, and stir thoroughly.
- One by one, dunk the salmon filets into the wet mixture, then roll them in the crushed pistachios, coating completely.
- Place the coated salmon fillets in the air fryer oven basket.
- Set the air fryer oven timer for 10 minutes.
- When the air fryer shuts off, after 10 minutes, the salmon will be partially cooked, and the crust begins to crisp. Using tongs, turn each of the fish filets over.
- Reset the air fryer oven to 350°F for another 10 minutes.

- After 10 minutes, when the air fryer shuts off, the salmon will be perfectly cooked, and the pistachio crust will be toasted and crispy. Using tongs, remove from the air fryer and serve.

731. Quick and Easy Air-fried Catfish

Preparation Time: 5 minutes
Cooking Time: 12 minutes
Servings: 4

Ingredients:
- 1 tbsp. chopped parsley
- 1 tbsp. olive oil
- ¼ C. seasoned fish fry
- 4 catfish fillets

Directions:
- Ensure your air fryer oven is preheated to 400°F.
- Rinse off catfish fillets and pat dry.
- Add fish fry seasoning to Ziploc baggie, then catfish. Shake the bag and ensure the fish gets well coated.
- Spray each fillet with olive oil.
- Add fillets to air fryer basket.
- Set temperature to 400°F, and set time to 10 minutes.
- Cook for 10 minutes. Then flip and cook another 2-3 minutes.

732. Tomato Parchment Cod

Preparation Time: 20 minutes
Cooking Time: 15 minutes
Servings: 5
- **Ingredients**
- 1 ¾ pound cod fillets
- ¼ tsp salt
- 1 tsp smoked paprika
- 1 tsp ground dried ginger
- ¼ cup pitted olives
- ¼ cup sundried tomatoes
- ¼ cup capers
- 1 Tbsp fresh chopped dill
- 1/3 cup keto marinara
- **Directions**
- Preheat your air fryer to 400 °F and line your air fryer tray with a long piece of parchment paper.
- Place the cod filets on the parchment and sprinkle with the salt, paprika, and ginger and rub the spices into the fish.
- Top the fish with the remaining ingredients and then wrap the parchment paper up around the fish filets, enclosing them completely.
- Place the tray in the air fryer and bake for 15 minutes.
- Remove from the air fryer, unwrap the parchment and serve while hot!

733. Oreganata Clams

Preparation Time: 10 minutes
Cooking Time: 10 minutes
Servings: 4

Ingredients:
- 1 cup of unseasoned breadcrumbs
- ¼ cup fresh, chopped parsley
- ¼ cup of grated Parmesan cheese

- 3 peeled and minced cloves of garlic
- 1 tsp of fresh lemon zest
- 1 tsp of dried oregano
- 4 tbsp of melted butter
- 24 shucked clams
- Coarse sea salt
- 2-3 fresh lemon wedges

Directions:
- Combine the breadcrumbs, parsley, Parmesan, garlic, lemon zest, and oregano in a bowl – toss to combine. Pour in the melted butter and mix until incorporated.
- Place 1 tbsp of the breadcrumb mixture on top of each clam.
- Fill an air fryer cake insert with coarse sea salt. Nestle the clams in the salt.
- Fry for 3-4 minutes at 400°F.
- Take the clams out of the air fryer and transfer them to a serving plate. Garnish with a few fresh lemon wedges.

734.   Ahi Tuna Steaks

Preparation Time: 15 minutes
Cooking Time: 30 minutes
Servings: 2

Ingredients:
- 1 tbsp of olive oil
- 1 tbsp of garlic powder
- 1 tsp of thyme
- ½ tsp of salt
- ½ tsp of black pepper
- 6 peeled and minced garlic cloves
- Ingredients for the Tuna
- 1-pound fresh Ahi tuna
- Wedges of fresh lime to serve

Directions:
- First, prepare the marinade. In a dish, combine the olive oil with the garlic powder, thyme, salt, black pepper, and minced garlic. Place the fish in the dish and transfer to the fridge to marinate for a minimum of 15 minutes.
- Remove the fish from the marinade, shaking off any excess and place it in the air fryer. Air fry for 8-10 minutes at 400°F until cooked to your preferred level of doneness
- Serve and enjoy with a squeeze of fresh lime juice.

735.   Hake in Creamy Red Pepper Sauce

Preparation Time: 10 minutes
Cooking Time: 20 minutes
Servings: 4

Ingredients:
- 4 frozen breaded hake fillets
- 1 large onion
- 1 large or 2 medium red pepper
- 200 ml of cooking cream
- Extra virgin olive oil
- Salt
- Ground pepper

Directions:
- Cut the onion and pepper in julienne and put it in a pan with a little extra virgin olive oil over medium-low heat to sauté.
- Place the hake fillets in the basket of the air fryer and paint with a silicone brush and oil.
- Select 180°C for about 20 minutes or so.
- While the hake fillets are made, return to the peppers. When they are tender, add the cream, salt, and pepper.
- Boil so that the cream reduces.

736.   Hake Fillet with Green Salad

Preparation Time: 10 minutes
Cooking Time: 20 minutes
Servings: 4

Ingredients:
- 8 hake fillets
- Flour, egg, and breadcrumbs for breading
- 1 lettuce
- 1 bag of canons
- Slices of cooked ham
- Extra virgin olive oil
- Sherry vinegar
- Salt

Directions:
- Season the hake fillets.
- Breaded, passed through flour, beaten egg and breadcrumbs.
- Place in the air fryer and paint with oil.
- Select 180°C, 20 minutes.
- Make hake fillets in batches.
- Prepare the salad; in a bowl, put the lettuce chopped with the canons and add salt, vinegar and oil.
- Bind and add the chopped cooked ham.
- Serve the hake fillets with the salad.

737.   Fish Sticks with Chili Ketchup Sauce

Preparation Time: 10 minutes
Cooking Time: 12 minutes
Servings: 4

Ingredients:
- 8 fish sticks, store-bought
- ½ cup tomato ketchup
- 1 tbsp Sriracha sauce
- 1 tbsp chopped fresh parsley to garnish
- Sliced pickles for serving

Directions:
- Insert the dripping pan into the bottom part of the air fryer and preheat the oven at Air Fry mode at 390°F for 2 to 3 minutes.
- Arrange the fish sticks on the cooking tray and fit them onto the middle rack of the oven. Close and set the timer for 12 minutes and cook until the fish sticks are golden brown and crispy.
- Meanwhile, in a small bowl, mix the tomato ketchup, Sriracha sauce, and parsley until well combined and set aside for serving.
- When the fish is ready, transfer onto serving plates and serve warm with the sauce and pickles.

738.   Baked Seafood Gratin

Preparation Time: 0 minutes
Cooking Time: 30 minutes
Servings: 4

Ingredients:

- 12 oz crab meat
- 1/2 cup mozzarella cheese, shredded
- 2 tbsp green onions, sliced
- 1 cup mayonnaise
- 6 oz shrimp
- 12 oz lobster meat

Directions:

- Spray the air fryer from the inside with cooking spray.
- Add all ingredients except mozzarella cheese into the air fryer and stir well.
- Sprinkle mozzarella cheese on top.
- Seal pot with air fryer lid and select bake mode, then set the temperature to 350°F and timer for 30 minutes.
- Serve and enjoy.

739.   Shrimp Fajitas

Preparation Time: 10 minutes
Cooking Time: 15 minutes
Servings: 4

Ingredients:

- 1 lb. shrimp, peeled and deveined
- 1/2 lime juice
- 1 1/2 tbsp taco seasoning
- 1 1/2 tbsp olive oil
- 3 bell peppers, sliced
- 1 medium onion, sliced

Directions:

- Line roasting pan with parchment paper and set aside.
- Insert wire rack in rack position 6. Select bake, set temperature 390°F, and timer for 15 minutes. Press start to preheat the air fryer.
- In a mixing bowl, toss shrimp with the remaining ingredients.
- Spread shrimp mixture on a roasting pan and bake for 12-15 minutes or until shrimp are cooked through.
- Serve and enjoy.

740.   Sea Bass and Fennel

Preparation Time: 30 minutes
Cooking Time: 20 minutes
Servings: 2

Ingredients:

- ¼ cup black olives, pitted and sliced
- 2 sea bass, fillets
- ¼ cup basil; chopped.
- 1 fennel bulb; sliced
- Juice of 1 lemon
- 1 tbsp. olive oil
- A pinch of salt and black pepper

Directions:

- In a pan that fits the air fryer, combine all the ingredients.

- Introduce the pan to the machine and cook at 380°F for 20 minutes, shaking the fryer halfway.
- Divide between plates and serve

741.   Horseradish Salmon

Preparation Time: 20 minutes
Cooking Time: 25-30 minutes
Servings: 2

Ingredients:

- 2 salmon fillets
- 1/4 cup breadcrumbs
- 2 tbsp olive oil
- 1 tbsp horseradish
- Pepper
- Salt

Directions:

- Place the dehydrating tray in a multi-level air fryer basket and place the basket in the air fryer.
- Place salmon fillets on dehydrating tray.
- In a small bowl, mix together breadcrumbs, oil, horseradish, pepper, and salt and spread over salmon fillets.
- Seal pot with air fryer lid and select air fry mode, then set the temperature to 400°F and timer for 7 minutes.
- Serve and enjoy.

742.   Oriental Shrimp Fried Rice

Preparation Time: 15 minutes
Cooking Time: 15 minutes
Servings: 2

Ingredients:

- 1 egg, lightly beaten
- 1/4 tsp ground ginger
- 1/8 tsp cayenne pepper
- 2 cups of water
- 1 small onion, chopped
- 1 1/2 tbsp soy sauce
- 1 1/2 tbsp olive oil
- Oz frozen shrimp, peeled
- 1 cup rice, rinsed and drained
- 1 cup frozen carrots and peas
- 3 garlic cloves, minced
- Pepper
- Salt

Directions:

- Add 1 tbsp oil to the air fryer and set the pot on sauté mode.
- Add egg into the pot and cook until scrambled.
- Transfer scrambled egg to a plate and set aside.
- Add remaining oil, garlic, onion and sauté for 2 minutes.
- Add carrots, peas, shrimp, rice, water, ginger, soy sauce, pepper, and salt. Stir well.
- Seal pot with lid and cook on manual high pressure for 5 minutes.
- Once done, then release pressure using the quick-release method, then open the lid.
- Add scrambled egg and stir well.
- Serve and enjoy.

743. Shrimp Mac and Cheese

Preparation Time: 15 minutes
Cooking Time: 20 minutes
Servings: 4

Ingredients:
- 1 1/4 cups elbow macaroni
- 1 tbsp butter
- 2/3 cup milk
- 1 bell pepper, chopped
- 15 shrimp
- 1 tbsp Cajun spice
- 1/2 cup flour
- 1 cup cheddar cheese, shredded

Directions:
- Add butter to the air fryer duo and set the pot on sauté mode at 360°F.
- Add bell pepper and sauté for minutes.
- Add water and pasta and stir well.
- Seal pot with lid and cook on manual high pressure for 3 minutes.
- Once done, then release pressure using the quick-release method, then open the lid.
- Add Cajun spices and flour and stir well.
- Set pot on sauté mode. Add shrimp and cook for 2 minutes.
- Add cheese and milk and stir well.
- Serve and enjoy.

744. Great Air-Fried Soft-Shell Crab

Preparation Time: 10 minutes
Cooking Time: 10 minutes
Servings: 2

Ingredients:
- 2 soft-shell crabs
- 1 cup of flour
- 2 beaten eggs
- 1 cup of panko breadcrumbs
- 1 tsp of onion powder
- 1 tsp of garlic powder
- 1 tsp of salt
- 1 tsp of black pepper

Directions:
- Preheat your air fryer to 360°F.
- Using a bowl, add the flour, pick a second bowl, add the eggs and mix properly. Then using a third bowl, mix the panko breadcrumbs and the seasonings properly.
- Grease your air fryer basket with a nonstick cooking spray and add the crabs inside.
- Cook it inside your air fryer for 8 minutes or until it has a golden-brown color.
- Thereafter, carefully remove it from your air fryer and allow it to cool off.
- Serve and enjoy!

745. Salmon Rice Pilaf

Preparation Time: 10 minutes
Cooking Time: 15 minutes
Servings: 2

Ingredients:
- 2 salmon fillets
- 1 cup chicken stock
- 1 tbsp butter
- 1/2 cup of rice
- 1/4 cup vegetable soup mix
- 1/4 tsp sea salt

Directions:
- Add all ingredients except fish fillets into the air fryer and stir well.
- Place steamer rack on top of rice mixture.
- Place fish fillets on top of rack and season with pepper and salt.
- Seal pot with lid and cook at 400°F for 5 minutes.
- Once done then, release pressure using the quick-release method, then open the lid.
- Serve and enjoy.

746. Cajun Shrimp Boil

Preparation Time: 10 minutes
Cooking Time: 15 minutes
Servings: 5

Ingredients:
- 2 lbs. Frozen shrimp, deveined
- 1 onion, chopped
- 1/2 tsp red pepper flakes
- 1 tbsp old bay seasoning
- 10 oz sausage, sliced
- 5 frozen half corn on the cobs
- 3 garlic cloves, crushed
- 1 cup chicken stock
- 1/2 tsp salt

Directions:
- Add all ingredients into the air fryer and stir well.
- Seal pot with lid and cook at 400°F for 15 minutes.
- Once done, then release pressure using the quick-release method, then open the lid.
- Stir and serve.

747. Crab Filled Mushrooms

Preparation Time: 20 minutes
Cooking Time: 25-30 minutes
Servings: 12

Ingredients:
- 1 tbsp Olive oil
- 4 ounces Lump crabmeat, fresh
- 2 tsp Lemon peel, grated
- 1 tbsp Butter, melted
- 2 tbsp Parmesan cheese, shredded
- ¼ tsp Salt
- Baby belle mushrooms, washed,
- 24 pieces of stems removed
- ¼ cup Breadcrumbs, crispy, plain panko
- ¾ cup Fontina cheese, shredded
- 2 tbsp Green onions, chopped
- 1 tsp Seafood seasoning mix
- 1 tsp Dill weed, fresh, chopped

Directions:

- Preheat the air fryer to 375°F. Mist cooking sprays onto a pan.
- Toss mushroom caps in olive oil before adding to the pan. Air-fry for twelve minutes.
- Combine melted butter and breadcrumbs. Stir in fontina cheese, green onions, lemon peel, salt, parmesan cheese, dill weed, seasoning, and crabmeat.
- Stuff mushroom caps with filling, then air-fry for another ten to twelve minutes.

748. Tuna Mushroom Pasta

Preparation Time: 10 minutes
Cooking Time: 5 minutes
Servings: 4

Ingredients:

- 1 can tuna, drained
- 15 oz egg noodles
- 3 cups of water
- 3/4 cup frozen peas
- 4 oz cheddar cheese, shredded
- 28 oz can cream of mushroom soup

Directions:

- Add noodles and water into the inner pot of the air fryer duo crisp and stir well.
- Add cream of mushroom soup, peas, and tuna on top of the noodles.
- Seal the pot with a pressure cooking lid and 400°F for 4 minutes.
- Once done, release pressure using a quick release. Remove lid.
- Add cheese and stir well and serve.

749. Garlic Chili Fried Fish

Preparation Time: 10 minutes
Cooking Time: 15 minutes
Serving: 2

Ingredients:

- Sauce:
- 1/4 cup oyster sauce
- /4 cup soy sauce
- 8 to 10 cloves garlic, minced
- 1 tbsp fish sauce
- 2 tbsp brown sugar
- 1/4 tsp black pepper
- 1 tbsp lime juice
- 3 red chilies, chopped
- For the Fish:
- 2 whole red snappers
- 1 handful of fresh coriander
- 1 handful of fresh basil
- 4 tbsp oil

Directions:

- Prepare the sauce by mixing all its Ingredients: in a bowl.
- Make a foil packet for each fish fillet and place a fillet in the pocket.
- Place the fish pockets in the Air fryer Duo and top them with prepared sauce.

- Put on the Air Fryer lid and seal it.
- Hit the "Air fry Button" and select 10 minutes of cooking time, then press "Start."
- Once the Air fryer Duo beeps, switch the Air fryer to Broil mode.
- Broil the fish for 5 minutes in the pot. Serve.

750. Sea Bay Tilapia

Preparation Time: 15 minutes
Cooking Time: 15 minutes
Servings: 2

Ingredients:

- ¾ cup cornflakes, crushed
- 1 (1-oz.) packet dry ranch-style dressing mix
- 2½ tbsp vegetable oil
- 2 eggs
- 4 (6-oz.) tilapia fillets

Directions:

- In a shallow bowl, beat the eggs.
- In another bowl, add the cornflakes, ranch dressing, and oil and mix until a crumbly mixture forms.
- Dip the fish fillets into the egg and then coat with the bread crumbs mixture.
- Press the "Power Button" of the Air Fry Oven and turn the dial to select the "Air Fry" mode.
- Press the Time button and again turn the dial to set the Cooking Time to 13 minutes.
- Now push the Temp button and rotate the dial to set the temperature at 356 °F.
- Press the "Start/Pause" button to start.
- When the unit beeps to show that it is preheated, open the lid.
- Arrange the tilapia fillets in greased "Air Fry Basket" and insert them in the oven.

751. Quick Crab Sticks

Preparation Time: 5 minutes
Cooking Time: 10 minutes
Servings: 4

Ingredients:

- Crab sticks (1 package)
- Cooking oil spray (as needed)

Directions:

- Take each of the sticks out of the package and unroll it until the stick is flat. Tear the sheets into thirds.
- Arrange them on the air fryer basket and lightly spritz using cooking spray. Set the timer for 10 minutes at 380°F.
- Note: If you shred the crab meat, you can cut the time in half, but they will also easily fall through the holes in the basket.

752. Italian Grilled Sardines

Preparation Time: 5 minutes
Cooking Time: 20 minutes
Servings: 4

Ingredients:

- 5 sardines
- Herbs of Provence

Direction:
- Preheat the air fryer to 160°C.
- Spray the basket and place your sardines in the basket of your fryer.
- Set the timer for 14 minutes. After 7 minutes, remember to turn the sardines so that they are roasted on both sides.

753. Caramelized Ginger Salmon

Preparation Time: 5 minutes
Cooking Time: 25 minutes
Servings: 4

Ingredients:
- 2 salmon fillets
- 60g cane sugar
- 4 tbsp soy sauce
- 50g sesame seeds
- Unlimited Ginger

Directions:
- Preheat the air fryer to 180°C for 5 minutes.
- Put the sugar and soy sauce in the basket.
- Cook everything for 5 minutes.
- In the meantime, wash the fish well, pass it through sesame to cover it completely and place it inside the tank and add the fresh ginger.
- Cook for 12 minutes.
- Turn the fish over and finish cooking for another 8 minutes.

754. Sea Salt Salmon

Preparation Time: 10 minutes
Cooking Time: 30 minutes
Servings: 4

Ingredients:
- 500g salmon fillet
- 1 kg coarse salt

Direction:
- Place the baking paper on the air fryer basket and the salmon on top (skin side up) covered with coarse salt.
- Set the air fryer to 150°C.
- Cook everything for 25 to 30 minutes. At the end of cooking, remove the salt from the fish and serve with a drizzle of oil.

755. Breaded Hake

Preparation Time: 15 minutes
Cooking Time: 12 minutes
Servings: 4

Ingredients:
- 1 egg
- 4 oz. breadcrumbs
- 2 tbsp vegetable oil
- 4 (6-oz.) hake fillets
- 1 lemon, cut into wedges

Directions:
- In a shallow bowl, whisk the egg.
- In another bowl, add the breadcrumbs and oil and mix until a crumbly mixture forms.
- Dip fish fillets into the egg and then coat with the bread crumbs mixture.
- Press the "Power Button" of the Air Fry Oven and turn the dial to select the "Air Fry" mode.
- Press the Time button and again turn the dial to set the Cooking Time to 12 minutes.
- Now push the Temp button and rotate the dial to set the temperature at 350 °F.
- Press the "Start/Pause" button to start.
- When the unit beeps to show that it is preheated, open the lid.
- Arrange the hake fillets in greased "Air Fry Basket" and insert them in the oven.
- Serve hot.

756. Potato Fish Cakes

Preparation Time: 5 minutes
Cooking Time: 10 minutes
Servings: 4

Ingredients:
- 8 oz. salmon, cooked
- 1 ½ oz. potatoes, mashed
- A handful of parsley, chopped
- Zest of 1 lemon
- 1 ¾ oz. plain flour

Directions:
- Carefully flakes the salmon. In a bowl, mix flaked salmon, zest, capers, dill, and mashed potatoes.
- For small cakes, use the mixture and dust the cakes with flour; refrigerate for 60 minutes.
- Preheat your air fryer to 350°F. And cook the cakes for 7 minutes. Serve chilled.

757. Prosciutto Wrapped Ahi Ahi

Preparation Time: 5 minutes
Cooking Time: 20 minutes
Servings: 2

Ingredients:
- 1-pound cod Ahi Ahi
- ¼ tsp salt
- ¼ tsp ground black pepper
- 2 oz prosciutto de Parma, very thinly sliced
- 2 Tbsp olive oil
- 1 tsp minced garlic
- 4 cups of baby spinach
- 2 tsp lemon juice

Directions:
- Preheat your air fryer to 325°F and line your air fryer tray with foil.
- Dry the cod fillets by patting with a paper towel the sprinkle with salt and pepper.
- Wrap the filets in the prosciutto, enclosing them as fully as possible.
- Place the wrapped filets on the prepared tray.
- Place the tray in the air fryer and bake for 10 minutes.
- Toss the spinach with the olive oil, garlic and lemon juice and remove the tray from the air fryer and place the spinach mix on the tray as well, around the wrapped cod.
- Place in the air fryer and bake for another 10 minutes. The spinach should be nicely wilted and the fish 145°F internally.

758. Prosciutto Wrapped Tuna Bites

Preparation Time: 5 minutes
Cooking Time: 10 minutes
Servings: 2

Ingredients:
- 1-pound tuna cut into 1" pieces
- ¼ tsp salt
- ¼ tsp ground black pepper
- 2 oz prosciutto de Parma, very thinly sliced
- 2 Tbsp olive oil
- 1 tsp minced garlic
- 4 cups of baby spinach
- 2 tsp lemon juice

Directions:
- Preheat your air fryer to 325 °F and line your air fryer tray with foil.
- Dry the tuna bites by patting with a paper towel the sprinkle with salt and pepper.
- Wrap the bites in the prosciutto, enclosing them as fully as possible.
- Place the wrapped bites on the prepared tray.
- Toss the spinach with the olive oil, garlic and lemon juice and place it on the tray as well, around the wrapped tuna.
- Place in the air fryer and bake for 12 minutes. The spinach should be nicely wilted and the fish 145 °F internally.
- Serve hot!

759. Black Pepper Flounder

Preparation Time: 5 minutes
Cooking Time: 8 minutes
Servings: 4

Ingredients:
- 1-pound flounder filets
- ¾ tsp black pepper
- ½ tsp salt
- ¼ tsp garlic powder
- 2 Tbsp softened butter

Directions:
- Preheat your air fryer to 450 °F and line your air fryer tray with foil.
- Place the flounder filets on the foil-lined tray.
- In a small bowl, combine the remaining ingredients and mix well to make a cohesive butter.
- Spread the seasoned butter over the fish filets.
- Bake the filets in the preheated oven for 8 minutes until nicely browned.
- Serve while hot.

760. Buttered Crab Legs

Preparation Time: 10 minutes
Cooking Time: 10 minutes
Servings: 4

Ingredients:
- 3 lb. crab legs
- ¼ cup salted butter, melted and divided
- ½ lemon, juiced
- ¼ tsp. garlic powder

Directions:
- In a bowl, toss the crab legs and two tbsp of the melted butter together. Place the crab legs in the basket of the fryer.
- Cook at 400°F for fifteen minutes, giving the basket a good shake halfway through.
- Combine the remaining butter with the lemon juice and garlic powder.
- Crack open the cooked crab legs and remove the meat. Serve with the butter dip on the side, and enjoy!

761. Foil Packet Salmon

Preparation Time: 5 minutes
Cooking Time: 10 minutes
Servings: 4

Ingredients:
- 2 x 4-oz. skinless salmon fillets
- 2 tbsp. Unsalted butter, melted
- ½ tsp. garlic powder
- 1 medium lemon
- ½ tsp. dried dill

Directions:
- Take a sheet of foil and cut it into two squares measuring roughly 5" x 5". Lay each of the salmon fillets at the center of each piece. Brush both fillets with a tbsp of bullet and season with a quarter-tsp of garlic powder.
- Halve the lemon and grate the skin of one-half over the fish. Cut four half-slices of lemon, using two to top each fillet. Season each fillet with a quarter-tsp of dill.
- Fold the tops and sides of the aluminum foil over the fish to create a kind of packet. Place each one in the fryer.
- Cook for twelve minutes at 400°F.
- Serve hot.

762. Parmesan Butter Flounder

Preparation Time: 5 minutes
Cooking Time: 8 minutes
Servings: 4
- **Ingredients**
- 1-pound salmon filets
- ½ cup fresh grated parmesan
- ¼ tsp black pepper
- ½ tsp salt
- ¼ tsp garlic powder
- 2 Tbsp softened butter

Directions:
- Preheat your air fryer to 450 °F and line your air fryer tray with foil.
- Place the flounder filets on the foil-lined tray.
- In a small bowl, combine the remaining ingredients and mix well to make a cohesive butter.
- Spread the seasoned butter over the fish filets.
- Bake the filets in the preheated oven for 8 minutes until nicely browned.
- Serve while hot.

763. Salmon & Eggs

Preparation Time: 10 minutes
Cooking Time: 10 minutes
Servings: 2

Ingredients:
- 2 eggs
- 1 lb. salmon, seasoned and cooked
- 1 cup celery, chopped
- 1 onion, chopped
- 1 tbsp olive oil
- Salt and pepper to taste

Directions:
- Whisk the eggs in a bowl. Add celery, onion, salt, and pepper. Add the oil to a round baking tray and pour in the egg mixture. Place in air fryer on 300°F. Let it cook for 10-minutes. When done, serve with cooked salmon.

764. Red Chili Mackerel

Preparation Time: 5 minutes
Cooking Time: 10 minutes
Servings: 4

Ingredients:
- 2 mackerel fillets
- 2 tbsp. red chili flakes
- 2 tsp. garlic, minced
- 1 tsp. lemon juice

Directions:
- Season the mackerel fillets with the red pepper flakes, minced garlic, and a drizzle of lemon juice. Allow sitting for five minutes.
- Preheat your fryer to 350°F.
- Cook the mackerel for five minutes before opening the drawer, flipping the fillets, and allowing it to cook on the other side for another five minutes.
- Plate the fillets, making sure to spoon any remaining juice over them before serving.

765. Buttered Thyme Scallops

Preparation Time: 5 minutes
Cooking Time: 10 minutes
Servings: 4

Ingredients:
- 1 lb. scallops
- Salt and pepper
- ½ tbsp. butter
- ½ cup thyme, chopped

Directions:
- Wash the scallops and dry them completely. Season with pepper and salt, then set aside while you prepare the pan.
- Grease a foil pan in several spots with the butter and cover the bottom with the thyme. Place the scallops on top.
- Pre-heat the fryer at 400°F and set the rack inside.
- Place the foil pan on the rack and allow to cook for seven minutes.

- Take care when removing the pan from the fryer and transfer the scallops to a serving dish. Spoon any remaining butter in the pan over the fish and enjoy.

766. Xinyan Cod

Preparation Time: 5 minutes
Cooking Time: 10 minutes
Servings: 2

Ingredients:
- 2 medium cod fillets; boneless
- 1 tbsp. light soy sauce
- 1/2 tsp. ginger; grated
- 1 tsp. peanuts; crushed
- 2 tsp. garlic powder

Directions:
- Put fish fillets in a heat proof dish that fits your air fryer, add garlic powder, soy sauce and ginger; toss well, put in your air fryer and cook at 350°F for 10 minutes. Divide fish on plates, sprinkle peanuts on top and serve.

767. Delicious Red Mullet

Preparation Time: 5 minutes
Cooking Time: 10 minutes
Servings: 8

Ingredients:
- 8 whole red mullets, gutted, and scales removed
- Salt and pepper to taste
- Juice from 1 lemon
- 1 tbsp olive oil

Directions:
- Preheat the air fryer to 390°F.
- Place the grill pan attachment in the air fryer.
- Season the red mullet with salt, pepper, and lemon juice.
- Brush with olive oil.
- Grill for 15 minutes.

768. Grilled Turbot

Preparation Time: 5 minutes
Cooking Time: 20 minutes
Servings: 2

Ingredients:
- 2 whole turbot, scaled and head removed
- Salt and pepper to taste
- 1 clove of garlic, minced
- ½ cup chopped celery leaves
- 2 tbsp olive oil

Directions:
- Preheat the air fryer to 390°F.
- Place the grill pan attachment in the air fryer.
- Flavor the turbot with salt, pepper, garlic, and celery leaves.
- Brush with oil.
- Cook in the grill pan for 20 minutes until the fish becomes flaky.

769.   Citrusy Branzini on the Grill

Preparation Time: 5 minutes
Cooking Time: 15 minutes
Servings: 4

Ingredients:
- 2 branzini fillets
- Salt and pepper to taste
- 3 lemons, juice freshly squeezed
- 2 oranges, juice freshly squeezed

Directions:
- Place all ingredients in a Ziploc bag. Keep it in the fridge for 2 hours.
- Preheat the air fryer to 390°F.
- Place the grill pan attachment in the air fryer.
- Place the fish on the grill pan and cook for 15 minutes until the fish is flaky.

770.   Cheesy Breaded Salmon

Preparation Time: 5 minutes
Cooking Time: 20 minutes
Servings: 4

Ingredients:
- 2 cups breadcrumbs
- 4 salmon fillets
- 2 eggs, beaten
- 1 cup Swiss cheese, shredded

Directions:
- Preheat your air fryer to 390°F. Dip each salmon filet into eggs. Top with Swiss cheese. Dip into breadcrumbs, coating the entire fish. Put into an oven-safe dish and cook for 20-minutes.

771.   Rice Flour Shrimps

Preparation Time: 20 minutes
Cooking Time: 20 minutes
Servings: 3

Ingredients:
- 3 tbsp rice flour
- 1-pound shrimp, peeled and deveined
- 2 tbsp olive oil
- 1 tsp powdered sugar
- Salt and black pepper, as required

Directions:
- Preheat the Air fryer to 325°F and grease an Air fryer basket.
- Mix rice flour, olive oil, sugar, salt, and black pepper in a bowl.
- Stir in the shrimp and transfer half of the shrimp to the air fryer basket.
- Cook for about 10 minutes, flipping once in between.
- Dish out the mixture onto serving plates and repeat with the remaining mixture.

772.   Sriracha and Honey Calamari

Preparation Time: 10 minutes
Cooking Time: 20 minutes
Servings: 2

Ingredients:
- 0.5 lb Calamari tubes - tentacles if you prefer
- 1 cup Club soda
- 1 cup Flour
- Salt - red pepper & black pepper
- ½ cup Honey + 1-2 tbsp. Sriracha

Directions:
- Fully rinse the calamari and blot it dry using a bunch of paper towels. Slice into rings: .25-inch wide). Toss the rings into a bowl. Pour in the club soda and stir until all are submerged. Wait for about 10 minutes.
- Sift the salt, flour, and red & black pepper. Set aside for now.
- Dredge the calamari into the flour mixture and set on a platter until ready to fry.
- Spritz the basket of the Air Fryer with a small amount of cooking oil spray. Arrange the calamari in the basket, careful not to crowd it too much.
- Set the temperature at 375°F and the timer for 11 minutes.
- Shake the basket twice during the cooking process, loosening any rings that may stick.
- Remove from the basket, toss with the sauce, and return to the fryer for two more minutes.
- Serve with additional sauce as desired.
- Make the sauce by combining honey, and sriracha, in a small bowl; mix until fully combined.

773.   3-Ingredient Air Fryer Catfish

Preparation Time: 5 minutes
Cooking Time: 15 minutes
Servings: 4

Ingredients:
- 1 tbsp. chopped parsley
- 1 tbsp. olive oil
- ¼ C. seasoned fish fry
- 4 catfish fillets

Directions:
- Preparing the Ingredients. Ensure your air fryer is preheated to 400°F.
- Rinse off catfish fillets and pat dry. Add fish fry seasoning to Ziploc baggie, then catfish. Shake the bag and ensure the fish gets well coated. Spray each fillet with olive oil. Add fillets to air fryer basket.
- Air Frying. Set temperature to 400°F, and set time to 10 minutes. Cook for 10 minutes. Then flip and cook another 2-3 minutes.

774.   Creamy Air Fryer Salmon

Preparation Time: 5 minutes
Cooking Time: 10 minutes
Servings: 2

Ingredients:
- ¾ lb. salmon, cut into six pieces
- ¼ cup plain yogurt
- One tbsp dill, chopped
- Three tbsp light sour cream
- One tbsp olive oil

Directions:

- Flavor the salmon with salt and put it in an air fryer. Drizzle the salmon with olive oil. Air-fry salmon at 285°F and cook for 10-minutes. Mix the dill, yogurt, sour cream, and some salt(optional). Place salmon on the serving dish and drizzle with creamy sauce.

775.   Barbecued Lime Shrimp

Preparation Time: 5 minutes
Cooking Time: 15 minutes
Servings: 4

Ingredients:

- 4 cups of shrimp
- 1 ½ cups barbeque sauce
- One fresh lime, cut into quarters

Directions:

- Preheat your air fryer to 360°F. Place the shrimp in a bowl with barbeque sauce. Stir gently. Allow shrimps to marinade for at least 5-minutes. Place the shrimp in the air fryer and cook for 15-minutes. Remove from air fryer and squeeze lime over shrimps.

776.   Spicy Air-Fried Cheese Tilapia

Preparation Time: 5minutes
Cooking Time: 10 minutes
Servings: 4

Ingredients:

- 1 lb. tilapia fillets
- One tbsp olive oil
- Salt and pepper to taste
- Two tsp paprika
- ¾ cup parmesan cheese, grated

Directions:

- Preheat your air fryer to 400°F. Mix the parmesan cheese, paprika, salt, and pepper. Drizzle olive oil over the tilapia fillets and coat with paprika and cheese mixture. Place the coated tilapia fillets on aluminum foil. Put into the air fryer and cook for 10-minutes.

777.   Pesto Scallops

Preparation Time: 10 minutes
Cooking Time: 7 minutes
Servings: 4

Ingredients:

- 1 lb. Scallops
- 3 tbsp heavy cream
- 1/4 cup basil pesto
- 1 tbsp olive oil
- Salt and Pepper

Directions:

- Spray air fryer multi-level air fryer basket with cooking spray.
- Season scallops with pepper and salt and adds them to the air fryer basket, and place the basket into the air fryer.
- Seal pot with air fryer lid and select air fry mode then set the temperature to 320°F and timer for 5 minutes. Turn scallops after 3 minutes.

- Meanwhile, in a small pan, heat olive oil over medium heat. Add pesto and heavy cream and cook for 2 minutes. Remove from heat.
- Add scallops into the mixing bowl. Pour pesto sauce over scallops and toss well.
- Serve and enjoy.

778.   Dijon Fish Fillets

Preparation Time: 10 minutes
Cooking Time: 3 minutes
Servings: 2

Ingredients:

- 2 halibut fillets
- 1 tbsp Dijon mustard
- 1 1/2 cups water
- Pepper
- Salt

Directions:

- Transfer water into the air fryer, then place the steamer basket
- Season fish fillets with pepper and salt and brush with Dijon mustard.
- Place fish fillets in the steamer basket.
- Seal fryer and cook at 400°F for 3 minutes.
- After the cooking is done, release pressure using the quick-release method, then open the lid.
- Serve and enjoy.

779.   Steamed Clams

Preparation Time: 10 minutes
Cooking Time: 3 minutes
Servings: 3

Ingredients:

- 1 lb. Mushy shell clams
- 2 tbsp butter, melted
- 1/4 cup white wine
- 1/2 tsp garlic powder
- 1/4 cup fresh lemon juice

Directions:

- Add white wine, lemon juice, garlic powder, and butter into the air fryer.
- Place trivet into the pot.
- Arrange clams on top of the trivet.
- Seal pot and cook at 400°F for 3 minutes.
- Once done then, allow to release pressure naturally, then open the lid.
- Serve and enjoy.

780.   Shrimp A La Boom

Preparation Time: 10 minutes
Cooking Time: 39 Minutes
Servings: 4

Ingredients:

- 1/2 cup mayonnaise
- 1 lb. raw shrimp
- 1/4 cup sweet chili sauce
- 1/4 cup flour
- 1 cup panko bread crumbs

- 1 tbsp. sriracha sauce
- 1 head of loose-leaf lettuce
- 2 green onions

Directions:
- Set an air fryer toaster oven to 400°F (200°C). Mix mayo, chili sauce, and sriracha sauce in a bowl until smooth. Reserve some boom sauce in a bowl for dipping, if needed. Put flour on a plate. Place panko on another plate. Coat shrimp first with powder, followed by mayonnaise mixture and then panko. Put coated shrimp on a baking sheet. Put shrimp in the air fryer toaster oven basket without overfilling. Cook it for 12 minutes or until your desired crispness. Do the same with the remaining shrimp. Eat-in lettuce wraps garnished with green onions.

781. Portuguese Bacalao Tapas

Preparation Time: 10-30 minutes
Cooking Time: 26 minutes
Servings: 4

Ingredients:
- 1 pound codfish fillet, chopped
- 2 Yukon Gold potatoes, peeled and diced
- 2 tbsp butter
- 1 yellow onion, thinly sliced
- 1 clove of garlic, chopped, divided
- 1/4 cup chopped fresh parsley, divided
- 1/4 cup olive oil
- 3/4 tsp red pepper flakes
- freshly ground black pepper to taste
- 2 hard-cooked eggs, chopped
- 5 pitted green olives
- 5 pitted black olives

Directions:
- Place the air fryer lid on, lightly grease the baking pan of the air fryer with cooking spray. Add butter and place the baking pan in the instant bowl.
- Close the air fryer lid and melt butter at 360°F. Stir in onions and cook for 6 minutes until caramelized.
- Stir in black pepper, red pepper flakes, half of the parsley, garlic, olive oil, diced potatoes, and chopped fish. For 10 minutes, cook at 360°F. Halfway through cooking time, stir well to mix.
- Cook for 10 minutes at 390°F until tops are lightly browned.
- Garnish with remaining parsley, eggs, and black and green olives.
- Serve and enjoy with chips.

782. Creamy Coconut Sauce on Jamaican Salmon

Preparation Time: 10-30 minutes
Cooking Time: 12 minutes
Servings: 2

Ingredients:
- 2 salmon fillets (6 ounces each)
- 1 ½ tbsp mayonnaise
- 2 tsp Caribbean jerk seasoning
- 1/4 cup sour cream
- 4 tbsp cream of coconut

- 1 tsp grated lime zest
- 4 tbsp cup lime juice
- 1/4 cup sweetened shredded coconut, toasted

Directions:
- Place the air fryer lid on, lightly grease the baking pan of the air fryer with cooking spray. Add salmon with skin side down. Spread mayo on top and season with a Caribbean jerk, then place the baking pan in the air fryer.
- Close the air fryer lid and cook at 330°F for 12 minutes.
- On medium-low heat, place a pan and bring lime juice, lime zest, cream of coconut, and sour cream to a simmer. Mix well. Transfer to a bowl for dipping.
- Serve and enjoy.

783. Garlic and Black Pepper Shrimp Grill

Preparation Time: 10-30 minutes
Cooking Time: 6 minutes
Servings: 2

Ingredients:
- One red chili, seeds removed
- Three cloves of garlic, grated
- One tbsp ground pepper
- One tbsp fresh lime juice
- 1-pound jumbo shrimps, peeled and deveined
- Salt to taste

Directions:
- Place the air fryer lid on and preheat the air fryer at 390°F.
- Place shrimps on the grill pan accessory inside the air fryer.
- Close the air fryer lid and grill the shrimps for 6 minutes.

784. Salmon with Lemon-Parsley Relish

Preparation Time: 10 minutes
Cooking Time: 25-30 minutes
Servings: 2

Ingredients:
- 2 salmon fillets
- Salt and black pepper
- 1 tbsp. olive oil
- For the relish:
- 1 tbsp. lemon juice
- 1 shallot
- 1 Meyer lemon
- 2 tbsp. parsley
- ¼ cup olive oil

Directions:
- Season salmon with pepper and salt, rub with 1 tbsp oil and place in an air fryer basket. Cook at 320°F for 20 minutes, flipping fish halfway.
- Mix shallot with lemon juice, a pinch of salt, and black pepper and stir, then leave it aside for 10 minutes.
- In a different bowl, mix marinated shallot with pepper, salt, lemon slices, parsley and ¼ cup oil, then whisk well.
- Divide salmon on plates, add lemon relish on top and serve.

785. Fried Stuffed Oysters on the Half Shell with Crawfish Stuffing

Preparation Time: 15 minutes
Cooking Time: 10 minutes
Servings: 8

Ingredients:
- Crawfish Stuffing:
- 4 ounces olive oil
- 1 1/2 cups onion, finely chopped
- 1 1/2 cups bell pepper, finely chopped
- 2 tbsp fresh garlic, minced
- 1-pound crawfish tails, chopped
- 1 tsp blackened seasoning
- 1/2 tsp Cajun seasoning
- 2 ounces garlic sauce
- 1/4 cup fresh parsley, finely chopped
- 1/4 cup green onions, minced
- 1 1/2 cups plain breadcrumbs
- Oysters:
- 24 oysters on the half shell
- 2 cups all-purpose flour
- 2 cups buttermilk
- 2 ounces of Cajun seasoning
- 1 package of fried fish mix

Directions:
- Place butter in the skillet, then add onions, bell pepper, garlic, and sauté.
- Add crawfish tails and cook for 3 minutes.
- Mix in blackened and Cajun spices.
- Remove the mix from heat and stir in garlic sauce.
- Stir in parsley, onion, and bread crumbs until crumbs begin to moisten.
- Wash and shuck oysters, leaving them on the half shell.
- Stuff each oyster with the crawfish mix.
- Place flour and fried fish mix in 2 separate bowls.
- In a 3rd bowl, mix together buttermilk and Cajun seasoning.
- Press oysters in flour, dip in buttermilk, then press in the fish mix to coat.
- Cook at 360°F for 10 minutes in your Philips.

786. Hawaiian Salmon

Preparation Time: 10 minutes
Cooking Time: 10 minutes
Servings: 2

Ingredients:
- 20 oz. Canned pineapple pieces and juice
- ½ tsp. ginger
- 2 tsp. garlic powder
- 1 tsp. onion powder
- 1 tsp. balsamic vinegar
- **2** medium salmon fillets
- Salt and black pepper

Directions:
- Season salmon with onion powder, salt and black pepper, garlic powder, rub. Add to the heat-proof dish and then add pineapple chunks and ginger and toss them gently.

- Drizzle the vinegar all over, put in your air fryer and cook at 350°F for 10 minutes.
- Divide everything into plates and serve.

787. Cod with Grape and Fennel Relish

Preparation Time: 20 minutes
Cooking Time: 25-30 minutes
Servings: 2

Ingredients:
- 2 black cod fillets
- 1 tbsp. olive oil
- Black pepper and Salt
- 1 fennel bulb
- 1 cup grapes
- ½ cup pecans

Directions:
- Sprinkle half of the oil over fish fillets, season with pepper and salt, rub well and place fillets in an air fryer basket. Then cook for 10 minutes at 400°F and put on a plate.
- Mix pecans with grapes, fennel, the rest of the oil, salt and pepper, and toss to coat in a bowl. Add to pan that fits air fryer. Cook at 400°F for 5 minutes.
- Share cod on plates, add grapes and fennel mix on the side, then serve.

788. Mahi Mahi in Dill Lemon Sauce

Preparation Time: 15 minutes
Cooking Time: 15 minutes
Servings: 2

Ingredients:
- 1/4 tsp. cracked black pepper
- 2 fresh or thawed Mahi Mahi fillets
- 1 Tbsp. lemon juice
- 1 Tbsp. olive oil
- 1/4 tsp. salt
- 2–3 fresh lemon slices
- 1 Tbsp. fresh dill – chopped

Directions:
- Mix together olive oil and lemon juice in a bowl
- Spread the fresh mahi-mahi fillets on a parchment paper
- Coat the 2 sides of the fillets with the mixture
- Add salt and pepper to season the fillet, and then drop the chopped fresh dill on it
- Put the Mahi Mahi fillets in the air fryer basket and cook at 350°F for 13-14 minutes
- Remove from basket and serve

789. Crab Rangoon

Preparation Time: 20 minutes
Cooking Time: 7-10 minutes
Servings: 6

Ingredients:
- 1/4 cup water
- 8 ounces room temperature cream cheese
- 8 ounces lump crab meat
- 1/4 cup olive oil
- 1 package Wonton on egg roll wrappers

Directions:
- Blend the crab meat and cream cheese together in a small bowl to make crab filling
- Put a tbsp of crab filling into the center of the wonton wrapper
- Fold it up and clip the 2 sides together and clip the other 2 sides together to make a pouch
- Put it in the air fryer basket, coat only outside with olive oil
- Set the air fryer to 300°F for 7 minutes, and it's done

790.   Scallops Gratin

Preparation Time: 20 minutes
Cooking Time: 10 minutes
Servings: 4

Ingredients:
- ½ cup half-and-half
- ½ cup grated Parmesan cheese
- ¼ cup thinly sliced green onions
- ¼ cup chopped fresh parsley
- 3 cloves garlic, minced
- ½ tsp kosher salt
- ½ tsp black pepper
- 1pound sea scallops
- For the Topping:
- ¼ cup crushed pork rinds
- ¼ cup grated Parmesan cheese
- Vegetable oil spray
- For Serving:
- Lemon wedges
- Crusty French bread (optional)

Directions:
- For the scallops: In a 6 × 2-inch round heatproof pan, combine the half-and-half, cheese, green onions, parsley, garlic, salt, and pepper. Stir in the scallops. In a container, combine the pork rinds or bread crumbs and cheese. Sprinkle evenly over the scallops. Spray the topping with vegetable oil spray. Then this will be inserted into the air fryer placed in a pan
- Set the air fryer to 325°F for 6 minutes. Set the I air fryer to 400°F for 3 minutes until the topping has browned. To serve: Squeeze the lemon wedges over the gratin and serve with crusty French bread, if desired.

791.   Pesto Fish Pie

Preparation Time: 20 minutes
Cooking Time: 15 minutes
Servings: 6

Ingredients:
- 2 tbsp prepared pesto
- ¼ cup half-and-half
- ¼ cup grated Parmesan cheese
- 1 tsp kosher salt
- 1 tsp black pepper

- Vegetable oil spray
- 1 (10-ounce) package of frozen chopped spinach
- 1pound firm white fish, cut into 2-inch chunks
- ½ cup cherry tomatoes, quartered
- All-purpose flour
- ½ sheet frozen puff pastry (from a 17.3-ounce package), thaw

Directions:
- In a small bowl, combine the pesto, half-and-half, Parmesan, salt, and pepper. Stir until well combined; set aside. Spray a 7 × 3-inch round heatproof pan with vegetable oil spray. Arrange the spinach evenly across the bottom of the pan. Top with the fish and tomatoes. Pour the pesto mixture evenly over everything.
- On a surface sprinkled with flour, roll out the puff pastry sheet into a circle. Put the pastry on top of the pan and tuck it in around the edges of the pan.
- The pan will be placed in the air fryer. Set the air fryer to 400°F for 15 minutes or until the pastry is well browned. Let stand 5 minutes before serving.

792.   Tuna Melt Croquettes

Preparation Time: 20 minutes
Cooking Time: 25-30 minutes
Servings: 6

Ingredients:
- 2 (5-ounce) cans tuna, drained
- 1 (8-ounce) package of cream cheese, softened
- ½ cup finely shredded cheddar cheese
- 2 tbsp diced onions
- 2 tsp prepared yellow mustard
- 1 large egg
- 1½ cups pork dust or powdered Parmesan cheese
- Fresh dill, for garnish (optional)
- For serving (optional):
- Cherry tomatoes
- Mayonnaise
- Prepared yellow mustard

Directions:
- Preheat the air fryer to 400°F.
- Make the patties: In a large bowl, stir together the tuna, cream cheese, cheddar cheese, onions, mustard, and egg until well combined. Place the pork dust in a shallow bowl.
- Form the tuna mixture into twelve 1½-inch balls. Roll the balls in the pork dust and use your hands to press it into a thick crust around each ball. Flatten the balls into ½-inch-thick patties.
- Patties will be put in the air fryer basket, leaving space between them. Cook for 8 minutes, or until golden brown and crispy, flipping halfway through. Garnish the croquettes with fresh dill, if desired, and serve with cherry tomatoes and dollops of mayo and mustard on the side.

CHAPTER 8: SNACKS, SANDWICHES & SAVORY BREADS

793. Pub Burgers

Preparation Time: 30 minutes
Cooking Time: 30 minutes
Servings: 8

Ingredients:
- 2-pound ground beef
- 3 green onions, chopped
- 1 tbsp. ketchup
- 8 slices of American cheese
- 8 Burger Buns, split
- 1/2 tsp. salt
- 1/4 tsp. pepper
- 10 ¾-ounce can chicken gumbo soup partially drained
- 10 ¾-ounce tomato soup
- 2 tbsp. mustard

Directions:
- Select Sauté on normal.
- Cook ground beef until no longer pink.
- Put in the rest of the ingredients except for cheese and bun to the Air fryer.
- Cook on High Pressure with Manual mode for 7 minutes.
- Spoon beef mixture onto buns.
- Add cheese slices to serve.

794. Buffalo Chicken Sliders

Preparation Time: 15 minutes
Cooking Time: 15-20 minutes
Servings: 6-12

Ingredients:

- 2.5 pounds boneless chicken breast cut into large pieces
- 4 tbsp. butter
- 3 green onions, diced
- 1/2 cup ranch dressing
- 12 sweet Hawaiian rolls
- 1/2 cup chicken broth
- 3/4 cup Frank's Buffalo Sauce
- 1 tbsp. dry ranch dressing mix
- 2 garlic cloves, minced
- 8 oz. cheddar cheese, shredded

Directions:

- Add chicken pieces, butter, dry ranch dressing mix, chicken broth, hot sauce, and garlic cloves to the Air fryer duo.
- Pressure Cook for 15 minutes.
- Shred chicken with forks.
- Let the chicken soak in the prepared sauce for a couple of minutes.
- Fill each roll with buffalo chicken, cheese, ranch, and green onions and serve.

795. Bacon Pizza

Preparation Time: 10 minutes
Cooking Time: 20 minutes
Servings: 4

Ingredients:

- Flour, for dusting
- Nonstick baking spray with flour
- 4 frozen large whole-wheat dinner rolls, thawed
- 5 cloves garlic, minced
- ¾ cup pizza sauce
- ½ tsp dried oregano
- ½ tsp garlic salt
- 8 slices precooked bacon, cut into 1-inch pieces
- 1¼ cups shredded Cheddar cheese

Directions:

- Set to 360°F Bake. On a lightly floured surface, press out each dinner roll to a 5-by-3-inch oval.
- Spray four 6-by-4-inch pieces of heavy-duty foil with nonstick spray and place one crust on each piece.
- Bake, two at a time, for 2 minutes or until the crusts are set but not browned.
- Meanwhile, in a small bowl, combine the garlic, pizza sauce, oregano, and garlic salt. When the pizza crusts are set, spread each with some of the sauce. Top with the bacon pieces and Cheddar cheese.
- Bake, two at a time, for another 8 minutes or until the crust is browned and the cheese is melted and starting to brown.

796. Mexican Style Pizza

Preparation Time: 10 minutes
Cooking Time: 10 minutes
Servings: 4

Ingredients:

- ¾ cup refried beans (from a 16-ounce can)
- ½ cup salsa
- 10 frozen precooked beef meatballs, thawed and sliced
- 1 jalapeño pepper, sliced

- 4 whole-wheat pita bread
- 1 cup shredded pepper Jack cheese
- ½ cup shredded Colby cheese
- ⅓ cup sour cream

Directions:

- Set to 370°F Bake. In a medium bowl, combine the refried beans, salsa, meatballs, and jalapeño pepper.
- Preheat the air fryer to 400°F for 3 to 4 minutes or until hot.
- Top the pitas with the refried bean mixture and sprinkle with the cheeses.
- Bake for 7 to 9 minutes or until the pizza is crisp and the cheese is melted and starts to brown.
- Top each pizza with a dollop of sour cream and serve warm.

797. Paprika Sweet Potato Chips

Preparation Time: 15 minutes
Cooking Time: 40 minutes
Servings: 4

Ingredients:

- 31-ounces of sweet potatoes, peeled and cut into chips
- ½ tsp salt
- 2 tbsp olive oil
- ½ tbsp paprika

Directions:

- Toss all the ingredients together in a bowl. Place in a pan inside your air fryer and cook for 40-minutes at 300°F.

798. Cheddar Muffins

Preparation Time: 15 minutes
Cooking Time: 15 minutes
Servings: 8

Ingredients:

- 2 cups all-purpose flour
- 1 ½ cup milk
- ½ tsp. baking powder
- ½ tsp. baking soda
- 2 tbsp. butter
- 2 cups melted cheddar
- 1 tbsp. sugar
- 2 tsp. vinegar
- Muffin cups

Directions:

- Combine the ingredients except milk to create a crumbly blend.
- Add this milk to the blend and make a batter and pour it into the muffin cups.
- Preheat the fryer to 300°F and cook for 15 minutes.
- Check whether they are done using a toothpick.

799. Kale Chips

Preparation Time: 15 minutes
Cooking Time: 6-10 minutes
Servings: 3-4

Ingredients:

- 6 cups packed kale leaves, de-stemmed.

- 1 tbsp extra-virgin olive oil
- 1 tsp soy sauce, low in sodium
- 1 tsp black sesame seeds
- 1/2 tsp dried garlic, minced
- Poppy seeds (optional)

Directions:
- Wash and dry kale leaves.
- Toss with olive oil and soy sauce in a bowl, ensuring the leaves are covered equally.
- Place piece of kale leaves in air fryer basket and cook at 188°C for 6 minutes or until fresh.
- Shake basket partially through cooking.
- Place kale leaves on a level sheet and sprinkle with sesame seeds, poppy seeds, and garlic.

800.   Mediterranean Turkey Burgers

Preparation Time: 30 minutes
Cooking Time: 16-18 minutes
Servings: 4

Ingredients:
- 1 lb. ground turkey
- ½ cup breadcrumbs
- ¼ cup Parmesan cheese, grated
- 1 egg, beaten
- 1 tbsp minced garlic
- 1 tbsp olive oil
- 1 tsp horseradish sauce
- 4 tbsp Greek yogurt
- 4 buns, halved
- 4 tomato slices

Directions:
- Preheat the air fryer to 380°F. Grease the air fryer basket with cooking spray.
- In a bowl, combine ground turkey, breadcrumbs, Parmesan cheese, egg, garlic, salt, and black pepper. Mix well. Form balls and flatten them to make patties. Brush them with olive oil and place them in the air fryer.
- Air Fry for 16-18 minutes, flipping once halfway through until nice and golden. Mix the yogurt with horseradish sauce. Assemble the burgers by spreading the yogurt mixture, then the patties, and finally top with fresh tomato slices. Serve immediately.

801.   Spiced Mixed Nuts

Preparation Time: 15 minutes
Cooking Time: 10 minutes
Servings: 6

Ingredients:
- ½ cup pecans
- ½ cup walnuts
- ½ cup almonds
- A pinch of cayenne pepper
- 2 tbsp sugar
- 2 tbsp egg whites
- 2 tsp ground cinnamon
- Cooking spray

Directions:
- Add cayenne pepper, sugar, and cinnamon to a bowl and mix well; set aside. In another bowl, mix pecans, walnuts, almonds, and egg whites. Add in the spice mixture and stir. Grease a baking dish with cooking spray. Pour in the nuts and place in the fryer. Bake for 6 minutes at 375°F. After, stir the nuts using a wooden vessel and cook further for 4 minutes. Pour the nuts into the bowl and let cool before serving.

802.   Tomato Quick Bread

Preparation Time: 15 minutes
Cooking Time: 25-30 minutes
Servings: 6

Ingredients:
- 1 and ½ cups flour
- 1 tsp cinnamon powder
- 1 tsp baking powder
- 1 tsp baking soda
- ¾ cup maple syrup
- 1 cup tomatoes chopped
- ½ cup olive oil
- 2 tbsp apple cider vinegar

Directions:
- In a bowl, mix flour with baking powder, baking soda, cinnamon and maple syrup and stir well. In another bowl, mix tomatoes with olive oil and vinegar and stir well. Combine the 2 mixtures, stir well, pour into a greased round pan that fits your air fryer, introduce into the fryer and cook at 360°F for 30 minutes. Leave the cake to cool down, slice and serve. Enjoy!

803.   Beef Jerky

Preparation Time: 30 minutes
Cooking Time: 60 minutes
Servings: 4

Ingredients:
- 1 cup beer
- 1/2 cup tamari sauce
- 1 tsp liquid smoke
- 2 garlic cloves, minced
- Sea salt and ground black pepper
- 1 tsp ancho chili powder
- 2 tbsp honey
- 3/4-pound flank steak, slice into strips

Directions:
- Place all ingredients in a ceramic dish; let it marinate for 3 hours in the refrigerator. Slice the beef into thin strips. Marinate the beef in the refrigerator overnight. Now, discard the marinade and hang the meat in the cooking basket by using skewers. Air fry at 200°F for 1 hour. Store it in an airtight container for up to 2 weeks.

804.   Hawaiian Pork Sliders

Preparation Time: 15 minutes
Cooking Time: 15 minutes
Servings: 8

Ingredients:
- Olive oil

- ½ cup crushed pineapple, drained
- 1-pound lean ground pork
- 1 tsp Worcestershire sauce
- ½ tsp garlic powder
- ½ tsp salt
- ½ tsp freshly ground black pepper
- Pinch of cayenne pepper
- 8 whole-wheat slider buns

Directions:
- Set to 370°F. Spray a fryer basket lightly with olive oil.
- In a large bowl, mix together the pineapple, pork, Worcestershire sauce, garlic powder, salt, and pepper.
- Form the mixture into 8 patties.
- Place the patties in the fryer basket in a single layer and spray lightly with olive oil. You may need to cook them in batches.
- Air fry for 7 minutes at 350°F. Flip the patties over, lightly spray with olive oil, and cook until the patties reach an internal temperature of at least 145°F, an additional 5 to 8 minutes.
- Place the cooked patties on the slider buns and serve.

805.   Beef and Blue Cheese Burgers

Preparation Time: 15 minutes
Cooking Time: 20 minutes
Servings: 4

Ingredients:
- Olive oil
- 1-pound lean ground beef
- ½ cup blue cheese, crumbled
- 1 tsp Worcestershire sauce
- ½ tsp freshly ground black pepper
- ½ tsp hot sauce
- ½ tsp minced garlic
- ¼ tsp salt
- 4 whole-wheat buns

Directions:
- Set the air fryer to 360°F. Spray a fryer basket lightly with olive oil.
- In a large bowl, mix together the beef, blue cheese, Worcestershire sauce, pepper, hot sauce, garlic, and salt.
- Form the mixture into 4 patties.
- Place the patties in the fryer basket in a single layer, leaving a little room between them for even cooking.
- Air fry for 10 minutes. Flip over and cook until the meat reaches an internal temperature of at least 160°F, an additional 7 to 10 minutes.
- Place each patty on a bun and serve with low-calorie toppings like sliced tomatoes or onions.

806.   Hoisin Turkey Burgers

Preparation Time: 40 minutes
Cooking Time: 20 minutes
Servings: 4

Ingredients:
- Olive oil
- 1-pound lean ground turkey
- ¼ cup whole-wheat bread crumbs
- ¼ cup hoisin sauce

- 2 tbsp soy sauce
- 4 whole-wheat buns

Directions:
- Set to 360°F. Spray a fryer basket lightly with olive oil.
- In a large bowl, mix together the turkey, bread crumbs, hoisin sauce, and soy sauce.
- Form the mixture into 4 equal patties. Cover with plastic wrap and refrigerate the patties for 30 minutes.
- Place the patties in the fryer basket in a single layer. Spray the patties lightly with olive oil.
- Air fry for 10 minutes. Flip the patties over, lightly spray with olive oil, and cook until golden brown, an additional 5 to 10 minutes.
- Place the patties on buns and top with your choice of low-calorie burger toppings like sliced tomatoes, onions, and cabbage slaw.

807.   Pepperoni Chips

Preparation Time: 5 minutes
Cooking Time: 8- 10 minutes
Servings: 5

Ingredients:
- 6 oz pepperoni slices

Directions:
- Place one batch of pepperoni slices in the air fryer basket.
- Cook for 8 minutes at 360°F.
- Cook remaining pepperoni slices using the same steps.
- Serve and enjoy.

808.   Caramel Popcorn

Preparation Time: 10 minutes
Cooking Time: 5-10 minutes
Servings: 8

Ingredients:
- 8 cups of popcorn
- 1 butter tablet
- 1 cup of sugar
- 1/3 cup whipped cream

Directions:
- Put a quantity of corn in a pan and put it into the air fryer. Drizzle with a little olive oil.
- Set the temperature at 240°F for 5 minutes.
- When the popcorn is ready, put it in a large bowl and set it aside while preparing the sauce.
- Mix butter, sugar and cream and heat over medium heat, stirring constantly. In a few minutes, the sauce should be boiling; continue boiling until the mixture reaches the softball stage 240°F.
- Remove mixture from heat and pour over popcorn, stirring until all popcorn is well coated. Be sure to serve it right away.

809.   Chicken Sandwich

Preparation Time: 20 minutes
Cooking Time: 7-10 minutes
Servings: 1

Ingredients:

- ⅓ cup chicken, cooked and shredded
- 2 mozzarella slices
- 1 hamburger bun
- ¼ cup cabbage, shredded
- 1 tsp. mayonnaise
- 2 tsp. butter
- 1 tsp. olive oil
- ½ tsp. balsamic vinegar
- 1/4 tsp. smoked paprika
- ¼ tsp. black pepper
- ¼ tsp. garlic powder
- Pinch of salt

Directions:

- Pre-heat your Air Fryer at 370°F.
- Apply some butter to the outside of the hamburger bun with a brush.
- In a bowl, coat the chicken with garlic powder, salt, pepper, and paprika.
- In a separate bowl, stir together the mayonnaise, olive oil, cabbage, and balsamic vinegar to make coleslaw.
- Slice the bun in two. Start building the sandwich, starting with the chicken, followed by the mozzarella, the coleslaw, and finally, the top bun.
- Transfer the sandwich to the fryer and cook for 5 – 7 minutes.

810.   Mushroom Pizza

Preparation Time: 15 minutes
Cooking Time: 10 minutes
Servings: 8

Ingredients:

- 1 vegan pizza dough
- 1 cup oyster mushrooms, chopped
- 1 shallot, chopped
- ¼ red bell pepper, chopped
- 2 tbsp. parsley
- Salt and pepper

Directions:

- Pre-heat the Air Fryer to 400°F.
- Cut the vegan pizza dough into squares.
- In a bowl, combine the oyster mushrooms, shallot, bell pepper and parsley. Sprinkle some salt and pepper as desired.
- Spread this mixture on top of the pizza squares.
- Cook in the Air Fryer for 10 minutes.

811.   Herbed Pork Burgers

Preparation Time: 30 minutes
Cooking Time: 45 minutes
Servings: 8

Ingredients:

- 2 small onions, chopped
- 21-ounce ground pork
- 2 tsp fresh basil, chopped
- 8 burger buns
- ½ cup cheddar cheese, grated
- 2 tsp mustard
- 2 tsp garlic puree
- 2 tsp tomato puree

- Salt and freshly ground black pepper, to taste
- 2 tsp dried mixed herbs, crushed

Directions:

- Preheat the Air fryer to 395°F and grease an Air fryer basket.
- Mix all the ingredients in a bowl except cheese and buns.
- Make 8 equal-sized patties from the pork mixture and arrange the patties in the Air fryer basket.
- Cook for about 45 minutes, flipping once in between and arrange the patties in buns with cheese to serve.

812.   Ham Pinwheels

Preparation Time: 15 minutes
Cooking Time: 10 minutes
Servings: 5

Ingredients:

- 1 puff pastry sheet
- 10 ham slices
- 1 cup Gruyere cheese, shredded plus more for sprinkling
- 4 tsp Dijon mustard

Directions:

- Preheat the Air fryer to 375°F and grease an Air fryer basket.
- Place the puff pastry onto a smooth surface and spread evenly with the mustard.
- Top with the ham and ¾ cup cheese, and roll the puff pastry.
- Wrap the roll in plastic wrap and freeze for about 30 minutes.
- Remove from the freezer and slice into ½-inch rounds.
- Arrange the pinwheels in the Air fryer basket and cook for about 8 minutes.
- Top with remaining cheese and cook for 3 more minutes.
- Dish out on a platter and serve warm.

813.   Sunflower Seed Bread

Preparation Time: 15 minutes
Cooking Time: 18-20 minutes
Servings: 4

Ingredients:

- 2/3 cup whole wheat flour
- 2/3 cup plain flour
- 1/3 cup sunflower seeds
- 1 cup lukewarm water
- ½ sachet of instant yeast
- 1 tsp salt

Directions:

- Preheat the Air fryer to 390°F and grease a cake pan.
- Mix together flours, sunflower seeds, yeast and salt in a bowl.
- Add water slowly and knead for about 5 minutes until a dough is formed.
- Cover the dough with a plastic wrap and keep it in a warm place for about half an hour.
- Arrange the dough into a cake pan and transfer it into an air fryer basket.

- Cook for about 18 minutes and dish out to serve warm.

814.   Bow Tie Chips

Preparation Time: 10 minutes
Cooking Time: 10-15 minutes
Servings: 5

Ingredients:

- 2 cups white bow tie pasta
- 1 tbsp olive oil
- 1 tbsp nutritional yeast
- 1½ tsp Italian seasoning blend
- ½ tsp salt

Directions:

- Cook the pasta for 1/2 the time called for on the package. Toss the drained pasta
- with olive oil or aquafaba, nutritional yeast, Italian seasoning, and salt.
- Place about half of the mixture in your air fryer basket if yours is small; larger ones may be able to cook in one batch.
- Cook on 390°F/200°C for 5 minutes. Shake the basket and cook 3 to 5 minutes more or until crunchy.

815.   Dinner Rolls

Preparation Time: 20 minutes
Cooking Time: 30 minutes
Servings: 12

Ingredients:

- 1 cup milk
- 3 cups plain flour
- 7½ tbsp unsalted butter
- 1 tbsp coconut oil
- 1 tbsp olive oil
- 1 tsp yeast
- Salt and black pepper, to taste

Directions:

- Preheat the Air fryer to 360°F and grease an Air fryer basket.
- Put olive oil, milk and coconut oil in a pan and cook for about 3 minutes.
- Remove from the heat and mix well.
- Mix together plain flour, yeast, butter, salt and black pepper in a large bowl.
- Knead well for about 5 minutes until a dough is formed.
- Cover the dough with a damp cloth and keep it aside for about 5 minutes in a warm place.
- Knead the dough for about 5 minutes again with your hands.
- Cover the dough with a damp cloth and keep it aside for about 30 minutes in a warm place.
- Divide the dough into 12 equal pieces and roll each into a ball.
- Arrange 6 balls into the Air fryer basket in a single layer and cook for about 15 minutes.
- Repeat with the remaining balls and serve warm.

816.   Shrimp Po'boy

Preparation Time: 35 minutes
Cooking Time: 15 minutes
Servings: 4

Ingredients:

- 1 tsp. creole seasoning
- 8 slices of tomato
- Lettuce leaves
- ¼ cup buttermilk
- ½ cup Louisiana Fish Fry
- 1-pound deveined shrimp
- 4 rolls
- Remoulade sauce:
- 1 chopped green onion
- 1 tsp. hot sauce
- 1 tsp. Dijon mustard
- ½ tsp. creole seasoning
- 1 tsp. Worcestershire sauce
- Juice of ½ a lemon
- ½ cup vegan mayo

Directions:

- To make the sauce, combine all sauce ingredients until well incorporated. Chill while you cook shrimp.
- Mix seasonings together and liberally season shrimp.
- Add buttermilk to a bowl. Dip each shrimp into milk and place in a Ziploc bag. Chill for half an hour to marinate.
- Add fish fry to a bowl. Take shrimp from marinating bag and dip into fish fry, then add to the air fryer.
- Ensure your air fryer is preheated to 400°F.
- Spray shrimp with olive oil. Cook 5 minutes, flip and then cook another 5 minutes.
- Assemble "Keto" Po Boy by adding sauce to lettuce leaves, along with shrimp and tomato.

817.   Smoked Bacon Bread

Preparation Time: 15 minutes
Cooking Time: 30 minutes
Servings: 6

Ingredients:

- 1 lb. white bread; cubed
- 1 lb. smoked bacon; cooked and chopped.
- 1/2 lb. cheddar cheese; shredded
- 1/2 lb. Monterey jack cheese; shredded
- 30 oz. canned tomatoes; chopped.
- 1/4 cup avocado oil
- 1 red onion; chopped.
- 2 tbsp. chicken stock
- 2 tbsp. chives; chopped.
- 8 eggs; whisked
- Salt and black pepper to taste

Directions:

- Add the oil to your air fryer and heat it up at 350°F
- Add all other ingredients except the chives and cook for 30 minutes, shaking halfway. Divide between plates and serve with chives sprinkled on top

818.   Mushroom Pie

Preparation Time: 15 minutes
Cooking Time: 10 minutes
Servings: 4

Ingredients:
- 6 white mushrooms; chopped.
- 3 eggs
- 1 red onion; chopped.
- 9-inch pie dough
- 1/4 cup cheddar cheese; grated
- 1/2 cup heavy cream
- 2 tbsp. bacon; cooked and crumbled
- 1 tbsp. olive oil
- 1/2 tsp. thyme; dried
- Salt and black pepper to taste

Directions:
- Roll the dough on a working surface, then press it on the bottom of a pie pan that fits your air fryer and grease with the oil
- In a bowl, mix all other ingredients except the cheese, stir well and pour the mixture into the pie pan
- Sprinkle the cheese on top, put the pan in the air fryer and cook at 400°F for 10 minutes. Slice and serve.

819.   Cheese and Tuna Sandwich

Preparation Time: 15 minutes
Cooking Time: 10 minutes
Servings: 3

Ingredients:
- 16 oz. canned tuna; drained
- 6 bread slices
- 6 provolone cheese slices
- 2 spring onions; chopped.
- 1/4 cup mayonnaise
- 2 tbsp. mustard
- 1 tbsp. lime juice
- 3 tbsp. butter; melted

Directions:
- In a bowl, mix the tuna, mayo, lime juice, mustard and spring onions; stir until combined.
- Spread the bread slices with the butter, place them in the preheated air fryer and bake them at 350°F for 5 minutes
- Spread tuna mix on half of the bread slices and top with the cheese and the other bread slices
- Place the sandwiches in your air fryer's basket and cook for 4 minutes more. Divide between plates and serve.

820.   Spicy Beet Chips

Preparation Time: 10 minutes
Cooking Time: 12 minutes
Servings: 2

Ingredients:
- 7 oz beets
- 1 tsp chili flakes
- ½ tsp red pepper
- 1 tsp olive oil
- ¼ tsp sage

Directions:
- Wash the beet carefully and slice it into the chips.
- Sprinkle the beet chips with chili flakes, red pepper, olive oil, and sage.
- Mix up the beet chips carefully.
- Preheat the air fryer to 360°F.
- Put the beet chips in the air fryer basket in one layer and cook for 10 minutes.
- Then shake the chips gently and cook for 2 minutes more.
- When the beet chips are cooked – let them chill till the room temperature and serve.

821.   Zucchini Chips

Preparation Time: 15 minutes
Cooking Time: 60 minutes
Servings: 6

Ingredients:
- 3 Zucchinis
- Salt and black pepper to taste
- 2 tbsp Olive oil
- 2 tbsp Balsamic vinegar

Directions:
- Mix vinegar, oil, salt, and pepper and whisk well. Add zucchini slices and toss to coat. Cook in the air fryer at 200°F for 1 hour. Shake once. Serve.

822.   Apple Chips

Preparation Time: 10 minutes
Cooking Time: 10 minutes
Servings: 1

Ingredients:
- 1 Apple, core & cut into half-moon slices
- ¼ tbsp Cinnamon
- Pinch of salt and sugar

Directions:
- Sprinkle apple slices with cinnamon, sugar and salt and place into the multi-level air fryer basket and place basket into the air fryer. Seal pot with air fryer lid. Select air fry mode and cook at 390°F for 12 minutes. Turn apple slices halfway through. Serve.

823.   Spiced Edamame

Preparation Time: 5 minutes
Cooking Time: 18 minutes
Servings: 2

Ingredients:
- 8 oz. Frozen edamame in a shell, defrosted
- 2 Garlic cloves, sliced
- 1 tsp Olive oil
- ½ tsp Paprika
- Pepper & salt, to taste

Directions:
- In a mixing bowl, toss edamame with the remaining ingredients. Add edamame into the multi-level air fryer basket and place the basket into the air fryer. Seal the pot with the air fryer lid. Select air fry mode and cook at 400°F for 18 minutes. Serve.

824. Cajun Peanuts

Preparation Time: 5 minutes
Cooking Time: 20 minutes
Servings: 4

Ingredients:
- 4 oz.Peanuts
- ½ tsp Cayenne pepper
- 1½ tsp Old bay seasoning
- 1 tbsp Olive oil
- Salt, to taste

Directions:
- In a mixing bowl, mix together the cayenne pepper, old bay seasoning, olive oil, and salt. Add peanuts and stir until coated thoroughly. Transfer peanuts into the multi-level air fryer basket and place the basket into the air fryer. Seal the pot with the air fryer lid. Select air fry mode and cook at 320°F for 20 minutes. Stir peanuts after 10 minutes. Serve.

825. Vegan Cornbread

Preparation Time: 10 minutes
Cooking Time: 30 minutes
Servings: 6

Ingredients:
- 2 tbsp ground flaxseed
- 3 tbsp water
- ½ cup cornmeal
- ½ cup whole-wheat pastry flour
- ⅓ cup coconut sugar
- ½ tbsp baking powder
- ¼ tsp sea salt
- ¼ tsp baking soda
- ½ tbsp apple cider vinegar
- ½ cup plus 1 tbsp nondairy milk (unsweetened)
- ¼ cup neutral-flavored oil (such as sunflower, safflower, or melted refined coconut)
- Cooking oil spray (sunflower, safflower, or refined coconut)

Directions:
- In a small bowl, combine the flaxseed and water. Set aside for 5 minutes, or until thick and gooey.
- In a medium bowl, add the cornmeal, flour, sugar, baking powder, salt, and baking soda. Combine thoroughly, stirring with a whisk. Set aside.
- Add the vinegar, milk, and oil to the flaxseed mixture and stir well.
- Add the wet mixture to the dry mixture and stir gently, just until thoroughly combined.
- Spray (or coat) a 6-inch round, 2-inch deep baking pan with oil. Pour the batter into it and bake for 25 minutes at 380°F, or until golden-browned and a knife inserted in the center comes out clean. Cut into wedges, top with a little vegan margarine if desired.

826. Taro Chips

Preparation Time: 5 minutes
Cooking Time: 15 minutes
Servings: 2

Ingredients:
- Cooking oil spray (coconut, sunflower, or safflower)
- 1 cup thinly sliced taro
- Sea salt

Directions:
- Spray the air fryer basket with oil and set it aside. Place the sliced taro in the air fryer basket, spread the pieces out as much as possible, and spray with oil. Fry for about 4 minutes at 350°F.
- Remove the air fryer basket, shake (so that the chips cook evenly), and spray again with oil. Fry for another 4 minutes at 350°F. If any chips are browned or crisp, remove them now.
- Remove the air fryer basket, shake again, spray again, and sprinkle lightly with salt to taste. Fry for another 3 to 4 minutes at 350°F. Remove all of the chips that are done, and cook any remaining underdone chips for another minute or until crisp. Please note that they may crisp up a tiny bit more as they sit at room temperature for a few minutes, but some may need extra time in the air fryer as they don't always cook at the same rate. You'll get the hang of how to test for doneness after you make a few batches.

827. Lime and Garlic Tortilla Chips

Preparation Time: 2 minutes
Cooking Time: 7 minutes
Servings: 3

Ingredients:
- 4 corn tortillas
- ½ tsp garlic granules
- ⅛ to ¼ tsp sea salt
- 2½ tsp fresh lime juice
- Cooking oil spray (coconut, sunflower, or safflower)

Directions:
- Cut the tortillas into quarters. Place in a medium bowl and toss gently with the garlic, salt to taste, and lime juice.
- Spray the air fryer basket with the oil, add the chips, and fry for 3 minutes at 360°F. Remove the air fryer basket, toss (so the chips cook evenly), and spray again with oil. Fry for another 2 minutes 360°F. Remove one last time, toss, spray with oil, and fry for 2 minutes 360°F, or until golden-browned and crisp. These may not all cook at the same rate, so as you go, be sure to remove the ones that are done. Let sit at room temperature for a few minutes to finish crisping up, and then enjoy.

828. English Muffin Tuna Sandwiches

Preparation Time: 10 minutes
Cooking Time: 5 minutes
Servings: 4

Ingredients:
- 1 (6-ounce) can chunk light tuna, drained
- ¼ cup mayonnaise
- 2 tbsp mustard
- 1 tbsp lemon juice
- 2 green onions, minced
- 3 English muffins, split with a fork
- 3 tbsp softened butter

- 6 thin slices of provolone or Muenster cheese

Directions:
- In a small bowl, combine the tuna, mayonnaise, mustard, lemon juice, and green onions.
- Butter the cut side of the English muffins. Grill butter-side up in the air fryer for 2 to 4 minutes at 360°F or until light golden brown. Remove the muffins from the air fryer basket.
- Top each muffin with one slice of cheese and return to the air fryer. Grill for 2 to 4 minutes or until the cheese melts and starts to brown.
- Remove the muffins from the air fryer, top with the tuna mixture, and serve.

829.   Rosemary Sweet Potato Chips

Preparation Time: 5minutes
Cooking Time: 12 minutes
Servings: 2

Ingredients:
- Cooking oil spray (coconut, sunflower, or safflower)
- 1 small-medium sweet potato, unpeeled, thinly sliced (about 1 cup)
- ¼ tsp dried rosemary
- Dash sea salt

Directions:
- Spray the air fryer basket with oil. Place the sweet potato slices in the basket, spreading them out as much as possible. Spray the tops with oil. Fry for 4 minutes at 375°F.
- Remove the air fryer basket, spray again with oil, and sprinkle the rosemary and sea salt on top of the potato slices. Spray again with oil and fry for another 4 minutes at 375°F.
- Remove the air fryer basket, shake, spray with oil, and fry for another 4 minutes, or until the pieces are lightly browned. Chips may cook at slightly different rates due to varying thicknesses, so remove any that are done before others that need more time. Also, they will usually crisp up once removed to a plate at room temperature for a minute, so if they look lightly browned, they're probably done. (Better to under-cook at this point—you can always pop them back in the air fryer if they don't crisp up at room temperature.) Continue to cook, often checking until all of the pieces are browned. Once crisp, you can serve—and continue cooking subsequent batches if you like.

830.   Salted Corn Nuts

Preparation Time: 20 minutes
Cooking Time: 35 minutes
Servings: 6

Ingredients:
- 14 ounces of giant white corn (such as Goya)
- 3 tbsp of vegetable oil
- 1 1/2 tsp of salt

Directions:
- Place the corn in a large bowl, cover with water and let sit for 8 hours to re-hydrate overnight.

- Drain the corn and spread it over a large baking sheet in an even layer. Pat dry with towels made from paper. Dry air for 20 minutes.
- The air fryer preheats to 400°F (200°C).
- Put the corn in a bowl. Season with oil and salt. Remove until the coating is even.
- Place the corn in batches in an even layer in the air fryer basket. Cook for a further 10 minutes. Shake the basket and continue cooking for another 10 minutes. Shake basket and cook for another 5 minutes, and transfer to a towel-lined sheet of paper. Repeat with leftover corn. Let the corn nuts cool down for about 20 minutes until crisp.

831.   Fish Finger Sandwich

Preparation Time: 20 minutes
Cooking Time: 15 minutes
Servings: 4

Ingredients:
- 4 small cod fillets (skin removed)
- salt and pepper
- 2 tbsp of flour
- 40g dried breadcrumbs
- spray oil
- 250g of frozen peas
- 1 tbsp of creme fraiche or Greek yogurt
- 10–12 capers
- Squeeze lemon juice
- 4 bread rolls or 8 small slices of bread

Directions:
- Preheat Air Fryer to 400°F.
- Take each filet of cod, season with salt and pepper and dust lightly in the flour. Then roll up in the breadcrumbs quickly. The idea is to have a light breadcrumbs coating on the fish rather than a thick layer. Repeat for each fillet of cod.
- Add a couple of oil spray sprays to the base of the fryer basket. Place the cod filets on top and cook for 15 minutes at a fish setting (200°C).
- While the fish is cooking, on the hob or in the microwave, cook the peas in boiling water for a few minutes. Drain and then add the creme fraiche, capers, and lemon juice to a blender to taste. Blitz until merged. Remove it from the Air Fryer once the fish has cooked, and start layering your sandwich with the bread, fish and pea puree. You can also add lettuce, tartar sauce and any other favorite toppings of your choice!

832.   Honey BBQ Bacon Sandwiches

Preparation Time: 10 minutes
Cooking Time: 7 minutes
Servings: 4

Ingredients:
- 1/3 cup BBQ sauce
- 2 tbsp honey
- 8 bacon slices, cooked and cut into thirds
- 1 red bell pepper, sliced
- 1 yellow bell pepper, sliced
- 3 pita pockets, halved
- 1 and ¼ cup butter lettuce leaves, torn
- 2 tomatoes, sliced

Directions:
- In a bowl, mix BBQ sauce with honey and whisk well.
- Brush bacon and all bell peppers with some of this mix, place them in your air fryer and cook at 350°F for 4 minutes.
- Shake fryer and cook them for 2 minutes more.
- Stuff pita pockets with bacon mix, also stuff with tomatoes and lettuce and spread the rest of the BBQ sauce.

833. Korean Burgers

Preparation Time: 40 minutes
Cooking Time: 15 minutes
Servings: 4

Ingredients:
- 1 pound (453.59 g) Lean Ground Beef
- 2 tbsp of gochujang
- 1 tbsp of dark soy sauce
- 2 tsp Minced Garlic
- 2 tsp of minced ginger
- 2 tsp of Sugar
- 1 tbsp of Sesame Oil
- 1/4 cup (25 g) of Green Onions
- 1/2 tsp (0.5 tsp) of Salt
- For the Gochujang Mayonnaise
- 1/4 cup (56 g) Mayonnaise
- 1 tbsp of gochujang
- 1 tbsp of Sesame Oil
- 2 tsp of Sesame Seeds
- 1/4 cup (25 g) of scallions, chopped
- 4 hamburger buns for serving

Directions:
- In a large bowl, mix the ground beef, gochujang, soy sauce, garlic, ginger, sugar, sesame oil, chopped onions, and salt and allow the mixture to rest in a fridge for 30 minutes or up to 24 hours.
- Divide the meat into four portions and form round patties with a slight depression in the middle to prevent the burgers from blowing out in a dome-shaped cooking process.
- Set your air fryer for 10 minutes at 360°F, and put the patties in the air fryer basket in a single layer.
- Make sure the Gochujang Mayonnaise: combines together the sesame oil, mayonnaise, gochujang, sesame seeds, and scallions when cooking the patties.

834. Garlic Cheese Bread

Preparation Time: 15 minutes
Cooking Time: 8-10 minutes
Servings: 3

Ingredients:
- 5 rounds of Bread slices - Round or baguette
- 5 tsp Sun-dried tomato pesto
- 3 Garlic cloves
- 4 tbsp melted butter
- 1 cup Grated Mozzarella cheese
- Garnish Options:
- Chili flakes
- Chopped basil leaves
- Oregano

Directions:
- Set the Air Fryer to reach 356°F.
- Slice the bread loaf into five thick slices.
- Spread the butter, pesto, and cheese over the bread.
- Put the slices in the Air Fryer for six to eight minutes.
- Garnish with your choice of toppings.

835. Pizza Hot Dog Buns

Preparation Time: 15 minutes
Cooking Time: 10 minutes
Servings: 2

Ingredients:
- 2 Hot dogs
- 4 slices of Pepperoni
- ½ cup Pizza sauce
- 2 Hot dog buns
- ¼ cup Mozzarella cheese
- 2 tsp Sliced olives

Directions:
- Warm the Air Fryer at 390°F.
- Make four slits down each hot dog and place them in the Air Fryer basket. Set the timer for 3 minutes. Transfer to a cutting board.
- Place a pepperoni half in each slit of the hot dogs. Portion the pizza sauce between buns and fill with the hot dogs, mozzarella cheese, and olives.
- Return the hot dogs back into the fryer basket and cook until the buns are crisp and the cheese is melted (2 min.).

836. Philly Chicken Stromboli

Preparation Time: 30 minutes
Cooking Time: 15-20 minutes
Servings: 4

Ingredients:
- 1 tsp Vegetable oil
- 0.5 Onion
- 1 lb. Chicken breasts
- 1 tbsp Worcestershire sauce
- 14 oz. Pizza dough
- Freshly cracked black pepper & salt
- ½ cup Cheese Whiz or your favorite cheese sauce
- 1½ cups Grated Cheddar cheese

Directions:
- Warm the Cheese Whiz in the microwave.
- Set the temperature to 400°F in the Air Fryer.
- Place the onion in the fryer for eight minutes – shaking gently halfway through the cycle. Thinly slice and add the chicken and Worcestershire sauce, salt, and pepper – tossing evenly. Air fry for another eight minutes – stirring several times. Remove and let the mixture cool.
- Lightly flour a flat surface and press out the dough into a rectangle of 11x13 (the long side facing you). Sprinkle half of the cheddar over the dough. Leave a one-inch border - topping it off with the onion/chicken mixture.
- Drizzle the warmed cheese sauce over the top, finishing with the rest of the cheddar cheese.
- Roll the Stromboli toward the empty corner (away from you). Keep the filling tight and tuck in the ends.

Arrange it seam side down and shape it in a "U" to fit into the basket. Slice four slits in the top with the tip of a knife.

- Lightly brush the top with a little oil. Set the temperature to 370°F.
- Spray the basket and add the Stromboli. Fry for 12 minutes – turning about halfway through the cooking process.
- Use a serving platter and invert the tasty treat from the basket. Arrange it on a cutting board and cut it into three-inch segments. Serve with ketchup for dipping.

837.   Chicken and Avocado Sliders

Preparation Time: 30 minutes
Cooking Time: 10-15 minutes
Servings: 4

Ingredients:
- ½ pound ground chicken meat
- 4 burger buns
- 1/2 cup Romaine lettuce, loosely packed
- ½ tsp dried parsley flakes
- 1/3 tsp mustard seeds
- 1 tsp onion powder
- 1 ripe fresh avocado, mashed
- 1 tsp garlic powder
- 1 ½ tbsp extra-virgin olive oil
- 1 clove of garlic, minced
- Nonstick cooking spray
- Salt and cracked black pepper (peppercorns) to taste

Directions:
- Firstly, spritz an air fryer cooking basket with a nonstick cooking spray.
- Mix ground chicken meat, mustard seeds, garlic powder, onion powder, parsley, salt, and black pepper until everything is thoroughly combined. Make sure not to overwork the meat to avoid tough chicken burgers.
- Shape the meat mixture into patties and roll them in breadcrumbs; transfer your burgers to the prepared cooking basket. Brush the patties with the cooking spray.
- Air-fry at 355°F for 9 minutes, working in batches. Slice burger buns into halves. In the meantime, combine olive oil with mashed avocado and pressed garlic.
- To finish, lay Romaine lettuce and avocado spread on bun bottoms; now, add burgers and bun tops. Bon appétit!

838.   Cheddar and Mustard Twists

Preparation Time: 20 minutes
Cooking Time: 20 minutes
Servings: 6

Ingredients:
- 2 cups cauliflower florets, steamed
- 1 egg
- 3 ½ oz oats
- 1 red onion, diced
- 1 tsp mustard
- 5 oz cheddar cheese
- Salt and black pepper to taste

Directions:
- Preheat Air Fry to 350°F, place the oats in a food processor and pulse until they are the consistency of breadcrumbs. Place the steamed florets in a cheesecloth and squeeze out the excess liquid.
- Place the cauliflower florets in a large bowl. Add the rest of the ingredients to the bowl. Mix well with hands to combine the ingredients completely. Take a little bit of the mixture and twist it into a straw.
- Place on a lined baking tray and repeat with the rest of the mixture. Cook for 10 minutes, turn over and cook for an additional 10 minutes.

839.   Basil Keto Crackers

Preparation Time: 30 minutes
Cooking Time: 15 minutes
Servings: 6

Ingredients:
- 1¼ cups almond flour
- Salt and pepper to taste
- ½ tsp baking powder
- ¼ tsp dried basil powder
- A pinch of cayenne pepper powder
- 1 clove of garlic, minced
- 3 tbsp heart-healthy oil

Directions:
- Preheat the air fryer to 325°F for 5 minutes.
- Mix everything in a mixing bowl to create a dough.
- Transfer the dough to a clean and flat working surface and spread out until 2mm thick. Cut into squares.
- Place gently in the air fryer basket. Do this in batches if possible.
- Cook for 15 minutes at 325°F.
- Serve and enjoy!

840.   Paprika Pickle Chips

Preparation Time: 10 minutes
Cooking Time: 10 minutes
Servings: 8

Ingredients:
- 36 sweet pickle chips
- 1 cup buttermilk
- 3 tbsp smoked paprika
- 2 cups flour
- ¼ cup cornmeal
- Salt and black pepper to taste

Directions:
- Preheat the Air Fryer function to 400°F. In a bowl, mix flour, paprika, pepper, salt, cornmeal and powder. Place pickles in buttermilk and set aside for 5 minutes. Dip the pickles in the spice mixture and place them in the cooking basket. Cook for 10 minutes.

841.   Cornbread with Pulled Pork

Preparation Time: 30 minutes
Cooking Time: 20 minutes
Servings: 6

Ingredients:
- 2½ cups pulled pork, leftover works well too

- 1 tsp dried rosemary
- 1/2 tsp chili powder
- 3 cloves garlic, peeled and pressed
- 1/2 recipe cornbread in box
- 1/2 tbsp brown sugar
- 1/3 cup scallions, thinly sliced
- 1 tsp sea salt

Directions:
- Preheat a large-sized nonstick skillet over medium heat; now, cook the scallions together with the garlic and pulled pork.
- Next, add the sugar, chili powder, rosemary, and salt. Cook, occasionally stirring, until the mixture is thickened.
- Preheat your air fryer to 335°F. Now, coat two mini loaf pans with a cooking spray. Add the pulled pork mixture and spread over the bottom using a spatula.
- Spread the previously prepared cornbread batter over top of the spiced pulled pork mixture.
- Bake this cornbread in the preheated air fryer until a tester inserted into the center of it comes out clean, or for 18 minutes. Bon appétit!

842.   Spicy Cheese Crisps

Preparation Time: 10 minutes
Cooking Time: 10 minutes
Servings: 3

Ingredients:
- 4 tbsp grated cheese + extra for rolling
- 1 cup flour + extra for kneading
- ¼ tsp chili powder
- ½ tsp baking powder
- 3 tsp butter
- A pinch of salt

Directions:
- In a bowl, mix in the cheese, flour, baking powder, chili powder, butter, and salt. The mixture should be crusty. Add some drops of water and mix well to get a dough. Remove the dough to a flat surface.
- Rub some extra flour in your palms and on the surface, and knead the dough for a while. Using a rolling pin, roll the dough out into a thin sheet. With a pastry cutter, cut the dough into your desired lings' shape. Add the cheese lings to the basket, and cook for 8 minutes at 350°F on the Air Fry function, flipping once halfway through.

843.   Chickpea Cauliflower Tacos

Preparation Time: 20 minutes
Cooking Time: 30 minutes
Servings: 4

Ingredients:
- 4 cups cauliflower
- 2 tbsp. olive oil
- 2 tbsp. taco seasoning
- 8 small tortillas
- 2 avocados sliced
- 19 oz. rinsed chickpeas
- 4 cups cabbage shredded
- Coconut yogurt to drizzle

Directions:
- Preheat of air fryer toaster oven to 390°F. Toss the cauliflower and chickpeas with olive oil and taco seasoning in a bowl. Place everything into the basket of your air fryer. Shaking the basket occasionally for 20 minutes or until cooked through. Serve the tacos with avocado slices, cabbage and coconut yogurt.

844.   Chili Cheese Curds

Preparation Time: 15 minutes
Cooking Time: 15 minutes
Servings: 4

Ingredients:
- 4 cups grated cheese
- 1 cup all-purpose flour
- 1 tbsp butter
- 1 tbsp baking powder
- ¼ tsp chili powder
- ¼ tsp salt, to taste
- 2 tbsp water

Directions:
- In a bowl, mix the flour and the baking powder. Add the chili powder, salt, butter, cheese and 1-2 tbsp of water to the mixture. Make a stiff dough.
- Knead the dough for a while and sprinkle about a tbsp of flour on the table.
- With a rolling pin, roll the dough to ½-inch thickness. Cut into any shape and cook for 6 minutes at 370°F.

845.   Orange Turkey Burgers

Preparation Time: 20 minutes
Cooking Time: 11-15 minutes
Servings: 4

Ingredients:
- 1 lb. Ground Turkey
- 1 tsp ground mustard seed
- 1 tbsp Grape nuts Nuggets
- ¼ tsp Chinese Five Spice
- 1 Diced scallion
- Orange Basting Sauce:
- ½ cup Orange Marmalade
- 1 tbsp Soy sauce
- 1 tsp Fish sauce
- 2 tsp Oyster sauce
- Orange Aioli:
- 1 tbsp Orange juice
- 1 tsp Orange zest
- ½ cup Mayonnaise
- 1 tsp ground chili paste

Directions:
- In a small bowl, whisk Orange Aioli ingredients and refrigerate.
- In another bowl, combine basting sauce and keep aside.
- Set the air fryer at 200°C and pre-heat for about 10 minutes.
- In a medium bowl, combine the burger ingredients and add 1 tbsp of basting sauce.
- Shape the mix into 6 patties and create an indentation at the center of the patties.

- Now lightly grease the surface of the air fryer basket with cooking oil and place the patties in the frying basket.
- Set the temperature to 180°C and cook for 9 minutes.
- Flip the burgers intermittently every 4 minutes.
- Baste the burger after every 2 minutes.
- After 9 minutes of cooking, baste the burger and cook a further 3 minutes.
- Serve hot along with Orange Aioli.

846.   Cheese Vegan Sandwich

Preparation Time: 10 minutes
Cooking Time: 12 minutes
Servings: 1

Ingredients:
- 2 slices of sprouted whole grain bread
- 1 tsp vegan margarine
- 2 slices of vegan cheese
- 1 tsp mellow white miso
- 1 medium-large garlic clove, minced
- 2 tbsp fermented vegetables, kimchi or sauerkraut
- Romaine lettuce

Directions:
- Preheat your Air Fryer to 392°F
- Spread outside of bread with Vegan margarine, place sliced cheese inside and close sandwich back up
- Transfer Sandwich to Air Fryer and cook for 6 minutes, flip and cook for 6 minutes more
- Transfer to plate and spread miso and garlic clove inside one of the slices, top with fermented veggies and lettuce
- Close sandwich and cut in half
- Serve and enjoy!

847.   Smoked Paprika Pumpkin Seeds

Preparation Time: 15 minutes
Cooking Time: 35 minutes
Servings: 4

Ingredients:
- 1½ cups pumpkin seeds
- Olive oil as needed
- 1½ tsp salt
- 1 tsp smoked paprika

Directions:
- Cut pumpkin and scrape out seeds and flesh
- Separate flesh from seeds and rinse the seeds under cold water
- Bring 2 quarters of salted water to boil and add seeds; boil for 10 minutes
- Drain seeds and spread them on a kitchen towel
- Dry for 20 minutes
- Preheat your fryer to 350 °F
- Take a bowl and add seeds, smoked paprika, and olive oil
- Season with salt and transfer to your Air Fryer cooking basket
- Cook for 35 minutes; enjoy it!

848.   Vegetable Tuna Melt

Preparation Time: 15 minutes
Cooking Time: 11 minutes
Servings: 2

Ingredients:
- 2 low-sodium whole-wheat English muffins, split
- 1 (6-ounce) can chunk light low-sodium tuna, drained
- 1 cup shredded carrot
- ⅓ cup chopped mushrooms
- 2 scallions, white and green parts, sliced
- ⅓ cup nonfat Greek yogurt
- 2 tbsp low-sodium stone-ground mustard
- 2 slices low-sodium low-fat Swiss cheese, halved

Directions:
- Place the English muffin halves in the air fryer basket. Grill for 3 to 4 minutes at 365°F, or until crisp. Remove from the basket and set aside.
- In a medium bowl, thoroughly mix the tuna, carrot, mushrooms, scallions, yogurt, and mustard. Top each half of the muffins with one-fourth of the tuna mixture and a half slice of Swiss cheese.
- Grill in the air fryer for 4 to 7 minutes, or until the tuna mixture is hot and the cheese melts and starts to brown. Serve immediately.

849.   Veggie Pita

Preparation Time: 15 minutes
Cooking Time: 12 minutes
Servings: 2

Ingredients:
- 1 baby eggplant, peeled and chopped
- 1 red bell pepper, sliced
- ½ cup diced red onion
- ½ cup shredded carrot
- 1 tsp olive oil
- ⅓ cup low-fat Greek yogurt
- ½ tsp dried tarragon
- 2 low-sodium whole-wheat pita bread, halved crosswise

Directions:
- In a 6-by-2-inch pan, stir together the eggplant, red bell pepper, red onion, carrot, and olive oil. Put the vegetable mixture into the air fryer basket and roast for 7 to 9 -minutesat 400°F, stirring once, until the vegetables are tender. Drain if necessary.
- In a small bowl, thoroughly mix the yogurt and tarragon until well combined.
- Stir the yogurt mixture into the vegetables. Stuff one-fourth of this mixture into each pita pocket.
- Place the sandwiches in the air fryer and cook for 2 to 3 minutes at 360°F, or until the bread is toasted. Serve immediately.

850.   Green Vegetable Pizza

Preparation Time: 11 minutes
Cooking Time: 20 minutes
Servings: 4

Ingredients:
- ¾ cup whole-wheat pastry flour
- ½ tsp low-sodium baking powder

- 1 tbsp olive oil, divided
- 1 cup chopped kale
- 2 cups chopped fresh baby spinach
- 1 cup canned no-salt-added cannellini beans, rinsed and drained
- ½ tsp dried thyme
- 1 piece of low-sodium string cheese, torn into pieces

Directions:

- In a small bowl, mix the pastry flour and baking powder until well combined.
- Add ¼ cup of water and 2 tsp of olive oil. Mix until a dough forms.
- On a floured surface, press or roll the dough into a 7-inch round. Set aside while you cook the greens.
- In a 6-by-2-inch pan, mix the kale, spinach, and remaining tsp of the olive oil. Air-fry for 3 to 5 minutes at 350°F until the greens are wilted. Drain well.
- Put the pizza dough into the air fryer basket. Top with the greens, cannellini beans, thyme, and string cheese. Air-fry for 11 to 14 minutes, or until the crust is golden brown and the cheese is melted. Cut into quarters to serve.

851.   Salmon Nachos

Preparation Time: 10 minutes
Cooking Time: 12 minutes
Servings: 5

Ingredients:

- 2 ounces (about 36) baked no-salt corn tortilla chips
- 1 (5-ounce) baked salmon fillet, flaked
- ½ cup canned low-sodium black beans, rinsed and drained
- 1 red bell pepper, chopped
- ½ cup grated carrot
- 1 jalapeño pepper, minced
- ⅓ cup shredded low-sodium low-fat Swiss cheese
- 1 tomato, chopped

Directions:

- In a 6-by-2-inch pan, layer the tortilla chips. Top with the salmon, black beans, red bell pepper, carrot, jalapeño, and Swiss cheese.
- Bake in the air fryer for 9 to 12 minutes at 400°F, or until the cheese is melted and starts to brown.
- Top with the tomato and serve.

852.   Turkey Quesadillas

Preparation Time: 7 minutes
Cooking Time: 8 minutes
Servings: 3

Ingredients:

- 6 low-sodium whole-wheat tortillas
- ⅓ cup shredded low-sodium low-fat Swiss cheese
- ¾ cup shredded cooked low-sodium turkey breast
- 2 tbsp cranberry sauce
- 2 tbsp dried cranberries
- ½ tsp dried basil
- Olive oil spray for spraying the tortillas

Directions:

- Put 3 tortillas on a work surface.

- Evenly divide the Swiss cheese, turkey, cranberry sauce, and dried cranberries among the tortillas. Sprinkle with the basil and top with the remaining tortillas.
- Spray the outsides of the tortillas with olive oil spray.
- One at a time, grill the quesadillas in the air fryer for 4 to 8 minutes at 400°F, or until crisp and the cheese is melted. Cut into quarters and serve.

853.   Salmon Jerky

Preparation Time: 2 hrs.
Cooking Time: 4 hrs.
Servings: 4

Ingredients:

- 1 lb. boneless skinless salmon
- ½ tsp. liquid smoke
- ½ tsp. ground ginger
- ¼ cup soy sauce
- ¼ tsp. red pepper flakes

Directions:

- Cut the salmon into strips about four inches long and a quarter-inch thick.
- Put the salmon in an airtight container or bag along with the liquid smoke, ginger, soy sauce, and red pepper flakes, combining everything to coat the salmon completely. Leave the salmon in the refrigerator for at least two hours.
- Transfer the salmon slices to the fryer, taking care not to overlap any pieces. This step may need to be completed in multiple batches.
- Cook at 140°C for four hours.
- Take care when removing the salmon from the fryer and leave it to cool. This jerky makes a good snack and can be stored in an airtight container.

854.   Creamy Salmon Pie

Preparation Time: 35 minutes
Cooking Time: 20 minutes
Servings: 8

Ingredients:

- 1 Tsp Paprika
- ½ Cup Cream
- ½ Tsp Baking Soda
- 1 ½ Cups Almond Flour
- 1 Onion, Diced
- 1 Tbsp Apple Cider Vinegar
- 1 lb. Salmon
- 1 Tbsp Chives
- 1 Tsp Dill
- 1 Tsp Oregano
- 1 Tsp Butter
- 1 Tsp Parsley
- 1 Egg

Directions:

- Start by beating your eggs in a bowl, making sure they're whisked well. Add in your cream, whisking for another two minutes.
- Add in your apple cider vinegar and baking soda, stirring well.

- Add in your almond flour, combining until it makes a non-stick, smooth dough.
- Chop your salmon into pieces, and then sprinkle your seasoning over it.
- Mix well, and then cut your dough into two parts.
- Place parchment paper over your air fryer basket tray, placing the first part of your dough in the tray to form a crust. Add in your salmon filling.
- Roll out the second part, covering your salmon filling. Secure the edges, and then heat your air fryer to 360°F.
- Cook for 15 minutes, and then reduce the heat to 355°F, cooking for another 15 minutes.
- Slice and serve warm.

855.   Pizza Egg Rolls

Preparation Time: 10 minutes
Cooking Time: 5 minutes
Servings: 4

Ingredients:
- 4 egg roll wrappers
- 4 Light Mozzarella String Cheese
- Cooking Spray
- 12 slices of small turkey pepperoni, thinly sliced
- Italian Seasoning or Parsley
- Parmesan Cheese

Directions:
- Preheat the air fryer to 350°F.
- Arrange an egg roll wrapper with the corners fixed vertically on a level work surface. Place three slices of turkey pepperoni in the center of the egg roll wrapper. Place the turkey pepperoni on top of the string cheese.
- Coat the egg roll wrapper's outside edges with cooking spray. That will help the corners hold together when you fold them in.
- Fold the wrapper bottom to the middle, over the filling. Now fold the left side of the wrapper to the center gently yet firmly, and then fold to the right side. Fold the top of the wrapper to cover the filling and use water to seal any loose ends; repeat with the remaining ingredients.
- Fill your air fryer basket with filled wrappers and lightly coat the tops of the egg rolls with cooking spray. After 5 minutes, remove the basket and flip the egg rolls over. Cook for an additional 3 minutes.
- Garnish with parmesan cheese and parsley or Italian seasoning.

856.   Chicken Skin Crisps

Preparation Time: 20 minutes
Cooking Time: 15 minutes
Servings: 4

Ingredients:
- 1 lb. Chicken Skin
- ½ Tsp Black Pepper
- 1 Tsp Dill
- ½ Tsp Chili Flakes
- 1 Tsp Butter
- ½ Tsp Sea Salt, Fine

Directions:
- Slice your chicken skin roughly, and then sprinkle it with your seasoning.
- Mix you're chicken skin, and melt your butter before adding it.
- Preheat your air fryer to 360°F, and then place your chicken skin in your air fryer basket.
- Cook for three minutes per side, and then serve warm or at room temperature.

857.   Rustic Mushroom and Pork Burgers

Preparation Time: 20 minutes
Cooking Time: 30 minutes
Servings: 4

Ingredients:
- 1 tbsp canola oil
- 1 onion, chopped
- 2 garlic cloves, minced
- 1-pound ground pork
- 1/2-pound brown mushrooms, chopped
- Salt and black pepper, to taste
- 1 tsp cayenne pepper
- 1/2 tsp dried rosemary
- 1/2 tsp dried dill
- 4 slices of Cheddar cheese

Directions:
- Start by preheating your Air Fryer to 370°F.
- In a mixing bowl, thoroughly combine the oil, onions, garlic, ground pork, mushrooms, salt, black pepper, cayenne pepper, rosemary, and dill.
- Shape the meat mixture into four patties.
- Spritz the bottom of the cooking basket with cooking spray. Cook the meatballs in the preheated Air Fryer at 370°F for 20 minutes, flipping them halfway through cooking.
- Top the warm patties with cheese and serve. Enjoy!

858.   Guilt-free Sloppy Joes

Preparation Time: 35 minutes
Cooking Time: 40 minutes
Servings: 4

Ingredients:
- 1 tbsp olive oil
- 1 shallot, chopped
- 2 garlic cloves, minced
- 1 bell pepper, chopped
- 1-pound ground pork
- 1 ripe medium-sized tomato, pureed
- 1 tbsp poultry seasoning blend
- Dash ground allspice
- Keto Buns:
- 1/3 cup ricotta cheese, crumbled
- 2/3 cup part-skim mozzarella cheese, shredded
- 1 egg
- 1/3 cup coconut flour
- 1/2 cup almond flour
- 1 tsp baking soda
- 1 ½ tbsp plain whey protein isolate

Directions:
- Start by preheating your Air Fryer to 390°F. Heat the olive oil for a few minutes.
- Once hot, sauté the shallots until just tender. Add the garlic and bell pepper; cook for 4 minutes more or until they are aromatic.
- Add the ground pork and cook for 5 minutes more, crumbling with a fork. Next step, stir in the pureed tomatoes and spices. Decrease the temperature to 365°F and cook another 10 minutes. Reserve.
- To make the keto buns, microwave the cheese for 1 minute 30 seconds, stirring twice. Add the cheese to the bowl of a food processor and blend well. Fold in the egg and mix again.
- Add in the flour, baking soda, and plain whey protein isolate; blend again. Scrape the batter onto the center of a lightly greased cling film.
- Form the dough into a disk and transfer to your freezer to cool; cut into 4 pieces and transfer to a parchment-lined baking pan (make sure to grease your hands). Bake in the preheated oven at 400°F for about 14 minutes.
- Spoon the meat mixture into keto buns and transfer them to the cooking basket. Cook for 7 minutes or until thoroughly warmed.

859. Croque Monsieur

Preparation Time: 20 minutes
Cooking Time: 15 minutes
Servings: 2

Ingredients:
- 4 slices of white bread
- 2 tbsp unsalted butter
- 1 tbsp all-purpose flour
- 1/2 cup whole milk
- 3/4 cup shredded swiss cheese
- 1/4 tsp freshly ground black pepper
- 1/8 tsp salt
- 1 tbsp dijon mustard
- 4 slices ham

Directions:
- Start by cutting crusts off the bread and placing them on a pan lined with parchment paper.
- Melt 1 tbsp of butter in a saucepan, then dab the top sides of each piece of bread with butter.
- Toast bread in the air fryer for 3-5 minutes at 350°F until each piece is golden brown.
- Melt the second tbsp of butter in the saucepan and add the flour; mix together until they form a paste.
- Add the milk and continue to mix until the sauce begins to thicken.
- Remove from heat and mix in 1 tbsp of swiss cheese, salt, and pepper; continue stirring until cheese is melted.
- Flip the bread over in the pan, so the untoasted side is facing up.
- Set two slices aside and spread Dijon on the other two slices.
- Add ham and sprinkle 1/4 cup swiss over each piece.
- Broil for about 3 minutes.
- Top the sandwiches off with the other slices of bread, soft side down.

- Top with sauce and sprinkle with remaining swiss. Toast for another 5 minutes or until the cheese is golden brown.

860. Pita Pizza

Preparation Time: 7 minutes
Cooking Time: 8 minutes
Servings: 6

Ingredients:
- 10 slices pepperoni
- ½ cup pitted black olives
- 1 large whole wheat pita flatbread
- 1 cup mozzarella cheese (shredded)
- 1 cup cheddar cheese (shredded)
- 2 tbsp marinara
- 2 tbsp of olive oil
- 4 to 6 sprigs of fresh basil
- salt and fresh ground black pepper to taste

Directions:
- Place the crisper plate in the Air Fryer drawer.
- Use non-stick cooking spray to spray the crisper plate.
- Preheat the Air Fryer to 400°F or 200°C. Use the Air Fry setting and set the preheat for 3 minutes to 5 minutes.
- Use olive oil to lightly coat one side of the pita bread.
- Place the pita bread, olive oil-coated side down, in the Air Fryer on top of the crisper tray.
- Set the Air Fryer for 4 minutes and use the Air Fry setting to start cooking the pita bread.
- When it is done, take the pita bread out of the Air Fryer. The side that was face down on the crisper will be nicely cooked.
- Place it on a cooling rack or plate on a cooling rack with the crisper side up.
- When the pita bread is cool enough to touch (not too cold, though, it should still be warm), spread marinara sauce generously over the base.
- Place the shredded mozzarella sauce over marinara sauce.
- Put the pepperoni on top of the mozzarella.
- Put the place olives on top of the pepperoni.
- Top generously with cheddar cheese.
- Set the Air Fryer for 8 minutes and use the Air Fry setting to start cooking the pita pizza.
- When it is done, remove the pita pizza from the Air Fryer using a spatula, and set it on a rack to cool down a bit.
- When you can touch it, cut it into serving sizes with the pizza cutter, garnish with fresh basil, and serve

861. Mexican Fish Quesadilla

Preparation Time: 10 minutes
Cooking Time: 12 minutes
Servings: 2

Ingredients:
- 2 6-inch corn or flour tortilla shells
- 1 medium-sized tilapia fillet, approximately 4 ounces
- ½ medium-sized lemon, sliced
- ½ an avocado, peeled, pitted and sliced
- 1 clove of garlic, peeled and finely minced

- Pinch of salt and pepper
- ½ tsp of lemon juice
- ¼ cup of shredded cheddar cheese
- ¼ cup of shredded mozzarella cheese

Directions:

- Preheat the Air Fryer to 350°F.
- In the oven, grill the tilapia with a little salt and lemon slices in foil on high heat for 20 minutes.
- Remove fish in foil from the oven, and break the fish meat apart into bite-sized pieces with a fork – it should be flaky and chunky when cooked.
- While the fish is cooling, combine the avocado, garlic, salt, pepper, and lemon juice in a small mixing bowl; mash lightly, but don't whip - keep the avocado slightly chunky.
- Spread the guacamole on one of the tortillas, then cover with the fish flakes, and then with the cheese. Top with the second tortilla.
- Place directly on the hot surface of the air frying basket.
- Close the air fryer lid. Set the Air Fryer timer for 6 minutes.
- After 6 minutes, when the Air Fryer shuts off, flip the tortillas onto the other side with a spatula; the cheese should be melted enough that it won't fall apart.
- Reset Air Fryer to 350°F for another 6 minutes.
- After 6 minutes, when the Air Fryer shuts off, the tortillas should be browned and crisp, and the fish, guacamole and cheese will be hot and delicious inside. Remove with spatula and let sit on a serving plate to cool for a few minutes before slicing.

862. Beef Empanadas

Preparation Time: 10 minutes
Cooking Time: 20 minutes
Servings: 4

Ingredients:

- 1 tsp. water
- 1 egg white
- 1 cup picadillo
- 8 Goya empanada discs (thawed)

Directions:

- Ensure your Air Fryer is preheated to 325°F. Spray basket with olive oil.
- Place 2 tbsp of picadillo into the center of each disc. Fold disc in half and use a fork to seal edges. Repeat with all ingredients.
- Whisk egg white with water and brush tops of empanadas with egg wash.
- Add 2-3 empanadas to the Air Fryer.
- Close the air fryer lid. Set temperature to 325°F, and set time to 8 minutes; cook until golden. Repeat till you cook all filled empanadas.

863. Pulled BBQ Beef Sandwiches

Preparation Time: 20 minutes
Cooking Time: 50 minutes
Servings: 6

Ingredients:

- 2 pounds – Beef of choice
- 2 cps – Water

- 4 cps – Finely shredded Cabbage (the secret ingredient, and you'll never know it's in there.)
- 1/2 cup – Of your favorite BBQ Sauce
- 1 cup – Ketchup
- 1/3 cup – of Worcestershire Sauce
- 1 tbsp. – Horse Radish
- 1 tbsp. – mustard
- 6 buns

Directions:

- Add and stir in ingredients to your Air Fryer.
- Lock the pressure-Cooking lid on the Air Fryer duo and then cook for 35 minutes. To get a 35-minutes of cook time, press the "Pressure" button and adjust the time.
- For a pressure release, use the natural release method.
- Remove the lid from the Air Fryer. Close the air fryer lid. Select AIR FRY, set the temperature to 390°F, and set the time to 15 minutes. Check after 10 minutes, cooking for an additional 5 minutes if the dish needs more browning.
- Set the beef aside. Set the Air Fryer to a "Sauté" mode; sauté the sauce until it reaches the desired consistency.
- Serve and Enjoy.

864. Indian Brunch Wrap

Preparation Time: 20 minutes
Cooking Time: 10 minutes
Servings: 4

Ingredients:

- Cilantro Chutney
- 2¾ cups diced potato, cooked until tender
- 2 tsp oil (coconut, sunflower, or safflower)
- 3 large garlic cloves, minced or pressed
- 1½ tbsp fresh lime juice
- 1½ tsp cumin powder
- 1 tsp onion granules
- 1 tsp coriander powder
- ½ tsp sea salt
- ½ tsp turmeric
- ¼ tsp cayenne powder
- 4 large flour tortillas, preferably whole grain or sprouted
- 1 cup cooked garbanzo beans (canned are fine), rinsed and drained
- ½ cup finely chopped cabbage
- ¼ cup minced red onion or scallion
- Cooking oil spray (sunflower, safflower, or refined coconut)

Directions:

- Make the Cilantro Chutney and set it aside. In a large bowl, mash the potatoes well, using a potato masher or large fork. Add the oil, garlic, lime, cumin, onion, coriander, salt, turmeric, and cayenne. Stir very well until thoroughly combined. Set aside.
- Lay the tortillas out flat on the counter. In the middle of each, evenly distribute the potato filling. Add some of the garbanzo beans, cabbage, and red onion to each on top of the potatoes.
- Spray the air fryer basket with oil and set it aside. Enclose the Indian wraps by folding the bottom of the tortillas up and over the filling, then folding the sides

in—and finally rolling the bottom up to form, essentially, an enclosed burrito.

- Place the wraps in the air fryer basket, seam side down. They can touch each other a little bit, but if they're too crowded, you'll need to cook them in batches. Fry for 5 minutes at 360°F. Spray with oil again, flip over, and cook an additional 2 or 3 minutes until nicely browned and crisp. Serve topped with the Cilantro Chutney.

865. Greek Spinach Parcels

Preparation Time: 15 minutes
Cooking Time: 10 minutes
Servings: 2

Ingredients:
- 1 lb. baby spinach leaves; roughly chopped
- 4 sheets of filo pastry
- 1/2 lb. ricotta cheese
- 2 tbsp. pine nuts
- 1 egg; whisked
- Zest from 1 lemon; grated
- Greek yogurt for serving
- Salt and black pepper to the taste

Directions:
- In a bowl, mix spinach with cheese, egg, lemon zest, salt, pepper and pine nuts and stir.
- Arrange filo sheets on a working surface, divide spinach mix; fold diagonally to shape your parcels and place them in your preheated air fryer at 400°F. Bake parcels for 4 minutes; divide them into plates and serve them with Greek yogurt on the side.

866. Polenta Pie

Preparation Time: 15 minutes
Cooking Time: 55 minutes
Servings: 6

Ingredients:
- 1 Egg, slightly beaten
- 2 cups Water
- ¾ cup Monterey Jack cheese, w/ jalapeno peppers, shredded
- 3/4 cup Cornmeal
- ¼ tsp Salt
- 15-ounce chili beans, drained
- 1/3 cup Tortilla chips, crushed corn

Directions:
- Preheat the air fryer to 350°F.
- Mist cooking sprays onto a pie plate.
- In a saucepan heated on medium-high, combine water, salt, and cornmeal. Let the mixture boil, then cook on medium heat for six minutes. Stir in egg and let sit for five minutes.
- Pour cornmeal mixture into pie plate and spread evenly. Air-fry for fifteen minutes and top with beans, corn chips, and cheese. Air-fry for another twenty minutes.

867. Black Bean Burger with Garlic-Chipotle

Preparation Time: 30 minutes
Cooking Time: 20 minutes
Servings: 3

Ingredients:
- ½ cup corn kernels
- ½ tsp chipotle powder
- ½ tsp garlic powder
- ¾ cup salsa
- 1 ¼ tsp chili powder
- 1 ½ cup rolled oats
- 1 can of black beans, rinsed and drained
- 1 tbsp soy sauce

Directions:

In a mixing bowl, combine all Ingredients: and mix using your hands.
- Form small patties using your hands and set them aside.
- Brush patties with oil if desired.
- Place the grill pan in the air fryer and place the patties on the grill pan accessory.
- Close the lid and cook for 20 minutes on each side at 330°F.
- Halfway through the cooking time, flip the patties to brown the other side evenly

868. Spiced Veggie Burger

Preparation Time: 30 minutes
Cooking Time: 15 minutes
Servings: 6

Ingredients:
- ¼ cup desiccated coconut
- ½ cup oats
- ½ pound cauliflower, steamed and diced
- 1 cup bread crumbs
- 1 flax egg (1 flaxseed egg + 3 tbsp water)
- 1 tsp mustard powder
- 2 tsp chives
- 2 tsp coconut oil melted
- 2 tsp garlic, minced
- 2 tsp parsley
- 2 tsp thyme
- 3 tbsp plain flour
- salt and pepper to taste

Directions:
- Preheat the air fryer to 390°F.
- Place the cauliflower in a tea towel and ring out excess water. Place in a mixing bowl and add all ingredients except the bread crumbs.
- Mix well until well combined.
- Form 8 burger patties with the mixture using your hands.
- Roll the patties in bread crumbs and place them in the air fryer basket. Make sure that they do not overlap.
- Cook for 10 to 15 minutes or until the patties are crisp.

869. Basil and Garlic Crackers

Preparation Time: 10 minutes
Cooking Time: 30 minutes
Servings: 6

Ingredients:
- ¼ tsp dried basil powder
- ½ tsp baking powder
- 1 ¼ cups almond flour

- 1 clove of garlic, minced
- 3 tbsp coconut oil
- A pinch of cayenne pepper powder
- Salt and pepper to taste

Directions:
- Preheat the air fryer to 325°F for 5 minutes.
- Mix everything in a mixing bowl to create a dough.
- Transfer the dough to a clean and flat working surface and spread out until 2mm thick. Cut into squares.
- Place gently in the air fryer basket. Do this in batches if possible.
- Cook for 15 minutes at 325°F.

870.   Lamb Burgers

Preparation Time: 15 minutes
Cooking Time: 10 minutes
Servings: 6

Ingredients:
- 2 pounds of ground lamb
- 1 tbsp onion powder
- Salt and ground black pepper, as required

Directions:
- In a bowl, add all the ingredients and mix well.
- Make 6 equal-sized patties from the mixture.
- Arrange the patties onto a cooking tray.
- Arrange the drip pan in the bottom of the Air fryer Plus Air Fryer Oven cooking chamber.
- Select "Air Fry" and then adjust the temperature to 360°F.
- Set the timer for 8 minutes and press the "Start."
- When the display shows "Add Food," insert the cooking rack in the center position.
- When the display shows "Turn Food," turn the burgers.
- When cooking time is complete, remove the tray from the Air fryer and serve hot.

871.   Mexican Chicken Burgers

Preparation Time: 10 minutes
Cooking Time: 10 minutes
Serving: 6

Ingredients:
- 1 jalapeno pepper
- 1 tsp. cayenne pepper
- 1 tbsp. mustard powder
- 1 tbsp. oregano
- 1 tbsp. thyme
- 3 tbsp. smoked paprika
- 1 beaten egg
- 1 small head of cauliflower
- 4 chicken breasts

Directions:
- Ensure your air fryer oven is preheated to 350°F.
- Add seasonings to a blender. Slice cauliflower into florets and add to blender.
- Pulse till the mixture resembles that of breadcrumbs.
- Take out ¾ of the cauliflower mixture and add to a bowl. Set to the side. In another bowl, beat your egg and set it to the side.

- Remove skin and bones from chicken breasts and add to blender with remaining cauliflower mixture. Season with pepper and salt.
- Take out the mixture and form it into burger shapes. Roll each patty in cauliflower crumbs, then the egg, and back into bits again.
- Place coated patties into the Oven rack/basket. Place the rack on the middle shelf of the Air fryer oven. Set temperature to 350°F and set time to 10 minutes.
- Flip over at a 10-minute mark. They are done when crispy.

872.   Mixed Vegetable Chips

Preparation Time: 20 minutes
Cooking Time: 10 minutes
Servings: 4

Ingredients:
- 1 zucchini
- 1 sweet potato peeled
- 1/2 tsp pepper
- 1 red beet, peeled
- 1 large carrot
- 1 tsp salt
- 1 tsp Italian seasoning
- A pinch of cumin powders

Directions:
- Preheat the air fryer in Dehydrate mode at 110°F for 2 to 3 minutes.
- Meanwhile, use a mandolin slicer to thinly slice all the vegetables and transfer them to a medium bowl. Season with salt, Italian seasoning, and cumin powder.
- In batches, arrange some of the vegetables in a single layer on the cooking tray.
- When the device is ready, slide the cooking tray onto the top rack of the oven and close the oven
- Set the timer to 7 or 9 minutes and press Start. Cook until the vegetables are crispy.
- Transfer the vegetables to serving bowls when ready and make the remaining in the same manner. Enjoy.

873.   Chocolate Banana Chips

Preparation Time: 5 minutes
Cooking Time: 7-10 minutes
Servings: 4

Ingredients:
- 5 large firm bananas, peeled
- ¼ tsp cocoa powder
- A pinch of cinnamon powder

Directions:
- Preheat the air fryer in Dehydrate mode at 110°F for 2 to 3 minutes.
- Meanwhile, use a mandolin slicer to thinly slice the bananas and coat them well with the cocoa powder and the cinnamon powder.
- In batches, arrange as many banana slices as possible in a single layer on the cooking tray.
- When the device is ready, slide the cooking tray onto the top rack of the oven and close the oven
- Set the timer to 7 minutes and press Start. Cook until the banana pieces are crispy.

- Transfer the chips to serving bowls when ready and make the remaining in the same manner. Enjoy.

874. Healthy Turkey Lettuce Wraps

Preparation Time: 15 minutes
Cooking Time: 10 minutes
Servings: 4
- **Ingredients**
- 250g ground turkey
- 1/2 small onion, finely chopped
- 1 garlic clove, minced
- 2 tbsp extra virgin olive oil
- 1 head lettuce
- 1 tsp cumin
- 1/2 tbsp fresh ginger, sliced
- 2 tbsp apple cider vinegar
- 2 tbsp freshly chopped cilantro
- 1 tsp freshly ground black pepper
- 1 tsp sea salt
- **Directions**
- Sauté garlic and onion in extra virgin olive oil until fragrant and translucent in your air fryer toast oven pan at 350°F.
- Add turkey and cook well for 5-8 minutes or until done to desire.
- Add in the remaining ingredients and continue cooking for 5 minutes more.
- To serve, ladle a spoonful of turkey mixture onto a lettuce leaf and wrap. Enjoy!

875. Ranch Pretzels

Preparation Time: 10 minutes
Cooking Time: 15 minutes
Servings: 4

Ingredients:
- 2 cups pretzels
- ½ tsp garlic powder
- 1 ½ tsp ranch dressing mix
- 1 tbsp melted butter

Directions:
- Preheat the oven in Air Fryer mode at 270°F for 2 to 3 minutes.
- In a medium bowl, mix all the ingredients until well combined, pour into the rotisserie basket and close to seal.
- Fix the basket onto the lever in the oven and close the oven.
- Set the timer to 15 minutes, press Start and cook until the pretzels are lightly browner.
- After, open the oven, take out the basket using the rotisserie lift and transfer the snack into serving bowls.
- Allow cooling and enjoy.

876. Dehydrated Strawberries

Preparation Time: 10 minutes
Cooking Time: 7-10 minutes
Servings: 4

Ingredients:
- 1 lb. large strawberries

Directions:
- Preheat the air fryer in Dehydrate mode at 110°F for 2 to 3 minutes.
- Meanwhile, use a mandolin slicer to thinly slice the strawberries.
- In batches, arrange some of the strawberry slices in a single layer on the cooking tray.
- When the device is ready, slide the cooking tray onto the top rack of the oven and close the oven
- Set the timer to 7 minutes and press Start. Cook until the fruits are crispy.
- Transfer the fruit chips to serving bowls when ready and make the remaining in the same manner. Enjoy.

877. Chili Cheese Sandwich

Preparation Time: 10 minutes
Cooking Time: 8 minutes
Servings: 3

Ingredients:
- 6 slices of sandwich bread
- 4 tbsp butter
- 1 cup grated cheddar cheese
- 2 small fresh red chilies, deseeded and minced
- ½ tsp salt
- 1 tsp garlic powder
- 1 tsp red chili flakes
- 1 tbsp chopped fresh parsley

Directions:
- Preheat the oven in Broil mode at 375°F for 2 to 3 minutes.
- Spread the butter on one side of each bread slice and lay it on a clean, flat surface.
- Divide the cheddar cheese on top and follow with the remaining ingredients.
- Lay 3 pieces of the bread on the cooking tray, slide the tray onto the middle rack of the oven and close the oven.
- Set the timer for 3 to 4 minutes and press Start. Cook until the cheese melts and is golden brown on top.
- Remove the first batch when ready and prepare the other three bread pieces.
- Slice them into triangle halves and serve immediately.

878. Cranberry Spinach Turnovers

Preparation Time: 20 minutes
Cooking Time: 12 minutes
Servings: 6

Ingredients:
- 4 ounces cream cheese, at room temperature
- 2 tbsp sour cream
- 1 cup frozen chopped spinach, thawed and drained
- ⅓ cup dried cranberries, chopped
- 3 (9-by-14-inch) sheets of frozen phyllo dough, thawed
- 3 tbsp butter, melted

Directions:
- In a medium bowl, beat the cream cheese and sour cream until blended. Stir in the spinach and cranberries until well mixed. Set aside.

- Place the phyllo dough on the work surface and cover it with a damp towel. Remove one sheet of phyllo and cut it into four 3½-by-9-inch rectangles.
- Place a tbsp of the filling at the bottom of one of the rectangles, with the short side facing you. Fold the phyllo into triangles (like you would fold a flag), then brush with butter to seal the edges. Repeat with remaining phyllo, filling, and butter.
- Set or preheat the air fryer to 375°F. Put 4 to 6 triangles in the air fryer basket in a single layer. Put the basket in the air fryer and bake for 11 to 12 minutes or until the triangles are golden brown, turning over halfway through cooking time. Repeat with the remaining turnovers. Serve.

879.   Mushroom Toast with Ginger and Sesame

Preparation Time: 20 minutes
Cooking Time: 8 minutes
Servings: 4

Ingredients:
- 2 tsp olive oil
- 2 (4-ounce) cans of sliced mushrooms, drained
- 3 scallions, sliced
- 1 tbsp grated fresh ginger
- 1 tbsp soy sauce
- 3 slices of whole-wheat bread
- 2 tbsp sesame seeds

Directions:
- Heat the olive oil in a medium saucepan over medium heat. Add the mushrooms and cook, often stirring, for 3 to 4 minutes or until the mushrooms are dry.
- Add the scallions, ginger, and soy sauce and cook for another 3 minutes or until the mushrooms have absorbed the soy sauce.
- Transfer the mixture to a blender or food processor and process until it forms a paste.
- Cut the bread slices into fourths, making triangles. Spread the mushroom mixture onto the bread triangles, dividing evenly, then sprinkle with the sesame seeds.
- Set or preheat the air fryer to 375°F. Working in batches, place the triangles in the air fryer basket in a single layer. Fry for 7 to 8 minutes or until the toast is crisp. Repeat with the remaining triangles. Serve.

880.   Thai Style Pizza

Preparation Time: 15 minutes
Cooking Time: 20 minutes
Servings: 4

Ingredients:
- 8 ounces frozen pizza dough, thawed, or Pizza Dough
- ⅓ cup peanut butter
- 3 tbsp vegetable broth
- 1 tbsp soy sauce
- 1 tbsp sesame oil
- 2 tsp chili sauce
- ¼ tsp garlic powder
- 1 cup sliced shiitake mushrooms
- ⅔ cup shredded carrots
- 1 yellow bell pepper, thinly sliced
- ¼ cup chopped salted peanuts
- 3 scallions, sliced

Directions:
- Cut out two rounds of parchment paper that fit into the air fryer basket. Divide the pizza dough in half and roll out each directly onto a round of paper. Place one round in the basket.
- In a small bowl, whisk together the peanut butter, broth, soy sauce, sesame oil, chili sauce, and garlic powder. Drizzle half this mixture over the dough in the basket.
- Top the pizza with half of the mushrooms, carrots, bell pepper, peanuts, and scallions. Place the basket in the air fryer.
- Set or preheat the air fryer to 400°F. Bake for 7 to 10 minutes or until the crust is crisp and the toppings are hot. Remove from the air fryer and place on a wire rack.
- Repeat with the remaining dough, sauce, and toppings. Cut the pizzas into wedges and serve.

881.   Green Tomato BLT

Preparation Time: 30 minutes
Cooking Time: 30 minutes
Servings: 4

Ingredients:
- 2 medium green tomatoes (about 10 oz)
- ¼ tsp pepper
- ½ tsp salt
- 1 cup panko (Japanese) bread crumbs
- ¼ cup all-purpose flour
- 1 large egg, beaten
- 2 green onions, finely chopped
- 1 tsp snipped fresh dill or ¼ tsp dill weed
- ½ cup reduced-fat mayonnaise
- 8 slices of whole-wheat bread, toasted
- 8 cooked center-cut bacon strips
- 4 Bibb or Boston lettuce leaves

Directions:
- Ensure that your air fryer is preheated to 350°F and spray the basket with some cooking spray.
- Make eight slices out of your tomato, each slice with a thickness of ¼ inch. Finally, sprinkle salt and pepper on the tomato slices.
- Get three separate shallow bowls and place the bread, flour, and egg in each. Dip the tomato slices in the flour, and shake to re-move excess, then into the egg, and finally the crumb mixture.
- You may divide the slices into batches.
- Place the tomato slices in the air fryer bas-ket to form a single layer, then spray with cooking spray.
- Allow to cook for about 8-12 minutes, turning halfway, and spritzing with addi-tional cooking spray. Remove when the golden-brown color is consistent, and keep warm. Do the same for the other tomato slices.
- While cooking the tomato slices, make a mixture of green onions, dill, and mayonnaise. On each of the four slices of bread lay two bacon strips, one lettuce, and two tomato slices in it. Then spread the mayonnaise mixture over the remaining slices of bread, and place over the top.
- Serve immediately.

882.   Cheese-stuffed Burgers

Preparation Time: 20 minutes
Cooking Time: 35 minutes
Servings: 4

Ingredients:

- 2 green onions, thinly sliced
- 2 tbsp minced fresh parsley
- ¼ cup cheddar cheese, cubed
- 3 tsp Dijon mustard, divided
- 2 tbsp ketchup & ½ tsp salt
- ½ tsp rosemary, dried and crushed
- ¼ tsp sage leaves, dried
- 3 tbsp dry bread crumbs
- 1 lb. lean ground beef (90% lean)
- 4 hamburger buns, split
- Optional toppings:
- lettuce leaves and tomato slices

Directions:

- Ensure that your air fryer is preheated to 375°F.
- Get a small bowl, and in it, make a mixture of green onions, parsley, cheddar cheese, and one tsp mustard.
- Get another clean bowl and make a mix-ture of ketchup, unused mustard, season-ings, breadcrumbs, and beef. Mix thoroughly but lightly.
- Portion the mixture into eight thin pat-ties. Using a spoon, add a little out of the cheese mix to the center of the four pat-ties. Top with the remaining patties while pressing edges together firmly to seal completely.
- Transfer the burger into the air fryer bas-ket, arranging them in a single layer. If you have several burgers, you may work in batches.
- Air fry each batch for 10 minutes, then flip and continue cooking for about 8-10 minutes again (until you have a reading of 160°F on your instant-read thermometer).

883.   Flax Mozza Wraps

Preparation Time: 10 minutes
Cooking Time: 5 minutes
Servings: 2

Ingredients:

- 1 cucumber
- 1 egg
- 3 oz. flax seeds
- 3 oz. mozzarella, grated
- 1 tbsp water
- ½ tbsp butter
- ¼ tsp baking soda
- ¼ tsp salt

Directions:

- Crack the egg into a bowl and whisk it.
- Sprinkle the whisked egg with the flax seeds, grated mozzarella, water, baking soda, and salt.
- Whisk the mixture.
- Preheat the air fryer to 360°F.
- Toss the butter in the air fryer basket and melt it.
- Separate the egg liquid into 2 servings.
- Pour the first part of the serving into the air fryer basket.
- Cook it for 1 minute on one side.
- Turnover and cook for another minute.

- Repeat the same steps with the remaining egg mixture.
- Cut the cucumber into cubes.
- Separate the cubed cucumber into 2 parts.
- Place the cucumber cubes in the center of each egg pancake.
- Wrap the eggs.

884.   Chives and Lamb Burgers

Preparation Time: 20 minutes
Cooking Time: 25-30 minutes
Servings: 2

Ingredients:

- 1-pound ground lamb
- 3 oz chive stems
- 1 tsp minced garlic
- 1 tsp salt
- ½ tsp chili pepper
- 1 tsp ground black pepper
- 1 large egg
- 2 tbsp coconut flour
- 1 tsp olive oil

Directions:

- Combine the ground lamb with the diced chives.
- Stir carefully and sprinkle the mixture with minced garlic and salt.
- Add chili pepper, ground black pepper, and coconut flour.
- Crack the egg into the mixture and mix with your hands.
- Place the mixture in the fridge for 10 minutes.
- Meanwhile, preheat the air fryer to 400°F.
- Make 6 large balls from the ground lamb mixture and flatten them to make the shape of a burger patty.
- Place the burgers in the air fryer rack and drizzle them with olive oil. Cook for 6 minutes.
- Turn them using a spatula. Cook the lamb burgers for 3 minutes.

885.   Kohlrabi Chips

Preparation Time: 7 minutes
Cooking Time: 20 minutes
Servings: 10

Ingredients:

- 1-pound kohlrabi
- 1 tsp salt
- 1 tbsp sesame oil
- 1 tsp smoked paprika

Directions:

- Peel the kohlrabi.
- Slice it into thin pieces.
- Sprinkle the kohlrabi slices with salt, smoked paprika, and sesame oil.
- Shake the mixture.
- Preheat the air fryer to 320°F.
- Put the kohlrabi slices in the air fryer rack and cook for 20 minutes.
- Stir during cooking.
- Cool before serving.

886. Sourdough Bread

Preparation Time: 20 minutes
Cooking Time: 20 minutes
Servings: 8

Ingredients:
- 1 cup sourdough starter
- 1 cup unbleached all-purpose flour
- ¼ cup whole-wheat flour
- 1 tbsp white sugar
- ½ tsp salt
- 1 tbsp canola oil

Directions:
- In the baking pan of a bread machine, place all the ingredients in the order recommended by the manufacturer.
- Place the baking pan in the bread machine and close with the lid.
- Select the Dough cycle and press the Start button.
- Once the cycle is completed, remove the paddles from the bread machine but keep the dough inside for about 4 hours to proof.
- Now, transfer the dough into a floured proofing basket and set it aside to rise for about 3 hours.
- Set the temperature of the air fryer to 390°F.
- Carefully arrange the dough onto the grill insert of an air fryer.
- Air fry for about 20 minutes, turning the pan once halfway through.
- Remove the bread from the air fryer and place it onto a wire rack for about 2-3 hours before slicing.
- Cut the bread into desired size slices and serve.

887. BBQ Vegetable Sandwich

Preparation Time: 15 minutes
Cooking Time: 30 minutes
Servings: 2

Ingredients:
- For Barbecue Sauce:
- 1 tsp olive oil
- 1 garlic clove, minced
- ¼ of onion, chopped
- ½ cup water
- ½ tbsp sugar
- ½ tbsp Worcestershire sauce
- ¼ tsp mustard powder
- 1½ tbsp tomato ketchup
- Salt and ground black pepper, as needed
- For Sandwich:
- 2 tbsp butter, softened
- 1 cup sweet corn kernels
- 1 roasted green bell pepper, chopped
- 4 bread slices, trimmed and cut horizontally

Directions:
- For the barbecue sauce: In a medium skillet, heat the oil over medium heat and sauté the garlic and onion for about 3-5 minutes.
- Stir in the remaining ingredients and bring to a boil over high heat.
- Reduce the heat to medium and simmer for about 8-10 minutes or until desired thickness.
- For the sandwich: in a skillet, melt the butter on medium heat and stir fry the corn for about 1-2 minutes.
- In a bowl, mix together the barbecue sauce, corn, and bell pepper.
- Spread the corn mixture on one side of 2 bread slices.
- Top with the remaining slices.
- Set the temperature of the Air Fryer to 355°F.
- Place the sandwiches in an Air Fryer basket in a single layer.
- Air Fry for about 5-6 minutes.

888. Fruit Soft Tacos

Preparation Time: 10 minutes
Cooking Time: 5 minutes
Servings: 2

Ingredients:
- 2 soft shell tortillas
- 4 tbsp strawberry jelly
- ¼ cup blueberries
- ¼ cup raspberries
- 2 tbsp powdered sugar

Directions:
- Set the temperature of the air fryer to 300°F. Lightly grease an air fryer basket.
- Arrange the tortillas onto a smooth surface.
- Spread 2 tbsp of strawberry jelly over each tortilla and top each with berries.
- Sprinkle each with the powdered sugar.
- Arrange tortillas into the prepared air fryer basket.
- Air fry for about 5 minutes or until crispy.
- Remove from the air fryer and transfer the tortillas onto a platter.
- Serve warm.

889. Hummus Mushroom Pizza

Preparation Time: 20 minutes
Cooking Time: 6-10 minutes
Servings: 4

Ingredients:
- 4 Portobello mushroom caps, stemmed and gills removed
- 1 tbsp balsamic vinegar
- Salt and ground black pepper, as required
- 4 tbsp pasta sauce
- 1 garlic clove, minced
- 3 ounces zucchini, shredded
- 2 tbsp sweet red pepper, seeded and chopped
- 4 Kalamata olives, sliced
- 1 tsp dried basil
- ½ cup hummus

Directions:
- Coat both sides of each mushroom cap with vinegar.
- Now, sprinkle the inside of each mushroom cap with salt and black pepper.
- Place one tbsp of pasta sauce inside each mushroom and sprinkle with garlic.
- Set the temperature of the air fryer to 330°F. Grease an air fryer basket.
- Arrange mushroom caps into the prepared air fryer basket.

- Air fry for about 3 minutes.
- Remove from the air fryer and top each mushroom cap with zucchini, peppers and olives.
- Then, sprinkle with basil, salt, and black pepper.
- Place back mushroom caps into the air fryer basket.
- Air fry for about 3 more minutes.
- Remove from the air fryer and transfer the mushrooms onto a serving platter.
- Top each mushroom pizza with hummus and serve.

890.   Burger Taco Wrap

Preparation Time: 15 minutes
Cooking Time: 5 minutes
Servings: 6

Ingredients:
- 6 (12-inch) flour tortillas
- 2 pounds cooked ground beef
- 12 ounces of nacho cheese
- 6 tostadas
- 2 cups sour cream
- 2 cups Bibb lettuce, shredded
- 3 Roma tomatoes, sliced
- 2 cups Mexican blend cheese, shredded
- Olive oil cooking spray

Directions:
- Arrange the tortillas onto a smooth surface.
- Divide each ingredient into 6 portions.
- Place 1 portion of beef in the center of each tortilla, followed by the nacho cheese, tostada, sour cream, lettuce, tomato slices and Mexican cheese.
- Bring the edges of each tortilla up over the center to look like a pinwheel.
- Set the temperature of the Air Fryer to 400°F. Grease an Air Fryer basket.
- Arrange taco wraps into the prepared Air Fryer basket, seam side down and spray each with cooking spray.
- Air Fry for about 2 minutes.
- Carefully flip the wraps and spray each with cooking spray again.
- Air Fry for about 2 more minutes.
- Remove from Air Fryer and transfer the wraps onto a platter.

891.   Smoky Cheeseburgers

Preparation Time: 20 minutes
Cooking Time: 10 minutes
Servings: 4

Ingredients:
- 1-pound ground beef
- 1 tbsp Worcestershire sauce
- 1 tsp Maggi seasoning sauce
- 3-4 drops of liquid smoke
- 1 tsp dried parsley
- ½ tsp garlic powder
- ½ tsp onion powder
- Salt and ground black pepper, as required
- Olive oil cooking spray
- 4 whole-wheat hamburger buns, split and toasted

Directions:
- In a large bowl, mix together the beef, sauces, liquid smoke, parsley, and spices.
- Make 4 equal-sized patties from the mixture.
- Set the temperature of the Air Fryer to 350°F. Grease an Air Fryer pan.
- Arrange patties into the prepared pan in a single layer.
- Using your thumb, make an indent in the center of each patty and spray with cooking spray.
- Air Fry for about 10 minutes.
- Remove patties from the Air Fryer.
- Serve hot on a bun with your favorite side dishes.

892.   Cinnamon Roasted Chickpeas

Preparation Time: 5 minutes
Cooking Time: 10 minutes
Servings: 2

Ingredients:
- 1 tbsp. sweetener
- 1 tbsp. cinnamon
- 1 cup chickpeas

Directions:
- Preheat the air fryer oven to 390°F.
- Rinse and drain chickpeas.
- Mix all ingredients together and add to the air fryer.
- Pour into the Oven rack/basket. Place the rack on the middle shelf of the Air fryer oven. Set temperature to 390°F, and set time to 10 minutes.

893.   Taco Bell Crunch Wrap

Preparation Time: 20 minutes
Cooking Time: 5-10 minutes
Servings: 6

Ingredients:
- 6 wheat tostadas
- 2 cups sour cream
- 2 cups Mexican blend cheese
- 2 cups shredded lettuce
- 12 ounces of low-sodium nacho cheese
- 3 Roma tomatoes
- 6 12-inch wheat tortillas
- 1 1/3 cups water
- 2 packets of low-sodium taco seasoning
- 2 pounds of lean ground beef

Directions:
- Ensure your air fryer is preheated to 400°F.
- Make beef according to taco seasoning packets.
- Place 2/3 C. prepared beef, 4 tbsp. Cheese, 1 tostada, 1/3 C. sour cream, 1/3 C. lettuce, 1/6th of tomatoes and 1/3 C. cheese on each tortilla.
- Fold up tortillas' edges and repeat with remaining ingredients.
- Lay the folded sides of tortillas down into the air fryer and spray with olive oil.
- Set temperature to 400°F, and set time to 2 minutes. Cook 2 minutes till browned.

894. Brussel Sprout Pizza

Preparation Time: 10 minutes
Cooking Time: 30 minutes
Servings: 4

Ingredients:
- 9 slices of pancetta
- 2 tsp. extra-virgin olive oil
- 2 cloves of garlic, minced
- Brussels sprouts, trimmed and thinly sliced
- 1½-inch pizza crust
- ½ tsp. fennel seed
- ½ tbsp. cheese

Directions:
- Place 1 tsp of olive oil in the inner pot with pancetta and set to Sauté mode for 5 minutes. Transfer pancetta to a plate lined with a paper towel.
- Pour the remaining oil and sauté garlic until fragrant for about 20 seconds and add the sprouts. Continue cooking for 5-10 minutes more until the sprouts turn brown. Transfer sprouts with garlic to a bowl and adds pancetta to the mixture. Add cheese and fennel seed to the bowl of sprouts and toss to coat.
- Line the air fryer with parchment paper and place the pizza crust at the bottom. Spread the Brussels sprout mixture to fill in the crust.
- Place the air fryer to the air fryer duo crust and attach the air fryer lid.
- Bake at 400°F for 10-15 minutes or until cheese is melted.
- Slice to serve.

895. Tofu Crunch Wraps

Preparation Time: 10 minutes
Cooking Time: 15 minutes
Servings: 2

Ingredients:
- 2 servings tofu scramble (or vegan egg)
- 2 large flour tortillas
- 2 small corn tortillas
- ⅓ cup pinto beans, cooked
- ½ cup classic ranchero sauce
- ½ avocado, peeled and sliced
- 2 fresh jalapeños, stemmed and sliced

Directions:
- Assemble the large tortillas on a work surface. Arrange the crunch wraps by stacking the following ingredients in order: tofu or egg scramble, jalapeños, ranchero sauce, corn tortillas, avocado, and pinto beans. You can add more ranchero sauce if desired.
- Fold the large flour tortilla around the fillings until sealed completely.
- Place one crunch wrap in the air fryer basket and set the basket on top of the trivet.
- Air-fry each crunch wrap at 350°F (or 180°C) for 6 minutes. Remove from the basket and transfer to a plate.
- Repeat steps 3 and 4 for the other crunch wrap.

896. Chili Cheese Dogs

Preparation Time: 15 minutes
Cooking Time: 15 minutes
Servings: 4

Ingredients:
- 4 hot dogs
- Spray oil
- 1 cup of chili
- 4 hot dog buns
- ½ cup of shredded cheddar cheese

Directions:
- Spritz the hot dogs with spray oil and then place them in the air fryer basket.
- Cook the hot dogs for 8-10 minutes at 380°F until hot through and just crisp on the outside. Flip the hot dogs over halfway through cooking and spritz with a little more spray oil if desired.
- While the hot dogs cook, reheat the chili either using a microwave or in a pan on the stovetop.
- Arrange a cooked hot dog inside each bun, top with a ¼ cup of warm chili, and sprinkle with cheddar cheese.
- Serve straight away.

897. Chicken Jerky

Preparation Time: 10 minutes
Cooking Time: 7 hrs.
Servings: 4

Ingredients:
- 1 1/2 lb chicken tenders, boneless, skinless and cut into 1/4-inch strips
- 1/2 tsp garlic powder
- 1 tsp lemon juice
- 1/2 cup soy sauce
- 1/4 tsp ground ginger
- 1/4 tsp black pepper

Directions:
- Mix all ingredients except chicken into the zip-lock bag. Add chicken and seal bag and place in the refrigerator for 30 minutes.
- Arrange marinated meat slices on the dehydrate basket in a single layer.
- Insert wire rack in rack position 4. Select DEHYDRATE, set temperature 145°F, timer for 7 hours. Press start.
- Dehydrate meat slices for 7 hours.

898. Mushroom Chips

Preparation Time: 10 minutes
Cooking Time: 5 hrs.
Servings: 3

Ingredients:
- 1 cup mushrooms, clean and cut into 1/8-inch thick slices
- Salt

Directions:
- Arrange mushroom slices on the dehydrate basket in a single layer. Season with salt.

- Insert wire rack in rack position 4. Select DEHYDRATE, set temperature 160°F, timer for 5 hours. Press start.
- Dehydrate mushroom slices for 5 hours.

899. Pear Chips

Preparation Time: 10 minutes
Cooking Time: 5 hrs.
Servings: 4

Ingredients:

- 2 pears, cut into 1/4-inch thick slices

Directions:

- Arrange pear slices on the dehydrate basket in a single layer.
- Insert wire rack in rack position 4. Select DEHYDRATE, set temperature 160°F, timer for 5 hours. Press start.
- Dehydrate pear slices for 5 hours.

900. Honey Mango Slices

Preparation Time: 10 minutes
Cooking Time: 12 hours
Servings: 6

Ingredients:

- 4 mangoes, peel and cut into ¼-inch slices
- 1/4 cup fresh lemon juice
- 1 tbsp honey

Directions:

- In a big bowl, combine together honey and lemon juice and set aside.
- Add mango slices to the lemon-honey mixture and coat well.
- Arrange mango slices on the air fryer rack and dehydrate at 135°F for 12 hours.

901. Dried Pineapple Chunks

Preparation Time: 10 minutes
Cooking Time: 12 hrs.
Servings: 2

Ingredients:

- 1 cup pineapple chunks

Directions:

- Arrange pineapple chunks on the dehydrate basket in a single layer.
- Insert wire rack in rack position 4. Select DEHYDRATE, set temperature 135°F, timer for 12 hours. Press start.
- Dehydrate pineapple chunks for 12 hours.

902. Dried Dragon Fruit Chips

Preparation Time: 10 minutes
Cooking Time: 12 hrs.
Servings: 4

Ingredients:

- 2 dragon fruit, peel & cut into 1/4-inch thick slices

Directions:

- Arrange dragon fruit slices on the dehydrate basket in a single layer.
- Insert wire rack in rack position 4. Select DEHYDRATE, set temperature 115°F, timer for 12 hours. Press start.
- Dehydrate dragon fruit slices for 12 hours.

903. Candied Pecans

Preparation Time: 10 minutes
Cooking Time: 30 minutes
Servings: 2

Ingredients:

- 1 cup pecan halves, soaked in water overnight
- 6 tbsp maple syrup
- Pinch of cinnamon

Directions:

- In a bowl, toss pecan with maple syrup and cinnamon and arrange on the dehydrate basket.
- Insert wire rack in rack position 4. Select DEHYDRATE, set temperature 105°F, timer for 25 minutes. Press start.

904. Meatloaf Wraps

Preparation Time: 15minutes
Cooking Time: 10 minutes
Servings: 4

Ingredients:

- 1-pound ground beef, grass-fed
- ½ cup almond flour
- ¼ cup coconut flour
- ½ tbsp minced garlic
- ¼ cup chopped white onion
- 1 tsp Italian seasoning
- ½ tsp sea salt
- ½ tsp dried tarragon
- ½ tsp ground black pepper
- 1 tbsp Worcestershire sauce
- ¼ cup ketchup
- 2 eggs, pastured, beaten

Directions:

- Place all the ingredients in a bowl, stir well, then shape the mixture into 2-inch diameter and 1-inch thick patties and refrigerate them for 10 minutes.
- Meanwhile, switch on the air fryer, insert the fryer basket, grease it with olive oil, then shut its lid, set the fryer at 360°F and preheat for 10 minutes.
- Open the fryer, add patties in it in a single layer, close with its lid and cook for 10 minutes until nicely golden and cooked, flipping the patties halfway through the frying.
- When the air fryer beeps, open its lid and transfer patties to a plate.
- Wrap each patty in lettuce and serve.

905. Shrimp Grilled Cheese Sandwich

Preparation Time: 10 minutes
Cooking Time: 5 minutes
Servings: 2

Ingredients:
- 1¼ cups shredded Colby, Cheddar, or Havarti cheese
- 1 (6-ounce) can of tiny shrimp, drained
- 3 tbsp mayonnaise
- 2 tbsp minced green onion
- 4 slices of whole-grain or whole-wheat bread
- 2 tbsp softened butter

Directions:
- In a medium bowl, combine the cheese, shrimp, mayonnaise, and green onion, and mix well.
- Spread this mixture on two slices of bread. Top with the other slices of bread to make 2 sandwiches. Spread the sandwiches lightly with butter.
- Grill in the air fryer for 5 to 7 minutes at 375°F or until the bread is browned and crisp, and the cheese is melted. Cut in half and serve warm.

906.   Fried Pork Quesadilla

Preparation Time: 20 minutes
Cooking Time: 25-30 minutes
Servings: 2

Ingredients:
- 2 6-inch corn or flour tortilla shells
- 1 medium-sized pork shoulder, approximately 4 ounces, sliced
- ½ medium-sized white onion, sliced
- ½ medium-sized red pepper, sliced
- ½ medium-sized green pepper, sliced
- ½ medium-sized yellow pepper, sliced
- ¼ cup of shredded pepper-jack cheese
- ¼ cup of shredded mozzarella cheese

Directions:
- Preparing the ingredients. Preheat the Air Fryer to 350°F. Close air fryer lid and select broil; set time to 20 minutes. Grill the pork, onion, and peppers in foil in the same pan, allowing the moisture from the vegetables and the juice from the pork to mingle together. After 20 minutes, remove pork and vegetables in foil. While they're cooling, sprinkle half the shredded cheese over one of the tortillas, then cover with the pieces of pork, onions, and peppers, and then layer on the rest of the shredded cheese. Top with the second tortilla. Place directly on the hot surface of the Air Fryer basket.
- Air frying. Lock the air fryer lid. Set the Air Fryer timer for 6 minutes. After 6 minutes, when the Air Fryer shuts off, flip the tortillas onto the other side with a spatula; the cheese should be melted enough that it won't fall apart, but be careful anyway not to spill any toppings!
- Reset the Air Fryer to 350°F for another 6 minutes.
- After 6 minutes, when the Air Fryer shuts off, the tortillas should be browned and crisp, and the pork, onion, peppers and cheese will be crispy and hot and delicious. Remove with tongs and let sit on a serving plate to cool for a few minutes before slicing.

907.   Spicy Shrimp Pizza

Preparation Time: 15 minutes
Cooking Time: 20 minutes
Servings: 8

Ingredients:
- ¼ cup Cilantro leaves, fresh, chopped

- 1 tbsp Sesame oil, toasted
- 1 cup Carrots, shredded
- 1 tbsp Soy sauce
- 0.5 Avocado, peeled, sliced thinly, sliced into thirds
- 11 ounces of Pizza crust, thin, refrigerated
- 20 pieces of Shrimp, medium, peeled, deveined, tail shells removed, uncooked
- 2 cups Mozzarella cheese, shredded
- 2 Green onions, thinly sliced, greens & whites separated
- 1 tbsp Sriracha sauce

Directions:
- Preheat the air fryer to 375°F.
- Mist cooking sprays onto cookie sheet. Press unrolled dough onto sheet and coat with sesame oil. Air-fry for eight to ten minutes.
- Toss shrimp with soy sauce.
- Spread on top of the crust the following: cheese (1 cup), carrots, green onion whites, shrimp mixture, and cheese (1 cup).
- Air-fry for seven to eleven minutes. Serve topped with avocado, cilantro, and green onion greens, then drizzled with sriracha.

908.   All Meat Pizza

Preparation Time: 15 minutes
Cooking Time: 15 minutes
Servings: 6

Ingredients:
- 1 (7-inch) pizza pie crust defrosted if necessary.
- 1/3 cup of marinara sauce.
- 2 ounces of grilled steak, sliced into bite-sized pieces
- 2 ounces of salami, sliced fine
- 2 ounces of pepperoni, sliced fine
- ¼ cup of American cheese
- ¼ cup of shredded mozzarella cheese

Directions:
- Preheat the air fryer oven to 350°F. Lay the pizza dough flat on a sheet of parchment paper or tin foil, cut large enough to hold the entire pie crust but small enough that it will leave the edges of the air frying basket uncovered to allow for air circulation. Using a fork, stab the pizza dough several times across the surface – piercing the pie crust will allow air to circulate throughout the crust and ensure even cooking. With a deep soup spoon, ladle the marinara sauce onto the pizza dough, and spread evenly in expanding circles over the surface of the pie crust. Be sure to leave at least ½ inch of bare dough around the edges to ensure that extra-crispy crunchy first bite of the crust! Distribute the pieces of steak and the slices of salami and pepperoni evenly over the sauce-covered dough, then sprinkle the cheese in an even layer on top.
- Set the air fryer timer to 12 minutes and place the pizza with foil or paper on the fryer's basket surface. Again, be sure to leave the edges of the basket uncovered to allow for proper air circulation, and don't let your bare fingers touch the hot surface. After 12 minutes, when the air fryer oven shuts off, the cheese should be perfectly melted and lightly crisped, and the pie crust should be golden brown. Using a spatula – or two, if necessary, remove the pizza from the air fryer basket and set it on a serving plate. Wait a few minutes until

the pie is cool enough to handle, then cut into slices and serve.

909. Waffle Cheese Fries

Preparation Time: 10 minutes
Cooking Time: 20 minutes
Servings: 4

Ingredients:
- 1 cup Swiss cheese, shredded
- 2 cups frozen waffle fries
- 2 green onions, sliced
- 2 tsp olive oil
- 1 red bell pepper, chopped
- ½ cup bottled chicken gravy

Directions:
- In a bowl, combine the waffle fries with olive oil. Toss well.
- Arrange the waffle fries in the air fryer basket. Put the air fryer lid on and air fry in the preheated air fryer at 375°F for 10 to 12 minutes. Shake the basket once when it shows 'TURN FOOD' on the air fryer lid screen during cooking time.
- Transfer the fries to a 6×6×2-inch baking pan and sprinkle the pepper, green onions and cheese on top. Put the pan into the air fryer basket and put the air fryer lid on. Air fry for 3 minutes until the vegetables are tender.
- Remove the pan from the basket and pour the gravy over the fries. Return the pan to the basket and air fry for 2 minutes more or until the gravy is hot.
- Allow cooling for 5 minutes before serving.

910. Creole Jalapeno Coins

Preparation Time: 10 minutes
Cooking Time: 5 minutes
Servings: 2

Ingredients:
- 1 egg
- 2-3 tbsp coconut flour
- 1 sliced and seeded jalapeno
- Pinch of garlic powder
- Pinch of onion powder
- Pinch of Cajun seasoning (optional)
- Pinch of pepper and salt

Directions:
- Preparing the Ingredients. Ensure your Air Fryer is preheated to 400°F.
- Mix together all dry ingredients.
- Pat jalapeno slices dry. Dip coins into the egg wash and then into the dry mixture. Toss to thoroughly coat.
- Add coated jalapeno slices to Air Fryer in a singular layer. Spray with olive oil.
- Air Frying. Lock the air fryer lid. Set temperature to 350°F, and set time to 5 minutes. Cook just till crispy.

911. Apple Turkey Burgers

Preparation Time: 5 minutes
Cooking Time: 30 minutes
Servings: 8

Ingredients:
- 1 pound ground turkey 85% lean / 15% fat
- ¼ cup unsweetened apple sauce
- ½ onion grated
- 1 tbsp ranch seasoning
- 2 tsp Worcestershire Sauce
- 1 tsp minced garlic
- ¼ cup plain breadcrumbs
- Salt and pepper to taste

Directions:
- Combine the onion, ground turkey, unsweetened apple sauce, minced garlic, breadcrumbs, ranch seasoning, Worchester sauce, and salt and pepper. Mix them with your hands until well combined. Form 4 equally sized hamburger patties with them.
- Place these burgers in the refrigerator for about 30 minutes to firm up a bit.
- While preparing for cooking, select the Air Fry option. Set the temperature to 360°F and the cooking time as required. Press start to begin preheating.
- Once the preheating temperature is reached, place the burgers on the tray in the air fryer basket, making sure they don't overlap or touch. Cook on for 15 minutes, flipping halfway through.

912. Creamy Mushroom Pie

Preparation Time: 10 minutes
Cooking Time: 50 minutes
Servings: 6

Ingredients:
- 4 eggs
- 2 tbsp parmesan cheese, grated
- 2 ounces fresh spinach
- 2 tsp olive oil
- 1 tsp garlic, minced
- 4 ounces mushrooms, sliced
- 1/2 cup mozzarella cheese, shredded
- 1/4 tsp nutmeg
- 1/2 tsp pepper
- 1/2 cup heavy cream
- 16 ounces cottage cheese
- 1 tsp salt

Directions:
- Heat oil in a suitable pan over moderate heat. Toss in garlic and mushrooms and sauté until soft. Stir in salt, black pepper, nutmeg, and spinach. Drain this mushrooms spinach mixture, then add spread it into a suitable pie dish. Whisk eggs with cream and cottage cheese in a bowl. Pour this egg mixture over the mushrooms and top it with cheese. Place the mushroom pie in the air fryer. Put on the Instant Air Fryer lid and cook on Bake mode for 50 minutes at 350°F. Once done, remove the lid and serve warm.

913. Cheese and Spinach Muffins

Preparation Time: 10 minutes
Cooking Time: 30 minutes
Servings: 4

Ingredients:
- 2 eggs

- 1/2 zucchini, grated
- 1/8 cup parmesan cheese, grated
- 1/4 cup feta cheese, crumbled
- 2 onion spring, chopped
- 1/4 cup coconut flour
- 1/4 cup spinach, cooked
- 2 tbsp butter, melted
- 2 tbsp parsley, chopped
- 1/4 tsp nutmeg
- 1/8 cup water
- 1/4 tsp baking powder
- 1/8 tsp black pepper
- 1/8 tsp salt

Directions:
- In a bowl, whisk together eggs, water, butter, and salt.
- Add baking soda and coconut flour and mix well.
- Add onions, nutmeg, parsley, spinach, and zucchini. Mix well.
- Add parmesan cheese and feta cheese and stir well. Season with pepper and salt.
- Pour batter into the silicone muffin molds and place in the air fryer basket. Place basket in the pot.
- Seal the pot with an air fryer basket and select bake mode, and cook at 400°F for 20-25 minutes. Serve and enjoy.

914. Zucchini Yogurt Bread

Preparation Time: 10 minutes
Cooking Time: 45 minutes
Serving: 6

Ingredients:
- 1 cup walnut halves
- 2 cups all-purpose flour
- 1/2 tsp baking powder
- 1/2 tsp baking soda
- 1/2 tsp salt
- 3/4 cup 2 tbsp sugar
- 2 large eggs
- 1/2 cup vegetable oil
- 1/2 cup plain Greek yogurt
- 1 cup zucchini, grated

Directions:
- Whisk baking powder, flour, salt, and baking soda in a medium bowl.
- Stir in eggs, vegetable oil, yogurt, and sugar, then mix well.
- Add flour mixture and mix well until smooth.
- Fold in walnuts and zucchini, then spread this batter in a greased baking pan.
- Place this pan in the Air fryer Duo.
- Put on the Air Fryer lid and seal it.
- Hit the "Bake Button" and select 45 minutes of cooking time, then press "Start."
- Once the Air fryer Duo beeps, remove its lid. Slice and serve.

915. Cream Cheese and Sausage Biscuits

Preparation Time: 5 Minutes
Cooking Time: 15 Minutes
Servings: 5

Ingredients:
- 12 ounces chicken breakfast sausage
- 1 (6-ounce) can of biscuits
- ⅛ Cup cream cheese

Directions:
- Form the sausage into 5 small patties.
- Place the sausage patties in the air fryer. Cook for 5 minutes at 380°F.
- Open the air fryer. Flip the patties. Cook for an additional 5 minutes.
- Remove the cooked sausages from the air fryer.
- Separate the biscuit dough into 5 biscuits.
- Place the biscuits in the air fryer. Cook for 3 minutes at 330°F.
- Open the air fryer. Flip the biscuits. Cook for an additional 2 minutes.
- Remove the cooked biscuits from the air fryer.
- Split each biscuit in half. Spread 1 tsp of cream cheese onto the bottom of each biscuit. Top with a sausage patty and the other half of the biscuit, and serve.

916. Eggs Benedict

Preparation Time: 5 Minutes
Cooking Time: 10 Minutes
Servings: 4

Ingredients:
- 4 English muffins
- 8 slices of Canadian bacon
- 4 slices cheese
- Cooking oil

Directions:
- Split each English muffin. Assemble the breakfast sandwiches by layering 2 slices of Canadian bacon and 1 slice of cheese onto each English muffin bottom. Put it on top of the other half of the English muffin.
- Place the sandwiches in the air fryer. Spray the top of each with cooking oil. Cook for 4 minutes at 380°F.
- Open the air fryer and flip the sandwiches. Cook for an additional 4 minutes.
- Cool before serving.

917. Parmesan and Scallion Sandwich

Preparation Time: 10 minutes
Cooking Time: 15 minutes
Servings: 1

Ingredients:
- 2 slices of wheat bread
- 2 tsp Low-fat butter
- 2 sliced scallions
- 1 tbsp. grated parmesan cheese
- 3/4 cup low-fat, grated cheddar cheese

Directions:
- Adjust the Air fryer to 356°F.
- Apply butter to a slice of bread. Then place it inside the cooking basket with the butter side facing down.
- Place cheese and scallions on top. Spread the rest of the butter on the other slice of bread. Then put it on top of the sandwich and sprinkle with parmesan cheese.
- Allow cooking for 10 minutes. Serve.

918. Portobello Pesto Burgers

Preparation Time: 10 minutes
Cooking Time: 26 Minutes
Servings: 4

Ingredients:
- 4 portobello mushrooms
- 1/4 cup sundried tomato pesto
- 4 whole-grain hamburger buns
- 1 large ripe tomato
- 1 log of fresh goat cheese
- 8 large fresh basil leaves

Directions:
- Start by preheating the air fryer to 400°F.
- Place mushrooms on a pan; round sides are facing up.
- Bake for 14 minutes.
- Pull out the tray, flip the mushrooms and spread 1 tbsp of pesto on each piece.
- Return to the air fryer and bake for another 10 minutes.
- Remove the mushrooms and toast the buns for 2 minutes.
- Remove the buns and build the burger by placing tomatoes, mushrooms, 2 slices of cheese, and a sprinkle of basil, then topping with the top bun.

919. Brunch Mini Sliders

Preparation Time: 5 minutes
Cooking Time: 10 minutes
Servings: 6

Ingredients:
- 1 lb. ground beef
- 6 slices of cheddar cheese
- 6 dinner rolls
- Salt and Black pepper

Directions:
- Adjust the air fryer to 390°F.
- Form 6 beef patties (each about 2.5 oz.) and season with salt and black pepper.
- Add the burger patties to the cooking basket and cook them for 10 minutes.
- Remove the burger patties from the air fryer; place the cheese on top of the burgers and return to the air fryer and cook for another minute.
- Remove and put burgers on dinner rolls and serve warm.

920. Air Fryer Sausage Wraps

Preparation Time: 5 Minutes
Cooking Time: 3 Minutes
Servings: 2

Ingredients:
- 8 pre-cooked sausages
- 2 pieces of American cheese
- 1 can of 8 counts refrigerated crescent roll dough

Directions:
- Cut each of the cheese slices into corners.
- Unroll eat the crescent roll.
- At the wide end of the crescent roll, put down 1/4 of cheese and 1 sausage.
- Starting at the wide end, roll the crescent up and tuck in the ends to cover the sausage and cheese.
- Preheat the fryer to 380°F.
- Put them in the basket and cook for about 3 minutes

921. Bacon and Brown Sugar Little Smokies

Preparation Time: 10 minutes
Cooking Time: 10 minutes
Servings: 6 to 8 people

Ingredients:
- 14 ounces of Little Smokies
- 2/3 ounce of Bacon
- 1/3 cup of Brown Sugar Substitute
- Toothpicks

Directions:
- Cut Bacon tips into thirds, and put the brown sugar substitute into a shallow dish that is enough to fit the bacon thirds.
- Place a slice of bacon into the brown sugar substitute and coat on both sides.
- Wrap one little smokie with a slice of brown sugar-coated bacon and pin it with a Toothpick.
- Repeat with the rest of the little smokies and then place them inside the air fryer basket.
- Cook at 350°F for about 10 minutes until the bacon is crisped, flip halfway through the cooking process.

922. Garlic Cheese Bread

Preparation Time: 15 minutes
Cooking Time: 10 minutes
Servings: 4

Ingredients:
- 1 large egg
- ¼ cup Grated parmesan cheese
- ½ tsp Garlic powder
- 1 cup shredded mozzarella cheese

Directions:
- Layer the air fryer basket with parchment paper.
- Mix parmesan cheese, mozzarella cheese, garlic powder, and egg in a suitable bowl.
- Set the mixture in a well-greased pan and place this pan in the fryer basket.
- Return the basket to the fryer.
- Leave them to cook for 10 minutes at 350°F on Air Fryer Mode.
- Slice and serve warm

923. Potato Bread Rolls

Preparation Time: 20 minutes
Cooking Time: 13 minutes
Servings: 8

Ingredients:
- 5 large potatoes, boiled and mashed
- 2 small onions, chopped finely
- 2 green chilies, seeded and chopped
- 2 curry leaves
- 8 bread slices, trimmed
- 2 tbsp vegetable oil, divided
- ½ tsp ground turmeric

- Salt, to taste

Directions:
- Preheat the air fryer to 390°F and grease an air fryer basket.
- Heat 1 tsp of vegetable oil in a skillet on medium heat and add onions.
- Sauté for about 5 minutes, and add green chilies, curry leaves, and turmeric.
- Sauté for about 1 minute, and add mashed potatoes and salt.
- Stir well until mixed and remove from heat.
- Make eight equal-sized oval-shaped patties from the mixture.
- Wet the bread slices entirely with water and press the bread slices to drain completely.
- Put a patty in a bread slice and roll it in a spindle shape.
- Seal the edges to secure the filling and coat with vegetable oil.
- Repeat with the remaining bread slices, filling mixture and vegetable oil.
- Place the potato rolls in the air fryer basket and cook for about 13 minutes.
- Remove from the air fryer and serve warm.

924. Grilled Gruyere Cheese Sandwich

Preparation Time: 5 Minutes
Cooking Time: 10 Minutes
Servings: 1

Ingredients:
- 2 ounces of thinly sliced Gruyere cheese
- 2 slices of whole-grain bread
- 1 tbsp of butter

Directions:
- Lay the Gruyere cheese between the 2 slices of bread.
- Butter up the outside of the bread slices.
- Place the cheese sandwich in the air fryer basket. You may need to use toothpicks to secure it.
- Air fry the sandwich for approximately 3-5 minutes at 360 °F until the cheese melts.
- Flip the sandwich over and turn the heat up to 380 °F until crisp.
- Continue to air fryer for approximately 5 minutes until the sandwich is to your desired texture. You will need to check continually that the sandwich doesn't burn.
- Set to one side to cool slightly before enjoying.

925. Mozzarella -Spinach Stuffed Burgers

Preparation Time: 5 minutes
Cooking Time: 20 minutes
Servings: 4

Ingredients:
- 1 ½ lbs. ground chuck
- 2 tbsp. parmesan, grated
- 2 cups fresh spinach
- ½ cup shredded mozzarella cheese
- Pepper and salt as desired

Directions:
- In a standard mixing bowl, join ground chuck and season accordingly. Then scoop about 1/3 cup of meat

mixture and shape into 8 patties about ½ inch thick. Set in refrigerator.
- Cook spinach at 350°F for a couple of minutes until the spinach wilts. Drain spinach and let it cool before squeezing out excess liquid.
- Move spinach to the cutting board and chop the spinach. Add spinach, mozzarella cheese, and parmesan to a separate mixing bowl. Stir all ingredients together.
- Take beef patties out of the fridge and scoop about ¼ cup of stuffing, and place in the center of 4 patties.
- Cover with remaining beef patties and press edges together firmly to seal the stuffing inside the patties. Round out the edges of the patties to create a single thick patty.
- Heat a pan or grill to medium-high and prepare stuffed burgers for 5 to 6 minutes on, grilling equally on each side.

926. Flax Chips

Preparation Time: 5 minutes
Cooking Time: 15 minutes
Servings: 4

Ingredients:
- 1 cup almond flour
- 1/2 cup flax seeds
- 1 1/2 Tsp seasoned salt
- 1 Tsp sea salt
- 1/2 cup water

Directions:
- Preheat the Air fryer toaster oven to 170°C. Combine almond flour, flax seeds, 1 1/2 tsp seasoned salt and sea salt in a container; Stir in the water up to the dough is completely mixed. Shape the dough into narrow size slices the size of a bite and place them on a baking sheet. Sprinkle the rounds with seasoned salt. Bake in preheated air fryer toaster oven up to crispy, about 15 minutes. Cool fully and store in an airtight box or in a sealed bag.

927. Cheesy-Bacon Stuffed Pastry Pie

Preparation Time: 5 minutes
Cooking Time: 15 minutes
Servings: 4

Ingredients:
- 1/2 cup bacon, cooked
- 1/2 cup cheddar cheese, shredded
- 1/2 cup sausage crumbles, cooked
- 5 eggs
- one box of puff pastry sheets

Directions:
- Scramble the eggs and cook.
- Lightly grease a dish that fits in your Air fryer with cooking spray.
- Evenly spread half of the puff sheets on the bottom of the dish.
- Spread eggs, cooked sausage, crumbled bacon, and cheddar cheese.
- Top with remaining puff pastry and gently push down with a fork.
- Cover the top of the dish with foil.

- For 8 minutes, cook at 330°F. Remove foil and cook for another 5 minutes or until the top of the puff pastry is golden brown.
- Serve and enjoy.

928.   Fish Chicharron

Preparation Time: 10 minutes
Cooking Time: 15 minutes
Servings: 2

Ingredients:
- ½ pound salmon skin
- 2 tbsp. heart-healthy oil
- Salt and pepper, as needed

Directions:
- Fix the temperature to 400°F and preheat the air-fryer for 5 minutes.
- Make sure the salmon skin is patted dry.
- In a bowl, add all components and combine well.
- Transfer the ingredients to the air-fryer basket and close it
- Allow it to cook for 10 minutes at a temperature of 400°F.
- Shake the items halfway through the Cooking Time to make sure that the skin is cooked evenly.

929.   Homemade Peanut Corn Nuts

Preparation Time: 5 minutes
Cooking Time: 20 minutes
Servings: 4

Ingredients:
- 6 oz dried hominy, soaked overnight
- 3 tbsp peanut oil
- 2 tbsp old bay seasoning
- Salt to taste
- **Directions**
- Preheat the air fryer to 390°F.
- Pat dry hominy and season with salt and old bay seasoning. Drizzle with oil and toss to coat. Spread in the air fryer basket and Air Fry for 10-12 minutes. Remove to shake up and return to cook for 10 more minutes until crispy. Transfer to a towel-lined plate to soak up the excess fat. Let cool and serve.

930.   Roasted Lima beans

Preparation Time: 5 minutes
Cooking Time: 40 minutes
Servings: 4

Ingredients:
- 1 (12 ounce) Can Lima beans
- 2 Tbsp coconut oil
- Salt
- Garlic salt (optional)
- Paprika (optional)

Directions:
- Dry the Lima beans with a kitchen towel to not wet them. In a bowl, mix the Lima beans with coconut oil and sprinkle with salt, garlic salt and paprika. Place the Air Fryer Basket onto the Baking Pan. Put the

assembled pan into rack Position 2. Arrange to Air Fry at 350°F for 40 minutes

931.   Garlic Mozzarella Sticks

Preparation Time: 1 hour and 5 minutes
Cooking Time: 10 minutes
Servings: 4

Ingredients:
- 1 Tbsp Italian Seasoning
- 1 cup Parmesan Cheese
- 8 String Cheeses, Diced
- 2 Eggs, Beaten
- 1 Clove of Garlic, Minced

Directions:
- Start by combining your parmesan, garlic and Italian seasoning in a bowl. Dip your cheese into the egg, and mix well.
- Roll it into your cheese crumbles, and then press the crumbs into the cheese.
- Place them in the fridge for an hour, and then preheat your air fryer to 375°F.
- Spray your air fryer down with oil, and then arrange the cheese strings into the basket. Cook for 8 to 9 minutes at 365°F.
- Allow them to cool for at least five minutes before serving.

932.   Seasoned Pork Rinds

Preparation Time: 5 minutes
Cooking Time: 10 minutes
Servings: 8

Ingredients:
- ½ Tsp Black Pepper
- 1 Tsp Chili Flakes
- ½ Tsp Sea Salt, Fine
- 1 Tsp Olive Oil
- 1 lb. Pork Rinds

Directions:
- Start by heating your air fryer to 365°F, and then spray it down with olive oil.
- Place your pork rinds in your air fryer basket, and sprinkle with your seasoning. Mix well, and then cook for 7 minutes.
- Shake gently, and then serve cooled.

933.   Chocolate-Covered Maple Bacon

Preparation Time: 10 minutes
Cooking Time: 5 minutes
Servings: 3

Ingredients:
- 8 slices of sugar-free bacon
- 1 tbsp. granular erythritol
- 1/3 cup low-carb, sugar-free chocolate chips
- 1 tsp. coconut oil
- ½ tsp. maple extract

Direction:
- Place the bacon in the fryer's basket and add the erythritol on top. Cook for six minutes at 350°F and

turn the bacon over. Leave to cook another six minutes or until the bacon is sufficiently crispy.

- Take the bacon out of the fryer and leave it to cool.
- Microwave the chocolate chips and coconut oil together for half a minute. Remove from the microwave and mix it before stirring in the maple extract.
- Set the bacon flat on a piece of parchment paper and pour the mixture over. Allow hardening in the refrigerator for roughly five minutes before serving.

934.   Dehydrated Candied Bacon

Preparation Time: 3 hours
Cooking Time: 4 hours and 10 minutes
Servings: 4

Ingredients:
- 6 slices bacon
- 3 tbsp light brown sugar
- 2 tbsp rice vinegar
- 2 tbsp chili paste
- 1 tbsp soy sauce

Directions:
- Mix brown sugar, rice vinegar, chili paste, and soy sauce together in a bowl.
- Add bacon slices and mix until all are evenly coated.
- Set aside for up to 3 hours or up until ready to dehydrate.
- Then put the bacon on the food tray.
- Set bacon on the air fryer 's wire rack, then insert the rack at mid-position in the air fryer toaster oven.
- Select the Dehydrate function on the Air Fryer at 130°F, set the time to 4 hours, then press Start.
- Remove the tray once done baking and let the bacon cool for 5 minutes, then serve.

935.   Taco Flavored Kale Chips

Preparation Time: 5 minutes
Cooking Time: 3 hours
Servings: 2

Ingredients:
- 3 whole kale leaves, cut into 2-inch squares
- 1 tbsp. Olive oil
- 1 tbsp. taco seasoning

Directions:
- Mix taco seasoning and olive oil in a small bowl.
- Combine taco seasoning mixture with kale leaves until all are evenly coated.
- Place kale leaves into the fry basket, then insert the fry basket at mid-position in the Air Fryer.
- Select the Dehydrate function, fix the time to 3 hours and temperature to 140°F, then press Start.
- Remove when done and serve.

936.   Ranch Flavored Kale Chips

Preparation Time: 5 minutes
Cooking Time: 3 hours
Servings: 2

Ingredients:
- 3 whole kale leaves, cut into 2-inch squares
- 1 tbsp. olive oil
- 1 tbsp. ranch seasoning

Directions:
- In a small bowl, mix the olive oil and ranch seasoning.
- Mix ranch mixture with kale leaves until all are evenly coated.
- Put the kale leaves into the fry basket, then insert the fry basket at mid-position in the Air Fryer.
- Select the Dehydrate function, fix the time to 3 hours and temperature to 140°F, then press Start/Cancel.
- Remove when done and serve.

937.   Corn Dogs

Preparation Time: 5 minutes
Cooking Time: 10 minutes
Servings: 4

Ingredients:
- 2 uncured All Beef Hot Puppies
- ½ cup All-Purpose Flour
- Half Cup Bamboo Broach (About 2 1/8 oz.) or 12 craft sticks
- 1 1/2 cups minced corn flakes cereal
- 2 large eggs, lightly beaten

Directions:
- Slice each hot dog half lengthwise each length. Cut each half into 3 equal pieces. Put a craft stick or bamboo skewer at 1 end of each piece of a hot dog.
- Place the dough in a shallow dish. Place the overwhelmed eggs gently in another shallow dish. Place the cornflakes in a 0.33 shallow dish. Dip the hot dogs in the flour, adding extra. Dip in eggs, allowing any excess to drip off. Dredge into cornflake pieces, pressing to adhere.
- Lightly grease the air fryer basket with cooking spray. Place 6 corn dog bites in a basket; Spray lightly with cooking spray. Cook at 375°F until the corn is golden brown and crispy; 10 minutes, cut the corn dog through cooking. Repeat with remaining corn dog bite.
- To serve, place three corn dog bites on each plate with 2 tbsp of mustard, and serve immediately.

938.   Spiced Lentils Nibblers

Preparation Time: 5 Minutes
Cooking Time: 12 minutes
Servings: 4

Ingredients:
- 15 ounces canned lentils, drained
- ½ tsp cumin, ground
- 1 tbsp olive oil
- 1 tsp sweet paprika
- Salt and black pepper to taste

Directions:
- Place all ingredients in a bowl and blend it well.
- Transfer the mixture to your air fryer and cook at 400°F for 12 minutes.
- Divide into bowls and serve as a snack -or a side, or an appetizer!

939. Chia Seed Crackers

Preparation Time: 15 minutes
Cooking Time: 45 minutes
Servings: 48

Ingredients:

- 1 Cup raw chia seed
- 3/4 Tsp salt
- 1/4 Tsp garlic powder
- 1/4 Tsp onion powder
- 1 cup cold water

Directions:

- Put the chia seeds in a bowl. Add salt, garlic powder, and onion powder.
- Pour into the water. Stir. Cover with plastic wrap. Store in the fridge overnight. Preheat the Air fryer toaster oven to 95°C. Cover a baking sheet with a silicone mat or parchment. Transfer the soaked linseed to a prepared baking sheet. Scatter it out with a spatula in a thin, flat rectangle about 1 cm thick. Rate the rectangle in about 32 small rectangles. Bake in the preheated air fryer toaster oven up until the chia seeds have darkened and contracted slightly, about 3 hours. Let it cool. Break individual cookies.

940. Baked Eggplant Chips

Preparation Time: 5 minutes
Cooking Time: 15 minutes
Servings: 4

Ingredients:

- 2 medium eggplant, cut into 1/4-inch slices
- 1/2 cup crushed cornflakes.
- 1/8 Tsp ground black pepper
- 2 Tbsp grated goat cheese
- 2 Egg whites

Directions:

- Preheat the Air fryer toaster oven to 200° C. Mix the crushed cornflakes, pepper and goat cheese in a small container. Set aside the egg whites in a different container. Dip the eggplant slices in the egg white and cover the crushed cornflakes mixture. Place on a greased baking sheet. Bake in the preheated air fryer toaster oven for 5 minutes, then turn and bake for another 5 to 10 minutes until golden yellow and crispy.

941. Toasted Coconut Flakes

Preparation Time: 10 minutes
Cooking Time: 5 minutes
Servings: 3

Ingredients:

- 1 cup unsweetened coconut flakes
- 2 tsp. coconut oil, melted
- ¼ cup granular erythritol
- Salt

Direction:

- Oil, granular erythritol, and a pinch of salt ensure that the chips are coated completely.
- Place the coconut flakes in your fryer and cook at 300°F for three minutes, giving the basket a good shake a few

times throughout the cooking time. Fry until golden and serve.

942. Buttered Bagels

Preparation Time: 8-10 minutes
Cooking Time: 6 minutes
Servings: 5-6

Ingredients:

- 2 bagels, make halves
- 4 tsp butter

Directions:

- Place your air fryer on a flat kitchen surface; plug it and turn it on. Set temperature to 370°F and let it preheat for 4-5 minutes.
- Take out the air-frying basket and gently coat it using cooking oil or spray.
- Add the bagels to the basket.
- Push the air-frying basket into the air fryer. Let your air fryer cook the added bagels for 3 minutes.
- Slide out the basket; spread the butter over the bagels, and cook for 3 more minutes.
- Serve warm!

943. Salt Roasted Hazelnuts

Preparation Time: 15 minutes
Cooking Time: 10 minutes
Servings: 8

Ingredients:

- 2 Cups dry roasted Hazelnuts, no salt added
- 2 Tbsp coconut oil
- 1 Tsp garlic powder
- 1 Sprig of Fresh Thyme, chopped
- 1 1/2 Tsp salt

Directions:

- Preheat the Air fryer toaster oven to 175°C. Mix the Hazelnuts, coconut oil, garlic powder and thyme in a bowl until the nuts are fully covered. Sprinkle with salt. Spread evenly on a baking sheet. Bake in the preheated air fryer toaster oven for 10 minutes.

944. Cheddar Mustard Toast

Preparation Time: 8-10 min.
Cooking Time: 15 min.
Servings: 2

Ingredients:

- 2 eggs, whites, and yolks
- 1 tbsp mustard
- 4 bread slices
- 2 tbsp cheddar cheese, shredded
- 1 tbsp paprika

Directions:

- Place your air fryer on a flat kitchen surface; plug it and turn it on. Set temperature to 355°F and let it preheat for 4-5 minutes.
- Add the bread slice to the fryer basket. Cook for about 5 minutes or till toasted.
- In a bowl of medium size, thoroughly whisk the egg whites.

- In a bowl of medium size, thoroughly mix the cheese, egg yolks, mustard, and paprika.
- Gently fold in the egg whites.
- Top the mustard mixture over the toasted bread. Cook for about 10 minutes.
- Slide out the basket; serve warm!

945. Yam Chips

Preparation Time: 10 minutes
Cooking Time: 20 minutes
Servings: 4

Ingredients:
- 2 Yams
- 1 Tsp seasoned salt, or more to taste

Directions:
- Preheat the Air fryer toaster oven to 175°C. Coating 2 baking trays with oil. Prepare a longitudinal cut in the inside of each yam. Cut the yams into pieces using a spiral slicer. Place the pieces in the Silpat. Coating with an oil. Spice collective with seasoned salt. Bake in the preheated air fryer toaster oven for 20 to 25 minutes up until the corners start to form into a curved. Season with more salt. Let cool for 10 minutes up to crispy.

946. Roasted Pine nuts

Preparation Time: 10 minutes
Cooking Time: 35 minutes
Servings: 6

Ingredients:
- 1 1/2 cups pine nuts
- 2 Tsp olive oil
- 1 Pinch salt

Directions:
- Mix the seeds in a bowl with olive oil and salt. Spread the seeds in a layer in a basket and Put the assembled pan into rack Position 2. Fix the Air Fry at 350°F for 35 minutes. Cook up to golden brown.

947. Cheesy Beef Puffs

Preparation Time: 20 minutes
Cooking Time: 30 minutes
Servings: 24

Ingredients:
- 6 oz raw beef
- 3 tbsp onion
- 1 clove garlic
- ¾ cup white whole wheat flour
- ¾ tsp baking powder
- 1/8 tsp salt
- 1/8 tsp crushed red pepper flakes
- ¾ cup skim milk
- 1 large egg
- 4 oz reduced fat sharp cheddar cheese

Directions:
- Preheat the oven to 350°F. Lightly mist a 24-count mini muffin tin with cooking spray
- Add ground beef to the baking dish, spray with oil, and cook in the fryer.

- When cooked, add the hamburger seasoning, chopped onion, and garlic and cook in the fryer.
- In a large bowl, stir together flour, baking powder, salt and crushed red pepper. Add the milk and egg and whisk together to thoroughly combine. Add the ground beef mixture and cheese and stir until combined.
- Divide the batter evenly amongst the prepared mini muffin tin cups.
- Bake in the fryer for 18-20 minutes until golden.

948. Pao de Queijo

Preparation Time: 15 minutes
Cooking Time: 20 minutes
Servings: 4

Ingredients:
- 2 cups all-purpose flour
- 1 cup Milk
- 2 eggs, cracked into a bowl
- 2 cups grated Parmesan Cheese
- ½ cup Olive Oil

Directions:
- Grease the crisp basket with cooking spray and set aside.
- Put the cooker on Medium and select Sear/Sauté mode.
- Add the milk, oil, and salt, and let boil. Add the flour and mix it vigorously with a spoon.
- Let the mixture cool. Once cooled, use a hand mixer to mix the dough well, and add the eggs and cheese while still mixing. The dough should be thick and sticky.
- Use your hands to make 14 balls out of the mixture, and put them in the greased basket. Put the basket in the pot and close the crisping lid.
- Select Air Fry, set the temperature to 380°F and set the timer to 15 minutes.
- At the 7-minute mark, shake the balls. Serve with lemon aioli, garlic mayo or ketchup.

949. Mac and Cheese Toast

Preparation Time: 10 minutes
Cooking Time: 5 minutes
Servings: 2

Ingredients:
- 1 egg, beaten
- 4 tbsp cheddar cheese, grated
- Salt and pepper to taste
- ½ cup macaroni and cheese
- 4 bread slices

Directions:
- Spread the cheese and macaroni and cheese over the two bread slices. Place the other bread slices on top of the cheese and cut diagonally. In a bowl, beat egg and season with salt and pepper. Brush the egg mixture onto the bread. Place the bread into the air fryer and cook at 300°F for 5-minutes.

950. Classic Tortilla Pizza

Preparation Time: 15 minutes
Cooking Time: 7 minutes
Servings: 6

Ingredients:

- 1 large whole wheat tortilla
- 1 tbsp black olives
- Salt and pepper to taste
- 4 tbsp tomato sauce
- 8 pepperoni slices
- 3 tbsp of sweet corn
- 1 medium, tomato, chopped
- ½ cup mozzarella cheese, grated

Directions:

- Preheat your air fryer to 325°F. Spread tomato sauce over the tortilla. Add pepperoni slices, olives, corn, tomato, and cheese on top of the tortilla. Season with salt and pepper. Place pizza in an air fryer basket and cook for 7-minutes. Serve and enjoy!

951. Pizza Margherita

Preparation Time: 5 minutes
Cooking Time: 13 minutes
Servings: 4

Ingredients:

- ½ cup pizza sauce
- 12 oz. pizza dough
- 2 tbsp parmesan, grated
- 3 oz. mozzarella, sliced
- ¼ cup basil leaves
- Olive oil

Directions:

- Grease a baking pan with olive oil and add pizza dough to the pan. Stretch the money to cover the pan and spray with oil.
- Position the baking pan in Rack Position 2 and select the Bake setting. Set the temperature to 400°F and the time to 5 minutes.
- Remove from the oven and flip. Add sauce to the middle and spread in a thin layer, and leave a 1" border for the crust. Add parmesan and top with mozzarella. Grease border with oil.
- Return the pan to the oven and cook for 8 minutes. Add basil on top. Serve.

952. Hawaiian Pizza

Preparation Time: 15 minutes
Cooking Time: 10 minutes
Servings: 3

Ingredients:

- 1 large whole wheat tortilla
- ¼ cup tomato pizza sauce
- ¼ cup pineapple tidbits
- ¼ cup mozzarella cheese, grated
- ¼ cup ham slice

Directions:

- Preheat your air fryer to 300°F. Place the tortilla on a baking sheet, then spread pizza sauce over the tortilla. Arrange ham slice, cheese, and pineapple over the tortilla. Place the pizza in the air fryer basket and cook for 10-minutes. Serve hot.

953. Bacon and Cheese Popcorn

Preparation Time: 15 minutes
Cooking Time: 30 minutes
Servings: 3-4

Ingredients:

- 3 cups of corn
- 3 tsp garlic puree
- 6 oz cheddar cheese, shredded
- 3 tbsp coconut oil
- 200g bacon, fried and crisp
- Salt

Directions:

- Select the Sauté button to heat the Air fryer, and add the coconut oil.
- After 5 minutes and once the oil is hot, add garlic, corn and salt.
- Cover the pot, and popping will start.
- Wait for 8-12minutes until all popcorn pops up. Remove from the pot and set aside.
- Turn on the air fryer and set it to sauté function. Heat the oil and add the bacon. Fry the bacon for 2-3 minutes at 400°F or until fried and crisp
- Put in a bowl and put the cheese and bacon on top.
- Serve.

954. Kalamata Mozzarella Pita Melts

Preparation Time: 10 minutes
Cooking Time: 5 minutes
Servings: 2

Ingredients:

- 2 (6-inch) whole-wheat pitas
- 1 tsp extra-virgin olive oil
- 1 cup grated part-skim mozzarella cheese
- 1/4 small red onion
- 1/4 cup pitted Kalamata olives
- 2 tbsp chopped fresh herbs such as parsley, basil, or oregano

Directions:

- Start by preheating the toaster oven to 400°F.
- Brush the pita on both sides with oil and warm in the oven for one minute.
- Dice onions and halve olives.
- Sprinkle mozzarella over each pita and top with onion and olive.
- Return to the oven for another 5 minutes or until the cheese is melted.
- Sprinkle herbs over the pita and serve.

955. Squash and Zucchini Mini Pizza

Preparation Time: 30 minutes
Cooking Time: 15 minutes
Servings: 4

Ingredients:

- 1 pizza crust
- 1/2 cup parmesan cheese
- 4 tbsp oregano
- 1 zucchini
- 1 yellow summer squash
- Olive oil

- Salt and pepper

Directions:
- Start by preheating the toaster oven to 350°F.
- If you are using a homemade crust, roll out 8 mini portions; if the crust is store-bought, use a cookie cutter to cut out the portions.
- Sprinkle parmesan and oregano equally on each piece. Layer the zucchini and squash in a circle – one on top of the other – around the entire circle.
- Brush with olive oil and sprinkle salt and pepper to taste.
- Bake for 15 minutes and serve.

956.   Seven-Layer Tostadas

Preparation Time: 15 minutes
Cooking Time: 5 minutes
Servings: 6

Ingredients:
- 1 (16-ounce) can of refried pinto beans
- 1-1/2 cups guacamole
- 1 cup light sour cream
- 1/2 tsp taco seasoning
- 1 cup shredded Mexican cheese blend
- 1 cup chopped tomatoes
- 1/2 cup thinly sliced green onions
- 1/2 cup sliced black olives
- 6-8 whole wheat flour tortillas small enough to fit in your oven
- Olive oil

Directions:
- Start by placing the baking sheet into the air fryer while preheating it to 450°F. Remove pan and drizzle with olive oil.
- Place tortillas on the pan and cook in the fryer until they are crisp; turn at least once; this should take about 5 minutes or less.
- In a medium bowl, mash refried beans to break apart any chunks, then microwave for 2 1/2 minutes.
- Stir taco seasoning into the sour cream. Chop vegetables and halve olives.
- Top tortillas with ingredients in this order: refried beans, guacamole, sour cream, shredded cheese, tomatoes, onions, and olives.

957.   Morning Pizza

Preparation Time: 10 minutes
Cooking Time: 11 minutes
Servings: 6

Ingredients:
- 6 oz. Cheddar cheese, shredded
- 5 oz. Parmesan cheese, shredded
- 1 tomato
- 3 oz chive stems
- 1 tsp paprika
- ½ tsp dried oregano
- ½ tsp salt
- ½ cup almond flour
- 1 egg
- 4 tbsp water
- 1 tsp olive oil

Directions:
- Beat the egg in the bowl and whisk it with the help of the hand whisker.
- After this, add the almond flour and water. Mix the mixture up carefully and after this, knead the non-sticky dough.
- Then roll the dough into a thin circle.
- Preheat the air fryer to 355°F.
- Spray the air fryer basket tray with the olive oil and place the pizza crust there.
- Cook it for 1 minute.
- After this, remove the air fryer basket tray from the air fryer.
- Slice the tomato and dice the chives.
- Sprinkle the pizza crust with the diced chives and sliced tomato.
- Then put the shredded Cheddar cheese and Parmesan cheese over the sliced tomatoes.
- Sprinkle the pizza with salt, paprika, and dried oregano.
- Place the pizza back in the air fryer and cook it for 10 minutes.
- When the time is over and the pizza is cooked – slice it into the servings and serve!

958.   Honey Ham and Cheese Bagels

Preparation Time:7 minutes
Cooking Time: 5 minutes
Servings:2

Ingredients:
- 2 bagels
- 4 tsp. honey mustard
- 4 slices of cooked honey ham
- 4 slices of Swiss cheese

Directions:
- Preheat the air fryer oven to 350°F.
- Spread honey mustard on each half of the bagel
- Add ham and cheese and close the bagel.
- Bake the sandwich until the cheese is fully melted, approximately 5 minutes

959.   Jackfruit Taquitos

Preparation Time: 6 Minutes
Cooking Time: 11 Minutes
Servings: 4

Ingredients:
- Four whole-wheat tortillas
- 1 cup roasted red beans
- 14 oz. jackfruit
- 3/4 cup water
- 1/2 cup Pico de Gallo
- Olive oil spray

Directions:
- Switch on the air fryer, place jackfruit and beans in the inner bowl, stir in pico de gallo sauce, pour in water, and shut with a lid.
- Then press the manual button and cook for 3 minutes at a low-pressure setting and, when done, release pressure naturally.
- Open the lid, mash the jackfruit mixture, and set aside until required.

- Switch on the air fryer, insert the fryer basket, then shut it with the lid, set the frying temperature to 370°F, and let it preheat for 5 minutes.
- Meanwhile, prepare tortillas and for this, place 1/4 cup of the bean-jackfruit mixture onto each tortilla and roll it up tightly, and prepare the remaining tortillas in the same manner.
- Open the preheated fryer, place tortillas in it in a single layer, spray with olive oil, and cook for about 8 minutes while covered until golden brown and cooked.
- When done, the air fryer will beep and then open the lid and transfer tortillas to a dish.
- Serve straight away.

960. Keto Air Bread

Preparation Time: 10 Minutes
Cooking Time: 25 minutes
Servings: 19
- **Ingredients**
- 1 cup almond flour
- ¼ sea salt
- One tsp baking powder
- ¼ cup butter
- Three eggs

Directions:
- Crack the eggs into a bowl, then, using a hand blender, mix them up. Melt the butter at room temperature. Take the melted butter and add it to the egg mixture. Add the salt, baking powder, and almond flour to the egg mixture and knead the dough. Cover the prepared dough with a towel for 10-minutes to rest. Meanwhile, preheat your air fryer to 360°Fahrenheit. Place the ready money in the air fryer tin and cook the bread for 10-minutes. Then reduce the heat to 350°F and bake the food for an additional 15-minutes. You can use a toothpick to check to make sure the dough is cooked. Transfer the bread to a wooden board to allow it to chill. Once the food has chilled, then slice and serve it.

961. Tomato Cake

Preparation Time: 20 minutes
Cooking Time: 25-30 minutes
Servings: 8

Ingredients:
- 1 and ½ cups flour
- 1 tbsp. cinnamon powder
- 1 tbsp. baking powder
- 1 tbsp. baking soda
- ¾ cup maple syrup
- 1 cup tomatoes
- ½ cup olive oil
- 2 tbsp. apple cider vinegar

Directions:
- Mix in flour with baking soda, baking powder, maple syrup and cinnamon in a bowl, then turn properly.
- Mix in tomatoes with vinegar and olive oil in another bowl and turn properly.
- Blend the 2 mixtures, turn properly, put them into the round pan, get into the fryer and cook at 360°F for 30 minutes.
- Allow to cool, divide.

- Serve.

962. Avocado Cinnamon Bread

Preparation Time: 20 minutes
Cooking Time: 25-30 minutes
Servings: 6

Ingredients:
- 3/4 cup (3 oz.) white wheat flour
- 1 tsp cinnamon
- 1/2 tsp kosher salt
- 1/4 tsp baking soda
- 2 ripe avocados, cored, peeled and mashed
- 2 large eggs, beaten
- 1 tsp vanilla extract
- 1/2 cup granulated sugar
- 1/3 cup plain yogurt
- 2 tbsp vegetable oil
- 2 tbsp toasted walnuts, roughly chopped
- Cooking spray

Directions:
- Take a 6-inch baking pan and layer it with parchment paper and cooking spray. Combine all-purpose flour, salt, baking soda, and cinnamon in a suitable bowl. Beat eggs in a bowl and mix them with avocado mash, yogurt, Sugar, oil, and vanilla. Now stir in the wheat flour mixture and mix until well incorporated. Spread the batter into the pan evenly, then top it with walnuts. Preheat your Air Fryer machine to 310°F. Cook for 35 minutes. Once done, allow the bread to cool. Slice and serve.

963. Quinoa Burger

Preparation Time: 20 minutes
Cooking Time: 30 minutes
Servings: 6

Ingredients:
- 1 cup quinoa red, white or multi-colored
- 1½ cups water
- 1 tsp salt
- black pepper, ground
- 1½ cups rolled oats
- 3 eggs beaten
- ¼ cup minced white onion
- ½ cup crumbled feta cheese
- ¼ cup chopped fresh chives
- Salt and ground black pepper, to taste
- Vegetable or canola oil
- 4 hamburger buns
- 4 arugula
- 4 slices of tomato sliced
- Cucumber yogurt dill sauce
- 1 cup cucumber, diced
- 1 cup Greek yogurt
- 2 tsp lemon juice
- ¼ tsp salt
- Black pepper, ground
- 1 tbsp chopped fresh dill
- 1 tbsp olive oil

Directions:

- Add quinoa to a saucepan filled with cold water, salt and black pepper and place it over medium high heat. Cook the quinoa to a boil, then reduce the heat, cover and cook for 20 minutes on a simmer. Fluff and mix the cooked quinoa with a fork and remove it from the heat. Spread the quinoa in a baking stay. Mix eggs, oats, onion, herbs, cheese, salt and black pepper. Stir in quinoa, then mix well. Make 4 patties out of this quinoa cheese mixture. Place the patties in the Air Fryer's Basket and spray them with cooking oil. Air fry the patties for 10 minutes at 400°F. Flip the patties once cooked halfway through. Meanwhile, prepare the cucumber yogurt dill sauce by mixing all of its ingredients in a mixing bowl. Place each quinoa patty in a burger bun along with arugula leaves. Serve with yogurt dill sauce.

964.   Chick Fil A Burgers

Preparation Time: 20 minutes
Cooking Time: 25-30 minutes
Servings: 4

Ingredients:

- 2 boneless chicken breasts
- 1/2 cup dill pickle juice
- 2 eggs
- 1/2 cup milk
- 1 cup flour, all-purpose
- 2 tbsp powdered sugar
- 2 tbsp potato starch
- 1 tsp paprika
- 1 tsp of sea salt
- 1/2 tsp black pepper
- 1/2 tsp garlic powder
- 1/4 tsp ground celery seed ground
- 1 tbsp extra virgin olive oil
- Cooking spray
- 4 hamburger buns, toasted
- 8 dill pickle chips

Directions:

- Set the chicken in a suitable Ziplock bag and pound it into ½ thickness with a mallet. Slice the chicken into three smaller pieces. Add pickle juice and seal the bag. Refrigerate for 30 minutes approximately for marination. Whisk both eggs with milk in a shallow bowl. Thoroughly mix flour with spices and flour in a separate bowl. Dip each chicken slice in egg and then in the flour mixture. Shake off the excess and set the chicken pieces in the Air Fryer basket. Spray the pieces with cooking oil. Set the fryer basket in the Air Fryer and cook on Air Fryer mode for 6 minutes, approximately at 340°F. Flip the chicken pieces and cook for another 6 minutes. Enjoy with pickle chips and a dollop of mayonnaise.

965.   Classic Cheese Pizza

Preparation Time: 20 minutes
Cooking Time: 12-15 minutes
Servings: 6

Ingredients:

- 2 (8-oz) packages of pizza dough

- 1 tbsp extra virgin olive oil, divided
- 1/3 cup crushed tomatoes
- 1 clove of garlic, minced
- ½ tsp oregano
- Salt, to taste
- Black pepper, to taste
- 1/2 (8-oz) mozzarella ball, cut into ¼" slices
- Basil leaves for serving

Directions:

- Spread each of the dough balls into 8 inches round over a floured surface. Brush one side of the prepared dough rounds with olive oil and place them on the working surface with their oil side up. Add crushed tomatoes, oregano, and garlic to a medium bowl. Mix well and divide the mixture on top of the pizza crust while leaving ½ inch around the rim. Finally, place half of the mozzarella slices on top of each pizza. Place one pizza in the Air Fryer basket and return it to the Air Fryer, then cook for 12 minutes at 400°F until the cheese is melted. Cook the other pizza in the same way. Slice and serve warm.

966.   Breaded Deviled Eggs

Preparation Time: 30 minutes
Cooking Time: 20 minutes
Servings: 3

Ingredients:

- 6 eggs
- 1 cup Hooters Wing Breading
- 2 eggs
- 1 tsp white vinegar
- 1 tbsp hot sauce
- 1 ½ cups panko breadcrumbs
- ¼ cup mayonnaise
- 1 tsp Dijon mustard
- Black pepper, to taste
- 1/8 tsp salt
- ¼ tsp chili powder
- 2 slices bacon, cooked and chopped
- Chopped cilantro to serve
- Hot sauce, to serve

Directions:

- Add 6 eggs to the Air Fryer basket and cook for 17 minutes at 250°F. Remove the eggs from the Air Fryer basket and transfer them to a bowl filled with cold water. Peel them and allow them to dry. Cut each egg in half lengthwise, remove their yolks, and transfer them to a bowl. Keep the egg whites on a plate. Spread breadcrumbs on a plate, hooter wings breading on another plate, and beat 2 eggs with a hot cause in a bowl. Coat all the egg whites with wing breading, then dip them in the egg mixture and finally coat with the breadcrumbs. Place the coated egg whites in the Air Fryer basket and spray them with cooking oil. Cook them for 4 minutes at 350°F until golden brown in color. Meanwhile, whisk mash egg yolks in a bowl and add mustard, vinegar, mayonnaise, salt, chili powder, and black pepper; mix them well. Add this mixture to a piping bag and pipe it into the center of Air Fried egg whites. Serve and garnish with bacon, cilantro, and hot sauce.

967. Garlic Cheese Rolls

Preparation Time: 15 minutes
Cooking Time: 8-10 minutes
Servings: 8

Ingredients:

- 2 tsp of grated Parmesan cheese
- 2 cups shredded mozzarella cheese
- Cooking spray
- 1 tsp of garlic powder,
- salt and black pepper
- 2/3 cup of almond flour
- 1/2 tsp Italian herb blend
- **Directions**
- With a parchment paper or a piece of aluminum foil, Line your air-fryer basket. After that, spray the foil with a small cooking spray.
- With little inches of water, fill up a small to the average pot, then bring to simmer.
- With your heatproof bowl that is huge enough to relax on the pot without underneath touching the water. Add1/2 tsp salt, mozzarella cheese, 3/4 tsp of garlic powder, and the almond flour. Position your bowl in a simmering water pot. Stir until cheese thaws, and the combination becomes a damp dough, like 6 minutes.
- Scrape the dough out on a cutting board, then allow cooling enough for 3-4minutes to touch. Knead your dough in a smooth ball, pat out, then cut the dough into 6 equivalent portions. Roll every portion in a smooth ball.
- With your small bowl, jointly whisk your dried herbs, the remaining 1/4 tsp of garlic powder, the Parmesan cheese, and 1/4 tsp of pepper.
- Dip every ball into the herb, followed by the cheese combination. After that, lay it in on the ready air-fryer basket. After that, allow baking for 8minutes at 400°F (200°C) until it becomes a golden-brown crust. Allow it to cool for 3minus, and then enjoy!

968. Provolone Egg Sandwich

Preparation Time: 10 minutes
Cooking Time: 5 minutes
Servings: 2

Ingredients:

- 4 slices of artisan bread
- 8 slices provolone cheese
- 2 fried eggs
- 2 tbsp butter

Directions:

- Spread butter on one side of both pieces of bread
- Lay the butter side down for both pieces of bread and add the cheese slices to one piece of bread
- Place it on the air fryer and set it to 350°F for 5 minutes
- Top the melted cheese with an egg.

969. Simple Shredded Beef Tacos

Preparation Time: 30 minutes
Cooking Time: 15 minutes
Servings: 5

Ingredients:

- 1–2 pounds of beef sirloin

- 1 package of flour tortillas
- Salt and pepper to taste
- Sour cream
- Olives

Directions:

- Season your steak with salt and pepper.
- Put it in the air fryer basket and let it cook for 5 minutes at 350°F. Turn it over and air fry for another 5 minutes
- When it's done, cut it into pieces and place them into your tortilla
- Then garnish with sour cream or olives

970. Cheesy Grape Pizza

Preparation Time: 20 minutes
Cooking Time: 35 minutes
Servings: 8

Ingredients:

- 2 cups red seedless grapes
- 1 tsp. sea salt
- ¼ tsp. pepper
- 2 Tbsp. olive oil divided
- 1 sprig rosemary
- 1 pizza dough
- ½ cup ricotta cheese
- ½ cup shredded mozzarella cheese

Directions:

- Mix grapes with pepper, salt, rosemary leaves, 1 tbsp of olive oil
- Wrap them in a baking sheet and bake at 450°F for about 15 minutes, until the skins start to open up
- Bring the grapes out and leave the air fryer on
- Brush the pizza dough with olive oil and sprinkle with a pinch of salt
- Spread on the ricotta, then sprinkle on the other cheese
- Carefully put roasted grapes onto the pizza to avoid excess cooking liquid on the pizza
- Put them into the air fryer and bake at 450°F for 10 minutes or until they lightly brown

971. Cashew Masala

Preparation Time: 5 minutes
Cooking Time: 10 minutes
Servings: 2

Ingredients:

- 1 cup of Unsalted Cashews
- ¼ tsp. of Paprika Powder
- ¼ tsp. of red chili powder (not spicy)
- 1/4 tsp. of Masala Powder
- ½ tsp. of black pepper powder
- 1 tsp. of ghee or clarified butter
- Pink salt as required

Directions:

- Add the cashews, dry spices and add 1 tsp. of melted ghee in a bowl
- Rub the cashews with the spices slowly and make sure the ghee is well coated to have equal roasting
- Then place them in the air fryer and roast at 180°C for 5 minutes

- Stir with a dry spoon and then reduce the temperature to 120°C; roast the cashews for another 2-3 minutes.
- Take them out and leave them to cool.

972.   Cajun Snack Mix

Preparation Time: 15 minutes
Cooking Time: 10 minutes
Servings: 5

Ingredients:

- 2 cups mini wheat thin crackers
- 2 cups peanuts
- 2 cups mini pretzels
- 4 cups plain popcorn
- ½ cups butter melted
- 2 tsp. Cajun or Creole seasoning
- CAJUN SEASONING:
- 1 tsp. Garlic
- 1 tsp. Paprika
- ½ tsp. oregano
- 2 tsp. Salt
- 1 tsp. cayenne pepper
- 1 tsp. Black pepper
- ½ tsp. Thyme
- ½ tsp. onion powder

Directions:

- Pre-heat the air fryer to 370°F.
- Mix the melted butter and the Cajun spice together in a bowl
- Mix together peanuts, pretzels, crackers, and popcorn in another bowl, then pour the butter on mix snacks and mix thoroughly. Fry the first batch by placing them into the air fryer basket and air fry for 9-10 minutes until toasted
- Shake the basket at least 4 times through the cooking time

973.   Apple and Ham Panini

Preparation Time: 20 minutes
Cooking Time: 25-30 minutes
Servings: 1

Ingredients:

- 2 slices of whole-grain bread
- 2 tsp Dijon mustard
- 1 ounce (28 g) cooked low-sodium ham, thinly sliced
- 2 thin slices of Cheddar cheese
- 3 thin slices of apple
- **Directions**
- Preheat the air fryer to 300°F (150°C). Spritz the air fryer basket with cooking spray.
- On a dish, brush the bread with Dijon mustard on both sides.

- Assemble the ham, cheese, and apple slices between the bread slices to make the panini.
- Arrange the panini in the air fryer basket and cook for 5 minutes or until the cheese melts and the bread slices are lightly browned.
- Transfer the panini to a plate and serve warm.

974.   Kenny Rogers Corn Muffins

Preparation Time: 10-15 minutes
Cooking Time: 15 minutes
Servings: 4-6

Ingredients:

- 2 cups all-purpose flour
- 1 ½ cup milk
- ½ tsp. baking powder
- ½ tsp. baking soda
- 2 tbsp. butter
- 1 tbsp. sugar
- 2 tsp. vinegar
- 1 cup boiled corn
- Muffin cups

Directions:

- Combine the ingredients except milk to create a crumbly blend. Add this milk to the blend and make a batter and pour it into the muffin cups. Preheat the fryer to 300°F and cook for 15 minutes. Check whether they are done using a toothpick.

975.   Mini Sweet Corn Pakodas

Preparation Time: 15 minutes
Cooking Time: 8-15 minutes
Servings: 4-5

Ingredients:

- 1 cup flour
- ¼ tsp. Baking soda
- ¼ tsp. Salt
- ½ tsp. Curry powder
- ½ tsp. Red chili powder
- ¼ tsp. turmeric powder
- ¼ cup of water
- 10 pc. baby corn, blanched

Directions:

- Preheat the Air Fryer to 400°F.
- Put aluminum foil on the Air Fryer basket to cover and coat with a light brushing of oil.
- In a bowl, combine all ingredients save for the corn. Stir with a whisk until well combined.
- Coat the corn in the batter and put it inside the Air Fryer.
- Cook for 8 minutes until a golden-brown color is achieved.

CHAPTER 9: DESSERTS

976. Lemon Blueberry Cake

Preparation Time: 30 minutes
Cooking Time: 30 minutes
Servings: 6-8

Ingredients:

- 2 cups unbleached all-purpose flour
- 2 tsp. baking powder
- 1 egg room temp
- 1 tsp. vanilla extract
- 1/2 cup buttermilk
- 2 cups blueberries
- 1/2 lemon juice
- 1/2 cup powdered sugar
- 1/2 tsp. salt
- 1 lemon zest
- 1/2 cup unsalted butter room temp
- 3/4 cup sugar

Directions:

- Grease and flour a dish for the Air fryer.
- Mix the flour, baking powder, and salt in a bowl.
- Reserve 2 tbsp of mixture.
- Blend zest, sugar, egg, vanilla, and room temperature butter.
- Add flour mixture and buttermilk to the sugared butter in the stand mixer.

- Mix blueberries with reserved flour and add to batter.
- Pour water into the Air fryer with a rack.
- Spoon half of the batter into the greased dish in the Pot.
- Set the Air fryer to 400°F for 30 minutes.
- Mix the half lemon juice with half cup powdered sugar and pour over the cake.
- Repeat with the second cake and serve.

977.   Pomegranate and Chocolate Bars

Preparation Time: 20 minutes
Cooking Time: 4-5 minutes
Servings: 4

Ingredients:
- ½ cup milk
- 1 tbsp. vanilla extract
- 1 and ½ cups dark chocolate
- ½ cup almonds
- ½ cup pomegranate seeds

Directions:
- Warm pan with milk over medium heat, put chocolate, turn for 5 minutes, remove heat, put half of the pomegranate seeds, vanilla extract and half of the nuts and turn.
- Put the mix into a lined baking pan, spray spread a pinch of salt, nuts, and remaining pomegranate, get in the air fryer and cook at 300°F for 4 minutes.
- Allow in the fridge for 2 hours, then serve.

978.   Red Wine Pears

Preparation Time: 30 minutes
Cooking Time: 10-15 minutes
Servings: 8

Ingredients:
- 8 pears, peeled
- 2 tbsp. lemon juice
- 1 sprig of fresh mint
- 4 cups dry red wine
- 1/2 cup orange juice
- 2 tsp. grated orange zest
- 1/4 cup sugar
- 1 cinnamon stick
- 1/2 tsp. ground cloves
- 1/2 tsp. ground ginger

Directions:
- Leave pear stalks on with cores removed.
- Coat pears with the lemon juice.
- Sauté the last 7 ingredients for 5 minutes at 330°F.
- Add pears to liquid.
- Sauté at low for 5 minutes.
- Low-Pressure Cook for 3 minutes.
- Serve pears with mint sprig.

979.   Peanut Butter Custard

Preparation Time: 10 minutes
Cooking Time: 21 minutes
Servings: 10

Ingredients:
- ½ cup of granulated sugar

- ¼ tsp of salt
- 4 cups of whole milk
- 1 cup of whipping cream
- Two tsp of vanilla extract
- 1 cup of caramel
- Four whole eggs
- Four egg yolks
- Eight tbsp of peanut butter, smoothened

Directions:
- Set an Air fryer to 350 °F for 15 minutes. Combine peanut butter with sugar, salt, milk, vanilla extract, eggs, and egg yolks in a saucepan. For about 6 minutes, cook on medium-high heat and transfer into a baking dish. Place the baking dish on the cooking tray. Insert the cooking tray in the Air fryer when it displays "Add Food." Remove from the oven when cooking time is complete. Whip the cream with caramel in another bowl and serve it with the peanut butter custard.

980.   Chocolate Peanut Butter and Jelly S'mores

Preparation Time: 5 minutes
Cooking Time: 5 minutes
Servings: 1

Ingredients:
- 2 chocolate graham cracker squares, divided
- 1 chocolate-covered peanut butter cup
- 1 tsp seedless raspberry jam
- 1 large marshmallow
- Cooking spray

Directions:
- Start the S' mores by putting the peanut butter cup on one graham cracker square. Spread the raspberry jam and marshmallow on top.
- Then spritz with cooking spray. Gently arrange the S' mores into the air fryer basket.
- Put the air fryer lid on and cook in the preheated air fryer at 400°F for about 1 minute or until the marshmallow is softened.
- Remove from the basket and top with the remaining graham cracker square to serve.

981.   Creamy Leche Flan

Preparation Time: 10-15 minutes
Cooking Time: 10-15 minutes
Servings: 4-6

Ingredients:
- ½ cup white sugar
- 2 tbsp. water
- 4 large eggs
- 14 oz. sweetened condensed milk
- 12 oz. evaporated milk
- 1 tsp. lemon zest

Directions:
- Microwave sugar and water for 3-4 minutes, stirring midway.
- Pour contents into an oven-safe dish.
- Mix eggs, sweetened condensed milk, evaporated milk, and lemon zest.
- Pour custard mixture into the dish.

- Add water and dish on a trivet to the pot.
- High-Pressure Cook for 8 minutes.
- Refrigerate overnight and serve.

982. Marbled Cheesecake

Preparation Time: 35 minutes
Cooking Time: 20 minutes
Servings: 6-8

Ingredients:

- 1 cup graham cracker crumbs
- 3 tbsp softened butter
- 1½ (8-ounce) packages cream cheese, softened
- ⅓ cup sugar
- 2 eggs, beaten
- 1 tbsp flour
- 1 tsp vanilla
- ¼ cup chocolate syrup

Directions:

- Set to 320°F. Bake For the crust, combine the graham cracker crumbs and butter in a small bowl and mix well. Press into the bottom of a 6-by-6-by-2-inch baking pan and put in the freezer to set.
- For the filling, combine the cream cheese and sugar in a medium bowl and mix well. Beat in the eggs, one at a time. Add the flour and vanilla.
- Remove ⅔ cup of the filling to a small bowl and stir in the chocolate syrup until combined.
- Pour the vanilla filling into the pan with the crust. Drop the chocolate filling over the vanilla filling by the spoonful. With a clean butter knife, stir the fillings in a zigzag pattern to marbleize them.
- Bake for 20 minutes or until the cheesecake is just set.
- Cool on a wire rack for 1 hour, then chill in the refrigerator until the cheesecake is firm.

983. Peanut Butter and Chocolate Cupcakes

Preparation Time: 10 minutes
Cooking Time: 10-15 minutes
Servings: 8

Ingredients:

- Nonstick baking spray with flour
- 1⅓ cups chocolate cake mix (from a 15-ounce box)
- 1 egg
- 1 egg yolk
- ¼ cup safflower oil
- ¼ cup hot water
- ⅓ cup sour cream
- 3 tbsp peanut butter
- 1 tbsp powdered sugar

Directions:

- Double up 16 foil muffin cups to make 8 cups. Spray each lightly with nonstick spray; set aside.
- In a medium bowl, combine the cake mix, egg, egg yolk, safflower oil, water, and sour cream, and beat until combined.
- In a small bowl, combine the peanut butter and powdered sugar and mix well. Form this mixture into 8 balls.
- Spoon about ¼ cup of the chocolate batter into each muffin cup and top with a peanut butter ball. Spoon the

remaining batter on top of the peanut butter balls to cover them.

- Arrange the cups in the air fryer basket, leaving some space between each. Bake for 10 to 13 minutes at 380°F or until the tops look dry and set.
- Let the cupcakes cool for about 10 minutes, then serve warm.

984. Low Sugar Spiced Plums

Preparation Time: 10 minutes
Cooking Time: 20 minutes
Servings: 6

Ingredients:

- 6 plums; cut into wedges
- 10 drops stevia
- Zest of 1 lemon, grated
- 2 tbsp. water
- 1 tsp. ginger, ground
- ½ tsp. cinnamon powder

Directions:

- In a pan that fits the air fryer, combine the plums with the rest of the ingredients, and toss gently.
- Put the pan in the air fryer and cook at 360°F for 20 minutes. Serve cold

985. Raspberries and Avocado Cake

Preparation Time: 15 minutes
Cooking Time: 40 minutes
Servings: 4

Ingredients:

- 2 avocados, peeled, pitted and mashed
- 4 oz. raspberries
- 1 cup swerve
- 1 cup almonds flour
- 4 eggs, whisked
- 4 tbsp. butter; melted
- 3 tsp. baking powder

Directions:

- Take a bowl and mix all the ingredients, toss, and pour this into a cake pan that fits the air fryer after you've lined it with parchment paper.
- Put the pan in the fryer and cook at 340°F for 30 minutes
- Leave the cake to cool down, slice and serve.

986. Dessert Fries

Preparation Time: 15 minutes
Cooking Time: 18-20
Servings: 3

Ingredients:

- 2 medium sweet potatoes peeled
- ½ tbsp of coconut oil.
- 1 tbsp arrowroot starch
- 2 tsp melted butter
- 1/4 cup coconut Sugar
- 2 tbsp cinnamon
- Powdered Sugar for dusting
- Dipping Sauces
- Dessert Hummus

- Honey or Vanilla Greek Yogurt

Directions:

- Slice the peeled sweet potatoes into long ½ thick strips. Toss these slices with arrowroot starch and ½ tbsp coconut oil in a large bowl. Spread the slices in the Air Fryer's Basket and return the basket to the fryer. Cook them for 18 minutes at 370°F by pressing the Start button. Toss them well once cooked halfway through. Whisk sugar with cinnamon in a small bowl. Toss the fried potatoes with 2 tsp butter and drizzle cinnamon on top. Serve with dipping sauces.

987. Deep Fried Cookie Dough Balls

Preparation Time: 20 minutes
Cooking Time: 5-10 minutes
Servings: 4

Ingredients:

- ½ cup all-purpose flour
- ½ cup all-purpose flour
- 1 tbsp sugar
- ½ tbsp brown sugar
- ½ tsp baking powder
- ¼ tsp xanthan gum
- 1 egg, beaten
- ½ tbsp butter, melted
- ½ tsp vanilla extract
- Pinch of cinnamon (optional)
- 3 tbsp mini sugar-free chocolate chips
- Coconut oil, for frying

Directions:

- Combine all the dry ingredients in a mixing bowl. Whisk in egg, vanilla, and melted butter. Mix well until smooth dough forms, then fold in chocolate chips. Roll the dough into a ball, then refrigerate until the air fryer is ready. Grease the Air Fryer's Basket with coconut oil and preheat the fryer to 375°F. Divide the dough into small cookie-sized balls and place them in the basket. Return the fryer basket to the air fryer and cook them for 3-5 minutes. Serve.

988. Dark Chocolate Muffins

Preparation Time: 15 minutes
Cooking Time: 20 minutes
Servings: 8

Ingredients:

- 2 cups all-purpose flour
- 1 ½ cup milk
- 3 tbsp. Dark cocoa powder
- ½ tsp. Baking powder
- ½ tsp. baking soda
- 2 tbsp. butter
- 1 tbsp. sugar
- Muffin cups

Directions:

- Mix the ingredients together and use your fingers to get a crumbly mixture.
- Add the baking soda to the milk and mix continuously.
- Add this milk to the mixture and create a batter, which you will need to transfer to the muffin cups.
- Preheat the fryer to 300°F for 5 minutes.

- You will need to place the muffin cups in the basket and cover it.
- Cook the muffins for 15 minutes and check whether or not the muffins are cooked using a toothpick.
- Remove the cups and serve hot.

989. Fudgy Brownies

Preparation Time: 20 minutes
Cooking Time: 20 minutes
Servings: 8

Ingredients:

- 1/2 cup flour
- 1/3 cup cocoa powder
- 1 cup sugar
- 1/2 cup butter; melted
- 2 eggs
- 1 tsp. vanilla extract
- 1 tsp. baking powder

Directions:

- Set the temperature of the Air fryer to 350°F. Grease a baking pan. In a large bowl, add the sugar and butter and whisk until light and fluffy. Add the remaining ingredients and mix until well combined. Place mixture evenly into the prepared pan, and with the back of a spatula, smooth the top surface
- Arrange the baking pan into an air fryer basket. Air fry pan for about 20 minutes
- Remove the baking pan from the air fryer and set it aside to cool completely. Cut into 8 equal-sized squares and serve.

990. Low-fat Mug Cake

Preparation Time: 10 minutes
Cooking Time: 13-15 minutes
Servings: 1

Ingredients:

- 1/4 cup self-rising flour
- 3 tbsp. coconut oil
- 3 tbsp. whole milk
- 1 tbsp. cocoa powder
- 5 tbsp. caster sugar

Directions:

- In a shallow mug, add all the ingredients and mix until well combined
- Set the temperature of air fryer to 392°F.
- Arrange the mug into an air fryer basket. Air fry for about 13 minutes. Remove from the air fryer and serve warm

991. Stuffed Apples with Vanilla Sauce

Preparation Time: 20 minutes
Cooking Time: 15 minutes
Servings: 4

Ingredients:

- For Stuffed Apples:
- 1/2 cup blanched almonds
- 1/2 cup golden raisins
- 4 small firm apples, cored
- 2 tbsp. sugar

- For Vanilla Sauce:
- 2 tbsp. sugar
- 1/2 tsp. vanilla extract
- 1/2 cup whipped cream

Directions:
- In a food processor, add raisins, almonds and sugar and pulse until chopped. Carefully; stuff each apple with raisin mixture. Set the temperature of air fryer to 355°F. Line a baking dish with a parchment paper. Now; place apples into the prepared baking dish
- Arrange the baking dish into an air fryer basket. Air fry for about 10 minutes. Meanwhile; for the vanilla sauce: in a pan, add the cream, sugar and vanilla extract over medium heat and cook for about 2 to 3 minutes or until sugar is dissolved, stirring continuously
- Remove the baking dish from the air fryer and transfer the apples onto plates to cool slightly. Top with the vanilla sauce and serve.

992. Strawberry Cream cheese Chimichangas

Preparation Time: 35 minutes
Cooking Time: 30 minutes
Servings: 6

Ingredients:
- 1 package of cream chees, kept at room temperature
- ¼ cup Sour cream
- ¼ cup + 1 tbsp Sugar
- 1 tsp Vanilla extract
- 1 tsp Lemon zest
- 6 (8-inch) soft flour tortillas
- 1+3/4 cups of sliced strawberries
- 1 tbsp Cinnamon

Directions:
- Beat the sour cream with the cream cheese, 1 tbsp of sugar, vanilla extract, and lemon zest in the container of an electric mixer fitted with the paddle attachment, scraping down the sides of the bowl as desired.
- Fold up the sliced strawberries in 3/4 cup.
- If you warm them up a little bit in the microwave, the tortillas can bend easier. Leave them in the kit and spend 30-45 seconds in.
- Divide the mixture evenly between the tortillas, slathering each portion of each tortilla in the bottom third.
- Then turn the two sides of each tortilla towards the middle and roll up the tortilla like a burrito, and protect it with a toothpick.
- The remaining tortillas replicate the rolling process.
- Take a deep bowl, add the remaining 1/4 cup sugar with the cinnamon and set them aside.
- Set the air fryer at 400°F.
- Place the chimichangas in the basket of an air fryer.
- Spray some cooking spray over the chimichanga.
- Set the timer within 6 minutes.
- Take out chimichangas from the basket after 6 minutes.
- Roll them out into the mixture of cinnamon and sugar.
- Remove the chimichangas from all the toothpicks and place them on the serving plates.
- Cover each slice of strawberries with chimichanga and serve immediately.

993. S'mores

Preparation Time: 5 minutes
Cooking Time: 5 minutes
Servings: 4

Ingredients:
- 4 graham crackers (each half split to make 2 squares, for a total of 8 squares)
- 8 Squares of Hershey's chocolate bar, broken into squares
- 4 Marshmallows

Directions:
- Put 4 squares of graham crackers on a basket of the air fryer.
- Place 2 squares of chocolate bars on each cracker.
- Place back the basket in the air fryer and fry on-air at 390°F for 1 minute. It is barely long enough for the chocolate to melt. Remove basket from air fryer.
- Top with a marshmallow over each cracker. Throw the marshmallow down a little bit into the melted chocolate. This will help to make the marshmallow stay over the chocolate.
- Put back the basket in the air fryer and fry at 390 °F for 2 minutes. (The marshmallows should be puffed up and browned at the tops.)
- Using tongs, carefully remove each cracker from the basket of the air fryer and place it on a platter. Top each marshmallow with another square of graham crackers.
- Enjoy it right away!

994. Fried Oreos

Preparation Time: 10 minutes
Cooking Time: 10 minutes
Servings: 4

Ingredients:
- ½ cup Pancake Mix
- ½ cup Water
- Cooking spray
- 9 Chocolate sandwich cookies
- 1 tbsp Confectioners' sugar

Directions:
- Blend the pancake mixture with the water until well mixed.
- Line the parchment paper on the basket of an air fryer. Spray nonstick cooking spray on parchment paper. Dip each cookie into the mixture of the pancake and place it in the basket. Make sure they do not touch; if possible, cook in batches.
- The air fryer is preheated to 400°F (200°C). Add basket and cook for 4 to 5 minutes; flip until golden brown, 2 to 3 more minutes. Sprinkle the sugar over the cookies and serve.

995. Cinnamon Fried Bananas

Preparation Time: 10 minutes
Cooking Time: 10 minutes
Servings: 4

Ingredients:
- 1 cup panko breadcrumbs
- 3 tbsp. cinnamon

- ½ cup almond flour
- 3 egg whites
- 8 ripe bananas
- 3 tbsp. vegan coconut oil

Directions:
- Heat coconut oil and add breadcrumbs. Mix around 2-3 minutes until golden. Pour into a bowl.
- Peel and cut bananas in half. Roll each banana half into flour, eggs, and crumb mixture. Place into the air fryer.
- Cook for 10 minutes at 280°F.
- A great addition to a healthy banana split!

996. Soft Doughnuts

Preparation Time: 20 minutes
Cooking Time: 10 minutes
Servings: 6

Ingredients:
- 1/2 cup sugar
- 2 ¼ cups white flour
- 1 tsp. cinnamon powder
- 2 egg yolks
- 1/3 cup caster sugar
- 4 tbsp. butter; soft
- 1 ½ tsp. baking powder
- 1/2 cup sour cream

Directions:
- In a bowl; mix 2 tbsp butter with simple sugar and egg yolks and whisk well
- Add half of the sour cream and stir.
- In another bowl; mix flour with baking powder, stir and also add to eggs mix
- Stir well until you obtain a dough, transfer it to a floured working surface; roll it out and cut big circles with smaller ones in the middle.
- Brush doughnuts with the rest of the butter; heat up your air fryer at 360°F; place doughnuts inside and cook them for 8 minutes
- In a bowl, mix cinnamon with caster sugar and stir. Arrange doughnuts on plates and dip them in cinnamon and sugar before serving.

997. Vanilla Bread Pudding

Preparation Time: 15 minutes
Cooking Time: 20 minutes
Servings: 2

Ingredients:
- 4 white sandwich bread slices
- 1 egg
- ¼ cup heavy cream
- 1 tsp vanilla extract
- 3 tsp butter
- ½ tsp ground cinnamon
- 1 tbsp almond flakes
- 2 tsp raisins
- ½ tsp olive oil

Directions:
- Take off the crust from the sandwich bread slices.
- Then spread every bread slice with the butter.
- Spray the ramekin with olive oil.

- Place the first bread slice in the ramekin.
- Then sprinkle it with the vanilla extract.
- After this, put the second bread slice in the ramekin and sprinkle it with the ground cinnamon.
- Add the third bread slice and sprinkle it with the raisins.
- Then put the last bread slice in the ramekin.
- Crack the egg into the bowl and whisk it.
- Add heavy cream and whisk it.
- Pour the egg mixture into the ramekin.
- Sprinkle the pudding mixture with the raisins.
- Preheat the air fryer to 360°F.
- Put the ramekin in the air fryer and cook it for 22 minutes.
- Serve the cooked pudding immediately.
- Enjoy!

998. Semolina Milk Cake

Preparation Time: 15 minutes
Cooking Time: 6 minutes
Servings: 2

Ingredients:
- 4 tbsp semolina
- 8 tbsp milk
- 1 tbsp flour
- 2 tbsp white sugar
- 1 tsp butter
- 1 egg yolk
- 1 tsp vanilla extract

Directions:
- Combine together semolina and milk.
- Whisk the egg yolk in a separate bowl.
- Add flour and white sugar.
- After this, combine together semolina mixture and the egg yolk mixture.
- Add butter and vanilla extract. Whisk it well.
- Preheat the air fryer to 400°F.
- Place the semolina mixture in the air fryer basket and cook it for 6 minutes.
- When the cake is cooked – it will have a golden brown surface.
- Enjoy it warm!

999. Snow White's Cake

Preparation Time: 10 minutes
Cooking Time: 40 minutes
Servings: 6

Ingredients:
- 4 tbsp of olive oil
- 1 tsp of vanilla extract
- 2 tsp of baking powder
- ½ cup of sugar
- ¼ tsp of cinnamon powder
- 1 cup of all-purpose flour
- 2 apples, one sliced and one diced
- 1 tbsp of lemon juice
- 1 egg
- 1 tsp of baking soda
- 2 cups of water
- 1 cup of ricotta cheese

Directions:

- Set the Air fryer to 355°F for 40 minutes. Cream together sugar, egg, ricotta cheese, olive oil, and vanilla extract in a bowl. Sieve the cinnamon powder, flour, baking powder, and baking soda in another bowl. Fold the cinnamon mixture into the sugar mixture. Arrange the apples in the cake tin and squeeze in the lemon juice. Pour the combined batter over the apples and place the cake tin on the cooking tray. Insert the cooking tray in the Air fryer when it displays "Add Food." Remove from the oven when cooking time is complete. Slice into desired pieces and serve warm.

1000. Caramel Muffins

Preparation Time: 10 minutes
Cooking Time: 12 minutes
Servings: 2

Ingredients:

- 1 oz caramel
- 1 egg
- 4 oz sour cream
- 1/3 tsp baking powder
- 4 tbsp flour
- 2 tsp white sugar
- 1 tsp butter

Directions:

- Beat the egg in the mixing bowl and whisk it.
- Add sour cream and baking powder.
- After this, add flour, white sugar, and butter.
- Use the mixer to make the smooth mass.
- Then pour the dough into the muffin molds.
- Fill the piping bag with the caramel.
- Fill the muffin dough with the caramel.
- Preheat the air fryer to 365°F.
- Place the muffins in the air fryer basket and cook them for 12 minutes.

1001. Cinnamon Churros

Preparation Time: 10 minutes
Cooking Time: 6 minutes
Servings: 2

Ingredients:

- ¼ cup water, hot
- 1 egg
- 1 pinch salt
- 1/3 cup flour
- 1 tbsp butter
- 1 tbsp brown sugar
- 1 tsp ground cinnamon

Directions:

- Combine together flour, butter, salt, and hot water.
- Mix the mixture until smooth.
- Then beat the egg in the flour mixture and mix it with the help of the hand mixer.
- Fill the piping bag with the dough.
- Cover the air fryer basket with the parchment.
- Make the small sticks (churros) from the dough.
- Preheat the air fryer to 400°F and cook the meal for 6 minutes.

- Meanwhile, combine together the brown sugar and ground cinnamon.
- Toss the cooked churros into the sugar mixture and coat well.
- Serve the dessert and enjoy!

1002. Chocolate Oatmeal Cookies

Preparation Time: 10 minutes
Cooking Time: 7 minutes
Servings: 2

Ingredients:

- 1 tbsp chocolate chips
- 3 tbsp flour
- 3 tbsp butter
- 1 tbsp oatmeal
- 1 tsp lemon zest
- ¼ tsp vanilla sugar

Directions:

- Melt the butter and combine it together with the chocolate chips and flour.
- Add oatmeal, lemon zest, and vanilla sugar.
- Mix the mixture carefully with the help of the spoon and then knead it with the help of the fingertips.
- Make the medium balls from the dough and flatten them gently in the shape of the cookies.
- Preheat the air fryer to 365°F.
- Place the cookies in the air fryer basket and cook for 7 minutes. The time of cooking depends on the size of the cookies.
- When the cookies are cooked – let them chill well and serve.

1003. Cashew Cookies

Preparation Time: 15 minutes
Cooking Time: 15 minutes
Servings: 2

Ingredients:

- 3 tbsp flour
- 1 tsp butter
- 1 tsp cashew, crushed
- ½ tsp vanilla extract
- 1 tbsp brown sugar
- ½ tsp cream

Directions:

- Make the butter soft and place it in the big bowl.
- Add flour and vanilla extract.
- After this, add brown sugar and cream.
- Knead the smooth and non-sticky dough.
- Roll the dough and make the cookies with the help of the cutter.
- Sprinkle every cookie with crushed cashews.
- Press the surface of the cookies lightly.
- Preheat the air fryer to 360°F.
- Put the cookies in the air fryer basket tray and cook the cookies for 15 minutes.
- When the cookies are cooked – let them chill briefly.

1004. Apricot Nutmeg Muffins

Preparation Time: 15minutes
Cooking Time: 12 minutes
Servings: 2

Ingredients:
- 1 tbsp apricot jam
- 2 apricots
- ½ tsp ground nutmeg
- 1 tsp lemon juice
- 5 tbsp flour
- 3 tbsp butter
- ½ tsp baking soda
- 1 tsp vanilla extract
- 3 tbsp brown sugar

Directions:
- Halve the apricots and remove the stones.
- Chop the apricots and combine them with the jam.
- Add brown sugar, lemon juice, ground nutmeg, baking soda, and vanilla extract.
- Mix the mixture up and add flour.
- Then melt the butter and add it to the ham mixture.
- Use the hand mixer to make the homogenous dough.
- Preheat the air fryer to 360°F.
- Fill ½ part of every muffin mold with the dough and place them in the air fryer basket.
- Cook the muffins for 12 minutes.
- When the muffins are cooked – let them chill briefly and remove them from the air fryer basket.
- Serve the muffins, and enjoy!

1005. Sugar Free Coconut Cookies

Preparation Time: 20 minutes
Cooking Time: 12 minutes
Servings: 8

Ingredients:
- 1 Egg
- 3 tbsp Dried coconut
- 3 oz. Butter
- 2 oz. Erythritol powdered
- 1 tsp Vanilla extract
- 2 oz. Chocolate, no sugar added
- 5 oz. Almond flour

Directions:
- In a bowl, beat butter and erythritol until fluffy. Add one egg and vanilla extract and stir to combine. Crush the chocolate into small pieces. Add them to the mixture. Roll small balls with your hands. Roll these balls in the dried coconut. Place balls on the baking sheet. Preheat the air fryer to 370°F. Bake coconut balls for 8 minutes. Shake once. Lower temperature to 280°F to 300°F and cook for 4 minutes more. Serve.

1006. Moist Chocolate Cake

Preparation Time: 20 minutes
Cooking Time: 30 minutes
Servings: 6

Ingredients:
- 3 Eggs
- ½ cup Sour cream

- 1 cup Flour
- 2/3 cup Sugar
- 1Butter stick, room temperature
- 1/3 cup Cocoa powder
- 1 tsp Baking powder
- ½ tsp Baking soda
- 2 tsp Vanilla

Directions:
- Preheat the air fryer to 320°F. Mix the wet ingredients in a bowl and the dry ingredients in another. Gradually pour the dry mixture into the wet. Lightly mix. Place in the air fryer basket. Cook for 25 minutes. Check if the cake is done; if not, then cook for another 5 more minutes. Cool on a wire rack.

1007. Healthy Pecan Brownies

Preparation Time: 15minutes
Cooking Time: 20 minutes
Servings: 6

Ingredients:
- ½ cup Almond flour
- ½ cup Powdered erythritol
- 2 tbsp Unsweetened cocoa powder
- ½ tsp Baking powder
- ¼ cup Unsalted butter, softened
- 1 Egg
- ¼ cup Chopped pecans
- ¼ cup Chocolate chips

Directions:
- Mix almond flour, baking powder, cocoa powder, and erythritol in a bowl. Stir in egg and butter. Fold in chocolate chips and pecans. Scoop the mixture into a baking pan and place the pan into the air fryer basket. Cook at 300°F for 20 minutes. Cool, slice and serve.

1008. Best Carrot Cake

Preparation Time: 30 minutes
Cooking Time: 45 minutes
Servings: 8

Ingredients:
- 5 ounces Flour
- ¾ tsp Baking powder
- ½ tsp Baking soda
- ½ tsp Cinnamon powder
- ½ tsp Allspice
- ¼ tsp Nutmeg ground
- 1 Egg
- 3 tbsp Yogurt
- ½ cup Sugar
- ¼ cup Pineapple juice
- 4 tbsp Sunflower oil
- 1/3 cup Carrots, grated
- 1/3 cup Pecans, toasted and chopped
- 1/3 cup Coconut flakes, shredded
- Cooking spray

Directions:
- In a bowl, mix flour, nutmeg, cinnamon, allspice, salt, baking soda, and powder and mix. In another bowl, mix the egg with coconut flakes, pecans, carrots, oil,

pineapple juice, sugar, and yogurt. Combine the two mixtures and mix well. Pour this into a greased springform pan. Place the pan in the air fryer and cook at 320°F for 45 minutes. Cool, slice and serve.

1009. Autumn Pumpkin Cake

Preparation Time: 30 minutes
Cooking Time: 30 minutes
Servings: 10

Ingredients:
- ¾ cup White flour
- ¾ cup Whole wheat flour
- 1 tsp Baking soda
- ¾ tsp Pumpkin pie spice
- ¾ cup Sugar
- 1 Banana , mashed
- ½ tsp Baking powder
- 2 tbsp Canola oil
- ½ cup Greek yogurt
- 8 ounces of canned pumpkin puree
- Cooking spray
- 1 Egg
- ½ tsp Vanilla extract
- 2/3 cup Chocolate chips

Directions:
- In a bowl, mix whole wheat flour, white flour, salt, baking soda, baking powder, and pumpkin spice and stir. In another bowl, mix egg, vanilla, pumpkin puree, yogurt, banana, oil, and sugar. Mix with a mixer. Combine the 2 mixtures, and add the chocolate chips. Pour this into a greased Bundt pan. Place in the air fryer and cook at 330°F for 30 minutes. Cool, slice and serve.

1010. Chocolate Zucchini Bread

Preparation Time: 20 minutes
Cooking Time: 30-35 minutes
Servings: 6

Ingredients:
- 1/2 cup of all-purpose flour
- 1/4 cup of cocoa powder
- 1/2 tsp of baking soda
- 1/4 tsp of salt
- 1 egg at room temperature
- 6 tbsp of packed light brown sugar
- 2 tbsp of butter melted and slightly cooled
- 2 tbsp of vegetable oil
- 1/2 tsp of vanilla extract
- ¾ cup of packed shredded zucchini
- 1/2 cup of semisweet chocolate chips divided

Directions:
- The Air Fryer is preheated to 310°F.
- Grease with shortening to a mini loaf pan. Deposit aside.
- Whisk the flour, cocoa powder, baking soda, and salt together in a medium mixing bowl. Deposit aside.
- Combine eggs, brown sugar, melted butter, oil, and vanilla in a larger bowl. Whisk smoothly until.
- Add the dry ingredients and mix them until just combined.

- Fold in the zucchini and most chocolate chips, setting aside some for the top.
- Transfer to mini loaf prepared pan.
- Sprinkle over the remaining chocolate chips.
- Bake for 30 to 35 minutes in the air fryer at 310°F, or until the toothpick test comes out clean.
- Remove from the air fryer and cool down on a wire rack until warm.
- Then remove from the loaf pan before storing in an airtight container and continue cooling on the wire rack.

1011. Moist Date Bread

Preparation Time: 15 minutes
Cooking Time: 20 minutes
Servings: 10

Ingredients:
- ¼ cup of butter
- 1½ cups of flour
- One tsp of baking powder
- ½ tsp of salt
- 2½ cup of dates, pitted and chopped
- 1 cup of hot water
- ½ cup of brown sugar
- One tsp of baking soda
- One egg

Directions:
- Set an Air fryer to 340°F for 20 minutes. Combine dates with butter and hot water in a bowl. Strain together brown sugar, flour, baking powder, baking soda, and salt in another bowl. Fold the brown sugar mixture and egg in the dates mixture. Place the dough on the cooking tray. Insert the cooking tray in the Air fryer when it displays "Add Food." Flip the sides when it shows "Turn Food." Remove from the oven when cooking time is complete. Slice into desired pieces to serve.

1012. Cherry Pie

Preparation Time: 30 minutes
Cooking Time: 30 minutes
Servings: 6

Ingredients:
- 2 rolls of refrigerated pie crust
- All-purpose flour for dusting
- 1 can of cherry pie filling 12.5-ounce
- 1 egg beaten
- 1 tbsp of water
- 1 tbsp of raw sugar

Directions:
- Defrost the crust of the refrigerated pie and place it on a flat, floured surface of work.
- Roll out the thawed pie crust, and reverse the dough with a shallow air fryer baking pan.
- Cut the pan around, making your cut a half-inch wider than the pan itself.
- Repeat with the crust of the second pie. Only make the cut the same size or slightly smaller than the pan.
- Layout the larger crust at the bottom of the baking pan, gently pressing into the dough to conform to the shape of the pan.

- Spoon in the filling of a cherry pie. Place the smaller piece of crust over the filling, and pinch each crust edge together.
- OR-cut the second piece into 1 "strips and weave in a lattice pattern before placing it over the top of the pie. Make a few cuts at the top of the dough. In a small bowl, whisk the egg and water together. Sprinkle the egg gently over the top of the pie. Sprinkle with the raw sugar and place the pan in the air fryer basket. Bake at 320°F for 30 minutes, until golden brown and flaky.

1013. Chocolate Chip Muffins

Preparation Time: 20 minutes
Cooking Time: 15 minutes
Servings: 8

Ingredients:

- 1/2 cup of self-rising flour
- 1/2 cup of all-purpose flour baking powder salt or use half tsp pinch
- 1 tbsp of cocoa Nesquik or powder
- 1/4 tsp of baking soda
- 1/4 cup of sugar
- 1 tbsp of honey
- 2 tbsps. of yogurt
- 4 tbsps. of milk
- 2 tbsps. of vegetable oil
- 1/2 tsp vanilla extract
- 1 tsp of apple cider vinegar (or regular vinegar)
- 2 tbsps. of chocolate chips

Directions:

- The air fryer preheats to 200°F.
- Remove 1 tbsp of flour from the 1/2 cup flour and add 1 tbsp of cocoa or Nesquick powder. This is to ensure that the dry component total is 1/2 cup. Attach the baking powder and salt if you use plain flour and do not collect flour on your own.
- Stir in baking soda and sugar and combine it with a fork.
- Whisk together milk, yogurt, oil, and vanilla extract in a measuring jug or small bowl, until combined.
- Make the dry ingredients well, and add the wet ingredients. Stir in vinegar.
- Stir to merge. Do not over-mix; at this stage, a few lumps of flour are ok. Blend into chocolate chips. Spoon the mixture into 6 silicone cupcake/muffin molds Position 4 at a time in the preheated air fryer wire rack.
- Set timer at 8 minutes, after which a skewer/tester can be inserted to see if it comes out cleanly. At this point, you can keep the second batch for baking.
- Remove for 5 minutes, then cool. Remove from molds, and cover or place in airtight refrigerator containers.
- You can store that in an airtight box for 4-5 days in the refrigerator.

1014. Tropical Bananas

Preparation Time: 15 minutes
Cooking Time: 12 minutes
Servings: 4

Ingredients:

- 4 ripe but firm bananas cut into thirds
- 1/2 cup of tapioca flour

- 2 large eggs
- 1 cup of shredded coconut flakes
- 1 tsp of ground cinnamon
- coconut spray

Directions:

- Cut each banana into thirds. Make an assembly line-Pour in a shallow dish the tapioca flour.
- Crack the eggs and whisk lightly into another shallow bowl.
- In the third shallow dish, mix the shredded coconut with the ground cinnamon. Blend well.
- Dredge the tapioca flour into the bananas and shake off the excess.
- Dip the beaten eggs into it. Make sure the egg wash is fully coated.
- To coat it fully, roll the bananas in the cinnamon–coconut flakes. Press it firmly to ensure the bananas adhere to the coconut flakes. Keep them in a flat dresser.
- Sprinkle the air fryer basket with coconut oil liberally.
- Arrange the bits of coconut-crusted bananas in the bowl for the fryer. Sprinkle with more spray on coconut.
- Air fry for 12 minutes at 270°F with soil cinnamon and serve warm or at room temperature with a low-carb ice cream scoop (optional)

1015. Apple Cider Donuts

Preparation Time: 30 minutes
Cooking Time: 10 minutes
Servings: 5

Ingredients:

- 4 large eggs
- 4 tbsp of coconut oil melted
- 3 tbsp of honey
- 2/3 cup apple cider vinegar
- 1 cup of coconut flour
- 1 tsp of cinnamon
- 1 tsp of baking soda
- pinch salt

Directions:

- Oven preheats to 350°F. Prepare a donut baking pan by spraying liberally with cooking spray or using coconut oil to grease well.
- Wish the eggs, salt, honey, apple cider vinegar, and melted coconut oil together in a small bowl.
- Sift cinnamon, baking soda, and coconut flour together in a separate bowl to disperse the dry ingredients well.
- Attach the dry ingredients to the wet ingredients until mixed thoroughly. The batter is going to be a bit humid. Transfer the batter to the baking pan for the donut and scoop the batter into the cavities. Use your fingers to evenly spread the batter inside the cavity.
- Bake for 10 minutes at 350°F, until golden around the edges.
- Remove from the oven and cool in baking for 5-10 minutes before flipping onto a removable wire rack. It's very important that these are cool before you remove them. Otherwise, they're going to fall apart. They need to be a little tough!

1016. Sugar Free Cheesecake

Preparation Time: 40 minutes
Cooking Time: 2minutes
Servings: 4

Ingredients:

- 8 ounces of cream cheese
- 1/2 cup of erythritol
- 4 tbsp of heavy cream, divided
- 1/2 tsp of vanilla extract
- 1/2 cup of almond flour
- 2 tbsp of erythritol

Directions:

- Allow the cream cheese to sit on the counter and soften for 20 minutes.
- Fits a paddle attachment stand mixer.
- Mix the softened cream cheese, 1/2 cup Erythritol, vanilla and 2 Heavy cream spoonfuls until smooth.
- Lined with parchment paper, scoop onto a baking sheet.
- Freeze for approximately 30 minutes until strong.
- In a small mixing bowl, combine the almond flour with the 2 Tbsp erythritol.
- Dip the bites from the frozen cheesecake into 2 Tbsp of cream, then roll into the almond flour mix. Set at 300°F, and place in an air fryer for 2 minutes.

1017. Sesame Banana Dessert

Preparation Time: 5 minutes
Cooking Time: 15 minutes
Servings: 5

Ingredients:

- 1 ½ cups flour
- 5 bananas, sliced
- 1 tsp salt
- 3 tbsp sesame seeds
- 1 cup of water
- 2 eggs, beaten
- 1 tsp baking powder
- ½ tbsp sugar

Directions:

- Preheat Cuisinart on Bake function to 340°F. In a bowl, mix salt, sesame seeds, flour, baking powder, eggs, sugar, and water. Coat-sliced bananas with the flour mixture. Place the prepared slices in the Air Fryer basket and fit in the baking tray; cook for 8-10 minutes. Serve chilled.

1018. Flourless Chocolate Coconut Cupcakes

Preparation Time: 20 minutes
Cooking Time: 25-30 minutes
Servings: 4

Ingredients:

- 3 tbsp. of butter
- 2 tbsp. of real maple syrup
- 1/2 cup of almond flour
- 1/8 tsp. of salt
- 1/3 cup of chocolate chips
- 1 egg beaten

Directions:

- For Air Fryer: Preheat at 320°C. Use cupcake liners with silicone.
- Add the chocolate chips, butter, and honey to a glass or stainless-steel bowl and heat over a double boiler for a few seconds only until the chocolate begins to melt. When the chocolate begins to melt, remove the bowl and start stirring until the butter, honey, and chocolate are well blended. Let it cool off (about 5-8 min.).
- In the cooled melted chocolate, add the remaining ingredients and stir well with a wooden spoon. Scoop the batter into the cupcake pan that was packed.
- Bake for about 15-18 minutes or until a toothpick inserted comes out clean. Bake for 8-12 minutes
- If the toothpick does not come out clean, then continue cooking at intervals of 3-4 minutes.
- Top with slivered almonds and unflavored shredded coconut. Sprinkle on and serve with powdered sugar.

1019. Lemon Sugar Cookies

Preparation Time: 20 minutes
Cooking Time: 12 minutes
Servings: 12

Ingredients:

- 1/2 cup of unsalted butter, softened
- 1 package (3.4 ounces) of instant lemon pudding mix
- 1/2 cup of sugar
- 1 large egg, room temperature
- 2 tbsp of 2% milk
- 1-1/2 cups of all-purpose flour
- 1 tsp of baking powder
- 1/4 of tsp salt
- ICING:
- 2/3 cup of confectioners' sugar
- 2 to 4 tsp of lemon juice

Directions:

- Cream butter, pudding mixture and sugar in a large bowl until light and fluffy. Beat in milk and egg. Whisk the flour, baking powder and salt in another bowl; beat gradually into creamed mixture.
- Divide the batter into half. Form each into a 6-in.-long roll on a lightly floured surface. Wrap it and allow it to chill for 3 hours, or until firm.
- The air fryer preheats to 325°F. Cross-section dough unwraps and cuts into 1/2 in. Sliced slices. Place the slices in a foil-lined fryer basket in a single layer. Cook for 8-12 minutes, until edges are light brown. Cool down for 2 minutes in a basket. Remove to wire racks to fully cool down. Repeat with leftover dough. Mix sugar from the confectioners and enough lemon juice in a small bowl to achieve drizzling consistency. Drizzle cookies over. Let's stand till set.
- To Make Ahead: Dough can be done 2 days beforehand. Put in a resealable container and wrap it in. Store it in the fridge.
- Freeze option: Place wrapped logs and freeze them in a resealable container. Unwrap frozen logs to use, and cut them into slices. Cook as directed, adding 1-2 minutes more time.

1020. Irish Butter Cookies

Preparation Time: 15 minutes
Cooking Time: 10 minutes
Servings: 4

Ingredients:
- 8 ounces of all-purpose flour
- 1 tsp baking powder
- A pinch of nutmeg, grated
- A pinch of coarse salt
- 2½ ounces sugar
- 1 stick butter, room temperature
- 1 tsp vanilla extract
- 1 large egg, room temperature.

Directions:
- In a mixing bowl, combine the flour with baking powder, grated nutmeg, coarse salt, and sugar. Set aside.
- Whip the butter, vanilla extract, and separated egg in another bowl. Set aside.
- Blend two bowls of the mixture and continuously stir until it becomes a soft and smooth dough.
- To make the cookies, on a lightly floured surface, roll the dough into 1-inch balls and press them with the tines of a fork to flatten.
- Arrange them in the air fryer basket lined with parchment paper. Put the air fryer lid on and bake in batches in the preheated air fryer at 350°F for 20 minutes.
- Remove the cookies from the basket and serve on a plate.

1021. PB & J Doughnuts

Preparation Time: 30 minutes
Cooking Time: 11-15 minutes
Servings: 6

Ingredients:
- Doughnuts:
- 1 1/4 cup of all-purpose flour
- 1/3 cup sugar
- 1/2 tsp of baking powder
- 1/2 tsp baking soda
- 3/4 tsp of salt
- 1 Egg
- 1/2 cup of buttermilk
- 1 tsp of vanilla
- 2 tbsp of unsalted butter, melted and cooled
- 1 tbsp of melted butter for brushing the tops
- Filling:
- 1/2 cup of Blueberry or strawberry jelly (not preserves)
- Glaze:
- 1/2 cup of powdered sugar
- 2 Tbsp milk
- 2 Tbsp peanut butter
- Pinch of sea salt

Directions:
- Air fried doughnuts with peanut butter glaze. Whisk together the flour, sugar, baking powder, baking soda and salt in a large bowl.
- The egg, melted butter, buttermilk, and vanilla beat together in a separate bowl.

- Create a well in the dry ingredient center and pour it into the water. Use a fork to mix, then finish stirring with a large spoon until the flour is added.
- Turn the dough out onto a surface well-floured. Note that, at first, it will be very sticky. Work the dough very slightly before they come together, and then pat it out to a thickness of 3/4. Cut out dough rounds and brush them with melted butter using a 3 1/2 "cutter. Cut off 2 pieces of baking paper (it doesn't have to be precise) and place each dough round on paper, then inside the air fryer. Work in lots according to how many will fit in your fryer.
- Fry for 11 minutes at 350°F. Use a squeeze bottle or pastry sac to fill each doughnut with jelly.
- Whisk the ingredients of the glaze together, then slice over each doughnut.

1022. Zebra Cake

Preparation Time: 20 minutes
Cooking Time: 30 minutes
Servings: 8

Ingredients:
- 115g butter
- 2 eggs
- 100g of castor sugar
- 100g self-rising flour sifted
- 30ml of milk
- 1tsp of vanilla extract
- 1 tbsp of cocoa powder

Directions:
- The air fryer preheats to 160°C. Line the 6 "baking tin base and grease the surface of the tray Beat butter and sugar in a mixer until fluffy Add eggs one at a time and add vanilla extract and milk. Mix well in the mixer. Add sifted flour and mix until half the batter is mixed and set aside. Add cocoa powder to a mixer and mix well. Scoop 2 tbsp of plain batter in the center of a baking tin. Place the baking tin in the air fryer and bake for 30 minutes at 160°C, or until the skewer appears clean.

1023. Roasted Pears

Preparation Time: 10 minutes
Cooking Time: 20 minutes
Servings: 2

Ingredients:
- 4 pears with rind well washed
- 50 g Raisins
- 2 tbsp jam without sugar
- 1 tsp honey
- 1 pinch of cinnamon powder

Directions:
- Pears are washed and hollowed out by extracting the heart.
- Separate the pulp
- Mix the jam chosen with the pulp of pears, honey and raisins and cinnamon
- Fill the pears with that mixture
- Place the pears in the fryer
- In the bowl, place a glass of water

- Cook for 20 minutes at 180°C
- Serve them alone or accompanied with a scoop of vanilla ice cream.

1024.　Chocolate and Ricotta Cake

Preparation Time: 10 minutes
Cooking Time: 40 minutes
Servings: 8

Ingredients:
- 250 g flour
- 200 g of sugar
- Eggs
- 350 g ricotta
- 120 g melted butter
- 1 sachet of yeast
- 50 g of chocolate chips

Directions:
- Add ricotta with sugar, and add eggs and melted butter. Add the sifted flour with the yeast and finally the chocolate chips.
- Butter and flour the basket and pour the mixture inside, smearing well.
- Set the temperature to 180°C and bake the cake for 40 minutes.
- Let cool and remove it from the basket; sprinkle with icing sugar.

1025.　Cardamom Tapioca Pudding

Preparation Time: 10 minutes
Cooking Time: 12 minutes
Servings: 4

Ingredients:
- 1 cup of whole milk
- ½ cup of sugar
- 50 g of tapioca pearls
- ½ tsp of cardamom powder
- ½ cup of almonds, roasted
- ½ cup of water

Directions:
- Set the Air fryer to 375°F for 12 minutes. Combine tapioca pearls with milk, sugar, cardamom powder, and water in a bowl. Pour the tapioca pearls mixture into a baking dish. Place the baking dish on the cooking tray. Insert the cooking tray in the Air fryer when it displays "Add Food." Remove from the oven when cooking time is complete. Serve garnished with almonds.

1026.　Chia Blackberry Jam

Preparation Time: 10 minutes
Cooking Time: 30 minutes
Servings: 12

Ingredients:
- 3 cups blackberries
- ¼ cup swerve
- 4 tbsp lemon juice
- 4 tbsp chia seeds

Directions:

In a pan that suits the air fryer, combine all the Ingredients: and toss.
- Put the pan in the fryer and cook at 300°F for 30 minutes.
- Divide into cups and serve cold.

1027.　Apple Dumplings

Preparation Time: 20 minutes
Cooking Time: 30 minutes
Servings: 2

Ingredients:
- 2 tbsp Raisins
- 2 small apples
- 1 tbsp Brown sugar
- 2 Puff pastry sheets
- 2 tbsp melted butter

Directions:
- Warm the Air Fryer to reach 356°F.
- Peel and core the apples. Combine the raisins and sugar. Place the apples on the pastry sheets and fill them with the raisin mixture.
- Fold the pastry over to cover the fixings. Place them on a piece of foil so they won't fall through the fryer. Brush them with melted butter.
- Air-fry until they're golden brown (25 minutes).

1028.　Banana Fritters

Preparation Time: 35 minutes
Cooking Time: 20 minutes
Servings: 6

Ingredients:
- 3 tbsp Vegetable oil
- ¾ cup Breadcrumbs
- 3 tbsp Cornflour
- 8 Ripe peeled bananas
- 1 Egg white

Directions:
- Warm the Air Fryer to reach 356°F.
- Use the low-heat temperature setting to warm a skillet. Pour in the oil and toss in the breadcrumbs. Cook until golden brown.
- Coat the bananas with the flour. Dip them into the whisked egg white and cover with the breadcrumbs.
- Arrange the prepared bananas in a single layer of the basket and place the fritter cakes onto a bunch of paper towels to drain before serving.

1029.　Chocolate Walnut Cake

Preparation Time: 30 minutes
Cooking Time: 50 minutes
Servings: 10

Ingredients:
- 4 medium eggs
- 225g caster sugar
- 100g butter
- 60g plain flour
- 2 tsp. baking powder

- 120g dark chocolate
- 100g chopped walnuts

Directions:
- Beat the eggs in a mixing bowl. Add sugar and beat until the mixture turns creamy. Add butter and keep mixing. Then add the flour and baking powder.
- In a double boiler, melt the chocolate, mix everything together and add walnuts.
- Grease the base and sides of the inner pot, add the mixture and smooth the top of the mixture to create a level finish.
- Touch the MULTI COOK menu to select the BAKE program, set the cooking time for 50 minutes and press START. Close the lid.

1030. Moist Vanilla Cupcake

Preparation Time: 30 minutes
Cooking Time: 18 minutes
Servings: 10

Ingredients:
- 2 ½ cups flour
- 2 ½ tbsp baking powder
- ¼ tbsp salt
- 8 tbsp butter at room temperature
- 1 ¾ cups sugar
- 2 large eggs at room temperature
- 2 ¼ tbsp vanilla
- Seeds from 1 vanilla bean
- 1 ¼ cup milk at room temperature

Directions:
- For cupcakes. Preheat the oven to 350°F. Line 2 muffin tins with cupcake wrappers. In a bowl, sift flour, baking powder, and salt together.
- In a bowl of a stand mixer, cream butter and sugar together for 3 to 5 minutes or until light and fluffy.
- Slowly add eggs one at a time until combined.
- Add vanilla and vanilla beans to milk.
- Add 1/3 of the dry ingredients to the egg mixture and beat with the mixer until well combined.
- Add 1/3 of the milk and the mix, repeat with the remaining ingredients, and scrape the bowl as needed.
- Pour batter into prepared pans and bake for 16 to 18 minutes or until the toothpick inserted comes out clean.

1031. Lemon Chiffon Cake

Preparation Time: 30 minutes
Cooking Time: 55 minutes
Servings: 10

Ingredients:
- 1½ cups sugar
- 2 cups Sifted Flour
- 3 tbsp baking powder
- 1 tbsp salt
- 1/2 vegetable oil
- 7 eggs separated
- 3/4 cup cold water
- 2 tbsp vanilla
- ½ tbsp lemon extract
- ½ cup vegetable oil
- Zest of 1 lemon

- 1/2 tbsp cream of tartar

Directions:
- In the bowl of the mixer, combine the 7 egg whites with the cream of tartar and mix with the whip attachment until the whites form very stiff peaks; this should take between 15 and 20 minutes.
- While the egg whites are mixing, in a separate mixing bowl, combine sifted flour, sugar, salt, baking powder, egg yolks, vegetable oil, vanilla, lemon zest and water. Mix the ingredients until they become batter-like.
- When egg whites are at the stiff peak stage, gently fold the egg whites with the egg yolk mixture with a rubber scraper until it is just blended.
- Pour into a prepared pan and bake at 325°F for 45 to 55 minutes.

1032. Honey Pineapples

Preparation Time: 15 minutes
Cooking Time: 20 minutes
Servings: 2

Ingredients:
- 1 tsp cinnamon
- 5 pineapple slices
- ½ cup brown sugar
- 1 tbsp basil, chopped for garnish
- 1 tbsp honey, for garnish

Directions:
- Preheat your Air fryer to 340°F.
- In a small bowl, mix brown sugar and cinnamon.
- Drizzle the sugar mixture over your pineapple slices and set aside for 20 minutes.
- Place the pineapple rings in the frying basket and cook for 10 minutes.
- Flip the pineapples and cook for 10 minutes more.
- Serve with basil and a drizzle of honey.

1033. Pink Champagne Cupcakes

Preparation Time: 20 minutes
Cooking Time: 25 minutes
Servings: 12

Ingredients:
- Cake:
- 1 box of white cake mix
- 1 cup pink champagne
- 1/2 cup vegetable oil
- Three eggs
- Frosting:
- 2 (8-ounce) packages of cream cheese
- 1 stick butter
- 4 cups powdered sugar
- 1/4 cup pink champagne

Directions:
- Separate eggs and discard the yolks. Mix cake mix, oil, champagne, and egg whites.
- Fill cupcake liners and place them on the wire rack in the fryer six at a time.
- Bake it using your air fryer at 320°F for 25 minutes.
- While waiting for the cupcakes to be baked, mix cream cheese and butter.

- Slowly mix in powdered sugar and champagne, alternating each one.
- For additional effect, you can mix in a few drops of red food coloring to turn the frosting pink.
- Allow the cupcakes to cool before adding frosting.

1034. Pumpkin Muffins

Preparation Time: 20 minutes
Cooking Time: 15 minutes
Servings: 8

Ingredients:
- 1 cup pumpkin puree
- 2 cups oats
- ½ cup Honey
- 2 Eggs
- 1 tsp Coconut butter
- 1 tbsp cocoa nibs
- 1 tsp Nutmeg
- 1 tbsp Vanilla essence

Directions:
- Using a blender, combine all the ingredients making it a smooth paste.
- Now fill the muffin mix in 12 muffin cases.
- Place it in the air fryer basket.
- Set the temperature to 180°C and cook for 15 minutes.
- Serve when it becomes cool.

1035. Apple Fries with Caramel

Preparation Time: 10 minutes
Cooking Time: 7 minutes
Servings: 4

Ingredients:
- 3 Pink lady apples
- 3 Eggs
- ¼ cup Sugar
- ½ cup Flour
- 1 cup Breadcrumbs
- 8 ounces Whipped cream cheese
- 1 cup caramel sauce
- Cooking spray as required

Directions:
- Wash apples in running water, peel skin, cut into 8 wedges, remove the core and keep aside in a large bowl.
- Put flour over it and toss to get a proper coating on the apple wedges.
- Beat the eggs in a medium bowl.
- Put the crumbs on a flat plate.
- Keep the apple wedges, beaten egg bowl and crumb plate in order.
- Dip the tossed apple wedges in the beaten egg and then dredge on the crumbs.
- Start frying by preheating the air fryer.
- Set the temperature at 190°C.
- Coat the air fryer basket with cooking spray.
- Place the dipped wedges in the air fryer basket by not over-layering.
- Set the timer for 5 minutes and start cooking.
- Flip the apple wedges intermittently every 2 minutes.
- When the cooking continues, let us make the caramel cream dip.

- In a bowl, combine half of the caramel sauce and whipping cream. Mix it thoroughly.
- Transfer the caramel cream dip into a serving bowl.
- When the apple wedges are cooking over, remove them into a serving bowl.
- Before serving, top it with the remaining caramel sauce.

1036. Cinnamon Peaches

Preparation Time: 5 minutes
Cooking Time: 7-10 minutes
Servings: 4

Ingredients:
- 4 ripe peaches, stoned and quartered
- 2 tbsps. butter, melted
- 2 tbsps. brown sugar
- 1 tbsp. lemon juice
- 1 tsp. cinnamon powder

Directions:
- Preheat Air Fryer to 360°F.
- In a small mixing bowl, combine together butter, sugar, and cinnamon powder. Mix well.
- Coat all peaches with butter mixture.
- Place the peaches in the Air Fryer cooking basket and cook for 5-7 minutes. Cool slightly.
- Transfer into a serving dish.
- Serve and enjoy!

1037. Apple Crumble

Preparation Time: 35 minutes
Cooking Time: 40 minutes
Servings: 6

Ingredients:
- For the stewed apples:
- 1½ lbs. apples, peeled, halved and cored
- 1 cup water
- 1/3 cup brown sugar
- 1 tsp. ground cinnamon
- For the crumble:
- 4 oz. cold butter
- 4 oz. flour
- 3 oz. ground almonds
- 3 oz. oats
- 1/3 cup brown sugar
- 1 tsp. cinnamon powder
- pinch of salt

Directions:
- Preheat your Air Fryer to 360°F.
- Cut the apples into small pieces.
- In a large saucepan, heat ¾ cup of water and bring to a simmer. Add the apple chunks, brown sugar, and cinnamon. Cook, stirring, for about 10 minutes or until apples are softened and the sauce has become thick. Set aside.
- In a food processor, process all ingredients for the crumble until combined well, and the texture turns crumbly.
- Place the stewed apples into a baking dish that can fit into the Air Fryer cooking basket. Then, top apples with crumble mixture. Cook for 25-30 minutes, or until golden brown. Let cool.

- Divide among 6 serving bowls.
- Serve and enjoy!

1038. Raisin and Cranberry Beignet

Preparation Time: 22 minutes
Cooking Time: 8-10 minutes
Servings: 8

Ingredients:

- 1 tsp active quick-rising dry yeast
- ⅓ cup buttermilk
- 3 tbsp packed brown sugar
- 1 egg
- 1½ cups whole-wheat pastry flour
- 3 tbsp chopped dried cherries
- 3 tbsp chopped golden raisins
- 2 tbsp unsalted butter, melted
- Powdered sugar, for dusting (optional)

Directions:

- In a medium bowl, mix the yeast with 3 tbsp of water. Let it stand for 5 minutes, or until it bubbles.
- Stir in the buttermilk, brown sugar, and egg until well mixed.
- Stir in the pastry flour until combined.
- With your hands, work the cherries and raisins into the dough. Let the mixture stand for 15 minutes.
- Pat the dough into an 8-by-8-inch square and cut it into 16 pieces. Gently shape each piece into a ball.
- Drizzle the balls with melted butter. Place them in a single layer in the air fryer basket, so they don't touch. You may have to cook these in batches. Air-fry for 5 to 8 minutes at 380°F, or until puffy and golden brown.
- Dust with powdered sugar before serving, if desired.

1039. Vanilla Almond Cookies

Preparation Time: 40minutes
Cooking Time: 40 minutes
Servings: 12

Ingredients:

- 8 egg whites
- ½ tsp almond extract
- 1 ⅓ cups sugar
- ¼ tsp salt
- 2 tsp lemon juice
- 1 ½ tsp vanilla extract
- Melted dark chocolate to drizzle

Directions:

- In a mixing bowl, add egg whites, salt, and lemon juice. Beat using an electric mixer until foamy. Slowly add the sugar and continue beating until completely combined; add the almond and vanilla extracts. Beat until stiff peaks form and are glossy.
- Line a round baking sheet with parchment paper. Fill a piping bag with the meringue mixture and pipe as many mounds on the baking sheet as you can, leaving 2-inch spaces between each mound.
- Place the baking sheet in the fryer basket and bake at 250°F for 5 minutes. Reduce the temperature to 220°F and bake for 15 more minutes. Then, reduce the temperature once more to 190°F and cook for 15 minutes. Remove the baking sheet and let the meringues

cool for 2 hours. Drizzle with the dark chocolate before serving.

1040. Latte Crème Brûlée

Preparation Time: 10 minutes
Cooking Time: 10 minutes
Servings: 3

Ingredients:

- ½ tsp of vanilla extract
- 3 tbsp of superfine sugar
- 1 cup of water
- 4 egg yolks
- 1 cup of heavy cream
- ½ tsp of coffee powder
- Pinch of salt
- ¼ cup of granulated sugar

Directions:

- Set the Air fryer on an Air fryer to 375°F for 10 minutes. Whip the egg yolks with granulated sugar, coffee powder, heavy cream, vanilla extract, and salt in a bowl. Pour this mixture into three ramekins. Place the ramekins on the cooking tray. Insert the cooking tray in the Air fryer when it displays "Add Food." Remove from the oven when cooking time is complete. Sprinkle the superfine sugar on the Crème Coffee Brûlée and refrigerate for about 2 hours. Use a blow torch to burn the sprinkled sugar to serve.

1041. Pecan Pie

Preparation Time: 30 minutes
Cooking Time: 35 minutes
Servings: 8

Ingredients:

- ¾ cup maple syrup
- 2 eggs
- ½ tsp salt
- ¼ tsp nutmeg
- ½ tsp cinnamon
- 2 tbsp almond butter
- 2 tbsp brown sugar
- ½ cup chopped pecans
- 1 tbsp butter, melted
- 1 8-inch pie dough
- ¾ tsp vanilla extract

Directions:

- Preheat the Air fryer to 370°F, and coat the pecans with melted butter. Place the pecans in the Air fryer and toast them for 10 minutes. Place the pie crust into an 8-inch round pie pan, and place the pecans over.
- Whisk together all remaining ingredients in a bowl. Pour the maple mixture over the pecans. Set the Air fryer to 320°F and cook the pie for 25 minutes.

1042. Cream and Coconut Cups

Preparation Time: 15 minutes
Servings: 6

Ingredients:

- 8 oz. Cream cheese, soft
- 3 eggs

- 2 tbsp. Butter; melted
- 3 tbsp. Coconut, shredded and unsweetened
- 4 tbsp. Swerve

Directions:
- Take a bowl and mix all the ingredients and whisk well.
- Divide into small ramekins, put them in the fryer, cook at 320°F and bake for 10 minutes.
- Serve cold

1043. Mixed Berries and Lemon Crumble

Preparation Time: 20 minutes
Cooking Time: 30 minutes
Servings: 6

Ingredients:
- 12 oz fresh strawberries
- 7 oz fresh raspberries
- 5 oz fresh blueberries
- 5 tbsp cold butter
- 2 tbsp lemon juice
- 1 cup flour
- ½ cup sugar
- 1 tbsp water
- A pinch of salt

Directions:
- Gently mass the berries, but make sure there are chunks left. Mix with the lemon juice and 2 tbsp of the sugar.
- Place the berry mixture at the bottom of a prepared round cake. Combine the flour with the salt and sugar in a bowl. Add the water and rub the butter with your fingers until the mixture becomes crumbled.
- Arrange the crisp batter over the berries. Cook in the Air fryer at 390°F for 20 minutes. Serve chilled.

1044. Citrus Sponge Cake

Preparation Time: 35 minutes
Cooking Time: 30 minutes
Servings: 8

Ingredients:
- 9 oz sugar
- 9 oz self-rising flour
- 9 oz butter
- 3 eggs
- 1 tsp baking powder
- 1 tsp vanilla extract
- zest of 1 orange
- Frosting:
- 4 egg whites
- Juice of 1 orange
- 1 tsp orange food coloring
- zest of 1 orange
- 7 oz superfine sugar

Directions:
- Preheat the Air fryer to 260°F and place all cake ingredients in a bowl and beat with an electric mixer. Transfer half of the batter into a prepared cake pan; bake for 15 minutes. Repeat the process for the other half of the batter.

- Meanwhile, prepare the frosting by beating all the frosting ingredients together. Spread the frosting mixture on top of one cake. Top with the other cake.

1045. Black and White Brownies

Preparation Time: 10 minutes
Cooking Time: 20 minutes
Servings: 8

Ingredients:
- 1 egg
- ¼-cup brown sugar
- 2 tbsp white sugar
- 2 tbsp safflower oil
- 1-tsp vanilla
- ¼ cup cocoa powder
- ⅓ cup all-purpose flour
- ¼ cup white chocolate chips
- Nonstick baking spray with flour

Directions:
- In a medium bowl, beat the egg with the brown sugar and white sugar. Beat in the oil and vanilla. Add the cocoa powder and flour, and stir just until combined. Fold in the white chocolate chips. Spray a 6-by-6-by-2-inch baking pan with nonstick spray. Spoon the brownie batter into the pan. Bake for 20 minutes or until the brownies are set when lightly touched with a finger. Let cool for 30 minutes before slicing to serve.

1046. Salted Caramel Beignets

Preparation Time: 10 minutes
Cooking Time: 15 minutes
Servings: 6

Ingredients:
- 1 large fresh egg (do not use eggs from the fridge)
- ½ cup salted caramel coffee creamer
- ½ cup all-purpose flour
- ¼ cup white sugar
- ½ tsp baking powder
- 1 pinch salt
- 2 tbsp confectioners' sugar
- 1 ½ tsp butter
- 8 tbsp of fresh filtered water
- ½ tsp vanilla extract
- ¾ cup chocolate coffee creamer
- 5 ounces dark chocolate chopped
- 2 tbsp sour cream

Directions:
- Preheat the Air Fryer to 370°F or 185°C. Use the Air Fry setting and set the preheat for 3 minutes.
- Use non-stick cooking spray to coat the silicone egg-bite mold.
- In a large bowl, sieve flour, sugar, baking powder, salted caramel coffee creamer, and salt together. Mix dry ingredients well.
- Separate the egg, place the egg white into a small bowl and the yolk into the flour mix.
- Melt the butter in the microwave or in a saucepan on the stovetop.
- Pour the melted butter into the flour mix.
- Whisk the ingredients together and combine them well.

- Beat the egg white into soft peaks.
- Fold egg whites into the flour batter and make sure the batter is smooth.
- Scoop the batter with a large spoon evenly into the egg bite mold.
- Place the egg bite mold into the Air Fryer drawer.
- Set the Air Fryer for 10 minutes and use the Air Fry setting to bake the beignets.
- While the beignets are cooking, make the chocolate dipping sauce:
- Chop the chocolate into pieces.
- In a microwave-safe bowl, add the chopped chocolate.
- Place chocolate in the microwave and melt for about 30 seconds to 1 minute on high.
- Once the chocolate is melted, add the chocolate coffee creamer and sour cream.
- Whisk together until smooth and creamy.
- After 10 minutes, the Air Fryer will switch off.
- Use the oven glove to remove the egg bite mold from the Air Fryer.
- Line a large bowl with parchment paper and pop the beignets onto it.
- Lift the parchment paper with the beignets and pop it back into the Air Fryer drawer.
- Set the Air Fryer for 5 minutes and use the Air Fry setting to finish baking the beignets.
- Once the beignets are cooked, remove the Air Fryer drawer and place it on the cooling rack or mat.
- Place a clean piece of parchment paper on the large dinner plate.
- Pop the beignets out of the Air Fryer basket and onto the parchment-lined, large dinner plate.
- Sprinkle confectioners' sugar over the top of them.
- Serve with the chocolate dipping sauce.

1047. Raspberry Cream Rolls

Preparation Time: 10 minutes
Cooking Time: 30 minutes
Servings: 4

Ingredients:
- 1 cup of fresh raspberries, rinsed and patted dry
- ½ cup of cream cheese, softened to room temperature
- ¼ cup of brown sugar
- ¼ cup of sweetened condensed milk
- 1 egg
- 1 tsp of corn starch
- 6 spring roll wrappers
- ¼ cup of water

Directions:
- Cover the basket of the Air Fryer with a lining of tin foil, leaving the edges uncovered to allow air to circulate through the basket. Preheat the Air Fryer to 350°F.
- In a mixing bowl, combine the cream cheese, brown sugar, condensed milk, cornstarch, and egg. Beat or whip thoroughly until all ingredients are completely mixed and fluffy, thick and stiff.
- Spoon even amounts of the creamy filling into each spring roll wrapper, then top each dollop of filling with several raspberries.
- Roll up the wraps around the creamy raspberry filling, and seal the seams with a few dabs of water.

- Place each roll on the foil-lined Air Fryer basket, seams facing down.
- Close the air fryer lid. Set the Air Fryer timer to 10 minutes. During cooking, shake the handle of the fryer basket to ensure a nice even surface crisp.
- After 10 minutes, when the Air Fryer shuts off, the spring rolls should be golden brown and perfect on the outside, while the raspberries and cream filling will have cooked together in a glorious fusion. Remove with tongs and serve hot or cold.

1048. Angel Cake

Preparation Time: 20 minutes
Cooking Time: 30 minutes
Servings: 10

Ingredients:
- ¼ cup butter, melted
- 1 cup powdered erythritol
- 1 tsp strawberry extract
- 12 egg whites
- 2 tsp cream of tartar
- A pinch of salt
- Preheat the Air Fryer for 5 minutes.
- Mix the egg whites and cream of tartar.
- Use a hand mixer and whisk until white and fluffy.
- Add the rest of the ingredients except for the butter and whisk for another minute.
- Pour into a baking dish.
- Place in the Air Fryer basket, close the air fryer lid and cook for 30 minutes at 400°F or if a toothpick inserted in the middle comes out clean.
- Drizzle with melted butter once cooled.

1049. Blueberry Turnovers

Preparation Time: 35 minutes
Cooking Time: 15 minutes
Servings: 6

Ingredients:
- Half cup of blueberries (fresh)
- ¼ cup of white granulated sugar
- 2 tsp of cornstarch
- ½ tbsp of ground cinnamon (Zest)
- 1 lemon juice
- Package of puff pastry (17 oz.), thawed
- 1 egg + 1 tbsp of water for egg wash
- ½ cup of sugar in rough.

Directions:
- The blueberries, butter, cornstarch, lemon juice, zest, and cinnamon are mixed in a medium dish.
- Place onto the work surface on a sheet of puff pastry and cut into four even squares. Place one to two spoons full of blueberry filling in the middle of a square and fold into a rectangle; press down to close the edges. Continue with three squares left and the second layer of puff pastry.
- Mix the egg wash and spray over the puff pastry, then cover the sides of the pastry again with the tines of the fork.
- Cut a small slice on top of each pastry using a paring knife, and then dust in the raw with sugar.

- Spray the air fryer with olive oil spray, then put two turnovers in the basket at a time, move the remaining turnovers to a tray and hold cooled. Click the bake/dessert position at 320°F and raise the time to 15 minutes or until a rich golden brown puff pastry is available.
- Remove the cooked turnovers and repeat the process with the others, making sure that the basket is sprayed in between each pan.
- Serve dry or at room temperature.

1050. Leche Flan

Preparation Time: 15 minutes
Cooking Time: 30 minutes
Servings: 4

Ingredients:
- 1 cup heavy cream
- 1 tsp vanilla extract
- 1/2 (14 ounces) can sweeten condensed milk
- 1/2 cup milk
- 2-1/2 eggs
- 1/3 cup white sugar

Directions:
- In a blender, blend well vanilla, eggs, milk, cream, and condensed milk.
- Lightly grease the baking pan of the air fryer with cooking spray. Add sugar and heat for 10 minutes at 370oF until melted and caramelized. Lower heat to 300°F and continue melting and swirling.
- Pour milk mixture into caramelized sugar. Cover pan with foil.
- Cook for 20 minutes at 330°F.
- Let it cool completely in the fridge.
- Place a plate on top of the pan and invert the pan to easily remove the flan.
- Serve and enjoy.

1051. Mint Baked Alaska

Preparation Time: 25minutes
Cooking Time: 20 minutes
Servings: 4

Ingredients:
- ¼ cup plus ⅓ cup granulated sugar, divided
- ¼ cup butter, melted
- ¼ cup brown sugar
- 2 large eggs, yolks and whites separated
- 1 tsp vanilla
- ½ cup all-purpose flour
- ¼ cup cocoa powder
- Pinch sea salt
- Unsalted butter, at room temperature
- 2 cups mint ice cream with chocolate chips

Directions:
- In a medium bowl, combine ¼ cup of granulated sugar, the butter, and brown sugar and mix well. Beat in the egg yolks and vanilla.
- Add the flour, cocoa powder, and salt and mix just until combined. Cover and refrigerate the egg whites.
- Grease a 6-by-2-inch round pan with unsalted butter. Cut a piece of parchment paper to fit the bottom of the

pan and grease it. Pour the brownie batter into the pan. Cover the pan with aluminum foil, crimping the edges to secure. Poke a few holes in the foil with the tip of a knife.
- Set or preheat the air fryer to 325°F. Put the pan in the air fryer basket. Bake for 12 to 17 minutes or until a toothpick inserted near the center comes out with only a few moist crumbs.
- Remove the pan from the air fryer and cool for 20 minutes on a wire rack; then, run a knife around the edges of the pan and invert the brownie onto the rack. Cool completely.
- Line a 5-inch bowl with plastic wrap. Add the ice cream, pressing to fit the bowl. Smooth the flat surface of the ice cream.
- Put the brownie on a 7-inch round cookie sheet or in a 7-inch springform pan.
- Invert the bowl onto the center of the brownie, pressing down gently, so the ice cream adheres to the brownie. Leave the plastic wrap around the ice cream. Cover the ice cream and brownie and freeze for at least 3 hours.
- While the ice cream and brownie freeze, make the meringue. In a very clean medium bowl, beat the cold egg whites until frothy. Gradually add the remaining ⅓ cup of sugar, beating until stiff peaks form. Move the brownie and ice cream from the freezer. Remove the plastic. Carefully "frost" the whole thing with the meringue, just barely covering the brownie part but frosting the ice cream thickly. Make swirls with your knife.
- Freeze again, uncovered, for at least 3 hours. When it's frozen solid, you can carefully cover it with plastic wrap. Remove the plastic before baking.
- When you're ready to eat, set or preheat the air fryer to 400°F. Lower the cookie sheet or pan into the air fryer basket using a foil sling or plate gripper. Bake for 2 to 3 minutes or until the meringue is golden brown in spots. Carefully lift the dessert out of the air fryer using tongs to grip the foil sling or using the plate gripper. Cut into fourths and serve immediately

1052. Coconut Chocolate Fondue

Preparation Time: 5 minutes
Cooking Time: 10 minutes
Servings: 4

Ingredients:
- 2 tsp of sugar
- 2 tsp of coconut essence
- 200 g of Swiss bittersweet chocolate (70%)
- 2 tsp of coconut milk powder
- 2 cups of water
- 200 g of coconut cream
- **Directions**
- Set the Air fryer on an Air fryer to 375°F for 8 minutes. Combine chocolate with coconut cream and sugar in a ramekin. Place the ramekin on the cooking tray. Insert the cooking tray in the Air fryer when it displays "Add Food." Remove from the oven when cooking time is complete. Stir in the coconut essence and coconut milk powder to serve in a fondue pot.

1053. Sweet Pumpkin Cream

Preparation Time: 10 minutes
Cooking Time: 30 minutes
Servings: 4

Ingredients:
- 1 cup yogurt
- 1 cup pumpkin puree
- 2 eggs, whisked
- 2 tbsp sugar
- ½ tsp vanilla extract

Directions:
- In a large bowl, mix the puree and the yogurt with the other ingredients, whisk well, pour into 4 ramekins, put them in the air fryer and cook at 370°F for 30 minutes.
- Cooldown and serve.

1054. Mixed Berries Cream Puffs

Preparation Time: 15minutes
Cooking Time: 25-30 minutes
Servings: 6

Ingredients:
- ½ cup raspberries
- ¼ cup chopped strawberries
- ¼ cup blueberries
- 1 tbsp honey
- 6 tbsp water
- ¼ cup butter
- ½ cup all-purpose flour
- Pinch sea salt
- 2 large eggs

Directions:
- Combine the raspberries, strawberries, and blueberries with the honey in a small bowl and mix gently; set aside.
- Combine the water and butter in a medium saucepan over high heat and bring to a rolling boil. Reduce the heat to medium and add flour and salt. Beat well until the dough forms a ball and pulls away from the sides of the pan.
- Remove the pan from the heat. Using an electric hand mixer, beat in the eggs, one at a time until the dough is smooth and shiny.
- Line a 7-inch round cookie sheet with parchment paper. Working in batches, spoon three rounded tbsp of the dough onto the cookie sheet (half the dough), 1 inch apart.
- Set or preheat the air fryer to 400°F. Put the cookie sheet in the air fryer basket. Bake for 18 to 24 minutes or until the cream puffs are puffed and golden brown. Remove the cream puffs and let cool on a wire rack. Repeat with remaining dough.
- Slice the cream puffs in half crosswise. Remove any loose strands of dough, and fill with the fruit.

1055. Holiday Gingerbread Cake

Preparation Time: 15 minutes
Cooking Time: 27 minutes
Servings: 6

Ingredients:
- 1 cup all-purpose flour
- 1 tsp ground ginger
- ½ tsp cinnamon
- ½ tsp baking soda
- ¼ tsp sea salt
- ⅛ tsp nutmeg
- ⅛ tsp ground cardamom
- ⅓ cup brown sugar
- ⅓ cup honey
- ⅓ cup milk
- 1 large egg yolk
- Unsalted butter, at room temperature

Directions:
- In a medium bowl, combine the flour, ginger, cinnamon, baking soda, salt, nutmeg, and cardamom and mix well.
- In another medium bowl, combine the brown sugar, honey, milk, and egg yolk and beat until combined.
- Stir the honey mixture into the flour mixture just until combined.
- Grease a 7-by-3-inch round pan with unsalted butter. Cut a piece of parchment paper to fit the bottom of the pan, and grease that. Pour in the batter. Cover the pan tightly with aluminum foil and poke a few holes in the foil with the tip of a knife.
- Set or preheat the air fryer to 325°F. Put the pan in the air fryer basket. Bake for 22 to 27 minutes or until a toothpick inserted near the center of the gingerbread comes out with only a few moist crumbs.
- Remove from the air fryer and cool on a wire rack for 20 minutes, then cut into wedges to serve.

1056. Triple Berry Pavlova

Preparation Time: 20 minutes
Cooking Time: 35 minutes
Servings: 4

Ingredients:
- 3 large egg whites
- Pinch sea salt
- ⅔ cup granulated sugar
- 1 tsp cornstarch
- 1 tsp apple cider vinegar
- ½ cup heavy (whipping) cream
- 2 tbsp powdered sugar
- ⅓ cup blueberries
- ⅓ cup raspberries
- ⅓ cup chopped strawberries
- 1 tsp honey

Directions:
- In a very clean mixing bowl, use a hand mixer to beat the egg whites and salt.
- When soft peaks start to form, beat in the granulated sugar, one tbsp at a time. Keep beating until the meringue is glossy and forms stiff peaks when the beater is lifted.
- Fold in the cornstarch and vinegar.
- Cut a piece of parchment paper the same size as the bottom of a 7-inch round pan. Put a dot of the meringue mixture on the bottom of the pan and add the parchment paper; this helps the paper stay in place.

- Put the meringue mixture on the parchment paper, forming it into a disc and flattening the top and sides with a spatula.
- Set or preheat the air fryer to 300°F. Place the pan in the air fryer basket and the basket in the air fryer and bake for 40 to 45 minutes or until the meringue is dry to the touch. Turn off the air fryer, pull the basket out about an inch, and let the meringue cool for 1 hour.
- Remove the meringue from the air fryer and cool completely on a wire rack.
- In a small bowl, beat the cream with the powdered sugar until soft peaks form.
- Turn the meringue over so the bottom is on top. Spread the cream over the meringue, then top with the blueberries, raspberries, and strawberries and drizzle with the honey. You can serve this immediately or cover and refrigerate it for up to 1 day.

1057. Chocolate Chip Cookies

Preparation Time: 10 minutes
Cooking Time: 15 minutes
Servings: 8

Ingredients:
- 1 cup chocolate chunks
- 1½ cup all-purpose flour
- ½ cup butter kept at room temperature
- ½ cup of sugar
- ½ cup brown sugar
- ½ tsp baking soda
- 1 egg
- 1 tsp vanilla extract
- ¼ tsp kosher salt

Directions:
- Let us preheat the Air fryer.
- In the AIR FRY mode, set the temperature to 350°F and timer for 5 minutes.
- Press START to begin preheating.
- Take two baking pans that can accommodate the air fryer and grease it.
- In a medium bowl, combine sugar, butter, and brown sugar.
- Add vanilla, egg, and whisk thoroughly.
- Stir in salt, flour, and baking soda.
- Finally, add chocolate chunks and combine them thoroughly.
- Transfer half of the cookie dough into one baking pan. The remaining portion you can transfer into the other baking pan.
- Press the cookie dough firmly to the bottom of the pan.
- Put the pan in the air fryer basket and place the air fryer basket in the inner pot of the Air fryer.
- Close the crisp lid.
- In the BAKE mode, the select temperature at 350°F and the timer to 12 minutes.
- Press START to begin baking and continue baking until it turns slightly brown.
- Once it is ready, allow it to cool down for 4-5 minutes.
- Slice and serve.

1058. Sweet Potato Dessert

Preparation Time: 5 minutes
Cooking Time: 18 minutes
Servings: 4

Ingredients:
- 2 sweet potatoes, medium size
- 1 tbsp arrowroot powder
- 2 tsp butter, melted
- ½ tbsp coconut oil
- ¼ cup of coconut sugar
- 1 tbsp ground cinnamon
- 2 tbsp sugar, powdered
- ½ cup vanilla yogurt
- ½ cup dessert hummus
- ½ cup maple frosting

Directions:
- Peel the potatoes, wash and pat dry.
- Julienne the peeled potatoes in half-inch thickness.
- Put the julienned potatoes in a large bowl and add coconut oil and arrowroot powder.
- Toss them to mix thoroughly.
- Transfer the coated julienned potatoes to a baking tray and put them in the inner pot of the Air fryer.
- Close the crisp cover and set the temperature to 370°F in the AIR FRY mode.
- Set the timer for 18 minutes.
- Press START to begin the baking process.
- Halfway through the cooking, open the crisp cover, and stir the potatoes.
- Close the crisp cover to resume baking for the remaining period.
- After cooking, transfer it into a bowl.
- Drizzle 2 tbsp of melted butter, and sprinkle the cinnamon powder and sugar powder. Toss it to mix thoroughly.
- Serve along with the dipping sauce.

1059. Lime Cheesecake

Preparation Time: 20 minutes
Cooking Time: 65 minutes
Servings: 6

Ingredients:
- 1 tbsp. butter, melted
- 1½ cups Graham cracker crumbs
- 24 oz. cream cheese, softened
- 1 tbsp. cornstarch
- 1 cup white sugar
- 3 large eggs
- 2 cups key lime juice
- 1 tbsp. lime zest, grated

Directions:
- Combine Graham cracker crumbs with butter and press the mix into the bottom of the air fryer basket lined with parchment paper. Refrigerate.
- Add the cream cheese, lime peel, sugar, and cornstarch to a large mixing bowl. Using an immersion blender, blend the ingredients until smooth and fluffy. Gradually add in eggs while continuously beating to blend until smooth. Also, add key lime juice with a mixer on low

mode. Finish mixing with your hand. Avoid over blending lest your cake will crack when baked.
- Pour batter over the prepared base.
- Place the basket inside the air fryer duo unit and use the air fryer lid to cover it. Secure and set to bake at 300°F for 65 minutes. Allow to cool and refrigerate overnight.

1060. Vanilla Oat Sandwiches

Preparation Time: 10 minutes
Cooking Time: 18 minutes
Servings: 6

Ingredients:
- 1 ½ cups plain flour
- 3.5 oz. butter
- 3 oz. white sugar
- ½ small egg beaten
- ¼ cup desiccated coconut
- ½ cup gluten-free oats
- 1/3 oz. white chocolate
- 1 tsp vanilla essence
- Filling:
- 3.5 oz. icing sugar
- 2 oz. butter
- 1/2 tsp lemon juice
- 1 tsp vanilla essence

Directions:
- Whisk butter with sugar in an electric mixer until fluffy.
- Stir in egg, vanilla essence, coconut, and chocolate, then mix well.
- Slow add flour and continue mixing until it forms a cookie dough.
- Make medium-sized biscuits out of it, then roll them in the oats to coat.
- Place the cookies in the Air Fryer Basket. Cook the cookies in batches to avoid overcrowding.
- Set the Air Fryer Basket in the Air fryer Duo.
- Put on the Air Fryer lid and seal it.
- Hit the "Air fry Button" and select 18 minutes of cooking time, then press "Start."
- Flip the cookies after 9 minutes, then resume cooking.
- Once the Air fryer Duo beeps, remove its lid.
- Air fry the remaining cookies in the same manner.
- Meanwhile, beat butter with icing sugar into a creamy mixture.
- Stir in vanilla and lemon juice, then mix well.
- Spread a tbsp of this filling in between two cookies and make a sandwich out of them.
- Use the entire filling to make more cookie sandwiches.
- Serve.

1061. Blueberry Cheesecake

Preparation Time: 10 minutes
Cooking Time: 15 minutes
Servings: 6

Ingredients:
- 6 digestives
- 2 oz. butter, melted
- 5 cups soft cheese
- 1 ½ cups caster sugar
- 4 large eggs
- 3.5 oz. fresh blueberries
- 2 tbsp Greek yogurt
- 1 tbsp vanilla essence
- 5 tbsp icing sugar

Directions:
- Take a 6-inch springform pan and dust it with flour.
- Crush digestive biscuits in a food processor and mix with melted butter.
- Spread the biscuit crumb in the pan and press it evenly.
- Beat cream cheese with sugar in an electric mixer until fluffy.
- Stir in eggs, vanilla essence, and yogurt, then mix well.
- Fold in chopped berries and mix gently with the filling.
- Spread the blueberry-cream filling in the crust evenly.
- Place the prepared pan in the Air Fryer Basket.
- Set the Air Fryer Basket in the Air fryer Duo.
- Put on the Air Fryer lid and seal it.
- Hit the "Air fry Button" and select 15 minutes of cooking time, then press "Start."
- Once the Air fryer Duo beeps, remove its lid.
- Allow the cake to cool down, then transfer to the refrigerator for 4 hours.
- Garnish with icing sugar.
- Slice and serve.

1062. Sweet Potato Cheesecake

Preparation Time: 20 minutes
Cooking Time: 10 minutes
Servings: 4

Ingredients:
- 4 tbsp spread, softened
- 6 ounces mascarpone, delicate
- 8 ounces cream cheddar, delicate
- 2/3 cup graham wafers, disintegrated
- ¾ cup milk
- 1 tsp vanilla concentrate
- 2/3 cup sweet potato puree
- ¼ tsp cinnamon powder

Directions:
- In a bowl, blend spread in with disintegrated saltines, mix well, push on the base of a cake dish that accommodates the air fryer cooker and keeps in the ice chest for the time being.
- In another bowl, blend cream cheddar with mascarpone, sweet potato puree, milk, cinnamon and vanilla and whisk truly well.
- Spread this over the covering, present in the air fryer cooker, cook at 300°F for about 4 minutes and keep in the cooler for a couple of hours before serving. Enjoy the recipe!

1063. Nutmeg Apple Jam

Preparation Time: 10 minutes
Cooking Time: 25 minutes
Servings: 4

Ingredients:
- 1 cup water
- ½ cup sugar
- 1-pound apples, cored, peeled and chopped
- ½ tsp nutmeg, ground

Directions:
- In a pot that suits your air fryer, mix the apples with the water and the other ingredients, toss, introduce the pan to the fryer and cook at 370°F for 25 minutes.
- Blend a bit using an immersion blender, divide into jars and serve.

1064. Currant and Plum Tarts

Preparation Time: 20 minutes
Cooking Time: 35 minutes
Servings: 6

Ingredients:
- ¼ cup almond flour
- ¼ cup millet flour
- 1 cup dark colored rice flour
- ½ cup genuine sweetener
- 10 tbsp margarine, delicate
- 3 tbsp milk
- For the filling:
- 1-pound little plums, pitted and divided
- 1 cup of white currants
- 2 tbsp cornstarch
- 3 tbsp sugar
- ½ tsp vanilla concentrate
- ½ tsp cinnamon powder
- ¼ tsp ginger powder
- 1 tsp lime juice

Directions:
- In a bowl, blend darker rice flour with ½ cup sugar, millet flour, almond flour, spread and milk and mix until you get a sand-like mixture.
- Reserve ¼ of the mixture, press the remainder of the batter into a tart container that accommodates the air fryer cooker and keep it in the refrigerator for 30 minutes.
- Meanwhile, in a bowl, blend plums with currants, 3 tbsp sugar, cornstarch, vanilla concentrate, cinnamon, ginger and lime; squeeze and mix well.
- Pour this over the tart outside layer, disintegrate the reserved mixture on top, present it in the air fryer cooker and cook at 350°F for about 35 minutes.
- Leave the tart to chill off, cut and serve. Enjoy the recipe!

1065. Red Velvet Cupcakes

Preparation Time: 20 minutes
Cooking Time: 12 minutes
Servings: 10

Ingredients:
- For Cupcakes:
- 2 cups refined flour
- ¾ cup icing sugar
- 2 tsp beet powder
- 1 tsp cocoa powder
- ¾ cup peanut butter
- 3 eggs
- For Frosting:
- 1 cup butter
- 1 (8-ounces) package of cream cheese, softened
- 2 tsp vanilla extract

- ¼ tsp salt
- 4½ cups powdered sugar
- For Garnishing:
- ½ cup fresh raspberries

Directions:
- For cupcakes: in a bowl, put all the ingredients and with an electric whisker, whisk until well combined.
- Place the mixture into silicone cups.
- Set the temperature of air fryer to 340°F.
- Arrange the silicon cups into an air fryer basket.
- Air fry for about 10-12 minutes or until a toothpick inserted in the center comes out clean.
- Remove the silicone cups from the air fryer and place them onto a wire rack to cool for about 10 minutes.
- Now, invert the cupcakes onto a wire rack to completely cool before frosting.
- For the frosting: In a large bowl, mix well butter, cream cheese, vanilla extract, and salt.
- Add the powdered sugar, one cup at a time, whisking well after each addition.
- Spread frosting evenly over each cupcake.
- Garnish with raspberries and serve.

1066. Fruity Oreo Cupcakes

Preparation Time: 15 minutes
Cooking Time: 10 minutes
Servings: 6

Ingredients:
- 1 pack of Oreo biscuits, crushed
- 1 tsp of cocoa powder
- 1 cup of milk
- ¼ tsp of baking soda
- 1 banana, peeled and chopped
- 1 tsp of fresh lemon juice
- ½ tsp of baking powder
- 1 apple, peeled, cored and chopped
- 1 tsp of honey
- A pinch of ground cinnamon

Directions:
- Set the Air fryer on an Air fryer to 325°F for 10 minutes. Combine biscuits, cocoa powder, baking soda, milk, and baking powder in a bowl. Pour this mixture into six muffin molds and place them on the cooking tray. Insert the cooking tray in the Air fryer when it displays "Add Food." Remove from the oven when cooking time is complete. Meanwhile, mingle apple, banana, honey, lemon juice, and cinnamon in another bowl. Top the muffins with apple-banana mixture to serve.

1067. Raspberry Cupcakes

Preparation Time: 15 minutes
Cooking Time: 15 minutes
Servings: 10

Ingredients:
- 4½ ounces self-rising flour
- ½ tsp baking powder
- A pinch of salt
- ½ ounce cream cheese, softened
- 4¾ ounces butter, softened

- 4¼ ounces caster sugar
- 2 eggs
- 2 tsp fresh lemon juice
- ½ cup fresh raspberries

Directions:
- In a bowl, mix well flour, baking powder, and salt.
- In another bowl, mix together the cream cheese and butter.
- Add the sugar and whisk until fluffy and light.
- Now, place the eggs one at a time and whisk until just combined.
- Add the flour mixture and stir until well combined.
- Stir in the lemon juice.
- Place the mixture evenly into silicone cups and top each with 2 raspberries.
- Set the temperature of air fryer to 365°F.
- Arrange the silicon cups into an air fryer basket.
- Air fry for about 15 minutes or until a toothpick inserted in the center comes out clean.
- Remove the silicone cups from the air fryer and place them onto a wire rack to cool for about 10 minutes.
- Now, invert the cupcakes onto a wire rack to completely cool before serving.

1068. Baked Apples

Preparation Time: 15 minutes
Cooking Time: 20 minutes
Servings: 4

Ingredients:
- ¼ cup water
- ¼ tsp. nutmeg
- ¼ tsp. cinnamon
- 1 ½ tsp. melted ghee
- 2 tbsp. raisins
- 2 tbsp. chopped walnuts
- 1 medium apple

Directions:
- Preheat your air fryer to 350°F.
- Slice the apple in half and discard some of the flesh from the center.
- Place into the frying pan.
- Mix remaining ingredients together except water. Spoon the mixture into the middle of the apple halves.
- Pour water into overfilled apples.
- Place pan with apple halves into the air fryer oven, and bake for 20 minutes.

1069. White and Black Brownies

Preparation Time: 10 minutes
Cooking Time: 20 minutes
Servings: 8

Ingredients:
- 1 egg
- ¼ cup brown sugar
- 2 tbsp white sugar
- 2 tbsp safflower oil
- 1 tsp vanilla
- ¼ cup cocoa powder
- ⅓ cup all-purpose flour
- ¼ cup white chocolate chips

- Nonstick baking spray with flour

Directions:
- In a medium bowl, beat the egg with the brown sugar and white sugar. Beat in the oil and vanilla.
- Add the cocoa powder and flour, and stir just until combined. Fold in the white chocolate chips.
- Spray a 6-by-6-by-2-inch baking pan with nonstick spray. Spoon the brownie batter into the pan.
- Pour the pan into the Oven rack/basket. Place the rack on the middle shelf of the Air fryer oven. Set temperature to 390°F, and set time to 20 minutes. Bake for 20 minutes or until the brownies are set when lightly touched with a finger. Let cool for 30 minutes before slicing to serve.

1070. Cocoa Banana Brownies

Preparation Time: 15 minutes
Cooking Time: 30 minutes
Servings: 12

Ingredients:
- 2 cups almond flour
- 2 tsp baking powder
- ½ tsp baking powder
- ½ tsp baking soda
- ½ tsp salt
- 1 over-ripe banana
- 3 large eggs
- ½ tsp stevia powder
- ¼ cup coconut oil
- 1 tbsp vinegar
- 1/3 cup almond flour
- 1/3 cup cocoa powder

Directions:
- Preheat the air fryer oven for 5 minutes.
- Combine all ingredients in a food processor and pulse until well combined.
- Pour into a baking dish that will fit in the air fryer.
- Place in the air fryer basket and cook for 30 minutes at 350°F or if a toothpick inserted in the middle comes out clean.

1071. Apple Empanadas

Preparation Time: 30 minutes
Cooking Time: 35 minutes
Servings: 12

Ingredients:
- 1 peeled, cored, and diced red apple
- 1 peeled, cored and diced green apple
- 2 tbsp of honey
- 1 tsp of vanilla essence
- ⅛ tsp of ground nutmeg
- 1 tsp of ground cinnamon
- 1 tsp of water
- 2 tsp of cornstarch
- 12 empanada wrappers
- Spray oil

Directions:
- Add the apples, honey, vanilla essence, nutmeg, and cinnamon to a saucepan over moderately high heat. Cook for 2-3 minutes until the apples have softened.
- In a small bowl, stir together the water and cornstarch. Add the cornstarch to the apple mixture and stir. Cook for 30 seconds. Take off the heat.
- Lay the empanada wrappers out on a clean work surface. Divide the apple mixture equally between the wrappers. Fold the wrappers in half to enclose the filling, creating half-moon shapes. Crimp the edge to seal.
- Arrange the prepared empanadas in the air fryer and cook for 8 minutes at 400°F. Flip the empanadas over and cook for another 10 minutes.
- Take out of the air fryer and allow to cool a little before serving.

1072. Sweetened Plantains

Preparation Time: 5 minutes
Cooking Time: 8 minutes
Servings: 2

Ingredients:
- 2 ripe plantains, sliced
- 2 tsp avocado oil
- Salt to taste
- Maple syrup

Directions:
- Toss the plantains in oil.
- Season with salt.
- Cook in the air fryer basket at 400°F for 10 minutes, shaking after 5 minutes.
- Drizzle with maple syrup before serving.

1073. Coffee Cake

Preparation Time: 10 minutes
Cooking Time: 15 minutes
Servings: 2

Ingredients:
- 1 egg
- 1 tsp cocoa powder
- 1/4 cup flour
- 1/4 cup sugar
- 1 tbsp black coffee
- 1/2 tsp instant coffee
- 1/4 cup butter

Directions:
- Spray a mini baking dish with cooking spray and set aside.
- In a bowl, beat egg, butter, and sugar. Add black coffee, instant coffee, and cocoa powder and beat well.
- Add flour and stir to combine.
- Pour batter into the prepared baking dish.
- Place steam rack into the air fryer, then place baking dish on top of the rack.
- Seal pot with air fryer lid and select bake mode, then set the temperature to 330°F and timer for 15 minutes.
- Serve and enjoy.

1074. Chocolate Smarties Cookies

Preparation Time: 10 minutes
Cooking Time: 15 minutes
Servings: 6

Ingredients:
- 5 oz. butter
- 5 oz. caster sugar
- 8 oz. self-rising flour
- 1 tsp vanilla essence
- 5 tbsp milk
- 3 tbsp cocoa powder
- 2 oz. nestle smarties

Directions:
- Whisk cocoa powder with caster sugar and self-rising flour in a bowl.
- Stir in butter and mix well to form a crumbly mixture.
- Stir in milk and vanilla essence, then mix well to form a smooth dough.
- Add the smarties and knead the dough well.
- Roll this cookie dough into a 1-inch thick layer.
- Use a cookies cutter to cut maximum cookies out of it.
- Roll the remaining dough again to carve out more cookies.
- Place half of the cookies in the Air Fryer Basket.
- Set the Air Fryer Basket in the Air fryer Duo.
- Put on the Air Fryer lid and seal it.
- Hit the "Bake Button" and select 10 minutes of cooking time, then press "Start."
- Flip the cookies after 5 minutes, then resume cooking.
- Once the Air fryer Duo beeps, remove its lid.
- Bake the remaining cookies in a similar way.
- Enjoy.

1075. Tangy Lemon Mousse

Preparation Time: 10 minutes
Cooking Time: 12 minutes
Servings: 2

Ingredients:
- 2 oz cream cheese, soft
- 1/2 tsp sugar
- 2 tbsp fresh lemon juice
- 1/2 cup heavy cream
- Pinch of salt

Directions:
- Spray 2 ramekins with cooking spray and set aside.
- In a bowl, beat together cream cheese, sweetener, lemon juice, heavy cream, and salt until smooth.
- Pour cream cheese mixture into the prepared ramekins.
- Place the dehydrating tray in a multi-level air fryer basket and place the basket in the air fryer.
- Place ramekins on a dehydrating tray.
- Seal pot with air fryer lid and select bake mode, then set the temperature to 350°F and timer for 12 minutes.
- Serve and enjoy

1076. Fudgy Nutella Brownies

Preparation Time: 10 minutes
Cooking Time: 20 minutes
Servings: 8

Ingredients:
- 2 eggs
- 1/2 cup all-purpose flour
- 1 1/4 cup Nutella chocolate hazelnut spread
- 1 tsp kosher salt

Directions:
- Spray a baking dish with cooking spray and set aside.
- In a mixing bowl, mix together eggs, Nutella, flour, and salt until well combined.
- Pour batter into the prepared baking dish.
- Place steam rack in the air fryer, then place baking dish on top of the rack.
- Seal pot with air fryer lid and select bake mode, then set the temperature to 350°F and timer for 20 minutes.
- Serve and enjoy.

1077. Toffee Cookies

Preparation Time: 10 minutes
Cooking Time: 12 minutes
Servings: 8

Ingredients:
- 1 egg
- 1/3 cup toffee chips
- 1/2 tsp baking powder
- 1 cup all-purpose flour
- 1 tsp vanilla
- 1/2 cup brown sugar
- 4 tbsp butter, softened
- 1/8 tsp salt

Directions:
- In a mixing bowl, beat butter and sugar until smooth.
- Add egg and vanilla and stir to combine.
- Add flour, baking powder, and salt and stir to combine.
- Add toffee chips and stir to combine. Place cookie mixture into the refrigerator for 1 hour.
- Place the dehydrating tray in a multi-level air fryer basket and place the basket in the air fryer.
- Line dehydrating tray with parchment paper.
- Make cookies from the mixture and place some cookies on the dehydrating tray.
- Seal pot with air fryer lid and select bake mode, then set the temperature to 350°F and timer for 9 minutes.
- Bake the remaining cookies using the same method.

1078. Marshmallow Turnovers

Preparation Time: 10 minutes
Cooking Time: 10 minutes
Servings: 4

Ingredients:
- 4 sheets of defrosted filo pastry
- 4 tbsp of chunky peanut butter
- 4 tsp of marshmallow fluff
- 2 ounces of melted butter
- Just a pinch of sea salt

Directions:
- Preheat your Air Fryer to a temperature of 360°F (182°C)
- Take one of your filo sheets and brush it up with butter.

- On top of your filo sheet, place another sheet and butter it up as well.
- Keep repeating until all leaves are used up.
- Cup the stalks into three pieces of 3x12 inch strips.
- Take about one tbsp of peanut butter and marshmallow fluff and add them under your filo strips.
- Hold the sheet and fold it over your mixture, forming a triangle, and then keep folding it in a zigzag manner until all of the fillings have been wrapped up.
- Take some butter and tighten.
- Add the sheets to your cooking basket and cook for about 3-5 minutes.
- Serve with a sprinkle of salt.

1079. Soft Sugar Cookies

Preparation Time: 10 minutes
Cooking Time: 12 minutes
Servings: 8

Ingredients:
- 1 egg yolk
- 1/4 tsp baking soda
- 1/2 cup + 2 tbsp all-purpose flour
- 1/2 tsp vanilla
- 1/3 cup granulated sugar
- 1/4 cup butter, melted
- Pinch of salt

Directions:
- In a bowl, stir together the egg yolk, vanilla, sugar, and butter until well combined.
- Add flour, baking soda, and flour and mix until dough is formed.
- Place the dehydrating tray in a multi-level air fryer basket and place the basket in the air fryer.
- Line dehydrating tray with parchment paper.
- Make cookies from the mixture and place them on dehydrating tray.
- Seal pot with air fryer lid and select bake mode, then set the temperature to 350°F and timer for 12 minutes.
- Serve and enjoy.

1080. Lemon Pound Cake

Preparation Time: 20 minutes
Cooking Time: 30 minutes
Servings: 6

Ingredients:
- 4 eggs
- 2/3 cup yogurt
- 1 tsp vanilla
- 2 tbsp fresh lemon juice
- 1 tbsp lemon zest, grated
- 1 cup Swerve
- 1/2 cup butter, softened
- 1 tsp baking powder
- 1 1/2 cups all-purpose flour
- 1/2 tsp salt

Directions:
- Spray bundt cake pan with cooking spray and set aside.
- In a medium bowl, mix together flour, baking powder, and salt.

- In a mixing bowl, beat together butter and sweetener until creamy.
- Add eggs and beat until well combined.
- Add flour mixture, vanilla, yogurt, lemon juice, and lemon zest and blend until smooth.
- Pour batter into the prepared cake pan.
- Place the steam rack into the air fryer, then place the cake pan on top of the rack.
- Seal pot with air fryer lid and select air fry mode, then set the temperature to 320°F and timer for 30 minutes.
- Serve and enjoy.

1081.   Strawberry Souffle

Preparation Time: 10 minutes
Cooking Time: 15 minutes
Servings: 4

Ingredients:
- 3 egg whites
- 1/2 tsp vanilla
- 1 tbsp sugar
- 2 cups strawberries

Directions:
- Spray four ramekins with cooking spray and set aside.
- Add strawberries, vanilla, and sugar into the blender and blend until smooth.
- In a large bowl, beat egg whites until medium peaks form. Add strawberry mixture and fold well.
- Pour batter into the prepared ramekins.
- Place the dehydrating tray in a multi-level air fryer basket and place the basket in the air fryer.
- Place ramekins on a dehydrating tray.
- Seal pot with air fryer lid and select bake mode, then set the temperature to 350°F and timer for 15 minutes.
- Serve and enjoy.

1082.   Puff Pastry Pears

Preparation Time: 10 minutes
Cooking Time: 15 minutes
Servings: 4

Ingredients:
- 4 puff pastry sheets
- 14 ounces vanilla custard
- 2 pears, halved
- 1 egg, whisked
- 2 tbsp. sugar

Directions:
- Put the puff pastry slices on a clean surface, add a spoonful of vanilla custard in the center of each, top with pear halves and wrap.
- Brush pears with egg, sprinkle sugar and place them in your air fryer's basket and cook at 320°F for 15 minutes.
- Divide parcels among plates and serve.

1083.   Vanilla Strawberry Mix

Preparation Time: 10 minutes
Cooking Time: 20 minutes
Servings: 10

Ingredients:
- 2 tbsp lemon juice
- 2 pounds strawberries
- 4 cups coconut sugar
- 1 tsp cinnamon powder
- 1 tsp vanilla extract

Directions:
- In a pot that fits your air fryer, mix strawberries with coconut sugar, lemon juice, cinnamon and vanilla, stir gently, introduce it to the fryer and cook at 350°F for 20 minutes.
- Divide into bowls and serve cold.
- Enjoy!

1084.   Apricot Blackberry Crumble

Preparation Time: 10 minutes
Cooking Time: 20 minutes
Servings: 9

Ingredients:
- 18 ounces of fresh apricot
- 5½ ounce of fresh blackberries
- ½ a cup of sugar
- 2 tbsp of lemon juice
- 1 cup of flour
- Salt as required
- 5 tbsp of cold butter

Directions:
- Take a knife and cut up your apricots into two.
- Remove the stones.
- Gently cut them up into cubical shapes and add them to a bowl.
- Add blackberries, lemon juice, and two tbsp of sugar to the mixture and mix everything thoroughly.
- Take a baking dish and grease it up nicely.
- Spread the mixture on your baking dish.
- Take another bowl and add flour, sugar, and salt.
- Mix well and add one tbsp of cold water, butter and rub everything until a crumbly mixture appears.
- Air Fryer to a temperature of 390°F (200 °C).
- Take your baking dish and add the crumbly mixture on top of your batter.
- Push it to your Air Fryer cooking basket and let it cook for about 20 minutes until golden brown. texture comes
- Serve!

1085.   Lemon Cupcakes

Preparation Time: 10 minutes
Cooking Time: 15 minutes
Servings: 12

Ingredients:
- 2 eggs
- 1 tbsp fresh lemon juice
- 1 tbsp lemon zest, grated
- 1/4 cup milk
- 1 tsp vanilla
- 3/4 cup sugar
- 1/4 cup butter
- 1 1/2 tsp baking powder
- 1 1/4 cups all-purpose flour
- 1/4 tsp salt

Directions:

- In a small bowl, mix together flour, baking powder, and salt and set aside.
- In a mixing bowl, beat together sugar and butter until well combined.
- Add eggs, lemon juice, lemon zest, milk, and vanilla and beat until combined.
- Add flour mixture and stir to combine.
- Pour batter into the 12 silicone muffin molds.
- Place the dehydrating tray in a multi-level air fryer basket and place the basket in the air fryer.
- Place 6 silicone muffin molds on dehydrating tray.
- Seal pot with air fryer lid and select bake mode, then set the temperature to 350°F and timer for 15 minutes.
- Bake the remaining cupcakes using the same method.

1086. Quick Oatmeal Cake

Preparation Time: 20 minutes
Cooking Time: 30 minutes
Servings: 8

Ingredients:

- 2 large eggs
- 1 cup powdered sugar
- 1 cup brown sugar
- 1/2 cup margarine
- 1 1/2 cups flour
- 1 tsp vanilla extract
- 1 1/2 tsp baking soda
- 1 tsp ground cinnamon
- 1 1/2 cups warm water
- 1 cup quick oats
- 1 tsp salt

Directions:

- Grease the baking dish with butter and set it aside.
- Insert wire rack in rack position 6. Select bake, set temperature 350°F, timer for 40 minutes. Press start to preheat the oven.
- Mix together quick oats and warm water. Set aside.
- In a mixing bowl, beat together sugar, brown sugar and margarine until creamy.
- Add eggs, salt, cinnamon, baking soda, vanilla, and flour mix until combined.
- Add oats and water mixture into the batter and fold well.
- Pour batter into the prepared baking dish and bake for 40 minutes.
- Slice and serve.

1087. Vanilla Crème Brulee

Preparation Time: 10 minutes
Cooking Time: 15 minutes
Servings: 8

Ingredients:

- 6 tbsp sugar
- 3 cups heavy whipping cream
- 7 large Egg Yolks
- 2 cups water
- 2 tbsp Vanilla Extract

Directions:

- In a mixing bowl, add the yolks, vanilla, whipping cream and half of the swerve sugar. Use a whisk to mix them until they are well combined.
- Pour the mixture into the ramekins and cover them with aluminum foil.
- Open the cooker, fit the reversible rack into the pot and pour in the water.
- Place 3 ramekins on the rack and place the remaining ramekins to sit on the edges of the ramekins below.
- Close the lid, secure the pressure valve and select Pressure mode on high for 8 minutes. Press Start.
- Once the timer has stopped, do a natural pressure release for 10 minutes, then a quick pressure release to let out the remaining pressure.
- With a napkin in hand, remove the ramekins onto a flat surface and then into a refrigerator to chill for at least 6 hours.
- After refrigerators, remove the ramekins and remove the aluminum foil.
- Equally, sprinkle the remaining sugar on it and return it to the pot. Close the crisping lid. Select Bake mode and set the timer to 4 minutes at 380°F. Serve the crème Brulee chilled with whipped cream.

1088. Baked Almond Donuts

Preparation Time: 10 minutes
Cooking Time: 15 minutes
Servings: 6

Ingredients:

- 2 eggs
- 1 1/2 tsp vanilla extract
- 3 tbsp maple syrup
- 1 cup almond flour
- 1/4 tsp baking soda

Directions:

- Spray the donut pan with cooking spray and set aside.
- Insert wire rack in rack position 6. Select bake, set temperature 320°F, timer for 15 minutes. Press start to preheat the air fryer.
- In a large bowl, add all ingredients and mix well until smooth.
- Pour batter into the greased donut pan and bake for 15 minutes.
- Serve and enjoy.

1089. Coconut Caramel Cream

Preparation Time: 10 minutes
Cooking Time: 15 minutes
Servings: 4

Ingredients:

- 1 cup heavy cream
- 3 tbsp caramel syrup
- ½ cup coconut cream
- 1 tbsp sugar
- ½ tsp cinnamon powder

Directions:

- In a bowl, mix the cream with the caramel syrup and the other ingredients, whisk, divide into small ramekins, introduce into the fryer and cook at 320°F and bake for 15 minutes.

- Divide into bowls and serve cold.

1090. Autumn Pumpkin Pie

Preparation Time: 20 minutes
Cooking Time: 30 minutes
Servings: 6

Ingredients:

- 3 eggs
- 1/2 cup cream
- 1/2 cup almond milk
- 1/2 cup pumpkin puree
- 1/2 tsp cinnamon
- 1 tsp vanilla
- 1/4 cup sugar

Directions:

- Spray a square baking dish with cooking spray and set aside.
- Insert wire rack in rack position 6. Select bake, set temperature 350°F, timer for 30 minutes. Press start to preheat the air fryer.
- In a large bowl, add all ingredients and whisk until smooth.
- Pour the pie mixture into the prepared dish and bake for 30 minutes.
- Remove from the air fryer and set aside to cool completely.
- Place into the refrigerator for 2 hours.
- Slice and serve.

1091. Tropical Rice Pudding

Preparation Time: 10 minutes
Cooking Time: 5 minutes
Servings: 8

Ingredients:

- 1 tbsp avocado oil
- 1 cup rice
- 14 ounces milk
- Sugar to the taste
- 8 ounces canned pineapple, chopped

Directions:

- In your air fryer, mix oil, milk and rice, stir, cover and cook at 400°F for 3 minutes.
- Add sugar and pineapple, stir, cover and bake for 2 minutes more.
- Divide into dessert bowls and serve.

1092. Rich Chocolate Pudding

Preparation Time: 10 minutes
Cooking Time: 20 minutes
Servings: 2

Ingredients:

- 2 tbsp water
- 1/2 tbsp agar
- 4 tbsp stevia
- 4 tbsp cocoa powder
- 2 cups coconut milk, hot

Directions:

- In a bowl, mix milk with stevia and cocoa powder and stir well.
- In a bowl, mix agar with water, stir well, add to the cocoa mix, stir and transfer to a pudding pan that fits your air fryer.
- Introduce in the fryer and cook at 356 °F for 20 minutes.
- Serve the pudding cold.

1093. Spiced Orange Slices

Preparation Time: 10 minutes
Cooking Time: 6 hours
Servings: 3

Ingredients:

- 2 large oranges, cut into ⅛-inch-thick slices
- ½ tsp ground star anise
- ½ tsp ground cinnamon
- 1 tbsp Choco-hazelnut spread

Directions:

- Dash seasonings on the orange slices.
- Place into the fry basket, then insert the basket at mid-position in the Air Fryer.
- Select the Dehydrate function, fix the time to 6 hours and temperature to 140°F, then press Start.
- Remove once done, and if desired, serve with chocolate hazelnut spread.

1094. Cinnamon Pear Crisps

Preparation Time: 10 minutes
Cooking Time: 25 minutes
Servings: 2

Ingredients:

- 1 cup flour
- 1 stick vegan butter
- 1 tbsp cinnamon
- ½ cup sugar
- 2 pears, cubed

Directions:

- Mix flour and butter to form a crumbly texture.
- Add cinnamon and sugar.
- Put the pears in the air fryer.
- Pour and spread the mixture on top of the pears.
- Cook at 350°F for 25 minutes.

1095. Spiced Mandarin and Apple Sauce

Preparation Time: 10 minutes
Cooking Time: 20 minutes
Servings: 4

Ingredients:

- 4 apples, cored, peeled and cored
- 2 cups mandarin juice
- ¼ cup maple syrup
- 2 tsp cinnamon powder
- 1 tbsp ginger, grated

Directions:

- In a pot that fits your air fryer, mix apples with mandarin juice, maple syrup, cinnamon and ginger,

- introduce it into the fryer and cook at 365 °F for 20 minutes
- Divide apples mix between plates and serve warm.

1096. Coconut-Coated White Chocolate Cookies

Preparation Time: 15 minutes
Cooking Time: 12 minutes
Servings: 8

Ingredients:
- 3½-ounce butter
- 1 small egg
- 5-ounce self-rising flour
- 1¼-ounce white chocolate, chopped
- 3 tbsp desiccated coconut
- 2¼-ounce caster sugar
- 1 tsp vanilla extract

Directions:
- Preheat the Air fryer to 355°F and grease a baking sheet lightly.
- Mix sugar and butter in a large bowl and beat till fluffy.
- Whisk in the egg, vanilla extract, flour and chocolate and mix until well combined.
- Place coconut in a shallow dish and make small balls from the mixture.
- Roll the balls into coconut evenly and arrange them onto a baking sheet.
- Press each ball into a cookie-like shape and transfer it into the air fryer.
- Cook for about 8 minutes and set the air fryer to 320°F.
- Cook for about 4 minutes and dish out to serve.

1097. Vegan Chocolate Vanilla Bars

Preparation Time: 10 minutes
Cooking Time: 7 minutes
Servings: 12

Ingredients:
- 1 cup sugar-free and vegan chocolate chips
- 2 tbsp coconut butter
- 2/3 cup coconut cream
- 2 tbsp stevia
- ¼ tsp vanilla extract

Directions:
- Put the cream in a bowl, add stevia, butter and chocolate chips and stir
- Leave aside for 5 minutes, stir well and mix the vanilla.
- Transfer the mix to a lined baking sheet, introduce it to your air fryer and cook at 356°F for 7 minutes.
- Leave the mix aside to cool down, slice and serve.
- Enjoy!

1098. Coconut Raspberry Bars

Preparation Time: 10 minutes
Cooking Time: 6 minutes
Servings: 12

Ingredients:
- ½ cup coconut butter, melted
- ½ cup coconut oil
- ½ cup raspberries, dried

- ¼ cup swerve
- ½ cup coconut, shredded

Directions:
- In your food processor, blend dried berries very well.
- In a bowl that fits your air fryer, mix oil with butter, swerve, coconut and raspberries, toss well, introduce it to the fryer and cook at 320°F for 6 minutes.
- Spread this on a lined baking sheet, keep it in the fridge for an hour, slice and serve.
- Enjoy!

1099. Sweet Blueberry Jam

Preparation Time: 10 minutes
Cooking Time: 11 minutes
Servings: 2

Ingredients:
- ½ pound blueberries
- 1/3-pound sugar
- Zest from ½ lemon, grated
- ½ tbsp butter
- A pinch of cinnamon powder

Directions:
- Put the blueberries in your blender, pulse them well, strain, transfer to your pressure cooker, add sugar, lemon zest and cinnamon, stir, cover and simmer on sauté mode for 3 minutes.
- Add butter, stir, and cover the fryer and 400°F for 8 minutes.
- Transfer to a jar and serve.

1100. Chocolate Avocado Pudding

Preparation Time: 2 hours
Cooking Time: 2 minutes
Servings: 3

Ingredients:
- ½ cup avocado oil
- 4 tbsp sugar
- 1 tbsp cocoa powder
- 14 ounces canned coconut milk
- 1 avocado, pitted, peeled and chopped

Directions:
- In a bowl, mix oil with cocoa powder and half of the sugar, stir well, transfer to a lined container, keep in the fridge for 1 hour and chop into small pieces.
- In your air fryer, mix coconut milk with avocado and the rest of the sugar, blend using an immersion blender, and cover the cooker and 400°F for 2 minutes.
- Add chocolate chips, stir, divide the pudding into bowls and keep in the fridge until you serve it.

1101. Autumn Fruit Bowl

Preparation Time: 10 minutes
Cooking Time: 35 minutes
Servings: 4

Ingredients:
- 2 cups cherries, pitted and halved
- 1 cup rhubarb, sliced
- 1 cup apple juice

- 2 tbsp sugar
- ½ cup raisins.

Directions:

- In a pot that fits your air fryer, combine the cherries with the rhubarb and the other ingredients, toss, cook at 330°F for 35 minutes, divide into bowls, cool down and serve.

1102. Summer Fruit Bowl

Preparation Time: 10 minutes
Cooking Time: 10 minutes
Servings: 4

Ingredients:

- 1 cup oranges, peeled and cut into segments
- 1 cup cherries, pitted and halved
- 1 cup mango, peeled and cubed
- 1 cup orange juice
- 2 tbsp sugar

Directions:

- In the air fryer's pan, mix the oranges with the cherries and the other ingredients, toss and cook at 320°F for 10 minutes.
- Divide into bowls and serve cold.

1103. Zesty Strawberry Jam

Preparation Time: 10 minutes
Cooking Time: 25 minutes
Servings: 8

Ingredients:

- 1-pound strawberries, chopped
- 1 tbsp lemon zest, grated
- 1 and ½ cups of water
- ½ cup sugar
- ½ tbsp lemon juice

Directions:

- In the air fryer's pan, mix the berries with the water and the other ingredients, stir, introduce the pan to your air fryer and cook at 330°F for 25 minutes.
- Divide into bowls and serve cold.

1104. Cream Cheese Stuffed Strawberries

Preparation Time: 10 minutes
Cooking Time: 10 minutes
Servings: 4

- **Ingredients**
- 1 lb. fresh strawberries
- 4 oz cream cheese
- ¼ cup powdered sugar
- ¼ tsp vanilla extract
- 1 full-sized low-fat graham cracker
- **Directions**
- Cut tops off strawberries.
- Remove the interior of each strawberry.
- Cook it for 5 minutes in Air Fryer.
- Take a bowl, add cheese, sugar, and vanilla and mix it in the mixer.
- Add this mixture to strawberries.
- Then coat the strawberries with crackers.

1105. Sweet Grape and Pear Compote

Preparation Time: 10 minutes
Cooking Time: 15 minutes
Servings: 4

Ingredients:

- 4 pears, cored and cut into wedges
- 1 tsp vanilla
- 1/4 cup apple juice
- 2 cups grapes, halved

Directions:

- Put all of the ingredients in the inner pot of the air fryer and stir well.
- Seal pot and 400°F for 15 minutes.
- As soon as the cooking is done, let it release pressure naturally for 10 minutes, then release the remaining using quick release. Remove lid.
- Stir and serve.

1106. Peanut Butter Bars

Preparation Time: 20 minutes
Cooking Time: 20 minutes
Servings: 20

- **Ingredients**
- 1 cup of peanut butter
- 2 tsp of vanilla extract
- 1 cup of peanuts
- 5 cups of Cheerios cereal
- 1/2 cup of white sugar
- 1/2 cup of corn syrup
- 1 scoop of vanilla powder
- 2 tbsp of mini chocolate chips

Directions:

- In a medium saucepan, mix together white sugar and light corn syrup.
- Bring to a boil.
- Add peanut butter, vanilla and protein powder.
- Mix until smooth.
- Place peanut butter, Cheerios, and peanuts in a large mixing bowl.
- Pour peanut butter mixture over Cheerios and peanuts. Stir until combined.
- Spread Cheerio mixture in a baking dish that has been greased with non-stick cooking spray.
- Cook for 20 minutes in Fryer.

1107. Cinnamon Cappuccino Muffins

Preparation Time: 10 minutes
Cooking Time: 25 minutes
Servings: 12

Ingredients:

- 4 eggs
- 1 tsp espresso powder
- 1 tsp cinnamon
- 2 tsp baking powder
- 1/4 cup coconut flour
- 1/2 cup Swerve
- 2 cups almond flour
- 1/2 tsp vanilla
- 1/2 cup sour cream

- 1/4 tsp salt

Directions:
- Preheat the color air fryer to 350°F.
- Add sour cream, vanilla, espresso powder, and eggs to a blender and blend until smooth.
- Add almond flour, cinnamon, baking powder, coconut flour, Swerve, and salt and blend to combine.
- Pour the mixture into the silicone muffin molds.
- Place molds into the air fryer basket and cook for 25 minutes. Cook in batches.
- Serve and enjoy.

1108. Dark Rum Cake

Preparation Time: 15 minutes
Cooking Time: 25 minutes
Servings: 6

Ingredients:
- ½ package yellow cake mix
- ½ (3.4-ounce) package Jell-O instant pudding
- 2 eggs
- ¼ cup of vegetable oil
- ¼ cup of water
- ¼ cup dark rum

Directions:
- In a bowl, add all the ingredients, and with an electric mixer, beat until well combined.
- Arrange a parchment paper in the bottom of a greased 8-inch pan.
- Now, arrange a foil piece around the cake pan.
- Place the mixture into the prepared baking pan, and with the back of a spoon, smooth the top surface.
- Arrange the drip pan at the bottom of the Air fryer Plus Air Fryer Oven cooking chamber.
- Select "Air Dry" and then adjust the temperature to 325°F.
- Set the timer for 25 minutes and press the "Start."
- When the display shows "Add Food," place the baking pan over the drip pan.
- When the display shows "Turn Food," do nothing.
- When cooking time is complete, remove the pan from the Air fryer and place it onto a wire rack to cool for about 10 minutes.
- Carefully invert the cake onto a wire rack to cool completely before cutting.
- Cut into desired-sized slices and serve.

1109. Toffee Apple Upside-Down Cake

Preparation Time: 10 minutes
Cooking Time: 30 minutes
Servings: 9

Ingredients:
- ½ cup walnuts, chopped
- 1 lemon, zest
- 1 tsp vinegar
- ¾ cup of water
- 1 ½ tsp mixed spice
- ¼ cup sunflower oil
- 1 tsp baking soda
- 1 cup almond flour
- 3 baking apples, cored and sliced

- 2 tbsp liquid Stevia, divided
- ¼ cup almond butter

Directions:
- Preheat your air fryer to 390°F. Melt the butter in a skillet, then remove from heat and add one tbsp Stevia and stir. Pour the mixture into a baking dish that will fit into your air fryer. Arrange the slices of apples on top and set them aside.
- Combine flour, baking soda, and mixed spice in a large mixing bowl. In another bowl, add water, vinegar, remaining tbsp of liquid Stevia, lemon zest, and oil, and mix well. Mix in the wet ingredients with dry ingredients and stir until well combined. Pour over apple slices and bake for 30-minutes.

1110. Creamy Vanilla Berry Mini Pies

Preparation Time: 10 Minutes
Cooking Time: 10 Minutes
Servings: 4

Ingredients:
- 4 pastry dough sheets
- 2 tbsp mashed strawberries
- 2 tbsp mashed raspberries
- ¼ tsp vanilla extract
- 2 cups cream cheese, softened
- 1 tbsp honey

Directions:
- Preheat fryer on Bake function to 375°F. Divide the cream cheese between the dough sheets and spread it evenly. In a small bowl, combine the berries, honey, and vanilla. Spoon the mixture into the pastry sheets. Pinch the ends of the layers to form a puff. Place the winds in a lined baking dish. Place the bowl in the toaster oven and cook for 15 minutes. Serve chilled.

1111. Tangerine Cake

Preparation Time: 10 minutes
Cooking Time: 20 minutes
Servings: 8

Ingredients:
- ¾ cup sugar
- 2 cups flour
- ¼ cup olive oil
- ½ cup milk
- 1 tbsp. cider vinegar
- ½ tbsp. vanilla extract
- Juice and zest from 2 lemons
- Juice and zest from 1 tangerine
- Tangerine segments

Directions:
- Mix in flour with sugar and turn.
- Mix oil with vinegar, milk, vanilla extract, tangerine zest and lemon juice, then beat properly.
- Put flour, turn properly, get the mix into a cake pan, get in the air fryer and cook at 360°F for 20 minutes.
- Serve with tangerine segments over.

1112. Sweet Walnut Fritters

Preparation Time: 20 minutes
Cooking Time: 15 minutes
Servings: 4

Ingredients:

- Cooking spray
- 1 cup all-purpose flour
- ½ cup walnuts, coarsely chopped
- ¼ cup white sugar
- ¼ cup milk
- 1 egg
- 1½ tsp baking powder
- 1 pinch salt
- 2 tbsp white sugar
- ½ tsp ground cinnamon
- Glaze:
- ½ cup confectioners' sugar
- 1 tbsp milk
- ½ tsp caramel extract
- ¼ tsp ground cinnamon

Directions:

- Preheat your Air Fryer Machine to 350°F. Layer the Air Fryer's Basket with parchment paper. Grease the parchment paper with cooking spray. Whisk flour with milk, 1/4 cup sugar, egg, baking powder, and salt in a small bowl. Separately mix 2 tbsp sugar with cinnamon in another bowl, toss in walnuts and mix well to coat. Stir in flour mixture and mix until combined. Drop the fritter mixture using a cookie scoop into the prepared Air Fryer's Basket. Air Fry them for 5 minutes. Flip fritters for 5 minutes until golden brown. Meanwhile, whisk milk, caramel extract, confectioners' sugar, and cinnamon in a bowl. Transfer fritters to a wire rack and allow them to cool. Drizzle with a glaze over the fritters.

1113. Chocolate Chip Bread

Preparation Time: 20 minutes
Cooking Time: 40 minutes
Servings: 6

Ingredients:

- 12 tbsp melted butter
- 2 cup buttermilk
- 2 tsp baking powder
- 2 tsp salt
- 4 cups all-purpose flour
- 1 cup sugar
- 6 eggs
- 2 tsp vanilla extract
- 1 cup chocolate chips
- 2 tsp baking soda

Directions:

- In a bowl, mix baking powder, baking soda, melted butter and salt
- Add vanilla extract, egg, buttermilk, sugar and mix properly
- Use non-stick cooking spray to spray the air fryer pan
- Add chocolate chips to the mixture

- Pour the mixture into the pan and set it into an air fryer basket. Air fry at 330°F for about 40 minutes, and it is done

1114. Soft Cinnamon Donuts

Preparation Time: 20 minutes
Cooking Time: 5-10 minutes
Servings: 5

Ingredients:

- 1/2 cup granulated white sugar
- Coconut oil spray
- 2 tbsp ground cinnamon
- 4 tbsp melted butter
- 16 oz refrigerated flaky jumbo biscuits

Directions:

- Take out biscuits from the can and put them on a flat surface
- Press the center of the biscuits with a 1-inch round biscuit cutter to make a hole at the center
- Mix cinnamon and sugar together in a bowl and put aside
- Use coconut oil to grease the air fryer basket
- Place the donut in a single layer in the air fryer basket
- Air fry at 360°F for 5 minutes
- Take them out and soak them in melted butter and then coat it with cinnamon sugar and serve

1115. Double-Dipped Mini Cinnamon Biscuits

Preparation Time: 30 minutes
Cooking Time: 10-13 minutes
Servings: 8

Ingredients:

- 2 cups blanched almond flour
- ½ cup sugar
- 1 tsp baking powder
- ½ tsp fine sea salt
- ¼ cup plus 2 tbsp (¾ stick) very cold unsalted butter
- ¼ cup unsweetened, unflavored almond milk
- 1 large egg
- 1 tsp vanilla extract
- 3 tsp ground cinnamon
- GLAZE:
- ½ cup sugar
- ¼ cup heavy cream

Directions:

- Preheat the air fryer to 350°F. Line a pie pan that fits into your air fryer with parchment paper.
- In a medium-sized bowl, mix together the almond flour, sweetener (if powdered; do not add liquid sweetener), baking powder, and salt. Cut the butter into ½-inch squares, then use a hand mixer to work the butter into the dry ingredients. When you are done, the mixture should still have chunks of butter.
- In a bowl, mix the almond milk, egg, and vanilla extract (if using liquid sweetener, add it as well) until blender. Using a fork, stir the wet ingredients into the dry ingredients until large clumps form. Add the cinnamon and use your hands to swirl it into the dough. Form the dough into sixteen 1-inch balls and place them on the prepared pan, spacing them about ½ inch apart. (If

you're using a smaller air fryer, work in batches if necessary.)

- Bake in the air fryer until golden, 10 to 13 minutes. Remove from the air fryer and let cool on the pan for at least 5 minutes.
- While the biscuits bake, make the glaze: Place the powdered sweetener in a small bowl and slowly stir in the heavy cream with a fork. When the biscuits have cooled, dip the tops into the glaze, allow it to dry a bit, and then dip again for a thick glaze. Serve warm or at room temperature. Store unglazed biscuits in an airtight container in the refrigerator for up to 3 days or in the freezer for up to a month. Reheat in a preheated 350°F air fryer for 5 minutes, or until warmed through, and dip in the glaze as instructed above.

1116. Peach Hand Pies

Preparation Time: 40 minutes
Cooking Time: 30 minutes
Servings: 5

Ingredients:
- Non-stick cooking spray
- 2 peeled and chopped peaches,
- 1 tbsp. fresh lemon juice (from 1 lemon)
- 3 tbsp. granulated sugar
- 1 tsp. Vanilla extract
- ¼ tsp. salt
- 1 tsp. cornstarch
- 1 package unbaked pie crust (2 crusts)

Directions:
- Mix together in a bowl peaches, lemon juice, sugar, vanilla, and salt and leave for 15 minutes; stir occasionally
- Drain peaches, reserve 1 tbsp liquid to Whisk in together with cornstarch stir into drained peaches.
- Measure 4 inches and cut the pie crust into 8 pieces circles and put 1 tbsp filling in the middle of each circle
- Rub edges of dough with water and fold the dough over the filling to make a semi-circle shape
- Press the edges with a fork to seal
- Cut 3 small slits on top of pies and spray with cooking spray
- Put 3 pies in one layer into the air fryer basket and cook at 350°F for 15 minutes or until golden brown
- Repeat with the remaining pies

1117. Moist Banana Bread

Preparation Time: 20 minutes
Cooking Time: 25-30 minutes
Servings: 6

Ingredients:
- 3 ripe bananas, mashed
- 1 cup sugar
- 1 large egg
- 4 tbsp (½ stick) unsalted butter, melted
- 1½ cups all-purpose flour
- 1 tsp baking soda
- 1 tsp salt

Directions:
- Coat the insides of 3 mini loaf pans with cooking spray. In a large mixing bowl, mix together the bananas and sugar. In a separate large mixing bowl, combine the egg, butter, flour, baking soda, and salt and mix well. Add the banana mixture to the egg and flour mixture. Mix well. Pour into pan.
- Set the mini loaf pans into the air fryer basket.
- Set the temperature of your air fryer to 310°F. Set the timer and bake for 22 minutes. Insert a toothpick into the center of each loaf; if it comes out clean, they are done. If the batter clings to the toothpick, cook the loaves for 2 minutes more and check again. When the loaves are cooked through, use silicone oven mitts to remove the pans from the air fryer basket. Turn out the loaves onto a wire rack to cool.

1118. Banana Foster

Preparation Time: 10 minutes
Cooking Time: 10 minutes
Servings: 1

Ingredients:
- 1 tbsp unsalted butter
- 2 tsp dark brown sugar
- 1 banana, peeled and halved lengthwise and then crosswise
- 2 tbsp chopped pecans
- ⅛ tsp ground cinnamon
- 2 tbsp light rum
- Vanilla ice cream for serving

Directions:
- In a 6 × 3-inch round heatproof pan, combine the butter and brown sugar. Place the pan in the air fryer basket.
- Set the air fryer to 350°F for 2 minutes, or until the butter and sugar are melted. Swirl to combine. Add the banana pieces and pecans, turning the bananas to coat.
- Set the air fryer to 350°F for 5 minutes, turning the banana pieces halfway through the cooking time. Sprinkle with the cinnamon. Remove the pan from the air fryer and place it on an unlit stovetop for safety. Add the rum to the pan, swirling to combine it with the butter mixture. Carefully light the sauce with a long-reach lighter. Spoon the flaming sauce over the banana pieces until the flames die out. Serve over ice cream.

1119. Middle Eastern Toast and Milk

Preparation Time: 20 minutes
Cooking Time: 50 minutes
Servings: 8

Ingredients:
- 1 cup sweetened condensed milk
- 1 cup evaporated milk
- 1 cup half-and-half
- 1 tsp ground cardamom, plus additional for garnish
- 1 pinch saffron thread
- 4 slices of white bread
- 2 to 3 tbsp ghee or butter, softened
- 2 tbsp crushed pistachios, for garnish (optional)

Directions:

- In a 6 × 4-inch round heatproof pan, combine the condensed milk, evaporated milk, half-and-half, cardamom, and saffron. Stir until well combined.
- The air fryer must be preheated to 350°F for 15 minutes, stirring halfway through the cooking time. Remove the sweetened milk from the air fryer and set it aside.
- Slice each bread into two triangles. Brush each side with ghee. The bread will then be placed in the basket of the air fryer
- Set the air fryer to 350°F for 5 minutes or until golden brown and toasty.
- Remove the bread from the air fryer. Arrange two triangles in each of four wide, shallow bowls. Pour the hot milk mixture on top of the bread and let soak for 30 minutes.
- Garnish with pistachios if using, and sprinkle with additional cardamom.

1120.   Spiced Pears with Honey Lemon Ricotta

Preparation Time: 10 minutes
Cooking Time: 8-10 minutes
Servings: 2

Ingredients:

- 2 large Bartlett pears
- 3 tbsp butter, melted
- 3 tbsp brown sugar
- ½ tsp ground ginger
- ¼ tsp ground cardamom
- ½ cup whole-milk ricotta cheese
- 1 tbsp honey, plus additional for drizzling
- 1 tsp pure almond extract
- 1 tsp pure lemon extract

Directions:

- Each pear must be peeled and cut in half lengthwise. Place the pear halves in a medium bowl, add the melted butter, and toss. Add the brown sugar, ginger, and cardamom; toss to coat. Place the pear halves, cut side down, in the air fryer basket.
- Set the air fryer to 375°F for 8 to 10 minutes, or until the pears are lightly browned and tender but not mushy. Then, combine the ricotta, honey, and almond and

lemon extracts. Be sure to mix it well by whisking it until it becomes fluffy and light. To serve, divide the ricotta mixture among four small shallow bowls. Place a pear half on top of the cheese. Drizzle with additional honey and serve.

1121.   Lemon Tart Macaroons

Preparation Time: 20 minutes
Cooking Time: 25-30 minutes
Servings: 8

Ingredients:

- 2 large egg whites, room temperature
- ⅓ cup Swerve confectioners'-style sweetener
- 2 tbsp lemon zest
- 2 tsp poppy seeds
- 1 tsp lemon extract
- ¼ tsp fine sea salt
- 2 cups unsweetened shredded coconut
- lemon icing:
- ¼ cup Swerve confectioners'-style sweetener
- 1 tbsp lemon juice

Directions:

- Preheat the air fryer to 325°F. Line a 7-inch pie pan or a casserole dish that will fit inside your air fryer with parchment paper. Place the egg whites in a medium-sized bowl and use a hand mixer on high to beat the whites until stiff peaks form. Add the sweetener, lemon zest, poppy seeds, lemon extract, and salt. Mix on low until combined. Carefully fold the coconut in with a rubber spatula. Use a 1-inch cookie scoop to place the cookies on the parchment, spacing them about ¼ inch apart.
- Place the pan in the air fryer and cook for 12 to 14 minutes, until the cookies are golden and a toothpick inserted into the center comes out clean. While the cookies bake, make the lemon icing: Place the sweetener in a small bowl. Add the lemon juice and stir well. If the icing is a little thin, add a dash of sweetener. If the icing is too thick, add a little more lemon juice. Remove the cookies from the air fryer and allow them to cool for about 10 minutes, then drizzle with the icing. Garnish with lemon zest, if desired.

CONCLUSION

Cheers! You made it! And if you have found your favorite Air Fryer recipes, then mark them down, put on your aprons and let's do some Air Frying!

This cookbook is centered around the idea of the Air Fryer, and with all the guaranteed health advantages, the method is considered much better than traditional frying to home-cook crispy, fried, and oil-free food. The need for the air fryer stems from the rising health problems of the day. High cholesterol, cardiac disorders, and obesity are some common issues that are becoming life-threatening due to the use of excessive oil in the food. Traditional frying, therefore, has been condemned by the health expert's society, and they all recommend food with lesser oil and fat content. Air Fryer came as a blessing for all those who were struggling to minimize their daily fat consumption. An Air Fryer is a kitchen miracle that can cook super crispy food but without the use of much oil.

In a nutshell, this Air Fryer cookbook is the right fit for all beginners who love to have crispy and healthy food on the menu. So, ditch the traditional messy deep-frying method and try some quality homecooked food with minimum effort by using an Air Fryer now!

INDEX

Ahi Tuna Steaks, 176
Air Fried Leeks, 37
Air Fried Shirred Eggs, 17
Air Fryer Sausage Wraps, 217
Air-fried Green Herbs Scallop, 172
Air-Fried Lemon Olive Chicken, 141
Air-fried Pork with Sweet and Sour Glaze, 118
Alaskan Cod with Apple Slaw, 169
Alfredo Chicken Wings, 146
All Meat Pizza, 214
Almond Crusted Shrimps, 169
Amish Baked Oatmeal, 30
Angel Cake, 246
Apple and Ham Panini, 228
Apple Chips, 194
Apple Cider Donuts, 238
Apple Crumble, 243
Apple Dumplings, 241
Apple Empanadas, 252
Apple Fries with Caramel, 243
Apple Turkey Burgers, 215
Apricot and Vanilla Porridge, 28
Apricot Blackberry Crumble, 255
Apricot Nutmeg Muffins, 236
Apricot-Glazed Turkey, 126
Apricots Stuffed with Walnuts, 41
Arancini with Jerked Tomatoes & Mozzarella, 58
Arugula and Beets Salad, 56
Asian Chicken and Peas Salad, 54
Asian Chicken Noodles, 122
Asian Steamed Salmon, 162
Asian Style Chicken Strips with Asparagus, 174
Asparagus Fries, 50
Asparagus Strata, 67
Autumn Fruit Bowl, 258
Autumn Pumpkin Cake, 237
Autumn Pumpkin Pie, 257
Avocado and Crispy Tofu Salad, 86
Avocado Asparagus Soup, 83
Avocado Cinnamon Bread, 225
Avocado Toast with Poached Eggs, 18
Avo-Eggs, 10
Baba Ghanoush, 49
Bacon and Brown Sugar Little Smokies, 217
Bacon and Cheese Jalapeno Poppers, 42
Bacon and Cheese Popcorn, 223
Bacon Carbonara, 114
Bacon Cheeseburger Dip, 34
Bacon Pizza, 189
Bacon Scallops, 43
Bacon Wrapped Hotdogs, 117
Bacon -Wrapped Onion Rings, 52
Bacon-Wrapped Filet Mignon, 96
Bahian Seasoned Chicken, 144
Baked Almond Donuts, 256
Baked Apples, 252
Baked Cod, 171
Baked Eggplant Chips, 221
Baked Eggs with Kale and Ham, 19
Baked Mushrooms, 46
Baked Parsnip and Potato, 69
Baked Root Vegetables, 72
Baked Seafood Gratin, 177
Baked Vegetables with Cheese and Olives, 70
Baked Yams with Dill, 46

Balsamic and Shallots Cod, 168
Balsamic Cherry Tomato Skewers, 55
Banana and Peach Bake Oatmeal, 30
Banana Foster, 262
Banana Fritters, 241
Bang Bang Shrimp, 168
Barbecued Lime Shrimp, 184
Basic Taco Meat, 106
Basil and Garlic Crackers, 205
Basil Keto Crackers, 198
BBQ Tofu, 73
BBQ Vegetable Sandwich, 210
Beans in Tomato Sauce, 51
Beef Adobo, 100
Beef and Avocado Pan, 99
Beef and Blue Cheese Burgers, 191
Beef and Napa Cabbage Mix, 99
Beef BBQ Cubes with Onions, 104
Beef Bolognese Sauce, 103
Beef Broccoli, 93
Beef Cabbage Rolls, 100
Beef Chimichangas, 93
Beef Empanadas, 204
Beef Hamburger Casserole, 101
Beef Jerky, 190
Beef Mozzarella, 95
Beef Mushroom Soup, 71
Beef Pot Pie, 95
Beef Roll-ups, 93
Beef Schnitzel, 91, 98
Beef Spanish Casserole, 104
Beef Taco Fried Egg Rolls, 103
Beef Tenderloin with Green Sauce, 99
Beef, Carrot and Herbs Meatballs, 102
Beer-Braised Short Loin, 97
Beer-Coated Duck Breast, 134
Bell Pepper and Tomato Sauce, 75
Bell Pepper Eggs, 11
Bell Pepper Gratin, 74
Berbere-Spiced Fries, 38
Berry and Nuts Granola, 27
Best Carrot Cake, 236
Black and White Brownies, 245
Black Bean and Sausage Soup, 88
Black Bean and Tater Tots, 129
Black Bean Burger with Garlic-Chipotle, 205
Black Bean Egg Rolls, 40
Black Pepper Flounder, 181
Blackberry-glazed Salmon, 152
Blackened Baked Chicken, 135
Blueberry Cheesecake, 250
Blueberry Turnovers, 246
Boneless Air Fryer Turkey Breasts, 143
Bourbon Peach Wings, 129
Bow Tie Chips, 193
Bratwurst Bites with Spicy Mustard, 121
Breaded Artichoke Fries, 39
Breaded Deviled Eggs, 226
Breaded Hake, 180
Breaded Okra, 42
Breaded Prawns, 155
Breaded Spam Steaks, 25
Breakfast Bagels, 18
Breakfast Blueberry Cobbler, 18
Breakfast Broccoli Muffins, 7

Breakfast Egg Pastries, 19
Breakfast Egg Puffs, 15
Breakfast Egg Sandwich, 14
Breakfast Hash, 15
Breakfast Quinoa, 7
Breakfast Spinach Quiche, 3
Breakfast Stuffed Poblanos, 11
Brined Turkey Breast, 136
Broiled Tilapia, 164
Brown Rice and Salmon Frittata, 22
Brunch Mini Sliders, 217
Brussel Sprout Pizza, 212
Buffalo Cauliflower Bites, 41
Buffalo Chicken Sliders, 188
Burger Taco Wrap, 211
Burrata-Stuffed Tomatoes, 87
Butter and Orange Fried Chicken, 124
Buttered Bagels, 221
Buttered Baked Cod with Wine, 158
Buttered Cod and Chives, 169
Buttered Crab Legs, 181
Buttered Filet Mignon, 96
Buttered Fish Scampi, 150
Buttered Garlic Squash, 74
Buttered Salmon with Dill, 166
Buttered Thyme Scallops, 182
Buttermilk Chicken, 146
Cabbage Diet Soup, 69
Cacao Banana Leather, 29
Caesar Marinated Grilled Chicken, 143
Cajun Lemon-Shrimp Kebabs, 164
Cajun Lobster Tails, 166
Cajun Peanuts, 195
Cajun Red Rice and Beans, 34
Cajun Shrimp Boil, 178
Cajun Shrimps, 160
Cajun Snack Mix, 228
Cajun Sweet Potato Tots, 42
Cali Breakfast Melt, 22
California Style Grilled Chicken, 135
Candied Pecans, 213
Caramel Muffins, 235
Caramel Popcorn, 191
Caramelized Carrot Soup, 62
Caramelized Ginger Salmon, 180
Caramelized Pepper Pork, 114
Cardamom Tapioca Pudding, 241
Caribbean Chicken Thighs, 127
Carrot and Potato Hash Browns, 21
Carrot Balls, 44
Cashew Cookies, 235
Cashew Masala, 227
Cauliflower and Avocado Toast, 7
Cauliflower Florets, 37
Cauliflower Fried Rice, 63
Cauliflower Fritters, 83
Celeriac Fries, 55
Celeriac Potato Gratin, 84
Cheddar and Mustard Twists, 198
Cheddar Cheese English Muffins, 21
Cheddar Cheese Sliced Cauliflower, 80
Cheddar Muffins, 189
Cheddar Mustard Toast, 221
Cheese and Broccoli Quiche, 5
Cheese and Crab Souffle, 151
Cheese and Salsa Mushrooms, 41
Cheese and Spinach Muffins, 215
Cheese and Tuna Sandwich, 194
Cheese Broccoli Pasta, 72
Cheese Herb Chicken Wings, 129
Cheese Scones, 6
Cheese Vegan Sandwich, 200
Cheeseburger Dip, 45
Cheese-stuffed Burgers, 209

Cheesy Beef Enchiladas, 107
Cheesy Beef Puffs, 222
Cheesy Breaded Salmon, 183
Cheesy Fennel, 55
Cheesy Fingerling Potatoes, 39
Cheesy Fish Balls, 165
Cheesy Grape Pizza, 227
Cheesy Ham Pastries, 12
Cheesy Lemon Rice, 54
Cheesy Pork Casserole, 117
Cheesy Sticks with Sweet Thai Sauce, 56
Cheesy Tomato and Egg, 4
Cheesy Turkey Calzone, 124
Cheesy Zucchini Frittata, 14
Cheesy Zucchini Fritters, 77
Cheesy-Bacon Stuffed Pastry Pie, 218
Cherry Pie, 237
Chery Tomato and Rutabaga Pasta, 75
Chia Blackberry Jam, 241
Chia Pudding, 22
Chia Seed Crackers, 221
Chick Fil A Burgers, 226
Chicken Alfredo, 124
Chicken and Avocado Sliders, 198
Chicken Breasts with Passion Fruit Sauce, 138
Chicken Bruschetta, 132
Chicken Buffalo Dip, 45
Chicken Coconut Meatballs, 127
Chicken Cordon Bleu, 147
Chicken Corn Zucchini Soup, 87
Chicken Curry, 130
Chicken Fillets, Brie & Ham, 142
Chicken Fried Rice, 130
Chicken Jalapeno Popper Dip, 44
Chicken Jerky, 212
Chicken Luncheon Salad, 149
Chicken Marinara, 127
Chicken Orzo Soup, 62
Chicken Parmesan Meatballs, 136
Chicken Pasta Salad, 127
Chicken Sandwich, 191
Chicken Sausage with Nestled Eggs, 123
Chicken Skin Crisps, 202
Chicken Tandoori, 132
Chicken Tenders, 140
Chicken Tikka Kebab, 139
Chicken with Chanterelle Mushrooms, 136
Chicken Wontons, 149
Chicken, Chive and Feta Frittata, 19
Chickpea Cauliflower Tacos, 199
Chickpea Chicken Stew, 148
Chickpea Fries, 38
Chili Cheese Curds, 199
Chili Cheese Dogs, 212
Chili Cheese Sandwich, 207
Chili Ground Beef, 101
Chinese Char Siu, 111
Chinese Duck Legs, 128
Chinese Five-Spice Pork Belly, 113
Chinese Orange Tofu, 66
Chinese Pork Dumplings, 118
Chinese Style Chicken Wings, 134
Chinese Style Meatballs, 113
Chive and Cheese Chicken Rolls, 132
Chives and Lamb Burgers, 209
Chocolate and Ricotta Cake, 241
Chocolate Avocado Pudding, 258
Chocolate Banana Chips, 206
Chocolate Banana Muffins, 24
Chocolate Cherry Oatmeal, 32
Chocolate Chip Bread, 261
Chocolate Chip Cookies, 249
Chocolate Chip Muffins, 238
Chocolate Oatmeal Cookies, 235

Chocolate Peanut Butter and Jelly S'mores, 230
Chocolate Smarties Cookies, 253
Chocolate Walnut Cake, 241
Chocolate Zucchini Bread, 237
Chocolate-Covered Maple Bacon, 219
Chorizo Parmesan Rolls, 14
Churro-Banana Oats, 16
Cinnamon Apple Pancakes, 12
Cinnamon Cappuccino Muffins, 259
Cinnamon Churros, 235
Cinnamon Fried Bananas, 233
Cinnamon Peaches, 243
Cinnamon Pear Crisps, 257
Cinnamon Roasted Chickpeas, 211
Cinnamon Rolls, 20
Citrus Balsamic Salmon, 169
Citrus Rosemary Chicken, 146
Citrus Sponge Cake, 245
Citrusy Branzini on the Grill, 183
Classic Beef Ribs, 92
Classic Beef Stroganoff, 97
Classic Cheese Pizza, 226
Classic Tortilla Pizza, 222
Cocoa Banana Brownies, 252
Coconut Blueberry Oatmeal, 23, 31
Coconut Caramel Cream, 256
Coconut Chicken Tenders, 130
Coconut Chocolate Fondue, 247
Coconut Cream Cheese Pancakes, 8
Coconut Curry Pork Roast, 118
Coconut Raspberry Bars, 258
Coconut Soup with Chive, 90
Coconut Tilapia, 151
Coconut-Coated White Chocolate Cookies, 258
Cod and Vegetable Gratin, 156
Cod in Jalapeno Sauce, 153
Cod Tortilla Wraps, 157
Cod with Grape and Fennel Relish, 186
Coffee Cake, 253
Coffee Rubbed Steaks, 93
Colby Potato Patties, 53
Coleslaw Stuffed Wontons, 40
Coriander Potatoes, 42
Coriander Shrimp Cakes, 157
Corn and Egg Salad, 49
Corn Dogs, 220
Corn Flakes Casserole, 25
Corn with Cheese and Lime, 45
Cornbread with Pulled Pork, 198
Cornflakes and Blackberries, 11
Cornmeal Battered Fish, 169
Cottage Cheese Chicken, 144
Cottage Cheese -Stuffed Chicken Breast, 131
Country Meatloaf, 115
Country Style Ribs, 111
Couscous with Raisins, 55
Crab Balls, 156
Crab Filled Mushrooms, 178
Crab Pastries, 156
Crab Rangoon, 186
Cranberry Bran Muffins, 22
Cranberry Bread Pudding, 24
Cranberry Pumpkin Oatmeal, 31
Cranberry Spinach Turnovers, 207
Cream and Coconut Cups, 244
Cream Cheese and Sausage Biscuits, 216
Cream Cheese Stuffed Strawberries, 259
Cream Cheese Zucchini, 85
Cream of Asparagus Soup, 65
Cream of Carrot Potato Soup, 80
Creamy Air Fryer Salmon, 183
Creamy Bacon Omelet, 13
Creamy Baked Cod, 173
Creamy Cajun Chicken, 131

Creamy Cauliflower Gratin, 83
Creamy Cauliflower Pasta, 65
Creamy Chicken Alfredo, 130
Creamy Coconut Chicken, 128
Creamy Coconut Sauce on Jamaican Salmon, 185
Creamy Eggplant Gratin, 82
Creamy Leche Flan, 230
Creamy Mac and Cheese, 29
Creamy Mushroom Pie, 215
Creamy Parsnip Soup, 63
Creamy Pork Curry, 120
Creamy Risotto, 9
Creamy Salmon Pie, 201
Creamy Turmeric Chicken, 139
Creamy Vanilla Berry Mini Pies, 260
Creamy Zucchini Mix, 76
Creole Jalapeno Coins, 215
Creole Veggie-Shrimp Bake, 165
Crispy Avocado Wedges, 37
Crispy Buttered Chicken, 142, 146
Crispy Fried Whole Chicken, 140
Crispy Halibut, 161
Crispy Noodle Vegetable Salad, 72
Crispy Pork Chops, 111
Crispy Ranch Fish Fillets, 168
Croque Monsieur, 203
Crunchy Almond & Kale Salad with Roasted Chicken, 48
Crunchy Curry Chicken Strips, 146
Crusted Fillet Mignon, 97
Cumin Tortilla Chips with Guacamole, 60
Cumin-Paprika Rubbed Beef Brisket, 98
Currant and Plum Tarts, 251
Curried Cauliflower Soup, 87
Curried Eggplant, 79
Curried Zucchini, 88
Curry Chicken Wings, 125
Curry Lentil Soup, 81
Curry Zucchini Soup, 71
Dark Chocolate Muffins, 232
Dark Rum Cake, 260
Deep Fried Cookie Dough Balls, 232
Dehydrated Candied Bacon, 220
Dehydrated Strawberries, 207
Delicious Beef Tips, 103
Delicious Red Mullet, 182
Dessert Fries, 231
Dijon Fish Fillets, 184
Dijon Lime Chicken, 129
Dijon Mustard 'n Parmesan Crusted Tilapia, 170
Dill Mashed Potato, 39
Dinner Rolls, 193
Disney Land Turkey Legs, 143
Doritos Chicken Bites, 143
Double-Dipped Mini Cinnamon Biscuits, 261
Dried Cranberry Farro, 31
Dried Dragon Fruit Chips, 213
Dried Pineapple Chunks, 213
Drunken Skewered Shrimp, Tomatoes 'n Sausages, 170
Dry-Rubbed Chicken Wings, 123
Duck and Tea Sauce Recipe, 134
Duck with Cherries Recipe, 132
Easy Cheese Sticks, 56
Easy Shrimp Paella, 168
Egg and Bacon Muffins, 4
Egg and Bacon Pie, 4
Egg and Ham Cups, 10
Egg and Sausage Casserole, 5
Egg Muffins, 6
Eggplant Boats, 74
Eggplant Caprese, 71
Eggplant Parmesan, 63
Eggplant Satay, 88
Eggplant stacks, 68
Eggplant Surprise, 38

Eggs Benedict, 216
English Muffin Tuna Sandwiches, 195
Espresso Oatmeal, 23
Falafel with Tahini Sauce, 43
Fennel Frittata, 7
Fennel Risotto, 79
Fiery Bacon Nibbles, 58
Fiery Cabbage, 77
Fiery Citrus Chicken, 141
Fiery Hasselback Chicken, 145
Fish Chicharron, 219
Fish Fillet in Pesto Sauce, 162
Fish Finger Sandwich, 196
Fish Sticks with Chili Ketchup Sauce, 176
Five Spicy Crispy Roasted Pork, 119
Flax Chips, 218
Flax Meal Porridge, 23
Flax Mozza Wraps, 209
Florentine Eggs, 9
Flourless Chocolate Coconut Cupcakes, 239
Flying Fish, 175
Foil Packet Salmon, 181
French Toast Sticks, 11
Fresh Shrimp Salad, 173
Fried Chicken Livers, 145
Fried Chicken with Salsa Verde, 142
Fried Duck Thighs, 141
Fried Oreos, 233
Fried Pork Quesadilla, 214
Fried Stuffed Oysters on the Half Shell with Crawfish Stuffing, 186
Fruit Soft Tacos, 210
Fruity Oreo Cupcakes, 251
Fudgy Brownies, 232
Fudgy Nutella Brownies, 253
Fusilli with Broccoli in Pesto, 89
Garam Masala Shrimps, 166
Garlic and Black Pepper Shrimp Grill, 185
Garlic Cheese Bread, 197, 217
Garlic Cheese Rolls, 227
Garlic Chili Fried Fish, 179
Garlic Honey Chicken, 122
Garlic Lemon Chicken with Green Olives, 130
Garlic Mashed Turnips, 43
Garlic Mozzarella Sticks, 219
Garlic Parsley Scallops, 171
German Pancakes, 5
Ginger-Orange Beef Strips, 106
Glazed Skirt Steak, 100
Goat Cheese and Figs, 44
Goat Cheese Balls, 58
Gorgonzola Stuffed Mushrooms with Horseradish Mayo, 53
Great Air-Fried Soft-Shell Crab, 178
Greek Egg Muffins, 15
Greek Kafta Kabobs, 92
Greek Lamb Patties, 94
Greek Spinach Parcels, 205
Green Beans and Mushroom Casserole, 78
Green Tomato BLT, 208
Green Vegetable Pizza, 200
Grilled Chicken and Radish Mix Recipe, 126
Grilled Endive with Yogurt Sauce, 59
Grilled Gruyere Cheese Sandwich, 218
Grilled Turbot, 182
Ground Beef Yuca Balls, 94
Haddock and Spinach, 167
Hake Fillet with Green Salad, 176
Hake in Creamy Red Pepper Sauce, 176
Halibut with Eggs and Veggies, 172
Ham Pinwheels, 192
Hamburger Pasta Casserole, 119
Hanger Steak in Mole Rub, 109
Hasselback Zucchini, 64
Hawaiian Pizza, 223
Hawaiian Pork Sliders, 190

Hawaiian Roasted Quail, 126
Hawaiian Salmon, 186
Healthy Banana Pancakes, 4
Healthy Beet Hummus, 44
Healthy Carrot Oatmeal, 12
Healthy Cheese Pockets, 66
Healthy Pecan Brownies, 236
Healthy Turkey Lettuce Wraps, 207
Herbed Fish Fingers, 163
Herbed Omelet, 12
Herbed Pork Burgers, 192
Herbed Pulled Beef, 98
Herbed Roast Chicken, 125
Hoisin Pork Loin, 117
Hoisin Turkey Burgers, 191
Holiday Beef Roast, 105
Holiday Gingerbread Cake, 248
Holiday Roasted Goose, 148
Homemade Peanut Corn Nuts, 219
Honey and Sriracha Calamari, 161
Honey BBQ Bacon Sandwiches, 196
Honey Dill Carrots, 46
Honey Glazed Chicken, 133
Honey Ham and Cheese Bagels, 224
Honey Lime Chicken wings, 145
Honey Mango Slices, 213
Honey Pineapples, 242
Horseradish Salmon, 177
Hot Bacon Shrimps, 172
Hot Mexican Bean Dip, 36
Hot Pumpkin Rendang, 90
Hummus Mushroom Pizza, 210
Hungarian Beef Goulash, 106
Indian Brunch Wrap, 204
Indian Spiced Fish Fingers, 168
Indian Spiced Okra, 47
Indian Style Sweet Potato Fries, 36
Indonesian Chicken Drumettes, 138
-Ingredient Air Fryer Catfish, 183
Irish Butter Cookies, 240
Italian Beef Meatballs, 95
Italian Eggplant Stew, 63, 75
Italian Fried Ravioli, 59
Italian Grilled Sardines, 179
Italian Parmesan Chicken Wings, 142
Italian Style Pork Chops, 116
Italian Tofu Steaks, 73
Jacket Potatoes, 33
Jackfruit Taquitos, 224
Jalapeno Breakfast Muffins, 25
Jalapeno Cheese Balls, 40
Jamaican Meatballs, 111
Japanese Steamed Tuna, 150
Japanese Tofu Omelet, 21
Juicy & Spicy Chicken Wings, 133
Juicy Turkey Legs, 145
Julienne Vegetables with Chicken, 74
Kalamata Mozzarella Pita Melts, 223
Kale and Black Olives, 52
Kale and Brussels Sprouts, 52
Kale and Cottage Cheese Omelet, 6
Kale Chips, 189
Kale Egg Muffins, 6
Kale Muffins, 29
Kenny Rogers Corn Muffins, 228
Keto Air Bread, 225
Khao Pad Fried Rice, 89
Kheema Burgers, 108
Kohlrabi Chips, 209
Korean Burgers, 197
Korean Cauliflower, 68
Korean Chicken Wings, 125
Lamb Burgers, 206
Lamb Kebabs, 91

Lamb Korma, 96
Lamb with Madeira Sauce, 107
Latte Crème Brûlée, 244
Lebanese Chicken, 135
Leche Flan, 247
Leg of Lamb with Brussel Sprouts, 95
Lemon Blueberry Cake, 229
Lemon Chiffon Cake, 242
Lemon Cupcakes, 255
Lemon Flavored Green Beans, 37
Lemon Lentils, 49
Lemon Parmesan Halibut, 164
Lemon Pepper Shrimp, 156
Lemon Pound Cake, 254
Lemon Sugar Cookies, 239
Lemon Tart Macaroons, 263
Lemon Tofu, 67
Lemongrass Tuna Steaks, 159
Lime and Garlic Tortilla Chips, 195
Lime Cheesecake, 249
Lime Coconut Breakfast Quinoa, 31
Lime-Chili Pork Tenderloin, 112
Loaded Disco Fries, 39
Lobster Wontons, 151
Louisiana Catfish, 159
Louisiana Chicken Drumettes, 139
Low Sugar Spiced Plums, 231
Low-fat Mug Cake, 232
Lunch Chicken Fajitas, 148
Mac and Cheese Balls, 52
Mac and Cheese Toast, 222
Mahi Mahi in Dill Lemon Sauce, 186
Marbled Cheesecake, 231
Marinated Rib Eye Steak, 102
Marshmallow Turnovers, 254
Meatless Ziti Pasta, 82
Meatloaf Wraps, 213
Mediterranean Turkey Burgers, 190
Mexican Avocado Fry, 88
Mexican Baked Potato Soup, 65
Mexican Beef Soup, 61
Mexican Black Beans and Corn, 54
Mexican Chicken Burgers, 206
Mexican Chicken Burrito, 128
Mexican Chilis Frittata, 30
Mexican Fish Quesadilla, 203
Mexican Fish Tacos, 157
Mexican Pork Carnitas, 110
Mexican Pork Chops, 113
Mexican Rice, 57
Mexican Salsa Eggs, 24
Mexican Style Pizza, 189
Mexican Waffles, 4
Middle Eastern Toast and Milk, 262
Milky French Toast, 13
Minestrone Soup, 89
Mini Peppers with Goat Cheese, 50
Mini Smoked Salmon Quiche, 21
Mini Sweet Corn Pakodas, 228
Mint Baked Alaska, 247
Mint Lamb with Red Potatoes, 99
Miso Trout, 153
Mixed Berries and Lemon Crumble, 245
Mixed Berries Cream Puffs, 248
Mixed Berries Muffins, 18
Mixed Berries Oatmeal, 13
Mixed Vegetable Chips, 206
Mixed Vegetable Frittata, 10
Moist Banana Bread, 262
Moist Chocolate Cake, 236
Moist Date Bread, 237
Moist Vanilla Cupcake, 242
Morning Burrito, 19
Morning Pizza, 224

Moroccan Beef Roast, 106
Moroccan Lamb Balls, 103
Moroccan Vegetable Stew, 69
Mozzarella and Cherry Tomato Pastries, 17
Mozzarella and Radish Salad, 86
Mozzarella -Spinach Stuffed Burgers, 218
Mozzarella Turkey Rolls, 125
Mushroom and Asparagus Cakes, 71
Mushroom and Beef Meatballs, 93
Mushroom and Cheese Hasselback Potatoes, 47
Mushroom and Leeks Frittata, 20
Mushroom Beef Steak, 101
Mushroom Chips, 212
Mushroom Frittata, 5
Mushroom Pie, 194
Mushroom Pizza, 192
Mushroom Soup, 82
Mushroom Toast with Ginger and Sesame, 208
Mushrooms and Sour Cream, 38
Mustard and Lemon Lamb Chops, 94
Mustard Chicken Fingers, 143
Mustard Salmon, 153
Mustard Tuna Cakes, 172
Noodle Ham Casserole, 119
Nutmeg Apple Jam, 250
Nutmeg Cranberry Scones, 10
Nutty Bread Pudding, 21
Nutty Carrot Soup, 80
Oat and Vanilla Pudding, 4
Okra Corn Medley, 88
Old Bay Chicken Wings, 143
Olive and Calamari Rings, 37
Onion and Cheese Omelet, 8
Orange Turkey Burgers, 199
Oreganata Clams, 175
Oriental Lamb Shoulder, 102
Oriental Pork Meatballs, 121
Oriental Red Snapper, 152
Oriental Shrimp Fried Rice, 177
Oriental Shrimps, 174
Outback Ribs, 112
Pakoras, 48
Panko-Crusted Tilapia, 157
Pao de Queijo, 222
Papaya Coconut Oatmeal, 31
Paprika Cucumber Chips, 56
Paprika Egg Souffle, 14
Paprika Fish Nuggets, 170
Paprika Pickle Chips, 198
Paprika Sweet Potato Chips, 189
Paprika-Cumin Beef Brisket, 101
Parmesan and Scallion Sandwich, 216
Parmesan Butter Flounder, 181
Parmesan Chicken Nuggets, 129
Parmesan Crusted Clams, 161
Parmesan Egg Clouds, 15
Parmesan Garlic Wings, 128
Parmesan Spiced Pork Chops, 112
PB & J Doughnuts, 240
Peach and Nuts Millet, 28
Peach Hand Pies, 262
Peanut Butter and Chocolate Cupcakes, 231
Peanut Butter Bars, 259
Peanut Butter Custard, 230
Peanut Butter Muffins, 15
Peanut Oats and Chia Porridge, 10
Pear and Walnut Oatmeal, 12
Pear Chips, 213
Peas and Bacon, 50
Pecan Pie, 244
Pepperoni Chips, 191
Perfect Scrambled Eggs, 8
Pesto and Almond Crusted Salmon, 154
Pesto Beef Rolls, 98

Pesto Fish Pie, 187
Pesto Lamb Ribs, 102
Pesto Omelet, 26
Pesto Scallops, 184
Pesto Tomatoes, 35
Pesto Zucchini Salad, 85
Philly Chicken Stromboli, 197
Pigs in a Blanket, 52
Pineapple French Toast, 24
Pineapple Spareribs, 115
Pine-Pumpkin Puree, 73
Pink Champagne Cupcakes, 242
Pistachio and Pineapple Oats, 28
Pistachio Crusted Salmon, 175
Pita Pizza, 203
Pizza Egg Rolls, 202
Pizza Hot Dog Buns, 197
Pizza Margherita, 223
Pizza Omelet, 26
Pizza Stuffed Chicken, 147
Polenta Pie, 205
Pomegranate and Chocolate Bars, 230
Porcini Risotto, 50
Pork Apple Meatballs, 120
Pork Brunch Sticks, 120
Pork Bun and Liver Souffle, 121
Pork Chops and Mushrooms, 112
Pork Chops in Lemon Sage Sauce, 111
Pork Egg Rolls, 114
Pork Fricassee, 114
Pork Kebabs, 117
Pork Neck with Salad, 115
Pork Posole, 120
Pork Sausage Ratatouille, 116
Pork Sausage with Mashed Cauliflower, 117
Pork Taquitos, 113
Portobello Mushroom Pizza, 37
Portobello Pesto Burgers, 217
Portuguese Bacalao Tapas, 185
Potato and Kale Croquettes, 57
Potato Bread Rolls, 217
Potato Fish Cakes, 180
Potato -Kale Croquettes, 52
Potato Parsley Soup, 87
Potato Poutine, 35
Prosciutto Wrapped Ahi Ahi, 180
Prosciutto Wrapped Asparagus, 45
Prosciutto Wrapped Tuna Bites, 181
Provolone Egg Sandwich, 227
Pub Burgers, 188
Puff Pastry Pears, 255
Pulled BBQ Beef Sandwiches, 204
Pumpkin Gnocchi, 83
Pumpkin Lasagna, 84
Pumpkin Muffins, 243
Pumpkin Spice Oats, 25
Quail in White Wine Sauce, 126
Queso Crumpets, 14
Queso Fundido, 33
Quick and Easy Air-fried Catfish, 175
Quick and Easy Lobster Tails, 163
Quick Crab Sticks, 179
Quick Oatmeal Cake, 256
Quinoa Burger, 225
Radish Hash Browns, 17
Raisin and Cranberry Beignet, 244
Ranch Fish Fillet, 163
Ranch Flavored Kale Chips, 220
Ranch Potatoes, 46
Ranch Pretzels, 207
Ranch Taco Wings, 145
Raspberries and Avocado Cake, 231
Raspberry Cream Rolls, 246
Raspberry Cupcakes, 251

Ratatouille Soup with Quinoa, 63
Red Cabbage Avocado Bowls, 85
Red Chard and Kalamata Olives, 84
Red Chili Mackerel, 182
Red Hot Chili Fish Curry, 154
Red Velvet Cupcakes, 251
Red Wine Pears, 230
Rice Flour Coated Tofu, 78
Rice Flour Shrimps, 183
Rich Chocolate Pudding, 257
Ricotta Balls, 42
Roast Beef Lettuce Wraps, 94
Roasted Bell Peppers with Spicy Mayo, 70
Roasted Brussel Sprouts with Parmesan, 35
Roasted Chicken with Tomato Salsa, 137
Roasted Corn on the Cob, 51
Roasted Duck Breasts with Endives, 125
Roasted Duck with Orange-Date Stuffing, 137
Roasted Garlic Zucchini, 47
Roasted Grape Dip, 59
Roasted Hot Corn, 54
Roasted Lima beans, 219
Roasted Paprika Carrots, 43
Roasted Parsley Cod, 171
Roasted Pears, 240
Roasted Pepper and Greens Salad, 50
Roasted Pine nuts, 222
Roasted Potato Salad, 34
Roasted Tomato Salsa, 59
Roasted Vegetable Pasta, 68
Roasted Veggie Tacos, 65
Rosemary and Garlic Fries, 47
Rosemary Sweet Potato Chips, 196
Rosemary Veggie Gratin, 71
Rotisserie Chicken, 142
Rumaki Balls, 60
Russian Beef Gratin, 105
Rustic Baked Halloumi with Fennel Salad, 84
Rustic Mushroom and Pork Burgers, 202
Salami and Prosciutto Omelet, 23
Salmon & Eggs, 182
Salmon in Honey Chili Sauce, 152
Salmon Jerky, 201
Salmon Nachos, 201
Salmon Rice Pilaf, 178
Salmon with Avocado Sauce, 152
Salmon with Carrots and Fennel, 159
Salmon with Kohlrabi and Asparagus, 173
Salmon with Lemon-Parsley Relish, 185
Salsa Eggplants, 78
Salt and Pepper Chicken Wings, 144
Salt Roasted Hazelnuts, 221
Salted Caramel Beignets, 245
Salted Corn Nuts, 196
Salted Tequila 'n Lime Shrimp, 171
Sausage Balls, 16
Sausage Quiche, 9
Sautéed Duck with Asian Vegetables, 137
Sautéed Pumpkin and Potatoes, 51
Savory Feta Oats, 27
Savory Pearl Barley, 23
Scallops Gratin, 187
Scallops with Spring Veggies, 160
Scotch Eggs with Spicy Pepper Sauce, 58
Sea Bass and Fennel, 177
Sea Bay Tilapia, 179
Sea Salt Parsnip Fries, 36
Sea Salt Salmon, 180
Seasoned Omelet with Croutons, 28
Seasoned Pork Rinds, 219
Semolina Milk Cake, 234
Sesame Banana Dessert, 239
Sesame Cabbage & Prawns Egg Roll Wraps, 162
Sesame Crusted White Fish, 167

Sesame Mustard Greens, 55
Sesame Tuna Steak, 157
Seven-Layer Tostadas, 224
Sherry-Braised Ribs, 118
Shrimp & Sausage Paella, 154
Shrimp A La Boom, 184
Shrimp Egg Rolls, 158
Shrimp Fajitas, 177
Shrimp Grilled Cheese Sandwich, 213
Shrimp Mac and Cheese, 178
Shrimp Nuggets, 155
Shrimp Po'boy, 193
Shrimp Stroganoff, 155
Shrimp Stuffed Peppers, 151
Shrimp with Palm of Hearts, 155
Sichuan Spiced Lamb, 98
Simple Broccoli Side Dish, 56
Simple Shredded Beef Tacos, 227
Simple Spiced Chicken Legs, 147
Smoked Bacon Bread, 193
Smoked Crispy Ribs, 105
Smoked Ham and Pears, 116
Smoked Paprika Pumpkin Seeds, 200
Smoked Salmon Omelet, 9
Smoky Cheeseburgers, 211
Snapper Scampi, 167
Snow White's Cake, 234
Soft Cinnamon Donuts, 261
Soft Doughnuts, 234
Soft Sugar Cookies, 254
Sourdough Bread, 210
Southern Buttermilk Biscuits, 23
Southern Chicken Stew, 133
Southern Fried Chicken, 128
Southern Pulled Pork, 115
Southwest Egg Rolls, 51
Spanish Greens, 76
Spiced Beef Fajitas, 92
Spiced Edamame, 194
Spiced Lentils Nibblers, 220
Spiced Mandarin and Apple Sauce, 257
Spiced Mixed Nuts, 190
Spiced Mozza Sticks, 36
Spiced Orange Slices, 257
Spiced Pears with Honey Lemon Ricotta, 263
Spiced Sweet Potato Soup, 81
Spiced Turnip Salad, 77
Spiced Veggie Burger, 205
Spicy Acorn Squash Wedges, 57
Spicy Air-Fried Cheese Tilapia, 184
Spicy Arancini, 53
Spicy Beef Spaghetti, 97
Spicy Beet Chips, 194
Spicy Cheese Crisps, 199
Spicy Lamb Balls, 99
Spicy Lamb Chops, 94
Spicy Lime and Basil Clams, 169
Spicy Mango Okra, 34
Spicy Pimento Cheese Dip, 35
Spicy Pork Meatballs, 117
Spicy Short Ribs in Red Wine Reduction, 92
Spicy Shrimp Pizza, 214
Spicy Steamed Mussels, 163
Spicy Tomato Chutney, 57
Spicy Vegetable Soup, 62
Spicy Vinegar Prawns, 171
Spinach and Cheese Toast, 27
Spinach Balls, 46
Spinach Cheese Pie, 25
Spinach Muffins, 20
Spring Salad, 43
Squash and Zucchini Mini Pizza, 223
Squash Oatmeal Muffins, 29
Squash Risotto, 72

Sriracha and Honey Calamari, 183
Sriracha Chicken Wings, 145
Steak & Bread Salad, 101
Steak A La Mushrooms, 105
Steamed Clams, 184
Steamed Salmon and Summer Greens, 162
Sticky BBQ Chicken, 140
Sticky Pork Ribs, 116
Strawberry Cream cheese Chimichangas, 233
Strawberry Dutch Pancakes, 3
Strawberry Parfait, 16
Strawberry Souffle, 255
Streusel Donuts, 26
Stuffed Apples with Vanilla Sauce, 232
Stuffed Eggplants, 62
Stuffed Okra, 78
Stuffed Pork Chops, 116
Stuffed Tomatoes, 76
Sugar Free Cheesecake, 239
Sugar Free Coconut Cookies, 236
Summer Fruit Bowl, 259
Summer Vegetable Soup, 81
Sunflower Seed Bread, 192
Sunny Lentils, 88
Super Cheesy Chicken Mac and Cheese, 139
Super Cheesy Hash Browns, 12
Super Nutty French Toast, 16
Suya-spiced Flank Steak, 107
Swedish Meatballs, 108
Swedish Meatloaf, 108
Sweet and Sour Chicken, 123
Sweet and Sour Lamb Chops, 100
Sweet and Spicy Pork Chops, 111
Sweet Blueberry Jam, 258
Sweet Corn Fritters, 53
Sweet Grape and Pear Compote, 259
Sweet Potato Casserole, 69
Sweet Potato Cheesecake, 250
Sweet Potato Dessert, 249
Sweet Potato Frittata, 30
Sweet Potato Hash, 11
Sweet Potato with Broccoli, 36
Sweet Pumpkin Cream, 248
Sweet Walnut Fritters, 261
Sweetcorn Risotto, 57
Sweetened Onions, 48
Sweetened Plantains, 253
Swiss Chard Salad, 76
Swordfish Steak with Avocado Salsa, 152
Szechuan Pork Soup, 64
Taco Bell Crunch Wrap, 211
Taco Flavored Kale Chips, 220
Taco Turkey Casserole, 141
Taiwan Cod Fillets, 165
Tangerine Cake, 260
Tangy Beef Steak, 106
Tangy Lemon Mousse, 253
Tangy Orange Chicken Wings, 138
Taro Chips, 195
Tender and Juicy Whole Chicken, 140
Tequila Orange Chicken, 134
Teriyaki Halibut Steak, 161
Teriyaki Salmon Noodles, 167
Tex Mex Peppers, 75
Tex Mex Stir-fried Chicken, 133
Texas Baby Back Ribs, 121
Texas Chicken Chili, 147
Thai Basil Pork, 119
Thai Chicken Satay, 123
Thai Fish Cake with Mango Sauce, 159
Thai Peanut Tofu, 77
Thai Style Pizza, 208
Thanksgiving Turkey with Mustard Gravy, 124
Thyme Chicken Balls, 136

Thyme Turkey Nuggets, 146
Tikka Masala Chicken, 131
Toad in the Hole, 17
Toasted Coconut Flakes, 221
Toffee Apple Upside-Down Cake, 260
Toffee Cookies, 254
Tofu Crunch Wraps, 212
Tofu Omelet, 8
Tofu Red Curry Noodle, 90
Tofu with Capers Sauce, 79
Tomato and Bell Pepper Soup, 86
Tomato and Fennel Stew, 64
Tomato Basil Tilapia, 165
Tomato Cake, 225
Tomato Corn Risotto, 85
Tomato Frittata, 8
Tomato Parchment Cod, 175
Tomato Quick Bread, 190
Tomatoes and Brussel Sprouts Mix, 77
Tortellini Pasta Salad, 35
Traditional Italian Rice & Parmesan Balls, 85
Triple Berry Pavlova, 248
Tropical Bananas, 238
Tropical French Toast, 5
Tropical Rice Pudding, 257
Tropical Shrimps, 160
Trout with Butter Sauce, 174
Tuna and Capers, 154
Tuna Au Gratin, 154
Tuna Melt Croquettes, 187
Tuna Mushroom Pasta, 179
Tuna Niçoise Salad, 164
Tuna Patties, 158
Tuna Stuffed Potatoes, 174
Tuna with Olives and Spinach, 153
Turkey Breast Rolls, 144
Turkey Breast with Maple Mustard Glaze, 148
Turkey Loaf, 124
Turkey Quesadillas, 201
Turkey Shepherd's Pie, 135
Turkey Wings with Collard Greens, 141
Turkey with Mushrooms and Peas Casserole, 131
Turkish Lamb Liver, 104
Turmeric Flavored Shrimps, 153
Turmeric Potatoes, 44
Tuscan Pork Chops, 119
Tuscan White Bean Soup, 87

Twice Baked Potatoes, 41
Vanilla Almond Cookies, 244
Vanilla Apple Quinoa, 27
Vanilla Bread Pudding, 234
Vanilla Crème Brulee, 256
Vanilla Oat Sandwiches, 250
Vanilla Steel Cut Oats, 13
Vanilla Strawberry Mix, 255
Vegan Chili and Cheese Fries, 70
Vegan Chocolate Vanilla Bars, 258
Vegan Cornbread, 195
Vegan Smoked Bacon, 86
Vegan Taco Bowls, 73
Vegetable and Fruit Skewers, 70
Vegetable Quiche, 20
Vegetable Spring Rolls, 45
Vegetable Tuna Melt, 200
Vegetable Wontons, 66
Vegetables and Couscous, 68
Veggie Pita, 200
Veggie Toast, 9
Vietnamese Pork Chops, 113
Waffle Cheese Fries, 215
Wasabi Crab Cakes, 158
Western Chicken Wings, 144
Wheat Berry Pilaf, 89
White and Black Brownies, 252
Wild Rice Spinach Balls, 38
Wine Poached Clams, 165
Wine Roasted Beef, 104
Winter Beef Soup, 79
Winter Vegetables & Lamb Stew, 96
Xinyan Cod, 182
Yam Chips, 222
Yuzu Soy Squid, 170
Zebra Cake, 240
Zesty Strawberry Jam, 259
Zucchini and Fruits Breakfast Plate, 28
Zucchini Chips, 194
Zucchini Curly Fries, 40
Zucchini Enchiladas, 67
Zucchini Fries, 47
Zucchini Fritters, 64
Zucchini Gratin, 7
Zucchini Muffins, 6
Zucchini Omelet, 26
Zucchini Yogurt Bread, 216

Printed in Great Britain
by Amazon

81848093R00160